Presented To:

_____

From:

_____

Date:

_____

Leading From

JOE TURNHAM

Our Knees

INSPIRING DAILY PRECEPTS
for leaders of faith

All Scripture quotations unless otherwise marked are taken from the King James Version of the Holy Bible.

Publishing services by Selah Publishing Group, LLC, Tennessee. The views expressed or implied in this work do not necessarily reflect those of Selah Publishing Group.

ISBN: 978-1-58930-232-7
Library of Congress Control Number: 2009901283

Acknowledgements

Better than wealth or beauty is the blessing to be born into a family of faith. Being reared by Christian parents, who value faith above all and make church attendance central to your life, is perhaps my greatest blessing. I give eternal thanks to my own parents, Pete and Kay Turnham, who set the right example and made sure that I was exposed to the teachings and fellowship of the Christian faith. Thanks to my sister Diane and my sister Ruthmary for helping to raise me and for praying for me and believing in me. My brother Tim has been a great friend and confidant in recent years and thanks for being a great 'big brother'.

I also give great acknowledgement and thanks to the many servant leaders in my early years of life that cared for me in nursery and in Sunday school. There are several teachers, pastors and mentors in my childhood and adolescent youth that instilled the principles and values needed to find and know the Savior. I pay tribute to each and every one of you, many of whom have already gone to their mansion in heaven.

The church families of Lakeview Baptist Church, Trinity United Methodist Church and First Baptist Church of Auburn are especially memorable and had positive spiritual impact on my life. Thanks to my pastors, Sunday school teachers, missions' committee friends, mission trip partners and many others who love and serve Christ in humble and purposeful ways and made me search more deeply in the faith.

I am especially grateful to my many political mentors in the great State of Alabama, including my own dad. Thanks to my right arm in the political arena for the last several years, Jim Spearman. Thanks also to those many volunteers, supporters, donors who allowed me to become a leader of faith. I also want to give thanks for my rivals, opponents and critics who, whether right or wrong, made me work harder and become a more disciplined and determined leader.

To my clients and benefactors and friends who in the past years hired me, believed in me and gave me meaningful work to do, I give thanks to each of you for rescuing me between my political romps. Leadership is not always profitable and having work to do for patient and understanding employers is a blessing from God.

Thanks to my Recession to Renewal Project partners and dear friends, Rick Carne, Jim Creaghan, Lydia LaFleur, and Ronnie Shows. You believed in me and this work and helped to make it a reality. Thanks also to Rhiannon Jackson and the team at Selah Publishing. Rhiannon's kind and efficient assistance made this journey so much smoother. Thanks to Christy Phillippe for the many hours of copy-edits done with professional precision. Thanks to my personal friends who have quietly affirmed my work.

Acknowledgements

To my wonderful wife and best friend, Paula, you never let me get too low or too high. Thanks for your critical eye and many hours of first edits. Thanks for putting up with my many idiosyncrasies and early morning and weekend hours of research and writing. My son Pete Matthew and my daughter Abby were so encouraging of their dad and put up with my early morning typing and bumping around in the dark to create this book. I love you all dearly and hope this book inspires something in your own life's faith and leadership journey.

Praise be to God for his love for me and for giving me this task to do. Many of the burdens and low points of my life and leadership journey were meant to be so they could be written down and shared with others in this book.

God forgives my many sins and shortcomings and quietly keeps me on the path. I give praise for the ever quiet whisper of the Spirit in my mind and heart as It nudged me out of bed in the early morning hours day after day. It is my miracle. I felt the call to write this book. I consider it one of my life's most meaningful achievements. But, regardless of how many people read these pages, I am forever changed spiritually for having written it and from having been given the call to share it with the world. Thanks, I love You Lord!

Contents

Foreword

Throughout generations people have combed the Holy Scriptures in search of meaning, purpose, solace and forgiveness. Its words give us new understanding of creation, history, prophecy and revelation: therein, we find the promise of the soul's salvation.

But my own burden and calling that led me to the writing of this book, *Leading From Our Knees*, revealed to me that the Holy Scriptures are also the ultimate collection of timeless leadership precepts. From Genesis to Revelation we encounter those many reluctant and imperfect characters that God chose to become leaders for holy tasks. God worked His providence and purpose through each of them and bids you also as a leader in this time to become a partner in building the Kingdom of God.

Leading From Our Knees is a daily roadmap to guide you as you tackle the tasks of leadership that God has given you to do. It will help you identify and understand your own calling more clearly and help you gain confidence from the fact that whatever situation or challenge you are going through in these days, the great saints of the faith experienced also.

Leading From Our Knees lists for you forty-seven categories of the faith experience with their corresponding lessons found within the book. Use this category listing as a resource to assist you in your own special time of need.

Special occasions of the calendar-year are noted and cross-referenced by page number so that you can find inspiration and new meaning for each of those notable dates.

Virtually every leader and supporting character of the Bible is portrayed through the daily lessons and can be located through the character index in the back of the book.

Use this book as a teaching or study guide or as your own personal daily devotional. Use it as a quick desk reference to help you confront and overcome the spiritual burdens that will arise in the course of your own leadership responsibilities.

Each daily lesson has its own title and sub-title that will provoke your spiritual curiosity. Every lesson is anchored in scripture. While the lessons were not written in chronological scriptural order, they are listed in sequence by chapter and verse in the book beginning with Genesis and proceeding through Revelation. This sequential placement of the lessons allows you quick access to your favorite character, story or scripture and gives you a chance to read a leadership lesson from all sixty-six books of the Bible.

Note that for each day's lesson there is a written featured scripture and a referenced background scripture for you to look up in your own Bible. By reading both the featured scripture and background scripture for each day, you will substantially read through the entire Bible over the course of the year.

The text of each lesson ties the scripture to an appropriate biblical precept and leadership lesson of faith. At the bottom of each page is a suggested prayer that relates to the day's lesson. Allow this daily prayer to unlock the Holy Spirit's voice within you as you read it. Each daily devotional can be read in as little as five minutes or when meditated upon and cross-referenced with your own bible, can be completed in about twenty minutes.

The creation of *Leading From Our Knees* was God's call to me and was written over the course of six and a half years. Many days I felt as if God was the author, and I was merely His scribe. As I studied and wrote, I could feel God extracting and intertwining the lessons I learned through forty years of Christian lay-study with my own personal leadership experiences. Insights for the lessons were drawn from my own leadership success and failure as well as from my observation of the hundreds of diverse leaders that I have encountered throughout my life.

I feel a kinship with so many of the characters and situations in the book. Some days I am that fallen and repentant leader and other days I am the brave warrior equipped with new hope and confidence. But in every circumstance I am a leader in constant need of Christ's daily power and special provision.

Often we are called to leadership battles for which we will never see the earthly victory. Yet through it all we have a holy obligation to serve others. And as we serve others faithfully, God affirmatively moves each of us into new roles of providential leadership for Him.

We are all imperfect and fragile. We will fail and make mistakes, even as we disappoint others and fall short of our goals. But we are capable of accomplishing so much more than our human mind can comprehend. For the God who calls us to our task of leadership is awesome, powerful, loving and redeeming. The Trinity of God is active in our life today and can be found in every human event and circumstance.

It is through the actions of leaders of faith, great and small alike, that the holy work of the heavenly purpose is unveiled. And if all that you do in your journey as a leader is grounded in humility, devotion and pure love towards our Savior and His children; then it will surely yield those fruits of eternal success and reward.

I give thanks and praise to God for allowing me to be part of this project. It was a humbling and life-changing experience for me to be the vessel that brings *Leading From Our Knees* to you today.

It is now my prayer and great hope that something in this work will comfort you, inspire you and lead you towards finding God's peace in your own life and leadership journey. Let each of us as leaders of faith allow Christ's love to be manifested in us so that we can shower it upon others through our humble acts of service each day. Remember, that as leaders of faith, we bring our sweetest praise to the Father, Son and Holy Spirit when we are obediently leading from our knees.

A Contract With Creation

"Leaders of All Descriptions Have a Sacred Contract with Creation"

"And God created great whales, and every living creature that moveth…and God saw that it was good…. And God remembered Noah, and every living thing…. I establish my covenant with you, and with your seed after you; And with every living creature that is with you…. Gird up now thy loins like a man; for I will demand of thee and answer thou me. Where wast thou when I laid the foundations of the earth? Declare, if thou hast understanding…. All things were made by him; and without him was not any thing made that was made."

Featured Scriptures: Genesis 1:21; 8:1; 9:9–10; Job 38:3–4; and John 1:3
Background Scriptures: Genesis 6—9:15; Job 38—41; Matthew 10:29; and Matthew 6:28–29

God is a Creator of design and intricacy. God is fiercely proud and protective of His creation. In fact, after finishing each great work, God went to great lengths to declare them good. Later, He commanded Noah to save them from the extinction of the Great Flood. After the Flood, God not only made a covenant with man that He would never destroy us in such a manner again, but He also made that same covenant with the creatures He had made.

In God's later speeches to Job (see Job 38—41), God declared that no man, even Job, could begin to fathom the complexity and miraculous design of crocodiles, hippos, goats, and the like. In the Book of Matthew, Christ said that not even a sparrow could fall without His knowledge. He also tells us in the Book of Luke that the lilies of the field, through no effort of their own, are more glorious than Solomon in all of his wealth and glory. Jesus tells us that the heavenly Father feeds the ravens. According to the Book of John, Christ Himself was an active participant in the creation of everything that was made.

God is serious about what He has made. God gave man dominion over His creation, but that gift and responsibility is itself a sacred trust, especially for leaders who in some way manage natural resources. What God entrusts to you, He will require an accounting for, especially from leaders of faith who are given explicit responsibilities. If God made a covenant with the creatures and gave us dominion over them, are we not then the very trustees of God's sacred creation?

Leadership of any kind will ultimately require us to interface with creation. Many times our decisions are tough, and the leadership choices in a demanding world and marketplace are not pleasant to make. As a single species vanishes, the very thumbprint of the Creator is wiped away. Leaders of faith should seek God's voice and guidance as we manage the precious assets created by the hand of God.

Keeping our contract with God to protect His creation will put us directly into conflict with man and institutions of power, money, and greed. It will require great courage to resist profits over protecting the vulnerable habitats and creatures that God made and declared good. God is watching and will judge each of us for how well we kept our part of the sacred contract to care for the things He has made.

Our Prayer: *Lord, Creator of heaven and earth, we marvel at what Your hand has created. We praise You that You have given us dominion over it. You said that not a single sparrow falls from the sky without Your knowledge. Help us to know that we are but the custodians of a sacred covenant You have with all You created.* **Amen.**

Generation To Generation

"PASSING OUR ORAL HISTORY AND LIVING LEGACY TO ANOTHER GENERATION"

"This is the book of the generations of Adam. In the day that God created man, in the likeness of God made he him; male and female created he them; and blessed them, and called their name Adam, in the day when they were created."

FEATURED SCRIPTURE: GENESIS 5:12

BACKGROUND SCRIPTURE: GENESIS 5

The passing down of the history of faith is illustrated in the fifth chapter of Genesis. From Adam to Noah, we see the longevity of man prior to the Great Flood. Patriarchs lived hundreds of years and were able to convey history and oral tradition to generations of new family members. Noah and his sons' future generations were then able to pass along God's history to Moses, the great author and leader of the faith, who recorded these accounts of in the Book of Genesis.

God has instilled into every generation of each family on earth the ability to pass along the traditions of our faith. Even amid great floods, wars, calamities, and genocides, the resilience of man and the miracle of the human spirit has passed the essence of history and faith to each of us. Each leader of faith is somehow the by-product of oral history and generational legacy passed down from our parents of old. It is especially incumbent upon each of us as leaders of faith to be purveyors of our own history.

Oral history and leadership examples must survive in each generation and be passed along. Sharing our stories and history with family and friends is part of keeping the chain alive. Identifying apprentices and instilling in our congregations and institutions the value of our history and our legendary leaders is tantamount to continued success. Leaders of faith today must be affirmative and prepare for the passing of history, knowledge, and faith to future generations. We should keep good written records, maps, photos, and, most especially, good oral tradition. Good storytelling etches into the soul like no other form of communication. When a mother or father tells a family story to a child over and over, it becomes part of that child's being. We find ourselves telling our children the same stories over and over until they become part of their souls.

God intended us to not only lead others, but to pass along the faith to future generations. It takes planning and discipline, but it is a requirement for truly successful leaders. Find new and imaginative ways to pass along the lessons of your life and work. Leave the clutter and competition of life's hustle and take a trip with your family or team members to a remote place. Tell stories around the table or in front of a warm fire. Use humor to pass a lesson along.

Pray for your children and followers. Honor those who have gone on before you. Honor the saints and give tribute to all generations. Make memorials and special occasions mean something special in your organization. Pay tribute to those who have sacrificed so that you may live. Honoring them is also part of passing on the faith. And passing on the faith is our solemn duty to God.

Our Prayer: *God of all generations, we give thanks for those who came before us. We give thanks for Adam, Abraham, Noah, and Moses. We give thanks for Ruth, Esther, Elisabeth, and Mary. We give thanks for our families and fellow workers. Instill in us a passion to pass along the faith and history of our lives and organizations to others. Make our passing of history be used to build the Kingdom of Heaven.* **Amen.**

Building To God's Specifications

"After Receiving the Call, We Must Execute According to God's Plan"

"Make thee an ark of gopher wood; rooms shalt thou make in the ark, and shalt pitch it within and without with pitch. And this is the fashion which thou shalt make it of: The length of the ark shall be three hundred cubits, the breadth of it fifty cubits, and the height of it thirty cubits. A window shalt thou make to the ark, and in a cubit shalt thou finish it above; and the door of the ark shalt thou set in the side thereof; with lower, second, and third stories shalt thou make it."

Featured Scripture: Genesis 6:14–16
Background Scripture: Genesis 6; and 2 Peter 3:1–7

Many persons who hear a call from God fail to follow the specifications for success. When we as leaders of faith receive a call from God for a holy task here on this earth, we should always pray to receive the full set of instructions before beginning the labor. When God called Noah to build the ark, God was clear to set forth the detailed specifications by which it was to be built. Noah followed God's specifications to the letter, and the mission was successful.

If Noah had cut corners and made the ark a little shorter or a little narrower, it would not have held all the species of animals that God wanted to save. If Noah had failed to build the window as God commanded, he would not have been able to release the dove to determine if dry land had been found. If Noah had not applied the pitch inside and outside the ark, water would have seeped into the ark, drowning Noah and his family.

Specifications matter! When we receive a call to do a job for God, we must follow the charts and rules. We must immerse ourselves in the technical and vocational training necessary to go and do what God wants us to do. We cannot preach without study of and meditation upon God's Word. We cannot lead a business without knowing the products and services we offer. We cannot lead governments and constituents if we do not know the laws and customs of our land. Leaders of faith should be consummate learners and seekers of knowledge. If we are faithful and search diligently for an instruction guide for our calling, we shall surely find it.

Those whom God calls to His service will be equipped with what they need to know. Be diligent and patient to take each new step and every new day with faith and purpose. Seek out elders and experts. Read the Scriptures and research your topics well. Get out among those you are called to serve; listen to them and garner their thoughts and opinions of how the organization needs to be built. Learn from your own mistakes and failures of the past. Use the successful examples of your competitors and rivals as a page of your new specification for success.

God will get you through the difficult process of construction. Pick the right team members and tools. Seek holy resources and work methodically on your task. When you follow God's specifications in your calling, you will survive the rain, the floodwaters, and the wind. God will send the dove back to tell you when the journey is ending successfully.

Our Prayer: *God of Creation, we praise You for creating us and saving us from the rains and the floods of this life. We give thanks for Noah and his obedience to follow Your specifications in building the ark and saving creation. Create in us, O Lord, a patience and ability to follow Your every instruction in our calling. Show us how to get through every task that You give us to do this very day.* **Amen.**

Altars To God

"LEADERS BUILD ALTARS TO GOD THROUGH CONTINUAL PRAISE AND GOOD WORKS"

"And Noah built an altar unto the LORD.… And the LORD smelled a sweet savor.…
And the LORD said unto Moses… An altar of earth thou shalt make unto me.… And
David built there an altar unto the LORD.… By Him let us offer the sacrifice of praise
to God continually, that is the fruit of our lips giving thanks to his name. But to do
good…for with such sacrifices God is well pleased."

FEATURED SCRIPTURES: GENESIS 8:20–21; EXODUS 20:24; 2 SAMUEL 24:25; AND HEBREWS 13:15–16
BACKGROUND SCRIPTURES: GENESIS 8:20–23; EXODUS 20; 2 SAMUEL 24; AND HEBREWS 13:7–16

Noah, Moses, and David all built altars to God. Noah built an altar to God in acknowledgment of God's deliverance of a remnant of man and each species of animal from the Flood.
Moses built an earthen altar without silver or gold. The earthen altar had no stairs and nothing
else that would allow the people to worship the materials instead of the God who had saved
them. Moses received the Law from God and offered this altar as holy ground. David bought
the threshing floor on Mount Moriah from Araunah for fifty shekels of silver and turned it
into an altar of intercession and repentance of his own sin of commanding a census. David's
altar on Mount Moriah staved off the angel of pestilence and became the site of the eventual
holy Temple of Jerusalem.

Altars are places where we offer sacrifices to God. Altars are places that commemorate God's
blessing and deliverance. Altars are holy points of reference where we can rally those we lead to
enter into a new state of relationship with a holy God. Leaders of faith in all ages are called to the
altar. The cross and empty tomb have become the altars of saints and leaders of faith. Today, we
are to offer God the sacrifice of continual praise and good works among those whom God has
called us to lead. The fruit of our lips should be the praise of Jesus. Building an altar of praise
pleases God, as did the altars of old.

We build our altars to God when we praise Him in both defeat and victory. We build altars to
God when we do something for a stranger in Jesus' name. Christ has already won our victory,
and no earthly event or life condition we endure can change the fact that Christ has overcome
the world. So it pleases God for our altars of today to be those spontaneous "hallelujahs" to God
for His gifts to us, as well as our service to those in need around us.

As a leader of faith, when we stop to acknowledge Christ in our work and give Him the glory
for our strength and achievement, we are building an altar to God. As we make Christ our
central focus in those institutions where we have been called to lead, we are building spiritual
altars to God that allows others to find their way to Jesus. Build your altar today. Praise God for
Christ, and perform your good works to those you are called to serve. Then, the savor from this
altar of faith will become a sweet-smelling fragrance to the Lord above.

Our Prayer: *Lord, we build an altar to You today as we pause to praise Your holy name and give
thanks for the unspeakable gift of Jesus. The sacrifice of Jesus is the last and best sacrifice, which
liberates us from all sin. We shout "Hosanna in the highest" on this day at this very place, and offer
all our good works upon this spiritual altar of the cross to You, God.* **Amen.**

The Babel Of Leadership

"Why God Confounds and Scatters Leaders and Followers"

"And they said, Go to, let us build us a city and a tower whose top may reach unto heaven; and let us make us a name, lest we be scattered abroad upon the face of the whole earth.… And the Lord came down to see the city and the tower, which the children of men builded.… And the Lord said… Go to, let us go down, and there confound their language, that they may not understand one another's speech. So the Lord scattered them abroad from thence upon the face of all the earth: and they left off to build the city."

Featured Scriptures: Genesis 11:4, 5, 6–8
Background Scripture: Genesis 11:1–9

The three sons of Noah and their descendants had the great responsibility to go out, be fruitful, and replenish the earth. It was their time to claim the promise and protection of God. They held the great covenant God made with Noah and the earth. But in today's lesson, we see how the people wanted something else. Somewhere in the plain between the Tigris and Euphrates rivers, the descendants of Noah decided to build a great city and a tower that would reach heaven itself. They did not want to scatter as God desired them to; they wanted collective power and achievement.

God railed at the thought that His people would choose the security and celebration of their own ingenuity and ideas over His plan and providence. God struck the people so that their single language disappeared, thus cutting them off from building their city. The acts of God confused them, forcing them to pick up, scatter abroad, and build in new, strange lands. God made sure that His commandment to the people to be fruitful and multiply throughout the earth was kept.

As leaders of faith, we often see the Babel of confusion in our own organizations, governments, and congregations. We relish in our own success and ingenuity. We even build buildings and monuments to celebrate our success. It is in those times that we begin to feel a sense of lordship over our own destiny. In order to protect our way of life, we build walls of security and shun new risks in order to protect what we have accumulated. It is in these times God will strike us with new confusion.

God will judge us and those we lead whenever we veer from the essence of His calling for us. As we lead others in God's providence, it requires that we separate, scatter, and try new things. It requires that we learn new ideas and travel to distant places. God wants us to scatter, and He multiplies His blessings as we minister in new ways to new people.

When our success has been stifled and our followers scattered, perhaps God is calling us into a new obedience. By our scattering and the multiplying of His gifts and the Good News, God assures that we are sharing the Kingdom of God with all the earth. Don't hoard or build towers to your own success and ingenuity. As leaders of faith in our own situations of Babel, exercise a new scattering and multiplying of Christ's gift of love and peace for all the earth to see.

Our Prayer: *Dear God, help us to know that when You make a covenant with us as leaders of faith, we must obey. Forgive us when we are timid to scatter and multiply our works with others. Forgive us and help us avoid the dreadful mistake of celebrating our own greatness or success. Make Your way known to us and give us the provision to be fruitful leaders who excel in multiplying good works for the faith.* **Amen.**

Leaving Home And The Familiar

"Answering the Call of Faith Sometimes Means Leaving Home and Family"

"Now the Lord had said unto Abram, Get thee out of thy country, and from thy kindred, and from thy father's house, unto a land that I will show thee: And I will make of thee a great nation, and I will bless thee, and make thy name great and thou shall be a blessing…. By faith Abraham, when he was called to go out into a place…obeyed; went out not knowing whither he went. By faith he sojourned in the land of promise, as in a strange country…."

Featured Scriptures: Genesis 12:1–2; and Hebrews 11:8–9
Background Scriptures: Genesis 11:27—12:5; Nehemiah 9:7–8; Acts 7:1–6; and Hebrews 11:8–12

The three great monotheistic faiths call Abraham their father. The faith progeny of Abraham are indeed many. Abraham's life and faith shine forth even in our world today as they have for centuries. However, the great impact of Abraham's life of faith begins with his answer to a difficult call, one of the toughest a person may ever receive. That call is the call of God to leave your own home, family, country, and inheritance and to go far away into the unknown in obedience and faith.

Many a missionary, soldier, student, diplomat, merchant, teacher, explorer, and pastor have heard this same call of God and answered it affirmatively. God calls some leaders of faith to leave home and family to go abroad and serve others. This call can be a painful one as it often involves leaving those we love the most to travel into the unknown. Writers throughout the Scriptures remember and praise the faith of Abraham in answering his call to leave home in obedience to God's call. But God never calls us away without having a great promise for us, a promise that will bless us and our work not only in this day, but throughout generations to come.

Sometimes our call is simply to leave our familiar surroundings and familiar routines. We are called to leave our community of friends and the certainties of this day for God's unknown promise of tomorrow. But we can claim dominion over the uncertainties of tomorrow through our faith in God's call and provision. Most leadership journeys of faith begin with the reality of leaving the certainty and comfort of old congregations and organizations behind us. It means going into a new field of work or a strange profession or embarking on a new educational experience. It may mean leaving behind the certainty of a pension, promotion, or "safe" career. Answering this call usually means leaving something behind.

The promise of Abraham was not realized overnight. He had to travel many treacherous miles over many days to get to his new land. He encountered obstacles and hostilities along the way. Our own call from God to leave home and the familiar will be full of setbacks and hardships. We will need constant faith and a daily prayerful reliance on God's provision to get us through to our next safe passage.

But God has already gone before us preparing the way. New friends and new opportunities await us. Blessings are already beginning to sprout up in that new place, which will affirm upon our arrival that we are the chosen and faithful of the Almighty and His holy call.

Our Prayer: *God of Abraham, You are our God and our salvation. We hear Your call to us today. Give us the faith and courage to answer Your call to leave home and the familiar. Prepare the way for us and bring us blessings and a new confidence as we obediently serve others in strange places in Your name.* **Amen.**

Delivered From Our Own Poor Choices

"Leaders with a Clear Mission Can Make Cowardly Mistakes and Still Fulfill a Promise of God"

"And I will bless them that bless thee, and curse him that curseth thee: in thee shall all families of the earth be blessed. So Abram departed, as the Lord had spoken unto him.… Say I pray thee, thou art my sister: that it may be well with me for thy sake; and my soul shall live because of thee.… And Abraham said of Sarah his wife, She is my sister, and Abimelech king of Gerar sent, and took Sarah."

Featured Scriptures: Genesis 12:3–4, 13; and 20:2
Background Scriptures: Genesis 12; 20; 21:1–3

Abram became Abraham with a promise from God that he would become the father of many nations. He was given the absolute blessing of God's anointing and protection. While Abraham was faithful, he made poor choices that caused him to stumble along the way. In Genesis 12 and 20, we read that Abraham lost his courage and made poor choices twice when confronted with seemingly life-threatening odds. However, God—true to His promise—protected Abraham and Sarah. Our lesson today shows us that we should claim God's power in all circumstances and not succumb to poor choices.

Abraham was the newly anointed leader of God's nation. Yet, along the way in his journey, his beautiful wife, Sarah, was noticed and became physically desired by Pharaoh and his sons. Later again, Sarah's beauty would be desired by King Abimelech. Our Scripture today shows us how Abraham told a half-lie to save his own life and get out of what appeared to be a hopeless situation. By passing his wife off as his sister, he hoped to not be killed, even though the choices he made could have foiled God's plan. However, God did not allow Abraham's fear or poor decision to affect His promise to Abraham. God delivered both Abraham and Sarah by His power.

God often delivers leaders of faith from their own bad choices. Often we are given a strong mandate and anointing by God to lead others. Yet, along the way, we suddenly find ourselves confronted head-on with seemingly impossible odds. It is in these times that we may feel compelled to make compromised choices. Instead of claiming God's promise and power in such impossible circumstances, we often make seemingly cowardly and meek decisions intended for self-preservation. But we, too, can save heart. God can still deliver us from our bad choices.

Abraham could have boldly declared Sarah to be his wife in both of these tough confrontations. When they stood in his way, Abraham could have told both Pharaoh and the king to move aside by God's power. God would have delivered him just the same. But to God, a promise is a promise. Like Abraham, all of God's chosen leaders are imperfect and will make poor choices from time to time. But we can still be blessed. God will work His plan in all our circumstances.

Be bold and fierce when confronted with the impossible circumstance. The promise and victory is already yours. Claim victory this day over every tough circumstance in Jesus' name!

Our Prayer: *O God, help us to know that Your promises of blessing and protection are all-powerful. Help us to claim those promises boldly and to never yield to fear when confronted with tough choices. We praise You and claim Your power. Forgive us when we make poor choices as leaders. Bless us even as You blessed Abraham. Empower us to serve others boldly in faith.* **Amen.**

Leaders In The Order Of Melchizedek

"Being Both a Leader and a Priest Called for a Special Purpose"

"And Melchizedek king of Salem brought forth bread and wine: and he was the priest of the most High God.... For every high priest taken from among men is ordained for men in things pertaining to God, that he may offer both gifts and sacrifices for sins: Who can have compassion on the ignorant, and on them that are out of the way; for he himself is compassed with infirmity."

Featured Scriptures: Genesis 14:18; and Hebrews 5:1–2
Background Scriptures: Psalm 110:4; and Hebrews 5:1–10; 7: 1–3

Christ Himself was both a king and a priest. Christ was from the tribe of Judah, not the Levites. The Levite tribe was the priestly tribe. Therefore, Christ was a chosen, ordained, eternal priest set aside by God Himself. Melchizedek came to Abram after a battle to offer bread and wine, which later became the sacraments of our faith. Melchizedek was not born into the line of priests; he was a leader who was given an even greater duty by God.

Jesus, like Melchizedek, did not have the proper pedigree to be an earthly priest. The calling of Jesus was to become *"a priest for ever after the order of Melchisedec"* (Hebrews 5:6). This unique line of priesthood is called for a special purpose. This line of priesthood is unique, without father or mother, without descent. This line is the line of sacrifice and offering. This line of priesthood is ordained to serve men for God's purposes. This line of priesthood is called to minister with compassion. These priests become suffering servants who will confront the evils of man and offer the gift of salvation to all.

Leadership journeys of faith are journeys of calling by God. If you are called by God to lead for His purposes; you, too, become a leader or priest not unlike Melchizedek. Most leaders of faith don't have leadership backgrounds or special pedigrees. Leaders of faith are called not to power, but to service and sacrifice for others.

When we answer a calling to leadership from God, we must be obedient to where that calling takes us. For some leaders, their journey is short and earthly in nature. But for us, in a priestly line of leadership, our journey is an eternal journey. For the things we do in our ministry of leadership have been ordained by God to yield eternal fruit. We may not know it, or realize it at the time we do it, but every action done under God's anointing in your leadership journey can become a priestly act to others in Christ's name.

You may not have known you could become a priestly leader in the order of Melchizedek, but you can—with God's calling and ordination! Jesus taught us how by His eternal sacrifice for mankind. Let us lead by that example in the order of Melchizedek.

Our Prayer: *Lord God, we praise You for giving us the Great Priest of Melchizedek, Your Son, Jesus. His example of sacrifice of privilege and position to come and minister to us guides us in our way. Give us the power and courage to become leaders in the order and example of Melchizedek, so we can give and sacrifice and add to Your eternal kingdom.* **Amen.**

Leaders Should Avoid Becoming Obligated

"LEADERS OF FAITH SHOULD AVOID UNHOLY GIFTS AND OBLIGATIONS"

"And Abram said to the king of Sodom, I have lift up mine hand unto the LORD, the most high God, the possessor of heaven and earth, That I will not take from a thread even to a shoe latchet, and that I will not take any thing that is thine, lest thou shouldest say, I have made Abram rich."

FEATURED SCRIPTURE: GENESIS 14:21–22
BACKGROUND SCRIPTURE: GENESIS 14:8—15:1

Abram, not yet Abraham, had gone to rescue his nephew Lot, who had been captured by a group of warring local kings. Lot and his people and possessions had been captured by an evil alliance. Lot had been living in the area of Sodom. When Abram heard his kinsman had been captured, he took his best servants, raised from his own house, and went out on a rescue mission. Abram's small army came, divided, and defeated the enemy. Abram rescued Lot, his goods, and his people. Mission accomplished.

The king of Sodom's army had been defeated by the same kings who had captured Lot. So by avenging for Lot, Abram had defeated the foes of the king of Sodom. Sodom was a place of sinfulness. But the king of Sodom came to Abram to offer him tribute for killing his enemies. He offered Abram payment of gifts for his efforts. Abram refused the king's request. Abram knew that by accepting the tribute and payment from the king of Sodom, he could be seen as being obligated to him. Abram wanted no one to ever attribute his wealth to an earthly king, especially to the king of Sodom.

Abram knew his provision was from God, and his obligation was solely to the Lord. Abram knew that his duty in this situation was to rescue his kinfolk. By refusing the riches of the king of Sodom, Abram lifted God up and showed faith in God's provision and His reward alone. Abram avoided a bad obligation that might later hurt his ability to lead.

As leaders of faith, we can learn a great lesson from Abram. When we are called to God's service and are anointed for His purposes, He alone is worthy of praise and He alone will make our provision and reward. When we allow unscrupulous persons and institutions to give us tribute and rewards for what we are already called to do in God's name, we can become obligated to the wrong persons for the wrong reasons. Had Abram taken tribute from Sodom, he would have been yoked with a sinful kingdom and his witness would have been diminished.

Even when we are running low on resources or are in need of affirmation from others, we should be careful to whom we allow ourselves to become obligated. Even sending the signal that our success is attributable to someone other than God, or that we are obligated to something or someone of questionable repute, can limit our effectiveness in leadership.

Our Prayer: *Lord, the possessor of heaven and earth, we are called to Your service. We lift You up as our sole caller and sustainer in this journey. Help us to resist the temptation to take gifts or accolades from sources that could obligate us or give false appearances. You are our shield and reward. May our witness be pure.* **Amen.**

Finding The Righteous Among The Evil

"God Helps Leaders Who Intercede to Salvage People and Projects"

"And the LORD said, Because the cry of Sodom and Gomorrah is great, and because their sin is very grievous; I will go down now, and see.… And Abraham drew near and said, Wilt thou also destroy the righteous with the wicked? Peradventure there be fifty righteous within the city: wilt thou also destroy and not spare the place for the fifty righteous that are therein? And the LORD said, If I find in Sodom fifty righteous within the city, then I will spare all the place for their sakes."

FEATURED SCRIPTURE: GENESIS 18:20, 23–24, 28
BACKGROUND SCRIPTURES: GENESIS 18:17–33; AND GENESIS 19

Abraham was freshly appointed in his role as the chosen leader of God's new nation. God and His angels were about to deal with the wickedness of Sodom and Gomorrah. Sodom and Gomorrah were known throughout the region in their time as being the most perverse and sinful places around. God was testing Abraham to see if he would be an intercessor on behalf of others.

Abraham did not disappoint. He indeed went to God to seek His mercy for the cities. Abraham offered to find the righteous among the wicked and appealed to God for their sake in hopes that He would spare the destruction He had planned. Abraham negotiated with God to find just fifty righteous, and if he could God agreed to spare the cities. In the end, Abraham could not find any righteous there. The cancer of sin had consumed the cities. Yet, Abraham pleased God, in that he showed love for the lost and the righteous by attempting to spare them from their assured destruction.

In our own leadership journeys of faith, we, too, come to points where we are merely doing salvage work with bad projects. The project or organization is so sick, so injured, that we must find what little good left in it to justify saving the whole. It often takes great love or commitment by us as leaders of faith to not destroy bad appendages of the organizations we lead. In these times, we should reach out to God for His guidance and providence as to how to find the righteousness left in the rottenness.

God cannot tolerate unrepentant sin. However, God desires that none perish. God sends leaders of faith into Sodom and Gomorrah situations every day to seek and glean what good and righteous thing may be left in dying places. Like Abraham, we may have to set the bar low in order to find righteousness and goodness, but the Lord desires that we try. Great leaders don't give up on hopeless situations before harvesting what is good and noble first. It is part of our calling as leaders of faith to find the righteous among the evil.

Our Prayer: *Dear Lord, Your eyes cry for the sin and debauchery in the world. You called Abraham, and You have called us as leaders of faith to go into bad places and situations to find what goodness may still exist in them. May we endeavor to be faithful to our calling, and seek the salvation of the lost, and lift up the righteousness we find, even among the evil.* **Amen.**

Giving Up On Your Most Precious Possession

"A Great Act of Love Is Giving Up Those You Love to the Service of Others"

"And he said, Take now thy son, thine only son Isaac, whom thou lovest, and get thee into the land of Moriah; and offer him there for a burnt offering upon one of the mountains which I will tell thee of.… And He said…now I know that thou fearest God, seeing thou hast not withheld thy son, thine only son from me.… In this was manifested the love of God, but that he loved us and sent his Son to be the propitiation for our sins."

FEATURED SCRIPTURES: GENESIS 22:2, 12; AND 1 JOHN 4:9
BACKGROUND SCRIPTURES: GENESIS 22:1–18; JOHN 3:16; AND 1 JOHN 4:7–10

Behind every leader-servant is a person who is making the ultimate gift in the name of service. Those persons are the mothers and fathers, spouses, family members, and special friends who send their loved ones into leadership and service for others each day. Like we read in today's Scripture lesson, it may mean the willingness to sacrifice the very life of your loved one for others. Or that sacrifice may mean lost time and missed joys with loved ones because they are off serving others.

The sacrifice in leadership journeys of faith begins in homes and in communities as people of great love send their most precious possessions off to military service, mission fields, or public service. The chain of leadership begins here with this offering of our loved ones to the service of others. God will bless those who give in this manner as part of a heavenly calling.

The *"Angel of the Lord"* who appeared to Abraham was the preincarnate Christ. Christ rewarded Abraham's faithfulness in his offering of Isaac. In the time to follow, this same Christ would leave the paradise of heaven and His heavenly Father to come to earth to serve us. God pronounced His satisfaction with the His offering of His only Son. God never asks us to make a sacrifice He has not already made for us. Just the obedience we show to God by allowing our loved ones to serve and lead others can bring blessings to our own families.

Leaders of faith should recognize from today's lesson that the answer to our own calling is significant, but that the sacrifice of our loved ones in giving us up for service is noble in itself. We should seek those loved ones out, thank them, acknowledge their selflessness in allowing us to serve. It may mean taking special time to love a child who gives up a mom or dad for a day or week or year. It may mean sacrificing your free time to reward them with a special event. It may mean one day giving them up to the service of others.

Giving up our prized possessions to the leadership and service of others is a profound act of love. *"In this was manifested the love of God toward us, because God sent his only begotten Son into the world that we might live through Him"* (1 John 4:9).

Our Prayer: *Dear heavenly Father, You showed us Your love by this great gift of Your only Son. We praise You! You also set an example for us to follow when we give our loved ones to the service and leadership of others. If we are the ones to leave, comfort our loved ones as we go away to serve. Protect them, reassure them, and cover them with Your love and assurance that their gift is worthy and appreciated and will become an eternal blessing to many.* **Amen.**

A Deal Is A Deal Regardless Of The Circumstances

"WHEN GOD CHOOSES YOU AND ORDAINS YOU FOR A TASK, HE KEEPS THE DEAL"

"And, behold, I am with thee, and will keep thee in all places wither thou goest, and will bring thee again into this land; for I will not leave thee, until I have done that which I have spoken to thee of.… And God appeared unto Jacob again.… And God said unto him, Thy name is Jacob, but Israel shall be thy name.…"

FEATURED SCRIPTURES: GENESIS 28:15; GENESIS 35:9–10
BACKGROUND SCRIPTURES: GENESIS 28:10–22; GENESIS 35:1–15

The life journey of Jacob provides a fascinating look at love, jealousy, deception, revenge, and courage. But most of all, the life of Jacob demonstrates how God keeps his promises; how He heaps blessings on those He chooses for tasks of leadership. With God, *a deal is a deal regardless of the circumstances* that come along.

Esau, not Jacob, was the rightful son to receive the blessing of Isaac. It was by deception and cheating that the birthright of Esau passed to Jacob. By selling his birthright for pottage and through Jacob and his mother's craftiness, Jacob received the blessing. Jacob later lived in guilt and fear as a result of these events, but he eventually reconciled with his brother and kept God's commandments. Through all circumstances, Jacob received the blessing of God.

Jacob's own sons committed some bloody deeds, and Jacob lived and traveled among some dangerous local inhabitants. His life was long and trying, but through all of it God was faithful to keep His promise to build a mighty nation through Jacob.

In our own journeys of faith, even when we feel the true calling from God for a leadership mission, circumstances can overwhelm us. We often see obstacle after obstacle come into our paths that seemingly pose for us insurmountable odds. Certain individuals in our lives can become vexatious and hostile to our success. It is in these times that many of us come to doubt our calling and wonder if God called us to fail rather than succeed.

In all circumstances God is there for us. We may not see His providence in bad situations, but He is there. God will find ways to validate His love and blessing to us just as He did with Jacob. Even if we don't have dreams and see angels, God will send messengers and events our way to give us assurance of His presence. He will speak to us as we seek Him in prayer and study. His still, small voice will speak to us when we need it most. The clouds will part and the sun will rise, and we will know that the God who called us to the task will complete it in us and through us by His might. With God, a deal is a deal through all life's circumstances.

Our Prayer: *Dear God, thank You for Jacob, and thank You for Israel. Thank You that Your promises and blessings are true and real. We pray for ongoing confirmation of Your calling for our lives. Forgive us when we doubt. Guide us and bless us through all unpleasant events and circumstances in our leadership journeys.* **Amen.**

Faith And Love Trump A Broken Deal

"How a Raw Deal Becomes a Blessing of a Nation Thanks to a Leader's Love and Faith"

"And Jacob served seven years for Rachel; and they seemed unto him but a few days, for the love he had to her…. And it came to pass, that in the morning, behold, it was Leah and he said to Laban, What is this thou has done unto me? Did not I serve with thee for Rachel? Wherefore then hast thou beguiled me?"

Featured Scripture: Genesis 29:20, 25
Background Scriptures: Genesis 28:10–22; and Genesis 29—30

Jacob, son of Isaac, had received God's covenant blessing and had journeyed to a new land to live with his extended family in the house of Laban. Jacob was a hard worker, and for Jacob's sake, God blessed the house of Laban. Jacob loved Rachel, Laban's younger daughter. Laban offered her to Jacob in marriage if he would but serve him for seven years. Jacob made a deal and served Laban seven years. But on Jacob's wedding night, Laban slipped his eldest daughter, Rachel's sister, Leah, into Jacob's bedchamber as a substitute wife. After seven years of service from Jacob, Laban broke the deal they had made.

How betrayed Jacob must have felt by this broken deal. Jacob had toiled hard for seven years to get to the final moment of love and fruition, but it brought him only disappointment and embarrassment. In our own leadership journeys, we, too, experience heartbreak from deals broken by those we trust. How should we react when that happens to us?

Laban, knowing he broke the deal, offered a weak excuse and promises to Jacob that he might have Rachel's hand, as well as handmaidens from both sisters. Laban's broken deal caused pain to his daughters and to Jacob. But because of the love and faith of Jacob, God kept a promise and made good come from seeming disappointment.

From the marriages of Leah and Rachel to Jacob, plus their handmaidens, sprang forth the twelve sons of Jacob, and thus the twelve tribes of Israel. God used the broken deal of Laban to create His great nation and fulfill His covenant because of Jacob's love, resolve, and faith.

The lesson today for leaders of faith is that if we remain in God's plan for our life of service, God can take our broken deals and the betrayal of others and use them to build His Kingdom. Like Jacob, we must be guided by true love, loyalty, and a sense that if we do what we are called to do, God Almighty will make it right in the end.

In our calling to the leadership of faith, many events will go amiss and, as it did for Jacob, hurt and embarrass many persons in the process. But when God's hand is upon your life and you remain faithful to Him, showers of blessings will come down upon every broken event and every misfortune.

Our Prayer: *Dear God of Jacob, help us to always know that You are a God who keeps promises and fulfills every covenant. Help us to know that we are to be true and serve You and others with great love and faith. You will bless us for Jacob's sake if we remain steadfast to the tasks You give us to do.* **Amen.**

Leading Through The Adversity of Betrayal

"Succeeding When Circumstances and People Betray Us"

"And it came to pass after these things, that his master's wife cast her eyes upon Joseph; and she said, lie with me. But he refused…as she spoke to Joseph day by day, that he hearkened not unto her, to lie by her, or to be with her…and she spoke…the Hebrew servant, which thou hast brought unto us, came in unto me to mock me. *But the Lord was with Joseph*, and showed him mercy, and gave him favor.…"

Featured Scripture: Genesis 39:7–8, 10, 17, 21

Background Scripture: Genesis 39

Joseph had had a long, arduous journey to his pinnacle of leadership. First, he was betrayed by his own brothers. He was sold into slavery by his brothers to a caravan of traders. He was sold again to the Egyptian officer Potiphar and his adulterous wife. Along each step of Joseph's journey, *"the Lord was with Joseph."* And in every tough circumstance, Joseph was obedient to those who had authority over him. But in Potiphar's wife's repeated attempts to cause Joseph to commit adultery with her, Joseph resisted the call to sin. Even when Joseph was propositioned numerous times by her, he was faithful to his tasks and loyal to his master, Potiphar, and God's commandments.

The refusal of Joseph to betray Potiphar made him the target of betrayal by Potiphar's wife, and ultimately Potiphar himself. It was Joseph's own goodness and loyalty to Potiphar and his obedience to God in resisting adultery that led to his imprisonment. *"But the Lord was with Joseph"* and He used Joseph's betrayal and a seemingly hopeless circumstance to bless him and elevate him to a higher cause and purpose. Because of these events, Joseph was imprisoned. While he was there, the keeper of the prison noticed Joseph's extraordinary gifts and bestowed upon Joseph the management control of the prison. *"The Lord was with Joseph,"* and that which he did, the Lord made it to prosper. While imprisoned, Joseph interpreted dreams. He then was introduced to Pharaoh and interpreted Pharaoh's dreams. Through these chains of events, Joseph subsequently earned the position of the highest leader of Egypt.

The story of Joseph is a classic story of God's providence toward His favored leaders and their life circumstances, even those of adversity and betrayal. In our own leadership journeys of faith, we, too, will experience the betrayal of friends and colleagues closest to us. Often that betrayal can land us into situations that seem to stifle us and yank the mantle of leadership from us. But if we are truly servant-leaders, faithful to God, He will use each and every act of betrayal against us as a launching point to an even greater good.

The story of Joseph teaches us that calm submission and obedience to earthly authority can actually place us in positions of power over our circumstances. It teaches us that resisting sin and temptation at the risk of alienation and imprisonment can become the liberating experience of our journey of faith. So lead on in your adversity. Don't let hurt, humiliation, or betrayal stop you from fulfilling your call from God.

Our Prayer: *We thank You, God, for leaders like Joseph, who though betrayed, remained obedient in Your blessing and power and thus achieved great things for the Kingdom. We know that in our lives and leadership journeys, we, too, will be let down, even betrayed by those closest to us. Help us to never lose the heart of faithful service to You in all circumstances. Bless us we pray, even while imprisoned in life's valleys.* **Amen.**

But God Meant It For Good

"When Bad Things Happen to Good Leaders"

"Now therefore be not grieved, nor angry with yourselves, that ye sold me hither: for God did send me before you to preserve life. But as for you, ye thought evil against me; but God meant it unto good, to bring to pass, as it is this day, to save much people alive."

Featured Scripture: Genesis 45:5; 50:20
Background Scriptures: Genesis 50:15–26; Genesis 37 and 45

Few stories in the Scriptures better illustrate the providence of God than the life journey of Joseph. One of the twelve sons of Jacob and his favorite, Joseph would be betrayed by his own brothers. After being sold into slavery and taken away from his home and family, Joseph would wind up a servant in Potiphar's house. He was betrayed by his master's wife, then thrown into prison. Joseph's journey took him to the palace of Pharaoh, where he ascended to interpreting dreams and ultimately overseeing the operations of the nation of Egypt.

Today's Scripture comes as Joseph lay on his deathbed. At 110 years old, he was dying and sharing his last words with his brothers, including the words of the featured Scripture above. Rather than expressing bitterness and remorse for the course of events in his life, Joseph celebrated God's plan and providence while praising the lives that were saved by his own arduous journey. Leaders of faith today often see the travesty in the lives of good people. We see situations and life events that come and spoil the tranquility and innocence of families. When bad things happen to good leaders and families, how do we respond?

For those of us who live in the totality of God's calling and providence, we must give to God the bad situations of life. Only God can understand and bring purpose from life's tragedies. Our duty is to be prayerful and to lead through all events of life. We must glean from every bad circumstance the love and grace of the Suffering Servant. We can cry, comfort, grieve with others, and assist them in all ways possible. But only in time and by the providential hand of God can we see the rainbows of goodness shine forth from life's tragedies.

In his own bad times, Joseph never lost faith. He was humble and hardworking in all situations, including slavery and imprisonment. In each situation he provided leadership. His talents and leadership qualities showed in each occasion, and he went on to serve God's purpose. You, too, must lead through bad happenings and tragedies. Seek to strengthen the weak around you. Bloom where you are planted, and build with the materials and tools around you. Most especially, forgive others who intend you harm, and give all of life's events to God so His providence and purpose can shine from them.

Our Prayer: *God of Providence, we give thanks for Joseph and his service. We, too, want to lead even when bad things happen to us. Help us, Lord, to always know that You are the God of circumstance, who can make beauty from tragedy and who can bring salvation from betrayal. Instill in us the heart of Joseph so we, too, can forgive and serve in complete obedience to Your calling.* **Amen.**

Leading Onto Holy Ground

"When God Is Present in our Work, Our Workplaces Become Holy Ground"

"And Moses said, I will now turn aside, and see this great sight, why the bush is not burnt. And when the Lord saw that he turned aside to see, God called unto him out of the midst of the bush, and said, Moses, Moses.... And He said, Draw not nigh hither: put off thy shoes from off thy feet, for the place whereon thou standest is holy ground.... And the captain of the Lord's host said unto Joshua, Loose thy shoe from off thy foot; for the place whereon thou standest is holy. And Joshua did so."

FEATURED SCRIPTURES: EXODUS 3:3–5; AND JOSHUA 5:15
BACKGROUND SCRIPTURES: GENESIS 3; AND JOSHUA 5:13–15

Moses had ascended onto Mount Horeb, or Sinai, to receive instruction from God concerning his mission. Joshua was trapped in battle at a riverside and came face-to-face with an angelic commander of the Lord's host army. In both of these places, where these two great leaders of our faith had traveled on their journeys and callings, they found themselves on holy ground. Holy ground is not just a predetermined place or a set place of worship; ground becomes holy when God's presence envelopes the workplace of leaders.

The sign of reverence and respect to God's presence was to bow and to remove your shoes from your feet. In both cases Moses and Joshua obeyed the instruction of God and His angel. What time, place, and station has God placed you in today? If the presence of the Lord has followed you into the workplace, you, too, may be walking on holy ground. God shows up when His servants are obedient to His commands and exercise bravery even in the face of tremendous odds. Be prepared to meet God in these places, and if need be, remove your shoes and show a new sense of honor and respect at work.

What God is also telling us is that the places we go to do His will can become special, maybe even holy places. As we perform the tasks we were given to do, God's Spirit and angelic beings will be in our midst. Be prepared to give thanks to God in all places and to remember proper behavior and decorum as you go about your leadership duties.

We think of temples or churches, not battlefields, as being holy ground. We often think we must go to a sacred shrine to find a holy site. But if our work is God's holy work, our office place or work site will become holy ground, too. For those called to work abroad, mission fields and places of war and poverty can become holy ground. Wherever we find ourselves working, let us maintain a holy awareness of God. When we sense His presence, let us claim that spot as holy ground. Just like Moses and Joshua, leaders of faith today will be met by God and His hosts right where we stand.

Our Prayer: *Dear Great I AM, Your holy presence goes forth with those You call for holy tasks. We praise You for calling great servants like Moses and Joshua and for protecting Your people. We pray, Lord, for Your presence here in our places of leadership. May we always be prepared to turn our workplaces into holy ground.* **Amen.**

Tell Them That I AM Has Sent You

"Called Leaders Can Expect Questions and Ridicule for Their Calling"

"And Moses said unto God, Behold, when I come unto the children of Israel, and shall say unto them, The God of your fathers hath sent me unto you; and they shall say to me, What is his name? What shall I say unto them? And God said unto Moses, *I AM THAT I AM:* and he said, Thus shalt thou say unto the children of Israel, *I AM* hath sent me unto you."

FEATURED SCRIPTURE: EXODUS 3:13–14
BACKGROUND SCRIPTURE: EXODUS 3:1–14

Those persons who are convinced they have been called into the service of God must be prepared to give the answer to others as to why they are serving. Leaders of faith who claim the promise and call of God will be thrust into a secular world that will not understand the spiritual call to service. Moreover, God chooses unlikely persons to serve and lead. Perhaps you are that unlikely person. Expect others to wonder why and how someone like you should lead. Expect ridicule and even scoffing at your answer as to why you are stepping forth to lead.

Moses found himself in such a predicament as he was called to be a liberating leader for God. Moses was tending the sheep of his wife's father when God came to give him his calling. In the light of the burning bush, Moses confronted God and asked the basic question: "When I do this thing You ask me to do, what will I say as to who sends me?" The "who are you" and the "why are you here" will be asked of you also. Moses was told to say that *I AM* had sent him. The theology of this command of God is very direct. We are always to acknowledge the basic fact that we as leaders of faith are called by the true God to service. The same *I AM* who called Moses to His service hearkens to us today.

While we may not be called to lead an entire nation of God's chosen people from the bondage of Pharaoh, we may be asked to lead a reluctant congregation or a rebellious classroom of children. We may be called to go to a strange community to take a new position of leadership among people of different backgrounds. We may be called to lead persons who are older and better educated than ourselves. They all may wonder who you really are and why you are the one in charge. It is your boldness and certainty of your calling that will make others listen. Others will see in you that your passion for a task is driven by something bigger than you—*I AM*.

Always be brave to admit that you feel the call of God in your life. Some will understand; many will not. But go forth with the assurance and promise that *THE GREAT I AM* goes before you to prepare the way. If He calls you, He will assure your success.

Our Prayer: *O GREAT I AM, we stand in awe of You, as Moses did that day when he saw the burning bush. We bow in stillness and humility to listen for Your call to us. Help us to be bold and assured in answering that call and fulfilling the task of leadership that You give us to do. Give us the confidence to always tell others that I AM has sent us to this service.* **Amen.**

When You Feel Unworthy To Lead

"GOD CALLS THE UNLIKELY AND EQUIPS THEM FOR HOLY SUCCESS"

"And Moses said unto the LORD, O my LORD, I am not eloquent…but I am slow of speech and of a slow tongue. And the LORD said unto him Who hath made man's mouth? Or who maketh the dumb, or deaf, or the seeing, or the blind? Have not I the LORD? Now therefore go, and I will be with thy mouth, and teach thee what thou shalt say."

FEATURED SCRIPTURE: EXODUS 4:10–12
BACKGROUND SCRIPTURES: EXODUS 3:1–14; AND EXODUS 4:1–17

Moses was a titan of the faith, the leader of the nation of Israel who delivered them from bondage. Because of Moses' prominence in our faith history, many falsely assume he was a charismatic, booming orator who moved masses with his words. The Scriptures clearly indicate that Moses did not possess the outward attributes of a deliverer. In fact, Moses was a reluctant leader, even to the point of arguing with God Himself about his insufficiencies as a natural leader of faith.

But Moses yielded to God's call and indeed fulfilled the tasks God asked of him. In God's call, He promised to become Moses' mouth and to teach him what he should say. In Moses' obedience, he became that hero, titan of the faith, and prolific author of Scripture.

God's call on Moses is not unlike His call on many of us. We are the unlikely leaders. We may not be handsome, eloquent, or powerful. But God sees something in us that He desires. We, like Moses, are called by God to a special leadership task of faith. Oftentimes we are asked to assume a role of leadership in our workplaces, congregations, or local communities. We may feel a call to offer ourselves for election to public office or to apply for a new job.

In many cases, God speaks to us and drafts us into new service through the actions and petitions of friends and associates. They are the ones who see the latent qualities of leadership in us and draft us into leadership for an important task at hand. God confirms this calling in our hearts as circumstances in our lives change. Be prayerful, humble, and expectant.

God will come to us, and like Moses, pull us out of your comfort zones to perform a task He especially wants us to do. The task of leadership for which God calls us may not be leading a nation from bondage, but it could entail a role of spiritual leadership in our places of worship, like becoming a Sunday school teacher or elder or missionary. It could be a call to become an officer in an organization or a chance to lead our own families or group of coworkers in an important and holy task.

If you consider yourself to be an unlikely leader, beware; God pursues those He needs for service. If you feel God's tug and call to leadership, know that He will equip you, as He equipped Moses, with what you need for success. Don't argue with God. Heed his call to leadership today. No matter how unworthy you feel, God is ready to be your mouth and work miracles through the call of an unlikely leader.

Our Prayer: *Lord, we often feel unworthy when we hear Your call to service and leadership. Thank You for Moses and for his obedience in answering Your call. Help us claim Your promise that You will equip us for any task You call us to do. May we honor You in all our service.* **Amen.**

When The Evil Pursue The Chosen

"LEADING MEANS RELYING ON GOD TO DELIVER US IN THE TOUGH SPOTS"

"And the LORD hardened the heart of Pharaoh king of Egypt, and he pursued after the children of Israel: and the children of Israel went out with an high hand. But the Egyptians pursued after them…and the children of Israel cried out unto the LORD. And Moses said unto the people, Fear ye not, stand still, and see the salvation of the LORD.…"

FEATURED SCRIPTURE: EXODUS 14:9–10, 13
BACKGROUND SCRIPTURE: EXODUS 14

Nothing can be as dangerous as the hardened hearts of evil kings and leaders. But our Scriptures today show how God can use the hardened hearts of evil persons to set up His miracles. Even after the plagues, the death, and the destruction wrought by God upon Pharaoh through Moses, Pharaoh pursued the Israelites. Even when we are God's chosen people and are serving the Lord, it seems that our tormentors keep pursuing us at every turn.

Moses had undertaken leadership of one of the toughest human migrations known in history. It had taken faith, miracles, and incredible planning and discipline to bring the people to this point. Now this migrating nation of God's chosen people faced potential mass slaughter as they sat peacefully camped at Pi-hahiroth. This encampment was the place where God told Moses to set up camp, a place entangled between a land mass and the sea.

Leaders of faith often embark on journeys of leadership where we have felt called to undertake a massive project. We have assembled resources, made intricate plans, and are in the midst of accomplishing something great. In our supposed time of peace, we awaken to find our congregation or organization exposed and vulnerable while we seem to face sudden defeat. It is in these moments that our competitors, our detractors, and the evil thoughts of our adversaries pursue us and seek to take advantage of our bad situations.

Moses was harangued by his own people as they lost faith in God and Moses and focused on what they believed to be a hopeless situation. Moses, however, never doubted the calling or the promise of God. Moses responded as a leader by lifting the situation to God and facilitating the miracle. God moved, the Red Sea parted, the people passed through safely. Pharaoh's army pursued and God caused them to drown in the sea. The chosen people had eluded defeat once more by God's providential hand.

Leaders of faith will inevitably come to their own Red Sea experience. The magnanimity of circumstance and the voracity of pursuit by evil adversaries may bring us to a water-parting moment. Will we keep the faith? While a literal sea may not open for us when we are trapped in a bad circumstance, God is still moving in the moment. When we are chosen for God's task and remain faithful, God will always shape the scene for our success and His purpose. Hearts will change and good will come from every tough moment when we rely fully and faithfully on our Lord.

Our Prayer: *O God of Moses, we praise You for keeping Your promise and covenant with Israel and the people You choose for your purposes. As leaders called to Your service, gird us with Your strength, power, and provision to withstand evil persons in our pursuit. In all our tough circumstances, even when there seems to be no way out, we pray that You will part the seas of our troubles so we may pass along to greater service for You and those You have called us to lead.* **Amen.**

When People Murmur Against You

"STAYING TRUE TO YOUR CALLING EVEN IN THE FACE OF CRITICISM"

"So Moses brought Israel from the Red Sea, and they went into the wilderness of Shur; and they went three days in the wilderness and found no water.… And the whole congregation of the children of Israel murmured against Moses and Aaron in the wilderness."

FEATURED SCRIPTURES: EXODUS 15:22; 16:2
BACKGROUND SCRIPTURES: EXODUS 15:22—17:7; AND LUKE 23:33–37

No leader of faith who has been called to travel a long road of service for God can escape the murmur of others against them. Others will doubt, mock, and confront God's chosen and their claim to leadership when the desert gets hot and the water runs out. It is in these moments that our faith must remain strong and our reliance on God must be firm. Even after a series of miracles and providential rescue, Moses and Aaron faced the murmuring chatter of the people as their sun got hot and their water ran out. Moses feared for his very life as his own people threatened to stone him to death.

The true test of leadership is trusting God each day, each step of the way, for our very next drink of water. It is difficult to store God's provisions because He wants us to rely on Him in a new way each day. Like Moses, we may lead our organization or congregation through a series of incredible events and success only to find ourselves on this day in danger of being sacked by our own followers. In these times we must reclaim our calling and seek God's power and sustenance. God will bring us to the rock that will yield water for our followers to drink.

Leaders of faith must guard against becoming bitter or downtrodden when those we lead gossip about us and undermine us through criticism. One day leaders may get the praise of the pundit, and tomorrow they may get the rant. Leadership often involves completing only one leg of a journey, which others will then pick up and follow. Murmuring from others sometimes comes because the outcome they expected did not happen. Godly leadership is part of an eternal plan, and we owe God our allegiance to be obedient even in the face of criticism.

God never fails those He calls and those who are faithful to fulfill His commandments. Water will be found. Problems will be solved. Mountains will be moved. God's timing and methods are not always known to us in advance. Leaders must be willing to venture out most days with an empty cup as we pray to find the sweet water. As the chatter and murmuring grows around you this day, know that every great leader of faith has traveled this same path and that the same Almighty God who called and delivered them is already coming to your rescue. Keep the faith, continue the search, offer a fervent prayer, and you will find your rock that flows with sweet water.

Our Prayer: *God of Moses and the saints, the people murmur against me today. They gossip and chatter and are turning on me as they turned on Your servant Moses. Lead me to the rock with the sweet water of provision that I need for the day ahead. I believe and trust in this very moment that Your power and provision is being prepared and that my leadership will be successful as I seek to serve those You have given to me. I praise and thank You, claiming it all in the name of Jesus.* **Amen.**

Leadership Manna Day By Day

"GOD EXPECTS LEADERS TO BE FAITHFUL DAY BY DAY FOR PROVISION"

Then said the LORD unto Moses, Behold, I will rain bread from heaven for you; and the people shall go out and gather a certain rate every day, that I may prove them, whether they will walk in my law, or no.... Give us this day our daily bread."

FEATURED SCRIPTURES: EXODUS 16:4; AND MATTHEW 6:11
BACKGROUND SCRIPTURES: EXODUS 15:22—17:7; AND MATTHEW 6: 5–15

Moses had a restless constituency. Today's Scripture tells of the constant complaints, or "murmurings," of the Israelites against Moses and God. What a tough leadership task Moses had in dealing with those constant complaints, doubts, and lack of faith from those he was leading. God Himself took note of this weakness in the people and offered a daily solution.

Manna, or bread, was essential to life. God had led the people out of bondage, but when they felt the first pangs of hunger, they began to doubt. God made a promise to Moses that He would provide manna from heaven, sufficient for the day as each family required. People could not hoard more than one day's supply. This arrangement by God made the people dependent and faithful day by day to God for their provision.

How often in your own leadership journey of faith have you led a group of people or an organization into new and promising areas of opportunity, only to find those same folks getting anxious as you encountered obstacles? We can do mighty deeds of leadership and take our team into promising bounds of new success, but when the hunger pangs hit or when the thirst of the moment overtakes those we lead, these same "murmurings" that Moses heard can infect our own followers and stifle good leaders.

Even our Lord Jesus taught us to pray for daily bread. As a leader of faith, you, like Moses, are called to a special task for God. God will not lead you to a wilderness point in your journey and not be prepared to rain your leadership manna of provision. Leaders and their followers often fail when they try to hoard blessings from God. When we attempt to hoard God's provisions, it sends a signal to God that we doubt His promise and pledge to give us exactly what we need when we need it.

Moses had to constantly remind his people that their complaining was sending the wrong signal to God. He had to remind them that faith is a daily walk of trust in the Lord's provision. Leaders don't get popular by leading one day at time, but it is what God requires of you. God provided fresh water, bread, quail, and ultimately a new land of milk and honey for His people. Let us strive to cease asking God for enough blessings to store up and start trusting Him for our daily leadership manna. Let us give thanks for our daily bread and praise Him for every bite.

Our Prayer: *Dear God of all gifts, we know that if we are called, You are faithful to provide our daily needs. Forgive us when we doubt and complain of not having enough. As leaders of faith, help us to instill in those we lead a strong faith and trust that You will feed us day by day.* **Amen.**

Gods Before Me

"When Our Time and Allegiances Get in the Way of God"

"I am the LORD thy God, which have brought thee out of the land of Egypt, out of the house of bondage. Thou shalt have no other gods before me … Ye shall not fear other gods, nor bow yourselves to them, nor serve them, nor sacrifice to them: But the LORD who brought you up out of the land of Egypt with great power and a stretched out arm, him shall ye fear, and him shall ye worship, and to him shall ye do sacrifice."

FEATURED SCRIPTURES: EXODUS 20:2–3; AND 2 KINGS 17:35–36
BACKGROUND SCRIPTURES: DEUTERONOMY 5:1–22; AND MATTHEW 6:19–21

How do you spend your time? What consumes your thoughts and resources? Given a free day or new resources, what would you choose to do? Leaders of faith can often be blinded to their growing tendency to become slaves to projects and institutions. The good causes we champion can themselves come to compete with our time spent and intimacy with our loving God. Some of those activities can be noble and just. But the first and most distinct commandment given by God to Moses and the people was the call to singleness of love, worship, and allegiance to the great *I AM*.

Our careers and professional ambitions can become god-like figures that consume us. Our ambition for wealth, power, and recognition can almost become an idol that even the best among us give too much affection. Our fear of failure or of need can drive us to become obsessed with our work to build earthly security. Leaders can find themselves so busy tending to a congregation and institutional responsibilities that the time set aside for communion, worship, and contemplation with God gets carved back. Our time and allegiances get in the way of God.

God's first command is that nothing is to come before Him. Our highest use of time and purpose should be to engage in worship and praise of our Lord. The sacrifice of all our time and money for work and pleasure means we are offering a tithe to the wrong god. God wants our time. He wants our complete attention each and every day. Time should be set aside for prayer and study, as well as service to others. We should pause to give thanks for every meal and the small blessings in our lives. We should never let our quest for leisure and pleasure become as gods placed before the true God.

Leaders of faith must set examples for others to follow in our own time management and in managing the resources of lives. How we make God the top priority and focus of our day can send powerful signals to those who follow us. God is a jealous God. He not only longs for our heart and loyalty, but also for our time and resources. Getting our priorities in order and placing God in the center of our daily existence shows our obedience to His first commandment. When we obey it, God blesses and multiplies our work in ways we could never imagine. Never allow the gods of this life to come before your love and worship of your Redeemer.

Our Prayer: *God, our hearts and souls rest in You alone. Forgive us when we have allowed outside influences and ambitions to steal time away from You. Forgive us when we have let our quest for pleasure and the seeking of power become too prominent in our lives. Make our lives a more passionate search to know You better and love You more. We give our praise and worship and our humble service as leaders to You alone.* **Amen.**

A Leader's Prayer Of Intercession

"Leaders Who Pray When Their Constituents Go Astray"

"And Moses returned unto the Lord, and said, Oh, this people have sinned a great sin, and have made them gods of gold. Yet now, if thou wilt forgive their sin; and if not, blot me, I pray thee, out of thy book which thou hast written."
Featured Scripture: Exodus 32:31–32
Background Scripture: Exodus 32

Leadership callings can be tough assignments. It is tough enough keeping yourself pure of heart and deed; however, it is especially tough when those you are called to lead commit blunders and ethical breaches that threaten the survival of the organization. It is in times like these that prayerful intercession is a leader's first, best choice to make.

The Hebrew people had become restless in Moses' absence. They went to the man in charge, Aaron, and insisted that he make gods for them to worship in Moses' absence. The people had lost their faith that Moses would return, and they felt they were stranded in the desert without supernatural powers. In building the golden calf, the people of God committed a great sin against the true God. As Moses returned, he heard God's anger and feared His wrath, and he found himself as the last, sole intercessor for constituents gone astray.

God told Moses that He would destroy them all, start over, and make of Moses a new and great nation. But Moses exemplified an extraordinary love and passion to save the Hebrew nation. Moses sought the Lord and reasoned with God by reminding Him of the covenant with Abraham, Isaac, and Israel. Moses even offered to be the sacrifice and asked the Lord to strike him down instead of the people as atonement for their sin.

In our own leadership journeys, we may return from a venture to find things going amiss. We may find our leadership team in dissension or find that ethical or even criminal activities have taken place without our knowledge. We may find that those we lead have lost the mission and purpose for which they were hired. We may find our team members working against the best interests of the organization. We know that we may survive as leaders, but without great prayerful intercession with God, our congregation or organization may fail. What do we do?

Moses reasoned with God that His promises to the forefathers of the Hebrews were still good. Moses offered his own goodness as a sacrifice. Moses asked for forgiveness for the sins that had been committed. In the end, people were punished, but the nation survived, thanks to the grace of God gained for them through the fervent intercession and prayer of a great leader of faith.

Be bold to pray and to intercede with God, and on behalf your constituents and followers who have gone astray. It may be your great calling in leadership.

Our Prayer: *God of Moses and all mankind, thank You for Your mercy and grace toward a sinful people. Thank You for great leaders of faith like Moses who refused to quit on their people, even in the depths of their sinfulness. Give us the courage to seek Your intercession for those we serve, even in the midst of turmoil.* **Amen.**

When Leaders Really Need To See God

"It Is Alright for Leaders to Pray for Reaffirmation of Their Calling"

"And Moses said unto the LORD, See thou sayest unto me, Bring up this people: and thou has not let me know whom thou wilt send with me. Yet thou hast said, I know thee by name, and thou hast also found grace in my sight.… If I have found grace in thy sight, shew me now thy way, that I may know thee, and that I may find grace in thy sight: and consider that this nation is thy people. And He said, My Presence shall go with thee and I will give thee rest."

FEATURED SCRIPTURE: EXODUS 33:12–14
BACKGROUND SCRIPTURE: EXODUS 33:12–23

Leaders of faith often come to those moments in the middle of their journey when an overwhelming need for reaffirmation of their calling must be met in order for them to continue with their work. We have taken great risks in our career to come to a critical juncture, only to wonder if it has been worth the cost. In these times, we really need to see God. We need a tangible sign from God Himself that confirms our calling and mission for life.

In today's lesson, Moses was at just that juncture of leadership. He had been halfway through the journey. He had led the people out of Egypt and fought off an army, hunger, and the elements of the desert, plus the sinful rebellion of those he led. God had charged him to go toward the great Promised Land. Yet, lying before him were some of the fiercest obstacles a leader could imagine. Moses wasn't afraid, for he knew God's provision was solid. But what Moses needed is to get a new glimpse of God to reassure his heart.

Leaders know that each time we slay the problems and obstacles that beset us, even more will follow. Leaders come to expect the unexpected. Leaders of faith, called by a living God, know that evil and temptation will come against those serving the purposes of the Almighty. Yet, there are those extraordinary moments when we need to seek God in a new way, as never before. We can pray boldly for God to reveal Himself to us, for if God calls us to the task, He will go with us and give us the signs, peace, and rest that will confirm our calling.

God granted Moses' request as He placed Moses in the cleft of a rock and let His glory pass by. Moses only saw the back part of God's Glory, but it was the backside of the great *I AM*. Moses had his confirmation.

We may not see the literal glory of God pass before our eyes, but when we pray for an appointment to see God, He always grants our request. God may confirm His presence with a warmth and peace of mind. He may send a child or stranger into our lives to reveal new miracles. God may come to us in a dream or leap at us through a Scripture, prayer, or sermon. But He will come. Make your appointment with God. Go to the cleft of the rock and wait. You will see God.

Our Prayer: *Great Jehovah, we need to see You. We pray that in these times as we confront the great work we are to accomplish along with the likely obstacles that come with it, You will reconfirm our callings. Give us Your assurance that Your presence will be with us in every difficult moment and task. We praise You for showing Yourself to us.* **Amen.**

Consecrating Those Who Succeed Us

"Elder Leaders Pave the Way for New Leaders by Tangible Gestures"

"And Moses said unto the congregation, this is the thing which the Lord commanded to be done. And Moses brought Aaron and his sons, and washed them with water. And he put upon him the coat, and girded him with the girdle, and clothed him with the robe, and put the ephod upon him…. And he poured of the anointing oil upon Aaron's head, and anointed him, to sanctify him."

Featured Scripture: Leviticus 8:5–7, 12
Background Scriptures: Leviticus 8:1–13; and Exodus 29:1–9

God commanded Moses to anoint Aaron and his sons as the successors to leadership. God told Moses exactly what to do and that he must do it in the presence of the people. These tangible signs of consecration were God's way of validating His choice to the people. Consecrating those who succeed us in leadership journeys of faith is also a sacred responsibility. If God has sent an apprentice to you and you feel the call to turn over responsibility, the example of Aaron's consecration may be one to consider.

Leaders of faith today may not be the deliverers of Israel, but even in our own organizations and congregations we can lift up future leaders to our followers by tangible gestures of affirmation. People are always looking for signs from trusted leaders as to what new paths to take. People sense when an elder leader is nearing the end of a journey. Successful elder leaders do a great service to those who follow them when they help identify and anoint new leaders who can take the helm.

Elder leaders have gained wisdom and knowledge during their journeys, and they can use their God-given abilities to find those who can perform and carry on a vital mission with integrity and honor. When new leaders come to fill the shoes of a beloved elder, people may not fully embrace them. The anointing of Aaron and his sons in front of the congregation was a holy service and exercise that utilized all the trappings of the priestly rights and gave the people confidence in them.

You can find many ways to publicly validate new leaders. Sometimes a ceremony and the endorsement of a new leader in the presence of senior statespersons send a great signal of confidence. Leaders should make sure their successors are present in meetings and in social settings with the appropriate institutional authorities. Allowing new leaders to take credit for new success helps others to begin gaining confidence in their leadership.

If you feel God's call to close this phase of your journey and you believe He has sent you someone to take over your tasks, pray to see if God wants you to publicly set the mantle of your blessing upon them. To consecrate a new leader in front of your followers can be one of the richest and most edifying experiences a leader of faith can perform. If your successor is ready and waiting, lift them up to others today.

Our Prayer: *Lord God, You have given me a wonderful and successful journey of leadership. You have sent others to begin taking over the mantle from me. Give me the wisdom to know when and how to consecrate them to Your service in the presence of others. Let me use my blessings and posture to lift these future leaders up so that others will follow them under the hand of Your blessing.* **Amen.**

Holy As I AM Holy

"Called to Lead and Called to Holiness"

"For I am the Lord your God: ye shall therefore sanctify yourselves, and ye shall be holy; for I am holy.... For I am the Lord that bringeth you up out of the land of Egypt, to be your God: ye shall therefore be holy, for I am holy."

Featured Scripture: Leviticus 11:44–45
Background Scriptures: Leviticus 19; 1 Peter 1:13–16; Galatians 2:20

When we are called by God to lives of leadership and service, we are called to perform holy tasks for a holy God. The radiance of God's holiness can never be spotted nor diminished. Therefore, in our calling we must become sanctified and holy servants in leadership. We are to become holy, even as God is holy.

How can the imperfect become holy? How can our flawed humanness aspire to God's holiness? Why would God call us to something that we can never truly obtain? Our lesson today takes us into deep theological waters of contemplation. Part of God's nature is one of love and mercy and grace. God is the great *I AM* who desires to shower blessings on those whom He created and loves. He desires for us to experience a transforming of the mind, body, and spirit, one that reflects His own holiness and perfection.

To those of us that are redeemed by Christ Jesus, it is no longer our own self that lives…but rather, it is Christ who now lives in us and through us. Christ exerts His will in our actions each day. The Lord can also bring us into new holiness through a change of our hearts and motivations. As God sends His Holy Spirit into our hearts and minds, humility replaces arrogance. Love replaces hate. Forgiveness replaces revenge. Purity replaces lust. Patience replaces aggression. And a passion for selfless service to the hurting souls around us replaces the raging ambition to attain wealth, power, and pleasure for ourselves.

Attaining holiness is a process that moves us toward the throne of God. Our character and constitution become governed by a different set of laws. Through silence, prayer, and meditation, our thoughts are washed clean. We are given a new set of priorities and objectives for living. The things that we deem as important will change as we become more attuned with a holy God.

Leaders of faith are chosen people. We have been summoned to God's throne and given important work to do. When God calls us, He creates within us a new capacity for holiness. We will still stumble along the way. We will still invariably experience failure and sin. Yet, we are still becoming new creatures, capable of an existence and future that is filled with power, wonder, and new truth. God doesn't dare us to be holy. He desires that we be holy. If you are called to lead, then you are called to be holy. Give in to that call this day and allow your heart and mind and soul to be transformed into a new vessel that reflects the holiness of a holy God.

Our Prayer: *Holy God, we are humbled and honored to be in Your presence. We are awed by Your call to holiness. Take our imperfections and sinful nature, and by Christ's redeeming power, make us new and holy creatures. Instill in us new thoughts and desires that reflect Your wonder. Shine Your love and holiness through our actions and service to those we meet today.* **Amen.**

Getting Your Rain In Due Season

"Obedience to God's Command Preserves, Protects, and Rewards"

"Ye shall keep my sabbaths, and reverence my sanctuary: I am the Lord. If ye walk in my statutes, and keep my commandments, and do them; then I will give you rain in due season, and the land shall yield her increase, and the trees of the field shall yield their fruit…and I will walk among you, and will be your God, and ye shall be my people."

Featured Scripture: Leviticus 26:2–4, 12
Background Scripture: Leviticus 26:1–12

The Book of Leviticus was given to Moses and the priestly tribe of the Levites. The lessons and laws of Leviticus were meant to be a specific guide for living, worship, and gaining atonement with God. The specifics within this long book of Scripture deal with many subjects, such as what to do with those who were diagnosed with leprosy, and what the people were to eat or not eat. These standards for living were specific and detailed. God knew that a chosen people must know and obey these commandments if they were to survive over time and retain their uniqueness as a covenant people.

To the generations of our day, the codes set forth in Leviticus may seem strange and obtuse. Indeed, our faith and culture has evolved beyond many of the arcane requirements for the people of Moses' day. However the entire theme of Leviticus and the crux of our lesson today give credence to this central truth: God still requires those whom He calls and sets apart for service to live to a higher standard of rule and conduct. We are to live our lives to a standard that honors the Sabbath day. We are to bring our first, best offerings of time, resources, and talents to God. We are to live in legal and sexual purity within our own families and communities.

Leaders of faith are called and set apart by God. Answering a call of God to leadership service summons us to higher ethical standards. We must die to our old daily routines. We can no longer seek many of the pleasures and personal liberties in which others immerse themselves each day. We must become cautious of what physical fulfillments we desire. We must sacrifice our personal time in order to serve those in need.

The price for living lives set apart in leadership and service may seem too high. But God promises a harvest of blessings to those who can keep His commands and follow His rules. He promises our rain in due season. Our rain may be in the form of a congregation, a business, or a project that survives over time through the storms of adversity. Our rain in due season may come in the form of the changed lives from those we serve. Our rain in due season may come in the form of newfound resources that supply our own family's needs.

God always keeps and preserves those who trust Him and obey His commands. Our Lord will walk with us in the midst of our every challenge. When our lives become hot and dry, He brings the refreshing, holy rain in due season as our reward for holy obedience.

Our Prayer: *O Lord, You called us and set us apart as Your servant-leaders. We are bound to a higher code and calling. We have many rules and commands to obey. Mold us into Your image and strengthen us as we strive to serve others and preserve Your promise. Walk with us each day and bring our rain in due season as we cling to the power of Your word.* **Amen.**

Success Means Delegating Authority

"GREAT LEADERS FIND THE WISE AND DELEGATE AUTHORITY TO OTHERS"

"And the Lord said unto Moses, Gather unto me seventy men of the elders of Israel, whom thou knowest to be the elders of the people, and officers over them; and bring them unto the tabernacle of the congregation, that they may stand there with thee. And I will come down and talk with thee there: and I will take of the spirit which is upon thee, and will put it upon them; and they shall bear the burden of the people with thee, that thou bear it not thyself alone."

FEATURED SCRIPTURE: NUMBERS 11:16–17
BACKGROUND SCRIPTURES: EXODUS 18:13–27; AND DEUTERONOMY 16:18–22

The nation of Israel was growing. Moses was doing a great job as leader. He was also a judge and arbitrator of disputes among the tribes. Like most leaders of faith, Moses was becoming overwhelmed and clearly needed help. God knew the great burden that Moses was under and commanded him to select officers and elders. God came down and blessed the elders to lead so as to free Moses of some of his great leadership burden.

The proper delegation of authority is a God-sanctioned plan for leaders of faith to follow. In order for organizations, businesses, or congregations to grow, great leaders must delegate authority to the wise coworkers around them. The old adage "delegate or stagnate" is true. However, many leaders of faith feel as if they must control all aspects of an organization. They lack the ability or willingness to empower others to take over tasks of responsibility. They allow the burdens of responsibility to slowly crush them.

God knows when we need help. God instructed Moses to go to the tabernacle and wait on His anointing of helpers. We, too, must call upon the Lord to send us wise and capable leaders to assist us in our callings. Many leaders flounder when they fail to tap the wealth of talent that exists around them by giving away authority to others. Leaders only become stronger when they appropriately delegate authority to wise and capable helpers.

Jesus Himself carefully chose and empowered disciples and apostles, bestowing upon them the ability to do great things in His name. Jesus even told His disciples that they would be given the authority to bind on earth and in heaven in His name. God and His Son set the example of delegation of authority. If our own power is derived from God and manifested in our special callings, we can never fail if we turn to God for His blessing and guidance in the delegation of our tasks to others in His name. It all belongs to Him.

Our Prayer: *Dear Lord, please send us wise and anointed helpers. Our burdens get heavy at times, and You ordained the gathering of officers to assist us in the tasks You call us to do. Remove our sense of ownership and pride that prevents us from delegating tasks and authority to those around us. Bless us as we strive to grow and build Your Kingdom.* **Amen.**

A Minority Report

"LEADING EVEN WHEN YOU DON'T HAVE THE VOTES"

"And Caleb stilled the people before Moses, and said, Let us go up at once, and possess it; for we are well able to overcome it...."
FEATURED SCRIPTURE: NUMBERS 13:30
BACKGROUND SCRIPTURE: NUMBERS 13—14:35

In positions of leadership, we often become obsessed with the principle of majority rule. Our leadership efforts often become a quest to build a majority consensus among our followers so we can lead our organization into the next mission. We can become frustrated or can even abandon good ideas because we don't have the votes to move forward. Our lesson today, however, focuses on leaders of faith who are called by God to accomplish His purposes in minority positions. They are called to lead even when they don't have the votes.

The twelve spies of Israel went on a scouting mission to view the land that God had promised to them. They were asked to go and observe and bring a verdict back to Moses and the people. After seeing the giants that inhabited the land of milk and honey, ten of the twelve said the task was too great and the land could not be taken. Only Caleb and Joshua came back with a message of hope: Let us go up and possess it, for we are able to overcome it. Caleb and Joshua were forced to give a minority report. They did not have the votes but knew that by God's might, the land could be taken.

Leaders of faith often stall the will of God when they seek majority opinion on all the great subjects of the day. God often calls us to be a Caleb or Joshua. We may need to give the minority report. God's wrath was great upon the ten spies who held to the majority opinion, as well as their tribes, for failing to believe God's promise. Only Caleb and Joshua lived to see and inhabit the Promised Land. The majority got it wrong, and their judgment was forty years of wandering in the wilderness—for all the people.

Daring leadership often puts us in a minority position. It often brings the scorn and rebuke of others. Leaders of faith should get used to the position of leading from a minority position. Yet, leaders of faith should be bold and courageous to inspire others to join them in claiming the promises of God. Delivering a minority report often means we must invoke others to believe in a cause greater than ourselves. It may mean that we must tackle an injustice alone and hope others follow. It may mean we risk our own resources and good reputation to follow God's directives.

God's purposes are not always achieved by majority opinion. They are achieved through the obedience and bravery exhibited by leaders of faith who lead on even through the skepticism of their own followers. Be a Caleb. Be a Joshua. When God calls you, inspire others "to go at once and possess it; for we are well able to overcome it."

Our Prayer: *Lord God, give me the courage of Caleb and Joshua. Lift me up to the seemingly impossible tasks You call me to do. Never let me fear being in the minority when I am called by You. Instill within me courage and an unbending spirit of commitment to fulfill Your calling. Help me to speak Your truths clearly and boldly, regardless of the earthly consequences. Give me Your peace in all circumstances.* **Amen.**

Intercession For Fallen Family And Friends

"GREAT LEADERS FORGIVE AND INTERCEDE TO GOD FOR FRIENDS WHO FALTER"

"And Aaron said unto Moses, Alas my lord, I beseech thee, lay not the sin upon us, wherein we have done foolishly, and wherein we have sinned. Let her not be as one dead, of whom the flesh is half consumed when he cometh out of his mother's womb. And Moses cried unto the LORD, saying Heal her now, O God, I beseech thee."

FEATURED SCRIPTURE: NUMBERS 12:11–13
BACKGROUND SCRIPTURES: NUMBERS 12; AND EXODUS 15:20–21

Moses was the chosen leader of God. Moses had unprecedented access to God, and God spoke directly to him as the prophet for His people. Miriam and Aaron were the sister and brother of Moses and were leaders in the hierarchy of the tribes of Israel. Miriam is thought to have been the sister who plucked Moses from the basket as he floated in the Nile River as a baby. But in today's story, jealousy and pride overcame Miriam and Aaron at Miriam's prompting.

It began with Miriam and Aaron speaking out against Moses for taking an Ethiopian wife. It continued as they challenged Moses' superiority as the supreme prophet of God. They told Moses that they, too, were the voices of God. God heard this accusation against Moses by Miriam and Aaron, and in great anger He came down in a pillar of fire. The Lord set the record straight. Moses was His prophet and He would speak directly to and through Moses. The Lord left, and Miriam was struck with leprosy as a result of her sin. Aaron saw Miriam and appealed directly to Moses for forgiveness.

In a great act of love and intercession, as well as forgiveness, Moses interceded for Miriam and cried out to the Lord for her immediate healing. The Lord heard Moses and agreed to heal Miriam after her seven-day banishment from the people. Moses set the example for leaders of faith who are betrayed by the ones they love. Family and friends may rebel and say hurtful things to you. They may plot your downfall. Family and friends are often the very ones who will scorn or doubt your leadership calling. They may scoff at your new powers of leadership and may seek to undermine or take undue advantage of your new exalted leadership role. Great leaders of faith should take their cue from Moses on how to react and respond to these crises.

When God ordains leaders, He instills into them levelheadedness and balance. God helps remove wrathful thoughts and gives leaders the wisdom to overcome jealousy and pettiness. If you remain humble and prayerful, you will be given an incredible capacity to forgive. When friends and family fall from grace or disrupt your mission, intercede to God on their behalf. Let love, forgiveness, and intercession be the shining qualities of your leadership pathway. God will judge, but God will also be merciful to those we love and pray for in intercession. Intercede for someone you love today and bring God's healing and the restoration of relationships into his or her life!

Our Prayer: *Lord God, we give thanks for Your chosen prophet Moses. We thank You for the spiritual leaders among us today. Help us to respect our leaders of faith. Help leaders of faith to have forgiving hearts. Make them intercessors, O Lord, for their friends and family members who need forgiveness and restoration. Forgive us, Lord, when we step out of line and assume authority we do not have. Bless us as we strive to serve You.* **Amen.**

Consequences Of A Disobeyed Order

"Leaders Who Deviate from God's Plan of Action Pay a Heavy Price"

"And the Lord spake unto Moses, saying, Take the rod, and gather thou the assembly together…and speak ye unto the rock before their eyes; and it shall give forth his water.… Hear now, ye rebels; must we fetch you water out of this rock? And Moses lifted up his hand, and with his rod he smote the rock twice: and the water came out abundantly.… Because ye trespassed against me among the children of Israel at the waters…because ye sanctified me not in the midst of the children of Israel…thou shall not go thither unto the land which I give the children of Israel."

Featured Scriptures: Numbers 20:7–8, 11; Deuteronomy 32:51–52
Background Scriptures: Numbers 20:1–13; Deuteronomy 32:48–52; Matthew 17:1–9

Moses was one of the most prolific heroes of the faith. He was the liberator of Israel and the great author of Scripture. Moses appeared again in the Book of Matthew during the Transfiguration of Christ before His disciples. Yet for all Moses' actions of faith, his unique calling, and the miracles he performed, one disobeyed order cost him dearly.

The people of Israel were once again restless. They were complaining and whining to Moses. Every leader of faith encounters the lack of faith and the negative whining from those they lead from time to time. But here in the wilderness, the water ran out and the people were stuck. Moses and Aaron went before God and prayed in the tabernacle for an answer. God heard their prayer and gave them a very specific order: Moses was to speak to the rock in front of the congregation, and the water would then pour out.

When Moses gathered the people together, instead of declaring God's salvation once again, he sarcastically rebuked the complainers, raised his rod, and twice struck the rock. The water still came forth, but Moses had disobeyed a direct order from God. This great general of the faith would pay a price. God's punishment would be that Moses and Aaron would not have the privilege of passing into the Promised Land. God allowed Moses to look over into the land, but not possess it, as a result of this disobeyed order.

Leaders of faith oftentimes go to their prayer closets, as did Moses, for answers in tough situations. God always shows us the way out. But do we always follow His instructions to the letter? Moses' great mistake was in making a spectacle before his disgruntled followers. In striking the rock with his rod, he gave the impression that his leadership, not God's, had provided the water.

In all things we accomplish in leadership, we must give God the glory and credit. We must follow God's instructions found in the Scriptures and in answered prayer. Every leader of faith will be held accountable for their actions. If God punished this great leader of faith, Moses, He will certainly hold us accountable. When God says "speak"…don't "strike"!

Our Prayer: *O holy God, when You call us to a task, You call us to obedience in every act. May we always endeavor to follow Your holy Word and every command You give us. Forgive us when we fail You. Help us to endure our punishment with reverent respect and an understanding that a holy God cannot be dishonored. Thank You for Moses, for his life, and for showing us how to live through examples both good and bad.* **Amen.**

Perversion Of Leadership

"A Leader Hired to Curse and Subvert Others Meets the Angel of the Lord"

"He sent messengers therefore unto Balaam…. Come now therefore, I pray thee, curse me this people; for they are too mighty for me…that we may smite them…for I wot that he whom thou blessest is blessed, and he whom thou cursest is cursed…. And God's anger was kindled because he went: and the angel of the Lord stood in the way for an adversary against him…."

Featured Scripture: Numbers 22:5–6, 22
Background Scriptures: Numbers 22—24; 31:1-17; 2 Peter 2:15–16; and Jude 11

The story of Balak, Balaam, and the children of Israel is a fascinating recollection of how God protects those He chooses, and how He will intervene in the lives of leaders. Balak was the king of the Moabites, and he saw and feared the coming of the people of Israel near his land. So fearful was King Balak that he hired a local diviner and man of reputed supernatural power (Balaam) to come with him and curse Israel so they would be killed. Balaam was offered treasure for the task, and even though he was conscious of God in this matter, he proceeded with his task.

Balaam and his donkey encountered the angel of the Lord and were turned away. The angel of the Lord in this portion of Scripture refers to the preincarnate Christ. Our Scriptures for today tell us that *"the angel of the Lord stood in the way for an adversary against him."* So often in our lives of leadership, we see others with power and connections hired to subvert our work. They may come in the form of consultants, rivals, experts, and professional operatives who intend to harm our work and hurt the people we lead. If we are truly called by God, the same Christ who stood as an adversary against Balaam will stand against those who mean us harm.

Each time Balaam was sent to curse Israel, by God's intercession, he actually blessed them. Only in later days was he able to entice some of the people of Israel to sin. God dealt strongly with this action, and Balaam was slain in battle by the troops of Moses. The acts of sin were punished, and the children of Israel were protected once more. The hired leader-diviner-sooth-sayer was destroyed. Leaders who use their skills and cunning to hurt God's people will always meet their destruction.

The perversion of leadership and power can lead people astray and hurt organizations and congregations of believers. Know that what God has ordained, He will protect. Leaders of faith should always be wary of the Balaams and Balaks in their midst. They come like the night to do us harm. Guard against the perversion of leadership and power in your own ranks and cling firmly to the promises of God.

Our Prayer: *Lord God, we praise You. You protect us by Your sword and by Your hand. Christ is the adversary of those who would oppose us. We give thanks for our calling and for Your protection. Gird our hearts and minds against the perversion of leadership and make us aware when people in our midst intend to subvert our mission. May we always call upon Your name for our protection.* **Amen.**

Following Legends In Leadership

"EVERY LEADER MUST SEIZE THEIR OWN MOMENT, FORSAKING COMPARISONS"

"And the LORD said unto Moses, Take thee Joshua the son of Nun, a man in whom is the spirit, and lay thine hand upon him.… And he laid his hands upon him, and gave him a charge, as the LORD commanded.… Now after the death of Moses the servant of the Lord it came to pass.… Moses my servant is dead; now therefore arise, go…."
FEATURED SCRIPTURES: NUMBERS 27:18, 23; JOSHUA 1:1–2
BACKGROUND SCRIPTURES: NUMBERS 27:12–23; JOSHUA 1:1–9

Even before Moses' death, God had appointed Joshua to lead. Numbers 27 shows God's appointment of Joshua by Moses. But it was not until the death of Moses that we see God telling Joshua it was time to arise, seize the moment, and lead His people. Joshua had the awesome task of following a legend in leadership. Moses is, even today, the towering giant of our faith. Moses is still the great leader of Israel. Moses, the servant of the Lord, had led God's chosen people out of bondage, given them the Law, and because of their disbelief, guided them through forty years in the wilderness. God, through Moses, had brought the people to the precipice of the Promised Land, and now it was Joshua's turn to lead. No doubt Joshua was ready to lead—but what a task, and what great expectations the people must have had for him. Some folks probably gossiped about their comparisons of Moses and Joshua.

Leaders of faith in every time and place will find themselves following the successful leadership of legends and successful leaders. Maybe we are the apprentice who gets to take over for the master. Leaders of faith must often follow in the footsteps of famous leaders, orators, and bigger-than-life visionaries who built congregations and organizations over many years. But how should we respond? Leaders of faith are called by God to lead in their own special situations. Just as God called Moses for the tasks of his day, God called Joshua to a new set of tasks. Joshua was not Moses. But Joshua, like we are today, was called for special tasks and was accountable to that calling. We are not called to the tasks of God in order to be remembered or to become famous. We are simply called to be faithful in dutifully performing those things God sets before us with full heart and effort.

Each of us is equipped with unique, God-given skills for our own moment of leadership. Joshua happened to be a soldier. He would need those skills as he entered Canaan. God tells Joshua *to be strong and of a good courage: as I was with Moses, so I will be with thee.* Joshua was called to lead within his own skin and through his own personality.

Your leadership journey of faith is measured in how you respond to God's great challenge of your own moments, not how you stack up against the record of other leaders. We can't all be a Moses or a Joshua, but God has called us to this place and time to do something special for the heavenly realm. Even as you follow legends in leadership, be bold in your own calling as you serve God and those in need around you.

Our Prayer: *Jehovah God, we give thanks for leaders of faith like Moses and Joshua, who against human odds achieved great things by placing their faith and future in Your hands. Help us in our own leadership journeys to never feel compelled to compare ourselves with others, but to simply, in measured devotion, carry out the assignments You give to us. Never let vanity, legends, or comparisons of greatness infect us or deter us.* **Amen.**

Backsliding When You Are Full

"Backsliding Leaders Can Break the Chain of Godliness"

"When thou hast eaten and art full, then thou shalt bless the Lord thy God for the good land which he hath given thee. Beware that thou forget not the Lord thy God, in not keeping his commandments, and his statutes, which I command thee this day.… Only take heed to thyself, and keep thy soul diligently, lest thou forget the things which thine eyes have seen, and lest they depart from thy heart all the days of thy life: but teach them thy sons, and thy sons' sons'.…"

Featured Scriptures: Deuteronomy 8:10–12; 4:9
Background Scriptures: Deuteronomy 4:1–10; Deuteronomy 8; Proverbs 3:1–5; and Proverbs 4:20–27

We rarely backslide in our faith when we are hungry and struggling leaders of faith. The diminishing habits of good prayer, study, worship, and service more often occurs when leaders are full and feel secure. Prosperity and security can cause leaders and the organizations and congregations they lead to atrophy. One dangerous outcome of backsliding is that we fail to teach our children and followers the miracle of our calling from God. We fail to adequately rejoice in the abundant mercy and grace from God, which is the foundation of our success.

Moses warned his followers, in their new fullness and abundance, to not forget God and to be diligent in keeping His statutes and commandments. Leaders of faith in the tribes of Moses were to teach each generation the stories of God's providence in their lives. As leaders of faith, we too, carry a heavy burden. Our own backsliding in faith and worship not only breaks our harmony with God, but it also endangers the missions to which we have been called.

Backsliding does not usually involve a steep slope upon which leaders quickly slide downward. Backsliding occurs in small doses. We may develop habits that are not conducive to great leadership. We fail to attend to the small details of our daily work, and this lack of attentiveness can cause an erosion of efficiency and service to our team. We begin to miss worship services, and our prayer life wanes. We begin to enjoy the fat of the table and the accolades of leadership success too often. In our prosperity we often fail to see the small cracks and leaks in our organizational structure that, when left unattended, can erode the foundation. We fail to see the needy around us.

Successful leaders of faith who enjoy longevity in service must guard mightily against backsliding in their personal lives and within the institutions they serve. Constant praise and thanksgiving to God must always be present in their lives. Humility and graciousness are noticeable in these leaders and organizations. Frugality and temperance are constant qualities of successful leaders.

If you are backsliding, it is time to address it with all seriousness—today. Go to God in prayer. Make a list of your bad habits. Enlist others in helping you to build a more disciplined agenda. Budget your time and resources more efficiently. And constantly remind those you lead of God's ownership of their lives and calling. Never let others believe we are successful from our own work alone. When our hearts are etched with God's thumbprint, backsliding is not an option.

Our Prayer: *Lord God, make me ever vigilant against backsliding in my personal walk with You and in my leadership calling. Make me ever mindful of Your presence and providence in my daily affairs. I will strive this day and every day to lift up Your name and remind those entrusted to my leadership that it is only by Your hand that we are redeemed and sustained.* **Amen.**

God Of A New Clean Slate

"God Picks Up Our Broken Dreams and Hews New Life in New Stones"

"At that time the Lord said unto me, Hew thee two tables of stone like unto the first, and come up unto me into the mount, and make thee an ark of wood. And I will write on the tables the words that were in the first tables which thou brakest, and thou shalt put them in the ark."

Featured Scripture: Deuteronomy 10:1–2
Background Scriptures: Deuteronomy 10:1–5; and Exodus 32:15–35

Moses did what God had commanded him to do. He had gone into the mountain and encountered God's presence. There, God gave to Moses and the people of Israel the Law and the commandments. With God's own finger, He inscribed the holy tablets. Moses took them back to the people. When Moses was delayed in returning, the people panicked and committed grave sins. When Moses arrived and witnessed their disobedience, he became angry and cast the holy tablets upon the ground and broke them.

The fingerprint of God was shattered by Moses in his frustration and anger at his followers. If this incident was the joint failure of a leader and his followers or if it is just an unfortunate event of human shortcoming is left to be debated. But our lesson today shows that God came back to Moses and gave him the chance to have a fresh, clean slate of tablets and a chance to start anew.

We as leaders of faith too often take the precious gifts and tools God has hewn for us and drop them. We break them through our own human frustrations and emotions. We may take a treasured relationship and destroy it through betrayal, neglect, or lust. We may take a healthy body and a keen mind and allow them to atrophy through addiction or neglect. Those we lead may take a holy and sacred calling and let selfish ambition and corruption seep into its foundation until the whole congregation and institution begins to crumble around us.

God, in His infinite mercy, love, and forgiveness, takes our broken dreams and shattered lives and bids us to come to Him. He summons us back to the mountain so He can rebuild relationships and rehabilitate our brokenness. He will even call us to build an ark of protection so His new creations in our lives will be protected from harm. If you or those you lead have failed in your journey of faith, maybe it is time you went back to the holy mount of God. Bring your own blank tablets to God. Let Him write a new message of hope upon your heart. Let Him build new support systems in your life to protect you.

Just as God gives you a chance to repair your life, you as a leader should give those in your care a second chance and a clean slate, restoring their hope. The new life that can be written on a fresh set of stones may erase all the past brokenness and make us all even better than before. So climb the holy mount and seek God and a clean slate of opportunity this very day.

Our Prayer: *God, You are a great God of clean slates and second chances. Just as You forgave Moses and the fallen people of Israel, forgive us today. Like Moses, we break rules and blow opportunities in anger and frustration. Forgive us and call us to come to You. Give us a clean slate and write Your words upon our hearts. Give us a fresh chance to serve You by leading and serving others in Christ's name.* **Amen.**

Leaving Something Behind

"Giving Others a Chance by Leaving Something Behind"

"When thou cuttest down thine harvest in thy field, and hast forgot a sheaf in the field, thou shalt not go again to fetch it: it shall be for the stranger, for the fatherless, and for the widow: that the Lord thy God may bless thee in all the work of thine hands."

Featured Scripture: Deuteronomy 24:19

Background Scriptures: Deuteronomy 24:17–22; and Ruth 2:1–7

Taking care of the poor, the widows, and the orphans is a concept that hearkens back to the Mosaic Law. In our study today, Moses explained to the Israelites that they were to take care of the hungry, the stranger, the widowed, and the fatherless by leaving some of the harvest of the field, the olive tree, and the grapevine behind so that others would have a chance to share in the abundance of God's blessings. The weakest among them could be fed and cared for by their merely leaving some of their bounty for others. God also promised a blessing to those who followed this command: "*to bless thee in all the work of thine hands.*"

The same principles apply to leaders of faith today. We are to share our own resources with those who are in need. We can budget part of our organization's funds to be given to the neediest in our own communities. We can offer scholarships to worthy youth. We can set aside part of our profits to use in the care of children and elderly persons who need heat and food and love. Moreover, we can set apart our time to minister to the needs of others who are lonely and in need of hope. Sometimes the hardest thing to set aside or leave behind is our time and personal attention to assist a person who could never repay us.

The law of leaving something behind was followed by Boaz in the story of Ruth and Naomi. Ruth and Naomi were widows in a new land, hungry and alone. While harvesting his fields, Boaz left something behind for them. The end result was not only hunger being fed, but love found between Ruth and Boaz. Marriage followed, and a child was born to them who became part of the bloodline of Christ through the obedience of Boaz to this principle. God doesn't just command us to leave something behind; God promises that if we obey this principle of helping others, every work of our hand will be blessed. Blessings follow obedience.

When we are charitable to others and give them a chance, we reap more rewards and have even more to leave behind tomorrow. Our Scripture reminds the owner of the field and vineyard that they, too, were once slaves in the hands of the Egyptians. God delivered them and expected them to be part of the deliverance of others. The more we are blessed, the more we should leave behind. The beneficiaries of our leftovers may become the leaders of faith of tomorrow. In all that you do as a leader of faith, however small or humble, leave something behind for others. God multiplies all the wheat and olives and grapes of love that others find left on our vines.

Our Prayer: *Heavenly Father, we give thanks for our harvest this day. We praise You for showing us how to leave something in the field for others. All that we have is from Your hand of blessing. We offer our lives, time, and possessions to others in Your name. Continue to bless the work of our hands as we leave part of our life in the field for others.* **Amen.**

From Harlot To Heroine Of Faith

"GOD DRAFTS THE UNLIKELY TO BECOME LEADERS OF FAITH FOR HIS PURPOSES"

"And Joshua sent two men to spy secretly, saying, Go view the land, even Jericho. And they went, and came into an harlot's house, named Rahab, and lodged there. But she brought them up to the roof of the house, and hid them with the stalks of flax…. And she said unto the men, I know that the Lord hath given you the land…then she let them down by a cord through the window: for her house was upon the town wall."

FEATURED SCRIPTURE: JOSHUA 2:1, 4, 9, 15
BACKGROUND SCRIPTURES: JOSHUA 2; 6:22–27; HEBREWS 11:31; AND JAMES 2:25

God had positioned His chosen people to subdue and conquer Canaan under Joshua's leadership. Joshua sent two spies to scout out the land before making an assault. The spies came across a house belonging to Rahab, whom the Scriptures tell us was a harlot in Jericho. Rahab had heard of the great God of Israel and believed He was the true God of heaven and earth. She kept the two spies safe and told them of the fear that her people had of the Israelites. She saved them from the king's scouts and helped them escape.

For her assistance, Rahab gained the promise of the spies that she and her family would have safe harbor when Israel came to destroy Jericho. They agreed and the deal was kept. The faith and works of Rahab are remembered throughout Scripture. Her story continues even into the writings of Matthew, the author of Hebrews, and James. The story of the enormous faith and saving works of this harlot of Canaan is a lesson of how God can use people of true heart and faith to accomplish His purposes.

Scholars give Rahab mention in the bloodline of King David and eventually Christ Himself. This harlot turned heroine turned leader of faith shows us that any person around us today—regardless of status, profession, or culture—can become something great for God. Rahab's assistance to Joshua's spies was also about kept promises. It tells us that good deeds done to assist God's leaders of faith will not go unremembered by those leaders or God.

Perhaps you have become a leader of faith in an unorthodox way. Maybe you were the most unlikely person to be chosen by God for a leadership journey of faith. God crushes all man's earthly assumptions about who is able to lead.

Our lesson today should put all persons on notice: You cannot hide behind your own sub-par profile, sinful past, or sordid profession. If God calls you to a holy task of leadership, He will lift you from all impossible circumstances to the rooftop of provision, protection, and blessing. If you or someone you know of humble rank is feeling the tug of God's call, you may do well to remember Rahab, and answer that call today.

Our Prayer: *Dear Lord, how we marvel at Your ability to choose persons like us to tackle holy tasks of leadership in Your name. We are humbled, yet honored, to have received the call. Just as You chose Rahab to help the nation of Israel, You have chosen us in our place, status, and time to accomplish feats of leadership both great and small for You. Bless us, protect us, and give us the provision we need to do Your will.* **Amen.**

The Inheritance Of Leadershiip

"The Inheritance of Leadership Is Carved Out from the Assets of Others"

"By lot was their inheritance, as the Lord commanded by the hand of Moses, for the nine tribes, and for the half tribe. For Moses had given the inheritance of two tribes and an half tribe on the other side of Jordan: but unto the Levites he gave none inheritance among them.... Command unto the children of Israel, that they give unto the Levites of the inheritance of their possession, cities to dwell in; and ye shall give also unto the Levites suburbs for the cities round about them."

FEATURED SCRIPTURES: JOSHUA 14:2–4; AND NUMBERS 35:2
BACKGROUND SCRIPTURES: NUMBERS 35:1–8; JOSHUA 14; AND JOSHUA 21

God kept His covenant with Israel. They had come into the land of promise and the inheritance was finally being divided. Each of the twelve tribes received their specific allotment, except the tribe of Levi. The Levites, as God commanded Moses, were to be given the cities and suburbs of every other tribe. The priestly tribe would receive these like a tithe, and the Levites would dwell in each city to oversee the temples and to lead the worship of all the people.

Because the assets of the Levites were carved from the inheritance of every other tribe, the Levites were given a special uniqueness and kinship with the entire nation of Israel.

Organizations and congregations blessed and called by God are to be led by leaders of faith. We as leaders of faith are set apart in a unique, priestly line of leaders who have been ordained for God's special purposes. Leaders of faith must come from the ranks of those whom they lead. Our claim to power or authority must be carved out from the assets of those followers and organizations we are called to lead.

An inheritance is bequeathed from the assets of others. As a leader in the spirit of the tribe of Levi, we are only allowed to have power as it is freely given and bestowed upon us by those we lead. When leaders of faith assume the reins of responsibility, know that they lead at the will of others and are the custodians of their spiritual assets. The wealth of the organizations we lead are God's own assets. Thus, leaders of faith, like the Levites, have a special and sacred responsibility to all others to be faithful, holy, and attentive to every tribe's needs as our special calling of God. We are part of their inheritance for God's sake.

As we think of the fulfillment of the covenant of God to the children of Israel, we see an inheritance that is special, sacred, and honorable. Let us treat our leadership positions as a special calling to protect the holy assets and the inheritance of God's Kingdom. As priestly leaders of faith, we should dwell among all the tribes of God's children in peace and prosperity.

Our Prayer: *Great God of All Tribes, You give each of us an inheritance in Your Kingdom. We praise and thank You for bestowing these blessings upon us. As leaders called by Your voice and purpose, we know that our position of leadership is carved from the inheritance and assets of those we are charged to lead. May we be ever mindful of our responsibility to be holy and good custodians of that which You and others have entrusted to us.* **Amen.**

An Exhortation For All Leaders To Remember

"Leaders Must Remember Why They Were Called and Whom They Serve"

"And Joshua called for all Israel, and for their elders, and for their heads, and for their judges, and for their officers, and said unto them: And ye have seen all that the Lord your God hath done unto all these nations because of you; for the Lord your God is he that hath fought for you.… Be ye therefore very courageous to keep and to do all that is written in the book of the law of Moses that ye turn not aside therefrom to the right hand or to the left.…"

Featured Scripture: Joshua 23:2, 6
Background Scripture: Joshua 23—24

Years earlier Moses had turned the reins of leadership over to Joshua at God's command. Joshua served nobly. He had brought the tribes of Israel into their Promised Land and divided the inheritance among them. For the time, they had subdued their enemies. When Joshua's time for death had come, he brought all the leaders of his day together to exhort them to *"remember where they came from"* and *"who it is that brought them"* and *"who it is that they are to serve"* and *"to warn them about deviating from God's law and purpose for Israel."*

The transitioning of power in a time of peace is a cause for celebration. In the case of Israel at the close of the leadership reign of Joshua, it was a time to bring all the leaders together to remind them of their calling and warn them of the consequences of disobedience. The chosen people of Israel had come a long way from their bondage in Egypt. The exceptional leadership of Moses and Joshua had brought the people to their land and inheritance. But what would the future leaders of Israel do? What will those who follow us in our leadership journey of faith do?

As leaders of faith, we stand on the shoulders and accomplishments of others. Our leadership journey is merely laying bricks upon a foundation that others dug and poured with the sweat of their brows, and through their own calling and obedience to God. For leaders of faith to maintain the success of others in an organization, a family, or a congregation, we must adhere to the solid principles of our calling and to the discipline of work that was exemplified by our elders.

Our calling to the leadership of faith entails a higher responsibility than just insuring the success of the organization. It means that we are to constantly remind those we lead to not break from the traditions or from the fundamentals of purity, honesty, and hard work. We cannot break from the reality that our success is a blessing from God, and God requires more from those He anoints for service. We, too, must exhort those we lead and who will lead after us, to stay true to the mission of our calling and to remember the God who sustains us. Just like Joshua, this last exhortation to your own successors may be your most important leadership responsibility in your own journey of faith.

Our Prayer: *Jehovah God, Your covenant with us is always true and pure. Help us as leaders of faith to exhort those who follow us to stay true to our side of the deal. Help us to always remember that it is You who called us and You who sustains us. Let us not deviate from Your commandments to the right or to the left. Thank You, Lord.* **Amen.**

Forgetting Where We Came From

"New Generations Fail When They Lose Faith and History"

"And Joshua died…and also all that generation were gathered unto their fathers: and there arose another generation after them, which knew not the Lord, nor yet the works which he had done for Israel. And the children of Israel did evil in the sight of the Lord, and served Baalim: and they forsook the Lord and served Baal and Ashtaroth."

Featured Scripture: Judges 2:8, 10–11, 13
Background Scripture: Judges 2:6–23

Joshua and the elders who followed him had led a nation of people who worshiped God and kept His commandments. They remembered their previous bondage and God's guiding hand of deliverance. They remembered the wandering in the desert and the crossing into a new and great land that God gave them. They remembered God's providence as He conquered their enemies. But once Joshua and the generation of elders who followed him died, the new generation that rose up betrayed their God and faith and searched after the idols of their new land. Alas, they lost the faith of their fathers and were judged. They had forgotten where they came from.

When our parents, grandparents, and elders pass away and our generation lets the stories, the traditions, and the bedrock of that faith journey cease to be known to our offspring, our children and grandchildren will fall prey to the false promises of this day. Even the institutions we serve as leaders of faith can atrophy and die from a lack of knowledge of our own history. It is our duty as leaders to keep the good traditions alive. It is our duty to ensure that the faithful labor of those who came before us is remembered. We should value the principles and discipline that built our strong structure; we must not allow sin to seep into our foundation and erode away God's past providential blessings toward our congregations and organizations.

When our children leave home and start their own lives, are they leaving equipped with a true sense of who they are and where they came from? Do those persons who graduate from our leadership care and tutelage go forth armed with a strong constitution and confidence? Each leader of faith has a solemn responsibility to be like Joshua and to instill the faith in a new set of elders. The elders must keep the tradition alive. The new generation of leaders must never succumb to the notion that all new things are true and right and cast away all they have been taught.

God wants to bless each new generation of leaders and their flock. But when we forget where we came from and whose hand it was that guided us to this place of blessing, we risk failure and the undoing of the good works of so many who came before us. Remain firm in the faith of our fathers and in the solid traditions of the great institutions that have nurtured us. Serve God and those He has given us to lead in truth and light. Be a protector of what is pure, and blaze a brave and bright trail. Never forget where you came from.

Our Prayer: *God of all generations, we give thanks for Your guidance and deliverance over the many years. We give thanks for our ancestors and predecessors who instilled the faith in us and who showed us how to lead and serve others. May we never forget our roots and where we came from, by Your grace and mercy.* **Amen.**

Awake, Awake! What Are You Waiting For?

"When You Feel Called, Get Up and Get Going"

"Awake, awake, Deborah: awake, awake, utter a song.… And Deborah said to Barak,
Up; for this is the day…is not the Lord gone out before thee…?"
FEATURED SCRIPTURES: JUDGES 5:12; 4:14
BACKGROUND SCRIPTURES: JUDGES 4; 5:1–12

We pray. We meditate. We ponder. We worship, and we wait on the word of the Lord to come to us. But there comes a time in every leadership experience to awake and get going. God's people were mightily oppressed by the Canaanites. The Israelites had prayed for mercy and deliverance; now, their time was at hand. The opportunity had come, and it was time for someone to lead. For the prophetess Deborah and her commander, Barak, the call was there. It was time to awake and seize God's promise.

Deborah had to get up from the shade tree from where she judged Israel and lead a new battle. Her routines of leadership would be shaken on this day and take a new turn. She had to attack a seemingly superior army. For twenty years, Jabin, the king of the Canaanites, had oppressed Israel. The call to action was now. Deborah had to heed the call and take a bold leadership risk in faith.

Are you at a juncture in your own leadership journey of faith? Have you prayed for deliverance or for a new opportunity? Are you seeking a miracle for a provision or providence to overcome a challenge? God may be calling you to simply awake, get up, and go to it. You may be in the midst of a call to get your general and go to the battle. If the Lord has gone into the battle ahead of you, you cannot fail. Often our routines and daily habits of leadership stifle our ability to hear God's call to battle.

The boldness of our actions as we awake and tackle the challenge of this day may inspire others to follow us in a bolder way. The courage of Deborah to seize the day and claim the promise of God broke the captivity of her people. When leaders develop an aversion to risk, they cease to be open to new calls of God. Breaking the captivity in your organization and congregation means you must awake today and do something different. Our captivity may be a chronic lack of resources. It may be a declining membership or falling sales. It may be a physical or health challenge. Whatever is holding us captive, God can deliver us if we will but seize the day and arise.

Leave the shade and comfort of your leadership chair today. Find your own Barak, and go into a battle today for the independence from those chains that are binding you. If you have prayed for deliverance, perhaps God is just waiting for you to get up and go to it. *Awake, awake! What are you waiting for?*

Our Prayer: *Lord God, we give thanks for Deborah and Barak. They seized the day and the opportunity You gave them. Their prayer had already been answered. Awaken us, Lord, from our self-pity and old routines. Awaken us from a lack of faith. Instill in us as leaders a new fearlessness and boldness to claim Your promise. Go before us, Lord, today and prepare the way as we ride into battle to become free.* **Amen.**

Threshing, Tending, Plowing, Fishing

"Called from Humble Tasks to Faithful Service"

"And there came an angel of the Lord…and Gideon threshed wheat by the winepress to hide it from the Midianites.… Wherefore Saul sent messengers unto Jesse, and said, Send me David thy son, which is with the sheep.… So he departed thence, and found Elisha…who was plowing with twelve yoke of oxen.… And Jesus, walking by the sea of Galilee, saw two brethren, Simon, called Peter, and Andrew his brother, casting a net into the sea: for they were fishers."

Featured Scriptures: Judges 6:11–12; 1 Samuel 16:19; 1 Kings 19:19; and Matthew 4:18
Background Scriptures: Judges 6:6–14; 1 Samuel 16:14–23; 1 Kings 19:15–21; and Matthew 4:18-21

Gideon, David, Elisha, Peter, and Andrew are names that appear in the Hall of Fame for leaders of faith. These prophets, kings, and apostles answered God's call to service. They were not called out of the great academies or universities of their time. They were not in the courts of kings when their call came. These humble servants were doing manual labor, even as the call of the Lord came to them.

Gideon was threshing wheat in a hiding place. David was tending the sheep for his father, Jesse. Elisha was in his father's field with twelve yoke of oxen plowing the ground for planting. Peter and Andrew were at sea, casting nets in hopes of making a catch of fish to sell. On each separate occasion, these leaders-in-waiting were going about the routine tasks of their day. The Lord comes calling on us when we least expect it, even as we labor away in our menial jobs. God calls the humble for the holy.

What are you doing today? Are you getting ready to go to your humble job or laboring away at some menial task? The key to becoming a leader of faith is being ready when God calls. Be ready to leave the press, leave the pasture, leave the field, and leave the boat. Each of the leaders above was summoned by angels, kings, prophets, and the Messiah Himself. Be ready for your pastor, boss, spouse, neighbor, or even a stranger to tap you on the shoulder and ask you to accept a leadership position of faith. God's Spirit moves across the face of the earth and touches pure hearts and brave souls, inspiring them to do the work of the Kingdom of God.

Many congregations and organizations are filled with leaders of faith who were called to God's service from factory floors, farms, classrooms, and even from retirement, to embark on an important mission of service to others. God uses the full retinue of the world's talent for His purposes. Never minimize your own worth to God. Be ready. If you are threshing, tending, plowing, or fishing, be ready. The Master may come by and tap you for heavenly service this very day.

Our Prayer: *Lord Jesus, You choose the most unlikely for the highest callings of service. Regardless of our status in life, we claim the promise that You can call us to leadership journeys of faith. We pray that we will be ready when that moment comes. Show us the task that You would have us do. In the meantime, let us work humbly and faithfully in the tasks, jobs, and professions we are blessed to do.* **Amen.**

When God Stacks The Odds Against Us

"GOD USES STACKED ODDS AS A WAY TO CREATE OUR RELIANCE UPON HIM"

"And the LORD said unto Gideon, The people that are with thee are too many for me to give the Midianites into their hands, lest Israel vaunt themselves against me, saying mine own hand has saved me."

FEATURED SCRIPTURE: JUDGES 7:2
BACKGROUND SCRIPTURE: JUDGES 6—8

Gideon was not only an unlikely leader, he was skeptical of his calling. After testing the call of God through the wet and dry fleece, Gideon finally heeded God's call to military leadership. When Gideon's call to the people of Israel went out, 32,000 responded. Their enemies, the Midianites, numbered 135,000 men. God then, through a series of commands, told Gideon to reduce the number of his troops. Gideon's task of service to God began with God stacking the odds against him.

God ultimately reduced Gideon's army to just three hundred chosen men. By following God's plan in faith, Israel prevailed as the enemy turned on each other in chaos and confusion. God often stacks the odds against us to teach us reliance on Him. He leads us into victory in impossible situations so that we may never claim the credit for ourselves. The miracle of Gideon's leadership victory was laid squarely at the altar of God. The confusion and routing of the Midianites shows us that God is not interested in numbers or odds.

As a leader of faith called to service today, do you feel God stacking the odds against you? Perhaps God is telling you to rely on His providence and not on your own skills or the assets of your institution. Perhaps God is telling you that talent, beauty, and skill are not necessary, but only your full measure of faith in His power. God may call you to blow trumpets and smash clay pitchers instead of using conventional methods of warfare. God is seeking humble reliance from those He calls. Gideon wisely gave Yahweh the glory and credit for the victory. Jewish history is replete with praise to God for His deliverance of Israel from captivity of the Midianites through the obedient leadership of Gideon. When the odds get stacked against you, begin seeking your own instruction from God.

Are the Midianites camped below your tent today? Are you hopelessly outnumbered in a tough life circumstance and can only see God subtracting from your resources? Maybe God is calling on you as a leader to get on your knees and give the situation to Him. If God be for us, who can be against us?

God brings provision and victory in many ways. God controls circumstances and resources. God brings confusion to our adversaries and causes chaos among our rivals. Only God can increase our power through subtraction. So find your three hundred chosen ones and go into battle. Try unorthodox methods through faith. Blow your trumpet, break your pitchers, let the lights shine, and claim victory even today as the odds are stacked against you.

Our Prayer: *Great Yahweh, only You can save us. Even as the odds are stacked against us, You call us to action and leadership for You. We claim Your power and await the miracle of our salvation. Show us what to do and what remnant of followers to take into the battles of our day. Victory is at hand through Your power alone. Mold us into Gideon leaders today.* **Amen.**

Beware Of Building A Dynasty

"CALLED LEADERSHIP IS NOT ALWAYS TRANSFERRABLE TO FAMILY AND FRIENDS"

"Then the men of Israel said unto Gideon, rule thou over us, both thou, and thy son, and thy son's son also: for thou hast delivered us from the hand of Midian. And Gideon said unto them, I will not rule over you, neither shall my son rule over you: the Lord shall rule over you.… Abimelech hired vain and light persons which followed him. And he went unto his father's house at Ophrah, and slew his brethren…and all the men of Shechem gathered and made Abimelech king.…"

FEATURED SCRIPTURES: JUDGES 8:22–23; 9:4–6
BACKGROUND SCRIPTURE: JUDGES 8—9

The story of the triumph of Gideon is part of the godly heroism found in the history of Israel. Gideon was an unlikely leader of faith called by God to deliver God's people from the oppression of the Midianites. Though vastly outnumbered, Gideon, by God's own provision, led a small army against a superior enemy. In the glory of victory, the people of Israel came to Gideon to anoint him and his sons rulers of Israel. Gideon flatly refused their offer. Gideon said neither he nor his sons would rule Israel, but God alone. Gideon shunned the making of his own leadership dynasty.

Yet Gideon's son Abimelech had other ideas. He felt a sense of entitlement to rule because he was the blood son of Gideon. Abimelech used murder and other treachery to gain a kingship. His rule would be troubled and cursed by God. His self-led quest for a leadership dynasty would end in utter ruin. The tragedy of this story can teach leaders of faith a thoughtful lesson. Godly leadership is not always transferrable to our family and friends. God sometimes ordains the transfer of leadership for some leaders, like King David to his son Solomon. But in the case of Gideon, a leadership dynasty was not to be built.

Leaders always want the best for their children and families. We want our friends and loyal associates to be rewarded in life. But we can fail God when we project leadership onto those whom God has not called. Gideon said that not he or his sons, but *the LORD shall rule over you.* God is perfectly capable of appointing your successor in leadership. It is most important that we be humble and attuned to God's voice in our own journey. God will bless our family and friends if we remain obedient and faithful to Him. Always beware that you do not push others into positions of leadership in order to protect your own ambitions or legacy. Abimelech's ruthless ambition cost many lives and caused much suffering.

Let your dynasty of leadership be built solely upon the rock of Christ's promises. Build your own leadership dynasty through love and service to others. The lineage of leadership that you will build through humility and selfless service will carry on as others seek to emulate your devotion to your own personal calling from an awesome God.

Our Prayer: *Heavenly Father, it is not me or those who follow me in leadership who rule. It is You, Lord, who is to rule over us. Instill in us as leaders of faith the humility and devotion to duty that will transcend any quest we may have for power or dynasty. Let our work and service to others speak for itself. We ask Your blessings on our families, friends, and associates also. Show them what tasks they can do for the Kingdom of God.* **Amen.**

A Last Shot At Leadership Redemption

"Leaders of Faith Can Be Restored for Final Acts of Strength for God"

"Now the house was full of men and women; and all the lords of the Philistines were there; and there were upon the roof about three thousand men and women that beheld while Samson made sport. And Samson called unto the Lord, and said, O Lord God, remember me, I pray thee, and strengthen me, I pray thee, only this once…. And Samson said, Let me die with the Philistines. And he bowed himself with all his might and the house fell upon the lords, and upon all the people that were therein. So the dead which he slew at his death were more than they which he slew in his life."

Featured Scripture: Judges 16: 27–28, 30
Background Scripture: Judges 13—16

Samson judged Israel for twenty years. Samson's mother pledged him before his birth to be a Nazarite, after having been visited by the angel of the Lord. Samson was to be set apart by God from birth to deliver Israel from the grip of the Philistines. Samson would receive superhuman strength during his lifetime and would become legendary in battle against the Philistines for his courage and power. Samson killed many Philistines and was greatly feared.

Later in Samson's life, he fell for the charms of the seductress Delilah. Delilah, with her pillow talk and evil conniving, lulled Samson into sharing the secrets of his strength and holy protection. Delilah sold Samson out to the Philistines and shared with the enemies of Israel Samson's secret of protection. Samson's head was shaved. He was captured, his eyes gouged out. He was imprisoned and made a jester for the Philistines. Mighty Samson had not only fallen, but he had been reduced to humiliation through his own sin.

Great leaders of faith can fall suspect to the same temptation of sin. In Samson's attraction and lust for the wrong women, he allowed himself to become seduced by their deceit. It cost him his position and his blessing, and it cost Israel a great leader. God, however, is a God of grace, and He gave Samson a last shot at leadership redemption.

Samson's last plea to God was heard as he regained his strength for one final act of revenge against his tormentors and the Philistine enemies of Israel. Leaders of faith must be ready at all times for any purpose if God calls, even a call for your redemption in leadership.

Leaders who are out of fellowship with God and out of power within their old institutions may be given new chances at leadership redemption. Leaders of faith should know that when they are called upon by God, they must be willing and prepared. God will show fallen leaders a great deed that can be done for His purpose if we will pray for new opportunities to serve God and those in need around us. Our strength and honor as leaders can be restored by our awesome God.

Our Prayer: *Dear God, redeem us as You redeemed Samson for one final act of strength. Help us as leaders of faith to not be seduced by the lure of the seductress. The seductions can come in many forms, but give us the courage to say no when tempted. Restore in those of us who fall short a purpose and task, with the strength to do it for You, even if for one last time.* **Amen.**

A Paid "Yes-Man" Who Can Bring Down A Leader

"Subverting Holy Advice for Your Own Purposes Can Invite Destruction"

"And Micah said unto him, Dwell with me, and be unto me a father and a priest, and I will give thee ten shekels of silver by the year, and a suit of apparel and thy victuals. So the Levite went in. Then said Micah, Now know I that the Lord will do me good, seeing I have a Levite to my priest."

Featured Scripture: Judges 17:10, 13
Background Scripture: Judges 17—18

The time recorded in the Book of Judges was a turbulent one for the tribes of Israel. It was also an evil time, as the Scripture states: *"…but every man did that which was right in his own eyes"* (Judges 17:6). This Micah of Judges (not the prophet Micah) was not a credible man. But he does provide us with a great example of how to sow the seeds of failed leadership. After stealing from his own mother, Micah took up with a wandering Levite named Jonathan.

As a Levite, Jonathan was of the priestly tribe of Levi, but nothing indicates that this Jonathan was himself a priest. Micah made Jonathan a deal to hire him as a personal priest. He would pay him a stipend each month, and would acquire for him all the clothes and trappings of an authentic, holy priest. Jonathan took the deal and Micah, in his own blindness and superstition, believed his actions would bring him the favor of God.

Micah not only used this paid, "yes-man" priest as a pretentious personal symbol, but when Micah was called to lead his tribe, he carried his "yes-man" forth into a tribal battle as a warrior priest and adviser. The sum effect of this tremendous leadership apostasy by Micah was that it allowed spiritual bankruptcy to develop among his tribe as they trusted in the graven images of idolatry.

Today it is not hard to see examples of failed leadership of similar proportions in our own institutions and communities. Failing leaders often surround themselves with advisers who are only in place to tell them what they want to hear. Their decisions may be expedient, but can bring long-term damage to those they lead.

Even leaders of faith can fall into the trap of Micah by putting the wrong people into the wrong places for the wrong reasons. To veer away from true holy places and the respected advice of our own real priests and real religion, searching instead for symbolic trappings of power and paid advice, can set the trap for your own demise.

Leaders of faith should always establish strong, stable, and diverse groups of confidants and advisers, including pastors, priests, and elders. Put people into place in your congregation and organization who will never tell you only what you want to hear. Surround yourself with advisers and confidants who will only give you the advice you need to know to have to serve God and others well.

Our Prayer: *Father, chasten us, but forgive us when we seek and take the wrong advice. Cleanse us from any false trappings of leadership. Bring to us calm comfort and protection by providing mentors and advisers of godly character and wisdom. Keep us in the right way, we pray.* **Amen.**

Where Loyalty Can Lead

"Leaders Should Be Loyal Because Loyalty Brings Blessings"

"And Ruth said, intreat me not to leave thee, or to return from following after thee; for wither thou goest, I will go; and where thou lodgest, I will lodge; thy people shall be my people, and thy God, my God."

Featured Scripture: Ruth 1:16
Background Scripture: Ruth 4:13–22

A senior leader once said that the greatest leadership sin is ingratitude. It happens by turning your back on those who love you in a time of trouble. It happens when we forget who helped us gain our success. But today's lesson takes another angle to that view. If ingratitude is a leadership sin, then leadership gratitude shown by loyalty is a virtue. No greater example of gratitude and loyalty can be found in Scripture than in the story of Ruth and Naomi. This story shows us where loyalty can lead.

The backdrop for this show of loyalty in today's lesson is set amidst a country's famine as two women grieved over the deaths of their sons and husbands. All of these tragedies took place in a strange land. As all seemed hopeless, Naomi and Ruth found themselves destitute and hungry. But Ruth's cleaving loyalty to her mother-in-law, Naomi, gave God a chance to work miracles as they returned to Bethlehem. The Book of Ruth tells one of the great love stories of the Bible.

The love of Naomi for Ruth, and the loyalty exhibited to Naomi by her daughter-in-law, Ruth, set the stage for a renewal of hope that would touch generations to come. This new hope of Ruth led to her marriage to Boaz and the birth of new life in Obed. Obed became the father of Jesse and the grandfather of David, thus part of the bloodline of Christ. Loyalty, love, and gratitude in our own poverty will bring hope and blessings and set off a chain reaction of God's providence.

Loyalty can put you in the right place at the right time. Loyalty in the face of hunger and destitution is one of life's greatest displays of love. Not only were Naomi and Ruth given food from the kindness of Boaz as he allowed them to glean his fields for leftover wheat, but Ruth found the love of this very same man. She would also find marriage and the blessing of a son. In this chain of events, Naomi herself was restored as the grandmother of new life.

Good leaders of faith will inspire loyalty. Inspiring the loyalty of others will unleash new power that can accomplish great tasks. As we are loyal in leadership, others become loyal to us. We, too, as leaders of faith, should reward loyalty in those who follow us. Leave a little grain on the ground for those persons who need assistance in your organization or congregation. Loyalty leads to the love of others and a newfound faith in the Almighty. God can work His plans as we watch and follow where loyalty can lead.

Our Prayer: *Heavenly Father, thank You for Ruth, Naomi, and Boaz. Thank You for Your loyalty to us, even when we fail You. Help us to live our lives so as to inspire the loyalty of others. Help us to reward the loyalty of those around us who quietly serve us each day. Give us the faith to see where loyalty can lead. We pray the loyalty around us will bring blessings to others and praise to You.* **Amen.**

Leaders Who Fail To Lead At Home

"GREAT LEADERS FAIL WHEN THEY FAIL TO LEAD AT HOME"

"Now the sons of Eli were sons of Belial; they knew not the LORD.… For I have told him that I will judge his house for ever for the iniquity which he knoweth; because his sons made themselves vile, and he restrained them not."

FEATURED SCRIPTURES: 1 SAMUEL 2:12; AND 3:13
BACKGROUND SCRIPTURES: 1SAMUEL 3:13—4; AND PROVERBS 22:6

True leadership is time-consuming, is demanding, and often requires untold sacrifice on the part of a leader of faith. In order to meet the needs of those whom God has given to us to serve, we must spend time away from our own families. Great leaders all sacrifice something of value in performing their tasks and duties. Many times that means we miss the chance to lead our own families at critical times in the lives of our children. Our lesson today warns us that even the great leaders of faith can fail when they fail to lead at home.

One of Scripture's greatest lessons can be found in the Book of 1 Samuel and the story of the prophet Eli and his two sons. The prophet Eli served the Lord and Israel for forty years and had much success. However, we find that his life as a father and a leader in his own home was lacking, and ultimately caused his family's own demise. The ungodly acts of his own two sons contributed to the end of his reign as an effective leader of Israel.

By scriptural account, Eli's two sons were *belial*, or the embodiment of all that was bad and evil. They were not trained in the knowledge of the Lord. They defiled the Temple and made mockery of the holy activities of worship. While Eli was leading Israel, his own sons were going astray. Eli failed to discipline them and teach them the ways of God. By failing to lead at home, Eli failed in his leadership of Israel. His people lost in battle and the Ark of the Covenant was taken from them. Eli, his sons, his daughter-in-law, and his unborn grandson all perished, and the succession of prophetic leadership was passed to another.

While we in our own leadership journey may never bear the responsibilities of the prophet of an entire nation, we can still cause damage to our own godly work by failing to take the time and attention to love, teach, discipline, and care for our families. Our children and spouses should never suffer from our absence or lack of instruction in the holy ways of God. Our institutional leadership effectiveness can suffer when our own families are neglected.

God wants leaders of faith to take the necessary time to follow His command to teach our children in the ways of the Lord. It may mean slowing down, missing some important congregational events, or the setting of new priorities. It may mean forgoing a promotion or not seeking higher office or greater power or wealth. Becoming a great leader of faith means we become a great leader within our own home. It may just be our greatest leadership calling!

Our Prayer: *Dear Father, You are our heavenly Father. You ordained and blessed us with families to love and cherish and to lead. Please make us always mindful to lead them and teach them Your ways. Show us how to balance our lives and time so we can first lead at home before attempting to lead in our communities. Also, forgive us when we don't, and help repair the damage that our failures may have caused.* **Amen.**

Substituting Superstition For Real Power

"Reducing the Power of God to Symbolism Can Bring Leaders Down"

"When the Philistines took the ark of God, they brought it into the house of Dagon, and set it by Dagon.… And it was so, that, after they had carried it about, the hand of the LORD was against the city with a very great destruction: and he smote the men of the city, both small and great, and they had emerods in their secret parts."

Featured Scripture: 1 Samuel 5:2, 9
Background Scripture: 1 Samuel 5—7:1–2

The people of Israel had fought the Philistines and lost. The Ark of the Covenant was taken by the Philistines. Eli, the judge and priest, dropped dead. The time was tough for Israel. But for the Philistines in their arrogance and superstition, the capture of the Ark for the sake of power and advantage over God's people would bring them to doom. They had perverted holiness and substituted superstition and symbolism associated with the Ark in a quest for power. This action constituted an abomination toward the true God.

Throughout history and even today, we see many leaders and seekers of power try to capture the symbols of faith and use them for political or military gain. Not only do they seize the sacred tablets or the cross of Christ as symbols, but by vain uses of Scripture or declaring a false anointing, they try through the symbols of faith to claim power over the minds of others. To those who are weak in faith or who do not have faith, these grabs of power through the use of holy symbols can seem amusing or even be interpreted as a positive thing. But clearly God will not be mocked, nor will He allow an imposter of true power to be successful by the substitution of symbolism for true faith. God will judge.

In our own leadership journeys of faith, we must be cautious in choosing symbolism over true substance of faith. The Scripture, the teachings, and the endorsement of elders should be carefully used so as to edify and glorify God and not to further personal agendas. When we see the misuse of symbols of faith, we should be bold to declare it. True power rests in our obedience and reliance on God's power and provision.

The Philistines paid a great price for their folly. The Ark housed the tablets hewn by the very finger of the Creator. The idols fell before it. Their cities were destroyed, and their men were struck with tumors. In the end, the Philistines hauled the Ark of the Covenant back to Israel, acknowledging that the real power did not rest in the ownership of symbols and superstition.

Leaders of faith who have answered the call of duty should report to work each day in all humility and reverence. We should never use the symbols and trappings of power and authority for any use but for completing the tasks that God has given us to do. True power rests in keeping our eyes focused on the living God and serving others.

Our Prayer: *Lord God, we stand in awe of You today. We pray that we will never misuse or abuse the faith or seek to capture the symbols of faith for selfish motive. Keep us humble and centered in Your will. May we approach every task You give us to do in faith and reverence.* **Amen.**

Five Smooth Stones

"Real Leaders Choose the Right Ammunition and the Right Challenges"

"And David said unto Saul, I cannot go with these; for I have not proved them. And David put them off him. And he took his staff in this hand, and chose him five smooth stones out of the brook, and put them in a shepherd's bag which he had, even in a scrip; and his sling was in his hand: and he drew near to the Philistine."
Featured Scripture: 1 Samuel 17:39–40
Background Scripture: 1 Samuel 17

The story of David and Goliath is one of the Bible's most remembered and most often invoked situational comparisons when people face daunting odds. However, there are many lessons of leadership to be learned from David and the people of Israel as they faced this life-and-death situation. In today's lesson David was chosen as Israel's representative to face the giant Philistine warrior champion, Goliath. This one-on-one duel would decide the fate of a nation. Besides being an unlikely gladiator, it was David's own choice of five smooth stones as his ammunition against the nine-foot-tall Goliath that holds wisdom for leaders of faith. David's own life experiences as a shepherd in wild places influenced his belief that he could, indeed, kill Goliath. It also influenced his choice of a sling and five smooth stones versus a sword and shield as the holy weapon and ammunition needed to defeat his foe.

David's faith and youthful confidence in the God of Israel was mocked by Goliath and the Philistines. The mocking of God and the Israelites by Goliath and an army that worshiped idols only emboldened David to action. First, David had to sell his credentials and life experience to King Saul as to why he should be chosen as Israel's representative to face Goliath and hold the fate of the nation in his hands.

As a leader of faith, you, too, may have to convince those in authority to give you a chance to attempt the great feat God has called you to do. You also must choose the right ammunition. Don't accept a sword and shield when you really need a sling and five smooth stones. Like David, be willing to accept those Goliath-like challenges that play to your own God-given strengths and abilities. Be ready to step into life's toughest battles with faith in the skills and assets you've attained through your own unique life experience. When the core beliefs and principles upon which we stand are mocked and challenged, we must respond, even to the seemingly insurmountable challenges. Accepting mismatched challenges in our leadership journeys of faith will certainly become part of our daily life as leaders. As God's chosen-elect, we will often appear to be the smaller and weaker warrior. But our God is great.

In every leadership task of life that God gives us to do, He will hone in us the skills that we will need to face the bigger challenges ahead. We can never pierce the armor of injustice, poverty, or sin by running from a challenge or choosing conventional weaponry. It will take all the faith and confidence gained through our own lonely night experiences to make us ready. Be ready to choose your own five smooth stones for the holy victory in your mismatched challenge this day.

Our Prayer: *Lord, how often we face the Goliaths of life only to see defeat and destruction ahead. How often we fail, not because we ran away, but because we chose the wrong weapon and the wrong fight. Help us, dear Lord, to have the courage and faith of Your servant David as we seek to slay the giants of injustice in our own leadership journeys.* **Amen.**

Jealousy Destroys Leaders

"ALLOWING THE PROWESS OF OTHERS TO FILL YOU WITH JEALOUSY CAN DESTROY"

"So the women sang as they danced, and said: Saul has slain his thousands, and David his ten thousands. Then Saul was very angry and the saying displeased him…so Saul eyed David from that day forward. And it happened on the next day that the distressing spirit from God came upon Saul.…"

FEATURED SCRIPTURE: 1 SAMUEL 18:7–10
BACKGROUND SCRIPTURE: 1 SAMUEL 18:1–16

Jealousy destroys good leaders. Jealousy is a cancer in leadership. It infects us when we look upon ourselves with great delight. For leaders of faith, self-congratulation mocks God. In the case of King Saul, the new leader, David, was rising and being noticed by the people. Instead of glorifying God and thanking Him for raising up a new, young leader, Saul viewed David with an eye of jealousy. David was a faithful servant to Saul. Even though David was not trying to displace Saul, the accolades that David was receiving drove Saul to anger. Once jealousy entered the heart of Saul, the Scripture says a *"distressing spirit from God came upon Saul."*

The story of Saul and David turned tragic as the great King Saul became obsessed with David. David was a leader and the future king, anointed by God's hand. But Saul's jealousy blinded him from seeing God's blessing. Jealousy is used by Satan to destroy our best works. Even the greatest leaders of faith must realize that others will be greater than they and that their time of leadership is finite. Leaders of faith should recognize and nurture the new and bright talent in their midst. Rather than being a mentor to David, Saul marred his own place in history through his blind jealousy toward God's servant David.

In our own lives of leadership, it is easy to slip into a mode of self-congratulation when times are good. Our self-admiration can lead to our jealousy of competitors and rivals. It is our duty to God to remain humble and prayerful and to maintain the presence of mind to give God the glory for all our achievements. We should become the mentors and cheerleaders of young and rising leaders. They, too, are part of God's plan to raise up the next generation of leadership. Any condescension toward rising leaders can breed jealousy.

When we as leaders of faith sense feelings of jealousy seeping into our thoughts and words, let us retreat to our prayer closets and seek God's forgiveness and guidance. Never let Satan's arrows pierce your good works through petty jealousies. Lift the new leaders among you. Never desire to be seen as better or more remembered than others. Let your life be lived so that the only accolade you desire to hear is from the judgment throne of God as He says: *"Well done my good and faithful servant"* (Matthew 25:23).

Our Prayer: *Lord Jesus, let Your Holy Spirit indwell me and purify me of all jealousy. Help me to stand guard against self-congratulation and the desire to be greater than others. Instead of a jealous leader, make me a teacher and mentor to rising stars and leaders of faith. Never let pride drive my decisions. Keep me safe and in a humble spirit of service for You.* **Amen.**

When Intercession Is Leadership

"We Become Leaders When We Intercede to Prevent Calamity"

"And David heard in the wilderness that Nabal did shear his sheep.... And when Abigail saw David, she hasted, and lighted off the ass, and fell before David on her face, and bowed herself to the ground, And fell at his feet, and said, Upon me, my lord, upon me let this iniquity be: and let thine handmaid, I pray thee, speak in thine audience, and hear the words of thine handmaid."

FEATURED SCRIPTURES: 1 SAMUEL 25:4; 23—24
BACKGROUND SCRIPTURE: 1 SAMUEL 25

The story of David and Abigail begins with a great act of courage and leadership. Abigail is described as a woman of good understanding and of a beautiful countenance. In today's lesson, Abigail teaches us the leadership principle of leadership through intercession. Sometimes leaders of faith will be called upon to get involved in bad situations as intercessors so as to avoid calamity. We may do this at great risk to ourselves.

Abigail's husband, Nabal, was described as a wealthy and arrogant man who had little regard for others. Nabal took David's sheep and sheared the wool off their backs while David was away on a trip. When confronted by David's messengers as to why he would do such a thing, he insulted David and would not acknowledge his wrongdoing. David was now set for revenge and retribution against Nabal and his clan. Blood would be shed, and innocent lives might be lost. But the heroine of faith, Abigail, stepped in the gap through intercession. Her understanding and quick decision in this volatile situation set the mark of great leadership.

Abigail seized the mantle of leadership from her drunken husband, Nabal. She prepared a peace offering and went to meet David just as he and his men approached Nabal's home. Abigail was an innocent party, yet she put herself into the middle of this dispute on behalf of her wicked husband and the innocent people of his household. It worked. David's anger was squashed by her humility, offering, and valor. Nabal died ten days later of a heart attack. David then married Abigail, and a great love story of Scripture was written.

The example of Abigail's intercessory leadership is a poignant reminder for leaders of faith today. In our own congregations, businesses, and organizations, our superiors and peers will often make poor decisions that stand to hurt others. We may see evil or corruption taking place in our midst. When we see these situations arise, we, too, may be called to lead by intercession. Intercessory leadership is risky. We can be blamed. We can be fired. We can be hurt. Unlike Abigail, we may not be rewarded by love and marriage. But if God calls us to intercessory leadership, He will never abandon us. Stay true to your calling, and He will stay true to you.

Our Prayer: *Dear God, thank You for Abigail and her heroism. May her example of bravery and intercession on behalf of others become our model for leadership. Bless us with the understanding and discernment to know when to intercede on behalf of others. Protect and bless our decisions and help us to keep the innocent from harm by Your power.* **Amen.**

A Mother's Faith Comes To Lead A Nation

"HANNAH'S PRAYER FOR A SON AND HER DEDICATION OF HIM TO
GOD'S PURPOSES SET AN EXAMPLE OF HOW A MOTHER CAN LEAD OTHERS"

"For this child I prayed; and the LORD hath given me my petition which I asked of him: Therefore also I have lent him to the LORD; as long as he liveth he shall be lent to the LORD. And he worshipped the LORD there."
Featured Scriptures: 1 Samuel 1:27–28; and Luke 2:51
BACKGROUND SCRIPTURE: 1 SAMUEL 1—2:10

Hannah was leading before she ever had a son. Hannah prayed for a child and was faithful to God so that her prayers could be answered. God sensed the true heart of Hannah and granted her petition. Hannah endured the bitterness, the wait, and the anxiety of barrenness and rebuke, but in the end she gave birth to Samuel, who would become the great prophet of Israel.

Nowhere is the purpose and plan of God as clearly revealed as it is through the mothers of each generation who devote themselves and their children to God's service. Hannah joins Ruth, Elisabeth, Mary, the mother of Jesus, and the other great women of faith who sensed that their humble, yet powerful commitment to devoted motherhood could change the world as they knew it.

Mothers today may not raise a great prophet, but all can raise great citizens and servants of God. Through a mother's leadership, communities are strengthened and the faith is passed along to each successive generation. A mother's leadership is seen in the daily instruction of respect and discipline and by showing love and forgiveness for others.

Mothers surely suffer as they see their children fail and fall. They suffer most when they know they must let them make their own mistakes and work their own way through the pain. And mothers give thanks and praise for even the smallest achievements and success of a child. Mothers uniquely know when to let their children go and entrust them to the Lord's keeping.

Mothers become leaders of faith when they take children to a place of worship and teach them to respect the institution of the Church. Mothers lead when they cherish education, fitness of body, and character. Mothers lead when they pray daily for their sons and daughters even as their children stumble, fall, and fail to meet expectations. Mothers lead when all humanity has lost hope in their children, but yet they pray on and on, hoping and expecting a miracle in their children's broken lives. Mothers lead when they push a good child to expand their boundaries and do even better.

Even if we cannot be a physical mother, we can mentor and care for a child in need of instruction, love, and advocacy. You, like Hannah, can endure the anxiety and uncertainty of motherhood and leadership if you will only trust that God can turn your commitment to Him into eternal greatness. Keep leading as a mother; our world depends upon you. God will bless your service.

Our Prayer: *Lord above, we praise You for mothers and the leadership they provide in many quiet ways. Bless mothers past, present, and future. Strengthen, we pray, the women of our world who need courage, hope, and a special portion of blessing today. Let the faith of mothers continue to bless our people and further Your Kingdom on this earth.* **Amen.**

Beware The Soothsayer

"Seek the Power of the Living God, Never Superstition or Magic"

"And when Saul enquired of the Lord, the Lord answered him not, neither by dreams, nor by Urim, nor by prophets. Then said Saul unto his servants, seek me a woman that hath a familiar spirit, that I may go to her, and enquire of her. And his servants said to him, behold, there is a woman that hath a familiar spirit at Endor.… Then said the woman, whom shall I bring up unto thee? And he said, bring me Samuel."

Featured Scripture: 1 Samuel 28:6–7, 11

Background Scriptures:1 Samuel 28; 31; and Deuteronomy 18:9–14

King Saul had come to the end of his wits. God had anointed David to be future king; the great prophet Samuel was dead; and Saul was surrounded by the Philistine army. Saul had turned from God, and in his own quest to hold on to his power, had been overcome with jealousy against David. God's blessing was removed from Saul, and he languished in panic. Instead of seeking forgiveness, Saul sought to force a sign from God. When Saul did not get an answer by his dreams or the prophets, he committed an even graver sin; Saul sought a soothsayer.

God's commandment against divinations and magic was well known to the people of Israel. In fact, King Saul had removed witchcraft from his kingdom. But now, in a panic, Saul sought a soothsayer to summon the dead prophet Samuel in order to predict his future. God allowed Samuel to be awakened from his death sleep to appear to Saul. Samuel did appear and scolded Saul, telling of his imminent death in battle and the nation's doom. Not only would Saul fall, but Israel would fall as well.

Saul's sad transformation from godly leader to a seeker of soothsayers portends many lessons to leaders of faith. We are called by and serve a living and holy God. His power and grace are sufficient for us. God's commandment against seeking magic is as clear for us today as it was in the time of Saul. Soothsaying and magic are in the realm of Satan. It is abominable to God for His chosen leaders to taint their judgment by seeking unholy advice from any unsavory source.

Leaders of faith should beware and protect themselves from the soothsayers of our day. We should never consult with the dead or fortune-tellers of the future. Christ is our light and salvation. We belong to the land of the eternal living and the redeemed. Our calling is to serve God by serving others. We have the Scriptures and unfettered access to God through prayer. We have the examples of the saints and prophets. We have the fellowship and intercession of fellow believers. When we obey Christ's commands and live in humble service, we have all the power we will ever need. As we seek the Savior, no soothsayer will ever be needed.

Our Prayer: *Lord Jesus, You are our salvation and our light. We never have need of any power other than Your power. Protect us from the evil one and from all temptation. Gird us and make us strong to withstand the assaults of those who would do us harm. Keep us in perfect peace as we lead others in Your name.* **Amen.**

Covenant Friendships Key To Leadership

"Showing Kindness to Friends by Rewarding Loyalty Is Notable"

"And David said, Is there yet any that is left of the house of Saul, that I may show him kindness for Jonathan's sake? Now when Mephibosheth, the son of Jonathan, the son of Saul, was come unto David, he fell on his face and did reverence.… And David said unto him, Fear not: for I will surely show thee kindness for Jonathan thy father's sake, and will restore thee all the land of Saul thy father and thou shalt eat bread at my table continually."

Featured Scripture: 2 Samuel 9:1, 6–7

Background Scripture: 1 Samuel 20

The friendship and loyalty between Jonathan and David is a great testimony of how love trumps jealousy, war, and tragedy. It also shows how a covenant friendship can extend beyond our time to future generations. Jonathan had risked his own life and his relationship with his father, King Saul, in order to protect his friend David. David was wanted and hunted by Saul, yet Jonathan provided David safe harbor and loyal friendship during one of David's toughest life challenges.

Saul, Jonathan, and two of his brothers were killed and mutilated in a battle against their fierce foe, the Philistines. Later David came to power, united the kingdom, and defeated all the foes of Israel. At his peak of power, King David thought back and remembered his old friend Jonathan. He demanded to know if anyone of the house of Saul still existed. The answer came back. Jonathan had a son who lived. His name was Mephibosheth. Mephibosheth was disabled (lame in his feet). David showed kindness to Mephibosheth, restoring the land of his grandfather Saul and his father, Jonathan, to him. David brought him into his own house for the rest of his years for Jonathan's sake and by doing so paid tribute to his old friend Jonathan. David's friendship with Jonathan was a covenant friendship that now spanned the generations.

Each of us develops covenant friendships in our own lives. What friend do you, as a successful leader of faith, need to look up and thank today? Who is a former ally or forgotten family member or friend that assisted you in your path toward leadership success? You, like David, can seek them out and in doing so restore a covenant friendship through this simple act of kindness.

The same grace, mercy, and blessing that God had bestowed upon King David and Israel, David bestowed upon the disabled son of his old friend and the grandson of his former nemesis. David's act of kindness to Mephibosheth embodies a great principle of leadership: remembering and rewarding loyalty and friendship. Great leaders today practice this same principle when they help persons who have helped them along the way.

Leaders inspire loyalty of others when they reach down to reward the friendship and love of those around them. David's act was not one of mere patronage or political payoff, for there was nothing that Mephibosheth could offer David but love and the memory of his dear old friend Jonathan. You must imagine that David shared with Mephibosheth the stories of his father, Jonathan, at meals and praised God for the blessing of friendship. Let us follow that same example as leaders of faith by honoring and rewarding our own covenant friendships today.

Our Prayer: *Father, help us to remember and celebrate the friendships of old. Help us to reward those who love us and are loyal to us. Let us seek to share grace, mercy, and kindness with others as You have shared it with us.* **Amen.**

Leading Even When Your Superiors Fail You

"Uriah's Devotion to Duty and Discipline Shine Above David's Sin"

"And Uriah said unto David, The Ark, and Israel, and Judah abide in tents; and my lord Joab, and the servants of my lord, are encamped in the open fields; shall I then go into mine house to eat, drink, and lie with my wife? As thou livest, and as thy soul liveth, I will not do this thing."

Featured Scripture: 2 Samuel 11:11
Background Scripture: 2 Samuel 11

David is one of the Scriptures' greatest heroes. In fact, David was *"a man after God's own heart"* (1 Samuel 13:14). However, in David's lustful, sinful act with the wife of Uriah, Bathsheba, it was Uriah who became the true leader in today's lesson.

David's attempt to cover up Bathsheba's pregnancy from their encounter together set the stage for testing the character of Uriah. Through David's deception, Uriah did not even know of Bathsheba's predicament, but he acted with the selfless, loyal duty and discipline of a leader as David sought to cover up his sin by tempting Uriah back to Bathsheba's bed.

In leadership, many times it is the soldiers and subordinates in organizations that set the true standard and example of leadership—even in the face of sin and failure by their own boss or commander. Uriah led by example in foregoing the pleasures of food, sex, safety, and love of family because duty and loyalty to those in his command called him to a higher realm of service. His loyalty and leadership cost him his life as David sent him into battle on the front line to die in order to finally cover up David's own sin. But God's plan was fulfilled through Uriah's act of courageous leadership.

Uriah led on in devotion even when his superior failed him. His obedience became part of God's bigger plan. Uriah's example of leadership is often lost in this bigger story. While Uriah gave his life in the service of King David and Israel, the sin of David was revealed and punished by God. David paid a price for his sin but was restored in the end by a forgiving God. The child born of the sin of David and Bathsheba died, but they were married and she would later give birth to Solomon, who would become part of the bloodline of Christ. God both rewards obedience and salvages the brokenness of our sinful lives to produce wisdom and beauty for His purposes.

Leading by the example of your devotion to your duty, even when others around you are failing, gives God a chance to redeem you and those around you. Through loyalty and by restoration, God can take our leadership discipline and failures along the journey of faith and mold them into a fabric of eternal success.

Our Prayer: *Jehovah, please give us the courage and devotion of Uriah to lead by example and duty even as circumstances around us unravel. Forgive us when we have sinned and allowed our subordinates and coworkers to be subjected to pain and suffering because of our actions. Redeem us all by Your might and mercy.* **Amen.**

Lamp For The Path Of Leadership

"God's Word Is the Lamp of Light for Our Leadership Journey"

"For thou art my lamp, O Lord: and the Lord will lighten my darkness.... Thy word is a lamp unto my feet, and a light unto my path.... And the light shineth in the darkness; and the darkness comprehended it not."

FEATURED SCRIPTURES: 2 SAMUEL 22:29; PSALM 119:105; AND JOHN 1:5
BACKGROUND SCRIPTURES: 2 SAMUEL 22:29–31; PSALM 119:103–106; AND JOHN 1:1–5

A journey of leadership will become a dark experience. In positions of responsibility we must make tough decisions that affect the lives and welfare of others. We must choose between dismal alternatives. We will be forced to take actions that cause us to lose the friendships and respect of old acquaintances. Christ tells us that in our dark moments of leadership, He provides a lamp that can guide us and comfort us.

Our lesson today tells us that this lamp is God's Word, given to us by way of inspired Scripture written over thousands of years. This lamp for the path of leadership is not just passages of Scripture, but the very promises of God. The gift of the Holy Spirit to leaders of faith enables us to search and seek supernatural meaning and comfort from the lamp of Scripture. The lamp of Scripture, its canonization and preservation over time and its many translations, is the great miracle of humankind.

Careful study of Scripture and the claiming of its promises can light up every dark leadership situation you encounter. The lamp of Scripture will exhort, warn, empower, and instruct us as to how we should lead others. It will convict us of our own shortcomings and reassure us as we make tough choices. Second Samuel 22:31 says: "As for God, his way is perfect; the word of the Lord is tried: he is a buckler to all them that trust him." The Book of Psalms tells us, "How sweet are thy words and through thy precepts I get understanding: therefore I hate every false way" (Psalm 199:103). John tells us that the darkness cannot comprehend the light of this lamp (see John 1:5).

The darkness in our moments of leadership is merely our call to open the Scriptures, and by careful study, allow the Holy Spirit to shine new understanding upon our situation. As Christ becomes centered in our work each day, His light conquers the darkness of our fear. So keep oil in your lamp by setting aside a quiet time each day to study, meditate, and pray. Don't trust your own understanding in times of darkness. Turn on your lamp and seek the confirmation of your holy inclinations.

God's Word is pliable and applicable to all of life's circumstances. It is a living and spiritual organism that is interpreted for the moment and for the person as the Holy Spirit prescribes. Never fear darkness when you hold the lamp. Use it well; claim its promises and truths as you use it for the completion of the tasks God has chosen you to do in these challenging days.

Our Prayer: *O Lord, You are indeed a lamp unto our feet and a light for our path. We praise You, Lord, for Your written Word and for the promises it holds for us. Jesus, You are the Light of the World. We should never fear the darkness of life, pain, or death. As leaders of faith, may Your Holy Spirit always keep the oil of our lamps full with prayer, praise, petition, and power.* **Amen.**

An Example In A Leader's Last Words

"Praising God for His Blessings and Keeping His Covenant"

"The Spirit of the Lord spake by me, and his word was in my tongue. The God of Israel said, the Rock of Israel spake to me, He that ruleth over men must be just, ruling in the fear of God…yet he hath made with me an everlasting covenant, ordered in all things, and sure: for this is all my salvation, and all my desire…."

Featured Scripture: 2 Samuel 23:—3, 5

Background Scripture: 2 Samuel 23: 1–7

On David's deathbed he praised God and lifted up the covenant of the Lord as his salvation. David had done the work the Lord had called him to do. David had great last words for future leaders of faith: *"He that ruleth over men must be just, ruling in the fear of God."* David's entire life's fulfillment was that he knew and claimed the salvation of God's holy promise.

In looking back on his life, David could see the perfect order of God's hand. David's great success as a leader was a kept promise from God. David knew that the plan God had for His people would never be thwarted by the hands of men. Those who tried would become "like thorns burned in a fire" (see 2 Samuel 23:6).

If leaders of faith today had the hindsight of this great leader of faith, David, to see God's order and steady hand in all situations, they would be bolder in our own leadership journeys. David had his own challenges as a leader. He was not perfect. He sinned and was chastened by God for his mistakes. But in all things, David was faithful, repentant, and fearful of God. David trusted God for the miracle when there was no other way out.

The dying David looked back at the harp-playing youth he had used to be, playing and learning at the feet of King Saul. He remembered his encounter with Goliath. He remembered his sins with Bathsheba and by numbering his people. David remembered the friendship of Jonathan and the betrayal of his own family. But in all these memories, David saw the guiding hand of God molding His covenant through the imperfection of His leaders.

As a leader of faith, you, too, can look back on your journey and see your triumphs and mistakes, your courageous moments and your moments of cowardice. You can see your successes and failures. But, like David, if you are called by God, fear Him, and stay in His plan and covenant for your life, you will be blessed. Those who try to steal your success for God will be stopped in their tracks.

Be just. Fear God. And let all you do as a leader of faith, be done in ordered ways in a covenant relationship with God and those you are called to lead.

Our Prayer: *God of Israel and David, thank You for great leaders of faith. We are thankful that You have provided examples of leadership through great servants like David. In our own journeys, Lord, bless us, forgive us, and restore us as we attempt to fulfill Your calling for us. We pray that at the end of our lives and leadership journeys, we will have done well as a faithful servant to a mighty God.* **Amen.**

Faithful Fathers Make Loyal Leaders

"Setting the Leadership Example As a Father Is the Most Important Calling"

"Now the days of David drew nigh that he should die; and he charged Solomon his son, saying, I go the way of all the earth: be thou strong therefore, and show thyself a man; and keep the charge of the Lord thy God, to walk in his ways, to keep his statutes, and his commandments, and his judgments, and his testimonies, as it is written in the law of Moses, that thou may prosper in all that thou doest...."

Featured Scripture: 1 Kings 2:1–3
Background Scriptures: 1 Kings 2:1–12; Matthew 1:18–25; Matthew 2:13–23; and Luke 15:11–32

No spiritual study of leadership would be complete without examining the role that faithful fathers play in the lives of their children. Faithful fathers and mothers make loyal leaders. God entrusts His most precious gifts to the care of fathers and mothers. Fulfilling your role as a parent is answering the call to a leadership journey of faith. Today's Scripture shows King David charging his son Solomon with the fatherly wisdom of the faith. As his life was coming to a close, David knew that his role as a father would not be successful unless he commanded his son to walk in the ways of God and keep His commandments.

Scripture is full of faithful fathers who obeyed the call of God by becoming great fathers. Noah protected his family in the ark. At an old age, Abraham obediently became the father of many nations. David battled through his adultery to raise a wise son named Solomon. The father of the prodigal son set for us an example of love and forgiveness as he forgave the sins of a rebellious son and welcomed him back into his home. Joseph, the earthly father of our Christ, obeyed the instructions of the angel, married the Virgin Mary, and protected the Messiah in His early years. From kings to carpenters, all were faithful fathers who became great leaders of our faith.

All leaders of faith must recommit themselves daily to becoming better fathers. At all ages, fathers should love and nurture their families. Fathers should be prayer warriors for their sons and daughters and extended families. Fathers should quietly set examples of faith and ethics through their own wholesome lifestyles. Fathers should set aside their most valuable asset, time, and freely shower it upon those they love. When children love and respect their fathers, others will notice. Those whom we are called to lead in our congregations and organizations will note that we are revered by our own children and will want to follow us all the more.

To those of us who are not fathers, we can become fathers to the orphaned, the lonely, and the forgotten. We can become advocates and mentors to the underdogs among us. Find a fatherly role to play and give of your heart and time to serve the needs of children everywhere. Like King David, let us exhort those in our care to follow the Lord God with all their hearts. Let us all be the faithful fathers and loyal leaders for the Kingdom of God.

Our Prayer: *Lord God, we give thanks for our fathers, past and present this very day. Your gift of earthly fathers has protected our faith and led us to a greater love and understanding of You. Forgive us when we have been absent and not attentive to our own children. Instill in us the desire to nurture and be a witness to those around us with fatherly love. Let us renew ourselves daily to becoming faithful fathers and loyal leaders who are inspired by our heavenly Father.* **Amen.**

Integrity Of Heart

"GOD'S FORMULA FOR LONGEVITY AND LEGACY IN LEADERSHIP"

"And if thou wilt walk before me, as thy father David walked, in integrity of heart, and in uprightness, to do according to all that I have commanded thee, and wilt keep my statutes and my judgments: Then I will establish the throne of thy kingdom forever...."

FEATURED SCRIPTURE: 1 KINGS 9:4–5
BACKGROUND SCRIPTURE: 1 KINGS 9:1–9;11:1–13

God is a God who measures heart and intention. He is a jealous God who demands that we abide within the confines of His commandments. In fact, Jesus used the keeping of commandments as the sign of true love for Him when He said: *"If ye love me, then keep my commandments"*(John 14:15). Leaders of faith are especially measured by heart and intention, and by how they follow the rules of Scripture.

In today's Scripture lesson, Solomon, the son of the great King David, was visited by God Himself. Solomon had successfully completed the great construction of the holy Temple of God as he was commanded to do. He had also built some of the greatest building works of that era of history. Yet while pleased with Solomon and his work, God did not measure Solomon's skill and résumé of earthly achievement as the mark of his legacy. The true test of Solomon's longevity as a leader of faith would be based on one simple and true test: integrity of heart. Early in his life, Solomon had chosen well when God offered him the gift of his heart's desire. Solomon chose wisdom, and for this choice God was exceedingly pleased. Solomon was then blessed by God, and his reward made him the wisest and wealthiest man of the ages.

Today we are blessed with the inspired writings of Solomon as we read Ecclesiastes and the Book of Proverbs. These books give us the benefit of the God-given wisdom that still inspires readers and leaders today. However, in the twilight of Solomon's life, his heart turned away from God and toward the trappings of wealth, success, and consumption. While outwardly he was still the epitome of leadership success, his full connection to God was lacking. Solomon became distracted, and in his attempts to please the whims of wives, princesses, and concubines, his integrity of heart became compromised. His quest to accommodate the foreign gods and earthly needs of others displeased his own heavenly Father.

In the end, for all the wisdom and glory Solomon had displayed as a leader, his legacy would be soured. The great Solomon's Temple would be destroyed. His sons would eventually lose the kingdom. Solomon's great legacy would be tarnished by a failure to hold true to God's command to maintain integrity of heart during the leadership journey. Solomon is remembered as a man of God and a successful figure of faith, but his legacy could have been even greater. When great leaders of faith lose discipline and integrity of heart, they wane and falter. Let your leadership journey be marked by integrity of heart and a quest to keep all God's commandments so your longevity and legacy of leadership will be noble and pure.

Our Prayer: *Lord God, instill in Your leaders of faith a sense of purity and integrity of heart. May we always be aware that true longevity and legacy in leadership rests not in our abilities alone, but in the full measure of our obedience to the call of righteous service. Give us the strength to guard against the compromising of principles and integrity in a quest to please others.* **Amen.**

Heeding The Old And Wise Counsel

"WISE LEADERS NEED BALANCED COUNSEL AND SAGE ADVICE"

"So Jeroboam and all the people came to Rehoboam the third day, as the king appointed.… But he forsook the counsel of the old men, which they had given him, and consulted with the young men that were grown up with him…and the king answered the people roughly…and spoke to them after the counsel of the young men.…"

FEATURED SCRIPTURE: 1 KINGS 12:8; 12—14

BACKGROUND SCRIPTURES: 1 KINGS 11:41–43; 1 KINGS 12

King Solomon was dead. His son Rehoboam had been chosen to rule in his place. In Rehoboam's first great test of leadership, he failed miserably. Our lesson today provides an abiding lesson in leadership. New leaders of faith should always heed the old and wise counsel. We need to have a diverse group of advisers and confidants, certainly. But when we seek the young adviser and new ideas exclusively and walk away from the advice of the gray-haired elders, we will surely fail.

Jeroboam was the spokesperson for a group of the king's subjects whowere placed under a heavy burden during the reign of King Solomon. Seeking a fresh start under the new king, they came to Rehoboam and sought concession and mercy. The old and wise counsel that had served in the power and splendor of Solomon's day advised the new king, Rehoboam, to accommodate the request of the people. They advised him to make some concessions to the people and in return, the people would serve him in peace. But in pride and hubris Rehoboam rejected the old and wise counsel and took on a new set of young advisers whom he had known as a child. They advised him to increase the burden on these oppressed people. Jeroboam took the advice of the young advisers over the old advisers. This poor decision brought insurrection from the oppressed people and a failed kingdom. God's hand was surely against Rehoboam as He used Rehoboam and his young advisers' arrogance and inexperience to hasten their downfall.

All leaders of faith need mentors and coaches. We all need experienced advice and counsel from people from various sectors of life. Successful leaders seek out the best advice from many sources to assure that they are informed and ready to perform their called duties. With whatever cabinet of advisers you choose to surround yourself with, make certain that you include some old and wise veterans of faith. God gives us elders to perpetuate the faith. Elders aren't always perfect; they can often seem old-fashioned and out of touch with the realities we face today. But in every elder adviser rests knowledge and understanding that new leaders cannot afford to miss.

Humble and godly leaders of faith know that they should seek the advice of persons with whom they may not agree. In our quest to have a fresh start in an organization or congregation, we may want to exclude the former leadership from the new discussions. But we should always strive to be on good terms with all people without surrendering our own thoughts and values. We will learn from both the past successes and failures of the old and wise counsel. So don't forsake the old for the new. Include them all. Heed old and wise advice and become a wiser leader.

Our Prayer: *God of the ages, thank You for sending the old and wise counsel to help us and advise us in our leadership journey. Help us to be humble enough and curious enough to seek out the best and most experienced advice. Protect us from our own arrogance and over-certainty in a position. Let us prayerfully and humbly search for meaning and understanding from all those gifted people You place in our path.* **Amen.**

When Leaders Are Down To Their Last Jar

"When Leaders Are Obedient, Provisions for Their Calling Never Run Out"

"For thus saith the Lord God of Israel, The barrel of meal shall not waste, neither shall the cruse of oil fail.... And she went and did according to the saying of Elijah and she, and he, and her house did eat many days. And the barrel of meal wasted not, neither did the cruse of oil fail, according to the word of the Lord, which He spake by Elijah."

Featured Scripture: 1 Kings 17:14–16
Background Scripture: 1 Kings 17:1–17

So many times in our leadership journeys we will find ourselves in the same predicament as the prophet Elijah. Our brook is dry and our bread is gone. We felt called by God and were obedient to the calling, but here we sit, broke and without savings or resource. Is this our time of doom, or just the setup for God to work His miracle in our lives?

The story of Elijah and the widow is one of Scripture's most beautiful accounts of God's miraculous provision for those He calls and for those who obey Him. Elijah did as the Lord commanded and went to the brook Cherith. His journey had begun. The ravens came and brought him bread and meat, and the brook provided water. All was well. But then a drought came and caused the brook to go dry. Just part of the way into his leadership journey, Elijah was thirsty again. What would this prophet do?

How often we, too, sit by the dried-up brook, confronted with the lack of resources to complete God's calling and wondering where to go next. Elijah never lost faith. He was obedient to the instruction of God to go to Zerephath and seek out the most unlikely source of help—a destitute widow. In our own journeys, perhaps we sit by the brook too long waiting for rain when we need be like Elijah. We need to get up and go to our own Zerephath to find God's new provision for our journey. God often sends the most unlikely persons into our paths to rescue us. Often we do not see them because they are not people of wealth or the methods of support that we suspect can save us.

In the home of the widow, God took her last bit of oil and meal and miraculously caused it to last, leaving Elijah and the widow with enough provision to survive. The jars never ran empty. In our leaderships journey of faith, we often are down to our last jar. God doesn't always send new jars, but in our faith He can keep the jar we have from running out. Our perception of what the miracles of provision will be and who will bring them is sometimes out of sync with God's methods. But through faithful obedience, without pretension, our needs will be met when we are called to do God's work in this life of leadership.

Our Prayer: *Lord God, we praise You for Your power to bring miracles into our lives. We thank You for Elijah and for an obedient widow. Help us in our own lives when we are destitute and without provision. May we rely on Your might and power to deliver us. Help us to know where to go and whom to see for help. Work a miracle for us. Like Elijah, we pray that our jars will never run out as we serve You.* **Amen.**

When We Are Pursued

"God Will Come and Save His Chosen from the Pursuers of Harm"

"But he himself went a day's journey into the wilderness, and came and sat down under a juniper tree: and he requested for himself that he might die; and said, It is enough; now, O Lord, take away my life; for I am not better than my fathers.… My soul is weary of my life; I will leave my complaint upon myself; I will speak in the bitterness of my soul."

Featured Scripture: 1 Kings 19:4; Job 10:1
Background Scriptures: 1 Kings 19:1–18; 2 Kings 2:1; Job 10:1–13; and Job 42: 12–17

Many leaders of faith will find themselves at their wit's end. You will find yourself pursued by rivals, by evildoers, and by betrayers. Chosen leaders will find themselves in situations of persecution and adversity. In today's Scripture, Elijah and Job recount their own exhaustion from their travails and pursuers. King Ahab and his evil wife, Jezebel, had destroyed the prophets and instituted the worship of idols in the land. They now were pursuing Elijah to the bitter end. Elijah had succeeded in salvaging a remnant of pure worshipers of God, but now he was paying the price. Elijah was exhausted by his pursuers.

Job, by God's allowance, was being tried and tortured by Satan himself. Job, like Elijah, coveted death rather than continuing to endure the tribulations of this life. But God was in absolute control of these situations. These two men of God still had work left to do and blessings awaiting them. Are you being pursued? Is your own leadership journey marked by crushing persecution and challenge? Has your calling exhausted and frustrated you to the point of wanting life itself to end?

Let God speak to you now. Even in your misery of the moment, His purposes are being accomplished in you. The Scriptures are full of examples of weary leaders who were only inches from the gold of success. Success often comes through persecution. And a new dawning in life will appear even as the pursuer arrives at your door. Ahab and Jezebel failed to destroy Elijah. The sufferings of Job were turned through his humility, repentance, and prayer for his friends. Elijah later anointed kings and his own successor. Rather than death, he was taken into heaven in a whirlwind. In the end, Job was more blessed than before his travails and went on to live a long and prosperous life.

As the pursuers come at you with newfound relentlessness, don't be afraid. Don't give up. Don't give in. Let the power and purpose of God be magnified in the tragedy of the moment. God chose you, and He will make His fruit appear on the tree of your service if you remain steadfast in constant prayer and faith. Your own Jezebels and evil pursuers are no match for God's power and providence. Keep the faith. You, too, are a chosen leader of faith, and God's chariot of deliverance is on its way to your rescue.

Our Prayer: *Lord God, we are overwhelmed by the pursuers who seek to harm us. Life's circumstances are beating us into a depressed and lonely state. Come to us now and lift us up. Help us to seize the power of Your throne and defeat the enemy. Just like You did for Elijah and Job, bless us and help us to be an example of faith for others to follow. We praise You now as You deliver the enemy into our hands.* **Amen.**

Becoming A Double-Portion Mentor

"The Greatest Leaders Are Selfless Mentors"

"So he departed from there and found Elisha…who was plowing with twelve yoke of oxen…then Elijah passed by him and threw his mantle on him. Elijah said to Elisha, Ask. What may I do for you before, before I am taken away from you? And Elisha said, please let a double portion of your spirit be upon me."

Featured Scriptures: 1 Kings 19:19; and 2 Kings 2:9
Background Scriptures: 1 Kings 19:19–21; 2 Kings 2

Great leaders are great mentors. They find persons to whom the mantle of leadership can be passed and nurture them. Many times, leaders of faith choose unlikely persons to tutor and give opportunity to learn and excel. The Scriptures have few greater examples of successful mentoring and leadership than those found in the stories of Elijah and Elisha. These two prophetic leaders performed many miracles and led God's people in unique and powerful ways.

God gave Elijah a word for choosing a successor. Often it is hard for leaders to understand and come to grips with their own mortality. It is difficult for some leaders to know when to give up the mantle of leadership and pass it along to another. Part of becoming a great leader of faith is acknowledging that it is time to select and groom another to take over your responsibilities. God gives leaders of faith good instincts in choosing successors. Elijah found a plowboy and put the cloak of leadership upon his back. Where is your Elisha?

Elijah's selection of a leader in the fields demonstrates how God utilizes the unlikely to achieve the impossible. Elijah did not go to the great halls of scholarship or the courts of kings in search of a successor. God led Elijah to a field to find a humble servant plowing in the soil of the earth. Who are the unlikely persons you encounter each day who need a chance to learn leadership? The Elishas of our day may be found in the humble places and professions. Let God lead you there.

Elijah gave Elisha the chance to receive a parting blessing. Boldly, Elisha asked for a double-portion of the great spirit of Elijah. In granting this wish, Elijah showed the real character and greatness of a leader of faith. Many average leaders would want to leave a greater legacy than others. They would not want their successors to outshine them in power or popularity. But the selfless and generous Elijah granted this request and imparted upon Elisha great power and spirit. In granting this wish, Elijah set the bar for leaders. Elijah became a double-portion mentor!

We can never truly reach our potential in our leadership callings of faith until we identify and nurture young leaders to replace us. God's Spirit should flow through us to new leaders in such a way that our organizations and congregations become greater. As your leadership journey matures, become a double-portion mentor to an unlikely pupil. Then you, too, can ride the chariot of God's love and grace into an eternity with the fulfillment of a job well done.

Our Prayer: *O Lord, make me a humble and selfless leader. Lead me to those unlikely persons You choose to follow me in leadership. Make me a double-portion mentor to a new leader of faith. Never let my own ego or quest for a legacy become a hindrance to serving others. Show me clearly when it is time for me to go. Bless my service and lead me to the fields to find my new Elisha to carry on the calling of faithful leadership.* **Amen.**

Leaders Who Covet And Use Power To Possess Will Collapse

"WHEN THE LUST FOR ANOTHER'S POSSESSIONS OR POWER BRINGS DISASTER TO LEADERSHIP"

"But Jezebel his wife came to him, and said unto him, Why is thy spirit so sad, that thou eatest no bread?... I spake unto Naboth the Jezreelite, and said unto him, Give me thy vineyard for money; or else, I will give thee another vineyard for it: and he answered, I will not give the my vineyard.... And Jezebel his wife said unto him, Dost thou now govern Israel? Arise and eat bread, and let thine heart be merry: I will give thee the vineyard of Naboth the Jezreelite."

FEATURED SCRIPTURE: 1 KINGS 21:5–7
BACKGROUND SCRIPTURES: 1 KINGS 21:1–29; 1 KINGS 22:37–40; AND 2 KINGS 9:35–37

Jezebel did the dirty work, but the seeds of King Ahab's destruction were sown by his coveting the possession of another person. The Ten Commandments tell us that to covet another's possessions is a sin. Yet, a greater sin as a leader of faith is to not only covet another's power or possession, but to use your God-given power and authority to attain it.

In the case of Ahab, Jezebel used the authority of the king's office to conspire, steal, and commit murder for the sake of satisfying an ungodly desire of her husband. The tale is tragic and has earned Jezebel one of the most reviled places in history. Their sin crumbled the legacy of Ahab and the future rule of his family in Israel. This story of Ahab issues a powerful message from God that leaders of faith should never abuse the sanctity of their position in order to pillage the property of another.

Granted, most leaders of faith are not married to Jezebel and do not commit murder for the sake of a piece of property, but many of us can use our God-given power to intrude upon another person's rights or privileges. Leaders of faith often covet a promotion or a higher position of power that another person possesses. Often we see leaders who sow the seeds of dissension or gossip in an organization in order to harm another person's reputation. We often see outright falsehoods spread in order to bring one person down and raise another up in the quest for more power.

Leaders can use networks or relationships to get special treatment and can, in fact, disadvantage the opportunities of others. No one begrudges leaders of faith from pleasure or the enjoyment of their position, but leaders of faith who are called to leadership service by a holy God must always remain vigilant, humble, and respectful of the rights, possessions, and power of others. We should endeavor to not allow our spouses, subordinates, or others to misuse our good name or position in the acquisition of goods or for special treatment. God will reward our faithfulness and bless our work if we stay within this cloak of righteousness.

Our Prayer: *God, our positions as leaders of faith are a gift and responsibility that You have empowered us to have. Please keep us ever mindful that we should never covet nor lust for the possessions or power of others. Help us to remain humble and content with the things You provide to us. In our humility and contentment may we serve our fellow man in true faith.* **Amen.**

Sights And Sounds Of The Throne

"The God Who Calls Us Has Majesty and Sits on a Heavenly Throne"

"I saw the Lord sitting on his throne, and all the host of heaven standing by him on his right hand and on his left.… I saw the Lord sitting upon a throne, high and lifted up, and his train filled the temple. Above it stood the seraphims…and one cried unto another and said Holy, holy, holy is the Lord of hosts: the whole earth is full of his glory…and, behold, a throne was set in heaven, and one sat on the throne…to look upon like a jasper and a sardine stone: and there was a rainbow round about the throne…and twenty four elders…and out of the throne proceeded lightings and thundering and voices…and before the throne was a sea of glass like unto crystal…and four beasts and they rest not day and night saying, Holy, holy, holy Lord God Almighty, which was, and is, and is to come."

Featured Scriptures: 1 Kings 22:19; Isaiah 6:1–4; and Revelation 4:2–6, 8
Background Scriptures: 1 Kings 22:1–40; Isaiah 6; John 12:37–50; and Revelation 4—5

Lest we think that the One who calls us is merely a bearded, triton-like, grandfatherly figure who floats in the air, let our lesson and Scripture today allow us to experience the sights and sounds of the throne of the Lord God Almighty, the One who called us!

The prophets Micah and Isaiah, as well as the apostle John, witnessed firsthand the throne of God and lived to write it down in the books of Scripture. Each of them saw a heavenly throne filled with unimaginable majesty. They saw God sitting upon that throne. They saw heavenly hosts and elders. They heard thundering and constant praises of holiness. The very train of God's garment filled the whole Temple. Rainbows, jasper, sardine, and seas of crystal were abundant and endless. God's glory filled not only the holy Temple but the whole earth.

God is unfathomable. His power and glory are not measurable. He is a Spirit who never sleeps, who is clairvoyant and universal. But in our Scripture today, God allows each of us to have a tiny glimpse of Him by way of these special servants. This majestic God is our Creator and Sustainer. He loves us very much, even more than we love ourselves. He watches us constantly and longs for us to succeed and be fruitful. He has called us for a special task of service straight from this holy throne.

When we think upon our work and our calling and become tired or confused or too weary to continue, it would do us well to envision the description of the habitation of the One who has called us. If this majestic God on this holy throne is for us, is watching us, and wants us to succeed, we must get up and get going with new zeal. We can't let Him down. His glory fills the earth and fills our every day. This same glory can overcome the poverty, violence, and depravity of humankind if we will let it shine through our service to others.

The sights and sounds of the throne of the Almighty are cheering you on to proclaim the Good News and serve others in God's love this day!

Our Prayer: *Holy, holy, holy, Lord God Almighty, which was, and is, and is to come, we praise You this moment. We stand in awe as we experience the sights and sounds of Your throne. Let Your glory and power overwhelm us and cover us in this day of our service to You.* **Amen.**

When Following Instructions Heals

"RECEIVING A MIRACLE THROUGH REPETITIOUS ACTS OF OBEDIENCE"

"Now Naaman, captain of the host of the king of Syria, was a great man…honorable…mighty man in valor, but he was a leper…so Naaman came and stood at the door of Elisha…and Elisha sent a messenger saying, go wash in the Jordan seven times…but Naaman was wroth and went away…but when he went down, and dipped himself seven times in the Jordan and he was clean."

FEATURED SCRIPTURE: 2 KINGS 5:1, 9, 11, 14
BACKGROUND SCRIPTURES: 2 KINGS 5:1–14; AND LUKE 4:24–27

The scourge of leprosy had struck the great soldier Naaman. In those days, contracting leprosy meant the loss of all things and essential banishment from society. Naaman was led to the great prophet Elisha by way of a Hebrew servant girl who knew of God's healing power. Naaman showed faith.

In hopefulness and desperation, Naaman traveled and sought out Elisha to inquire as to how he could be healed. Elisha gave him specific instructions: "*Go and wash yourself seven times in the Jordan River.*" Naaman was taken aback by such unorthodox instructions. Perhaps Naaman wondered why Elisha couldn't heal him by just giving the word or waving a hand. There were other rivers that were closer by than the Jordan. Why not go there and save time and travel? Naaman nearly walked away from a miracle because he failed to follow the instructions of the great prophet.

How often we as leaders of faith come to God asking for healing and deliverance and yet fail to follow the instructions. We, too, walk away from miracles because of our failure to become active participants in our own healing miracles. The receiving of a miracle more often than not requires our active involvement through faith. We may want to wash one time, not seven times. We may pray for the provision for our journeys, only to cease searching for new opportunities. We may want success to come in one year, not seven. We may want to be healed without experiencing pain or changing our lifestyles.

God wants to heal us, but He has some specific instructions for us to follow through His Word and through our patience in faith. Miracles come through our repetitious acts of obedience in our daily living. To receive God's miracle may mean we must change our behaviors and attitudes toward others. It means we must be humble in our response to God's command and instruction. It may mean giving up power, or forgiving others, before we can be forgiven.

Naaman nearly walked away in indignity from a miracle because the instructions to receive it seemed burdensome. But when he washed seven times in the Jordan River as he was instructed, he became clean again. Listen to God's instructions through Scripture, prayer, and the advice of mentors and friends. Then go and wash seven times and be made clean again this very day.

Our Prayer: *Lord, You are a God of miracles. How often we want a miracle but are too busy to listen to Your instructions for us. We are too impatient, Lord, to hear You. Humble us and make us listen to Your voice and instructions. Forgive us when we are impertinent and self-important. We need a miracle today, O Lord. We need to be healed. Tell us where to go and what to do.* **Amen.**

When Ego And Trappings Warp Good Leaders

"How the Sin of a Good Leader Goes Unconfessed and Leaves a Legacy of Ruin"

"And Isaiah said unto Hezekiah, Hear the word of the Lord. Behold, the days come, that all that is in thine house, and that which thy fathers have laid up in store unto this day, shall be carried into Babylon: nothing shall be left, saith the Lord.... Then said Hezekiah unto Isaiah, Good is the word of the Lord which thou hast spoken. And he said, Is it not good, if peace and truth be in my days?"
Featured Scripture: 2 Kings 20:16–17,19
Background Scripture: 2 Kings 20

By all accounts Hezekiah was a good king of Judah who ruled for twenty-nine years. The son of David, Hezekiah, was described as someone who *"did right in the sight of the Lord, according to all that David his father did"* (2 Kings 18:3). Hezekiah won miraculous victories over the Assyrians, accumulated great wealth, and oversaw great feats of engineering and construction. But as with many good leaders, ego and his satisfaction in his accomplishments and wealth overtook the old and sick Hezekiah to the detriment of all he and his fathers had done.

The flattery lavished on Hezekiah by his rivals caused him to entertain a delegation of Babylonians into his court. They had feigned concern about the health of Hezekiah and now were his guests. Hezekiah showed them every part of the wealth of Judah, as well as his personal stash of gold, silver, ivory, armor, and every other precious thing. Isaiah the prophet knew the heart of Hezekiah and confronted him. Hezekiah admitted what he had done, but he failed to see the sin in it. Isaiah told the king of God's coming judgment as a result.

Hezekiah's response to the dreadful prophecy of Isaiah was to say, *"Is it not good, if peace and truth be in my days?"* A great leader had fallen victim to his own ego in the peace and prosperity of the moment. But what about tomorrow?

Leaders of faith must guard each day against reveling in their accomplishments and accumulated wealth and honor. These can erode your sense of good judgment and can bring about the wrath of God. Showing off our wealth or achievement for the sake of bragging or vanity gives the sense that the legacy of achievement is ours and not God's. It sends the signal that "all is well with me," but not the right signal: that whatever good we have or do is by the grace, might, power, and blessing of the Almighty God.

The days after Hezekiah's reign are very tragic, indeed. His great career of leadership was tarnished in the end by self-absorption and he left his heirs only poverty and slavery. As a leader of faith, God gives us these stories in the Scripture to remind us that our blessings are conditional. We must remain in humility and reliance on God. When we are caught in our sin, let us confess and change our ways, and God, who is generous, will forgive us and restore our blessing.

Our Prayer: *Lord, how we can become vain and prideful. Even great leaders can allow themselves to fall into ruin by seeing achievement and wealth as a museum of their own greatness. Forgive us when we revel in our own self-worth. Help us to constantly acknowledge You as the Giver and Sustainer of all good things in our lives. Keep our eyes on You we pray.* **Amen.**

Reviving By Ridding

"Leaders Revive Organizations by Ridding Them of Idols and Evil"

"Moreover the workers with familiar spirits, and the wizards, and the images, and the idols, and all the abominations that were spied in the land of Judah and in Jerusalem, did Josiah put away, that he might perform the words of the law, which were written in the book that Hilkiah the priest found in the house of the Lord."

Featured Scripture: 2 Kings 23:24
Background Scripture: 2 Kings 23:1–25

Josiah was one of the bright and great kings of Israel. But Josiah came on the scene during a period of history when the leaders before him had failed to honor God and live by His laws. Ascending to the throne at a young age, Josiah lived and ruled in the spirit of his ancestor King David. Josiah knew that to revive Israel as the chosen people of God, he must rid his kingdom of the cancerous presence of idols and evil.

Past kings and priests had corrupted and defiled the holy places. The worship of Jehovah God had been supplanted by Baal worship and the perversion of the Temple. The entire land was rife with altars to sin and debauchery. Josiah's passion was to turn his people back to God and to make sure that all the symbols of false worship were ceremoniously destroyed. The passion and zeal Josiah displayed in his leadership greatly pleased the Lord.

Many leaders of faith today take over new projects or new positions of leadership only to find their congregations or organizations strewn with the idols and evil of our day. We may find ourselves in the midst of a leadership task in which our coworkers are serving themselves and not those they are employed to help. We may find that the resources of our congregations and organizations are given over to self-consumption and not put to the wisest use of helping those who are hurting. What should we do? How can we learn from King Josiah?

Idolatry and evil comes not just in the form of golden images and blasphemous priests. Idolatry and evil can take the forms of gluttony, a loss of mission, or a need to constantly seek pleasure. It can come in the form of envy or a burning need for revenge. It can come in the loss of vision and heart for serving others while we merely "make time" and "just get by." Waste, neglect, and corrupt practices usually point to the presence of idolatry and evil within an organization.

When you are faced with this situation, go to God in prayer. Ask for the vision, strength, and bravery to confront the cancer in your path. Get about the task of instituting new procedures and bringing the people you lead back to their core mission and purpose. Set the example of discipline and focus on service and selflessness. Give others the sense that God is praised only when we serve others in selfless love and holy sacrifice.

Our Prayer: *Jehovah God, we confess the sin around us and seek Your forgiveness. Even in our day and in our service, we see signs of idolatry and evil. Empower us to confront it and to revive our organization by ridding it of all semblances of sinful behavior. Bless the work of our hands that it might restore us to a new and meaningful relationship with You and those You give us to serve.* **Amen.**

Surrounding Yourself With Good People

"Successful Leaders Find and Reward Brave and Loyal Captains"

"These also are the chief of the mighty men whom David had, who strengthened themselves with him in his kingdom, and with all Israel, to make him king, according to the word of the Lord concerning Israel.… Now three of the thirty captains went down to the rock to David, into the cave of Adullam; and the host of the Philistines encamped in the valley of Rephaim.… And the three brake through the host of the Philistines, and drew water out of the well of Bethlehem…and brought it to David: but David would not drink of it, but poured it out to the Lord."

Featured Scripture:1 Chronicles 11:10, 15, 18

Background Scripture: 1 Chronicles 11

Part of the anointing of David as king over Israel was the appointing of great captains to serve and defend both the king and the nation. The captains and servants of David were chosen well. They were brave and loyal. They feared and worshiped the God who called them. David's success as a godly king was in no small measure due to the fact that he surrounded himself with good people. Not only did he surround himself with these great captains who would slay his enemies and rescue him from danger, but David also recognized and gave tribute to their service and to the God who had called them.

None of us as leaders of faith can succeeds in our calling all alone. Regardless of the tasks we are called to do for God, it will be necessary to surround ourselves with people of like mind and heart. If God has called us to service, He will send us captains to defend and assist us in the task. Be sure that you know when and where to find loyal assistants. And when you find them, be sure to recognize their service and to give praise to God for them. We make a grave error when we are not constantly building the corps of captains within our congregations and organizations.

Surrounding ourselves with good people who love God and have a heart for service is a skill we must develop. Often we must give others a chance to prove themselves. We may find the most courageous captains in the most unlikely places. The bravest captains may not always be the youngest and strongest. Leaders of faith can find great help from all ages, races, and backgrounds. Seek those with humble hearts who brim with enthusiasm and passion. Find those who are selfless in their service to others. Those faithful qualities will speak volumes about their character.

Be sure to set aside time to converse with those around you. Those who love you and serve you will often tell you the things that you may not want to hear, but they are the things that might save you. Be sure to find ways to reward the loyalty of others and help them reach their own potential in leadership. David showed us that surrounding ourselves with loyal and brave people and then giving tribute to them and to God is a mighty formula for leadership success. Now go find your loyal captains and love them and give thanks for them.

Our Prayer: *Lord God, we give thanks for the captains in our leadership journeys. We have been blessed with brave and loyal servants. Show us how to give thanks for them and how we can better validate their love for the cause. Instill in us the instinct to find new captains and to become better mentors to them. We give praise for the many untold acts of others on our behalf in our own leadership journeys. Reward them in Your own way, O Lord.* **Amen.**

Provoked To Be Sifted

"Beware: Satan Seeks to Destroy God's Chosen Leaders"

"And Satan stood up against Israel, and provoked David to number Israel.… Simon, behold, Satan hath desired to have you, that he may sift you as wheat: But I have prayed for thee, that thy faith fail not."

Featured Scriptures: 1 Chronicles 21:1; and Luke 22:31–32
Background Scriptures: 1 Chronicles 21; 1 Samuel 13:14; Matthew 4:1; Matthew 16:18; and James 4:7

David was a man after God's own heart. Peter was the rock upon which Christ would build His Church. Jesus Himself after His baptism was led straight into the wilderness to be tempted. Does Satan dare exploit the called and holy of the Almighty God? Our lesson today tells us that not only did Satan desire to destroy the witness and leadership of David, Peter, and our Savior, but he also provokes leaders of faith today as he seeks to sift them as wheat.

Satan provoked David to issue a census of God's people. The godly counselor to David, Joab, warned David against offending God with a census. David's issue of the census was boastful. Peter was tempted to physically interfere with Christ's calling and mission to go to the cross. Satan came to Christ as He began His ministry, attempting to cut a deal if Christ would only worship him.

What is your calling? What great cause or project has God given you to do? In the midst of your own good works will come those times of seemingly harmless temptation to drift away from your mission. We lose our discipline or do something against our better judgment. The result can be devastating to our progress and can hurt those we serve. Beware! Satan seeks you and desires to sift your good works and holy call into a powder of failure. Jesus told Peter that He prayed for him, that he would not fail when confronted by the evil one. David and Israel had to pay a price for David's succumbing to Satan's provocation, but in the end they were redeemed because of David's contrite heart. Christ rebuked Satan in the wilderness with Scripture. Leaders of faith should pray for each other. We should pray that the Father, Son, and Holy Spirit protect us and give us discernment to overcome the evil one. Scripture tells us "*to resist the devil, and he will flee*" (James 4:7).

Are you in a jam today? Has Satan seemingly infiltrated your congregation or organization? Don't be surprised! The greater your call for good, the greater the evil pursuit will be. God desires for you to succeed, and Christ's power is sufficient to help you escape the grasp of the evil one. Christ has overcome the world. Death has already been conquered. Leaders of faith who stay grounded in Christ's love and power can also resist and overcome the provocations and temptations Satan sets before us.

Our lesson tells us to be alert. Be on guard and watch that you don't drift from your calling. Bathe your own life with prayer, study of the Word, and fellowship with other believers. Let humility and discipline be your compass. Become more selfless and forgiving and refuse to allow pride and hubris to seep into your work. With your eyes focused firmly on Christ and the service to the precious children of God, you cannot fail.

Our Prayer: *Lord Jesus, keep us safe from the evil one. Hold us in the palm of Your hand. Instill in us an alertness and holiness that can identify and resist the temptations that would destroy our mission for You. Forgive us for our failures when we succumb to temptation. Restore us and bless us, we pray.* **Amen.**

A Perfect Heart And A Willing Mind

"Serving God with Purity of Heart and Openness of Mind"

"And thou, Solomon my son, know thou the God of thy father, and serve him with a perfect heart and with a willing mind: for the Lord searcheth all hearts, and understandeth all the imaginations of the thought; if thou seek him, he will be found of thee; but if thou forsake him, he will cast thee off forever."

Featured Scripture: 1 Chronicles 28:9

Background Scriptures: 2 Chronicles 1; 2 Kings 20:1–11; and Jeremiah 17:10

No greater inheritance can a son or daughter receive than that of their parents' faith. Today's lesson features the admonition of David to Solomon to know God and to serve Him with a perfect heart and a willing mind. David told Solomon that God could not be fooled. God searches our hearts and knows our every thought. Developing a perfect heart and a willing mind is a providential process that begins with humble acceptance of God's grace and mercy. It moves forward as we yield ourselves to God's calling us to service.

Success in our leadership journey of faith requires that we develop a pure heart and willing mind. As we perfect our hearts for service to others, we should pray and ask God to wash away any bitterness and unresolved anger that we may harbor toward others. We need to cleanse ourselves of selfishness and personal ambition. To achieve a perfect heart, we must become the repository for God's light and love. To develop a willing mind, we must be prepared to develop new habits and gain new spiritual insights as we study the Scriptures. We must be open to trying new things for God. We must surround ourselves with elders and mentors who can impart new knowledge to us. We must obtain a mental willingness to take to the road of attempting the impossible for God. We must retain mental toughness while incurring the criticism of others.

God searches our hearts and minds continually. Yet His power and peace are available to us in this process. He gives freely to us according to our needs and deeds. God is forgiving when we fall short if we are serving Him with perfect hearts and willing minds. Don't ever forsake Him. When you fail, keep coming back to God. We can be successful and live great lives of accomplishment in our calling if we continually seek Him and serve Him with perfect hearts and willing minds.

When the Lord searches your thoughts, what does He find? Does He sense doubt, or does He see resolve? Does He sense your goodwill toward others or jealousy of a peer? Does He sense a yearning within you to live a more holy life, or does He see your dark thoughts of lustful desire? Seek Him. Trust Him and pray for the indwelling of a new spirit within you. Love and intimacy with God will lead you toward attaining the perfect heart and willing mind that David desired for Solomon and that Christ desires for all those who hear His voice.

Our Prayer: *O Lord, purify our hearts and open our minds that we may become Your faithful servants. Pierce our soul and cleanse us from selfish and sinful thoughts. Wash away our bitterness and anger and sense of worthlessness. Grant us wisdom and knowledge. Empower us to answer Your call to leadership with a perfect heart and willing mind.* **Amen.**

Be Strong, And Do It

"When God Gives You a Task, You Will Have What You Need—Now Do It"

"And David said to Solomon his son, Be strong and of good courage, and do it: fear not, nor be dismayed: for the Lord God, even my God, will be with thee; he will not fail thee, nor forsake thee, until thou hast finished all the work for the service of the house of the Lord."

Featured Scripture: 1 Chronicles 28:20

Background Scripture: 1 Chronicles 28

There comes a time in the life of a person of faith when he or she no longer needs to ponder, pray, and meditate over a matter. There comes a time when God tells us: *Be strong, and do it.* The sanctuary needed to be built. God gave David the plans in a dream. Now David was entrusting Solomon to build it. No more guessing, no more hesitation. It was time to cast away fear and doubt. The provisions were ready, and the people were ready to follow. Solomon merely needed to gird himself with courage and go about the task of his calling. It was time to go to work.

Leaders of faith today may be at just that same crossroad. You have prepared all your life for leadership. You have been trained and educated. You have received life experience from previous tasks. Perhaps God is telling you today to just *be strong, and do it.* When you are called to a leadership task, it is akin to building a small sanctuary for God. You are putting a stone in place or mixing the mortar of service for Christ's Kingdom right here and now. If you have felt God's tug upon your heart to attempt some task of leadership or service, but you have failed to respond, perhaps you need to heed today's lesson by answering God's call right now.

First Chronicles 28 is full of good theology. David's strong spiritual instruction to his son Solomon is also timeless advice to leaders. God chooses different people for different tasks. While David was given the dream and plans for building the Temple of God, God did not desire that David build it himself. God knew that David was a man of war who had shed much blood, and He desired that Solomon, a more peaceful king, would build it. Sometimes it is the son, the apprentice, or the understudy who is more appropriate for a task. God utilizes different saints for different jobs.

Our lesson today also shows the resolute and immovable purpose of God. When God designates that something be done, even if it takes much gold and resources, it will be accomplished! Give thanks to God for your calling. Don't be hesitant. *Be strong, and do it.* Take your first step toward building your sanctuary to God this very day.

Our Prayer: *Heavenly Father, You bless us when You call us to a task. We give thanks for David and Solomon and the many saints who answered the call of service. Instill in us, O Lord, the courage and certainty of our calling. We claim this day all the provision that will be needed for this task in Your holy name.* **Amen.**

Recipe to Rebuild a Nation

"Ingredients Include Humility, Prayer, a Fervent Search for God, and Changed Ways"

"If my people, which are called by my name, shall humble themselves, and pray, and seek my face, and turn from their wicked ways; then will I hear from heaven, and will forgive their sin, and will heal their land."

Featured Scripture: 2 Chronicles 7:14

Background Scriptures: 2 Chronicles 7:12–22; 2 Chronicles 6:28–30; and James 4:7–10

God never sleeps. He wanders to and fro every moment taking the measurement of the hearts of His people. Second Chronicles 6:30 tells us that" *for thou only knowest the hearts of the children of men."* The verse just before our featured Scripture today is a comforting invitation from God: *"If there is no rain; if locusts devour the land; or if pestilence is among the people—then try the recipe in the scripture above, and your land will be healed"* (2 Chronicles 7:13).

The recipe for rebuilding a nation is also good theology for rebuilding lives and institutions. As a leader of faith, you should commit this recipe to heart and use it often. When our hearts are humble and our lives are full of devoted prayer and adherence to God's rules, we have full power to change our situation. If we have strayed afield, fellowship can be restored and healing can occur when we repent and change our behavior. God, who knows our hearts, will sense when we are ready to have the pestilence removed from our lives.

The drought, the locusts, and the pestilence of 2 Chronicles can also come to our congregations and organizations. The drought may be the financial hardship caused from a lack of faithful tithing and stewardship. The locusts may be the selfish and corrupt members of our teams. The pestilence may be the apathy and the misdirected judgment of leaders who have lost the zeal for their calling. Whatever the sin and pestilence that has caused our work to fall short, God can remove it according to the recipe above.

As leaders of faith, we must set the example. By changing our hearts and by becoming humble in our power, it will move us to prayer and to search anew for God. Our followers will sense our change of heart and our willingness to change our self-destructive behaviors. We can call our team to a time of collective prayer and praise. Our changed hearts will be sensed by our God, as He begins to fulfill His promise to remove our obstacles and heal our institutions. God wants restored relationships. He wants nations and congregations to be full of blessing. Take God up on His offer.

Changed ways involve action and change of habit. They require new discipline and the practice of a new work ethic. It means we must instill in our followers a strict code of holy ethics so hearts will be in tune with God. The recipe for rebuilding means we must get all the pots and utensils for baking a healed life out of the drawers. We must fire up the ovens and get prepared to bake. We must return to worship and the study of Scripture. We must immerse ourselves in selfless love and service to others as we add the ingredients of humility, prayer, searching and changed ways. Once the above are done; the rebuilt life and nation just need time to cook.

Our Prayer: *God of love, You desire to heal our nation and institutions by removing the pestilence in our lives. We claim Your promise this day with changed hearts. In humility we pray and search for You. We commit to change our ways. Heal us. Heal our hearts and brokenness. Call all sinners to come home to You, O Lord.* **Amen.**

Shall We Go To Ramothgilead?

"Know When to Ignore the Prevailing Opinion and Trust the Lone, Wise Prophet"

"Therefore the king of Israel gathered together four hundred prophets and said unto them, shall we go to Romothgilead to battle, or shall I forbear? And they said, go up; for God will deliver it into the king's hand. But Jehoshaphat said, is there not here a prophet of the Lord besides, that we might inquire of him? And the king of Israel called for one of his officers, and said, fetch quickly Micah…and Micah said, as the Lord liveth, even what my God has saith, that will I speak…I did see all Israel scattered upon the mountains as sheep that have no shepherd: and the Lord said, these have no master; let them return therefore every man to his house in peace."

Featured Scripture: 2 Chronicles 18:5–6, 8, 13, 16
Background Scriptures: 2 Chronicles 18—19; and 1 Kings 22:1–40

Good King Jehoshaphat of Judah had become close to Ahab, king of Israel, through a series of events and by way of Ahab's gifts to him of sheep and oxen. In this newfound relationship, Ahab solicited Jehoshaphat to join alliances with him and bring the divided kingdoms together to battle the Armenians at the city of Ramothgilead. To buttress his case for battle, Ahab assembled four hundred prophets to give testimony and affirmation that if they went to battle, they would be victorious. So… *shall we go to Ramothgilead?*

But Jehoshaphat wanted to hear one more opinion from another prophet. Reluctantly, Ahab sent for Micah the prophet. Micah never told Ahab what he wanted to hear, and Ahab feared that Micah would be a dissenter regarding this battle. Micah came before the kings after seeing a vision from the throne of God. It revealed that a spirit of deception had entered the words of the other four hundred prophets. He told them they would lose the battle and he could see all Israel scattered with no shepherd. Ahab threw Micah into prison for this prediction and forged ahead into battle. Ahab died in battle, but Jehoshaphat survived by God's hand and used this life-changing event to repent and to bring new integrity to the judges of Israel.

Good leaders of faith can get sucked into making bad decisions by following the "group-think" of advisers. Like Ahab, we often want to gather advisers around us who will tell us what we want to hear. The four hundred advisers were, indeed, the prophets of Israel. But they had become deceived by an evil spirit. Good advisers can give bad advice. Jehoshaphat was wise to seek another opinion. As we work in the heavenly realms of our spiritual battles, in all our humility, we should seek the Micahs of our day for counsel.

Sometimes the logical and obvious choices before us may not be God's will for our lives. Our families, friends, and closest confidants may be telling us to go forward with a job, investment, project, or major life decision. Go to God in prayer. Then seek out a wise elder, pastor, or mentor for a second opinion. Seeking God through secondary advice from the holy voices around us may just save our missions and keep us on the proper courses in our calling. Are you struggling with your own decision about going to Ramothgilead? Seek God, fetch your Micah, and let the right spirit guide your decision.

Our Prayer: *Lord God, we seek the true spirit of knowledge from Your throne. Guide us to make the right choices, even when they seem illogical and go against the good advice of others. Bring us a Micah. Bless us and protect us by Your holy might.* **Amen.**

Standing Still In The Face Of Battle

"Stillness and Worship in Our Times of Trouble Bring Victory"

"Ye shall not need to fight in this battle: set yourselves, stand ye still, and see the salvations of the Lord with you, O Judah and Jerusalem: fear not, nor be dismayed; tomorrow go out against them: for the Lord will be with you.... And when they began to sing and to praise, the Lord set ambushments against the children of Ammon, Moab, and Mount Seir, which were come against Judah; and they were smitten."

Featured Scripture: 2 Chronicles 20:17, 22
Background Scriptures: 2 Chronicles 17; 20:1–30

Knowing when to fight and when to worship can mean the difference between victory and defeat. As leaders of faith, we will have enemies come against us and seek to do us harm. These enemies often bring seemingly overwhelming odds against us. When we are surrounded by these enemies, our first instinct may be to devise a plan of escape or ready ourselves to fight with all our might. But our lesson today teaches us that sometimes we win by *not* fighting. We win by becoming still and falling before God in worship and praise!

The enemies of Judah had come together in an alliance against the people of God. Wise King Jehoshaphat continually sought God's presence and guidance in all matters. In the face of this cataclysmic battle, Jehoshaphat heard the call not to battle, but to stillness and worship in the face of danger. Heeding the leadership call of their king, all of Judah and Jerusalem fell before the Lord in worship and praise. They would fight the next day.

When we face challenges in life, praise and worship may seem like odd or inappropriate actions to take. Our earthly instincts tell us to act differently. How about a prayer of desperation? How about striking out immediately to fight the battle? But as we praise and worship God in tough situations, we unleash the Lord's power. We set ourselves up for a miracle because we know only by God's might and intercession can we prevail. Our Scripture today tells us that when people sing and praise the Lord, He sets traps and ambushes our enemies. God was going before the army of Jehoshaphat even while the people were worshiping Him.

Taking the time to acknowledge the majesty of God in our time of trouble is appropriate and necessary for leaders of faith. As we seek stillness and wait upon the Lord to appear to us in our worship, God is already at work preparing our way and setting the traps for our enemies. It gives God great pleasure when our hearts are continually set upon Him. Jehoshaphat did not fling himself on God in a prayer of desperation. He led his people to stillness, praise, and worship—and then to triumph. Try this leadership lesson in your trials and troubles today. Even as you do, God is going before you with gladness and victory.

Our Prayer: *Lord of Jehoshaphat, hear our prayer of praise to You this very day. Set our hearts to continually seek You. We now stop our worrying and become still before You, God. We fall on our faces in praise and adoration of Your wonder and love for us. In our worship we give up all our troubles to You. We trust that You go before our very enemies as we worship You now.* **Amen.**

Word Gets Around

"RIGHTEOUS LEADERSHIP WILL GET YOU NOTICE FROM YOUR ADVERSARIES"

"And the fear of God was on all the kingdoms of those countries, when they heard that the LORD fought against the enemies of Israel. So the realm of Jehoshaphat was quiet: for his God gave him rest round about.... And the men of Bethshemesh said, Who is able to stand before this holy LORD God.... And they sent messengers to the inhabitants of Kirjathjearim, saying, The Philistines have brought again the ark of the Lord; come ye down, and fetch it up to you."

FEATURED SCRIPTURE: 2 CHRONICLES 20:29–30; AND 1 SAMUEL 6:20–21
BACKGROUND SCRIPTURE: 2 CHRONICLES 20; AND 1 SAMUEL 5—7:2

The holy purposes of God cannot be perverted. When leaders are obedient and remain in true fellowship with God, He becomes their awesome protector. God's direct intervention in the life of the leader Jehoshaphat came in the form of God slaying the enemies of Judah. In the time of Samuel, God interceded for His people after the Ark of the Covenant was stolen in battle. The curse of God upon the Philistines brought the enemies of Israel to their knees. The word had gotten around: For those whose God was the Lord, they were to be left alone.

The faithfulness of Jehoshaphat and Samuel are examples of spiritual leadership that invoked God's direct intervention. Through God's public and dramatic actions, enemies were destroyed and peace was established in the land. In the lives of these two leaders, the word had gotten around so that they no longer had to deal with the invaders. While we may never see our protection from God strike people dead on our behalf, we may see the providential hand of God intervene in our dire circumstances to keep our critics away.

There are many examples in which God sends the word to others by way of His working miracles for our benefit. Righteous leaders project the call and dignity of a holy God. People will know of our determination. We go into a task with bravery and an assurance of heavenly protection. Our adversaries will hear and know of our cloak of protection sent from above. Leaders of faith perform best when the man-made odds are completely against them. It creates the perfect stage for God to execute His righteousness.

Clinging to the hem of God's robe of righteousness gets us noticed. Even unbelievers will sense we are different. God has given us immense power to finish the tasks He has called us to do. Never doubt Him, and never cease to be courageous to complete each assignment without fear of consequence. Some of our rivals may even see in our lives a God they want to get to know. Others may want to share in fellowship with an awesome Lord who is jealous and protective of those He loves. Let the word get around. Let the word go forth: Those whom God calls, He loves. Those whom He loves, He protects.

Our Prayer: *Lord God, You are our Protector and Deliverer in all situations. We call upon Your name in the face of our adversities and in the presence of our enemies. Come and deliver us for Your name's sake. We give You praise and honor and worship. Let the word go forth that we belong to You and You are able to defend those You choose. May others want to come to the grace of salvation of this same God.* **Amen.**

When Prepared Hearts Can Trump The Rules

"HELPING UNLIKELY FOLLOWERS EXPERIENCE GOD BY BENDING THE RULES"

"For there were many in the congregation that were not sanctified…for a multitude of the people…had not cleansed themselves, yet they did eat the Passover otherwise than it was written. But Hezekiah prayed for them, saying, the good LORD pardon every one that prepares his heart to seek God…though he be not cleansed according to the purification of the sanctuary. And the LORD hearkened to Hezekiah, and healed the people."

FEATURED SCRIPTURE: 2 CHRONICLES 30:17–20
BACKGROUND SCRIPTURES: 2I CHRONICLES 30; AND EXODUS 12:43–51

The divided nation of Israel was reawakening under the leadership of King Hezekiah. At this moment in their history, the chosen people of God came together en masse to praise God through the celebration of the Passover and the Feast of Unleavened Bread. The many tribes were gathered for the observance, but there was a problem. The rules and rituals of purification and sanctification of the Passover could not be met by the masses that had come to worship.

Our Scripture and lesson today show us how a leader of faith petitioned God to bend the rules in order for the masses of people to experience the Lord in worship. King Hezekiah knew well the Law of Moses and the requirement for persons to undergo purification before receiving the Passover rites. But on this day Hezekiah sensed that the prepared hearts and humble spirits of his followers needed to trump the rules. Hezekiah petitioned God to allow the unsanctified people to participate in the sacred ritual of the Passover. Hezekiah interceded for his people to God in prayer, and God granted his wish, healing and blessing the people.

Leaders of faith need to sense those times when peoples' hearts are moving toward God. Leaders need to develop a holy discernment of the hearts of those they lead. The masses that followed Hezekiah were preparing their hearts for a better life. The nation was repenting and ridding itself of idols and sin. While not technically pure enough by the Law to receive Passover, the followers of Hezekiah were moving in the right direction and needed to experience healing. When have you as a leader of faith faced a similar situation? Do you encounter persons whom many observers would say are not clean or refined enough to enter into acts of worship, yet you know their hearts are preparing to experience God? We may need to prayerfully seek God's intercession for the unsanctified among us. We may need to ask that institutional authorities suspend some rules to allow those we lead to be offered a second chance in life. We may need to petition our elders to allow the imprisoned, the sick, and the outcast to become part of our congregations.

When the hearts of people we lead are tilted toward God in preparation for a new beginning, we must find ways to lead them to God's altar, even if it means bending the rules. Great movements of the Holy Spirit should never be stifled by regulations or rigid codes of conduct. Let God's love and grace abound in every situation. Like He did following King Hezekiah's petition for his people, God will allow the rules to bend to His will and glory when we lead prepared hearts to Him.

Our Prayer: *Lord God, instill in us as leaders of faith the sense to know when hearts are prepared to find You. Help us to lead others to Your throne of grace and salvation. Even when the rules and regulations of man and faith seem to stifle us, let us petition You for intercession. Let every humble and prepared heart find Passover and salvation in Christ's love.* **Amen.**

Refusing To Hear God From The Unlikely

"God Often Speaks to Us Through Unlikely Persons and Circumstances"

"When Josiah had prepared the Temple, Necho king of Egypt came up to fight against Carchemish by Euphrates: and Josiah went out against him. But he sent ambassadors to him, saying, what have I to do with thee, thou king of Judah? I come not against thee this day but against the house wherewith I have war: for God commanded me to make haste: forbear thee from meddling with God, who is with me, that he destroy thee not. Nevertheless Josiah would not turn his face from him, but disguised himself, that he may fight with him, and hearkened not unto the words of Necho from the mouth of God, and came to fight."

Featured Scriptures: 2 Chronicles 35:20–23
Background Scripture: 2 Chronicles 35:20–27; and Proverbs 16:1–9

Even as a young king, Josiah sought after the God of his grandfather David and did what was right in the eyes of God. Josiah rid the nation of idolatry, rebuilt the Temple, and found the lost Scriptures. He even reinstated the observance of the Passover. Josiah's reign was blessed by God even as the nation itself had been sentenced to be punished by God for its past transgressions. The prophetess of Judah had said that upon Josiah's death, the nation would fall and the people would become captives. Today's lesson highlights the events leading up to Josiah's death. However, in his final act as king, Josiah failed to hear God's message because it came from a most unlikely source and through a sensational circumstance.

The pharaoh of Egypt, Necho, needed safe and peaceful passage through Judah so Egypt could join a battle at Carchemish against Nebuchadnezzar and the Babylonians. Judah was not part of this battle, but God had appeared to the Egyptian pharaoh and commanded him to move with haste through Judah. If Josiah agreed to his peaceful request, there would be no battle with Judah. Josiah would not agree and came to oppose Egypt. However, Josiah was killed and his army was defeated. Egypt moved on and the captivity of Judah would soon follow. Even in our godly success, we leaders of faith can harden our hearts and minds to the fact that God can speak to us through unbelievers or even our enemies. God may come to us in the most unlikely circumstances and desire for us to hear His voice. Our Scripture today tells us for certain that God spoke to the pharaoh. Why didn't God also speak these words to Josiah in a dream, in a vision, or through a prophet? Leaders of faith must be humble and open their minds to hear the mighty voice of God in those persons we see and encounter each day.

Leaders of faith can fail when they go into their own life battles without taking the time to hear what others around us are saying. Josiah was certain that the former oppressor of the Hebrews could not be trusted. Josiah could not imagine celebrating Passover on one day and allowing the pharaoh's army to march through Judah the next. Every circumstantial instinct probably proved Josiah correct. Yet his failure to acknowledge that God was truly speaking through Necho cost him his life and hastened the fall of Judah. Josiah's great faith and works would stand forever, but his failure to hear God from an unlikely person and circumstance brought his life to a premature end. Listen for God in all people, places, and circumstances. Even the godless and vexatious persons among us may be conduits of lessons we need to hear.

Our Prayer: *God of Josiah, we give thanks for this great king who sought after You and accomplished so much. Yet even his greatness was compromised by close-mindedness. Open our hearts and minds as leaders, Lord, to hear Your voice in every unlikely person and circumstance.* **Amen.**

Lobbyists Hired To Subvert Your Purpose

"Working Through the Adversity of Bad Publicity"

"Then the people of the land weakened the hands of the people of Judah, and troubled them in the building, And hired counselors against them, to frustrate their purpose, all the days of Cyrus king of Persia, even until the reign of Darius king of Persia."

Featured Scripture: Ezra 4:4–5
Background Scripture: Ezra 3—6:18

After seventy years of captivity in Babylon, God had restored His people back to Israel. After a census and reorganization, the Jewish people became as one and began to rebuild their Temple in Jerusalem. When the adversaries of Judah and Benjamin heard of this construction project, they approached them falsely wanting to become part of the project as a way to subvert the unity and spirit of oneness of the Jews.

The Jewish leaders recognized this effort to weaken their people and rebuffed these corrupt offers of assistance. Their refusal to be subverted in building the Temple prompted their adversaries to launch a public relations campaign meant to doom their project. The enemies of the Jews hired counselors to subvert the Temple construction by appealing to the Persian kings through various means of persuasion. This subversive activity went on for many days and through the reigns of two kings. But the eye of God was upon the elders of the Jews.

How many great projects of great repute have been started with the unity and help of good people, only to be subjugated to the grind of organized, paid opposition? If you are a leader of faith, you either have seen or will see such an occurrence, just as the Jews of Ezra's day did. Any time you attempt to do something good, opposition will arise. The opposition will often come from within your own organization in the form of persons who do not want to attempt new or bold things. It may come in the form of pessimists, who fear failure or who fear that other people will be emboldened if the project is successful.

The Jews of Ezra's day kept going forward. Their leaders did not let the organized opposition stop them. Indeed, they had to deal in faith with the efforts against them, it slowed them down, it most likely increased the time of completion, but it did not stop them. God's Temple would be built. It took prophets, workers, leaders, kings, and the like—all working together—to get the Temple built in the face of hired opposition.

Great projects big and small require leaders of faith who can persevere through the adversity of hired and organized opposition. You may have to survive the work of lobbyists who work against you. It will require your every skill. It will require you asking God for an added portion of patience and provision. And it will require bringing forth the collaborative teamwork of laity, clergy, and sympathizers in authority who believe that your own temple must be built. Keep on building as you are building unto the Lord!

Our Prayer: *Lord, all great projects we attempt for You will attract opposition from others. Help us to work as a team in our church and organizations to build the temples You ask us to build. Help us to know that through faith, hard work, and patience, all things are possible by Your might. We give thanks that the people of Ezra's day kept on building in the face of great odds.* **Amen.**

A Long Prayer And A Short Prayer

"Constant Supplication to God Yields Answers and Opportunity"

"And it came to pass, when I heard these words, that I sat down and wept, and mourned certain days, and fasted, and prayed before the God of heaven..... Then the king said unto me, For what dost thou make request? So I prayed to the God of heaven."

Featured Scriptures: Nehemiah 1:4; and 2:4
Background Scripture: Nehemiah 1—2:10

When Nehemiah's brother brought him the news of the dreadful condition of his beloved people and the city of Jerusalem, Nehemiah's heart was burdened to action. Exiled in the court of Persian King Artaxerxes, Nehemiah's first inclinations upon hearing of the tragedy of the Jews were to weep, mourn, fast, and pray before the God of heaven. These acts of penitence and the offering of long prayers were followed by his petition to God for his people's restoration. The first act of a great leader in a desperate situation should always be one of a humble spirit and fervent communication with God. In pureness of heart, we should always place our needs and requests before the throne of the Almighty.

As the cupbearer of the king, Nehemiah held a trusted position. Even in exile, Nehemiah was able to interact with the king. On this day as Nehemiah brought forth the king's wine, his countenance was sad. His grief was noticeably apparent following the bad news he had received and his long time of mourning, prayer, and intercession. As Nehemiah came before the king on this special day, King Artaxerxes sensed his sadness and inquired as to its source. That very moment was created by God for His purpose. Our Scripture today tells us that before Nehemiah answered the king, he said a prayer to the God of heaven. Nehemiah's short prayer stirred God to give him just the right words to say to the king.

A long prayer followed by a short prayer by this leader of faith set into motion the providential events that would begin the restoration of God's people and the holy city. Leaders of faith should be warriors of prayer. Sometimes we need those extended times of weeping, mourning, fasting, and prayers of confession. These extended moments are often born out of a great calling and challenge. We should set aside time to seek God in this way. But there also come moments when all we can do is offer a short prayer to God. In response to all of our prayers, God goes before us to prepare opportunities and circumstances so His power can move others to action.

In our own leadership journeys of faith, we, too, should say quick prayers and send our silent thoughts up before God. As leaders we can tap into the vastness of God's wisdom and receive the quick and instinctive answer we need for a moment of crisis. Long prayers and short prayers both have the power to change our conditions. Nehemiah's long and short prayers were answered, and the king granted his wish to return to his people and begin a leadership journey of restoration for the hurting people of Jerusalem. Keep knocking on God's door in prayer. He hears you and will send the answer and the very opportunity you need to help serve others in His name.

Our Prayer: *God of heaven, we seek You as Nehemiah sought You in humility, confession, and supplication. We know that we have fallen short and those we lead are imperfect. Open up for us, dear Lord, the opportunity to leave our current circumstances and begin a process of restoration. We pray this prayer and all prayers to You, O God, with the confidence that You have gone before us, already setting up the circumstances of our deliverance. **Amen.***

A Mind To Work

"INSTILLING A GOOD WORK ETHIC IN THOSE YOU ARE CALLED TO LEAD"

"So built we the wall; and all the wall was joined together unto the half thereof: for the people had a mind to work…. Yet now be strong O Zerubbabel, saith the LORD; and be strong, O Joshua, son of Josedech, the high priest; and be strong, all ye people of the land, saith the LORD, and work: for I am with you, saith the LORD of hosts."

FEATURED SCRIPTURES: NEHEMIAH 4:6; AND EZRA 2:4
BACKGROUND SCRIPTURES: NEHEMIAH 4:1–6; EZRA 3; AND HAGGAI 1—2:9

Rebuilding the Temple, as well as rebuilding Jerusalem in Jewish history, took great leadership, courage, and hard work. The single-mindedness and faithful execution of God's command to rebuild the holy places required teamwork and leadership that instilled a great work ethic in people who had been exiled from their home. The ability to motivate others to a single purpose and to extract from them a commitment to hard work is one of the most fundamental requirements for a leader of faith.

God goes before us and God is with us, but God requires that we do the work. The prophets Ezra, Nehemiah, and Haggai each had a special calling from God. Each was leading a remnant of people who would be charged with the task of rebuilding the former majesty of Israel. Motivating others to work in the midst of rubble, despair, and adversity means leaders must reach out in great faith to a mighty God.

Today, we are called to rebuild organizations and congregations that are mere remnants of their former selves. We are called to take over unprofitable or bankrupt ventures and motivate employees, volunteers, customers, and coworkers to accomplish tasks they have never done before. Leaders of faith must bring others to understand and believe in causes greater than themselves. Often we must work in environments where people ridicule us and seek to disrupt our efforts.

Our minds can never truly turn to work until they turn to God. People of faith will do work and tackle jobs that others may feel are beneath them. People of faith will gain a mind to work when they know that every wall we build and every meal we serve is done in the name of Christ. As we work and sweat together, our teamwork and camaraderie grows and tasks can become fun and fulfilling. Leaders should constantly remind those who work under them of the importance and meaning of their labor.

If God calls us to work for Him, He will sustain us and multiply our blessings. Our obedience to the task at hand will no longer seem like hard work, but part of a holy calling that will reap heavenly rewards. So get a mind to work. The Lord of hosts is with you and watching you today. Your labor will not be in vain.

Our Prayer: *Lord of hosts, give us a mind to work for You. We know that much work needs to be done in Your name this very day. You have called us to lead others and to serve others. Let Your Spirit and the love of Christ move among those we lead so that they will gain a mind to work in obedience and service to You. May every wall and temple and church we build be consecrated to the edification of the Kingdom of God.* **Amen.**

Leaders In Waiting

"CRITICAL SITUATIONS BRING UNLIKELY LEADERS TO THE FOREFRONT"

"For if thou altogether holdest thy peace at this time, then shall their enlargement and deliverance arise to the Jews from another place; but thou and thy father's house shall be destroyed: and who knoweth whether thou art come to the kingdom for such a time as this?"

FEATURED SCRIPTURE: ESTHER 4:14
BACKGROUND SCRIPTURE: ESTHER 3—8:2

Who knows whether you have come to the Kingdom for such a time as this? Leaders of today were once leaders-in-waiting. Esther was a leader-in-waiting. Mordecai, her cousin and mentor, challenged Queen Esther in this time of crisis to consider whether God had placed her in this position at this time in history to save God's people. Here was Esther, a Jewish orphan of incredible God-given beauty and charm, placed into the harem of King Ahasuerus. Esther claimed the heart of the king and became his wife and queen. But now she must step out and risk it all for the salvation of her people.

The evil assistant to King Ahasuerus was Haman. Haman was wroth with Mordecai and was devising an evil plot to destroy both Mordecai and the Jewish people. Mordecai discovered the plan and appealed to Esther to intercede with the king. For Esther to intercede without being summoned by the king could, by law, result in her death. Yet boldly, Esther answered the call. She went directly to the king, uninvited. She bloomed in her moment, telling the king of the true plot, the betrayal of Haman, and the unrewarded loyalty of Mordecai. This leader-in-waiting, through bravery, seized her moment of leadership. Through Esther's intervention, the king acted and God's people were saved. Esther claimed her time and calling by God and became a heroine of our faith.

Are you a leader-in-waiting? Has God blessed you with beauty, talent, and grace? Have you been given a set of unique skills? Have you been strategically placed in a town, congregation, or organization with special access to the halls of power? God equipped Esther with assets and placed her in the right circumstances to be a leader-in-waiting. In His divine plan of faith, God situated her in just the right place at the right moment to step up and lead.

While the balance of a nation may not rest upon your shoulders, you may still be a leader-in-waiting. God may have given you the talents and opportunity to be placed in a unique situation to serve Him and others. When you see a situation and feel a tug in your heart to take action on behalf of others, it may well be God calling you to a leadership task of faith. In humility and bravery, be ready, like Esther, to step up and seize the moment. Your time to come to the forefront of human events may be now. Who knows whether God placed you in all of eternity in the Kingdom for a moment such as this? Answer the call!

Our Prayer: *Lord God, help me to be brave and courageous like Esther. Send a Mordecai to mentor me. Make me aware that a whole life of preparation for leadership can come down to an extraordinary moment to act on the call You give to me. Create a situation and moment to seize for You, O Lord. May I always rely on Your power to see me through every opportunity to step up and lead others in Your name.* **Amen.**

When Bad Things Happen To Good Leaders

"When Leaders Shun Victim Status to Claim Victory"

"And the Lord said unto Satan, Hast thou considered my servant Job, that there is
none like him in the earth, a perfect and an upright man, one that feareth God, and
escheweth evil? Then Satan answered the Lord, and said, Doth Job fear God for nought?"
FEATURED SCRIPTURE: JOB 1:8–9
BACKGROUND SCRIPTURES: JOB CHAPTERS 1, 3, AND 42

Job's story is one of the most pondered subjects of Scripture. Job's travails have even spawned secular phrases such as *Jobish experience*. This term refers to when a series of bad things happen to the same person for no apparent reason.

In the study of Job, however, we can glean much theology and many leadership lessons from the negative events of his life. We are given a glimpse into the ways of God and see how good people can be tested through bad circumstances. Job's story begs the question of why bad things happen to good people. Job was a leader in his community. He was blessed with wealth and a large family. He was upright and faithful to God. Job seemingly was a good man, doing good things. If all this was true, then why would God allow him to be so harshly tested by Satan?

Satan and other creatures of the heavenly order obviously have access and ongoing communication with the Lord. The Lord inquired of Satan as he was searching the earth for a man to tempt and prompted him to "consider my servant Job." Satan said that Job had no reason to be disobedient to God because he possessed all the blessings of this life. "Who wouldn't praise the Lord when they are so blessed?" Satan said of Job.

When Satan asked God's permission to test Job, it was given. Job went on to suffer the loss of family, personal possessions, his health, and his good standing in the community…he seemingly lost it all at Satan's hand. In addition, Job received bad advice from friends who advised him to curse God and die. But Job never did. Job went through a laborious recounting by others as to why these bad things happened to a seemingly innocent person. Yet God speaks to us mightily in the Book of Job about how His ways are not our ways.

Job ultimately repented of his own self-pity and ceaseed to challenge God. He acknowledged God's omnipotence and his own powerlessness. God ceased Job's travails and blessed him when his heart and prayers became focused upon others. Job 42:10 says: *"And the Lord turned the captivity of Job, when he prayed for his friends: also the Lord gave Job twice as much as he had before."*

The lesson of Job in life and leadership is straightforward: Bad things happen to good leaders. We will be tested. We will suffer loss. Yet we should praise God in all of life's circumstances. We should never blame God or others for our earthly travails. When we remain steadfast and devoted to God, repent of our sense of entitlement, and put others first in prayer and deed, God will deliver us and bless us. Job was restored by God and died an old, wealthy, beloved leader because he ultimately followed that same plan.

Our Prayer: *Lord, thank You for the lesson of Job. When we are tested, give us strength, faith, and a sense of selflessness and praise. As did Job, may we pray for the welfare of others before seeking blessings for ourselves. In all things we acknowledge that Your ways need no justification.* **Amen.**

Callers For Justice And Pleaders For Truth

"HOW TO DISCERN WHO IS RIGHT AND WHO IS WRONG IN GREAT DEBATES"

"For the congregation of hypocrites shall be desolate, and fire shall consume the tabernacles of bribery. They conceive mischief, and bring forth vanity, and their belly prepares deceit.... None calleth for justice, nor any pleadeth for truth: they trust in vanity, and speak lies; they conceive mischief, and bring forth iniquity."

FEATURED SCRIPTURES: JOB 15:34–35; AND ISAIAH 59:4
BACKGROUND SCRIPTURES: ISAIAH 59:1–8; PSALM 7

In leadership there will come times when we must join great debates. And great questions will arise as to who is on the righteous side. In every debate, skillful orators come forward with the skill and cunning to sway the congregation or audience their way. But how do we as leaders of faith discern who is right and who is wrong in these debates? Our Scripture lesson today tells us that we must look for who is truly calling for justice and who is pleading for truth for the innocent.

The great issues and debates of our day in which we ourselves will participate should always propel us to the side of justice and truth. We may even find ourselves building alliances with unpopular persons or unlikely interests. And often, those forces opposing us may on the surface appear to be taking the noble and correct course. We may even begin to question our own values and methods. But God tells us that in the fire of justice and truth lies our redemption. In Psalm 7, King David appealed to God for judgment his positions in the great debates he faced. His enemies appeared to be victimized by David, but in the end David was protected because his positions were just and true and his heart rests with God.

In every congregation and organization, leaders of faith will confront some great debate that divides the people. The great debate may take the form of changing a mission or tackling a controversial subject or calling out a popular figure for reprimand. How should we approach it, and what side should we take? First, we must measure the motives of the debaters. Who stands to gain from the prevailing side and what motivates them? We should also look at who will ultimately become the innocent victim of each side of the debate. Which side seeks justice for the weak and which speaks the truth in the matter at hand?

These debates can be hard-hitting and can cause us to lose friends and supporters. By taking the side of justice and truth, we may be criticized and our own motives may be called into question. But God is the ultimate judge and jury. His sole measure is basic and fundamental: Is it just and is it true? It is better to be on this prevailing side of justice and truth than to win the mortal debate in the court of public opinion.

Leaders of faith were not called to win debates, but to change hearts and serve others in justice and truth. If we do, our work and debates, whether won or lost, will manifest themselves for the edification of all those whom we were called by God to serve.

Our Prayer: *Lord God, our enemies and rivals come after us with artful debate and false causes. Empower us to be strong and pure in these times and battles. Let us debate for the sake of justice and truth. Protect us from those who would do us harm for the sake of wealth, vanity, or power. As we serve others, steer us clear of man's vengeance and let justice and truth prevail.* **Amen.**

Stop, Think Upon This Thing, Be Still...Selah

"CLEARING YOUR HEART AND MIND TO HEAR THE EMPHASIS OF GOD'S CALL"

"O ye sons of men, how long will ye turn my glory into shame? How long will ye love vanity, and seek after leasing? Selah. Stand in awe, and sin not: commune with your own heart upon your bed, and be still. Selah...I cried unto the Lord with my voice, and he heard me out of his holy hill. Selah."

FEATURED SCRIPTURES: PSALM 4:2, 4; AND PSALM 3:4
BACKGROUND SCRIPTURE: PSALM 82:1–4

Our deliverance from God, as well as the hearing of a special call, usually comes to us as part of a three-step process. First, we must cease from our fretting and activity. When we are still and open to hear God's voice speaking to our minds and hearts, we will regain a sense of awe of His presence within us. As we achieve a holy state of mind, the Spirit convicts us of the vanity and self-centeredness that overtakes our lives. And in our quietness, we then cry out to God in His holy place, and He will hear us and come to us.

The Hebrew word *Selah* is used several times in the Psalms as a special notation telling the reader or singer of a psalm to pause and make special note of what they are reading or singing. It is a call to measure, to weigh, to think upon this special thing before moving ahead. All leaders of faith need to stop...pause...and be still.... *Selah*. Are you too busy going about your daily tasks to pause to hear God's voice?

Summoning the holy presence of God into our lives requires that we cease from the busyness of our travels and daily duties in order to hear Him. The Father, Son, and Holy Spirit are freely available to us. The Trinity of God longs to commune with us. But we must first practice *Selah*. We must pause and stop...even in the midst of the stress and emergencies of our lives. God wants our undivided attention. To offer God anything less disrespects the relationship. What power and peace we often forfeit because we cannot stop and become still before God. *Selah*.

The psalmist tells us that he found God in the stillness and quietness upon his bed as he lay still in awe of his Creator. We, too, may best find God in the stillness of our own bed or in a quiet place on bended knee. We may go to an unspoiled place in the woods or walk beside a stream. Or we can pause and be still right where we are this day.

We need to hear from God. We need to stay true to the calling and mission that God has planned for us. Most often it is not our work ethic or our abilities that grind us to a halt; it is failing to pause amidst the flurry of our activities to hear God's voice. Lock out the world around you this very day. Yes, we have holy work to do, but we must first hear the affirmation and admonition of our Lord. *Selah*. Practice the holy art of pausing, stopping, and meditating upon the words of God and upon the sacred events of life before moving on. God will richly bless you when you do. *Selah*.

Our Prayer: *Father, Son, and Holy Spirit, we stop, we pause, we ponder Your majesty in awe, trembling, and honor. Give us a sign. Come to us. Purify us this day for new purpose and renewal. Protect us and provide for us by Your might. Make us a blessing to others.* **Amen.**

A Gaze That Humbles, Empowers

"Star-Gazing Is a Powerful Way to Calibrate a Leader's Purpose and Goals"

"When I consider thy heavens, the work of thy fingers, the moon and the stars, which thou hast ordained; What is a man, that thou are mindful of him? And the son of man, that thou visitest him? For thou hast made him a little lower than the angels, and hast crowned him with glory and honor. Thou madest him to have dominion over the works of thy hands; thou hast put all things under his feet.…"

Featured Scripture: Psalm 8:3–4
Background Scripture: Psalm 89: 3–7

On a clear night, in a remote place, each of us has had some opportunity to gaze at the heavens. Star-gazing is as old a pastime as humanity itself. The psalmist in today's Scripture also was drawn to the heavens. But just as God awes us to our seeming insignificance in the light of the power of His creation, He compels us into action, into acknowledging our worth to Him as custodians of what He has made. The awesomeness of the heavens calls leaders of faith into humility and into action. The gaze that awes us empowers us into service to our Creator.

Many people facing huge tasks or decisions have taken a walk under a starlit sky seeking inspiration from the heavens. As technology grows more powerful each year, we can see farther into God's universe, literally seeing billions of galaxies and an infinitesimal sphere of creation. God's universe has no end, no limits.

The brilliance of the heavens is God's way of showing us how valuable we are to Him as His creatures. He has made us a little lower than the angelic beings. As leaders of faith, we should see God's order and the infinity of His power as bringing new possibilities into our lives. Those situations we face that seem unsolvable and hopeless can be given new perspective when put into heavenly alignment. What humbles us should soon empower us to attempt even greater things for God.

Plant a tree for which you will never live to enjoy its shade. Begin trusting that your small, unnoticed acts of service, when done with great love, will yield great returns in God's heavenly realm. If the heavens are so ordered for us to see, should we ever doubt that the human and spiritual failure around us is anything but a new canvas to sketch a portrait of God's power?

When star-gazing, try a small technique. Look up, and as you see the awe of it, inhale its wonder deeply. Next, hold your breath a moment, and feel God's wonder inside of you. As you exhale, feel empowered by God's own strength to attempt new things as mighty as His heavens are vast. Let the insurmountable love, power, mercy, grace, and forgiveness of an almighty Creator unleash itself in your own leadership journey of faith.

Our Prayer: *God, Creator of the heavens and the earth, Giver of all life, it is in awe that we give You thanks for it all. The heavens do declare Your glory, and the firmament shows us Your handiwork. Make us aware of our value as Your creation. Humble us, then empower us to dare to do mighty things to build Your Kingdom in our own lives and leadership journeys.* **Amen.**

Surrounded By Death And Ungodly Men

"Invoking God's Presence in the Midst of Our Horrors"

"The sorrows of death compassed me, and the floods of ungodly men made me afraid. The sorrows of hell compassed me about: the snares of death prevented me. In my distress I called upon the Lord, and cried unto my God: he heard my voice out of his temple, and my cry came before him, even into his ears.… And he rode upon a cherub, and did fly: yea, he did fly upon the wings of the wind"

Featured Scripture: Psalm 18:4–6, 10
Background Scriptures: Psalm 18; Joshua 1:9; and Psalm 27:1

The hero in this passage, David, admitted what every warrior experiences: He was afraid in the battle. As great soldiers say, "War is hell and hell is war." The call to leadership of faith places many men and women in the bowels of war, death, hell, and fear. David was forthright in his words to us: *"The sorrows of death compassed me, and the floods of ungodly men made me afraid. The sorrows of hell compassed me about."*

The stress of leadership journeys of faith is not always the organizational spats and interpersonal struggles of peers and followers; often, they are death and the hell of war about you. But for those leaders called by God, there is good news! He is there with you and will never forsake you. He will hear your voice and will come to you. God sometimes needs leaders of faith to be placed in the midst of horror for His purpose. Many a leader of faith in their call to service will find that they are surrounded by death and enemies who mean them harm. For these persons and these special callings: God not only hears your cry and appreciates your sacrifice, but Psalm 18:10 tells us, *"He will fly to you on the wings of the wind."*

David was the chosen king and warrior of God. David was a man after God's own heart. Unlike David's son Solomon, David was called to battle and sorrow for the Lord. Warriors experience the loneliness and fear and the floods of ungodly men in battle. Leaders in war zones know the ruthlessness of the enemy. God's measure and helping of comfort for you in these times is immense, as described in the Scriptures. Call upon God; He is a buckler to all those who trust Him, a very Rock of salvation.

The battle experiences of David and all of God's warriors are unique and sometimes too horrific to recall. Even after the battles, the sorrows and recollections of them can haunt you. Give them to God in prayer and meditation. Remember and repeat the words of David, the warrior and psalmist, in Psalm 18:45, 49: *"The strangers shall fade away… He delivereth me from mine enemies: yea, thou liftest me up above those that rise up against me: thou hast delivered me from the violent man."*

Our Prayer: *Lord God of hosts, You are the Rock of salvation. You are our Deliverer. You come to us in our times of trouble. Even in the midst of the horror of war, You are there with us. Even though we are afraid as we are surrounded by death and ungodly men, we will call out to You and You will fly to us on the wings of the wind and deliver us. Praise be to the Lord God Almighty.* **Amen.**

Acceptable Input And Outputs

"What We Read, Watch, and Meditate Upon Should Be Acceptable to God"

"Let the words of my mouth, and the meditation of my heart, be acceptable in thy sight, O Lord, my strength, and my redeemer."
Featured Scripture: Psalm 19:14
Background Scriptures: Joshua 1:8; Psalm 119:15–16; and Philippians 4:8

The minds and hearts of leaders of faith are delicate and sensitive and can become targets of evil. So much information, so many sensations, so many problems come before us each day. We as leaders need to temper that influx of stimuli to our minds, bodies, and souls with an antidote for negative thoughts and feelings. Acceptable and positive inputs in our lives each day become good, acceptable outputs. In Philippians 4:8, the apostle Paul told us to think on things *"that are true; honest; just; pure; lovely; of good report, and if there be any virtue, and if there be any praise in them…think on these things."*

God expects and desires that all persons, especially leaders of faith, take time for personal relaxation and meditation. Jesus Himself did this very thing. For us, it is critical that we consciously monitor our time and habits, lest we fall into poor patterns of routine that can become bad habits. Avoid the pitfalls of the flesh by letting lustful input trickle into your stream of thought. Don't become captive to secular entertainment that focuses on human voyeurism or the lustful lives of others.

A good first step to monitoring for acceptable input in your life is to copy our featured Scripture today and post it next to the communication devices that you use each day. As you communicate with others, you can be reminded of the psalmist's words: *"Let the words of my mouth, and the meditation of my heart, be acceptable in thy sight, O Lord, my strength, and my redeemer."*

Try positive inputs of stimuli like a walk in the woods to clear your mind of clutter. Engage in the playfulness of a child. Work with your hands in physical labor to keep your heart humble. Enjoy the fellowship with saintly mentors and friends, with whom you can be your true self and share your deepest thoughts. Physical exercise kills stress and makes us calmer and more able to ward off temptation. Healthy relationships make hearts healthy and minimize our need for lustful input.

Reading Scripture and finding daily meditations that stretch our minds and souls are foremost in developing healthy inputs. Never underestimate the power of song and daily laughter. The best things in life are usually free, and there really is no place like home. You don't have to travel or spend financial resources to find godly inputs upon which to meditate.

Each of us every day is constantly allowing the stimuli around us to have input in our lives. Whether we admit it or not, we do meditate on something almost every waking moment. Make sure that your inputs and meditations are edifying to your soul and serve to build character so that you can serve others with greater zeal, purity, and purpose. Acceptable inputs create holy outputs.

Our Prayer: *Lord, may the words of our mouths and the meditation of our hearts be acceptable to You. Teach us to put healthy inputs into our minds and souls so that we become more holy each day. Help us to break bad habits that can become chains around our shoulders. Teach us, we pray.* **Amen.**

Feasting On Blessings As Your Enemies Watch

"Finding Blessing in the Midst of Your Greatest Adversity"

"Thou preparest a table before me in the presence of mine enemies: thou anointest my head with oil; my cup runneth over."

Featured Scripture: Psalm 23:5
Background Scripture: Psalm 23

The Twenty-Third Psalm is one of Scripture's most quoted and beloved passages. It is often recited at funeral services and read during times of great struggle. Soldiers and servants facing life-threatening odds often recite this psalm as a last rite before death. Whatever the circumstance, this psalm is chockful of great theology for leaders of faith.

David was a warrior and a king. David knew great triumphs and blessings, but David was constantly under duress and often faced life-threatening circumstances in his own journey of leadership. David's enemies were numerous, and they relentlessly sought to destroy him. In penning this psalm, David alluded to the faith and comfort he had in God for His ultimate protection and provision. Even the death and destruction around him were made to become still in the presence of the Great Shepherd. David, even in his trouble, was made to feel as if he were lying down in a green pasture or walking with God beside still waters.

In our featured Scripture today, we learn that in what appears to be our moments of imminent destruction by the hand of our enemies, God is preparing a table of blessing for us—right in the very presence of those who seek to do us harm. Leaders of faith who are bathed in prayer and God's purpose will see their most stressful moments as a time for the unleashing of God's blessing. When our adversaries are knocking at our door is when the Lord's ultimate protection and provision will be made known to us.

God finds ways to anoint us in our times of trouble. He covers our very heads with heavenly oil and blankets our circumstances with His grace. He makes our cups of resources to become so full that they run over with provisions of blessing. When the enemy knocks at the door of your organization or congregation, God will cause your panic to turn to power. He will make the seemingly insurmountable obstacle to become a stairway to personal renewal. Darkness will become light.

As leaders of faith, we often miss the blessings and power promised by God through Psalm 23 because we allow ourselves to see death, challenges, and enemies as evil. God sees these turbulent times as opportunities for His love and power to conquer all. Even if death comes, eternal life in Paradise waits for us. Even when setbacks occur, God is planting the seeds of rebirth of a greater good. Even when the enemy knocks, God smiles and prepares His best meal for us, and evildoers watch us consume the blessings of the eternal Father. Surely goodness and mercy will follow true leaders of faith all the days of their lives, and they will dwell in the house of the Lord forever.

Our Prayer: *Our Lord and Great Shepherd, may the Twenty-Third Psalm become our cloak and mantra of faith. Grant us the faith of Your great servant David. Instill in us a sense of power and provision even in the presence of our enemies, even as they seek to devour us. May our faith in You bring praise and glory to the throne of Grace. Help us and guide us in all our valleys of leadership. Make us an example for other leaders to follow.* **Amen.**

Youthful Indiscretions Given To God

"Leaders of All Ages Should Give the Past Sins of Youth to God"

"Remember not the sins of my youth, nor my transgressions: according to thy mercy remember me for thy goodness' sake, O Lord.... Rejoice, O young man, in thy youth; and let thy heart cheer thee in the days of thy youth, and walk in the ways of thine heart, and in the sight of thine eyes: but know thou, that for all these things God will bring thee into judgment."

Featured Scriptures: Psalm 25:7; and Ecclesiastes 11:9
Background Scriptures: Jeremiah 3:22–25; Ecclesiastes 11:8–10; and Psalm 25

The great hope for many older leaders of faith is that God will not remember the sins of their youth. In Psalm 25, David appealed to God's tender mercies and His loving-kindness as he asked God to forget the sins of his youth. David was providing this prayer for us, as well. In the Book of Ecclesiastes, Solomon told young people to enjoy their youth but to also be careful; God would bring even youthful indiscretions into judgment.

David and his son Solomon were leaders from their youth. Both were chosen to do great things for God. God calls persons of all ages into leadership journeys for Him. God gives even the very young specific tasks to do. While youth are endowed with health and a vibrancy of life, they can succumb easily to youthful indiscretions that haunt them for a lifetime. It is often the very hand of God that guides young people through the danger and peril of the mistakes and poor decisions they make that put them into risk.

For those leaders of faith who committed youthful indiscretions, God is able to forgive and blot them from your past. For some, the punishment of the mistakes of youth have molded them and saved them from utter destruction. Some leaders still hold deep, dark secrets from their youth that need to be confessed to God. God is able to forgive and remember them no more. If we have been delivered from the foolishness of our youth, we have a sacred obligation to not repeat these mistakes. We also have an obligation to become mentors and teachers of the young, especially those whom sin and bad circumstances have already attacked.

Many times we may laugh and dismiss unconfessed sin as simply a "youthful indiscretion," but God wants us to come clean with Him. Give your past and your secrets to God. As we cleanse our lives of the mistakes of youth, we become empowered and emboldened to complete our calling for God with cleanness of heart and spiritual vigor.

Our Prayer: *Lord God, we bring the past of our youth to You for inspection. We confess our youthful indiscretions to You and ask You to cleanse our sins and remember them no more. Use our past experiences of youth to propel us and not hinder our leadership calling. Help us to take our newfound forgiveness and work harder and with greater purpose each day. Help us by Your Spirit to be an example and mentor to the youth of today as they struggle with their own temptations and youthful indiscretions.* **Amen.**

Hidden In Our Time Of Trouble

"God's Cloak of Protection Often Found in Strange Places"

"The Lord is my light and my salvation; whom shall I fear? The Lord is the strength of my life; of whom shall I be afraid?... For in the time of trouble he shall hide me in his pavilion: in the secret of his tabernacle shall he hide me; he shall set me up upon a rock."

FEATURED SCRIPTURE: PSALM 27:1, 5
BACKGROUND SCRIPTURE: PSALM 27

We often move along through life unaware of the danger and snares around us. In our own calculations, we may seek a new position or make a life decision without full knowledge of its consequences and without spiritual confirmation. Sometimes our lives stall and it seems we have missed the opportunities of success. Part of God's providence is that He is protecting us without our even knowing. We are hidden in our time of trouble as God safely positions us away from harm, evil, and tribulation.

God is the God of every circumstance. Even the evil ones were created for God's own purposes. All mature leaders of faith can honestly look back in life and see where their lives stalled or where a relationship failed and set them back. In analyzing the stall, the failure, and the setback, we see that it was really God protecting us from harm. The job we did not get could have led us down the wrong career path and away from our true ministry. The broken relationship occurred so we could meet the spouse God had chosen for us. The business sale we lost might actually have destroyed our organization had we been able to make the deal.

Our Scripture lesson tells us that God hides us in His pavilion and in His temple. It tells us that God sets us upon a rock for our own protection. Have you encountered a setback that was actually God protecting you from something destructive? Was your sickness, incapacitation, or incarceration the hard rock upon which God placed you for a time so that your life could be spared? Sickness and prison hardly seem like places of protection, but God uses even the adversity in our lives as a refuge from life's storms. It was upon our sickbed that we were still enough to contemplate what was truly important in life and to hear God's voice. It took an arrest and imprisonment to intercede and rescue us from a life run amok in sin, excess, and addiction.

Not every hard place and situation is God's refuge. But for leaders of faith involved in life-long journeys for God, we most often see God's protection in hindsight. Our answer to a call of heavenly purpose brings us squarely into spiritual warfare and peril that our finite minds cannot comprehend. It takes our all-powerful and sovereign God to set us in the places of protection that will assure our preservation and ultimate success for Him.

God is our light and our salvation. He is our very help in time of trouble. It is in His pavilion, in His Temple, and upon His rock that we will be hidden in our times of trouble. Praise the Lord this day for His cloak of grace and salvation in all the strange places.

Our Prayer: *God of life, You sustain us. You protect us. You hide us from our troubles and our own self-destruction. Help us to understand that setbacks, failures, and broken relationships are often Your way of preserving us from demise. Give us confidence this day that if we remain steadfast in Your light and will, we have nothing to fear.* **Amen.**

Taking Our Own Advice

"Be Careful to Listen to Yourself and Heed Your Own Instruction"

"Come, ye children, hearken unto me: I will teach you the fear of the Lord.... Keep thy tongue from evil, and do good; seek peace, and pursue it.... Finally, be ye all of one mind, having compassion one of another, love as brethren, be pitiful, be courteous: not rendering evil for evil.... For the eyes of the Lord are over the righteous, and his ears are open to their prayers: but the face of the Lord is against them that do evil."
Featured Scriptures: Psalm 34:11, 13–14; and 1 Peter 3:8–9, 12
Background Scriptures: Psalm 34:11–22; and 1 Peter 3:8–12

Leaders of faith are called to counsel, preach, teach, instruct, demonstrate, and explain. Almost every calling to leadership in faith requires that we impart what we know to others. It requires that we share our unique understanding of God's plan revealed to us for the edification of the institution and congregants we serve. We are, in essence, God's modern-day messengers. Our advice is valuable and highly sought. Yet our truest measure of success as a leader may just lie in how successful we become in taking our own advice.

Our Scripture today is taken from the words of King David and the apostle Peter. They were living examples of leaders who took their own advice. These two great faith leaders taught us how to be successful and remain in favor with God and man: Don't speak evil. Do good works. Pursue peace. Be unified in mind and have compassion on each other. Love each other as brothers and sisters. Be courteous to all and never repay evil for an evil.

Leaders heed their own words when we become the living example of the lessons we preach to others. Over time in leadership it can become easy and comfortable to preach and teach to others without being self-reflective. Great leaders should be the toughest self-critics. The more wisdom we share, the wiser we should become.

Are we meeting the mark that we set for others? We can't teach purity of speech if we gossip. We can't preach the pursuit of peace if we have unresolved conflict within our own families. We can't preach unity and harmony when we allow exclusive cliques to form in our congregations. We can't impart the value of love and courtesy to all when we harbor old prejudices and revel in another's misfortune. We might be saying all the right things as leaders but not listening to ourselves and heeding our advice. Don't let the fundamentals of your faith become stale and trite in your daily walk. The simple advice is timeless, solid, and powerful.

The Scripture says that the Lord's eyes are continually over the righteous and that His ears are constantly open to our prayers and requests of intercession. God abhors evil, especially from those chosen to lead others in the ways of right living. God expects us to be His living examples. If you have fallen short in your example, you can begin anew today by taking your own advice.

Some of the best advice you will ever receive as a leader is the advice you give yourself in your full submission to the living Lord.

Our Prayer: *Lord Jesus, You are the true example of word and deed. You called us to lead others. Help us to live the lessons we teach to others. Let us become a model of what You desire us to be. Let us listen to our own thoughts and words and remain righteous.* **Amen.**

Working Through Discouragement

"Discouragement Should Give Way to Praise and Work"

"And I will say unto God my rock, why hast thou forgotten me? Why go I mourning because of the oppression of my enemy? Why art thou cast down, O my soul? And why are thou disquieted within me? Hope thou in God: for I shall yet praise him, who is the health of my countenance, and my God. Yet the Lord will command his lovingkindness in the daytime, and in the night his song shall be with me, and my prayer unto the God of my life."

Featured Scripture: Psalm 42:9, 11, 18
Background Scripture: Psalm 42—43

Discouragement can be numbing. It can wrest control of our lives and paralyze our souls. The psalmist of today's lesson felt this same discouragement and vividly described his own "disquieted" soul. The poetic writing of Psalm 42 and 43 speaks to the writer's exile and separation from his home in Jerusalem and his desire to return to worship in the holy Temple. His self-pity, however, ultimately gave way to praise, and his sunken heart gave way to song and a healthy countenance as he worked his way through his own discouragement.

Our lesson today suggests that a bout of discouragement requires our active self-involvement to cure our doldrums. As we begin the process, God's presence and love will birth new hope and song within us. Discouragement has long been a tool of Satan to disable leaders of faith. The psalmist felt the pursuit and oppression of an earthly enemy that caused his separation from the people and places he loved. His physical mourning was a result of discouragement and a series of dreadful events. Regardless of our positions or status in life, discouragement will come to us as life's circumstances and situations from time to time will turn against us.

The psalmist's enemy was a military and political one. Today we may face the enemies of illness, financial distress, betrayal by a friend, or a string of unsuccessful ventures. Whatever the cause, discouragement grabs hold of us and grips our lives, threatening to stall our missions of service to God. Like the psalmist, we may begin to question if God has abandoned us or if we have been foolish to embark on this "false calling" that now seems to have ensnared us in our trouble. Begin working your way out of discouragement by praising God and seeking Him in new ways. Let your longing for His presence turn your mourning into poetry and song.

As we become active participants in defeating discouragement, new power and mercies from God begin to appear. God's love and promise is always constant and available to us. It is sometimes necessary for us to become cuffed to a bad life problem before we can truly and earnestly attain the humility and proper heart to communicate with a holy, righteous, and all-powerful God. If you are discouraged today, praise; don't panic. God has already equipped you with all the tools you need to work your way out of your own discouragement. Start digging.

Our Prayer: *God, our Rock and Salvation, I am discouraged today. Life's circumstances and my competitors seek to overtake me and do me harm. My heart aches and I am paralyzed with sorrow. But at this very moment, Lord, I praise and seek You. I sing my faint song of thanksgiving for Your manifold mercies. I pray that You will give me new strength. I begin right now to work my way out of despair by Your power. Pour your loving-kindness out upon my soul and create a new spirit in me this very moment, I pray.* **Amen.**

Losing Our Souls

"Seeking and Trusting in the Wrong Things Steals Our Souls"

"Hear this, all ye people; give ear, all ye inhabitants of the world.… My mouth shall speak of wisdom; and the meditation of my heart shall be of understanding … They that trust in their wealth, and boast themselves in the multitude of their riches; none of them can redeem his brother, nor give to God a ransom for him.… For what is a man profited, if he shall gain the whole world, and lose his own soul? Or what shall a man give in exchange for his soul.… But if from thence thou shalt seek the Lord thy God, thou shalt find him, if thou seek him with all thy heart and with all thy soul."
Featured Scriptures: Psalm 49:1–3, 6; Matthew 16:26; Deuteronomy 4:29
Background Scriptures: Deuteronomy 4:27–31; Psalm 48; and Matthew 16:24–28

Losing your soul is not something that happens instantaneously. The souls of men and women often die slowly from the culmination of a lifetime of bad choices and decisions. They often die one day at a time as they seek the wrong things in life. Our Scripture lesson today includes the words of Moses, David, and Christ Himself. They conclusively tell us that nothing we gain in this world is worth losing our souls. Nothing we accumulate in our earthly existence can redeem our souls from God. But God is merciful, and our souls can be redeemed and saved if we seek Him with all our hearts and with all our souls.

Some people lose their souls by becoming captive to the world and sensations around them. The mere quest for human survival in a material world is diversion enough for many of us to fail to seek true wisdom and understanding. Some of us lose our souls as we seek pleasure, power, and the admiration of peers and friends. We idolize the successful and the rich and famous.

Some of us can be saved and redeemed, but we allow our souls to suffer and be confined to sadness because we do not seek or meditate on the right things each day. Souls are living creations that must be fed. Some are fed with carnal pleasure, earthly sensations, and worldly ambition. But the wise feed their souls with prayer, study, worship, fellowship, and service. Feeding your soul the wrong way intoxicates it into a momentary high, only to bring you crashing to the ground. Feeding the soul the right way brings you peace in the arms of the Savior.

Leaders of faith should be protectors of souls. We are fishers of men. Our callings have a common thread. We care about the souls of others and desire that all persons seek and find truth, wisdom, mercy, grace, forgiveness, and eternal fellowship with the living God. We do this through our godly service, prayer, and tithes. We especially do this through our leadership example to others.

How's your soul doing today? Are you seeking the right things? Are you outwardly happy but internally restless and hopeless? Maybe God is speaking to you today. God wants all souls reconciled to Him. He is your Creator, and He loves you even more than you love yourself. Nothing you can attain in this world is worth neglecting your eternal soul. Seek God with all your heart and soul today. He is lovingly waiting for you, and you will surely find Him!

Our Prayer: *God of our souls, we need You, O Lord. Forgive us when we have sought the wrong things in this life. Outwardly we seem successful, but our souls long to know You more. This day and at this very hour we seek You, God. Redeem our souls and claim us, we pray.* **Amen.**

Renew A Right Spirit Within Me

"God Can Renew the Spirits of Fallen Leaders"

"Make me to hear joy and gladness; that the bones which thou hast broken may rejoice. Hide thy face from my sins, and blot out all mine iniquities. Create in me a clean heart, O God; and renew a right spirit within me."

Featured Scripture: Psalm 51:8–10
Background Scriptures: Psalm 51; 2 Samuel 11—12

The Fifty-First Psalm is a masterpiece written by a leader who needed to renew a right spirit with God. For all David's greatness, he, too, sinned. His sins were great, including adultery, deceit, and arranging the death of his loyal servant Uriah. David's passion for renewal and his desire for communion with God drove him to pen this prayer and appeal in Psalm 51. David set the example for leaders of faith who have fallen, yet who desire to renew a right spirit with God.

All leaders, including leaders of faith, will falter along the trail of service. Some fall by pride and arrogance. Some fall from succumbing to a simple temptation. Others fall from neglect and a lack of spiritual discipline and focus on the tasks at hand. Whatever the cause and however great the sin, leaders can renew a right spirit if they burn with a passion for God and His fellowship. Renewal of spirit does not mean that we won't pay a penalty for sin. David certainly did. But in our renewal we can find new success and a resurrected usefulness for God. God can use our own forgiven sin for new acts of grace.

The beginning of renewal starts with a sober acknowledgment of your failures. It begins with a broken heart. We, like David, must take our brokenness to God on bended knee and with praise and appeal. If God called us to His service, He wants to forgive us. His mercy and grace is sufficient for us if we seek Him with the earnestness of David. Our sins may not be as dramatic as sending an innocent person to their death, but it may entail the small betrayal of a friend, colleague, or spouse. It may be the compromising of principles, ethics, or standards of behavior. It may involve the acknowledgment of our own laziness or lack of giving a job our best.

Whatever has caused a broken spirit within you can be fixed. If you feel your conscience and heart ache, go to God today. Leaders with broken spirits need repair before they can do the work of the Master. God wants us to experience that joy and gladness from our souls. He wants to blot out our iniquities and create in us a clean heart and a right spirit. Go to Him today. He is waiting for you.

Our Prayer: *O Lord, create in us a clean heart. Forgive our iniquities and remember them no more. Blot out our failures as leaders and give us a renewed spirit so we can do the work of the Kingdom today. Give us the heart of David and the passion to desire ultimate fellowship with You. Bless the works of our hands that they may please You and be a blessing to others in need today.* **Amen.**

Becoming Early And Earnest Seekers Of God

"Great Leaders Pray Early and Earnestly in Solitude with God"

"O God, thou art my God; early will I seek thee: my soul thirsteth for thee, my flesh longeth for thee.… And in the morning, rising up a great while before day, he went out and departed into a solitary place, and there he prayed."

Featured Scriptures: Psalm 63:1; and Mark 1:35
Background Scriptures: Matthew 26:36–45; and Genesis 3:8

Today's two examples of early risers and earnest seekers of God are none other than David and Christ Himself. David and Jesus knew the power that they could harness for the long day ahead by getting up before the day started and, in all earnestness, seeking God's presence. David described his need as if he physically thirsted in longing to be with God. Even as both God and man, Jesus felt the need to arise before daylight and, in solitude, enter into prayer. What better models of success do leaders of faith need?

Leaders of faith who would reach their full God-given potential must develop habits of prayer, study, and meditation. When we arise early to do these tasks, it shows respect and a sense of priority to God. It sets our hearts and mind apart and puts them into the proper placement to brace us for the winds of life that will howl against us during our day.

In the case of David, he was constantly under duress from his enemies. They sought him day and night. David's solace in Psalm 63 was to seek and find protection in the shadow of the wings of God. Jesus' days at the height of His ministry would require many feats of healing, teaching, and the casting out of demons. He would have to evade the wrath of the religious leaders and guard against the attacks of the devil. These early times of seeking God, communicating with Him, and invoking His power and blessing were crucial to David and Jesus' success each day.

The stillness that occurs during the transition from night to dawn also has a great power of its own. Genesis 3:8 tells what Adam and Eve heard in the early cool of the garden: *"And they heard the voice of the Lord God walking in the garden in the cool of the day.…"* God never sleeps nor slumbers. He is always ready to hear from us. But when we seek Him early and earnestly, we, too, shall find Him in the garden.

As we make lifestyle adjustments to become early and earnest seekers of God, our prayer and study will expand exponentially. As we rise each day, let us think on David and Jesus and imagine they are rising with us. By becoming early and earnest seekers of God, we set ourselves up to receive the full measure of power and love from the Almighty Father, who longs to see us coming to Him early in our day.

Our Prayer: *Dear heavenly Father, You never sleep. You are awaiting us if we will but come to find You. Help us to become disciplined leaders of faith so that we may become early and earnest seekers of You. Like David and Christ, may our hearts desire You first thing each day. May we find You in prayer, meditation, and study in the stillness of every morning.* **Amen.**

Him That Hath No Helper

"A Universal Call to Serve Christ's Most Precious Constituency"

"Yea, all kings shall fall down before him: all nations shall serve him. For he shall deliver the needy when he crieth; the poor also, and him that hath no helper."
FEATURED SCRIPTURE: PSALM 72:11–12
BACKGROUND SCRIPTURES: PSALM 72; JOB 29:12; MATTHEW 11:4–6; MATTHEW 25:40; AND REVELATION 19:11–16

The psalmist in our Scripture today was writing of the coming Christ. But his writing also gives us unique insight into the nature of our Lord. The King of kings and Lord of lords is foremost the deliverer of "*him that hath no helper.*" The greatest of all kings is the helper of the least. We serve a Savior whose core constituency includes those persons who seemingly have no hope and no advocate in this life.

If we are called by God for service and leadership, we inherit Christ's constituency of those who have no helper. Leaders of faith may also be called to serve abandoned congregations, organizations, and institutions in states of ruin that have no helper and no leader. It is the innocent and most vulnerable whom Christ gives to us in order to share His eternal hope and love. The measure of our power begins with our capacity to defend the defenseless in every walk of life.

Many times those without a helper are absent and invisible to us. We just don't see them in our everyday walks of life. Sometimes they are around us but are silent and anonymous, suffering quietly without anyone knowing. Part of our spiritual duty as leaders of faith is to seek those congregations and individuals and to offer our hand of service. Sometimes those who have no helpers are the hardest to help. They may be a stranger or someone we sit next to at our place of work. They may smell bad, be addicted, or be of another race or religion. They may be imprisoned. They may even be our rival or competitor.

We must find them. They are Christ's constituency. Their cry of need can be heard if we will listen. The world is full of poverty, injustice, and unresolved burdens. It is part of the Lord's harvest. Whatever our call to service may be, it must include an interface to "*him that hath no helper.*" We may help with a prayer and a tithe. Some of us may become volunteers or short-term missionaries. Others may choose the way of political action or activism through governments or religious institutions.

Whatever our personal leadership mission statement may be, it can never be complete without a clause to be the helper to "*him that hath no helper.*" Incorporate this precept of our Lord into all your daily activities and reap new power and blessing. Kings and obstacles will fall before those who are the defenders of Christ's constituency.

Whom are you seeking and helping today? Is there a child who needs you? Maybe a family member or an old friend needs some time out of your busy day. God may send a stranger into your path who has prayed her last prayer and found no one to assist her. Will you be the one who answers that prayer today? Be a leader; be Christ's friend to "*him that hath no helper.*"

Our Prayer: *Lord Jesus, all kings bow before Your power and majesty. Yet You are foremost the friend to "him that hath no helper." You are our salvation and assurance. Give us this precious constituency of souls to protect, love, help, and serve in Your name and for Your sake.* **Amen.**

Increasing Our Capacity For Compassion

"Leaders Should Pray for the Ability to Lead with Compassion"

"But thou, O Lord, art a God full of compassion, and gracious, longsuffering, and plenteous in mercy and truth. O turn unto me, and have mercy upon me; give thy strength unto thy servant.… But ye, beloved building up yourselves on your most holy faith, praying in the Holy Ghost, Keep yourselves in the love of God, looking for the mercy of our Lord Jesus Christ unto eternal life. And of some have compassion, making a difference.…"

Featured Scriptures: Psalm 86:15–16; Jude 20–22

Background Scriptures: Lamentations 3:21–26; Romans 9:13–16; Matthew 5:6–7; and Matthew 18:21–35

One great dread that leaders of faith should have is a loss of their capacity for compassion. Often, leaders of faith are bombarded with the problems and misery of those around them. The tragedy of poverty, war, hunger, and the brokenness of the human condition can make us shrivel and shrink into a callousness of existence. We must guard greatly against the loss of compassion in leadership. The loss of compassion for others signals a sagging fellowship with God through the Holy Spirit.

We ourselves must rely on God's Spirit to fill us with His compassion and new mercies each day. In his prayer to God, David asked for God to turn to him and give the mercy and strength of compassion, longsuffering, and truth. Jude tells us to build ourselves in the Holy Ghost through prayer; keeping ourselves in the love of God, looking for the mercy of the Lord Jesus and giving that compassion to those who need it. Leaders of faith thus become the conduits of compassion from on high.

As leaders of faith we must constantly remind ourselves that our callings and positions are the fruits of God's grace and compassion to us. No amount of hard work or righteous living could ever entitle us to the salvation or leadership positions we are given. Therefore, as we are products of compassion, we should lead in compassion for others. It may mean forgiving our enemies. It may mean doing kind things to those who may not appear to deserve it. If your heart is hardened and unmoved by the pain and suffering of others, you should go now to your prayer closet and confess it to God.

Jude tells us to pray in the Spirit and to ask for a new portion of God's love. When you are washed in the Spirit of God's love, the compassions and mercies of the Lord Jesus will flow from you anew, like a fountain. Others will see it and be attracted to the Father of mercy. Increase your capacity for compassion in leadership today. Hurting souls who cry out to God need leaders like you to become the hands, feet, and advocates of their answered prayers.

Our Prayer: *Lord of mercy and compassion, forgive us when our hearts grow hardened to the pain and poverty around us. Thank You for Your compassion and mercy to us. Create in us, O Lord, a new and larger capacity for compassion. Make us a channel and conduit of Your love and mercy to those we lead and to those in need. Equip us with the patience and the resources to share Your compassions generously with those we encounter in our leadership journey of life.* **Amen.**

Numbering And Measuring Our Days

"Our Time in This Life Is Fading Fast, So We Must Plan and Manage It Wisely"

"Lord, thou hast been our dwelling place in all generations.... So teach us to number our days, that we may apply our hearts unto wisdom.... Lord, make me to know mine end, and the measure of my days, what it is; that I may know how frail I am."
FEATURED SCRIPTURES: PSALM 90:1, 12; AND PSALM 39:4
BACKGROUND SCRIPTURE: PSALM 90

What would you do if you knew that you only had one year to live? How about one month? Would you change your spiritual priorities? Would you quit the work you are doing today and pour yourself into family, friends, prayer, and reconciliation of broken relationships? Leaders of faith should hearken to the words of Moses and David in our Scripture from the Psalms today. Of all people, leaders of faith should be holy time managers. Our calling to do holy tasks of service for God is urgent and immediate. Life is fragile, and to mismanage time is to fail the Lord who calls us.

Numbering and measuring our days is our tithe and a gift of our most precious resource to God. Time is the great equalizer in life. Each person is blessed with different talents, beauty, wealth, and knowledge; however, the hours of the day are equal to us all. The psalmists petition God to teach us to number our days, to make us to know our end and to help us to measure our days. We have vital work to do for God. We should value each day of life as a precious and perishing commodity by setting clear priorities.

Numbering and measuring our remaining days begins with purifying our own hearts in prayer, worship, and fellowship with God, as well as seeking out fellow believers. It means forgiving others who have hurt us and seeking the restoration of our own broken relationships. It means turning our ambition for accumulating material possessions and professional accolades into a burning quest to love others in Christ's name and to share His redemptive love story in both word and deed.

Holy time management requires a reassessment of all that you do in a given day. Mindless entertainment and gatherings for careless gossip must be purged. Neglected friends and family members must be given new priority. If you truly love them, show them by giving them some of your time. A disciplined time for prayer, Bible study, and exercise must be set aside every day. Clean up your personal space and conquer the physical clutter in your life. Don't waste precious time due to a lack of organization. Find persons who are in need and consider small ways to shower Christ's love upon them. Give in to that tug and calling that has haunted you for months or years and say yes to God today.

As we succeed in numbering and measuring our days wisely, life will become richer and blessings will abound around us. Every moment, every event of life will bring us into greater fellowship with our timeless Creator.

Our Prayer: *O God, number and measure our days so that we can serve You with full heart and impact. Let us cease from wasting time on things that are not edifying to the Kingdom of Heaven. Show us how to manage our time, set goals, and wean ourselves from the clutter and busyness of life. Even in our frailty and the short time we have to spend on earth, use us in a mighty way, O Lord.* **Amen.**

Come Unto Him With Thanksgiving

"Communion and Communication with God Begins with Our Thankfulness"

"O come let us sing unto the LORD: let us make a joyful noise to the rock of our salvation. Let us come before his presence with thanksgiving.... Enter into his gates with thanksgiving, and into his courts with praise: be thankful unto him, and bless his holy name."

FEATURED SCRIPTURES: PSALM 95:1–2; AND PSALM 100:4
BACKGROUND SCRIPTURES: PSALM 95; PSALM 100; PHILIPPIANS 4:6; AND REVELATION 7:11–12

We should prepare our hearts before we seek communion with God. That preparation begins as we seek the Holy Spirit and let Him fill us with a great sense of thanksgiving to God. Coming to God in praise and thanksgiving establishes a holy, respectful tone of communication before the throne of God. The psalmist says that singing to the Lord and making a joyful noise is one way to kindle thanksgiving to God. Coming to God in thanksgiving should be more than a once-a-year celebration or holiday. It must mark the way we commune daily with our heavenly Father. When pure thanksgiving dwells within us, God unleashes even greater blessings. Before we offer our hurts and needs in prayerful petitions, we must bring our thanksgiving to God.

Leaders of faith must be leaders of thanksgiving. Our institutions should become zones of constant thanksgiving. In every circumstance and through every event of life, regardless of its hardship, we lead most effectively when we first give thanks to God. We should even give thanks for our challenges and sorrows, then lay them at the feet of the Almighty and ask Him to use them for his holy purposes.

Thanksgiving is a part of true worship. It establishes our Father-and-child relationship with God and helps purify us for real communion. Even the poorest and sickest among us can practice thanksgiving. Organizations and congregations will falter when they lose their sense of thankfulness. Thankfulness is our affirmation that all we are, all we have, and all that we will become are the pure gifts of our Creator. Coming to God with thanksgiving moors us and tethers us tightly to the merciful provision of our Maker. Don't fret about thanking God before requesting your provision. God knows your needs. He knows your pain and your sin. He knows your desires and longings, and you are in His care.

By giving thanks first and foremost in our prayers, we open the conduit for God to grant the provisions we need. Too often our prayer lives consist of constant pleading for help and deliverance, and they are not centered on thanksgiving and praise. Today is a great time to commit ourselves not only to a greater sense of thankfulness, but to a new reverence in the way we approach God. Those persons we lead will see hope through our thanksgiving and will want to follow us all the more. Those in need around us will come to know that thanksgiving is more about an eternal relationship than the current plight of the human condition. They may see our thanksgiving and want to find that same God whom we praise. So become a greater leader of faith by becoming a more fervent leader of thanksgiving. Enter into His gates with thanksgiving and into His courts with praise.

Our Prayer: *Almighty God and Creator, we come to You with thankful hearts, giving You praise for who You are. We give eternal thanks for every blessing, and especially for the gift of our salvation in Christ. In thanksgiving, praise, and humility, we cast our crowns and lives before You.* **Amen.**

Rejoice And Be Glad!

"REJOICING AND GLADNESS ARE BORN IN OUR TROUBLES"

"The LORD reigneth; let the earth rejoice; let the multitude of the isles be glad.... Let all those that seek thee rejoice and be glad in thee: and let such as love salvation say continually, Let God be magnified.... Rejoice and be exceedingly glad: for great is your reward in heaven: for so persecuted they the prophets which were before you.... This is the day which the LORD hath made; we will rejoice and be glad in it."

FEATURED SCRIPTURES: PSALM 97:1; 70:4; MATTHEW 5:12; AND PSALM 118:24
BACKGROUND SCRIPTURES: PSALM 40; PSALM 70; MATTHEW 5:1–12; AND REVELATION 19:1–7

Rejoicing and gladness are byproducts of our faith and salvation. They are found not in our success, but in our trials and tribulations. The psalms in today's lesson invoked rejoicing and gladness, yet they were written as David was surrounded by troubles. To rejoice and to be glad in all situations unleashes the power and salvation of a great God. The spiritual war has already been won. Jesus told us to rejoice and be exceedingly glad in persecution.

Most of the world awakens to trouble, poverty, hardship, and some form of unmet human need every day. As leaders of faith, we, too, awaken today with challenges and obstacles before us in our own leadership journeys. In all these troubles, the Scripture tells us not to wail and cry, but to rejoice and be glad. Each day and each circumstance of life is a gift. Heaven and earth rejoice and are glad together. As God is magnified through rejoicing and gladness, our troubles and needs are met. The rejoicing and gladness of the prophets were accompanied by persecution. The rejoicing and gladness of Christ Himself was surrounded by rejection and the cross of persecution.

To cultivate a faith of success, we must develop the daily practice of rejoicing and gladness. Today is the day the Lord hath made; we will rejoice and be glad in it. To start our day with these words on our lips melts the dread and fear of what is coming our way. God's ability to take all our circumstances and use them for His purposes is unlimited. When our rejoicing and gladness is focused solely on God's salvation and eternal deliverance, we become invincible to the travails of the world.

Cultivate a time of rejoicing and gladness in your prayer and quiet time each day. Praise God and lift your voice to Him. Hear the birds sing. Let the warm rays of the sun touch your face. Take a deep breath of air after a summer rain. Share a laugh with an old friend. The rejoicing and gladness of leaders is contagious and can set great examples for those we lead. When our organizations and congregations are rejoicing and glad, God will move powerfully in our midst, regardless of the troubles that encompass us. Rejoice. Be glad.

Our Prayer: *O Lord, we praise You and rejoice with gladness in the light and victory of Your salvation. You told us to rejoice and be exceedingly glad. In our victory over death and despair, we sing unto You, O Lord. Today is the day You have made for us; let us rejoice and be glad in it. Melt our troubles and sorrows away as the power and glory of Your majesty is magnified through our rejoicing and gladness.* **Amen.**

Bountifully Delivered

"GOD'S BOUNTY APPEARS TO US IN OUR DISTRESS AND SUPPLICATION"

"The sorrows of death compassed me, and the pains of hell gat hold upon me: I found trouble and sorrow. The LORD preserves the simple: I was brought low, and he helped me. Return unto thy rest, O my soul; for the LORD hath dealt bountifully with me."

FEATURED SCRIPTURE: PSALM 116:3, 6–7
BACKGROUND SCRIPTURES: PSALM 13; PSALM 116; PSALM 142; PSALM 119:17; AND 1 CORINTHIANS 2:9

Leadership journeys of faith often lead us into our own sorrows and hellish situations. We often feel imprisoned by our circumstances. Our rivals and troubles seemed poised to win the day. It is in these times that we must lay all our distress upon the Lord, who loves us and calls us to service. In our prayers and supplications, God will come to us at the very moment we seem defeated. When our only hope is a miracle of God, He will come to us and bring His bounty to us. We will be bountifully delivered.

The psalmist speaks on four occasions of bountiful deliverance, which appears to the chosen in times of their imprisoned despair. God's love toward us knows no boundaries and no limits. It pleases God to bless us and deliver us from our dire circumstances. Leaders of faith often find themselves halfway through a project only to discover they suddenly face insurmountable odds. The money runs out, and old friends become scarce. Markets go sour. Mistakes and misfortune abound. Our critics and creditors seem to have finally prevailed over us. We have played all of our cards, and our only hope is to give it all up to God.

God brings us to these points in our journey of faith so we can see the providence and salvation of His hand most clearly. When we have no more breath left to pray and we lay our heads down in total submission, we encounter the bountiful deliverance of our Lord. We awake to a new day and find a simple opportunity in front of us. An old friend finally returns our call. The rival we faced yesterday turns into a new alliance of hope and prosperity. When God calls us to His service, we have deposited into our heavenly account a bounty of blessing. God withdraws it for us and sends it to us when we need it most and often when we are at our weakest and lowest moments.

As we are bountifully delivered, our souls connect to our Lord in new and richer ways. The bond gets stronger, and our faith becomes bolder. The bountifully delivered leaders of faith will attempt to do even greater things in service for others. When all we have is stripped away and God's bountiful blessings arrive, we should start anew by shedding old perceptions and unfounded fears. Follow God in your exhaustion and empty yourself into every task before you. Bountiful deliverance will find you over and over again as you trust and serve the King of kings and Lord of lords.

Our Prayer: *Lord God, I am empty and imprisoned in my circumstances of despair. There is no escape but into Your arms. Take me, Lord, and deliver me, I pray. Like Your servant David, I pray for a bountiful deliverance and blessing. As Your bounty comes and covers me, make me a new vessel who is more faithful and more obedient. Let my bounty be shared with others in service and love and mercy to all those I encounter this very day.* **Amen.**

Leaders Value The Moment, The Day, The Season

"Mastering the Gift of Time and Season Is to Fathom God's Purpose"

"This is the day which the Lord hath made; we will rejoice and be glad in it.… To every thing there is a season, and time to every purpose under the heaven.…"
Featured Scriptures: Psalm 118:24; and Ecclesiastes 3:1
Background Scripture: Ecclesiastes 3

As a youth I was given an important saying to remember: "You can't kill time without damaging eternity." From that moment on, whenever someone remarked to me that they "were just killing time," the words recoiled in my heart. God had convicted me that the appreciation and appropriate use of the moment, the day, and the season is both a gift and command from the Creator. As leaders of faith, we must master the gifts of time and season in order to fulfill God's calling in our leadership journeys.

The one resource that kings and paupers alike are given in equal measure is the day at hand; not tomorrow, and not next year—but today. Today is the day the Lord has made. Time is the great equalizer in life. But to fail to recognize the purpose of each season is to also waste the resources of God.

Time, purpose, and the seasons of life can be artfully managed to achieve a beautiful service to God. This artful management is not merely wise planning, although organization is crucial; God will thwart the carefully made plans of man. Artful management of time, purpose, and season begins first and foremost with a sense of praise and thanksgiving to God for the gifts of the moment, day, and season. Training yourself to repeat today's featured Scripture can itself become your prayer of praise and thanksgiving upon awakening each day. People who are called by God can pray to be graced by the Holy Spirit with a new sense of purpose that will become their compass for time management. You will sense when your day or activities are getting off track.

As leaders of faith, we also are mindful that we should be graceful in the changing seasons of life, not holding on too tightly to the diminishing abilities of youth, but to embrace the wisdom that age, infirmity, or even death can teach us. Seizing the moment will mean taking greater risks and setting higher goals. It also means offering the tenderness of a hug, a shared laugh, or a smile in special moments. Because God makes everything beautiful in His time, we should never become cynical over well-doing, even when we don't see the finished project.

The circumstances will bend our way when God calls us to His service. The work of our hands, the meditations of our hearts, and each deep breath we take can become our praise to God. Value every moment, day, and season as each intersects with His holy and eternal purpose.

Our Prayer: *O God, today is the day that You have made. I will rejoice and be glad in it. To everything there is a season, and time to every purpose under the heavens. Help us to be wise stewards of time. Allow us to enjoy each moment as we bask in the knowledge that we are part of a wonderful eternal purpose.* **Amen.**

Both Inspiration And Obstacles

"The Mountain That Gives Us Inspiration May Become Our Obstacle of Faith"

"I will lift up mine eyes unto the hills, from whence cometh my help.… For verily I say unto you, If ye have faith as a grain of mustard seed, ye shall say unto this mountain, remove hence to yonder place; and it shall remove and nothing shall be impossible to you."

Featured Scriptures: Psalm 121:1; and Matthew 17:20
Background Scriptures: Psalm 121; and Isaiah 40:1–4

The view of a mountain or snow-covered peak has inspired many a person over time. As we sit and stare at the majesty of God's creation, we are prompted to cast our thoughts upon the Creator who placed it there. The psalmist tells us that he lifted up his eyes to the mountain and found his help from its Creator. In Scripture we see God's dwelling place in the holy mountain. Both Abraham and Moses sought God there. Jesus went into a mountain to pray. The mountain can become our inspiration. But the mountain can also become our test of faith and the very obstacle to our next phase of success in leadership.

The majesty of a mountain to a leader of faith is symbolic of those things that both inspire us to service and challenge us along the way. We will all face mountains of inspiration and obstacles in leadership. The mountain that inspires us to prayer may suddenly become an insurmountable task and our problem to solve. For example, we see mountains of underserved people in our community and they inspire us to want to help others. But often those who need our help may not readily accept us, and the mountaintop experience of service becomes rife with conflict and problems.

The cycle of inspiration to action followed by obstacles to success is God's process of keeping us in His divine will and dependent on His daily provision. The people in our congregations or organizations whom we love and who inspire us to action can often become our greatest heartaches when they criticize us and undermine our actions. But Jesus tells us that the mountain in front of us can be moved with faith as small as a mustard seed. Let the challenges before us as leaders inspire us to action and make us go to work shoveling the mountain of obstacles away. By confronting the obstacles with the mustard seed of faith, we may inspire others to action. We may become their mountains of inspiration through our courage to tackle seemingly impossible obstacles.

What is your mountain of inspiration? Is it children who have not heard the name of Christ? Is it a church family or institution that has become divided and ineffective because of feuding and lost vision? Whatever mountain inspires you, know that it can become your great obstacle to move in Christ's name. What inspires us to serve must challenge us to lead boldly. God never gives us a dream or inspiration without giving us the ability to move the obstacles in our way. Keep dreaming, but go to work with the faith that God's mountaintops of inspiration and obstacles are still holy places.

Our Prayer: *Lord, I lift my eyes to the mountains from which I know You will answer me. Give me the courage and faith to be both inspired and committed to serve others this day. Help me to move mountains of obstacles with new faith and zeal this day. I am inspired because You have placed this beautiful opportunity in my view. Let me continually seek You, God, in the holy mountains of leadership.* **Amen.**

Tending The Temple

"Our Bodies Are God's Temples, and Leaders Should Set the Right Example"

"I will praise thee; for I am fearfully and wonderfully made…. Know ye not that your body is the temple of the Holy Ghost which is in you, which ye have of God, and ye are not your own? For this is the will of God, even your sanctification, that ye abstain from fornication: that every one of you should know how to possess his vessel in sanctification and honor…."

Featured Scriptures: Psalm 139:14; 1 Corinthians 6:19; and 1 Thessalonians 4:3–4
Background Scriptures: 1 Corinthians 6:11–20; 1 Thessalonians 4:1–8

When we lead, we lead in mind, body, and soul. The mind, body, and soul are inexorably linked together to create a vessel of God's love. In fact, our Scripture lesson today tells us that the bodies of believers become the very temples and dwelling places of the Holy Spirit. Great leaders of faith are leaders who respect and value the presentation and condition of their own bodies. We should lead by example in the food and beverages we consume and the general fitness of our bodies and minds. To prolong our lives and to present our bodies as living and holy sacrifices to God is the right thing to do, our obedience to a command.

The Bible does not call us to beauty or physical prowess. But it does call us to care for the frame and vessels we have been given. Some of us may have physical frailties or disabilities, but by caring for these we set an example. Leaders of faith should care about grooming and the presentation of their bodies. We should eat and drink in moderation. Our minds and thoughts should be disciplined and given to honorable exercise. We should know the right and healthy way to live.

God may have called you to a task that requires physical endurance. He may have called you to a task that requires increased physical strength or a new and special skill. The body is destined to deteriorate and to die. Yet we as people of God must care for this gift and prolong our lives and health as long as possible so we can communicate the love of Christ in word and deed for as long as God gives us breath. When we, through our own abuse or neglect of our bodies, cut our lives or efficient functions short, we cut God short.

Our lesson today should call us out to tend the temple of our bodies. If the very Spirit of God dwells in us, we should make this home a happy and healthy one. We have within our power to build better bodies. We should seek medical advice. We should pray for the courage to tackle addictions and poor habits. We should pray for the instinct to eat healthy portions of healthy foods, as well as control our weight and begin an exercise routine. We should flee casual adultery and the offering of our bodies for ungodly behaviors. Let others see a change in us and know it is our commitment to God that drives us to that new end.

Our bodies, however humble, are all we have in this physical presence of life. We should treat these temples of God with care and thanksgiving. Every movement of eyes or hands or lips should be edifying to the Creator and bring Him praise. Let our temples illuminate the love and salvation of Christ Himself. Start tending your temple in a new and better way today.

Our Prayer: *Lord God, we give thanks and praise for the temple of these bodies of ours. We are the very dwellings where Your Holy Spirit abides. Let us today, O Lord, be committed to making our own bodies healthier and happier vessels. We pledge to become more disciplined to care for these vessels You have given us and to use them as instruments of Your love.* **Amen.**

Acknowledging God Even In Small Decisions

"God Desires That We Acknowledge and Seek Him Even in Small Matters"

"Trust in the Lord with all thine heart; and lean not unto thine own understanding.
In all thy ways acknowledge him, and he shall direct thy paths."
Featured Scripture: Proverbs 3:5–6
Background Scripture: Proverbs 3:1–7; 1 Chronicles 28:10; and 1 Corinthians 1:26–27

As persons of faith become more intimate with God, they develop an inner communication with Him that is thought-based and instinctive. We randomly carry on a mind-chat with God inside our brains. Sometimes God comes to us by the piercing of our conscience or a sudden, inexplicable intuition that we would not otherwise experience. Often we spontaneously approach God in a "thought-prayer" asking advice or seeking strength or new knowledge. Not only does God desire this kind of intimate communication, He longs for it and commands us to have it with Him.

As leaders of faith grow more comfortable in their journeys and callings, it may become easy to make small decisions without the value of prayer or meditation. But locking God out of small decisions can set a dangerous pattern. In fact, it can crack our reliance on God's guidance. The apostle Paul tells us in 1 Corinthians 1:27 that "*God has chosen the foolish things of the world to confound the wise and the weak things of the world to confound the things that are mighty.*" We should revel and glory in God's desire for this level of constant intimacy with us, rather than be sucked into sudden trouble for failing to turn to Him in all matters.

Leaders must make many decisions each day. But decisions and choices involving relationships, purchases, or the allocation of our time should be lifted to God in a short thought or prayer. He hears you and knows your thoughts; after all, He made you. When you let Him in your thoughts, His power will flow through you and make your choices more valuable and safe.

Even acknowledging God before a small choice can be edifying. What to wear and whom to call are choices. Whom to see and how to schedule your day are decisions. How we respond to an angry friend or family member is a choice. God wants our submission and obedience, but even more He wants to bless our every action and deed if it is done in His measured way.

We should acknowledge God when watching a sunset or smelling a new fragrance. We should acknowledge Him when we smile at the playfulness of children. We should acknowledge Him when we hear the grimace of pain uttered by a stranger. Acknowledge Him when you have a sinful thought and ask for forgiveness on the spot. You will unlock massive amounts of power, praise, healing, and blessing from the Almighty when you do. It takes changing your patterns and habits, but God is waiting to enter a new phase of relationship with you. Acknowledge Him; find Him today.

Our Prayer: *Heavenly Father, we acknowledge You now. We seek You now. We desire to enter into a more intimate relationship with You this moment. Instill in us, O God, the desire and ability to yield our thoughts and ways to You each day and to communicate with You constantly. We claim awesome blessings and new miracles in our lives as You dwell in us more perfectly.* **Amen.**

When Lust Leaves Leaders Empty

"Succumbing to Lust As a Leader Can Bring You Down"

"Say unto wisdom, Thou art my sister; and call understanding thy kinswoman: That they may keep thee from the strange woman, for the stranger which flattereth with her words.... He that troubleth his own house shall inherit the wind: and the fool shall be servant to the wise of heart."

FEATURED SCRIPTURES: PROVERBS 7:4–5; AND PROVERBS 11:29
BACKGROUND SCRIPTURES: PROVERBS 6:20–35; PROVERBS 7; PSALM 51; AND MATTHEW 5:27–28

Lust and adultery are sensitive subjects, and often leaders of faith are reluctant to discuss them. All of us are subject to the temptations of our humanity. Leaders and those in places of power, authority, or wealth are often disproportionately put into circumstances that can lead to bad outcomes. Succumbing to lust as a leader can place into jeopardy all that you have been called to accomplish. It can harm your witness and hurt others, including innocent people.

Leaders highlighted throughout the Scriptures in all ages have struggled with lust and adultery. Some leaders survived the fall, like David, and some didn't, like Samson. In every case, however, succumbing to lust leaves leaders empty and damaged. Forgiveness is available, but the consequences of illicit affairs and relationships can scar and damage leadership journeys in significant ways.

It is possible to end them. It is possible to avoid them. But in every way, leaders of faith must be vigilant to protect themselves, their families, and colleagues from situations and persons that can tip them over the line. Temptation is to be expected and immoral propositions are likely. Leaders of faith should develop healthy relationships and marriages that edify and satisfy the human need for love and affection, all within the confines of God's law and order.

The words of Proverbs are clear: we must avoid situations and circumstances in which flattery and temptation can overcome us. We must constantly remain mindful of the consequences of succumbing to lust. Proverbs 11:29 tells us that *"those who trouble their own home and family by succumbing to temptation can inherit the wind from their action. We can become the fool who must serve the wise of heart."*

By clinging to our God-given wisdom and by maintaining true understanding in all situations and circumstances, we as leaders of faith can resist the temptations that come our way. And when we do, God will reward our faithfulness and protect the works we have wrought in this leadership journey of faith.

Our Prayer: *Dear Lord, we know that the temptations and lusts of the flesh will come our way from time to time. Give us a full portion of wisdom and understanding to be able to resist them. Forgive us when we have failed. Help all leaders of faith to be protected from situations that could jeopardize their witness and leadership. Cloak us in Your love and grace for all seasons.* **Amen.**

Wages Of Our Ways

"Bad Habits of Good Leaders Bring Wages We Don't Want to Collect"

"There is a way which seemeth right unto a man, but the end thereof are the ways of death.... What fruit had ye then in those things whereof ye are now ashamed? For the end of those things is death. For the wages of sin are death; but the gift of God is eternal life through Jesus Christ our Lord."

Featured Scriptures: Proverbs 14:12; and Romans 6:21, 23
Background Scriptures: Romans 6:15–23; and 1 Peter 1:3–9

The redeemed are surely forgiven. Believers in Christ are washed clean of sin. By grace we are saved—not of ourselves. Our faith in Christ gives us eternal salvation, and we are God's sheep. A place is being prepared for us in heaven. Praise God! We are no longer subject to the wages of eternal death. However, leaders of faith can develop ways and habits that may not kill their souls, but that can quicken their bodily and leadership decline. Regardless of our callings and faith, each of us must account for our ways.

Great leaders can develop awful habits. We can develop ways of living that are destructive to our bodies and to our work. These ways can retard our spiritual growth and limit us from reaching our full leadership potential for God. We can be following the call of God obediently, yet still be practicing habits and ways that are neither edifying nor healthy for our lives or for the Kingdom. We will give an account for our every action. We as leaders of faith are called to a higher standard and a greater course of discipline in our personal and professional lives. Even the best of us can improve. Proverbs tells us that ways and habits that may seem acceptable to us can actually be bringing us down. The Book of Romans tells us that when these bad habits come home to roost in our lives, we will find no good fruit in them. As we tune in to God, the Holy Spirit will show us our bad ways. He will convict us of poor habits and destructive behavior. Listen intently, and pray for the strength to right your ways and correct your lives.

Leaders of faith should start with an honest evaluation of their health. Are we eating and exercising properly? Are we overweight? Is an unhealthy lifestyle threatening to cut our lives and work short of what God desires? God wants us to be strong in mind, body, and soul. Have we adopted habits of consumption and addictions that are destructive? Are we failing to read and study the Bible each day? Have we choked our own intellectual curiosity with prideful confidence? Are our prayer lives undisciplined and in disarray? Have we lost our true zeal for praise and worship?

Poor habits and bad ways start as small behaviors that become vines that can choke our lives and routines. They become sin when they separate us from God's holiness and fellowship. Have you become detached and estranged from others because of your habits? Do you need greater financial discipline in your daily affairs? Is lust for flesh or money seeping into your routine? Let God slay the habits and ways that bind you. Seek help from trusted friends and professionals. God desires that He never have to pay a wage that hurts you. Let Christ's grace and power separate you from your bad ways for good.

Our Prayer: *Heavenly Father, we all have ways and habits that are destructive and require payment of wages. Convict us, forgive us, and give us courage to confront them. Show us how to improve our lives and substitute healthy and holy behavior for those things that constrict our leadership journeys.* **Amen.**

Fear And Fear Not

"Fear of the Lord Gives Birth to Power and Fearlessness to Serve Christ"

"The fear of the LORD is the instruction of wisdom; and before honor is humility....
And when I saw him, I fell at his feet as dead. And he laid his right hand upon me,
saying unto me, Fear not: I am the first and the last."

FEATURED SCRIPTURES: PROVERBS 15:33; AND REVELATION L:17
BACKGROUND SCRIPTURES: ISAIAH 11:2–3; PROVERBS 22:4; GENESIS 15:1; LUKE 2:10; AND LUKE 12:6–8

The Scripture is clear: It tells us to fear the Lord. The Scripture is also clear: It tells us to fear not. So which is it: to fear or to fear not? The wise king Solomon writes that the fear of the Lord is the beginning of true knowledge and fellowship with Him. As we grow in the knowledge, love, and wisdom of God, we receive the grace, mercy, and salvation of Christ.

Yet it is Jesus Himself who tells us to fear not. When we love and obey Christ, we are no longer His servants, but we become His friends. Fear of God is exemplified by our awe, stillness before Him, and respect. It is the realization that God is our Creator and the Giver and Sustainer of all life. It is defined by that fundamental understanding that He controls our destiny and existence and is alone worthy of our love and worship.

Fearing not is not the absence of the fear of God, but it is the liberation and blessed assurance we have received as God's redeemed children. As recipients of salvation and power through God's unspeakable gift of Christ, we are moved beyond our fear of death and evil to an eternity of unfathomable joy and peace.

As leaders of faith we exercise our fear of God through our daily awe and worship of the Trinity of God. And as we acknowledge our frailties and place our dependence solely upon God each day, He cleanses our hearts from pride and instills a humility that equips us for His service. We need not fear not as leaders of faith when we claim the protection, promise, and power of the resurrected Christ.

In our Scripture today, the apostle John became the revealer and author of Revelation. His physical encounter with the risen and glorified Christ humbled John to utter humility, fear, trembling, and speechlessness. However, in this same encounter, Christ (discerning John's fear and purity of heart) placed His hand upon John with love and told him to fear not. John's fear-and-fear-not encounter with Christ opened his eyes to an eternal knowledge and gave him the ability to see and write the eternal truths that we read today in his apostolic writings.

Fearing God leads to our fearlessness to do God's bidding as a leader of faith. Leaders of faith must stay humble and bowed until we feel Christ's hand upon us. As we hear His command to *fear not*, we can arise and stand tall as we lead others with a new fearlessness, full of God's power and purpose.

Our Prayer: *Lord God, we bow before You in fear, trembling, and awe of Your majesty. We are Your creation and owe our lives and everything we have to You. Save us, forgive us, and create in us a clean heart of love and humility. O Lord, place Your hand of anointing and salvation upon us. Unleash in us a new fearlessness to lead and serve others in Your holy name.* **Amen.**

Parents Protecting The Promise

"GOOD PARENTS ARE GOD'S GREATEST LEADERS AND PRESERVE FAITH AND THE FUTURE"

"Train up a child in the way he should go: and when he is old, he will not depart
from it.... Honor thy father and mother; (which is the first commandment with
promise) that it may be well with thee, and thou mayest live long on the earth."
FEATURED SCRIPTURES: PROVERBS 24:6; AND EPHESIANS 6:2–3
BACKGROUND SCRIPTURES: DEUTERONOMY 5:1–22; LUKE 15:18–24; EPHESIANS 6:1–4; COLOSSIANS 3:20–21

No true treatise on leadership would be complete without holding up parents as some of the greatest leaders of societies. The family unit is the most fundamental and basic organization. Extended families have elders and leaders. Parents, grandparents, aunts, and uncles teach, admonish, lead, and protect the promise of God's future. The "parent commandment" of the Ten Commandments comes with a promise: that our days will be prolonged. Not only will a child live longer if he or she obeys, but mankind and the faith will endure.

The godly design of parents as leaders should be a clarion call to us all to excel at parenting or mentorship. Parents and children should develop lifelong bonds. Parents can continue leading a family by example well beyond the years when their children are in the home. The deeper and richer relationship that develops between adult children and parents is one of life's richest blessings. Parents protect the promise by instilling the faith to children and quietly living that faith out by worship and service to others. Parenting transfers love, acceptance, and constant forgiveness. It teaches tolerance, kindness, discipline, and call to duty. It sets forth the values of education and physical fitness, and it hones a moral compass.

Parents set the ultimate example for leaders of faith as they lead their congregations and organizations. When the teams we lead are "family-like" units, love abounds and respect among peers develops. When we must punish one another, it is done with love. When we encourage each other, it is done with sincerity. Parents show leaders that humble, quiet leadership is often best. Parents don't need credit and glory. They relish in the accomplishments of those entrusted to them. Parents teach leaders that sacrificing for those you serve is noble and instinctive. Parents are prayer warriors who never give up on the wayward, the addicted, or those who have made mistakes. Parents know that failure can be turned around with new beginnings in each new day.

The Scripture is full of stories of parents of faith, from Abraham to Mary, the mother of Jesus, who changed hearts and protected the promise of God. Let us lift up parenting as leadership and celebrate its proper place and example in our own leadership journeys. Let us give pause to say a prayer of thanksgiving for a parent or grandparent who is gone, and recommit ourselves to loving and respecting the ones still with us. Let our own leadership journeys of faith find new ways to emulate good parenting and be true to protecting the promise by encouraging, nurturing, and mentoring new and struggling parents. When we do, we keep the promise of faith and live longer, more enriching lives.

Our Prayer: *Lord Jesus, we give thanks for good parents. You ordained that parents were to be the great leaders of our faith and society. We give praise and thanks for our parents and grandparents who led us by example. We pray for those parents who fail and struggle. Help us as leaders of faith to lift up parents everywhere and transfer the holy call and example of good parenting into our own tasks of leadership today.* **Amen.**

Lazy Leaders Lose

"God Will Reward Your Faithful Labor of Love, But the Slothful Will Fail"

"I went by the field of the slothful, and by the vineyard of the man void of understanding; and, lo, it was all grown over with thorns, and nettles had covered the face thereof, and the stone wall thereof was broken down.... For God is not unrighteous to forget your work and labor of love…that ye be not slothful, but followers of them who through faith and patience inherit the promises."
Featured Scriptures: Proverbs 24:30–31; and Hebrews 6:10–11
Background Scriptures: Proverbs 24:30–34; and Hebrews 6:9–15

Our fields and vineyards are grown over with thorns and weeds. We have failed to adequately nurture and train our workers and volunteers. Our record-keeping has gotten shoddy. Our buildings are in need of repair and the cleanliness of our work environments is not up to par. Good leaders who become lazy leaders can lose. Don't become discouraged in working hard and putting forth your best each day. God will reward work, but slothfulness will overwhelm you.

Those of us who fight against becoming lazy and slothful in our daily affairs can cling to the promise of God in these words from Hebrews: *"God is not unrighteous to forget your work and labor of love."* God's promise to leaders who are faithful and patient in their hard work is that they will inherit the promises. To those of us who have let our congregations and organizations become infested with thorns, we show a lack of understanding as to the real meaning of God's promises.

Laziness can creep upon us as we fail to see results in our labor or when we feel unrewarded. Laziness also comes with complacency or from too much enjoyment of the successful abundance reaped from yesterday's work. When we take it easy after a hard laboring success, we can succumb to a slothful attitude. Great dangers lie in wait for slothful leaders as our enemies and rivals quietly labor and build better plans and tools. Small thorn branches, when left unattended, can begin to choke the very essence of our work. As leaders of faith, we must always be moving forward and tending our gardens with all diligence and duty.

Let your labor be done each day as an offering to God. Let every project you undertake or problem you attempt to solve be your daily tithe to the Master. Our accumulated labor of love to God can become as a cable of steel, impervious to thorns. Let God convict us this very day of the areas of our lives where slothfulness or laziness has seeped into our routines. In prayer and supplication, let us recommit ourselves to daily activities marked by fervent labor and patient and cheerful effort.

God is watching us. Too many hearts are broken and too many hurting souls require assistance for us to succumb to laziness in our work. If we will work harder each day, our labor will not be in vain. Our time is short, and there is no time to be slothful. Tend to the fields and vineyards God has given you; blessings await the hard labor put forth in your calling.

Our Prayer: *Righteous God, You have given us heavenly work to do. Help us to never be slothful or lazy in answering the call and performing the tasks we are given to do. Never let us become weary in our labor. Bless the work of our hands this day. Forgive us when we don't perform our best for You each day. Help us to work hard and labor away for the Kingdom of Heaven, where our eternal reward awaits.* **Amen.**

Searching For Your Own Glory

"Leaders Who Search for Glory Have Lost Control of Their Own Spirits"

"It is not good to eat much honey: so for men to search their own glory is not glory. He that hath no rule over his own spirit is like a city that is broken down, and without walls."

Featured Scriptures: Proverbs 25:27–28
Background Scriptures: Proverbs 25:25–28; and Proverbs 16:31–33

Today's lesson consists of a proverb. Leaders who use their power and assets to seek their own glory shall surely fail. Leaders of faith have been given responsibility over tasks and people by God, and reveling in their accomplishments or seeking the vain glory of others is a snare of a trap. Our Scripture lesson tells us that when leaders begin seeking their own glory, they have lost control over their own spirits. Leaders out of control and on a path of raw ambition can render a congregation or organization vulnerable to collapse, "*like a city that is broken down, and without walls.*"

God is the architect of all human events. For those who love God, no circumstance occurs without a purpose or design. When leaders of faith see good things happen, they should give God the glory. God exudes glory and honor. As we take our own crowns of human accomplishment and lay them before the throne of God, we are empowered to do even greater things. God wants our praise and He desires that we bring the glory to Him. When God is praised and glorified, the radiance of His goodness is multiplied to all.

If we sense ourselves openly seeking an award or some adulation in our role as a leader, we should stop and confess it to God. Humble servant-leaders have no need for glory or honor. Our pleasure is in spreading the love and grace of Christ to those in need. God tells us that our rewards in both heaven and on this earth will be immeasurable when we serve this way. Too much honey, too much praise, can intoxicate a leader. The sweetness of man-given praise can create in us an evil addiction to want more and more glory without doing the good works.

There is nothing wrong with leaders of faith being recognized and given accolades. But they should be unsolicited and received in humility and gratefulness of heart. When we receive a special honor appropriately, it is a gift from God and can inspire those we lead to do greater work. When our pleasure is derived from pleasing God through obedience to His call and commandments, we will be too happy to want much more.

When we are in God's will, we are in control of our spirits. Disciplined leaders who are under control and motivated to serve others can accomplish great tasks for the Kingdom of God. Heaven will be all the glory we need!

Our Prayer: *Heavenly Father, we bring all praise and glory from our leadership to Your throne. May all the good we do and the fruit we bear be given to You as an offering of thanksgiving. Radiate Your brilliance and light back to us by giving us the provision and peace to carry on for You. Forgive us when we have eaten too much honey of this world and desire more than we should. Keep our spirits in control and centered in Your will and protection.* **Amen.**

Finding And Fostering Friendship

"LEADERS NEED TO FIND AND NURTURE HEALTHY FRIENDSHIPS"

"Ointment and perfume rejoice the heart: so doth the sweetness of a man's friend by hearty counsel.... A friend loveth at all times, and a brother is born for adversity.... A man that hath friends must show himself friendly: and there is a friend that sticketh closer than a brother."

FEATURED SCRIPTURES: PROVERBS 27:9; PROVERBS 17:17; AND PROVERBS 18:24
BACKGROUND SCRIPTURES: JOHN 15:13–15; AND JOB 42:10

Leadership can make a person lonely. Leaders of faith are especially susceptible to finding themselves in tough and lonely positions as they channel God's vision and execute holy tasks. Our peers and followers may not fully understand what we are doing, and we may find ourselves all alone during times of difficult decisions. It is imperative that leaders of faith find and foster friendships and avail themselves to be a friend to others. Jesus talked of friendship, and He desires that we be His friend. Finding and fostering healthy friendships must become a disciplined and selfless way of life. True friendship may begin with the situations and circumstances we share with others. It may come as we become part of a team or network of persons working toward a common goal. Friendships can begin with random acts of kindness and courtesy toward others. Friendship can begin with a smile or gesture of goodwill. Close and long-term friendships require that we expend time and care toward another person.

Leaders of faith are stronger and more effective when they possess strong friendships. According to Proverbs, friends are like an ointment and perfume that make the heart rejoice. Friends love you all the time and are available to you in your adversity. Friends can provide the wise and honest counsel that others are afraid to share. Friends can hold you accountable for your actions and wrong behavior, all while accepting and forgiving you for your transgressions. Friends rejoice with you as you experience life's blessings and great events.

Friends are gifts from God. In order to have friends, we must practice being friends to others. We must show ourselves to be friendly. Many leaders find themselves with little time for meaningful visits with old friends. But friendships can wane and fade if they are not nurtured. Leaders of faith must take time each day to interact with a friend. It is good for the spirit and makes our hearts glad. Pray for your friends daily. And on this day, remember a special friend and reach out to them without desiring anything in return. Visit an old friend whom you have not seen or spoken with in years. Seek out a friend who is experiencing heartache or may be facing a debilitating adversity. Find a friend who has fallen or has had a recent failure and lift them up and bring a smile back to their face.

As we find and foster friendships, God works miracles in our own lives, for it takes the focus off ourselves and places it on the needs of others. In the process, we become better leaders, as well. Let your friendship with Jesus shine in your friendships with others as you strive to serve in selfless love.

Our Prayer: *Lord Jesus, Friend of the weak and the sinner, we give praise for You and Your love for us this day. We pray for strong and healthy friendships, and we desire more fellowship with those we love. Convict us when we don't make the time and effort to find and foster friendships in the way we should. Let our love for You shine in our friendships with others.* **Amen.**

Showing Favoritism Is A Snare; Beware

"God Has No Regard for Favoritism and Neither Should Leaders"

"To favor one side is not fair—to sin, bribed by a piece of bread…. Teacher, we know that you are true and teach the way of God truthfully…for you do not regard the position of man"

Featured Scriptures: Proverbs 28:21; and Matthew 22:16
Background Scriptures: James 2:9; and Acts 10:34–36

To avoid showing favoritism can be one of the hardest tasks for a leader. True service to God means we must assume the same posture as Christ. Christ saw everyone He encountered as a precious child of the living God—and so should we. The stories of Jesus are filled with lepers, harlots, tax collectors, and the poor, as well as persons of title and earthly status. He healed them, loved them, and judged them all, equally and fairly.

Leaders of faith are called to follow that example. Leaders who are swayed in their daily duties by the promise of a reward if they favor a person or a position fail God. It is easy to evaluate the status and position of those we encounter each day. We should always be respectful of power and authority, but godly leaders must stay true to their call by serving all persons in Christ's name. It is easy to render service to the kind and beautiful persons. Our time and efforts are more easily expended on behalf of the well-connected and those who can return our favors. They, too, are important, but do we deprive others in need in order to serve our favorites?

It is often hardest to serve those who are rude and angry. It is very hard to serve and pray for our enemies, but God calls us to do it. It is easy to carry a burden the second mile for a friend or a loved one. But can you rise early to help someone who criticizes you and is unappreciative of your efforts? Christ knew that by loving and healing all God's children equally, He validated the worth of every member of creation. He also knew that serving the undeserving or the undesirable conveyed a love and power that no earthly power could match.

Serving others without favoritism and without regard to their status sets leaders of faith apart. It embodies the essence of Christ's love in our daily activities. When we cannot be bribed for a piece of bread, we exemplify a faith that others want to emulate. When we can see Jesus in the faces of those we are called to serve, we can turn the undesirable into the redeemed and the unlovable into the sanctified.

We all have prejudices to overcome. We all have a sense of reluctance to help certain persons. But our call to God's service requires our obedience to the command to not regard the position of man. Love and serve the lepers, the poor, the unruly, the ignorant, and the arrogant, just as Christ served those He encountered each day. Our actions will bear fruit and bring others into a new understanding of a merciful and loving Lord.

Our Prayer: *Jesus, You taught us how to serve and love all persons. We give thanks that You loved the sinner and the lowly. We, too, would be unworthy of redemption if You had not called the imperfect to lead and serve others. Help and strengthen us this day so that we can perform our calling without favoritism and with equality to all Your children.* **Amen.**

A Leader's Anger Disrupts God's Plan

"Great Leaders Set Aside Anger and Wrath in God's Stillness and Love"

"Scornful men bring a city into a snare, but wise men turn away wrath…. Be not hasty in thy spirit to be angry: for anger resteth in the bosom of fools…. Let all bitterness, and wrath, and anger, and clamour and evil speaking, be put away from you, with all malice…. A soft answer turneth away wrath: but grievous words stir up anger."

Featured Scriptures: Proverbs 29:8; Ecclesiastes 7:9; Ephesians 4:31; and Proverbs 15:1
Background Scripture: Romans 12:19; 1 Corinthians 13:5; and 2 Corinthians 12:20

Anger is a natural emotion. Anger comes to us in varying degrees. However, a leader of faith must control, channel, then dismiss anger and all its symptoms or risk leadership disaster. Sudden outbursts of anger have doomed many a person. Otherwise rational and upstanding people have allowed the demon of anger to overwhelm them. Anger causes rash action. Anger makes us speak unkind words, even to those we love. If we make a strategic decision under its spell, it can doom our families, organizations, or institutions.

The Scripture is clear about anger, and it gives us some good recipes for dispensing it from our daily walks with God. As leaders of faith, anger management should be one of the top skills we develop and practice each day. Vengeance against every injustice will take place in God's way and time. We can rest assured that God will not let evil go unpunished. Neither will God let the anger that we exercise under His calling go unpunished. Our anger will turn around and wield its ugliness against us.

Leaders can manage and control anger in many ways. When we stay grounded in stillness, prayer, and the humility of love, anger has a tough time overcoming us. Being slow to react to provocation and using gentle words can turn away the anger of others and protect us from feeling that same anger. But letting bitterness and scorn for others stay in our memories can unleash our anger. Feeling victimized by others instead of tapping the wellspring of power available to us as called leaders of faith can lead to anger. We are eternally redeemed and loved of God, not made to channel anger.

Scorn, wrath, and anger can bring our organizations or congregations to ruin. Find a trusted and wise mentor with whom you can share your feelings. Walk away, give it time, sleep on it…but don't make decisions in rash moments of anger. Those who control their anger will control their situations. Those who are called of God and refuse to let anger control their actions will win most confrontations through a spirit of love and forgiveness. Bathe your soul each day in the soothing waters of God's grace and mercy, and the dirt of malice and anger will be washed away as God's peace rests in your soul.

Our Prayer: *Merciful Father, we pray that all anger and wrath that we harbor within us will be washed away by Your Spirit. Help us as leaders of faith to guard against the temptation of succumbing to anger. We pray that those unjust things done to us and those we love will be judged by You in Your way and time. Make us creations of peace, love, and forgiveness. Let Christ's easy yoke be upon us always.* **Amen.**

Virtuous Women, Virtuous Leaders

"The Honor and Dignity of Womanhood Sets Qualities for Leadership"

"Who can find a virtuous woman? For her price is far above rubies. Give her the
fruit of her hands; and let her own works praise her in the gates."
Featured Scripture: Proverbs 31:10, 31
Background Scripture: Proverbs 31:10–31

One day as a child I was walking down the hall of our home and noticed a new framed
picture of my great-grandmother, Nanny, hanging on the wall. Contained in the frame under-
neath her picture was a calligraphy text of today's Scripture from Proverbs 31. My Nanny had
passed away several years earlier at a ripe old age and had been a great love of my mother. She
was a gracious, talented lady who loved each grandchild very much and spent a long life of quiet
and faithful service to God and others.

The wall hanging's comparison of my Nanny to the Scripture's reference of a "virtuous
woman" sealed into my heart a new idea of who should qualify for such an honor. It helped
teach me at a tender age how a humble, yet talented family matriarch could become the epitome
of a biblical heroine. Many leaders of faith can fondly reminisce of the virtuous women, virtuous
leaders in their own families. Many of them taught us the faith and instilled their values in us.
The solid and godly qualities of those virtuous women, virtuous leaders even today are etched
into our own leadership decisions and actions.

In identifying talent and leadership for new projects, leaders of faith often overlook the most
obvious choice—the virtuous woman. She is all around us. She is a survivor. She is often too
busy to ask for another assignment. She is often unnoticed because the tasks she performs are so
necessary to daily life that she can seem invisible. But the qualities of a virtuous woman should
be sought as we look for new leaders of faith. So, who is she, and how do we recognize her?

This woman is, first, *fearful and faithful to God*; this guides her every task. She is *wise and
kind of tongue*. She is *not idle* and is *organized*. She *takes care of her family*. She is *honorable* and
rejoices when good things happen. She works with her hands and creates beautiful things. She is
entrepreneurial and *knows how to make an honest living*. She is *studious* and *understands current
events*. She is *kind to the poor* around her and *unafraid* to bear their burdens. Her *children and
husband praise her*.

In any successful home, organization, or institution lie the fingerprints of the virtuous women
who became virtuous leaders. Most virtuous women do not advertise or seek recognition. Women
of virtue are not celebrated enough around the globe, nor are they given the leadership opportunities they so richly deserve.

Yet their good works praise them in the gates, and their fruit of reward should never be
denied them.

Our Prayer: *Lord of hosts, we give thanks for the virtuous women of our lives who, by their faith
in You and by their godly qualities, have helped families and communities to survive and succeed.
Bless them—past, present, and future. We pray that You will raise them up in our leadership journeys
and protect them by Your might.* **Amen.**

Blessed Mothers Are The Repository Of Our Faith

"Through the Pure Hearts and Unheralded Service of Mothers, Great Leaders Arise"

"Her children arise up, and call her blessed.... Can a woman forget her sucking child, that she should not have compassion on the son of her womb? Yea, they may forget, yet I will not forget thee."

Featured Scripture: Proverbs 31:28; and Isaiah 49:15
Background Scriptures: Genesis 21:1–3; Exodus 2:1–10; and Luke 1:26–56

Both humanity and the Christian faith have endured because of blessed mothers. God entrusts mothers with new life and new promise. The mothers referenced today in our background Scripture include Sarah, the mother of Isaac; Jochebed, the mother of Moses; Elisabeth, the mother of John the Baptist; and Mary, the mother of Jesus. Through blessed mothers the great leaders of faith were born and raised. From Isaac came many nations. From Moses came the deliverance of God's chosen people and many words of Scripture. From John the Baptist the way of the Lord was prepared. And from the blessed Mother Mary came the Prince of Peace and salvation for mankind. From blessed mothers we have received many virtuous leaders of the faith.

On one special day each year, we take time to salute mothers of the past, present, and future. Most of these blessed mothers are never mentioned in print or glorified by public proclamation. Only God knows the contributions and blessings that have been yielded from the faith, virtue, and leadership of mothers. A hurting child, a wounded soldier, and a dying old man can all be heard to be calling the name of a blessed mother. Great leaders of faith today are most influenced today not by the sages of our time, but by the values learned at their mothers' knees. The collective survival of each new generation is dependent on the faith, ethics, and a sense of love and fairness that only a mother can teach.

Mothers are God's real and best leaders. They lead quietly. They teach and instruct. They accept our imperfections, yet demand our best. They stand watch for danger, then give us refuge in their care. They know the values of humility, hard work, loyalty, selflessness, fairness, and forgiveness, and it is from these values that great leaders emerge. By their example, mothers impart the essence of the faith, giving children pause to know that God is Lord and that we are to be thankful and obedient to His call.

As people everywhere honor mothers on this special day of the year, let us give thanks to God for mothers. Let leaders of faith do all they can to empower and lift up mothers. Let us all pray for mothers, as well as for the restoration of broken relationships and the renewal of love and commitment in families. *Let us rise and call them all blessed.*

Our Prayer: *Lord, we thank You for the blessed mothers of all generations. May we strive to honor them by becoming better leaders of faith. We pray now for mothers everywhere, that You would give them the strength and provision to do Your will. We give honor and thanks to You and our mothers, who serve as our role models. We pray for an eternal reunion in heaven with those who have gone before us, O God.* **Amen.**

That Which Makes You Mourn Makes You Lead

"Mourning and Grieving Is the Genesis of Great Action"

"And I gave my heart to seek and search out by wisdom concerning all things that are done under heaven.… For in much wisdom is much grief: and he that increases knowledge increases sorrow.… Blessed are they that mourn: for they shall be comforted."

Featured Scriptures: Ecclesiastes 1:13, 18; and Matthew 5:4
Background Scriptures: Ecclesiastes 1:12–18; Matthew 5:1–12; and Isaiah 53:3

What is it that God would have you do? What is your great spiritual calling in life? Have you accessed your talents and gifts through an educational degree? What are your interests and hobbies? Whom do you admire and what person can help you find new opportunities to use your unique abilities? Many future leaders seek their calling from God by answering these types of questions.

However, today's lesson focuses on a different way to learn the quest of hearing God's call for your life. What pierces your heart with sorrow today? What travesty in life has made you grieve? What injustice around you makes you mourn for the loss of innocence of God's children? Take that which makes you mourn and let it help you lead. Lead to solve inequity. Lead to bring about justice. Lead to feed the hungry and comfort the lonely. Lead to broker peace where rivalry and bitterness exist. Let your mourning become your vocation.

Both Solomon and Jesus speak in our Scripture today. The more knowledge the great and wise Solomon gained, he wrote, the more sorrowful he became. His wisdom concerning heavenly and earthly matters made him grieve. Jesus was the Man of Sorrows who was acquainted with grief. Yet Christ tells us that we are blessed when we mourn for the hurt, pain, and injustice around us. He also tells us that if we mourn, we will be comforted.

Could this comfort in sorrow come from taking action to comfort others who hurt? Could the blessing of our mourning be a heavenly call to leadership? Find a problem and solve it. Find a need and fill it. Find a hurt and shower it with love. Find the untouchable and embrace them. Forgive the seemingly unforgivable. Our greatest callings can come from our deepest hurts and sorrow. Our great mission of success can rise from the embers of our burned failures in life.

The more we learn and succeed in leadership, the more challenges of life we encounter. God often places us in positions of leadership only for us to find the odds of success virtually insurmountable. The lost and impoverished lives around us can seem like seas of hopelessness. Yet to God they are fields ripe for harvest. As God nurtures us through our leadership journeys, He will inevitably bring us to those times of mourning and grief in order to grant us increasing wisdom and to expand our calling to heavenly service. So mourn and grieve this day as you must, but allow that which makes you mourn and to cause you to lead with new resolve today.

Our Prayer: *Man of Sorrows, we come into Your presence this day with grief and mourning. Our lives are heavy with burdens and sorrow of the events and circumstances around us. Take our mourning and bless us. Turn our grief into service and our tears into new purpose. Let us share one another's burdens and lead with new strength and power by Your blessing and provision this day.* **Amen.**

Casting Our Vanity Aside

"Success and Wealth Gained Through Leadership Is Vanity Unless God Uses and Blesses It"

"So I was great, and increased more than all that were before me in Jerusalem; also my wisdom remained with me…and whatsoever mine eyes desired I kept not from them…my heart rejoiced in all my labour…then I looked on all the works that my hands had wrought…all was vanity and vexation of spirit…for God shall bring every work into judgment, with every secret thing, whether it be good or whether it be evil.

FEATURED SCRIPTURES: ECCLESIASTES 2:9–11; AND 12:14
BACKGROUND SCRIPTURE: ECCLESIASTES 12:9–14

When given the choice of a blessing from God, Solomon requested the gift of wisdom, and it was granted to him. Solomon's request pleased God. As a result, Solomon became a wealthy man and a successful leader. But despite Solomon's wisdom and successful leadership, he mounted his own quest for personal pleasure. At the end of his journey, Solomon had compromised his mission through consumption and the accommodation of his many wives' idolatrous faiths. Even with all his wealth and the trappings of power, Solomon came to realize the folly and vanity of it all. God will bring our every work, public or private, good or bad, into His holy judgment.

Casting our vanity aside is our signal to God and those we lead that we acknowledge the omnipotence of our Creator. All our accumulation of power and earthly wealth leads to naught unless it is part of God's eternal plan. Leaders who are called by God and blessed by God must hold themselves to different standards. You, like Solomon, may be blessed with gifts and the rewards of success in your leadership journey. No doubt, you may enjoy the earthly fruits of your labor and leadership. Yet you must guard against the snare of self-congratulatory indulgence that the perks and pleasures from power bring. To relish in your own accomplishments to excess leads to vanity and the self-consumption that tarnishes God's real purpose for your life and leadership.

Are you feeling good about your congregation and organization? Have you stopped to revel in your accomplishments and prosperity? By slaying your vanity today and by casting your crowns of personal achievement at God's feet, you will allow God to bless your work and service for holier purposes and to be judged worthy so your works will have eternal significance.

God's leaders are part of a vast heavenly plan that only the Creator Himself understands. In our lifetimes of leadership service, we are but one grain of sand on the endless beach of eternal purpose. We should build our grains of sand with humility and a sense of great calling, knowing that our every work—good or bad—will be subject to God's judgment.

Like Solomon, as we cast aside the vanities of our own life's work, God is then able to bless, magnify and multiply our humble service towards others into a holy and eternal significance.

Our Prayer: *Dear heavenly Father, You called us to service in leadership. Help us to stay grounded in Your commandments and with the knowledge that our every task is holy work that should be dedicated to You and the betterment of others. Keep us rooted in humility and protect us from evil as we labor by Thy might.* **Amen.**

Every Work Into Judgment

"Our Every Thought and Deed Should Be Measured and Wise"

"For God shall bring every work into judgment, with every secret thing, whether it be good, or whether it be evil.… But I say unto you, that every idle word that men shall speak, they shall give account thereof in the day of judgment. For by thy words thou shalt be justified, and by thy words thou shalt be condemned."

Featured Scriptures: Ecclesiastes 12:14; and Matthew 12:35–36
Background Scriptures: Ecclesiastes 12:9–14; and Romans 2:1–16

Nothing is wasted on eternity. Every day and every moment has importance. Our lives are brief, and our leadership journeys are even briefer. Our lesson today from the words of Solomon and Christ Himself tell us that every thought, word, and work of our hands will be brought into judgment on their own merit. We must realize that every task and daily chore we undertake is of eternal significance. Every decision we make and every human encounter we experience should be saturated with care, love, and seriousness.

Our good words and our good works will justify us in our time of judgment. Leaders of faith are held to an even higher standard. As persons called to leadership tasks of holy purpose, we must undertake each project and deal with every situation, no matter how small, as if the heavenly hosts are watching. We should be patient with the impertinent and gentle with the mean-spirited. In all things we should be prayerful and careful. Our works should be showered each day with the meekness of Christ's Spirit, yet filled with the boldness of His power. We should treat others as we want to be treated and in all things lift up the name of God. We should be always thankful and constantly lift others to a higher and better place through our own selfless service.

As we as leaders of faith grow in our relationship with God, our conscience and spirits will become more attuned with the Master. When we make poor judgments that hurt others, we will often feel it in our own hearts immediately. When we don't do our best work, we will convict ourselves. When we say careless things and make idle chatter that is more gossip than truth, our own spirits should tell us to tame our tongues and be more righteous in our discussions with others. We should be quick to ask for forgiveness from God and others when we know that our works have been unfaithful.

If you have lost this internal ability of self-conviction, you may need to take a sabbatical of purification so that your moral settings can get into alignment with God. All that we do will come into the light and holiness of God's perfection. No one is perfect, and all will stumble. But all are forgiven and cleansed from sin and failure through Christ.

As the redeemed of God, we have a great example to set. Our every word and work should reflect the love and sacrifice of our Redeemer. God delights in our righteous works. We should never fear judgment when we strive to fulfill our callings in faith and humility and keep God's commandments. When we are busy serving others through Christ's love, our every work will justify us and be pleasing to God in that day of judgment and glory.

Our Prayer: *Lord, we know that every thought, word, and work in our lives will be brought before the judgment throne. We appeal to Your mercy and grace for forgiveness when we fall short. We pray for Your cleansing power to tackle each day and each new work with a holy conscience. Cleanse us from all impurity so that our every work will be pleasing in Your sight.* **Amen.**

Bed Undefiled

"Leaders Can Enjoy Physical Passion by Channeling It Correctly"

"Let him kiss me with the kisses of his mouth: for thy love is better than wine.... Marriage is honorable in all, and the bed undefiled.... Let thy fountain be blessed: and rejoice with the wife of thy youth."
Featured Scriptures: Song of Solomon 1:2; Hebrews 13:4; Proverbs 5:18
Background Scriptures: Proverbs 5; the Book of Song of Solomon

The title of today's lesson, Bed Undefiled, is provocative, but the study is both exhilarating and liberating to leaders of faith who follow God's word correctly. Physical passion and sexual fulfillment are part of God's blessing and gift to men and women of all times. When these desires and passions are channeled correctly, leaders of faith can be made stronger, more complete leaders. Leaders who can tame their physical desires by channeling them into wholesome and healthy relationships become less vulnerable to the external temptations of lust and illicit affairs. Leaders who find and sustain romance and satisfaction through healthy, thriving marriages set great examples to others.

The most passionate and erotic work in all literature is found in the Song of Solomon. The phrases "love that is better than wine" and the "bed undefiled" call leaders into new physical passion and fulfillment through a long-term commitment to another person. Even as we age, we can take pleasure in the spouse of our youth. We should value the deepening and enriching love and pleasure found in a marriage partner. It helps protect us from adultery and focuses our efforts each day on the needs of others. To those of us who have not yet found this love, our lesson gives hope. To those who are in poor marriages or marriages without physical passion, our lesson gives us a challenge to cultivate new sparks of romance. To those who have had love and lost it through death or betrayal, we can give thanks for the passion we enjoyed and pray that love will find us again. Healthy lovers make heartier leaders of faith. Through our example of practicing passionate monogamy and disciplined personal lives, we can serve as beacons for those who are struggling with how to correctly channel physical passion into a successful relationship.

Reaching the apex of a passionate, successful love life within a vibrant marriage is difficult to achieve and maintain. It requires mutual respect and the setting of personal boundaries. It means avoiding and fleeing temptation, while aging gracefully. It means celebrating every tender moment and valuing a spouse as a trusted friend. It is always harder to betray a friend than a lover. When your lover is your best friend and confidant, the bond only gets stronger.

Don't shy away from acknowledging the gift of passion and physical pleasure. People of faith too often consider this subject a taboo topic of discussion. As our fulfillment from passion and pleasure makes us more self-realized and self-confident persons, our leadership abilities will increase and our hearts will more easily overflow to serve others. As we nurture that "love that is better than wine," let us praise the Author of love and the Sustainer of life.

Our Prayer: *Lord, thank You for love and passion and for the commitment of another person. Your blessing of a bed undefiled through a marriage that is strong is worthy of praise. We pray mightily that broken lives and relationships can be made whole and that those who search for love in this life will find it. More especially, Lord, we pray that the love of Christ will find us all and permeate our relationships with others.* **Amen.**

When True Love Leads Leaders In A Right Direction

"Those Who Can Commit to Another in Love Are More Stable to Lead"

"Set me as a seal upon thine heart, as a seal upon thine arm: for love is strong as death; jealousy as cruel as the grave: the coals thereof are coals of fire, which hath a most vehement flame. Many waters cannot quench love, neither can the floods drown it: if a man would give all the substance of his house for love, it would utterly be condemned."

Featured Scripture: Song of Solomon 8:6–8
Background Scriptures: The Book of Song of Solomon; and 1 Kings 11:1–13

King Solomon's appetite for many women ultimately contributed to his undoing. In fact, toward the end of his life, the Scripture tells us he had seven hundred wives, princesses, and three hundred concubines. It tells us that "his wives turned away his heart" (1 Kings 11:3). To accommodate his many women, Solomon compromised his faith by allowing them to bring their idols and false gods into his home. This accommodation of the women's desires helped bring the judgment of God upon Solomon.

In our lesson today, however, we see a different Solomon. We see a Solomon bitten with true love for the Shulammite woman. The Song of Solomon is a short love story, full of romantic dialogue, but it shows us that true love and commitment to a good marriage can have great benefits for a king—or for any leader of faith.

To win the Shulammite woman's heart, Solomon put off his royal persona and came to the woman's family vineyard to win her heart. The love that he found in her created a bond, a passion, and ultimately a commitment. Leaders in love are unique in that their position and status is healthily shed in the pursuit of love. When pretension and power are subjugated for the basic necessities of companionship, courtship, and love, a new person can be created; a stodgy leader can become new again. In sum, true love is a godly experience that can move the leader in a new and wholesome direction in life.

Leaders of faith who are in committed relationships and marriages make better leaders. Some of us need to rekindle the love of a spouse or friend today. Some of us need to become better, more romantic, attentive partners. If Solomon could have been contented with and committed to this one woman, what a different outcome his career might have had. Let the creation, nurturing, and rekindling of your love for another person in a wholesome relationship become your goal as a leader of faith. It will make you happier, healthier, and a better servant to those God has called you to lead. If you can love and commit to another in the home, you are more likely to stay strong and committed in your institution of leadership and service. Shed your royal robes and go to the vineyard of your true love today.

Our Prayer: *Loving Father, You ordained loving, committed relationships. The Church itself is the Bride of Christ. Thank You for marriage and for the power of love. Help us, Lord, to rekindle our relationships and to become better partners. Help us to value the love of another and to show more romance and passion in life. You gave us the love of another as a gift. May we enjoy it and use it to make lives stronger.* **Amen.**

Nothing Common Or Unclean

"No One Whom God Calls and Cleanses Is Ever Again Common or Unclean"

"Then said I, Woe is me! For I am undone; because I am a man of unclean lips, and I dwell in the midst of a people with unclean lips: for mine eyes have seen the King, the Lord of hosts. Then flew one of the seraphims unto me, having a live coal in his hand, which he had taken from off the altar: and he laid it upon my mouth and said…thine iniquity is taken away, thy sin is purged…but God hath shown me that I should not call any man common or unclean.… But the voice answered me again from heaven, what God hath cleansed, that call not thou common."

Featured Scriptures: Isaiah 6:5–7; Acts 10:28; and Acts 11:9
Background Scriptures: Isaiah 6; 1 Corinthians 6:9–11; Acts 1; and Acts 11:1–18

A great impediment to our becoming true leaders of faith is not the absence of God's voice within us harkening us to service. It is often our reticence to hear that voice that stems from our own sense of unworthiness or the idea that we could ever do anything holy. Our lifestyles and our past are marked by failure and lack of accomplishment. Maybe our lives are marked by legal action, divorce, bankruptcy, or contempt toward organized religion. But today, God's message to us is clear: The one whom God calls and cleanses is no longer common or unclean.

Both the prophet Isaiah and the apostle Peter show us the sanctifying effect of God's providential hand. God called Isaiah and then cleansed him for service from the holy coals of the heavenly altar. Peter's Gentile recruits of the early Church were considered unclean and unworthy to lead others by the religious authorities of their day. It was Peter who witnessed these newly called and salvation-cleansed Gentiles and saw the Holy Spirit rest upon them.

Each of us today who hears God's voice softly speaking to our hearts can claim that same cleansing and redemptive power in our lives as we answer our calls to faith. Through the ages, God has called the unclean to do the holy. We are all flawed and scarred by failures. Yet the redemptive blood and sacrifice of Christ has forever cleansed humankind from our unrighteous state. When we claim new life through Christ's love, grace, and mercy, He changes us. First Corinthians 6:11 tells us, "But ye are washed, but ye are sanctified in the name of the Lord Jesus, and by the Spirit of our God."

Our calling and redemptive cleansing should bring us new confidence that not only are we worthy to perform the holy tasks God asks us to do, but we are to no longer to see ourselves as too common or unfit to lead others in the faith. Likewise, we should never doubt that those unlikely or fallen people around us can also be transformed to do great things in Christ's service. The coals of God's altar and the blood of the Lamb are sufficient to make you and those you lead clean and able to report for duty in God's army of love, hope, and service.

Our Prayer: *Our Lord and our God, by Your love and grace You call us and have cleansed us from all unrighteousness. You wash us clean from our past and our frailty. Equip us to serve You and instill in us new worth and confidence to do mighty things for others in Your holy name.* **Amen.**

Prepare And Execute God's Call

"In Every Call Comes A Time For Precise Execution Of God's Plan"

"Prepare the table, watch in the watchtower and anoint the shield. For thus hath the LORD said unto me, go, set a watchman, let him declare what he seeth…. Set up the standards upon the walls of Babylon, make the watch strong, set up the watchmen, prepare the ambushes…. Prepare war, wake up the mighty men…beat your plowshares into swords, and your pruning hooks into spears: let the weak say, I am strong…. Pass through the host, and command the people, saying, Prepare you victuals; for within three days ye shall pass over Jordan, to go in to possess the land, which the LORD your God giveth you…."

FEATURED SCRIPTURES: ISAIAH 21:5; JEREMIAH 51:12; JOEL 39:10; AND JOSHUA 1:11
BACKGROUND SCRIPTURES: JOSHUA 1:1–11; ISAIAH 21:1–10; JEREMIAH 51; AND JOEL 3

Our time has come. After praying and searching, our call has come to us. We've received the call of God to become a leader of faith, and it is time to begin our journey. Now we must undertake the work to accomplish the mission. Our Scripture lesson today teaches us that in the course of every leadership journey comes the time to prepare and execute God's call.

Every call of God will require the necessity of meticulous, warlike planning and execution. It will require that we find the best talent around us and inspire the weakest among us to believe they can achieve greater things. Leadership calls us to be resourceful; the Israelites were to beat plows into swords and pruning hooks into spears. It means we must wade into environments and cultures that are unfamiliar to us and learn to speak new languages and practice new customs. We will need to learn and master new technical skills for which, until we answered our call, we did not know or understand.

Leadership is about action. Our Scripture today features Joshua leading the Israelites into the Promised Land. After years of wandering, doubt, and backsliding, it took preparation and execution to finally walk across the Jordan River and possess the land. The prophets Isaiah and Jeremiah spoke of the call to battle against Babylon, of getting the weapons ready and ambushes set. Joel wrote prophetically about preparing for a holy battle. Going into battle against seemingly superior forces, heavenly or earthly, can test our faith and calling. But these prophets knew that God's specific call required leaders to execute specific plans of action.

What great tasks lie before you? Are you preparing your congregation and organization to execute new projects? Are you developing new budgets and fundraising techniques? Are you organizing and upgrading your buildings and physical plants? Are you getting your own body into proper physical condition to better perform the new jobs that your leadership call requires? God doesn't just call us to contemplation; He calls us to action. We must show ourselves worthy of our leadership call by putting forth the effort to meticulously prepare and execute the tasks God gives us to do. God has already gone before us. All we must do is prepare and then execute our call and claim the victory.

Our Prayer: *Great God, You have called us by Your name to be a leader of faith. Give us courage to know when it is time to prepare and execute Your will through specific action. Grant us the wisdom and knowledge to prepare wisely and to execute accurately as we serve those in need today. We know that the victory is won as we go into today's battle of life.* **Amen.**

Certainty of Christ

"THE AGES OF PROPHECY AND THE HISTORY OF CHANGED LIVES EMPOWER US"

"He will swallow up death in victory; and the LORD God will wipe away tears from off all faces; and the rebuke of his people shall he take away from off all the earth: for the LORD hath spoken it. And it shall be said in that day, Lo, this is our God; we have waited for him, and he will save us: this is the LORD; we have waited for him, we will be glad and rejoice in his salvation."

FEATURED SCRIPTURE: ISAIAH 25:8–9

BACKGROUND SCRIPTURES: GENESIS 3:15; GENESIS 49:10; NUMBERS 24:17–19; DEUTERONOMY 18:15, 18; PSALM 2:7; PSALM 22; PSALM 69:21; ISAIAH 7:14; ISAIAH 42:2–3; ISAIAH 52:13—53:12; MICAH 5:2; ZECHARIAH 12:10; ISAIAH 25:8; MALACHI 3:1; MICAH 4:1–4; AND ISAIAH 11:10

From Genesis to Zechariah, dozens of verses by different authors foretell the coming of Christ. So detailed and specific are the fulfilled predictions that all mathematical probabilities against the factual existence of Christ are broken. The net effect is the certainty of Christ. Just as the prophets predicted, Christ came among us and reigns today. The certainty of Christ is then manifested in the gospels and acts of the leaders of the early Church. Today the certainty of Christ is shown in the changed lives and devotion of the countless souls who call upon Christ as Lord. As leaders of faith, the certainty of Christ is manifested in our own answer to His calling as we serve others in His name this very day.

Christ lives and rules and is active in the everyday affairs of humankind. His presence and glory can be felt in the most innocent of persons and in the smallest acts of love shown by one person to another. Part of our mission as leaders of faith who have been called by Christ is to lend our own testimony each day to the certainty of Christ. Scholars, historians, archaeologists, and theologians will debate the time and scope and even the historical existence of Christ. Skeptics and scoffers will seek to relegate Christ to earthly irrelevance as they supplant the holy and eternal with faulty logic and fleshly misunderstanding.

Leaders of faith need not be debaters of religion, but instead should be the vessels from which the truth and love of Christ's Spirit and teachings flow. If we lead in confidence and certainty, others will surely find the pathway to light and salvation. Confidence that comes from conviction emits that certainty that Christ indwells our work and our lives. Our bold example of accepting a calling to a journey of faithful leadership in our community testifies to the fulfillment of the Scriptures we read today.

Let the certainty of Christ give us new power and courage to tackle the challenges of this new day. Victory has already been won, and we are the laborers in a field of harvest that we did not even plant. Study and pray and gain confidence in the Lord you serve. Death is swallowed up in victory. All tears will be wiped away. The rebuke of God is removed. We are saved. All that we have waited for is found. Lead others today with new rejoicing in the certainty of Christ.

Our Prayer: *Christ of our salvation, we give joyous praise and thanksgiving for Your love for us. The certainty of Your victory over death, sorrow, human failure, and eternity gives us new voice and new life even now. May we take the certainties of our faith and calling to new heights as we strive to follow You and lead others in Your name.* **Amen.**

Wilderness And The Solitary Place

"GOD'S CREATION TEACHES US STILLNESS, PATIENCE, AND THE POWER OF SEASONS"

"The wilderness and the solitary place shall be glad for them; and the desert shall rejoice, and blossom as the rose. It shall blossom abundantly, and rejoice even with joy and singing…. And the parched ground shall become a pool, and the thirsty land springs of water.…"

FEATURED SCRIPTURE: ISAIAH 35:1, 2, 7
BACKGROUND SCRIPTURE: ISAIAH 35

After a hard rain, deep in the woods of a new spring season, wildflowers are sprouting and rushing water crashes down from a canyon wall. Leaves glow a bright green and birds sense the dawn of the new season as they sing. As weary and troubled leaders, we need to seek these places and in patience wait on the Lord to speak to us. We must allow God to command our stillness in this solitude. We must wait in that stillness as He inspires us to awe and wonder of His natural order.

Our Scripture today captures the essence and the hope for the return of Christ as the giver of new life in His new Kingdom to come. But it also speaks to leaders of faith today. The winter, bitter cold, drought, and fire of our own leadership journeys cannot still the hand of God as it regenerates new life in our lives through new beauty and form. If God ordains seasons and commands wildflowers to come forth from the rocky soil, He can renew our strength and can help leaders of faith bloom again.

Perhaps you are coming out of the winter of your own leadership journey. Your past leadership season of frost and the blasts of bitter cold from your critics may have caused you to believe that you have failed in your mission of faith. But the Scripture tells us that the desert shall rejoice and the parched ground shall become a pool.

The same order of the natural wilderness is set forth over our lives and leadership service to God. There will be seasons of change. There will be winters and there will be springs. The heat of the summer day will yield to the afternoon rain and the cool night. New actions that come forth like wildflowers from a renewed leader can be more beautiful and fragrant than any tended garden. The quenching waters that plunge over the jagged rocks in the wilderness are more pure and clean.

Go and seek God in a wild place in solitude. Clear your mind of the clutter of this life. Allow God to show Himself to you in the intricacies of creation. No leaf, no rock, no flower is out of place. The connectedness of every grain of soil and drop of water is an example of the active Spirit of the Creator who called us to our leadership tasks. Where can you blossom again? Be still and know that He is God and will renew you in His time and perfect season. Have confidence in your faith that new energy and vitality will spring forth from you if you will seek God in the wilderness and the solitary place.

Our Prayer: *Creator of Heaven and Earth, we give thanks for the order and majesty of nature. Call us into a wild place so that You can speak to us through the miracle of rebirth in the spring of life. Help us to always know that we can bloom again if we will stay rooted in the soil of our faith, even during the cold and drought of life's circumstances. Renew our spirits and attitudes. Instill in us a commitment to serve You in a more vibrant way.* **Amen.**

Sing A New Song

"God Deserves New Songs of Praise and New Acts of Faithfulness"

"Sing unto the Lord a new song, and his praise from the end of the earth, ye that go down to the sea, and all that is therein; the isles, and the inhabitants thereof.... Praise ye the Lord. Sing unto the Lord a new song, and his praise in the congregation of saints."

Featured Scriptures: Isaiah 42:10; and Psalm 149:1
Background Scriptures: Psalm 33:3; Psalm 96:1; and Psalm 98:1

How God must grieve as He blesses us each day with breath and life and sustenance, only to find us singing old trite songs of thanksgiving back to Him. Not only do we not praise and thank God often enough, but when we do bother to go to Him in praise and thanksgiving, it is usually in a bland and ritualistic way. God wants to hear our new songs. He wants to hear them everywhere and in new ways. He desires that we become fresh and vibrant in our faithfulness each day.

Song and praise are almost synonymous. A song can also be a new act of faithfulness done with glee. Leaders of faith should become the conductors of praise by leading our organizations in new songs and in new acts of faithfulness. We leaders can set the tone and tenor of an organization just by our demeanor. The whistle and quick step of a leader can become contagious among those we lead. When leaders of faith inspire others to a new sense of thankfulness and charity, we are singing new songs to God. When we motivate our followers to adopt a more giving spirit and undertake a charitable enterprise, we are singing a new song. When we sow the seeds of hope over despair and selflessness over selfishness, we are singing a new song to the Lord.

Examine your own personal spiritual life today. What rituals of study and prayer do you need to energize with a new song? Small actions and subtle changes of habit can lead to the singing of new songs of praise. Take some quiet time and go outside to different venues. Attend a class of preschool children at your place of worship and join in their song time. Attend new places of worship and experience new cultural ways of praise and song. Practice new, small acts of kindness as if you were singing a song of praise to God or a song of love to the recipient of your kindness.

In our leadership, let us find new ways to express our appreciation to our coworkers. Let us schedule more time for fellowship and social interaction with those we lead. Find new ways to approach the tasks of monotony and dread in your organization and turn them into meaningful and appreciated activities so as to lift people up with a new song.

God wants you to find new ways to fellowship with Him. He wants your praise and thanksgiving. As we find new songs to sing to God, God finds new ways to bless us and shower us with His love. Sing your new song today and open heaven's light.

Our Prayer: *God of love, we lift our voices to You this day with a new song of praise and thanksgiving. We sing through the clutter and difficulty of our own earthly circumstances to recognize Your sovereignty and beauty. Open our hearts and souls until new songs of praise and new acts of faithfulness come flowing out of us like a stream to You, O Lord.* **Amen.**

Fully Redeemed, Not Fatally Flawed

"LEAD IN POWER WITHOUT FEAR, BOLDLY CLAIMING GOD'S PROMISE"

"But now thus saith the LORD that created thee, O Jacob, and he that formed thee, O Israel, Fear not: for I have redeemed thee, I have called thee by thy name; thou art mine. When thou pass through the waters, I will be with thee; and through the rivers they shall not overflow thee: when thou walkest through the fire, thou shall not be burned; neither shall the flame kindle upon thee."

FEATURED SCRIPTURE: ISAIAH 43:1–2
BACKGROUND SCRIPTURE: ISAIAH 43:1–12

"Thou art mine." God formed us. He chose us. He calls us by our names for His purposes. We belong to God. We are created for His glory. God is not a passive observer in our lives. He is the single omnipotent force and sole designer of who we are and what we are to do. But do we truly claim His full redemption? Do we pray pitifully and live timidly without ever summoning the true power and protection that is offered to the fully redeemed? As leaders of faith, we are called to lead as if we are fully redeemed, not fatally flawed.

Fully redeemed leaders are not perfect. We fall short. We sin. We fail. So did Israel. Yet God loved her and saved her and protects her even today. Living as fully redeemed leaders means we must see ourselves as God's living vessels. Claiming our redemptive power means we must let go of all fear of life's challenges and tribulation. Redeemed leaders will not be drowned by water or burned by fire. Being redeemed does not mean that the raging waters of trouble will not find us. They will. It does not mean that hot fires of adversity will not break out around us. They will. It simply means that in every circumstance, God allows us to escape life's traps without being destroyed by them.

Being fully redeemed is not a get-of-jail-free card. It does not entitle us to become slothful or lack caution in our dealings with others. However, being fully redeemed should propel us to attempt bold initiatives without hesitation and confront our enemies without reservation. It should empower us to get up and try again after we have been knocked down. It should cause us to seek out new alliances and networks of provision in our times of trouble. God gathers us together to these places so He can work mighty miracles in our lives even though these places can seem unlikely spots for a mighty work.

Fully redeemed leaders in times of trouble will be given the quiet confidence in their hearts that tells them everything will be alright. We will be the last to panic and the first to offer hope in every situation. We will always find the resources from the ruins to begin again.

Yes, we are God's. We belong to Him and exist for His pleasure and glory. Therefore, our call to leadership is nothing less than a holy endeavor. As we claim the words of Isaiah today, let us arise anew with all boldness and fearlessness as we lead others as fully redeemed servants of the Lord Jesus Christ.

Our Prayer: *God of Jacob, we belong to You. You formed us and created us for Your glory. You have redeemed us and empowered us to do great things. You have called us for a special purpose. Let us claim this promise with boldness, confidence, and power today. Let us dare to slay the problems and circumstances that tangle our lives and keep us from serving You fully.* **Amen.**

When A Remnant Becomes Your Constituency

"How God Calls Leaders to Lead Valuable Remnants of People"

"Hearken unto me, ye that know righteousness, the people in whose heart is my law; fear ye not the reproach of men, neither be ye afraid of their reviling.... Therefore the redeemed of the LORD shall return, and come with singing unto Zion; and everlasting joy shall be upon their head: they shall obtain gladness and joy; and sorrow and mourning shall flee away."

FEATURED SCRIPTURE: ISAIAH 51:7, 11
BACKGROUND SCRIPTURE: ISAIAH 51

Isaiah spoke with joy and exhortation as he described the return of the Remnant, those Israelites who had survived the exile and captivity of the Babylonians. They saw much misery and despair, but they never lost the faith. God promises protection and blessings for His Remnant who have not forgotten God and His Law.

One day after I had accepted a difficult leadership assignment that would certainly put me under great duress, a fellow believer and dear friend said to me, "You have been called to lead the remnant of that organization." Indeed, she was right. But her words became as the voice of God within me as I realized how God puts us into the right places to gather and lift the broken remnant of movements and people and put them back together.

Just as the Jewish nation had been stripped of its home, seen its people deported, and been made to adopt new rules and laws of a conquering power, we see organizations, churches, and institutions today get torn apart by strife, evildoers, and the selfishness of others. In these circumstances, years of great tradition, a good reputation, and milestones of achievement can be tossed to the wind as the organization is exiled and hauled away by oppressors.

In each organization to which this happens, there usually remains a remnant of those persons who in their own hearts carry the oral history, the integrity, and the purpose of the founders. In the ashes of every situation is found those persons of great faith, hope, and purpose who did the right things, yet saw their works burn up around them.

Leaders of faith are often called into these situations by God to lead and nurture those who have built the wall, only to see it fall around them. What a blessing to be called to by God for such a task. It could be a call to heal a broken congregation or civic club. It could be a call to mentor a broken family. It could be a call to take over a failed business or charity. You may be called to take a group, a remnant of brokenhearted persons, and ask them to rebuild a wall with worn-out tools. But if you are called to lead a remnant, God will make your provisions known and will bless the work.

Our Prayer: *Our Jehovah, You never forget the faithful, the remnant of every broken circumstance. If we will but acknowledge and trust in Your name, You will make provision for us to rebuild the brokenness around us. As leaders of faith, call us to find ways to lead the broken to the healing power of the Great Physician.* **Amen.**

The Irony Of Ironies And The Prince Of Peace

"THE PRINCE OF PEACE EMBODIES GOD'S UNIQUE WAY OF REACHING US"

"For he shall grow up before him as a tender plant, and as a root out of a dry ground: he hath no form, nor comeliness; and when we see him, there is no beauty that we should desire him. He is despised and rejected of men; a man of sorrows, and acquainted with grief: and we hid as it were our faces from him; he was despised, and we esteemed him not."

FEATURED SCRIPTURE: ISAIAH 53:2–3
BACKGROUND SCRIPTURE: ISAIAH 53

The more we experience God's providence, the more we must understand that God's ways are not our ways. What appears to be an irony of human circumstance is the fingerprint of a God we cannot truly fathom. Nowhere do we see the purpose of God reflect this irony more poignantly than in the fulfillment of prophecy through the coming of the Prince of Peace. His life, His resurrection, and His control over eternity is the irony of ironies to mortal man, but it is the path to peace, knowledge, and eternal life to the redeemed among us.

If we try to form preconceived notions of God's plan and methods, we set ourselves up to miss His wonder. In fact, many people of Jesus' day missed Him because they were looking for the wrong thing. God gives us the Scriptures to guide us so we don't miss the Master when He comes into our lives. Many in the time of Christ looked for a Messiah who would deliver them from the oppression of Roman rule. They looked for a dashing warrior of earthly, royal stock. They looked for a handsome, learned scholar and political leader who could rally the masses for the cause of liberation; not for the son of a carpenter.

Dozens of passages of Scripture lent prophetic knowledge of the coming life and eternal purpose of Christ. Christ Himself has told us what to expect in this life and beyond. Are we missing Christ because we are looking for something different? Do we see human irony when we should see holy visions and prophecy fulfilled? Others may see our leadership calling as an irony, but let us see it as an expression of God's unique purpose fulfilled in us.

Christ was humble, born to a teenage virgin. Jesus came from Nazareth, a lowly place. Jesus, the Scripture says, was not handsome, dashing, or of eloquence. He was not an earthly king or patriarch. Jesus was not wealthy and was not a soldier or politician. He could have done anything He wanted, for He was both God and man. But He used His powers to heal, teach, and touch others, not to raise an army against Rome. He preached salvation and forgiveness to the poor and brokenhearted, and He did not cavort with the privileged. He died of His own free will. He conquered death and brings eternal life to all. He changed history forever by becoming the irony of ironies, God with us.

Are we as leaders of faith missing Christ's power in our leadership journeys because we are failing to emulate His life and mission? Do we set notions of our own success only to miss the miracles God can bestow upon us? Let God turn the apparent human ironies in our lives into miracles of service for Him.

Our Prayer: *Prince of Peace, Savior, we praise Your holy name and lift up Your life and purpose for the salvation of mankind. Thank You for loving us and redeeming us. Help us to drop our notions of how we think You should respond to us. Help us to only trust and obey in God's plan for us.* **Amen.**

Silence From The Unspeakable Gift

"THE TIME FOR GREAT LEADERS TO GO SILENT"

"He was oppressed, and he was afflicted, yet he opened not his mouth: he is brought as a lamb to the slaughter, and as a sheep before her shearers is dumb, so openeth not his mouth.… Then said Pilate unto him, Hearest thou not how many things they witness against thee? And he answered him to never a word; insomuch that the governor marveled greatly.… Thanks be unto God for his unspeakable gift."

FEATURED SCRIPTURES: ISAIAH 53:7; MATTHEW 27:13–14; AND 2 CORINTHIANS 9:15
BACKGROUND SCRIPTURE: MATTHEW 27:11–26

The apostle Paul described Jesus as God's Unspeakable Gift. No words can adequately describe the Son of the Trinity and the Creator and Sustainer of life. In the Passion Story, our Redeemer came to this moment of history as one despised and rejected of men. It is in this moment, standing before the Roman Governor Pontius Pilate (with the masses having chosen not to release Christ, but to release Barabbas) that the true majesty of Jesus confronted the sin and ignorance of man through its silence. It is in this moment of silence from our Lord that the prophecy of Isaiah would be fulfilled.

The Spirit of God must have ached as He watched this scene unfold. Didn't anyone at the trial remember Jesus' healing of the blind man or His raising of Lazarus from the dead? Didn't anyone in the crowd that day recall how the demons obeyed Jesus when He exorcised them from so many tormented souls? Didn't anyone remember the many lepers who were cleansed? Hadn't someone there heard His Sermon on the Mount or received bread and fish to eat from Christ's own miraculous hand? Had His mission and works been for naught as He stood silently before Pilate in this sham of a legal proceeding?

As leaders of faith we may ourselves come to these moments when all we stand for and all we have given our lives for seem to have gone unnoticed and unappreciated by those we have led and served. The Passion of Christ reminds us that when God calls us to a holy task of service for Him, those around us may not appropriately acknowledge our service. This seemingly devastating ending for Christ was but a part of the fulfillment of prophecy and necessary for the glorious plan of salvation that would come to billions of souls.

To be falsely accused in leadership for things you did not do is almost a certainty. For faithful leadership service to go unnoticed and unrewarded is a daily occurrence. In our own leadership journeys of faith, it is sometimes our own silence before our accusers that we display the most power. Let God do your talking in your silence through the spiritual fruits your work will bear. Never lose the faith that what you do for God in obedience to His calling will be proven true and worthy. Let us place our work and hope for success before the Unspeakable Gift in our silence and awe and wonder.

Our Prayer: *Unspeakable Gift and Lord, we stand silently with You as You stood before Pilate. We praise You for the gift of salvation and for taking the sins of the world upon Your own back. Thank You for the example You set in this moment for leaders of faith. How often we in our journeys are falsely accused and unappreciated. How often we feel our works have come to naught. In these moments may Your Spirit come upon us and render us silent, yet powerful before our accusers.* **Amen.**

Contrite And Humble Spirits

"GOD DESIRES CONTRITE AND HUMBLE SOULS TO DWELL WITH HIM"

"For thus saith the high and lofty One that inhabiteth eternity, whose name is Holy; I dwell in the high and holy place, with him also that is of a contrite and humble spirit, to revive the spirit of the humble, and to revive the heart of the contrite ones…. For he hath regarded the low estate of his handmaiden: for behold, from henceforth all generations shall call me blessed."

FEATURED SCRIPTURES: ISAIAH 57:15; LUKE 1:48
BACKGROUND SCRIPTURES: ISAIAH 57:14–21;LUKE 1:46–56

God can't say it more clearly. He loves and desires the company of contrite and humble spirits. To be contrite is to grieve and constantly give penance for your sin and shortcomings. Humility is that state of heart and mind that says all your existence and provision comes from God and you are His creation, made for His purpose. You submit all you are and all you have to Him. Our Scripture today says that to those souls that attain this level of the Spirit, He will revive their hearts.

Contrite and humble spirits can make great and effective leaders. The high and holy place of heaven above is filled with the contrite and humble. If we are to have any heaven on earth, in its midst must exist those persons who are constantly aware and confessing of their sin and short-comings and who give God the glory for their very lives. Leaders of faith who would become effective servants for the Lord should note the statement of Mary as she received her call. She said that God regarded the low estate of His handmaiden. Mary's heart and spirit was contrite and humble, thus ready for the highest purposes of God.

It is in our contriteness and humility that we are apt to hear the call to service and leadership. Those who are proud and arrogant may hear that false call to leadership. But before people of faith can truly be ready to do great heavenly tasks for God, our souls must be in the low estate of Mary. Contriteness and humility can be obtained through confession and prayer. We need to ask for forgiveness of God and from those around us whom we have hurt. We should diligently perform small tasks with great love for others. We should find someone who can never repay us and do something kind for them today.

If your spirit is low and broken, God promises that He revives the heart of the contrite and the humble. God desires to be with you and to bless you. Strive to be contrite and humble, and expect miracles to come into your life soon.

Our Prayer: *Holy God, create in us a contrite and humble spirit. We want to dwell with You in the high and holy places of eternity. We bow before You today, asking for forgiveness and casting our cares upon You. In humility we seek to serve You. Revive our broken hearts and empower us to shine Your love and light to all we encounter.* **Amen.**

Right and Wrong Fasting

"God Discerns Our Real Motives and Desires That We Act Instead of Fast"

"Is not this the fast that I have chosen? To loose the bands of wickedness, to undo the heavy burdens, and to let the oppressed go free, and that ye break every yoke? Is it not to deal thy bread to the hungry, and that thou bring the poor that are cast out to thy house? When thou seest the naked, that thou cover him; and that thou hide not thyself from thine own flesh?"

Featured Scripture: Isaiah 58:6–7
Background Scriptures: Isaiah 58; and Zechariah 8:19

Fasting is a way of denying ourselves the basic sustenance of food in order to make our voices heard on high. It is our symbol of self-sacrifice as we attempt to become one with the atoning of the Suffering Christ. In times of the Old Covenant, fasting was required on the Day of Atonement. But in today's lesson we see examples of how certain persons fast for their own self-righteousness and find pleasure in what should be a sacrificial act. We are given new instructions for a new fast.

The prophet Isaiah tells us that while some acts of fasting in self-denial may be right, true fasting is faith through our affirmative action of service to others. Real fasting is our quest to tackle injustice and free the oppressed. Real fasting occurs when we ease the burdens of our families and neighbors and give food to the local food bank. Our fast for Christ should be in clothing a needy schoolchild or bringing a lonely senior citizen into our home for a hot meal.

In our own leadership journeys of faith, we will encounter those persons who will want to be recognized for their piousness by way of their outward signs of self-sacrifice. Some will openly fast, while others will burden themselves with symbols of affliction in order to garner the approval of others. It is better to eat your food and share with others than fast falsely alone. Let your actions of love toward others become your new fast as you undertake new and sacrificial acts of service today.

As our lives become centered in service and ministry to the hurting around us, God says the light will break forth as the morning and our righteousness shall go before us, and the glory of the Lord shall be our reward. As we fulfill God's purpose through our calling, the prophet Zechariah tells us our fasting shall be turned to feasting.

Fasting in humility and solidarity with Christ and fellow believers as praise to God is good fasting. But God truly desires that we pour our own abundance of food, love, grace, mercy, and time onto those in need around us. That action of service represents the best and right kind of fasting and unleashes the free-flowing fountain of God's blessings to all. Now go and fast!

Our Prayer: *Heavenly Father, in the privacy of our hearts we fast by our humility and awe of you. We fast through our actions of love and service to others. We fast when we seek to lighten the burdens and ease the oppression of the innocent. Forgive us when we fast or sacrifice for the notice and praise of man. May our sole focus be to praise You by fulfilling our call of service and ministry to Your children in this world.* **Amen.**

Like A Watered Garden

"Our Garden of Leadership Requires Life-Sustaining Water"

"And the Lord shall guide thee continually, and satisfy thy soul in drought, and make fat thy bones: and thou shalt be like a watered garden.… Therefore they shall come and sing in the height of Zion, and shall flow together to the goodness of the Lord…and their soul shall be as a watered garden.…"

Featured Scriptures: Isaiah 58:11; and Jeremiah 31:12
Background Scriptures: Isaiah 58:11–12; Jeremiah 31:1–12; Genesis 2:6–10; John 18:1–11; and John 19:41–42

In the dryness of a hot summer afternoon, I observed a garden of vegetables as it began to show signs of stress. However, after a nice evening shower, I revisited that same garden the next morning to find new color and new life in each leaf and vine. To witness a watered garden reminds us of our own connection to God. Without water, all the cultivation, planting, and care put into a garden are for naught. Just as a garden is dependent on water, our own lives and leadership journeys of faith yearn for the living water of God's blessing.

Our Scripture lesson today from the great prophets Isaiah and Jeremiah liken the restored soul to a watered garden. Whether He was restoring the people of Zion or the soul of a weary believer, God is the lifeline of heavenly water. God is also the God of gardens. From the creation story of Genesis and the Garden of Eden, to the garden of love in the Song of Solomon, to the Garden of Gethsemane, site of Jesus' most fervent prayer, God has used the garden to illustrate life's journey. Our own leadership experience is like a garden. Our calling is like a new field to be cleared and worked. Our service to others means we must plow and plant for future harvests of good results. In all that we do, we are dependent on God's miracle of water and provision.

How is your leadership garden doing today? Is it a watered garden, or is it dry and parched? Is it suffering from lack of attention? Have you prayed for rain or drilled a well to water your plants? Does your organization or congregation suffer because it has not been fertilized with new training and higher ethical standards? Our leadership gardens require our active involvement in every phase of its life. We must take the initiative to get our gardens ready so that all they need is a heavenly watering. Even God's soothing and soaking rain cannot rescue a garden that is choked with weeds and neglect. Seeds that were never planted cannot sprout after a rain.

God desires that we cultivate our leadership gardens with purpose, passion, and faith. When we do our part, God's watering will come. Our leadership gardens contain the vegetables and produce meant to rescue a hungry and dying community around us. Healthy, watered organizations can employ new workers and create new wealth for the needy. Our leadership gardens are places where new leaders are cultivated and then planted in new and bigger gardens. As our leadership gardens grow each year, the soil gets deeper, allowing those who come behind us to plant in richer ground. Let your soul, life, and leadership journey become God's watered garden. Prepare daily and pray for rain. God desires that we bear much fruit and find glory and satisfaction in the harvest of our callings in leadership.

Our Prayer: *God of all gardens, water our souls and water the work of our hands this day. Help us to be ready when the rain comes. Lord, let our garden of leadership yield life-sustaining sustenance for the hurting and weary souls around us. Bless our gardens and all who consume the bounty it produces from Your heavenly water.* **Amen.**

The God-Given Value Of Pro-Life Leaders

"Before We Were Formed in our Mothers' Wombs, God Knew Us"

"Then the word of the Lord came unto me, saying, Before I formed thee in the belly
I knew thee; and before thou camest forth out of the womb I sanctified thee, and I
ordained thee a prophet unto the nations."

Featured Scripture: Jeremiah 1:4–5
Background Scriptures: Jeremiah 1:1–10; Isaiah 49:1–5; Luke 1:12–17; and Galatians 1:15–16

The calling and ordination of the great prophet Jeremiah did not take place in the middle of Jeremiah's life. The Scripture today tells us that before Jeremiah was ever conceived in the body of his mother, God knew him. And even while Jeremiah was being formed in his mother's womb, God sanctified and ordained him to be a prophet to the nations. The Scripture is a great testimony to the value of the unborn and the unconceived life. Life is not created by physical acts of men and women and science, but it comes by the very hand of God.

God has called you from the beginning of time to be His servant. Before you were even born, He knew you and loved you. If God so meticulously called and ordained leaders like Jeremiah, how can we doubt our own calling? Moreover, if God knew us and called us in ages past, how can we doubt that we will not succeed in our tasks for Him? If we cling to the Creator and Giver of all life, we will absolutely succeed!

Jeremiah was called to prophesy to the Jews in Judea and to the remaining Jews in captivity. His calling was a tough task in very tough times. God knows that tough situations require sanctified and ordained leaders. Many of these leaders of faith were called and ordained from the bellies of their mothers' wombs for godly service.

The lesson of Jeremiah's calling should also give us pause to consider the unborn and the unconceived. These souls may just be the next Jeremiahs of our time. They may be the chosen leaders of faith who have been called to the final fulfillment of the Great Commission. The call of Jeremiah is also the call to value the sanctity of all life, both born and unborn. The value of life is more than a political argument; it is the essence of our faith.

Be a leader of faith who celebrates life in all its forms. Become a leader who does not allow the unborn, the poor, the disadvantaged, or the disabled among us to be left out of God's plan for leadership. Cherish the God-given value of pro-life leadership that our Creator sanctified and ordained before the earth itself was formed. Let every human soul be afforded worth and dignity as a child of the living God.

Our Prayer: *God, Our Creator, You are our Maker. You knew us before we were even conceived. In our mothers' wombs, You loved us and made great plans for us. Instill in us, O Lord, a new respect and awe for life in all its forms. Create in us hearts of love and forgiveness and passion to create a culture that celebrates and protects life. Forgive us when we have taken a life or tossed people aside who were poor, addicted, or in some other way unsavory to us. By Your guiding Hand, let us find the good and the redeemable in every living soul that You created as an act of our appreciation to You, our God and Our Creator.* **Amen.**

What Seest Thou?

"Our Directive from God Is Often Our Simple View Expanded to a Holy Vision"

"Moreover the word of the LORD came unto me, saying, Jeremiah, What seest thou? And I said, I see a rod of an almond tree. Then said the LORD unto me, Thou hast well seen: for I will hasten my word to perform it. And the word of the LORD came unto me a second time, saying, What seest thou? And I said, I see a seething pot; and the face thereof is toward the north"

FEATURED SCRIPTURE: JEREMIAH 1:11–13
BACKGROUND SCRIPTURE: JEREMIAH 1

How will I know? What sign will come to me? When can I know that this insight and passion that has been filling my soul is, indeed, a holy vision from God? It is not only the leaders of faith of our day who wrestle with how to take a simple view and turn it to God's holy vision. In today's lesson, the great prophet Jeremiah was seeing something but did not know what it meant. God came to him twice and asked him: *"What seest thou?"* God reassured Jeremiah that He was, indeed, with him and expanded Jeremiah's view to holy prophecy.

The rod of an almond tree and a northward pointing seething pot shown in our Scripture today may not seem like the makings of prophecy, but to servants called by God for a heavenly task, such God-inspired views may be all they need to know. God often speaks to leaders of faith in visions, intuitions, parables, and unique circumstances. It is our task to take the small view before us and translate it into God's bigger vision. God took the simple vision Jeremiah was seeing and through it reassured Jeremiah of His presence; then He showed him the coming of the Babylonian invasion.

God may have placed a hurting community or a needy family in your line of view. God may be giving you a mental image of a new product or service that can help humankind. God may be placing within you a restlessness that says you need to move on to another vocation, a fresh relationship, or a new educational opportunity. Following those simple views to God's greater vision may lead to great mission work, personal fulfillment, or business success. It may lead you to new heights of service to others as a pastor or lay-leader in your faith.

When our hearts are still and prayerfully attuned with God's Spirit, we will be given views and visions of life that can be transforming. It is imperative that we get into positions of humble submission and yielding spirits if we want God to take us to another level of understanding of His will. Don't discount the words and mental images that come into your heart and mind. Your own small view of the rod of an almond tree or seething pot facing north may become God's vision of greater service to others. God may be giving you the new vision for your organization or congregation as you obediently seek and serve.

Our Prayer: *God, we give thanks to You for the prophets and the visionary leaders of faith who obediently took a view and turned it into Your vision. Create in us, O Lord, pure and humble hearts and minds so we, too, can see Your vision of the future in our own lives. Help us to lead others in truth and light. Show us how to take the fledgling signs and inclinations in our hearts and turn them into bold visions of faithful leadership by Your hand.* **Amen.**

Wrath Great Leaders Cannot Spare

"The Greatest Leaders Cannot Always Contain God's Judgment on Evil"

Then said the Lord unto me, Though Moses and Samuel stood before me, yet my mind could not be toward this people: cast them out of my sight and let them go forth.… And like unto him was there no king before him, that turned to the Lord with all his heart, and with all his soul, and with all his might.… Notwithstanding the Lord turned not from the fierceness of his great wrath, wherein his anger was kindled against Judah, because of all the provocations that Manasseh had provoked him withal."

Featured Scriptures: Jeremiah 15:1; and 2 Kings 23:25–26
Background Scriptures: Jeremiah 15:1–4; 2 Kings 23:4–27; and 2 Kings 21

The introduction of idolatry into Judah came at the hands of King Manasseh. Manasseh's evil ways brought the worship of the idol Baal into the holy land. The sins of Manasseh perverted the holy places and the Temple. The sins of this king and of the people of Judah greatly kindled the wrath of God. which would not be contained. Our Scripture today points to an important fact in leadership of faith. The prophets tell us that even the intercession of Moses, Samuel, and Josiah could not stop the judgment of God for the debauchery caused by Manasseh.

Moses, Samuel, and Josiah were, indeed, three titans of faith. Each served God faithfully, and their deeds are recorded in Scripture. Josiah's mighty deeds sought to rid Israel of the idols and evil planted by Manasseh. God praised Josiah for it, but He did not spare the land of Judah from ultimate punishment. Great leaders can only do so much to protect those they are called to serve. For all his good works and humble heart, Josiah could not undo what evil had been wrought before his time of service.

The greater lesson for us today is that we are not the masters of destiny. Even the greatest leaders and saints of faith cannot dictate nor change the wrath and judgment of God upon our own people. There are many examples where God was moved by the appeals of leaders like Moses or David. In the case of Judah, it could not be done. There are limits to our own abilities in the realms of God. The holiness and sanctity of God are not to be defiled, and such defilement will not go unpunished.

Great leaders of faith are often put into seemingly impossible situations. Josiah inherited a land of idols and evil in his kingdom. We, too, can be called to lead in the most horrific of circumstances where corruption and evil abounds. Like Josiah, we must be faithful and do the right things. Josiah's reforms, including the purging of idols and evil, were successful and they fulfilled his calling to God. We, too, can successfully fulfill our calls to God even without stemming the ultimate judgment and accountability others must face for their actions.

Lead on in every situation and let God be God. Today we have the blood of the Lamb that washes away all sin, but we still must let God be the judge. Keep leading and don't be discouraged.

Our Prayer: *Lord God, You are holy and perfect. You cannot tolerate sin in us or in those we lead. Your Son's sacrifice paid the eternal price for us. We know that idolatry and evil exists today, yet You call us to lead in the midst of it. May we be obedient and do Your will and not be discouraged when we cannot save others from judgment. Be merciful and gracious to us and let the love and salvation of Christ be our hope.* **Amen.**

False Leaders Of Faith Like False Prophets

"Not Everyone Who Claims to Be a Leader of Faith Is Called of God"

"I have seen folly in the prophets of Samaria; they prophesied in Baal, and caused my people Israel to err. I have seen also in the prophets of Jerusalem an horrible thing: they commit adultery, and walk in lies: they strengthen also the hands of evildoers, that none doth return from his wickedness.… Thus saith the LORD of hosts, Hearken not unto the words of the prophets that prophesy unto you: they make you vain: they speak a vision of their own heart and not out of the mouth of the LORD."

FEATURED SCRIPTURE: JEREMIAH 23:14
BACKGROUND SCRIPTURE: JEREMIAH 23:9–40

Not everyone who claims to be a leader of faith is called by God for that purpose. God's prophets of old were known by their sheer reliance on the Word of God. They were known by their good habits and lifestyles. The real prophets very seldom told the flock of the Lord what they wanted to hear. In fact, many of the prophecies that the true prophets spoke were admonitions to flee from evil and return to God. They were pronouncements of judgment and promises of restoration for those who repented from sin.

Jeremiah tells us that the false prophets invoked the idolatry of Baal and caused God's chosen people to err in their ways. The false prophets lied, lived lives of adultery, and strengthened the position of the evildoers around them, probably by taking bribes. There appeared to be a vanity in the false prophets, and the vision they shared with the people was most likely a concoction of a message that the people wanted to hear, rather than the warnings of the Lord of hosts. False prophets never repent; they don't feel guilt.

People are hungry for leadership. People are hungry for a prophetic word and visionary insights for their future. People can become vulnerable to the allure of false prophets and false leaders, especially those who claim a special calling from God.

How can we identify the false leaders of faith among us today? False leaders of faith claim a false calling. They live lifestyles that are not grounded in the Word of God. They will appear overly ambitious and lack humility. False leaders of faith will commiserate with the wrong persons. False leaders are usually telling people what they want to hear and setting forth a vision of prosperity, when a vision of God-fearing reliance on the Lord is the real message of hope. False leaders are usually unable to admit their faults or their mistakes, but they move ahead with reckless abandon, often hurting others in the process.

True leaders of faith must be careful to spot and expose these false leaders. God is clear in His loathing of them and promises their actions will not go unpunished. True leaders of faith must guard against actions that could mistake them for a false leader. The true calling of leaders of faith will be manifested in the love they have for others and their sole reliance on God, as well as the lifestyles they live.

Our Prayer: *Lord of hosts, we know that there will be false prophets and false leaders to come among us. We pray that You will show us whom to follow and how to spot the evildoers who seek to lead us astray. Please strengthen the true leaders of faith You have called so they may live and lead in a manner consistent with Your Word and calling.* **Amen.**

Turning Our Captivity With A New Hope

"Leaders Held Captive by Circumstance Are in Need of New Hope"

"For I know the thoughts that I think toward you, saith the Lord, thoughts of peace, and not of evil, to give you an expected end. Then shall ye call upon me, and ye shall go and pray unto me, and I will hearken unto you. And ye shall seek me, and find me, when ye shall search for me with all your heart. And I will be found of you, saith the Lord: and I will turn away your captivity, and I will gather you from all the nations...."

Featured Scripture: Jeremiah 29:11–14
Background Scripture: Jeremiah 29:1–14

Dire circumstances can overwhelm the best of leaders. Bad things happen to good leaders, often in waves and with growing intensity. In every leadership journey, there comes a time when we sit and wonder if we have the courage to go on. We may lose hope and feel abandoned. Even after we have faithfully answered and fulfilled what we felt to be the call of God, we feel anxiety about our lives. We are captives of our circumstances and in dire need of new hope.

The God of Israel, who spoke through His prophet Jeremiah, knew that the exiled leaders in captivity in Babylon were at such a point of losing hope. Jeremiah wrote to the remnant of leaders there, sending a message of new hope to a discouraged and captive people. The circumstances in our lives can become so dire and so depraved that we may ponder aloud if God still knows we exist and if He really cares. The resounding answer from our lesson today is that not only does He care, but He desires to give us peace and good things if we will seek Him heartily. He wants to break the captivity of our circumstances, but He needs us to be active participants in the process.

The end of captivity was growing near for the people of Israel. God promised to gather them back together. They had been scattered, but He would reunite and bless them again. God told the people that if they searched for Him with all their hearts, they would surely find Him. We should search and not mope. We should seek to find God in the new places and opportunities we encounter. God is waiting somewhere for you where you don't expect to find Him. He is armed with a special blessing of deliverance for you if you will persevere.

By searching for God, we put feet to our prayers. We become active participants in finding the new hope for which we pray. Take your present dire circumstances and rattle their cage for new possibilities. Try God out. Let Him prove what He says: He has good thoughts toward you for a desired outcome. He promises that He will turn our captivity from present circumstances and will deliver us to a better outcome. Start searching now.

Our Prayer: *Lord God, we will search for You with a new heart and with true earnest this day. We will seek You even in our dire circumstances. Help us to find new hope and experience the blessing we know You hold now for us in Your very hand. Give us the courage to try again and with new resolve. Bless us as we begin. We want to find You, and we know our circumstances are changing as we pray just now.* **Amen.**

Leaving A Written Legacy

"Leaders of Faith Should Record and Write About Their Journeys"

"Thus speaketh the Lord God of Israel, saying, write thee all the words that I have spoken unto thee in a book…. And the Lord said unto Moses, write thou these words: for after the tenor of the words I have made a covenant with thee and with Israel…. Blessed is he that readeth, and they that hear the words of this prophecy, and keep those things which are written therein: for the time is at hand."

Featured Scriptures: Jeremiah 30:2; Exodus 34:27; and Revelation 1:3
Background Scriptures: Jeremiah 30:1–5; Luke 1:1–4; Revelation 1:1–3; and Exodus 34:27–28

The great leaders of our faith were also the God-inspired authors of our Scriptures. Moses was not just the great liberator of the chosen people; he was the author of the written history and laws of God. Jeremiah was not just a prophet; his prophetic writings were commanded of God so as to give hope to the people. Luke and John were not just apostles. Their unique visions of the future and recollections of the life and teachings of Christ preserve the great Gospel story as well as the acts of the early Church. They are unique in all of Scripture and were commanded by Christ to give hope and blessing for all generations through God's Word.

The letters of Paul, the psalms of David, and the proverbs of Solomon are greater than all the literature, poetry, and treatises ever written. Not only are the lives and ministries of these leaders of faith our example, but their call to write about their journeys should serve as inspiration to record a written legacy of our own lives and callings. Our own written records of our humble callings can also serve to chronicle the faith and inspire others in the future to know God in a new way.

Even the act of writing letters can become a great theological endeavor. Leaders of faith should keep journals, write editorials, and leave notes to loved ones that give praise to God and encourage others in their walk with Christ. As we lead congregations and organizations, we should offer periodic written messages and bulletins to those in our care to help train and motivate our fellow servants to greater faith and work for God.

Many great leaders come to the end of life and regret that they have not kept a written log of their journey. If we are called by God for His heavenly tasks here on this earth, they are worthy to record in a written record. No one can ever know the power of the inspired and written word when it is penned for the purposes of Kingdom of God. Let the Spirit of truth flow through you. If you feel God's tug to write, sit down today and put your thoughts on paper. The time may be at hand. Others may be blessed from our written words, and God's eternal presence may continue to flow through them long after we have gone on to be with the Lord.

Our Prayer: *Heavenly Father, we give thanks for the inspired and written words of the titans of our faith. Inspire us to write words today that can bless others. Any person called to a task for You has material worthy to write. Regardless of how small and seemingly insignificant we may feel our words to be, give us the discipline to write and record the faith. We want to leave a written legacy that, by Your Spirit, can bless and inspire others in the days and years to come.* **Amen.**

Kindly Acts To Your Enemies Get Remembered

"Respect and Mercy Shown Toward Your Rivals Can Make History"

"Evil-merodach king of Babylon in the first year of his reign lifted up the head of Jehoiachin king of Judah, and brought him forth out of prison, And spake kindly unto him, and set his throne above the throne of the kings that were with him in Babylon, And changed his prison garments: and he did continually eat bread before him all the days of his life."

FEATURED SCRIPTURE: JEREMIAH 52:31–33
BACKGROUND SCRIPTURES: 2 KINGS 24:8–16; AND JEREMIAH 52:24–34

Jehoiachin, king of Judah, had been in prison for thirty-seven years. He had been a young king who, early in his reign, did evil in God's sight and surrendered Jerusalem, allowing the people and wealth of the city to be sacked. He has now spent most of his life imprisoned by the Babylonians. Evil-merodach was the new king of Babylon. In one of his first acts, he took mercy upon Jehoiachin and brought him into his presence. He gave him new clothes and fed him in his court. He restored to him some dignity and worth for a short while.

Evil-meodach only ruled Babylon for two years. Tradition says that he was murdered by his brother-in-law and his throne seized. He performed no significant act worthy of remembrance other than what was recorded the passage considered today. The only real achievement of this idolatrous king was in a kindly act to an old enemy. However, this act of mercy was so important that the prophet Jeremiah recorded it in the final words of the great Book of Jeremiah. Today's Scripture and lesson should cause leaders of faith to ponder the power that exists in practicing kindness to our enemies.

Being kind to your rivals and adversaries in life and in business does not mean that you are weak or that you are surrendering your principles. Kindness to a rival means that you set yourself apart and practice a level of behavior that gives you an advantage and causes you to stand out to others. Acts of kindness to competitors can help disarm the brutality we often see in what should be friendly competitions. Oftentimes when we compete for business, votes, power, or positions, we can become vindictive, not kind.

God expects those called by His name into leadership positions of faith to show kindness to their rivals and enemies. Our enemies may be imprisoned in jail or in a prison of evil behavior or addiction. Practicing kindness to them can demonstrate the love of God that inspires us to our own tasks of leadership. Kindness to our enemies also shows forgiveness and mercy, traits of the Lord Himself. In your journey of leadership, find ways to practice kindness to your opponents, enemies, and rivals. Pray for God to use that kindness for His good purpose.

Our Prayer: *Lord Jesus, help us to be kind to others, even our enemies. Help us to practice kindness where others would not expect it. Strengthen our hearts and minds so that we are confident that kindness can be a tool of power and not weakness. Guide us in every moment so we may know when and how to use kindness for Your purpose.* **Amen.**

Leading Amidst Defeat And Destruction

"Finding the Richness of God's New Mercies and Promise in Our Travails"

"It is of the Lord's mercies that we are not consumed, because his compassions fail not. They are new every morning; great is thy faithfulness. The Lord is my portion saith my soul; therefore will I hope in him."

Featured Scripture: Lamentations 3:22–24
Background Scriptures: Isaiah 33:2–6; and Malachi 3:3–6

Defeat and destruction are never the desired outcome for a leader. But if you lead long enough, you will find yourself faced with the circumstances of a defeat or the destruction of your work in your journey of faith. It is how we respond and lead during these times of great calamity that shows forth our true and holy character. Often God tests us in these dark moments to see if we can summon praise, hope, joy, and faith as we lead amidst our own defeat and destruction.

The loss of power, whether in battle or in an election, will ultimately come to all leaders. The perils of nature, war, corruption, and economic travail will visit nations and institutions when we least expect it. Those constituencies that we are entrusted to lead often make mistakes, and the consequences of their actions can be dire. They may put us into seemingly hopeless situations with few good choices at hand. We ourselves can make gross errors in judgment that take our congregations or organizations from prosperity to failure. Our callings from God may actually be to shepherd those souls obliterated through human acts of violence or nature's pestilence.

Sometimes it is only in our defeat and the ashes of our own destruction that we are able to see the tiniest of God's mercies or the brilliance of a budding new promise. The great prophets of the Old Testament, like Jeremiah and Isaiah, certainly knew of defeat and destruction, yet in all they experienced, they constantly sought God's mercies and blessing. The writer of Lamentations witnessed two years of surrounded embattlement of his people in Jerusalem. He knew that defeat, pillage, exile, and humiliation were ahead for his people. Yet this writer and prophetic leader of faith knew that his true success rested not in outward accomplishments, but in the fervent seeking of God's compassions and new mercies.

Sometimes hope, compassion, love, and faithfulness are all we can offer those we lead. True leaders of faith must trust in God's eternal providence and unmeasured grace. Godly leaders know that if all they can do is sow hope and faith for a better day for future generations, they can still be successful in God's eyes. Those coming behind us will reap the fruit of our obedience as we search for God's new mercies.

Wait and see what God can do, and do all you can do right now. Dry a tear. Dress a wound. Hold a hand. Find encouragement in each new sunrise. Watch as the Lord's small mercies come to you anew morning by morning, bringing with them new hope and new joy. Let us praise the Lord continually, and His blessings will rain down upon us even as we lead others amidst defeat and destruction. Fret not, for Christ has already overcome the world!

Our Prayer: *O Lord, when we as leaders of faith are humbled by the circumstances of our defeat and destruction, be gracious unto us. Be our arm of strength every morning, and be our salvation in every time of trouble. Help us to bestow Your hope of new mercies to those You entrusted us to lead, even when we lead in the darkest of valleys, and we will claim victory in Your name.* **Amen.**

Called To Lead The Stiff Hearted

"Not Everyone Whom God Calls Us to Lead Will Like What They Get"

"And the spirit entered into me when he spake unto me…Son of man, I send thee to a rebellious nation that hath rebelled against me…. For they are impudent children and stiffhearted…. And they, whether they will hear, or whether they will forbear, yet shall know that there hath been a prophet among them."

FEATURED SCRIPTURE: EZEKIEL 2:2–5

BACKGROUND SCRIPTURES: EZEKIEL 2; ISAIAH 6:9–12; JEREMIAH 1:17–19; AND LUKE 16:19–31

Not everyone called to leadership journeys of faith will be met with joy by those they lead. Many of us who are called to lead will be given tough tasks, like the ones given to the great prophets of the Old Testament. Ezekiel and his counterparts, Isaiah and Jeremiah, were called to bring the Word of God to rebellious and stiff-hearted constituents. In Ezekiel's case, he was to bring the message that God had not forgotten the exiled and suffering Israel. Ezekiel was to let them know that they deserved their plight, but also how they could become redeemed and restored.

God told Ezekiel that the people might not want to hear him. God called His people impudent, cocky, and bold. God did not assure Ezekiel that the people would heed the words he told them. But God told Ezekiel not to be afraid or dismayed by rejection, for God wanted people of all ages to hear His words and He needed a reliable prophetic leader of faith to bring the message of our Lord to them.

God wants the truths of the faith spoken boldly by His chosen modern-day prophets, who without fear or discouragement will deliver the holy message clearly. If your desire as a leader of faith is to always be liked, be careful to see if this desired outcome is truly the call of God. Tough leadership tasks almost always involve taking people where they don't want to go and coaxing them into doing things they don't want to do. Our success in leadership will not always be measured by the popularity we garner from our followers, but by the measure of our obedience to God's call. Ezekiel was a Levite priest who heard his calling while camped by the river Chebar. The glory of God came to him, and God chose Ezekiel for the tough task. God knew that Ezekiel loved Him and loved the nation of Israel. The tough love and strict obedience that Ezekiel displayed through the tough times for his nation are now a centerpiece of our faith.

The ability to succeed in tough tasks is centered in loving God and loving those around you, even the stiff-hearted. The ability to love and serve stiff-hearted persons may mean that God will use you in very special ways. Don't become discouraged or dismayed when those you try to serve reject you. Sometimes God just desires that we lay the message out there, whether people accept it or not. So be obedient, and know that God will reward your faithfulness to the call of leading the stiff-hearted.

Our Prayer: *Dear God, oftentimes You call us to lead stiff-hearted people who do not want us there and will not listen to us. Fill us with love and toughness to be able to tell them what they need to know. Give us the Word and the courage to tell it. Protect us from their assaults back at us. May those we lead repent of wrongdoing and find fellowship in Your bosom. Restore and redeem us all, we pray.* **Amen.**

The Days Are At Hand

"LEADERS MUST TELL FOLLOWERS THAT GOD'S WORD AND WARNINGS WILL COME TO PASS"

"Son of man, what is that proverb that ye have in the land of Israel, saying, The days are prolonged, and every vision faileth? Tell them therefore, Thus saith the LORD God; I will make this proverb to cease, and they shall no more use it as a proverb in Israel; but say unto them, The days are at hand, and the effect of every vision…there shall none of my words be prolonged any more, but the word which I have spoken shall be done, saith the LORD God."

FEATURED SCRIPTURE: EZEKIEL 12:22–23, 28
BACKGROUND SCRIPTURE: EZEKIEL 11—12

There comes a time when God's promises, prophecies, and warnings are fulfilled in every life and every generation. The prophet Ezekiel was faithful to tell the people he led the truth about God's call to repentance and obedience. Ezekiel mightily and boldly told the people of Israel about their coming doom, yet the people did not believe it would happen in their generation. They continued to build homes and go about their business with a false sense of security. They even scoffed at their leader, Ezekiel, saying, "You keep preaching doom to us, yet it has not happened." But today, God's days are at hand.

Leaders of faith in our generation can also be prophets. We lead others by a calling from God and with the special provision of divine help and motivation. Our leadership is grounded in the Word of our Lord, and the service we render to others is done by His love and grace. Just as God commanded Ezekiel to warn his flock of God's coming judgment, we, too, must be prepared to warn those we lead that God's words and commands must be followed. We must speak our truth clearly as we set an example of holiness in our deeds.

Part of a successful leadership journey is bearing news that our bad behavior has brought the days of judgment upon us. We must tell those we lead that there will be certain consequences from the neglect of God in our lives. The people of Ezekiel's day put God in a box and limited their view of the Almighty. They never thought the judgments predicted by Ezekiel would happen to them. Congregations and organizations we lead today can also become skeptics and mockers. Leaders of faith can find themselves in a lonely place as they attempt to lead others in God's truth, only to see that God's days are at hand.

As leaders of faith, we are only called to lead in truth and spirit. We cannot always make others heed God's words and warnings. When we have done all we can do, we must let God's purposes work themselves out in all situations. Even in God's judgment, there is the light of hope and redemption for those who would repent and follow God anew. Lead as God speaks to you. Be truthful with the flock God has given you, for God's days are at hand.

Our Prayer: *Lord God, give us the courage and understanding to lead others in the truth of Your Word. We know that Your purposes, prophecies, and judgments will be fulfilled in their due time. Show us clearly when it is our task as leaders of faith to speak Your judgments clearly and to warn those we lead that the day of the Lord is at hand. Forgive us and redeem us by Your grace and mercy for a new day.* **Amen.**

Prophesying Against The Prophets

"Real Leaders May Be Called to Purge False and Sinful Leaders"

"And the word of the Lord came unto me, saying, Son of man, prophesy against the prophets of Israel that prophesy.... They have seen vanity and lying divination, saying, The Lord saith: and the Lord hath not sent them: and they have made others to hope that they would confirm the word.... Because with lies ye have made the heart of the righteous sad."

Featured Scripture: Ezekiel 13:1–2, 6, 22
Background Scripture: Ezekiel 13

The call to the son of man in today's lesson was clear: He was to prophesy against the prophets. False prophets and false leaders rise up when our people become restless and lacking in faith. People compromise principles, listen to new voices, and follow new leaders when they become desperate. The prophet Ezekiel saw the people of Israel being led away from the truth by false leaders. These leaders claim to be speaking for God, but our Scripture today says that through their lies have made the heart of the righteous sad.

These prophets and leaders were claiming divine power, but they were practicing sorcery and the occult. They were falsely claiming to channel messages from God, but they were strengthening the hand of the wicked and stifling the faith of the righteous. God's anger was greatly kindled against them as they made a mockery of the righteous and holy calling of a prophet of God. Godly leaders are set apart by a true heavenly calling. Their works should be noble and their hearts clean and pure. Many self-professed leaders will arise and claim the mantle of leadership, but God will judge them severely as they commit sin in His holy name.

Your call to service from God may be one that involves exposing and rooting out corrupt and false leaders in your own organization or congregation. You may be called to give testimony against the powerful persons who are falsely and destructively leading innocent people. You may be called to prophesy against the prophets. This calling may be one of the most difficult of all. Prophesying against the prophets in power can bring strong and violent reaction against you. You may become the subject of rejection or ridicule as false leaders attempt to discredit you. You may be subject to false legal action or severed from your resources and finances.

When God calls you to lead against false leaders, He will protect you and miraculously open doors for you. Those whom you are chosen to lead may resist and rebuke your leadership at the outset, but the righteous and good people God sent you to lead will eventually come to your assistance. The righteous-hearted persons whose hearts have been made sad by false prophets and leaders will see the true hand of God in your efforts. They will rally to your side. As you see injustice and false leadership in your organization, you may be sensing a new call and purpose. You may be hearing God's voice to prophesy against the prophets. Answer that call today.

Our Prayer: *Lord God, You are the great* I AM. *When false prophets and false leaders arise and claim Your name and power in order to hurt others and cover their own sins, Your great wrath is kindled against them. Lord, You may be calling me to prophesy against the prophets. Give me the wisdom to hear Your call to root out the false leaders in our midst. Protect me as I tackle the powerful earthly and demonic powers that are an abomination to Your name. Give me strength and courage to perform every task with heavenly anointing.* **Amen.**

Pride Of A Prince Brings God's Wrath

"Leaders Who Become Self-Congratulatory Belittle God's Blessing"

"Thus saith the Lord God; Because thine heart is lifted up, and thou hast said I am a God, I sit in the seat of God.... Therefore thus saith the Lord God; Because thou has set thine heart as the heart of God; Behold, therefore I will bring strangers upon thee, the terrible of the nations: and they shall defile thy brightness."

Featured Scripture: Ezekiel 28:2, 6–7
Background Scriptures: Ezekiel 28:1–19; Proverbs 16:5, 18, 19

The power of leadership can become intoxicating. The ability for a leader of faith to summon people and resources to accomplish great tasks is a blessing from God, yet over a period of time the exercise of power and authority can become a trap for some. When leaders of faith take the pageantry, the accolades of accomplishment, and the adoration of others and turn it inward to their sense of self-worth, pride can begin covering their souls like a fungus.

The pen of Solomon in the Proverbs is crystal-clear on the danger of pride. *"Every one that is proud in heart is an abomination to the Lord and pride goeth before destruction; and a haughty spirit before a fall"* (Proverbs 16:5).In fact, the anointed cherub who covered the radiance of God was the one who ultimately symbolized pride and the fall. Satan himself was created for beauty and holiness by God. Satan was the cherub who carried praise and glory to the throne of God. It was in the midst of God's glory and beauty that Satan began admiring himself. The trappings of power and status, and the sense that he himself was a god, caused his fall and his eternal judgment.

Leaders of faith must at all time guard against pride. Harvesting humility and turning all accolades and gains of this life over to the throne of God in praise and thanksgiving is the inoculation against pride. Pride does not mean we can't gain pleasure or satisfaction from our work. God certainly wants His chosen ones to feel a sense of warmth and good spirit, which is derived from doing His will. And if we remain in His love and the love of others, the light of selflessness will rule our agendas, and we will be fine.

In our lesson today, the prince of Tyre grew intoxicated with his wisdom, power, and riches, and he became god-like in his own heart. The Scripture is clear: Like the prince, we, too, will be laid low by our pride. Pride causes leaders to make poor judgments. It gives them a false sense of invincibility. It causes them to become vindictive and gain a sense of entitlement from others. When you feel a sense of revenge for others and become angry when others do not pay you the homage and protocol you feel you deserve, watch out! Pride seeps in like moisture through a crack in a solid foundation until it causes an otherwise stable house to tilt.

Our Prayer: *Dear God, please protect us against the sin of pride. Keep our hearts humble and our hands busy doing the work You have called us to do. Help us to be motivated by love and the desire to serve others, and not to be self-congratulatory or to accumulate wealth. Forgive us and cleanse us today of all the pride that has built up in us and make us clean for Your service.* **Amen.**

Being A Good Upstream Leader

"GOD IMPLORES US TO CONSIDER HOW OUR ACTIONS AFFECT OTHERS"

"Seemeth it a small thing unto you to have eaten up the good pasture, but ye must tread down with your feet the residue of your pastures? And to have drunk of the deep waters, but ye must foul the residue with your feet? And as for my flock, they eat that which ye have trodden with your feet and drink that which ye have fouled with your feet…therefore…I will judge…."

FEATURED SCRIPTURE: EZEKIEL 34:18–20

BACKGROUND SCRIPTURES: EZEKIEL 34:17–22; GENESIS 1:28, 31; LUKE 16:1–5

Upon completing His creation, God pronounced everything that He had made *good*. It was flawless and meant to be left just as He had made it. Creation is also interdependent, and each component of it is delicately interrelated. God gave man dominion over all the living things. This dominion implied responsibility and accountability. In our lesson today, the prophet Ezekiel wrote about those who shirk the responsibility of their creation custodianship and trample upon their neighbors by way of callous disregard for natural resources. God commands us to be good, upstream neighbors and promises to judge those who are not.

A leader of faith is especially charged by God to be a good upstream leader. How we care for the resources entrusted to our care is of high importance. Societies often ravage the natural resources around them without concern as to how this behavior affects a downstream neighbor whom they might not ever see. Ezekiel warned that the evil among us trample their pastures with their feet and make them muddy. They drink of the deep and pure water, only to foul it with their feet and send polluted water downstream for others to use and drink.

States and nations are situated along rivers and bodies of water. Do the upstream nations use and pollute water and send it to the poorer nations downstream? Do we destroy our best wet-lands and pastures and cause our waste products to become poison for other communities? Are our own congregations and organizations doing all they can to reduce their negative resource footprints in the world today? You as a leader of faith with dominion over God's creation are held in judgment as to how well you perform this task of sacred stewardship.

Creation stewardship requires each of us to evaluate how our consumption and behavior affect our neighbors. As leaders of faith, we should ask those we lead to examine every facet of our lifestyles, from what we eat and drink to how we travel and where we live. How much of the good pasture do we destroy? Are we consuming too much deep and pure water so that none is left for others? Is the residue of our pastures clean and pristine, or is it compromised?

We have a solemn calling to be custodians of God's creation. Set an example for others to follow. It may mean sacrifice and the burden of responsibility, but it is commanded and expected by our God. Let being a good upstream leader become part of your praise and worship to God. Those living downstream from you will see your higher standard and sense in it the love and service that emanates from a God and Creator whom they will desire to know.

Our Prayer: *God and Creator, we give You praise for all You have made. Instill in us a burning passion to be Your custodian of the good pasture and the deep water. May our stewardship of creation become a beacon of light and love that draws others to want to know You.* **Amen.**

Leading By Your Lifestyle Choices

"Leaders Lead Well When They Make Good Personal Lifestyle Choices"

"But Daniel purposed in his heart that he would not defile himself with the portion of the king's meat, or with the wine which he drank: therefore he requested of the prince of the eunuchs that he might not defile himself.... Prove thy servants, I beseech thee, ten days; and let them give us pulse (vegetables) to eat, and water to drink."

Featured Scripture: Daniel 1:8, 12
Background Scripture: Daniel 1

I fondly remember the story of Daniel and his friends from my childhood Sunday school class. The story in Daniel 1 is often used as a biblical admonition to get children to eat their vegetables. It certainly made an impression on me! But the story of Daniel, Hananiah, Mishael, and Azariah is more than a story of boys who made the conscious decision to eat the right foods; it is the story of exemplifying leadership by making good lifestyle choices. You as a leader of faith in a secular world have the same opportunities Daniel and his friends had to set the example for others to follow in your lifestyle choices.

Nebuchadnezzar and the Babylonians had conquered Judah and the king had ransacked Jerusalem. Nebuchadnezzar charged the master of his eunuchs to find and fetch young men of the king of Judah's lineage and bring them into his own house to train. The four young men whom the eunuch found were *"children in whom was no blemish, but well favored and skilful in all wisdom, and cunning in knowledge, and understanding science, and such as had ability in them to stand in the king's palace and whom they might teach the learning and tongue of the Chaldeans"* (Daniel 1:4).

The king appointed a daily portion of meat and wine for these four boys to eat, but Daniel, showing great judgment and leadership, refused to defile himself and his companions with the largess of Nebuchadnezzar. Daniel demanded a diet of healthy foods and water instead of meat and wine. Thus, Daniel exemplified to the master of the eunuchs and the king that, indeed, he and his friends were set apart by their choice. God blessed the choice of Daniel and endowed him and his three friends with great wisdom and understanding, more than ten times than all the magicians and astrologers that were in the king's realm. Daniel led by making good lifestyle choices.

In our own leadership journeys, we have many chances to make personal lifestyle choices in full view of others. Do we make the right ones? People are watching us closely. Not only should we make choices that result in our own good personal health—regular exercise, clean living, a healthy diet—but we should refrain from habits and choices that demean our calling as leaders of faith. Like Daniel, God will bless your good personal lifestyle choices by setting you apart and giving you wisdom and understanding. Your good choices now may lead to greater opportunities to serve God!

Our Prayer: *Lord God, even in captivity Daniel and his friends kept the faith and made the right lifestyle choices. You blessed them and through their faith set an example for others to follow. Give us the wisdom and courage to make the right personal lifestyle choices each day in our own leadership journeys.* **Amen.**

Give Us A Miracle Or Give Us Death

"Asking for Miracles or Martyrdom in Lieu of Serving Idols"

"Shadrach, Meshach, and Abed-nego, answered and said to the king, O Nebuchadnezzar, we are not careful to answer thee in this matter. If it be so, our God whom we serve is able to deliver us from the burning fiery furnace, and he will deliver us out of thine hand, O king. But if not, be it known unto thee, O king, that we will not serve thy gods, nor worship the golden image which thou hast set up."

Featured Scripture: Daniel 3:16–18
Background Scriptures: Daniel 2:46–49; and Daniel 3

These three young men had been captured and brought with Daniel from Judah as spoils of war. They had all been faithful along with Daniel to the true God. They were skilled and had proven themselves to be wise managers and leaders in this new land of Babylon. Daniel had just intervened with King Nebuchadnezzar on their behalf and was promoted to oversee the affairs of the province of Babylon.

However, the king, in his self-sanctified glory, had constructed a ninety-foot tower of a golden image to serve as god over Babylon. The king gathered all the princes, rulers, governors, judges, sheriffs, and counselors of the land to come and see this new golden image. Then King Nebuchadnezzar commanded that upon the sound of the king's music, all of them bow down and worship the idol. This commandment was intended to make all leaders of the land subservient to the king and his golden idol. To refuse to worship the image would result in immediate death by burning in the fiery furnace.

Shadrach, Meshach, and Abed-nego were also called to come and worship the idol of the king. They steadfastly refused. They told the king that their true God would deliver them, but if He did not, they would rather face death than betray Him. At that moment, these young leaders of faith cast their hopes on a miracle or martyrdom for the Lord. Resoluteness and unmovable decisions by leaders like these set forth the standards for our faith. They were cast into the furnace, but the angel of the Lord came to them as they danced together inside. They were delivered, indeed. In the end, the king was moved toward God, and they were restored to power.

As leaders of faith today, we may also face life-or-death decisions as others try to force us to abdicate our faith or principles. We may also be asked by our superiors to commit unethical acts or participate in sinful activities by way of an order. We may become socially ostracized among our peers at work for failing to adhere to some hedonistic practice. How would you respond? If your heart and soul is entwined with the living God, you must be resolute and willing to risk your position, employment, or even your personal safety on behalf of your faith.

Knowing who you are and what you stand for is the beginning of great leadership for God. Let the furnace burn in the face of idols. Our God is able to deliver us from the blast of idolatry and the foolishness of godless kings and leaders who seek our worship.

Our Prayer: *Lord Jesus, we are often asked to participate in idolatrous acts by the foolish of this world. Help us to recognize the sinfulness of lending ourselves to any activity except what You have called us to do. Give us a miracle or give us death. Be with us in the fiery furnaces of faith. We give thanks for the martyrs of God. May we always choose the right path, O Lord.* **Amen.**

The Writing Is On The Wall

"Revelry, Partying, Irreverence, and Mockery Find a Leader Wanting"

"And the king, and his princes, his wives, and his concubines, drank in them. They drank wine and praised the gods of gold, and of silver, of brass, of iron, of wood, and of stone…in the same hour the fingers of a man's hand appeared and wrote opposite the lamp stand on the plaster of the wall…. You have been weighed in the balances and found wanting.…"

Featured Scripture: Daniel 5:3, 4, 27
Background Scripture: Daniel 5:1–32

Belshazzar was a king in Babylon during the time of the Jewish captivity there. God's prophet Daniel was called upon to interpret the meaning of an image of writing that appeared on the wall during the king's party. Daniel went before Belshazzar and gave it to him straight. He told the king that God had measured him and he had been found wanting. From this Scripture comes the age-old saying regarding a new reality: The writing is on the wall.

Revelry, partying, irreverence, and the mockery of things that are holy will find leaders wanting. Not only were Belshazzar and his guests engorging themselves in consumption, they were drinking from the sacred cups and vessels of the holy Temple as a mockery of the living God. Even as they mocked God, they praised the idols. When the Lord of lords observed this behavior, He called for immediate judgment.

Leaders of faith must guard against the runaway debauchery of wildness and revelry. We should flee from events that mock God and offend others. While we may never attend a party of the scale of King Belshazzar's, we are often invited to events that become lavish affairs, celebrating man's wealth and accomplishment at the expense of others. Beware of revelries that praise man while mocking God. As leaders of faith, we acknowledge that all blessings of this life are gifts from God. Our celebrations should always be done with care, humility, and a spirit of thankfulness. We can still have fun while respecting what is holy.

Leaders should celebrate the accomplishments and the great events of life. God certainly ordains celebrations. Our Savior performed His first miracle at the wedding reception of a friend. Have fun and celebrate on good occasions, but take care that you do so in moderation. Our enemies and opponents lurk behind the curtains waiting to capitalize on our excesses of revelry. Belshazzar's story reminds us to be holy leaders in all circumstances. We should never flaunt our wealth, power, or symbols of earthly gain before others or use them as a way to mock another. We should never allow those in our presence to desecrate the sacred vessels of God or the innocent lives of any of God's children.

God sees all and knows all. Always seek to temper the excess of ceremonies and celebrations with a thankful heart and humble respect and praise for all blessings of life. Never let God find you wanting, for God alone is worthy to be praised in all occasions of life.

Our Prayer: *God of Daniel, we give You praise and thanks for the blessings of life. Teach us how to celebrate life and special occasions without excess, revelry, or irreverence. Even amidst the wealth and power around us, let us seek to meet the needs of others and give You credit for all good accomplishments. Let us never be a part of any activity that mocks what is holy. We pray, O Lord, that You will never find us wanting.* **Amen.**

When Good Leaders Are Set Up To Fall

"Keeping Your Faith in the Lions' Den of a Rival's Jealous Plot"

"Then this Daniel was preferred about the presidents and princes, because an excellent spirit was in him; and the king thought to set him over the whole realm. Then the presidents and princes sought to find occasion against Daniel concerning the kingdom; but they could find none.... Then said these men, We shall not find any occasion against this Daniel, except we find it against him concerning the law of his God."

Featured Scripture: Daniel 6: 3–5
Background Scripture: Daniel 6

Leaders of faith who are called by God for special tasks will often find themselves in the company of ambitious people. Leaders of faith may find that they must share leadership responsibilities with persons who do not hold to the same set of godly principles or who are not believers. They may see something in you that sets you apart. It may invoke envy, jealousy, or hatred in them toward you. Those same persons may even plot to set you up for a fall because of the faith you exhibit in your daily tasks.

In his service to King Darius, Daniel was superb. His great ability was noticed, and the success he had was secure because David was honest and ethical in every way. But Daniel was clearly set apart by his faith and calling from God. His rivals knew this and used his blessing as a trap for him, a story that went on to become known as Daniel and the Lions' Den. This prophetic and intriguing lesson shows how good leaders can be falsely accused. David was trapped as his rivals fooled the king. But Daniel never lost faith, even in the den of hungry lions, and he was miraculously protected. The plot of Daniel's accusers was revealed, and the king threw them to the same lions. It was they who were devoured.

As a result of Daniel's faithfulness and God's mercy, King Darius and many others declared the greatness and dominion of God. Daniel was the boy captured and reared into great leadership through conviction, courage, and faith. The vision and purity in Daniel's life of service conquered the evil that his rivals set before him.

If you haven't been tested yet by jealous or hateful rivals, get ready. It will happen. Leaders of faith will become targets of evildoers because of their purity and unwavering adherence to God's way. The qualities of your faith will exude from you, and certain success will come to you, even as it does not come to others. Jealous rivals will want to attain your success, but they will try to do so through the wrong means.

Be firm in your purpose and remain steady in your faith, just like Daniel did. The God who called you to the lions' den for His sake will never let you be devoured by the evil conspiracies that attack you. Dare to be a Daniel; dare to stand alone; dare to have a purpose firm; dare to make it known.

Our Prayer: *Lord God, protect us from our enemies and from those in our leadership journeys who seek to do us harm. Keep us faithful to the task You have called us to do. Even in the lions' den of trouble, don't allow our enemies to prevail over us as they set a trap for our downfall. Keep us in perfect peace as we keep the faith like Your servant Daniel.* **Amen.**

Waiting On The Vision And Answers To Prayer

"God's Vision and Answers to Prayer Will Come Clearly in Time"

"In those days I Daniel was mourning for three full weeks…. Yet heard I the voice of his words: and when I heard the voice of his words, then was I in a deep sleep on my face, and my face towards the ground…. And he prayed again, and the heaven gave rain, and the earth brought forth her fruit."

Featured Scriptures: Daniel 10:2, 9; and James 5:18
Background Scriptures: Daniel 10; and James 5:13–18

Daniel was a great leader and a prophetic voice of our faith. Daniel's visions and insights came from God in various ways. Even the archangel Michael came to bring a special word to Daniel. The prophetic words of Daniel are of great value to all people of faith. Today's lesson will focus on the heart and patience of Daniel, and how God brings vision and answers to prayer to those who patiently seek Him in humility, truth, and purity of heart.

Daniel's leadership journey of faith was marked by consistency and obedience. Daniel was given the ability, call, and opportunity to interpret the dreams of others. Daniel was placed in stressful situations where he had to deliver interpretations of God's messages by way of dreams and signs. In today's Scripture Daniel was waiting on the Lord through fervent prayer, fasting, and self-denial. Daniel had mourned for three full weeks. He had eaten no pleasant bread, meat, or wine during this time as he was waiting on a word from God.

Leaders of faith who are called to great tasks for God do well to follow Daniel's example. We can become impatient and impose man-made deadlines on heavenly visions and immediate answers to our prayers. We can often endanger our holy mission by acting first before knowing where God wants to take us next. But if we, like Daniel, will set our hearts to truly understand what it is God wants us to know, we shall surely find it. God loves us and wants us to succeed. He knows our hearts, and His visions and answers will come to us in time if we wait with patience, humility, and perseverance.

God came to Daniel while he was sleeping on his face upon the ground by a river. God does not always answer when we are on our knees or in the sanctuary. He chooses His time and His way to appear to us. God often uses unique and unorthodox ways to speak to us. He may come to us in a dream or in quiet thought. He may send messages to us with a roar during a worship service or through the quiet voice of intercession from a friend or elder. God's voice may come to us in the candor of a child's remark or through a spouse's encouraging word. Like He did with Daniel, God may even come to us by a riverbank while we mourn. But rest assured: He will come. Pray again, listen for His words, and the rain will come that will bear much fruit.

Our Prayer: *Lord, thank You for Daniel and the other prophets and saints who shared Your visions and words through their faith and true hearts. Lord, set our hearts as leaders of faith to understand what it is that we are to do next. Come to us in time with a vision and answers to our prayers. May we seek You in all humility, sacrifice, and yearning.* **Amen.**

Set Your Heart Understand

"GOD MEASURES THE INTENT OF OUR HEARTS, THEN COMES TO US"

"And he said unto me, O Daniel, a man greatly beloved, understand the words that I speak unto thee, and stand upright: for unto thee am I now sent…. Then said he unto me, Fear not, Daniel: for from the first day that thou didst set thine heart to understand, and to chasten thyself before thy God, thy words were heard, and I am come for thy words."

FEATURED SCRIPTURE: DANIEL 10:11–12

BACKGROUND SCRIPTURE: DANIEL 10

God loved Daniel greatly. Daniel had been a captive in a strange land since his boyhood. In his seeming tragedy and misfortune, Daniel bloomed and became one of the faith's greatest leaders. In today's lesson, Daniel was given prophetic words from God via an angel. The angel who came to David revealed to him and to us all a great spiritual truth: When we discipline ourselves, seek God in purity and earnestness, and truly set our hearts to understand, He will come to us.

God measures the hearts and the intentions of leaders. In order to become pure of heart, we must purge ourselves of our tainted views and worldly influences. In order to hear from God, we must set ourselves apart both physically and mentally from our daily tasks and troubles. For us to hear God, we, too, must display our own repentance and cleansing process until we become helpless before our Creator.

Setting our hearts to understand can take time. Daniel had been in mourning for three weeks as he lay by the river on the day the angel came to him. The angel sent to Daniel told him of God's immense love and affection for him. When answers to our prayers and petitions don't come right away, it is important for us to hold on. Waiting faithfully is part of our soul's purification process. God's timing is always perfect.

Leaders of faith often face issues so big or situations so difficult that it drives us to our knees in search of an answer from our Lord. As you are confronted with leadership decisions in your own congregation or organization, set your heart to understand, and then wait patiently. The messenger of understanding who comes to you from God may be a real angel. But the messenger may also come in the form of a colleague, friend, or trusted mentor who gives you a new word. Sometimes the message may be revealed through the innocent observations of a child or by way of the voices of hurting persons crying out around us.

Whatever problems that confront us today, setting our hearts to understand God is our first step toward leadership success. Leaders of faith must lead in the midst of the spiritual warfare around us. The angel who visited Daniel had been delayed because he first had to overcome the deceivers and evildoers in another land. As we seek understanding during our own tough times, it may be necessary for us to remain by our own rivers of mourning until we feel the calm and gentle hand of God upon our shoulders. It is in that moment of peace that our portal of spiritual understanding will open.

Our Prayer: *Lord God, I stand before You in purity of heart. I purge my soul of all selfish thoughts and worldly understanding. Come to me in this time as I set myself apart and earnestly seek Your holy understanding. Come to me, O Lord, and give me the words I need to hear.* **Amen.**

False Leadership Obtained By Flattery

"Evil Leaders Seduce Many with Flattery, Then Rule with Contempt"

"And in his estate shall stand up a vile person, to whom they shall not give the honor of the kingdom: but he shall come in peaceably, and obtain the kingdom by flatteries…. And such as do wickedly against the covenant shall he corrupt by flatteries: but the people that do know their God shall be strong, and do exploits."

Featured Scripture: Daniel 11:21
Background Scriptures: Daniel 11:21–35; and Malachi 2:6–8

Restless people who long for a better day often fall prey to the promises and flattery offered by opportunists and would-be leaders. World history is replete with tragic stories in which downtrodden and humiliated people succumb to the smooth flattery of evil rulers and consent to their leadership. People of faith must resist such suitors and be on guard against persons who would take advantage of our tough situations. The real goal of such persons is only to loot and corrupt what goodness exists.

Today's lesson from the prophetic pages of the Book of Daniel features Antiochus Epiphanes, who was a descendant of one of the generals of Alexander the Great. This perverted leader came to power in Palestine peaceably through flattery, through bribery, and by self-proclamation. He then invaded and conquered much of Egypt and was ultimately stopped by the Roman Empire. His disgraced retreat back to Jerusalem provoked his great persecution of the Jews and the brutal desecration of the Temple of God. His short rule led to armed Jewish revolt and Roman intervention. A short but evil rule in history was marked by a king who came to power through flattery.

True leaders of faith are marked by strong character and by the respect they display to those they lead. Evil supplanters of power can sense when there exists a void of leadership. They see hopelessness and restlessness and consider it an opportunity to exploit others. God often calls leaders of faith to confront such evil plots. These exploiters and flatterers emerge in many organizations and congregations. Their initial appearance and words may seem sincere, but their actions will ultimately defy good intention. Unfortunately for many groups, much damage can be inflicted before the group realizes it has been corrupted from within.

Many brave Jewish leaders took action against this evil king. Many became martyrs rather than defile their faith and holy places. It is their show of courage and resistance that made for this great and inspiring account. We, too, as leaders of faith must seek out the evildoers among us and expose them. We must be brave to confront the false flattery and bribery with the sword of God's Word and the truth. Let us always endeavor to find floundering and desperate people and situations and insert the providence of Christ's love, power, and peace into them lest they fall to flattery.

Our Prayer: *Lord, we pray for the insight to find the false leaders who pervert others through flattery and evil seduction. We are ready to answer Your call to stand firm against those who would seek to destroy others by selfish intent. Guide us and direct our actions as we travel along the paths of our callings.* **Amen.**

Alliances That Compromise Leaders

"WHEN LEADERS RELY ON PROTECTION THROUGH ALLIANCES RATHER THAN ON GOD"

"Yea, though they have hired among the nations, now will I gather them, and they shall sorrow a little for the burden of the king of princes. Because Ephraim hath made many altars to sin, altars shall be unto sin. I have written to him the great things of my law, but they were counted as a strange thing."

FEATURED SCRIPTURE: HOSEA 8:10–12
BACKGROUND SCRIPTURE: HOSEA 7—8

Israel was God's chosen nation. God had led them and protected them. Though they were surrounded by troubles, time and time again the Most High God delivered them. Israel was surrounded by many nations and powers. Their land was strategic for travel and trade, yet Israel was small compared to the powers around her. Others nations wanted to acquire the land Israel for themselves.

The prophet Hosea wrote that the leadership of Israel had decayed. Rather than stay fully devoted to the Law of God and solely relying on His protection, they had entered into alliances with Egypt and Assyria for military protection. These alliances meant Israel had to pay tribute to the Assyrian monarch. Hosea brought the message of the judgment of God to Israel.

Leaders of faith can often seem outnumbered or ill-prepared for the challenges ahead. In our own organizations, congregations, or leadership projects, we may be tempted to turn to unlikely alliances for help. Not all alliances are bad, but leaders of faith must never supplant their reliance on God for the security of man-made alliances. These agreements meant they invited the allies' idolatry into their midst. It meant that they had to pay the price of tribute to a foreign king. They had compromised, through an unholy alliance, their covenant relationship with the Almighty God.

Have you ever formed alliances, mergers, or joint ventures with others unadvisedly? In your leadership journey of faith, have you ever relied on the power, the financial strength, or the network of others for your provision rather than going to God in prayer? If your alliances are the result of a lack of faith, sinful practice, or lazy leadership, you may be setting yourself up for a fall. Leaders called by God for service must never forget that they are set apart, not like other leaders. What may seem like a logical alliance to non-believers may morph into sinking sand for a leader of faith.

God is always able, and His calling and plans never deviate. Even when we are called by God for a leadership task, our missteps and foolish alliances with others who do not share our calling or values can entrap us. Like the princes of Israel, we may be subject to corrective action by God. Keep the faith, even in seemingly dire circumstances. God is setting you up for a miracle, and He is the only alliance you ever truly need.

Our Prayer: *Lord of Hosts, help us to know that if You call us for Your purposes, it does not matter who surrounds us or comes to destroy us. Your provision is sufficient. You, O Lord, are the only alliance we need. Give us discernment as leaders of faith to know when and when not to ally ourselves with others, and forgive us when we fail You.* **Amen.**

Rend Your Heart And Not Your Garments

"God Wants Hearts to Change and Not Gestures of Change"

"Therefore also now, saith the LORD, turn ye even to me with all your heart, and with fasting, and with weeping and with mourning: And rend your heart, and not your garments, and turn unto the LORD your God: for he is gracious and merciful, slow to anger, and of great kindness, and repenteth him of evil."

FEATURED SCRIPTURE: JOEL 2:12–13

BACKGROUND SCRIPTURES: JOEL 2:12–17; GENESIS 37:34–36; 2 SAMUEL 1:11–16; AND PSALM 34:18–19

The rending or tearing of one's clothing was for many years a religious sign of grief, mourning, and sorrow. It was a public display so that others would know of the person's changed condition. Great spiritual leaders such as Jacob and David were known to rend their garments in their own sorrow and grief. The prophet Joel, however, told the people of Judah during this time of drought and pestilence to turn to God, and to rend their hearts, not their garments.

God is a God who wants to see broken hearts given to Him. When life's circumstances tear our spiritual and mental fabric, we are to give our brokenness to Him. Whether our calamity was self-induced through our own sinful behavior or came to us in an unforeseen circumstance, God stands ready to be gracious, merciful, kind, and forgiving to us. Broken hearts given to God heal faster and with a greater capacity for openness than before.

Leaders of faith in their own life journeys will encounter times of extreme sorrow and mourning. We will fail and find ourselves broken and at a loss for words. In our leadership duties we will come to find our own congregations or organizations in the midst of sorrow and tragedy. What should we do? How should we respond? God expects us to mourn and to weep. He expects us to seek a new closeness to Him in these times through fasting and prayer. But what God really wants to see in times of brokenness are the hearts, souls, bodies, and minds that are fixed upon Him in holy submission, humility, and petition.

When we lead quietly and reverently by giving our deepest emotions up to God, we unleash His fountain of comfort and courage to get on with our lives and leadership. Too often those who find themselves caught in sin or a dire moment play to the crowd with outward signs of sorrow and contrition before they rend their hearts before the Lord. Brokenness that is not given to God can never heal. We can elicit sympathy for ourselves from others or receive a human pardon for wrongdoing. The pain of sin or tragedy may lessen with time, but new life and fresh starts will only come to those who lay their life's sorrows at the altar of the living God.

Our God is an awesome God of unlimited grace and kindness toward us. He longs to dry our tears and set us on a new path of peace and love. Rend your heart before Him and let the process of healing and rebirth in your life and in the lives of those you lead begin today.

Our Prayer: *Mighty God, we rend our hearts before You this day. The sin and calamity around us is more than we can bear. We lay it upon Your altar seeking forgiveness, mercy, kindness, love, and restoration. Show us how to lead others to true confession and restoration this day.* **Amen.**

Cosmic Disturbances

"EVEN EVENTS OF HEAVENLY SPACE ARE PART OF GOD'S PLAN AND OUR FUTURE"

"And I will show wonders in the heavens and the earth…and all the host of heaven shall be dissolved, and the heavens shall be rolled together as a scroll…the stars shall fall from heaven and the powers of the heavens shall be shaken…and I will show wonders in heaven above, and signs in the earth beneath.…"

FEATURED SCRIPTURES: JOEL 2:30; ISAIAH 34:4; MATTHEW 24:29; AND ACTS 2:19
BACKGROUND SCRIPTURES: ISAIAH 34:1–4; JOEL 2:28–32; MATTHEW 24:1–31: ACTS 2:14–21; AND REVELATION 6:12–17

The image of the entire cosmos being rolled together as a scroll gives us one of the most poignant descriptions of the awesome and total power of the living God. The prophets Isaiah and Joel, as well as the apostles Matthew and Luke, wrote of these cosmic disturbances. Jesus Himself described the sign of His Second Coming in terms of a cosmic disturbance. The prophetic and apocalyptic signs of the end of days may cause great panic and fear among unbelievers. Skeptics and scoffers ridicule it as religious science fiction. But to leaders of faith who are called by the God who made and commands the heavens, it should give great assurance that we are an integral part of this eternal plan. As humankind's understanding of the cosmos grows, our awe of its infinitesimal nature overwhelms even the scientist and theologian.

The formation and dying of stars in galaxies far away are merely the heavenly dances being performed for the return of Christ. The Big Bang of creation and the subsequent rolling up of the scroll of the cosmos is God's will and order at work. If these cosmic disturbances are so ordered and so orchestrated for God's purposes, then why should we doubt the strange events and circumstances of our heavenly call? Our mission for God will expand and contract like the universe itself. It can be shaken one day and called to order the next.

Our experiences in our call and our daily work is ordered and measured by the Creator. We serve the Christ who will return after all cosmic events unfold. We are blessed to share His very love and grace with those we serve each day. The small and seemingly insignificant chores we obediently perform each day are every bit as important to the fulfillment of God's plan as the cosmic disturbances millions of light years away.

The more astronomers learn about space, the more they must unlearn their previous assumptions about the size and function of the universe. Similarly, as leaders of faith learn more about the ways of God, the more we are forced to drop our old assumptions about the size and function of the Creator's call and purpose in our own lives. As each day unfolds in our lives, we see new manifestations of God's power and His unpredictability through twisting events.

Our world is often rocked by tragedy and human failure. We will find our world upended through conflict and loss of resources. But God will show us new wonders. God will take all the cosmic disturbances in our own lives and mold them and shape them into new creations of spiritual life and faith in Him. Watch in awe as God transforms you into the leader and person He desired for you to be from the beginning of time.

Our Prayer: *God of the Universe, we watch in awe as we behold the cosmic disturbances that are ordained for the coming of our Lord. Use us as Your heavenly instruments to bring others into a new life and hope in Christ.* **Amen.**

What's That Drowning Sound?

"GOD'S JUDGMENT AND RIGHTEOUSNESS ARE PURE, MIGHTY, AND EVER-FLOWING"

"I hate, I despise your feast days, and I will not smell in your solemn assemblies. Though ye offer me burnt offerings and your meat offerings, I will not accept them.... Take thou away from me the noise of thy songs; for I will not hear the melody of thy viols. But let judgment run down as waters, and righteousness as a mighty stream."

FEATURED SCRIPTURE: AMOS 5:21–24
BACKGROUND SCRIPTURE: AMOS 4—5

The imagery of flowing waters off the high rocks and the raging and mighty stream provides a human perspective of God's power. The prophet Amos gives us the language of God's judgment and righteousness that runs down as waters and a mighty stream. The drowning sound of them conquers all evil and injustice in our world today. Judgment and righteousness are consistent qualities of God. Man must always bend to God's measurements.

The people of Israel to whom Amos prophesied had oppressed the poor and failed to acknowledge God in their prosperity. They had become callous to the laws and holiness of the One True God. Even in their sin, they still came to God in false worship and with the rituals of sacrifice and offerings. But on this day, they were found sorely lacking. God refused their feast days and their solemn assemblies. He did not accept their burnt offerings or their songs. The drowning sound of the judgment and righteousness of God would not be polluted with the people's unclean hearts and unrepentant souls.

The flowing waters of judgment and the mighty stream of righteousness flow from the very throne of God. As leaders of faith, we are to be respectful and honor the holy and consistent nature of our Creator. Going through the motions and rituals of worship, sacrifice, song, and offerings as believers, even as we live sinful and unrepentant lives, is an affront to God. When we as leaders see injustice in our midst and the trampling upon the poor and innocent, yet we do nothing, we become as unacceptable to God as the people to whom Amos preached.

These waters are sweet and refreshing to leaders of faith who seek to right the wrongs and confront the injustice around them. Just as God was sickened by the false offerings of the unrepentant, He longs to bless the leaders and institutions that seek judgment and righteousness for the evils in our day.

Because we are called by God for holy tasks, we become the conveyers of God's love and righteousness through service to His children. Claim the flowing waters of God's judgment and the mighty streams of righteousness as your own as you lead today. The drowning sound of judgment and righteousness that comes from God's throne will overcome all the evil, prejudice, and injustice we will ever face.

Our Prayer: *Lord God, from Your throne we can hear the drowning sounds of judgment and righteousness. The waters and streams that flow from the holy throne bring relief to the poor, the oppressed, and the victims of man's sin against them. As a leader called by Your name, make me a seeker of justice and righteousness in all situations and for all people. Drown out the sounds of sin out Your judgment and righteousness.* **Amen.**

Saying The Right Thing At The Right Place

"CALLED TO MAKE BOLD PROCLAMATIONS TO POWERFUL PEOPLE IN SACRED PLACES"

"Then Amaziah the priest of Beth-el sent to Jeroboam King of Israel, saying, Amos hath conspired against thee in the midst of the house of Israel: the land is not able to bear all his words…. Also Amaziah said unto Amos, O thou seer, go, flee thee away into the land of Judah…. But prophesy not again any more at Beth-el: for it is the king's chapel, and it is the king's court."

FEATURED SCRIPTURE: AMOS 7:10, 12–13
BACKGROUND SCRIPTURES: AMOS 1:1–2; AMOS 7

Amos was not a trained prophet. In fact, he was a shepherd and a gatherer of fruit. God came to Amos as he tended his flock and gave him a specific call to leave his land of Judah, He was to go prophesy unto the people of Israel at the king's chapel at Beth-el with a bold message. For such a layman as Amos to leave his home and go to a different land to declare judgment against a king and nation in their sacred place was unusual, but Amos answered this holy call.

Not only are we as leaders of faith to be true in answering our calls, we are called to say the right thing at the right place to the right people. We must disregard our lack of pedigree and be bold enough to step into foreign territory and declare mighty things for God. God did not ask Amos to write a letter or to go to the Temple in Judah and from there prophesy against King Jeroboam of Israel. God told Amos to go directly to the king's own court and tell him the truth of the coming judgment. To the king's chief priest, Amaziah, Amos's action was conspiracy. To Amos, it was obedience to God.

Judah and Israel were divided kingdoms, but they were prosperous in the day of Amos. Yet for all their prosperity, the people of these nations had become decadent, corrupt, and idolatrous in their holy lands. God's judgment was imminent. It is often hardest to prophesy against and lead others in their times of prosperity. People don't want to hear bad news when they are enjoying the revelry of life. Corrupt kings and priests don't want to hear judgments of doom from a lowly shepherd or fruit gatherer who claims to have been given a word from God to share.

Like it did for Amos, God's call comes to us while we are performing the humble tasks of life. God asks us to bear His word to others, to be His lay-emissaries who go to rich and powerful congregations and organizations to bring the word of truth and justice. Amos preached against injustice and indifference to the poor. He lashed out against greed, waste, and corruption. He cautioned the powerful that their blasphemy against God and their idolatry would be brought under God's judgment. Do these conditions exist in places and institutions that you witness today? Maybe God is calling you to leave your flock, your comfort zone, to go and speak the right thing at the right place to the right people. Be bold. Be an Amos. Answer that call boldly today.

Our Prayer: *Lord of the prophets, give us Your bold calling today. Just as You called Amos to go to another nation and say the right thing at the right place to the right people, You call us to action against idolatry and injustice in our own communities. Give us, O Lord, the courage to face the powerful people in powerful places and to share Your words of truth with them.* **Amen.**

Rejoicing In Another's Destruction

"Leaders Who Revel in a Rival's Misfortune Come into Judgment"

"In the day that thou stoodest on the other side, in the day that the stranger carried away captive his forces, and foreigners entered into his gates, and cast lots upon Jerusalem, even thou was as one of them.... For the day of the Lord is near upon all the heathen: as thou hast done, it shall be done unto thee: thy reward shall return upon thine own head."

Featured Scriptures: Obadiah 11; and Obadiah 15
Background Scripture: The Book of Obadiah

The Edomites were the descendants of Esau, Jacob's twin brother. Esau was the elder of the two brothers, but through a series of actions by Jacob and his mother and by the providence of God, Jacob, not Esau, became the heir and birthright of Israel. The rivalry between the descendants of Esau and Jacob carried on for centuries.

Through history, the Edomites opposed Moses, Saul, David, and Solomon. They reveled in Israel's losses. Edomites participated in the looting of the sacred city of Jerusalem. The Edomites had become a strong and fierce people. They settled in the clefts of Petra, an impenetrable area protected by mountain walls. They were joined in a confederacy of tribes that also offered them protection. But on this day, their pride, as well as centuries of sin against God and their brothers and sisters in Israel, were about to be judged.

How often we see how longtime leadership rivalries can grow into grudges. We see blind partisanship grow into a viral infection that clouds the judgment of otherwise good leaders of faith. Just as the Edomites despised all the descendants of Jacob, we see the sin of jealousy and covetousness against leadership rivals bleed into our daily habits. This sin compounds itself as we relish and take enjoyment in the failure and demise of others.

Our lesson today from the Edomites and from the prophet Obadiah is that God does not condone our negative attitudes and actions of aggression against our rivals. To wish for another's destruction is not in the character of leaders of faith who have been called by God to redeem those who are lost. God told the Edomites: *as thou hast done, it shall be done unto thee: thy reward shall return upon thine own head."*

What joy and fellowship the Edomites missed over the years by not embracing the descendants of Jacob and following God Almighty. God's patience lasted several centuries, but His judgment did eventually come. Do you have your own rivalry or grudge that you need to confess? Have you wished the demise of another person for the wrong reason? Let Obadiah's message today bring all leaders of faith into confession and caution about reveling in a rival's destruction. All kingdoms and people are the Lord's.

Our Prayer: *Dear Lord, as leaders of faith, we do develop rivalries that become grudges. Convict us of our sinful thoughts and actions. Keep us from reveling in the failure of others, even if they are not good persons. Help us to stay grounded in Your love and meekness and power. May our example of love and charity to all, even our enemies, be the signs we send to others.* **Amen.**

Nineveh Or Tarshish

"Reluctant Leaders Cannot Escape God's Call to Action"

"Now the word of the Lord came unto Jonah…arise and go to Nineveh, that great city and cry against it…but Jonah rose up to flee unto Tarshish from the presence of the Lord…"

Featured Scripture: Jonah 1:1-3
Background Scripture: Jonah Chapters 1-4 & II Kings 14:23-29

The call was clear: "*Arise and go to Nineveh.*" God's call to a leader of faith is always clear. You, like Jonah, are the vessel God has chosen for a task of heavenly importance. Like Nineveh, the place where He calls you to serve may not be where you want to go. The message of Jonah holds great truths for those who are called to leadership journeys of faith. What is God calling you to do? Where is He telling you to go? Are you prepared to go to Nineveh?

The call to leadership is not always met with acceptance and excitement. Some of us run. Some of us plunge ourselves into obscure roles in life to avoid God and His call. Our lesson today tells us that what God wants, and those whom He calls, He gets. The people of Nineveh needed to hear God's word to them. God chose Jonah for the task. Jonah was a reluctant leader whom God tamed for the task at hand.

God's love for His people is constant and merciful. God doesn't desire that His people come to harm or perish. The people of Nineveh needed to hear the word of God through Jonah, yet Jonah fled from his calling. Jonah's flight from God toward Tarshish was met with great trials and tribulations. God was not taking no as an answer from Jonah. The purposes of God are more important than the comfort zones of reluctant leaders. We may not want to go to Nineveh, but if that is where the love of God needs to be shared, then we must go. To resist God is to risk the belly of the fish.

The trials and tribulations in our lives may sometimes represent the consequences of our unaccepted callings. When we resist or flee the voice and calling of God, He lets us know it. He makes us uncomfortable. He shakes our world until we submit. The storms of our lives are often the result of us not being in the will of God. It may take a big fish of life circumstances to transport us to the Nineveh of our calling.

As a result of Jonah's preaching, people were saved from God's wrath. Your calling is for a higher purpose. It is of eternal significance. God will provide your needs and will give you rest in the shade from the hardships you will face in accepting the call. The rewards for faithful leadership are great. Quit resisting the call. Go to Nineveh today. Hurting souls are waiting for a word of hope and a hand of rescue from God through His new leader of faith.

Our Prayer: *Lord, forgive us for resisting Your call. Help us to hear our call clearly and to see the task before us. Bless us with courage and excitement. Purge all reluctance from us. Instill in us an excitement to be part of an eternal plan and design. As we accept Your call to a leadership journey of faith, prepare the hearts of those we go to serve that they may accept the free gift of life everlasting.* **Amen.**

Getting Angry With God

"When Obedient Leaders See Outcomes They Don't Like"

"And God saw their works, that they turned from their evil way; and God repented of the evil, that he had said he would do unto them; and he did it not. But it displeased Jonah exceedingly, and he was very angry."

Featured Scripture: Jonah 3:10—4:1
Background Scripture: Jonah 3—4

Jonah did not want the assignment in the first place. He resisted his call from God. But God had his own reasons for calling Jonah into service. God wanted Jonah to go to Nineveh and preach against their wickedness. Nineveh was an enemy of Israel, and it was only through God's providence that Jonah went to Nineveh. Yet the people of Nineveh responded to Jonah's warning of their destruction. They repented, and God spared Nineveh.

A large metropolis heard God's message through Jonah and was saved. This outcome of deliverance should have been cause for celebration to most missionaries, but not to Jonah. Jonah once again stuns the reader of Scripture by shunning fellowship with God because of his anger over God's decision to spare Nineveh. Have you ever been angry with God? Has God ever given you a task to do, but when you did it, the outcome was not what you expected? Have you ever said, *Why, God?*

God's ways are not our ways. He calls the unlikely person for the unorthodox task. Even the most obedient of servants can misinterpret God's motives. In the case of Nineveh, God's love for the sinful people there was greater than His wrath. Every person counts to God. Leadership journeys of faith can seem to us to resemble tours of duty at Nineveh. We are reluctant to go, and we often find ourselves in consternation once we get there. Our view of a situation and God's view of a situation may not be compatible. But God commands our obedience, not our concurrence.

God may call us into a contest or a battle as a participant. We may accept the call to the contest with the expectation of winning. When we don't win, we get angry with God. God may have called us to play, but not to win. Our fellowship with God can be disrupted through our own anger, bitterness, and self-pity. Leaders of faith are blessed through our humility and obedience to the call and not our interpretations of the outcomes.

Let the God of the ages take care of judging Nineveh and our own institutions. Let us speak God's message of hope and repentance to those whom God has called us to lead. When we are busy serving others in need and rescuing those in danger, we will not have to question God. God's love for the sinful people of Nineveh was greater than Jonah's capacity to love his enemy. It should give us all great hope that a God of such great love, mercy, and forgiveness would call the least of us to noble tasks of leadership in faith.

Our Prayer: *God of love and forgiveness, show us where to go. Teach us to never be angry when You choose to spare Your wrath on our enemies. Make us obedient and humble servants who answer Your call to action with faith and assurance. Take our resentment and anger and wash them away in Christ's flood of love.* **Amen.**

Waiting And Winning

"God Often Calls Us to Stillness and Waiting Rather Than Action"

"Therefore I will look unto the Lord; I will wait for the God of my salvation: my God will hear me. Rejoice not against me, O mine enemy: when I fall, I shall arise; when I sit in darkness, the Lord shall be a light unto me.... But those that wait upon the Lord shall renew their strength; they shall mount up with wings as eagles; they shall run, and not be weary; and they shall walk, and not faint."

Featured Scriptures: Micah 7:7–8; and Isaiah 40:31
Background Scripture: Isaiah 40

A leader's natural tendency is to make something happen with speed and action. Even when under duress, a leader wants to intervene or charge forward into action to change the bad conditions. Our Scripture lesson today teaches leaders of faith that their call to action may, indeed, be a call to waiting. Waiting becomes action. God longs for and demands our reliance on Him. He wants us to acknowledge His supreme omnipotence over all time, circumstances, and events. He wants us to be humbled by His majesty and awed by His love and providence over His creation.

As leaders of faith, we can never be filled with the true power of God until we master the ability to worship God in awe and wonder and stillness. We must cease from our wanderings and reliance on our personal abilities. God will not come to us until we are still. He desires for us to wait for Him. It is only when we are sitting in darkness that we can see the light of God come. Sometimes that darkness may be the hopelessness of a situation. It may be the absence of resources and the dwindling hope for a better day. But waiting for God in our own darkness is our call to action today; God's light and strength are coming.

In Isaiah 40, the prophet told the people of Israel that God was in control and His strength was available to them if they would wait on Him. For God's strength to become our strength requires that we become still by waiting on His deliverance. Waiting does not mean that circumstances change right away. Waiting does not make the pain and suffering immediately disappear. Waiting does, however, allow the perfect timing and purpose of God's eternal plan to be revealed in our lives.

Leaders of faith must become leaders of patience. We must become leaders who call our followers to times of calm and patient waiting. Waiting in awe and worship sends out a holy call for deliverance. Don't wait in desperation. Wait in confidence that God is in control and that He loves you and desires for you blessings greater than you can ever imagine. Today your call to action is a call to wait in wonder and anticipation of the coming salvation of God. As you wait, you will become renewed with God's strength instead of your own. You will soar again on eagle's wings. You will run and not be weary, and you will walk again in victory and not be faint.

Our Prayer: *We wait for You, O Lord, in awe and wonder. You command us to be still in the darkness and wait. Our enemies may laugh at our inaction or the blind faith we have for our deliverance, but we wait on You in supreme confidence that salvation and victory are assured. As we wait, renew our strength, O Lord. Renew our hearts, minds, and bodies for Your service. Give us victory over every challenge in our way for Your sake.* **Amen.**

Litmus Test For Leadership Decisions

"Becoming a Micah 6:8 Leader"

"He hath showed thee, O man, what is good; and what doth the Lord require of
thee, but to do justly, and to love mercy, and to walk humbly with thy God…"
Featured Scripture: Micah 6:8
Background Scripture: Micah 6:1–8; Deuteronomy 10:12; Isaiah 1:17; Hosea 6:6; and Genesis 18:19

The demand to make sound daily decisions in leadership can put stress on leaders who are not grounded in something stronger than their own intuition. For leaders of faith, crafting sound decisions fluidly each day requires that we have an imbedded spiritual compass that guides us in that process. The Law and the prophets of the Old Testament were consistent in what that should be. The Lord spoke through Micah and laid out that litmus test for leaders.

Micah wrote about what the Lord required of a leader and what was good: *"Do justice; love mercy; and walk humbly each day with God."* The prophet Hosea said to *"desire mercy not sacrifice and knowledge more than burnt offerings."* Isaiah said to *"seek judgment; relieve the oppressed; judge the fatherless and plead for the widow."*

Doing the right thing with all humility before God is the modern-day equivalent of these instructions. Become merciful, not sacrificial. It is better to desire to know the real truth, by God's grace, than it is to later make amends when things go wrong. Seek fair judgment for others while also relieving their oppression. Seek justice for the orphans and plead for the well-being of the most vulnerable among us.

Wiring your spirit with the compass of Micah 6:8 will take more than desire and will-power; it will take prayer and anointing by God's grace. It will mean that as a leader of faith, you will have to sort through the false expectations of others before coming to the right conclusion. It may require that you leave your associates and take a lonely, but righteous stand in rendering a *Micah 6:8 Decision* as a leader. It may mean that you choose an underdog over a donor or a widow over a connected friend. It may mean you are subjected to ridicule within your own peer group.

God was repeatedly reminding earthly kings and rulers of what the holy litmus test of leadership should be. He laid it out in Genesis and Deuteronomy and reiterated it through the prophets. Jesus Himself would live out the litmus test of leadership and ask us to follow us as well. The result of making the right decisions using God's holy litmus test will bring peace, justice, and prosperity for many. It will bring blessings on those we lead and set an example for those leaders who follow us. Pray for and install your decision-making compass, the *Micah 6:8 Model.*

Our Prayer: *Lord God, be with all leaders of faith that we may make decisions based on the simple but real holy precepts that You set forth for us in the Scripture. May we do justice, love mercy, and walk with You each day in the humility of leadership and love. Forgive us when we seek the path of least resistance in our decision-making. Cover us with Your blessings as we strive to live by Your Law and Christ's example.* **Amen.**

Something To Know About The One Who Calls You

"God Is Good and Strong and Knows Those Who Trust in Him"

"The Lord is slow to anger, and great in power, and will not at all acquit the wicked: the Lord hath his way in the whirlwind and in the storm, and the clouds are the dust of his feet…. The Lord is good, a strong hold in the day of trouble; and he knoweth them that trust in him."

Featured Scripture: Nahum 1:3, 7

Background Scriptures: Nahum 1:1–7; Psalm 111:10; Proverbs 22:4; and 2 Timothy 2:19

Before you answer your call and go to work, it might be a good idea to get to know something about the One who has called you. In his prophecy against Nineveh, Nahum took time in his writings to tell us something about the nature of God. It is prudent and wise for us to learn more about the nature of the God we are called to serve.

A reading of Nahum tells us quickly that our God is great and powerful, a stronghold in our time of trouble. God also knows intimately those whom He has called and those who trust in Him. But God is also a jealous God and protective of His own. If He calls you, He desires your allegiance and full measure of devotion. Moonlighting on God's time is not acceptable.

God is unyielding in His pursuit of wickedness. While Nahum depicted God as wrathful against His enemies, it is actually comforting to know that God's sense of justice is absolute. If we are part of His plan for goodness and love, we should have no fear. Leaders who witness first-hand man's inhumanity to man should find solace in God's unchanging character. Though evil may seem to go unpunished, the Scripture tell us that darkness will pursue His enemies.

On the other hand, God is also slow to anger. He is patient and gives those who have gone astray a time and a way to come home. Before exercising His judgment, He gives the evildoers a chance to repent. Even in the midst of storms in our lives, God maintains His design and purpose for us. The Scriptures can instill into a leader a healthy fear, respect, and admiration of God. No injustice can ever stand up to God's indignation. No act or thought or deed will ever escape His judgment.

Our heavenly employer is certainly demanding. But His love, care, and protection for us is eternal and all-encompassing as we serve others in His name. His character is pure and beyond our own comprehension. When we follow Him and live in His care, we can unlock mysteries and summon new abilities that we never knew existed. If you trust Him, He will know it. He will be your stronghold in trouble, and your service will be rewarded.

Our Prayer: *God, You are our stronghold in the day of trouble. Your character is perfect and beyond our human comprehension. Teach us to trust You even more and unleash the power that is freely available to us. Be slow to judge us and quick to forgive us, O Lord. Let all we do bring glory to the Kingdom of Heaven.* **Amen.**

Silent Before Him

"Communication and Communion with God Begins with Our Silence"

"But the Lord is in his holy temple: let all the earth keep silence before him…. Be
silent, O all flesh, before the Lord: for he is raised up out of his holy habitation."
Featured Scriptures: Habakkuk 2:20; and Zechariah 2:13
Background Scripture: Psalm 4:4; 33:8; 68:5; Isaiah 57:15–16; and Matthew 7:7–11

We are troubled on many fronts. We have great needs. Our hearts are heavy and desperation
is setting in. We need to have a serious talk with God. It is a spiritual emergency…

Every leader of faith will experience moments when they come to their wits' end and must
petition God for assistance and relief. Surely the God who called us to this great task of service
for Him understands our need to shout aloud to Him. But while God longs to commune with us
and is able and willing to hear our cries, prayers, and petitions, we often falter in our relationship
with Him because we never cease our pleas and become silent before Him.

Being silent before Him means we must empty our minds and hearts of any personal thought.
We must find a way to mentally and spiritually kneel silently alone before His throne. We must
bow before Him, in awe and wonder. Let all anxiety flow out of your body. Let your entire being
rest upon Him in reverent silence. Stay in that silence and awe until God acknowledges you and
allows your thoughts and words to flow to Him. This act of silence before Him will empower you
and allow the Holy Spirit to petition the right things to God on your behalf.

God already knows you better than you know yourself. He knows your darkest sins and
your deepest desires. He knows your heart and your future. What God longs for is your silence,
your worship, and your faithful trust in His loving care for you. Our silence before Him is one
way to acknowledge His omnipotence and glory. His holy habitation is a place for the humble
and the contrite. When we come to Him in humility, contrition, and silence, we are coming
home to where we belong.

The ongoing practice of becoming silent before God empowers us in ways we never imagined. Once we have given God His holy silence, He can open our eyes and hearts to new revelations
and understanding. Becoming silent before God is not an easy task for many of us. Our lives are
crammed with busyness and activities, and our time before God becomes compromised. But we
must find silence before Him. When we cannot seem to find that silent place, we should stop our
thought processes and simply let our minds clear before God in meditation.

Sometimes our silence before God leads us to conviction of an unconfessed sin. It may
unlock a new love for a spouse or friend. It may prompt us to want to pray and petition God for
His providence with regard to a stranger or a world event. It may lead to a new call to service or
allow God to show us a vision of the future. Or, more simply, our silence before God may bring
silence back to us. God's silence does not mean that He did not hear us or that He does not want
speak to us. It simply means that we were obedient. God will always come to us if we remain
silent before Him.

Our Prayer: *O Lord, I am now still and silent before You…* **Amen.**

When All You Have Is Stripped Away, Rejoice!

"OUR JOY IN BARRENNESS UNLEASHES GOD'S STRENGTH"

"Although the fig tree shall not blossom, neither shall fruit be on the vines; the labor of the olive shall fail, and the fields shall yield no meat; the flock shall be cut off from the fold, and there shall be no herd in the stalls: yet I will rejoice in the LORD, I will joy in the God of my salvation. The LORD God is my strength…and he will make me to walk upon high places."

FEATURED SCRIPTURE: HABAKKUK 3:17–19
BACKGROUND SCRIPTURE: HABAKKUK 3

It is in our poverty and hardship that our worship and praise to God must sound sweetest to Him. When all seems lost and earthly ruin is all around us, we must rejoice. The prayer of the Old Testament prophet Habakkuk may seem out of place in a world where people measure God's blessings by earthly prosperity, power, and privilege. However, Habakkuk shows us how in our utter barrenness we can fall into God's arms through praise and adoration. This rejoicing in our barrenness can unlock new dimensions of God's love, comfort, and power.

Dead trees, fruitless vines, no cattle in the field, and no hay in the barn—all of these are temporary conditions. Our eternal salvation is assured, and the Author of our future is a God of immeasurable capacity and strength. When the barns are full, when life is great and money is in the vault, it is easy to raise our hands to heaven and rejoice. We unleash the power of the throne of God when we rejoice in our barrenness and tribulation.

Bad things will happen to great leaders. The plagues of this life will no doubt visit you. But when life feels empty and our fortunes are turning sour, God may be seeking our praise the most. In the time of our own barren fields, we need to see God clearly and feel His love toward us the most. God longs to hear our praise and thanksgiving in all situations. He longs to give us grace and blessing, as well. When your fields are bare, God can replant His failure resistant crops. Sometimes nothing but a clean slate will unleash our creativeness and willingness to try new and bold things.

God desires for us to walk upon the high places. From the barren soil of life's disasters, new careers, congregations, and organizations can be built. From the fruitless vine, a new crop can be planted that will yield the sweeter fruits of new friendships and restored relationships. From the poverty of our empty barns come a new purpose and a new entrepreneurial zeal. But it all begins with our humility and reliance on God alone. It all begins when we rejoice in our barrenness!

Our Prayer: *Lord, when the chips are down, when our lives seem stripped of all joy, help us to rejoice in You. You are worthy of praise in all of life's situations and circumstances. We rely on You alone and place every day and moment in Your hands. From our own barrenness, we praise You and lift our voices to You. Make us to be reborn and walk in the high places through Your grace and blessing.* **Amen.**

Gathered For A Solemn Assembly

"The Righteous, the Meek, and the Sorrowful Can Be Fully Restored"

"Seek ye the Lord, all ye meek of the earth, which have wrought his judgment; seek righteousness, seek meekness: it may be ye shall be hid in the day of the Lord's anger…. I will gather them that are sorrowful for the solemn assembly, who are of thee, to whom the reproach of it was a burden. Behold, at that time I will undo all that afflict thee…."

Featured Scriptures: Zephaniah 2:3; and 3:18–19
Background Scripture: Zephaniah 2—3

Regardless of the doom predicted by the prophets, hope still existed for the righteous, meek, and sorrowful. Zephaniah wrote that those among us who seek righteousness and meekness in times of trouble will not only be spared, but be gathered together in the end for a solemn assembly. Those who are called by God can have hope that He will, indeed, save us and reunite us with the saints in this life or the next.

The festivals of the people of Israel were seven-day affairs. On the eighth day, a solemn assembly of praise and worship to God was held. The people were set apart from all else for the solemn assembly of God's elect. Leaders of faith who answer a call to duty are also set apart to perform special tasks for God. We often perform those tasks in the midst of turmoil and conflict. War, injustice, or poverty may seem so cruel that we cannot see how the final outcome could ever be positive, yet God has comfort for those who seek righteousness and meekness in these times.

God provides a cleft of protection for those who must serve in situations that appear to be hell on earth. He hides us, protects us, and allows us to survive and serve another day. Our work is not in vain. As leaders, we, too, must create sanctuaries and refuges for our followers who step out in service. We should reward others in our own solemn assemblies by gathering and rewarding the sorrowful. Congregations and institutions of faith must become sacred and solemn assemblies that reserve the right to accept the righteous, the meek, and the sorrowful.

We should lift up the downtrodden and provide a second chance and a fresh start for the repentant. People whose hearts are changed by their lowly circumstances often need their own solemn assembly in order to be made whole. Those who have been imprisoned or fought off addiction may need our safe refuge. Those who have experienced broken hearts and relationships may need a solemn assembly of new friends and new acceptance.

What afflicts you? What sorrows do you have that need to be comforted? How can you become a better leader in righteousness and meekness? God promises us that when hearts are right toward Him as we seek Him, we can be set apart in a solemn assembly with those He has gathered. As God offers it to us, let us offer it to others. Our institutions can be covered with God's love and forgiveness and become solemn assemblies of the redeemed where all afflictions of life are undone.

Our Prayer: *Lord God, You are a God of love and forgiveness. We seek refuge from judgment with righteous minds and meek hearts. Protect us from evil and gather us into safe places. Gather us into the solemn assemblies where we can be set apart from the afflictions of this life. Help us, Lord, in our own leadership to make solemn assemblies of healing and hope for the hurting around us.* **Amen.**

From Contentment To Work In Obedience

"When God Calls a Leader and People to a Task, Start Building"

"Thus saith the Lord of hosts; Consider your ways. Go up into the mountain, and bring wood, and build the house; and I will take pleasure in it, and I will be glorified, saith the Lord."

Featured Scripture: Haggai 1:7–8
Background Scripture: Haggai 1—2

The Temple construction that had begun around fourteen years earlier had been halted. The people of Judah were still in Babylonian captivity, but they had become content, enjoying their homes and lives in a new land. These chosen people of God were not convinced that it was time to start rebuilding the Temple. But God had other plans.

The Lord came to the prophet Haggai and instructed him to go to the governor of Judah, Zerubbabel, and the high priest, Joshua, the son of Josedech, and tell them that the Lord of hosts wanted them to go to work and build the house.

Even though the people of Judah were surviving, they were not prospering due to the economic conditions of the day. God was causing the labor and savings of the unmotivated flock of Judah to waste away due to their disobedience. Haggai wrote:*"Ye looked for much, and lo it came to little; and when ye brought it home, I did blow upon it. Why…because of mine house that is waste…."* If the Lord's house was left to rot and languish, the people would not prosper.

Do we see signs of contentment in the congregations and organizations we lead today? How often do leaders of faith and the people they lead put off the tough projects and instead seek to enjoy the fruits of their earlier success. You know what great challenges lie ahead, but you are content to stay in your nice home and wait for a better day. The message of the Lord of hosts through Haggai is simple: If God calls a leader and those who follow to a task, they must go to work now. Don't put off for tomorrow what the Lord calls you to do today.

When the remnant of God's people heeded His call and began to build the Temple, God took care of their needs. Haggai 2:4 says: *"Yet now be strong O Zerubbabel, saith the Lord; and be strong, O Joshua, son of Josedech, the high priest; and be strong, all ye people of the land, saith the Lord, and work: for I am with you, saith the Lord of Hosts!"* Nowhere in Scripture does God call us to a mighty task without giving us the provision to complete our portion of it.

God instructed the prophet, who informed the governor and high priest, who asked the people to go to work for the Lord. Leaders of faith are part of such a chain of responsibility and are to be held accountable for the work that needs to be done for the Kingdom of God. You may not be building a temple, but you do need to tackle a holy task the Lord has for you to do today.

Our Prayer: *O Lord of hosts, give us work to do for Your Kingdom. Help us as leaders of faith to hear that call and to lead our people to accomplish Your objectives in this world. Help us to move out of our comfort zones and heed that call today. We claim Your promise that You will take care of our needs if we answer Your call to go to work today for the Kingdom.* **Amen.**

Me, Satan, And Filthy Garments Before the Lord

"God Redeems, Cleanses, and Anoints Us Regardless of Circumstance"

"And he showed me Joshua the high priest standing before the angel of the Lord, and Satan standing at his right hand to resist him. And the Lord said unto Satan, The Lord rebuke thee…. Now Joshua was clothed with filthy garments and stood before the angel…. Behold, I have caused thy iniquity to pass and I will clothe thee with change of garment…thus saith the Lord of hosts; If thou wilt walk in my ways and if thou wilt keep my charge, then thou shall also judge my house.…"

Featured Scripture: Zechariah 3:1–4, 7
Background Scriptures: Zechariah 3; and Revelation 12:10

As leaders of faith, many of us must have felt like Joshua the high priest when we received our callings from God. Our lives were a wreck, filled with sin. Our lifestyles were not admirable. The devil and his influence had run amok in our daily lives. But God saw something worth redeeming in us; He called us before His throne, claimed us, and anointed us into His holy service. Just as God called Joshua the priest to lead and judge Israel, God calls us all out of our own filthy garments and imperfection into heavenly service.

The angel of the Lord in today's Scripture is the preincarnate Christ. It was Jesus who ultimately came and claimed His people through His gifts and ministry on earth. The power of this prophecy and the fulfillment of that promise gives all leaders of faith hope for the future. God claims and cleanses us from our failures and sets us into positions where we can lead and serve others. Our Lord tells us, as He told Joshua the priest, that if we walk in His ways and keep His charge, He will help us lead and provide us with access to the very throne of God.

What filthy garment do you wear today? Is it pride or bitterness? What lifestyle choices do you cling to that would prevent you from serving God to the fullest? What demon holds you back as you seek to serve God? Is it a selfish, personal pursuit, or unbridled ambition, or a poor personal habit or addiction? Is it an unrepaired relationship? Each of us brings our own personal brokenness into leadership callings of faith. Yet we, too, can be wiped clean as we petition God to rebuke our devils and set us on the true path of new life with Him.

We also must refrain from casting judgment upon others who are called into service. We may encounter other unlikely leaders of faith who have filthy garments and lead questionable lives, God calls the imperfect for the most holy of tasks. God takes us and our filthy garments and redeems all that is lost; He claims what He loves. Let His immeasurable grace clothe you with new brilliance and confidence as you lead today.

Our Prayer: *O Lord, we come before the throne of grace in our imperfection, sin, and filthy garments and fall before You. The devil seeks to sift us as wheat and spoil our lives and ministries. We give it all to You, O Lord. Like Joshua the priest, we need new garments, renewed hope, and access to Your redemptive love. Help us to walk in Your ways and keep the charge of our callings so we can be good witnesses for Your Kingdom.* **Amen.**

Cheerful Givers Make Trusted Leaders

"Cheerful Generosity in Giving Is a Good Measure of a Great Leader"

"Bring ye all the tithes into the storehouse…and prove me now herewith, saith the Lord of hosts, if I will not open you the windows of heaven, and pour you out a blessing, that there shall not be room enough to receive it…. Every man according as he purposeth in his heart, so let him give; not grudgingly, or of necessity: for God loveth a cheerful giver. And God is able to make all grace abound toward you; that ye, always having all sufficiency in all things, may abound to every good work."

Featured Scriptures: Malachi 3:10; and 2 Corinthians 9:7–8
Background Scriptures: 2 Corinthians 9:6–15; Deuteronomy 14:22—15:8; and Luke 6:38

The Scriptures certainly command the people of God tithe of their bounty and income. But today's lesson is not as much about the command to tithe, as it is about how to develop the heart of a cheerful giver. God promises to open a storehouse of blessings upon those who perfect the art of cheerful giving. The selfless giving of time and resources by a leader is a sign that that leader has a deep love and affection for God and those he or she leads. Cheerful givers make trusted leaders.

God speaks to us today in our Scripture by asking us to take His challenge of cheerful giving to heart. God gave this challenge: to prove Him, bring in the tithes to the storehouse; and He will pour out blessings that are so great, we can't even count them. God also promises cheerful givers that they will receive all the grace and sufficiency they need. God sees the many begrudging hearts who make a tithe or donation out of a sense of obligation. How God's own heart must ache as He provides blessings and provisions to us, only to see us give back to Him out of duty instead of with cheerful love.

Leaders of faith who are blessed to have been called to holy service for God should become the epitome of the cheerful giver. If your heart is not overflowing with a joyful need to help others and give freely of your time and resources, you should reassess your life and work. People whom you lead will sense quickly whether or not you are a cheerful giver. Cheerful givers inspire others to give and serve. Cheerful givers reflect the personality of God, who gives to us all in such abundance that we can scarcely fathom His love for us. It was God who gave us the Unspeakable Gift of His only Son.

If your organization is lagging behind, begin to follow the cheerful giver principle. Organizations that are thriving are usually being led by cheerful givers. Make your heart right with God. Pray for joy and thankfulness to rain down upon you and those you lead. Bring your tithes into God's storehouse and watch His blessing pour out upon the purpose for which you have been called …for God loves a cheerful giver!

Our Prayer: *Gracious God, make us cheerful givers. Help us, O Lord, to take the challenge You laid out for us by trying to outgive You. Even in our poverty and personal struggles, make us cheerful givers. Never let our faith wane as we freely give of our time and resources back to You and Your children. Anoint leaders of faith with loving, generous, and cheerful hearts.* **Amen.**

Wise Men And Wicked Kings

"Both Good and Evil Forces Will Surround Our Miracles"

"Now when Jesus was born in Bethlehem of Judaea in the days of Herod the king, behold there came wise men from the east to Jerusalem, saying, where is he that is born King of the Jews for we have seen his star in the east, and are come to worship him. When Herod the king had heard these things, he was troubled, and all Jerusalem with him.… And he sent them to Bethlehem, and said, go and search diligently for the young child; and when ye have found him, bring me word again, that I may come and worship him also."

FEATURED SCRIPTURE: MATTHEW 2:1–3, 8
BACKGROUND SCRIPTURE: MATTHEW 2

The greatest gift and miracle of all time is the gift of Christ through His incarnation into our world. The timeless Christmas story of the wise men from the East following the bright star and bearing gifts for the newborn Savior is one of the wonderful images of that blessed season. But intricately tied into the story of the wise men is the story of a wicked king who sought to destroy this miracle of our salvation.

In the midst of the miracles of our faith exist both good and evil. Wise men and wicked kings will surround all that we do in service to our Savior. The plight of Christ was predicted centuries before it happened. Our own fate, too, lies in the eternal plans of an awesome God. The reality that both good and evil appear in our own times of miracles ties us more closely to our faith and should strengthen our reliance upon and obedience to God. Joseph and the wise men listened to the voice of the angel in the midst of the miracle and thus saved the life of Christ for all time.

In leadership journeys of faith, we can often see cycles when we are imperiled by danger and miraculously delivered. Once delivered, we often quickly see danger return. Our congregations and organizations can experience great times of revival that quickly give way to tragedy or controversy. We may experience great personal triumphs or blessings only to witness our rivals become overwrought with jealousy and wield their maliciousness against us.

How are we to respond when wise men and wicked kings appear simultaneously in the midst of our miracles? Do we retreat or go forward? The story of the wise men, Herod, and Jesus tells us that both good and evil persons lend testimony to great things. One wants to worship and the other wants to destroy. Satan's plan is to destroy and diminish our good works and great miracles. Like Herod the king, powerful people may seek us out with apparent good intent, but in reality they have come to steal our joy and happiness.

If we are called by God to serve others, then our miracles become part of the heavenly realm and are subject to seizure by the evil one. But we, too, like those called in the lesson today, are under God's holy cloak of protection. We are to be discerning, cautious, and obedient in our joy, especially when our miracles appear.

Our Prayer: *Lord of Wonder, we give praise and thanksgiving for the gift of the Baby Jesus. We are joyful when we read of the wise men bringing gifts to our newborn King. Protect us in our own time of miracles. Make us discerning and obedient so we may escape the evil plots that seek to destroy our work and witness for Christ.* **Amen.**

From Triumph To The Wilderness Of Temptation

"Temptations and Struggles Wedge Themselves Amidst a Leader's Success"

"And Jesus, when he was baptized, went up straightway out of the water: and, lo, the heavens were opened unto him , and he saw the Spirit of God descending like a dove, and lighting upon him: And lo a voice from heaven, saying, 'This is my beloved Son, in whom I am well pleased.' Then was Jesus led up of the Spirit into the wilderness to be tempted of the devil."

Featured Scripture: Matthew 3:16—4:1
Background Scripture: Matthew 3:16—4:11

A highlight in the earthly life of Christ is the moment of His baptism by John the Baptist. This triumphant event marked the beginning of His formal ministry. A reluctant John (who felt unworthy) performed the requested task when asked by Christ. As Jesus was baptized, the heavens opened and the Spirit of God Himself descended upon Christ. What a glorious moment of victory for Jesus as the Spirit of God descended like a dove and the Father pronounced that: *"This is my beloved Son, in whom I am well pleased."*

After this glorious moment in the faith, one would expect there to be a celebration or at least a sermon. We might expect there to be a revival or a shared meal in which Jesus told John and his disciples the wondrous plan of God. It was not to be. At this most glorious moment, Christ was called immediately by the Spirit into temptation in the wilderness. His triumph led Christ to encounter Satan in the wilderness.

How often do we as leaders experience a triumph, victory, or glorious achievement only to see an ensuing trial or tribulation lurking ahead? Often at our times of greatest achievement, we become saddled with crushing burdens and temptations. Is this a sign of failed leadership, or merely a part and portion for us of the same wilderness journey that Christ traveled in God's bigger plan?

Jesus was hungry and thirsty as the devil tempted Him. Yet Jesus prevailed by the very Word of God. Even though He was weak and exhausted, He triumphed and moved along to the next phase of His earthly mission. It is the very nature of leadership to go continually from triumphs to trials to triumphs again.

Leaders of faith should expect wilderness experiences. We should expect that our triumphs will lead to trials and back to triumph as we stay in the call and hand of God. Bad news will often follow good news. Wilderness trials will often come to us at a happy time as the devil seeks to disrupt our positive momentum in our leadership journeys of faith.

Be ready as temptation takes you to a new wilderness experience. But remember the example of Christ in His wilderness experience. He was armed with God's Word, a sense of mission, and total reliance upon the provision of the heavenly Father. You, too, will prevail in your triumphs and temptations this day if you rely on Christ as your sole provision!

Our Prayer: *Lord Jesus, nurture us as we go into the wilderness and trials of our own leadership callings of faith. Help us to know that our triumphs are merely setups for more temptations and trials. Arm us with Your strength and the knowledge of Your Word. When we hunger, feed us. As our callings and missions in life take us to the wilderness, go with us and sustain us, so we can become a blessing to others.* **Amen.**

Rubbing Salt, Shining Light

"SEASON WITH SALT UNTIL IT ALMOST BURNS, BUT SHINE LIGHT UNTIL ALL CAN SEE"

"Ye are the salt of the earth: but if the salt has lost his savor, wherewith shall it be salted? It is thenceforth good for nothing, but to be cast out, and to be trodden under foot of men. Ye are the light of the world…. Let your light so shine before men, that they may see your good works, and glorify your Father which is in heaven."

FEATURED SCRIPTURE: MATTHEW 5:13–14, 16

BACKGROUND SCRIPTURES: MATTHEW 5:13–16; JOHN 8:12; AND COLOSSIANS 4:5–6

Images of salt and light can stimulate the senses; taste, smell, sight, pain. The words of Christ tell believers to be spiritual salt and light. Just as salt seasons and preserves food, we must become the spiritual salt that preserves and seasons those we lead. Just as light shows us where to walk and how to see, we must become leaders of the light of truth and life.

As leaders of faith, we will be large purveyors of both salt and light in our own congregations and organizations. We must become leaders who give our institutions the flavor and understanding of the mission. We must also become leaders who rub salt on the resources of our institutions so they will be preserved and last through time and adversity. Salt in the right amount can flavor food, or in the wrong amount render it inedible. It can bring pleasure to the tongue or make a wound burn.

As we provide light as leaders, we become beacons by which others find their roles to play and the proper work to do. Light is not only vision and planning; light is accountability that shines in the dark places where others are scared to go. Leaders of light must illuminate the truth and justice of life's events and circumstances. Leaders of light must seek the dark places of despair as they rescue others with the light of new opportunity and hope.

Christ cautions us that our salt can lose its savor and that our lights can be hidden under bushels. Even though we are the recipients and custodians of salt and light, we can be cast aside if we do not share our blessings with others. Leaders of faith who are called to God's service are given an abundance of salt and light. The task of our calling is both heavenly and awesome. Salt and light are our assets. Leaders of faith season every situation with the salt of humor, the flavor of love, and the preserving power of wisdom. Leaders of faith attract others with the light of their charisma, character, integrity, and skill.

Pray that God helps you to exercise good judgment in using your salt and light. As you rub your salt and shine your light each day, know that you are Christ's own instrument of love and service to others. For spiritual salt and light to retain its qualities, it must be placed in the care of the Master and replenished with prayer, study, and humility. Let your salt bring flavor to the hurting, and let your light bring hope to the lost.

Our Prayer: *Lord Jesus, You are the salt of our salvation and the Light of the World. We give thanks for salt and light in our spiritual walk. Lord, make us servants and leaders of both salt and light. Craft us so that our lives and service bring flavor and hope to the hurting and the lost. Protect us so that we never lose our savor or hide the light within us.* **Amen.**

Anxious About Provisions

"GOD PROVIDES THE DAILY RESOURCES FOR THOSE CALLED TO HIS SERVICE"

"Therefore take no thought, saying, what shall we eat, or what shall we drink, or wherewithal shall we be clothed? For your heavenly Father knoweth that ye have need of all these things. But seek ye first the kingdom of God, and his righteousness; and all these things shall be added unto you."

FEATURED SCRIPTURE: MATTHEW 6:31–33
BACKGROUND SCRIPTURE: MATTHEW 6:25–34

Those heeding the call of God to His service will almost immediately be confronted with a large question of faith: Where will the resources come from to complete this great task? God often calls us before we are shown the funds, education, networks, or a clear road map to complete the journey. It can be awe-inspiring to hear the call to service, but it can be equally daunting to see the challenge of completing the mission.

Becoming a leader of faith by accepting a heavenly task defies conventional worldly thinking. Doing something for God often means venturing out on faith alone. We will immediately hit the roadblocks and hear the questions and criticism from our friends and family members. How will you pay for it? You aren't even trained in that area. Who can open those kinds of doors for you? Certainly there are others more qualified than you? You don't have any experience doing that, and besides, it is very dangerous.

In today's Scripture, Christ tells us that our journeys of faith will require constant and daily reliance on God's provision. Not only will our callings and early work be challenged, but at every point in the journey, we will need to look to heaven for our daily bread. This childlike dependence on God creates humility and maintains a constant connection to the Almighty. Were God to show us the cache of blessings all at once, we all might fall into self-reliance and think that it was our skill instead of God's hand that paves the way for us each day. Seeking God and His will each day allows our lives to be spiritual vessels instead of merely earthly bodies.

Anxiety over our circumstances can lead to depression and cause us to step outside of God's divine plan. Anxiety over provision is a breeding ground that allows Satan's influence into our daily affairs. When we praise God when the cupboard is bare, miracles begin to happen. When we walk on the next mile without knowing if we will be able to return, angels fly to our rescue. When we accept the call of God to do something great and announce it to the ridicule of others, Christ Himself takes us by the hand to lead us along the way. Don't be anxious about your next meal, an unpaid bill, or doors slammed in your face; these are merely faith hurdles to leap so you can complete a heavenly race. Glory and reward await you at the finish line if you will seek God first and let your needs be met in God's time.

Our Prayer: *Heavenly Father, we praise You for calling us to service this day. Our bank accounts ares low, our hearts are heavy, our challenges are steep, but we seek Your will and keep moving ahead. We know our provision has already been secured and opportunities will abound that this moment we cannot yet see. Give us the strength, confidence, and courage to continue. Never let us become anxious or downhearted about our present circumstances. Renew our hearts and minds this moment to Your service.* **Amen.**

Splinters And Logs

"LEADERS MUST LOOK INWARD AND ACKNOWLEDGE THEIR OWN FAULTS FIRST"

"And why beholdest thou the splinter that is in thy brother's eye, but considerest not the log that is in thine own eye?"
FEATURED SCRIPTURE: MATTHEW 7:3
BACKGROUND SCRIPTURES: MATTHEW 7:1–5; AND LUKE 6:37, 41–42

Honest, inward, and constant self-evaluation is crucial to maintaining healthy character. For leaders of faith, confession and self-improvement are necessary for success. When we are called to holy tasks for God, new spiritual power becomes available to us. God instills into us a conscience and a compass for self-reflection that cleanses our hearts. Leaders only stumble when they take that reflective ability and project it outward into the quick judgment of others.

Our Scripture lesson today talks about the splinters and logs of fault, failure, and sin. The splinter of imperfection is a fault we find in our friends, coworkers, and competitors. Jesus warns us strongly to be very careful in evaluating and judging the sins and faults of others while failing to acknowledge the logs of sin protruding from our own lives. Judging others brings us into God's judgment. If we will concentrate our efforts on removing the faults from our own lives, we will have no time nor need to judge others.

A splinter-and-log theology of leadership can help us stifle our desire to judge others. By resisting the need to judge others, we become better friends and leaders. As we work toward our own self-improvement, we develop a heart of forgiveness and empathy toward others. We see that sin and imperfection abound not only in our lives, but in the lives of others. Every leader will make mistakes and poor decisions. Our empathy and compassion grows for others as we recognize the difficulty of living a pure life.

Leaders of faith fail when they become hypocrites. Leaders who judge others are leaders who eventually fail. Jesus was harder on the hypocrite than the original sinner. The Savior reminds us that judgment is His department and that purity of heart and intention matters most of all. The splinter in the eye of our neighbor is easily plucked out when we love them, not judge them. When we as leaders of faith are totally focused on cleansing our own lives of sin, others notice.

Removing the logs from our eyes involves kneeling and hard confession to God. It involves seeking the forgiveness of others. It involves tackling each new day with a fresh resolve to be a more benevolent and merciful leader of faith. Harvest your own logs, and Jesus will pluck the splinters from others so we all may see the light of God's love more clearly.

Our Prayer: *Lord Jesus, forgive us when we have been judgmental of others. Forgive us when we fail to see our own sins and shortcomings as leaders. Create in us a heart for acceptance of others as we confess our faults and bad habits to You. Judge us mercifully with Your everlasting love. Make us pure and more able to do Your will in all things each day.* **Amen.**

Getting Just What We Needed

"GOD ALWAYS GIVES US WHAT WE NEED, BUT WE MUST SEEK AND FIND"

"Ask and it shall be given you; seek, and ye shall find…what man is there of you whom if his son ask bread, will he give him a stone: Or if he ask a fish, will he give him a serpent?"

FEATURED SCRIPTURE: MATTHEW 7:7, 9
BACKGROUND SCRIPTURES: MATTHEW 7:7–11; AND LUKE 11:1–13

In today's lesson we hear the words of the Master Himself as He talked about prayer and how we should ask freely of God for all our provisions. Jesus also used some sarcasm to get His point across. As leaders of faith, don't we sometimes deserve the butt of this sarcasm of Christ?

Oftentimes leaders pray in earnest, but without true faith for the provision. Do we really believe that in the difficulties of our own leadership journeys, when we pray for the bread for our task, God will give us a stone? However, many times the bread we pray for and that Jesus promises to us does not come to us as hot baked bread. It comes to us in the form of wheat for us to harvest, or flour for us to mix and bake, or yeast for us to sprinkle and bring the raw dough to rise.

When we ask for a fish, we will not get a serpent, but Jesus may also be telling us to cast our nets on the other side of the boat. He may be sending us the hook and the bait for us to go out and catch the fish He promised. Our Scripture today refers to asking, seeking, and finding. Heavenly provision is made available to us when we put feet to our prayers and when we work and search, as well as pray and ask.

Christ tells us that even evil men who are fathers will not give their own sons things that will hurt them. When the sons of evil men ask their own fathers for bread or fish, their evil fathers will give it to them. Are the called of God not more precious to our heavenly Father than these?

God wants good things for His children. He is faithful to give us what we pray for and what we need. What joy God must have when we as leaders of faith accept difficult tasks at His calling. What pleasure God must glean when we take secular missions and, by His hand, turn them into heavenly works of art that bring blessings to many others. Rest assured that what God called us to do will be confirmed with the provisions of answered prayer and blessings beyond our own imaginations.

Keep praying, keep asking, and keep seeking. The bread and fish for our leadership journeys today will ultimately be found if we obediently look for them in the right places. God is smiling and anxious to provide all we need, all we want, and much more. Open up in faith and action to His mysteries and miracles of provision.

Our Prayer: *Dear Jesus, thank You for teaching us how to pray and for showing us the fundamentals of faith. Forgive us when we lack the faith or simply don't seek the blessings that are lying in our path, already made available to us. May we serve others with the assurance that whatever resources we need will be provided to us, if we but ask the Master. We love You, Lord.* **Amen.**

I Never Knew You

"Beware the Leader Who Professes a Calling to Lead Without Authority"

"Many will say to me in that day, Lord, Lord, have we not prophesied in thy name?
And in thy name cast out devils? And in thy name done many wonderful works?
And then I will profess unto them, I never knew you: depart from me, ye that work
iniquity. For he taught them as one having authority, and not as the scribes."
Featured Scripture: Matthew 7:22–23, 29
Background Scriptures: Matthew 7:21–29; John 15:16; 1 Corinthians 13:2; and 2 Timothy 2:19

False teachers came along frequently in the time of the early Church. They come into the midst of our organizations and congregations even this day. Searching for notoriety and status, these false leaders hope to invoke the name of Christ in their actions for self-gain by manipulating others. Some self-proclaimed leaders claim spiritual authority over others through tradition or corrupt institutional backing. In today's lesson, Jesus was clear and powerful in His teaching that not every leader is called and endowed with godly authority.

In the end time of judgment, those self-proclaimed leaders who have worked in the name of God without having been chosen and given the authority of God will find that Christ never knew them. Working and leading in Christ's name without a true anointing and calling can actually work iniquity and do harm to others. Jesus said that in order to know Him, we must heed His words and teachings. Build your leadership journey on the solid rock and foundation of Christ's teachings and by prayerful petition, because all other foundations of authority are like sinking sand.

Those whom God calls to leadership will know their call is true through affirmations. God pursues those whom He calls. God pursues us by placing us in the right situations to hear His voice. God brings mentors and intercessors our way. He speaks to our hearts and minds through the reading of His Word. He presents answers to prayer and opens new doors to us. God's calling will slay our spirits with humility, repentance, love, and a burning passion to serve Him and others. He will create restlessness in us until we embark on a mission for Him. Our every thought will become praise and obedience to the task at hand. You, my friend, may be hearing His call in your life today.

Called leaders of faith will exude authority and peace. They are kind and loving, not full of conceit or vainglory. Beware the leader who professes authority without presenting a servant's spirit. Beware a leader whose words and lifestyle are not consistent with the teachings of Christ. The storms of life will test all leaders, both true ones and false ones. As adversity strikes an authentic true leader, their rocklike foundation is firm, and you will see them blossom even in tragedy. False leaders will crumble under deceit and false doctrine. They will sink in the sands of their own sinful manipulation. Know Christ, and know your calling through Him.

Our Prayer: *Lord Jesus, we have felt Your call on our lives. The Holy Spirit has struck us and called us to Your service. Our hearts are heavy and full of love, and our minds are strong and able to work. Help us all to discern and identify the false teachers and leaders who would deceive others and work iniquity in Your name. Keep us immersed in Your Word and love, and protect us from evil.* **Amen.**

Moved With Compassion

"We Can Never Lead Others in Christ's Power Until We Have Compassion"

"But when he saw the multitudes, he was moved with compassion on them, because they fainted, and were scattered abroad, as sheep having no shepherd.... Finally, be ye all of one mind, having compassion one of another, love as brethren...."

FEATURED SCRIPTURES: MATTHEW 9:36; AND 1 PETER 3:8
BACKGROUND SCRIPTURE: MATTHEW 9:35–38; 1 PETER 3:8–12; AND ROMANS 9:14–15

As the Son of the Trinity of God, Christ had the unique capacity to love those He encountered with the love of a Creator. As God incarnated into the body of a man, Christ had the ability to empathize with those He encountered as a man confined by the same limitations of the flesh. Christ knew hunger. He knew weariness. He knew pain. But Christ also sensed in the people who sought after Him their great need for a Shepherd-Leader of faith who could show them the way to God.

As the promised Messiah, Jesus discerned the condition of the heart. He could see purity and meekness of spirit in those who followed after Him. He knew that the people described in our Scripture fainted not only of physical need, but from their confused longing for God. The ability of Christ to be moved with compassion testifies to the character of God and sets the example for leaders of faith. We can never truly lead others in the spirit and power of Christ until we are moved with compassion for the people God has called us to serve.

Compassion means that love abounds in you. Empathy and an overwhelming sense to meet the needs and fill the emptiness of those around you shows that you are ready to be used by God for something special. When we as leaders of faith are moved with compassion, our actions will astound others and lend testimony that our journeys of leadership are guided by a higher authority. Acting out of compassion to others also gives God a chance to work miracles in the lives of those we serve. The hearts of people we encounter will repent and seek forgiveness when our unsolicited love and mercy is showered upon them. Love and kindness spreads and multiplies as those who receive mercy become merciful to others.

The ability to be moved with compassion in situations of leadership must come from God's Holy Spirit in your own life. Pray with a heart of compassion for the physical and spiritual plight of others. Jesus was moved with compassion as He saw the multitudes who followed Him. Is there a situation in your leadership journey that is overwhelming you and stirring your heart to compassion? Perhaps God is leading you to act and perform great works in the lives of others.

As we lead others each day, let us transform the monotony and our bland routines into movements of compassion for the brokenhearted and the fragile souls around us. People are in need of shepherds and leaders who feel their pain and can shower them with Christ's love and mercy.

Our Prayer: *Heavenly Father, You are the giver of mercy. You show compassion and mercy to us each day. As our Savior was moved with compassion toward those You gave to Him, let us also be moved with the compassion of His same Spirit in our own leadership journeys of faith. Let us become vessels of your love and grace as we shepherd and lead others in Your name.* **Amen.**

Works Give Testimony To A Mighty Calling

"By the Fruits of Your Works, People Will Know You Have Been Called"

"Jesus answered and said unto them, Go and show John again those things which ye do hear and see: The blind receive their sight, and the lame walk, the lepers are cleansed, and the deaf hear, the dead are raised up, and the poor have the gospel preached to them."

Featured Scripture: Matthew 11: 4–5

Background Scriptures: Isaiah 29:18; Isaiah 35:4–6; Isaiah 42:6–7; Malachi 3:1; and Malachi 4:6

Jesus loved John the Baptist very much. They were cousins. Their mothers were pregnant with them at the same time. John was the new Elijah who prepared the way for the Lord. John had great success in preaching the message of repentance, for the time of the Lord was at hand. John's ministry had been prophesied in Malachi 3:1. In our featured Scripture, Jesus sent word to John, who was in prison, of the news of the fulfillment of prophecy—that He was, indeed, the long-awaited Messiah.

When Jesus sent this word to John, He told John's disciples to tell of the works and miracles they had seen. Jesus knew that if John heard of these works and the fruit they bore, he would know that Jesus was, indeed, the Messiah. The promise of God had been fulfilled, and the works of the Lord gave testimony to it.

Leaders of faith usually don't have to write a paper or use a commercial to convince others that they have been called to a particular task of leadership. The proof of their calling will be declared in their works. People know that great leaders have been raised up by observing their selfless service to others. They see signs and wonders of a new leader's outstanding work on projects. They see the evidence in the coworkers who willingly gather to work under their direction. In fact, leaders of faith often don't realize they are truly leaders until those wise observers around them declare that God has anointed them for leadership service.

Leaders of faith are usually drafted or nominated by others because people see God-given gifts and talents proven out in the humility of their everyday work. The anointing of new leaders will seep out through the talents and signs they exude. You should recognize these works and deeds in others and reward their service.

We are called to heal the sick and bind up the brokenhearted. The prophetic signs of Isaiah, Malachi, and Matthew attested to both John and Jesus' calling and were proven by their good works. As each of us seeks to find a hurt and heal it, find a problem and solve it, seek justice for the oppressed, cast out evil, and preach the Gospel to the poor, we, too, will prove our own callings from God. If you are called by His grace to lead and serve others, God will let your works bear testimony to your calling.

Our Prayer: *Dear Lord, we give thanks for the fulfillment of prophecy, for saints like Elijah and John, and for the arrival of our Messiah. Please prove our callings as leaders of faith by allowing the fruits of our good works to shine forth. Bless us and guide us in this journey for Your name's sake.* **Amen.**

Where Weary Leaders Can Find Rest

"Developing a Complete Reliance on the Real Elixir for Weariness"

"Come unto me, all ye that labour and are heavy laden, and I will give you rest. Take my yoke upon you, and learn of me; for I am meek and lowly in heart: and ye shall find rest unto your souls."

Featured Scripture: Matthew 11:28–29
Background Scriptures: Matthew 11:25–30; Galatians 6:9; and 1 Thessalonians 3:13

For years these words of Jesus found in the Book of Matthew have comforted those whose lives were burdensome and overwhelming. Some people are heavy with troubled relationships, sickness, poverty, or personal brokenness. In today's lesson, Christ gives us the recipe for overcoming our weariness, a map to find our rest.

Leaders of faith can easily become weary when confronted daily with our called tasks for God. The crushing responsibilities of leadership can zap the spirit and strength from us and put us into a weary state that separates us from God's true power and purpose. What are we to do when this overwhelming weariness from our work takes hold of us and stifles our creativity and very desire to lead?

Jesus anticipates weariness in His followers and apostles. He knows that those with righteous hearts can often find the cold winds of this life to be more than they can bear. God gave Jesus the weary of this world as His flock. Jesus calls the weary unto Him. Prior to the day of Christ, keeping the covenant of the old law with all its demands could make a soul weary. Christ is the fulfillment of the Law and the strength by which leaders of faith can continue in service to others.

For us to become weary in our leadership is to veer from the source of our calling and power. The yoke Christ refers to is the hitching point for pulling a heavy load. The yoke was the frame by which a beast of burden might hook up to a heavy wagon to pull. By assuming Christ's meekness and calmness, and remaining assured that whatever we do in His name shall be blessed, our weariness begins to evaporate.

Weariness is more than a byproduct of physical exertion. It is the very weight that builds as we sense the difficulty of our tasks and our own inability to get the work done. Weariness is the burden of experiencing the obstacles of daily existence. It is in our moments of frustration and weariness that Jesus commands us to give it up to Him.

Through prayer and meditation, let us daily give our burdens, sins, and tasks left unfinished to Christ. Let us feel His arms embrace us and hear His words to us: "My yoke is easy; My burden is light." It is in recognizing who made us, called us, and sustains us that our weariness begins to lift. If we remain in His arms, tied to His yoke, nothing we do for His sake can ever fail. Let weariness be gone!

Our Prayer: *Precious Lord, take our burdens and make the weariness go away. Help us to give all our stress and heaviness to You and allow You to make something special with it. Help us to take Your yoke and rely on Your power to sustain us in every situation of this life. We praise You for being the Savior who takes away the weariness of all mankind.* **Amen.**

Followers Are Like Different Soils

"Some Followers Will Never Catch the Vision"

"Behold, a sower went forth to sow; And when he sowed, some seeds fell by the way side…some fell in stony places…some fell among thorns…. But other fell into good ground, and brought forth fruit, some an hundredfold, some sixtyfold, some thirtyfold."

FEATURED SCRIPTURE: MATTHEW 13:3–8
BACKGROUND SCRIPTURES: MATTHEW 13:1–11, 19; GENESIS 26:12; AND ISAIAH 6:9–10

Many people found the words and ministry of Jesus lacking. Some did not want to hear at all, preferring the world as it was; some heard the message, but wanted instead to hear a political and military message; some wanted to hear, but their own emotions and attraction to the world caused the message to fade away; and finally, the enlightened heard, and the message took root and changed their lives forever.

This parable of Jesus represented those persons He encountered in His ministry. The disciples also would encounter these types of persons in their ministries. Can we as leaders of faith today see these same persons in our daily service for God? It is hard for everyone to grasp the vision of goodness and hope. If it was hard for those who met Jesus to receive the hope of glory and salvation, rest assured our task will be equally hard.

In our leadership journeys of faith today, we see those would-be followers who are attracted for a brief moment to our congregational mission, but the distractions of pleasure and leisure pluck them away quickly. Some followers are like stony soil. Seeds of hope and success sprout quickly, but they soon fade away because they expect wealth and success in a short time. The winds of discouragement and the quest for the instant gratification of the world cause them to lose interest. Some followers have good soil, and the seed of hope takes good root and grows well. But thistles of corruption, blind ambition, and the hope for promotion without honest work eventually choke them with failure.

So how do we as leaders of faith sow to the good soil? First, we must realize that our leadership journeys will take us to fields of all type of soils. But we must keep plowing. Many a person in whom we invest our time, love, and energy will never reach their potential. While we must keep searching to find the good soil, we must also care for and nurture every seed and give God a chance to let them grow in their own season. God will show us the fertile fields of service and will provide the followers who will help it to bear its spiritual fruit.

Never be discouraged. If God called you to sow His message of love, hope, and salvation among the lost and hurting, He will bring the followers to your vision and cause. Keep planting and watering, and God will give the increase.

Our Prayer: *Lord, we give You praise and honor for being the God of new growth. We are humbled to be called into leadership. Help us to plant seeds of hope, love, and salvation in our leadership journeys of faith. Keep us strong and never let us become discouraged when our seeds die in bad soil or when others are plucked away from us by sin or earthly desire. Let our service yield a harvest of goodness for eternity.* **Amen.**

Tares Sown Among Us

"Weeds of Dissension Are Found Planted by Evil in Our Institutions"

"Another parable put he forth unto them, saying, The kingdom of heaven is likened unto a man which sowed good seed in his field: But while men slept, his enemy came and sowed tares among the wheat, and went his way. But when the blade was sprung up, and brought forth fruit, then appeared the tares also…. Let both grow together until the harvest: and in the time of harvest I will say to the reapers, Gather ye together first the tares, and bind them in bundles to burn them: but gather the wheat into my barn."

Featured Scripture: Matthew 13:24–26, 30
Background Scripture: Matthew 13:24–32, 36-43

Leaders of faith are part of God's Kingdom and have been called among the humanity of their own communities. In Christ's Parable of the Tares, He shows us how to deal with adversity when it is planted to choke our harvest of work. A tare is a grass that resembles wheat in its early stage of growth. But unlike wheat, a tare bares no fruit. Tares compete with wheat for nutrients and are susceptible to disease. They are planted to suck nutrients from the wheat and attract destruction for all.

In the Kingdom of God, Satan plants his evil seed among the good seed. In our spiritual journeys, we, too, will encounter evil tares sown among our good seeds. Every congregation or organization will have dissension sown in its midst by persons who do not want us to succeed or who through selfish motives want to hijack our efforts to serve others in Christ's name. The tares and dissenters of today often blend in with our good flock of followers. In the beginning they may appear kind and helpful and look like good team members. However, as time elapses and our work progresses, they not only will not bear fruit, but they will bring evil into our daily activities. They attract the disease of corruption and rivalry.

The lesson of Christ to His disciples years ago rings true for leaders of faith today. The tares sent by Satan to thwart our harvest of service for God should be allowed to grow until they are distinguishable from the good shoots of wheat. We can tell the difference in the selfless versus the selfish and the loving actions of our good followers versus the sinister acts of jealous backbiters. We can then harvest and rid the evildoers from our institutions through exposure to light, accountability, and disciplined action.

All our work and our service belong to God. It is His congregation and His mission we have been called to lead. God is the owner of our fields of harvest, and He will know when we need to separate the wheat from the tares. Be ready to endure a growing season with weeds of evil sown in the midst of the good you do. But be faithful and patient; God will fill your barns with the good wheat of your labor and destroy the evil sent to harm you.

Our Prayer: *Jesus, You own the fields in which we work today. We sow good seed and righteous work in the world in which we live. We know Satan will come and plant evil tares among us. Give us the patience and ability to distinguish the good from the evil and harvest it according to Your will. May all we do in our fields of service today build Your heavenly Kingdom.* **Amen.**

Meeting Both The Physical And Spiritual Needs

"FOLLOWING CHRIST'S EXAMPLE TO CARE FOR ALL THE NEEDS OF THOSE WE SERVE"

"And Jesus went forth, and saw a great multitude, and was moved with compassion towards them, and he healed their sick. And when it was evening, his disciples came to him, saying, This is a desert place, and the time is now past; send the multitude away, that they may go into the villages, and buy themselves victuals. But Jesus said unto them, They need not depart; give ye them to eat."

FEATURED SCRIPTURE: MATTHEW 14:14–16
BACKGROUND SCRIPTURES: MATTHEW 14:13–21; AND 15:29–39

Jesus was the Messiah. He came to preach salvation and to show the people the way to God in heaven. His priority was that none should perish, but that all have eternal life. If Christ's mission was an eternal one, why did He do so much to meet the physical needs of those around Him? Even if He fed them one day, they would hunger again.

The disciples reminded Jesus that they were in a remote place and He should let the people go away to find food because dark was coming soon. But Jesus told the disciples to give them something to eat. They searched among the people and found only five loaves of bread and two fish, hardly sufficient to feed the mass of people assembled to see Christ.

It was the love Jesus had for people in His ministry on earth that moved Him to compassion to heal them, feed them, and comfort them. Jesus knew the heart of every man and woman, yet, while He knew they needed spiritual salvation, He time and again stepped up to meet their immediate physical needs first. Jesus set an example of leadership that should be followed. Those we wish to serve have real needs. Can we sell a new project to those we lead if they are in financial peril, under duress, or have overwhelming obstacles in their personal lives?

Part of becoming a great leader is sensing and finding the needs in the lives of those persons who follow you. Sense their needs in your own spirit. Reach out to them and minister to their unspoken pains. We may not be able to turn five loaves and two fish into enough to feed a multitude, but we can offer kind gestures of care to our coworkers. We can offer an employee a day off to take care of a child or attend to a personal need. We can be an ear of sympathy to a follower struggling with family failures. We can find the funds to help a person who has lost their job or spouse.

When Jesus healed the sick and fed the hungry, He showed God's love for every person. But He also knew that by meeting the physical and emotional needs of those who followed Him, those same persons could move with new faith to help their own neighbors in need. The window to the eternal offering is found in meeting the needs of those here and now in Christ's name. Whom can you serve in a physical and spiritual way this very day?

Our Prayer: *O Great Physician, You healed so many in Your ministry and through the eons of time. Your power to heal us, feed us, and meet our every need is manifested anew in our lives each day. We praise You for Your grace and blessings to us. Give us that same desire to meet the physical as well as the spiritual needs of those we serve. Help us to minister to them in the compassion and love of Your Spirit.* **Amen.**

Breaking Our Own Momentum

"Risk Assessment on a Mission of Faith Can Sink Us"

"And Peter answered him and said, Lord, if it be thou, bid me come unto thee on the water. And he said, Come. And when Peter was come down out of the ship, he walked on the water, to go to Jesus. But when he saw the wind boisterous, he was afraid and beginning to sink, he cried, saying, Lord, save me."

Featured Scripture: Matthew 14:28–30
Background Scripture: Matthew 14: 22–33

Peter was the apostle with the greatest outward passion for the Lord. When Jesus surprised His disciples by walking on water, Peter asked the Lord if he could come on the water to Him. Jesus replied and bid him: "*Come.*" At that moment, Peter was completely focused on his Master. Peter's request to come to Jesus accompanied a longing to go somewhere he had never been before. But it also came with the beginnings of a newfound faith and ability to do the miracles Jesus longed for him to do.

How proud Jesus must have felt that Peter wanted to do something in faith he had never done before. Perhaps Peter was sensing the power and mission that was meant for him and the other disciples from the beginning of time. Peter excelled at expanding his boundaries and seeing a daring vision of something new. He wanted to plug into the true power of the Master and, indeed, he did. But like many leaders of faith, Peter's success and momentum sank the moment he took his eyes off the Master and made a mortal assessment of the peril that existed in the wind and waves around him. Peter began to assess where he was instead of where he was going. Peter broke his own momentum.

How often we attempt to do bold things in leadership by stepping out of our comfort zones and moving forward with zeal of faith and a sense of purpose that others do not possess. When we do, others are inspired to follow us, and great things are accomplished. But the instant we stop walking in faith toward success and start to calculate the cost of failure, we begin to sink. It is in these very moments that we break our own momentum and yield the special power Christ has afforded to us.

When Jesus tells us to come to Him or asks us to perform tasks never before accomplished, we can never sink. He will supply the power and provision even in the midst of the storms, wind, and waves. But if we break our own momentum in these times, we may not be able to recapture the vision and courage it took for us to get out of the boat. When Christ harkens us to a task, let us never waver as we stay focused on the Master.

Our Prayer: *Dear Jesus, like Peter, we want to get out of the boat in faith and come to You. We want to get on the water and move toward a leadership vision that we never dreamed we could accomplish until You inspired us to try. Help us to try again and to trust that You will never let us sink if our eyes are fixed solely upon You.* **Amen.**

The Rock And The Devil

"Leaders of Faith on Occasion Can Be Both Good and Evil"

"And Simon Peter answered and said unto him, Blessed art thou, Simon Barjona: for flesh and blood hath not revealed it unto thee, but my Father which is in heaven…thou art Peter, and upon this rock I will build my church…then Peter took him, and began to rebuke him, saying, Be it far from thee, Lord: this shall not be unto thee. But He turned and said unto Peter, Get thee behind me, Satan; thou art an offense unto me: for thou savourest not the things that be of God, but those that be of men."

Featured Scripture: Matthew 16:16–18, 22–23
Background Scriptures: Matthew 26:33–41; Mark 14:66–72; and John 21:15–17

Few heroes of our faith are as fascinating as the apostle Peter. Peter was one of Christ's closest disciples; he was emotional, passionate, and powerful. After Jesus ascended to heaven, Peter was a leader of the new mission movement that spread the Gospel around the world. He was an authority in the new Church. Peter performed miracles, drove out demons, and tutored the new generation of apostles. Peter was one of Scripture's greatest leaders of faith.

How could a man of Peter's stature and calling be used of the devil? On two striking occasions in the Gospels, Peter's zest of his own understanding, his earthly view, and his failure to stay in the Spirit caused him to be used of Satan. In one moment Peter was declared the "Rock" upon which Christ would build His Church, and the next moment he was rebuked, with Christ saying, *"Get thee behind me, Satan."* Leaders of faith can be vessels of both good and evil when they take their eyes off the Master.

During the Passion Week, Peter was with Christ at the Last Supper and the Garden of Gethsemane, but as Christ predicted, Peter denied Him three times, and then the rooster crowed. But, after Jesus rose from the dead, He visited with his beloved disciple Peter and redeemed him in a special encounter. On three occasions Christ asked Peter if he loved Him. Peter responded emphatically each time that, indeed, he loved Christ. Jesus said that if Peter loved Him, he must feed His sheep. Peter made the vow, and the relationship was restored.

Peter went on to incredible service for the Kingdom. However, Peter's susceptibilities to evil influences can only mean that we as leaders of faith will also encounter temptation to channel evil. We as leaders of faith must remain constantly by Christ's side in prayer and study. We must always keep an eternal view of all that we do. We cannot ever substitute our own agendas for a heavenly agenda. When we fail to acknowledge Christ and execute His plan, we, too, can be used by Satan for evil intent.

The good news is that Jesus forgives and redeems whose whom He ordains. He protects and empowers us to do great things. Just as Christ could easily have written Peter off, He knew that the heart and calling of Peter were pure and that Peter would become the Rock of the faith. Those of us who are called by this same Christ will also prevail if we cling to the promises of Christ even as we feed His sheep.

Our Prayer: *Dear Jesus, thank You for Peter, the Rock. Thank You for the lessons You teach us through him. Protect us from Satan in our leadership journeys that we may remain true to Your heavenly business and be grounded in Your love. In all that we do, O Lord, may we feed Your sheep.* **Amen.**

Cross-Bearers, Not Crown-Wearers

"Leadership in Faith Means Bearing Burdens, Not Harvesting Privileges"

"Then said Jesus unto his disciples, If any man will come after me, let him deny himself, and take up his cross, and follow me…. We then that are strong ought to bear the infirmities of the weak, and not to please ourselves…. Bear ye one another's burdens, and so fulfill the law of Christ. And they compel one Simon a Cyrene to bear his cross"

Featured Scriptures: Matthew 16:24; Romans 15:1; Galatians 6:2; and Mark 15:21
Background Scriptures: Matthew 20:25–28; and Matthew 27:27–32

Often leaders of faith will innocently insert themselves into the midst of chaos and controversy on behalf of others. What begins as our heartfelt sympathy for a stranger's plight leads us into a morass of problems that we feel called to tackle for an oppressed person or group. How do we get into these dilemmas? Are we like Simon of Cyrene, who was compelled to carry the cross of Jesus on the way to Golgotha? Breathe deeply and know that you are chosen of God. Leaders of faith are called to be cross-bearers, not crown-wearers.

Along with your call to God's service come new spiritual instincts that will lead you into the path of hurting souls. We find ourselves attracted to those persons and situations where injustice has been done or where people need an advocate. Bearing another's burden is what Christ calls "taking up your cross each day." By transmitting your time, love, and efforts toward solving the crises of others, we radiate the brilliance of Christ's power in all situations. Our friends, family members, and associates may wonder why we always seem to be attracted to difficulty and disaster. We may even endure ridicule and criticism from those we love. But by bearing another's burden, we bear the cross of Christ. And through that experience we find meaning in life.

God never calls us to a mission of burden-bearing activity without equipping us for the task. The Holy Spirit, who brings these hopeless situations and hurting souls into our paths, also goes ahead of us to move mountains and petition God for showers of blessings for our journeys. At each impasse along the way, small miracles will occur and unlikely allies will come to our assistance. Cross-bearers find strength and talents they never knew they had as they face each obstacle along the way. The hopelessness of a situation will turn into empowering movements of people. Broken lives will become resuscitated with hope and purpose. God's grace and mercy begin to explode around us as we fight for the freedom and deliverance of others.

Many persons shy from leadership when they find that their futures seem paved with cross-bearing and not crown-wearing. When one sees that the call to leadership is bearing the cross of adversity rather than a crown of entitlement, many would-be leaders leave the scene. But if you are one whom God has called to service and you see burdens and crosses as tools of glory, then come along. Our Savior has something wonderful in store for you this day. In heaven's Book of Life, the names of the crown-wearing royalty fade and forever give way to the names of the cross-bearing leaders!

Our Prayer: *Lord Jesus, You bore the cross for us all. Even now, You bear our burdens each day. We give praise and honor and glory for the cross and claim it for ourselves this very day. May Your Spirit guide us and motivate us to want to bear the burdens of the hurting souls around us. Equip us with Your power so that we, too, can become cross-bearers, not crown-wearers.* **Amen.**

Making Taxes Trivial

"How Leaders Allow Money to Obscure Their View of the Master"

"They that received the tribute money came to Peter and said, Doth not your master pay tribute?.... What thinkest thou Simon?.... Go thou to the sea, and cast a hook, and take up the fish that first cometh up; and when thou hast opened his mouth, thou shalt find a piece of money: that take, and give unto them for me and thee."
FEATURED SCRIPTURE: MATTHEW 17:24–27
BACKGROUND SCRIPTURE: MARK 12:16–18

What an encounter! What an exchange! This Scripture passage is chronicled as a miracle of Christ, yet its lesson yields an eternal insight for leaders. An attempt by the self-righteous leaders of the Temple to tax the Son of God unveils sobering truths about the greed and jealousy of man versus the calm measure of wisdom and holiness of God.

The apostle Peter was confronted by the Temple leaders as he and Christ arrived in the town of Capernaum. No doubt, these same leaders were following the disciples and the Son of Man in order to accuse them of wrongdoing. In doing so, they hoped to cripple their soaring ministry and find them afoul of the Jewish or Roman law. What better way to test Christ than asking Him to pay His fair share of the Temple tax? Taxing the Son of God? They had asked the Giver of all life to pay a tax on His own goodness to those who sought to destroy Him. Jesus calmly responded with a command to Peter and provided the miracle that forever made taxes trivial.

In all of Scripture scarcely any verse shows that Jesus ever touched, handled, or even concerned Himself with money or material possessions. To insist that the Creator of the universe pay a tax was blasphemous enough for God to have called the angels to destroy the Temple leaders. Yet Christ, through Peter, shows us that leadership of faith is not about the authority of man but the grace of God, who will supply our every need. By producing the shekel of Temple tax for Himself and for Peter from the mouth of a fish, Jesus shows us who really owns it all. He also tells us that the provision for our taxes and the provision to lead others will be provided to us in miraculous ways if we follow Christ's command and have faith.

We as leaders of faith often panic when confronted by authority. In these times we must dissect the sacred from the secular. When confronted with obstacles and by adversaries who would seek to devour you through taxes, legalism, and seemingly insurmountable obstacles, remember this lesson of Christ today. When you have a need or a crisis, take it to Christ. He may just send you out to fish for the provision. If He sends you, you will catch the fish and find your own coin of sustenance. The Savior who makes taxes trivial will never fail us!

Our Prayer: *Lord Jesus, we love You. How we long to fellowship with You and learn these lessons of faith. We give You praise for having made taxes trivial and the burdens of this life bearable. We need provision today, dear Lord. Show us where to fish to find the miracle we need right now. Bless us as we attempt to lead and serve others in Your name.* **Amen.**

Practicing Seventy-Times-Seven Leadership

"Leaders of Faith Must First Become Leaders of Forgiveness"

"Then came Peter to him and said, Lord, how oft shall my brother sin against me, and I forgive him? Till seven times? Jesus saith unto him, I say not unto thee, Until seven times: but, Until seventy times seven."

Featured Scripture: Matthew 18:21–22
Background Scripture: Matthew 18:21–35

This exchange between Peter and the Christ regarding forgiveness gives us some of the best theological insight into the issue of forgiveness ever written. We as leaders of faith are flawed but forgiven leaders ourselves. We have been redeemed by the love and blood of Christ. Our forgiveness has been purchased with the greatest price of all. Redeemed and forgiven leaders of faith should become living examples of Christ's forgiveness theology as we practice seventy-times-seven leadership and forgive others in our own leadership journeys.

Forgiving others is not just a proverb or admonition; it is a commandment. It is also a conditional command, meaning that when we forgive others, we are then forgiven by God. God expects the redeemed to become champions of forgiveness. Practicing forgiveness the way Christ taught us is the opposite of what the world teaches. The world says don't forget: retaliate and get even. When we don't act in the predictable ways of the world, many in our workplace will criticize us as being weak-minded or lacking courage. But the ability to forgive others unleashes the power of God not only in our own lives, but in the lives of others.

Forgiveness practiced appropriately multiplies itself as the Holy Spirit convicts people of their wrongdoing. Leaders of faith who hold grudges and aim to settle scores will become bitter and ineffective. They let the wrongs done to them control their own minds and actions through the sin of revenge. Leaders of faith transcend and control their opponents and adversaries as they forgive those who hurt them. It is the power that Christ alone gives to us.

Leaders of forgiveness don't let evil circumstances control them. Even the hurt and pain caused by the actions of others is released when we forgive. It is turned into new power and authority over our circumstances as we wash away the debts of others with our forgiveness. The forgivers claim authority over the evil done to them through the power of the cross itself. Jesus told us to carry the burden of others for the second mile, even when we are required to go only one mile.

Peter thought forgiving a brother seven times was sufficient. But Jesus said not seven times, but seventy times seven. Jesus said forgiveness should be infinite. Becoming a seventy-times-seven leader of faith requires that we lean upon our own forgiveness story: *"In that, while we were yet sinners, Christ died for us"* (Romans 5:8). When we forgive others, the wellspring of forgiveness from God to us becomes eternal and constant. It will empower and protect us as a leader from evil and allow us to soar above every hurt we experience.

Our Prayer: *Lord Jesus, Your sacrifice for us at the cross changed all eternity for us. We praise and thank You for offering forgiveness to us by giving Yourself as a ransom for our sins. Help us to practice forgiving others and to become seventy-times-seven leaders of forgiveness. Unleash upon us great power as we forgive the often horrid acts perpetrated against us by others. May our example be edifying for the Kingdom and bring others into the light, mercy, and forgiveness of Jesus.* **Amen.**

The Greatest Act Of Leadership Is Instilling Faith In A Child

"If We Don't Teach Them, How Will They Know?"

"But Jesus said, Suffer little children, and forbid them not, to come unto me: for of such is the kingdom of heaven…. Train up a child in the way he should go: and when he is old, he will not depart from it."

FEATURED SCRIPTURES: MATTHEW19:14; AND PROVERBS 22:6
BACKGROUND SCRIPTURE: LUKE 2:39–52

Many persons in the hustle of life, business, and government overlook the simple principle that our greatest responsibility as leaders of faith is to inspire and train children in the faith. That responsibility falls on a parent or family member of a child, but God calls all leaders of faith to this responsibility. Christ described the very Kingdom of Heaven as being made up of innocent children. If Christ raised the importance of teaching and loving children during His ministry on earth, what are you doing today as a leader of faith to be true to His words?

One can only imagine that Christ remembered His own childhood and His rearing in the faith by Mary and Joseph. Jesus remembered His times during the Passover Feasts at Jerusalem, perhaps the time He was lost from His parents as He stayed behind to learn and teach in the Temple. Mary and Joseph knew that they had a great responsibility as parents of the Son of God to immerse Jesus in the Scripture and teachings of the Jewish faith. Are we doing the same with our own children and the young people in our communities?

Leaders of faith should support the institutions that teach children, such as our schools, places of worship, museums, and the like. However, the essence of the spiritual well-being and welfare of children falls squarely on leaders of faith in the family and beyond. It may mean we become mentors in our communities or volunteer for a church's Bible school or nursery. It may mean taking time off to travel to see a grandchild and share the love of Jesus with them. It may mean loving and interceding for a child in trouble or children who seem unlovable. It may mean caring for children with special needs or relieving their parents for a time of rest.

Leaders of faith should also become prayer warriors for the children of the world. Tens of millions of them live in danger, poverty, and despair. By praying and then putting feet to our prayers on behalf of children, we build the Kingdom of God. Our covenant with children comes with a promise of Scripture. If we train children in the way they should go, when they are old, they will not depart from our teachings. Also, children who honor their parents are promised long and fruitful lives.

Find a child today to love and mentor. Maybe that child is your own! Love them; teach them the faith and the stories of Jesus, so that they, too, may expand the Kingdom of God.

Our Prayer: *Father, how we quickly forget that in the midst of all our important tasks in life, teaching faith to a child is the most sacred leadership responsibility of all. Help us to balance our time, and like Your example, make loving and leading children a solemn task in our daily leadership journeys.* **Amen.**

The Lord Hath Need Of Them

"LEADERS OF FAITH SHOULD ASK BOLDLY FOR THE PROVISIONS THEY NEED"

"Go into the village over against you, and straightway ye shall find an ass tied, and a colt with her: loose them, and bring them unto me. And if any man say ought unto you, ye shall say, The Lord hath need of them; and straightway he will send them."
FEATURED SCRIPTURE: MATTHEW 21:2–3
BACKGROUND SCRIPTURES: MATTHEW 21:1–11: LUKE 10:3–4: ZECHARIAH 9:9

Jesus sent two of His disciples to fetch the colt upon which Jesus would make His triumphal entry into Jerusalem. The prophet Zechariah had predicted the entry of the Messiah into Jerusalem in just such a way: *"Rejoice greatly, O daughter of Zion; shout, O daughter of Jerusalem: behold, thy King cometh unto thee: he is just, and having salvation; lowly, and riding upon an ass, and upon a colt, the foal of an ass"* (Zechariah 9:9).

The task that Jesus asked these two disciples to do on this day was no routine errand for the Master, yet it was in itself part of the fulfillment of the Holy Scripture. Nothing in the Scripture tells us how earthly preparations were made for securing these two animals. They would have had significant monetary value, and the two disciples were essentially telling their owner that they were taking them for Jesus without compensation.

Jesus anticipated the need. He instructed the disciples in what to say as they found and loosened the animals to bring them to the Lord. Jesus simply told them, if asked, to say: that the Lord had need of them. The power of God is all the legal tender you will ever need.

Today's story is yet another miracle, another perfect piece of an eternal puzzle that fits divinely together. What God has planned and called to be will happen. If we are part of a calling to leadership for Him, He will make the provisions available to us for our every task. In your leadership journey of faith, be bold in asking others for provisions.

These two men had learned that when Jesus gave them a task and told them what to do, they should just do it. They didn't ask Jesus what to do if the man with the animals said no. The presentation of these two animals for the fulfillment of Scripture had been made ready since the beginning of time. If the Lord needs it, we shall have it.

Leaders of faith at all levels who attempt to do something great will encounter the need for provisions they do not have. In these times we should be bold to know that if God calls us to the task, He will make the provision known to us. As we pray and search for provision, let us, too, like these disciples, boldly declare to others that *"the Lord hath need of them,"* and it shall be provided just as Christ said.

Our Prayer: *Lord Jesus, we praise You as the triumphal Christ of all ages. Thank You for fulfilling Scripture and for Your gift of salvation. We claim Your promise of provision in our own leadership journeys. If we are called by Your name and for Your purpose, the ass, the colt, and all provisions we need will be made ready to us if we claim them for Your Kingdom.* **Amen.**

When Pure Places Are Perverted

"Showing Righteous Indignation When Institutions Are Corrupted"

"And Jesus went into the temple of God, and cast out all them that sold and bought in the temple, and overthrew the tables of the moneychangers, and the seats of them that sold doves, And said unto them, It is written, My house shall be called the house of prayer; but ye have made it a den of thieves."

Featured Scripture: Matthew 21:12–13
Background Scriptures: Isaiah 56:7; Jeremiah 7:11; and Matthew 21:12–17

The Gospels record that on at least two occasions Jesus came to the Temple to find the corrupt buying and selling of sacrificial animals. Christ became indignant that His Father's house of prayer had become a den of thieves. In His exchange with the moneychangers at the holy Temple, we can see the righteous indignation of our Lord. Rather than seeing anger as a fault, Jesus set an example that leaders of faith must emulate when pure places are perverted.

It wasn't just the commerce happening in the Temple that drove Jesus to anger; it was the perversion of the very institution of the Temple that brought out such deep emotion in the Lord. The poor could only afford the lowly dove for a sacrificial animal. The merchants, in collusion with the religious authorities, were there to make a profit on these poor worshipers who had traveled to this sacred place to seek remediation for their sin. The coins of Caesar were traded for Temple coins so that the rich could earn a profit from the poor.

The one place where people had to go to pray, worship, and find spiritual hope was now an organized marketplace of profiteering predators. How often as a leader of faith do you see the precious institutions of faith, government, and service organizations become corrupted not only by profiteers, but by those who selfishly make the institution an extension of their own lust and selfish ambitions? How do you respond to such behavior?

When an institution has created barriers and lost its purity through corrupt practice so that those it was set up to serve may no longer find safe refuge within it, we, too, like Christ, must drive the thieves away with all that is within us. Many of the poor and repentant people we serve (like those who came to the Temple in Jesus' day) need to know that they can count on leaders of faith and sacred institutions to find hope and restoration.

Jesus became the eternal sacrifice, and His body would be the temple that others sought to destroy. It was torn down and rebuilt in three days by His death and resurrection. Jesus taught us that the sanctity and holiness of the temples and institutions we serve are worth protecting. Like Christ, we must tackle with great emotion the decay and sin within them. Every leader of faith must show righteous indignation against injustice and restore integrity to the holy places of God.

Our Prayer: *Father, Your Church and places of worship are holy ground. Help us to protect the sanctity and holiness of the institutions that You ordained. May the house of prayer be purified so that all who enter may find safe refuge there. Forgive us when we fail to tackle corruption and sin in the institutions You called us to serve. Give us grace and courage to do the right things.* **Amen.**

Leading Without Permission

"Leaders Called to Serve Should Seize the Moment Without Permission"

"Now when he came into the temple, the chief priests and the elders of the people confronted him as he was teaching, and said, by what authority are you doing these things? And who gave you this authority?"

Featured Scripture: Matthew 21:23
Background Scriptures: Matthew 21:23–27; and Acts 4:1–22

In our lesson today we find Jesus in the Temple teaching and revealing God's true nature. Jesus' role as the Messiah placed Him in direct conflict with a centuries-old religious system. The Temple was God's house, and Jesus, the Son of God, needed no man's permission to fulfill His calling and reveal the promises of Scripture. He was the fulfillment of prophecy and His very presence in the world changed eternity for us all. When we are called by God to serve others, we can lead without the permission of others.

The earthly institutions that govern our lives are filled with structure and a hierarchy of leaders who are protective of any new outside influences affecting the norm. Leaders of faith who are called by God will invariably encounter resistance when it comes our time to fulfill our own callings. Most of us must work within the structure of organizations and congregations. But if we are called to leadership tasks of faith, we must never wait to be granted man's permission to begin our journeys.

Leading without permission means we lead by seizing the moment and tackling problems that need to be solved. It means we step forward and volunteer to accept challenges. It means we undertake, without being asked, a humble job that needs to be done. Others will see our example and join in. In our world today, new leaders rise up who may be simple persons without credentials. Many are unskilled in oration or the mechanics of politics. But people rise to leadership because they are responding to the needs in the world around them.

New leaders may often sense ostracism or subtle rebuke from others. In every generation the followers of Christ are challenged as to who authorized them to lead in the name and power of Jesus. *"By what authority are you doing these things, and who gave you this authority?"* Find a need and fill it. Sense a hurt and cover it with care and love. Seek a stranger and comfort him. Find injustice and seek to right it. Find the good in others and inspire them to action to make our communities even better.

If you feel God's call to a leadership task, you have all the authority and permission you need. If you are serving others with love and humility, don't ever wonder if you have stepped out of line. Only God truly knows the heavenly harvest reaped by leaders who answered the call of faith and led others without asking the world's permission.

Our Prayer: *Jesus, thank You for coming into the temple of my heart and calling me to Your service. If You called me to lead others in Your name, that is all the permission I need to begin. Create in me a humble heart to know when You are calling me to do something bold for You. Even when others resist my leadership, grant me courage and strength to complete the task You ask me to do.* **Amen.**

Inviting The Univited

"The Call to Leaders to Seek and Find a New Constituency"

"The kingdom of heaven is like unto a certain king, which made a marriage for his son, and sent forth his servants to call them that were bidden to the wedding: and they would not come…. Then saith he to his servants, the wedding is ready, but they that were bidden were not worthy. Go ye therefore into the highways, and as many as ye shall find, bid to the marriage."

Featured Scripture: Matthew 22:2–3, 8–9
Background Scripture: Matthew 22:1–14

In this parable of Christ, we learn that those to whom Christ came to reveal Himself did not receive Him. The life and incarnation of Christ was then given to all who would believe and receive Him. The life and times of Christ are also an example of how God loves the unwanted and the uninvited of our world. God turns rejection into a blanket of grace to any and all who would receive it. To leaders of faith, our attempt to lead others through our callings may involve rejection and resistance from the very persons we hope to serve. Our lesson today shows us that when we are rejected, we are to lead on by building a new constituency in service.

The parable of the wedding feast also shows that we as leaders can prepare ourselves and our organizations for action, only to find that people will not follow us. Those persons we expected to join us don't show up and fail to participate. All our efforts may seem to have been in vain. Every leader of faith at some point in their journeys will see the food at their feasts go to waste. The king in the wedding feast parable scrapped the original guest list and sent an open invitation to all those in the highways of life.

Oftentimes in leadership, those we expect to do the most will do the least. And those we expect to do the least will do the most. When all our preparation and great plans fail to garner followers, it may be time to build a new constituency. Great leadership means cobbling together unlike and dissimilar persons to believe and work toward a common objective. We often must recruit the unqualified and the unlovable to achieve great things for God. Our lesson also teaches us that people in the highways and byways of life have value to God as He extends His invitation of grace, forgiveness, and salvation to us all.

Invite the uninvited into your organization or congregation today. Build new constituencies of service. Fill your table up with new persons who have never had an opportunity to feast at a great event or learn a new lesson. Drop your assumptions and open your heart to loving and mentoring people who may never get to know the light and love of God unless you invite them to do so.

Our Prayer: *Lord Jesus, we praise You for inviting us to dine at the table of Your salvation and to feast upon Your grace and love for us. As leaders of faith, help us to make ourselves available to serve those who have never had an opportunity or who have been left out. Help us to broaden the tent and bring people in to hear a message of hope and to experience Your love through our service to them.* **Amen.**

Status, Title, And Honor Can Tangle A Leader

"Leaders Who Allow the Title and Status of Leadership to Heighten Their Sense of Self-Worth Can Come Unraveled"

"But all their works they do for to be seen of men: they make broad their phylacteries, and enlarge the borders of their garment, And love the uppermost rooms at feasts, and the chief seats in the synagogues, And greetings in the markets, and to be called of men, Rabbi, Rabbi."

Featured Scripture: Matthew 23: 5–7
Background Scriptures: Matthew 23:1–12; and Mark 12:38–40

Jesus had great contempt for the pompousness of the scribes and Pharisees who reveled in their power, prestige, and position of authority. Jesus warned others of the vanity they displayed by the way they wore the garments of prestige. They expected the best seats at the feasts and the chief seats in the synagogues. They enjoyed having others bow and greet them in the streets of the marketplace calling out to them, "Rabbi." As leaders enjoy status, title, and honor, they can become tangled in a web self-deceit and be set up for a fall.

The great leaders of faith who have enjoyed longevity and success in their careers have all exhibited humility and meekness of heart. They are not demanding and don't have expectations of special privilege by virtue of their office or position. When leaders of faith called by God begin embellishing their God-given power and privilege, they can be entangled in a sense of false pride. That false pride can lull a leader into thinking they themselves are superior or entitled. When this happens, God gets less glory, thanks, and praise. People whom you lead will notice this attitude, and their trust in you as a leader can begin to wane as a result.

God will not allow His leaders to act in such a way. God will bring low the proud. Leaders of faith make themselves vulnerable when they accept gifts that break ethical boundaries or make questionable alliances.

Successful leaders of faith should never feel the need to wear a special garment or gain a special title in order to feel worthy to serve. You will know great leaders by their works and by the aura of respect that surrounds them. You know will know them by their humility and quiet displays of power. You will know them by the loyalty and love others hold for them. Their status will only be magnified by their self-denial of special privileges. God multiplies His blessings on those leaders of faith whose only desire is to honor Him and serve others in love.

Our Prayer: *Dear God, to be chosen by You for a task of leadership is all the accolade we need. Keep us humble and focused on doing good works for others in Your name. Forgive us when we have used our title or status to gain an advantage over others. May all we have be used for Your Kingdom and for service to those in need.* **Amen.**

Signs Of The Times

"Leaders of Faith Should Know the Prophetic Signs of These Days"

"And Jesus answered and said unto them, Take heed that no man deceive you. For many shall come in my name, saying, I am the Christ; and shall deceive many. And ye shall hear of wars and rumors of wars: see that ye be not troubled: for all these things must come to pass, but the end is not yet…. For nation shall rise against nation…and there shall be earthquakes in divers places, and there shall be famines and troubles: these are the beginnings of sorrows"

Featured Scriptures: Matthew 24:4–6; and Mark 13:8
Background Scriptures: Mark 13; and Luke 21:5–28

These words of Christ concerning the future have been recorded in three of the four Gospels. Some of these words concerned the destruction of the Temple, but others foretell His Second Coming and are being fulfilled in living events today. Leaders of faith should discern that Christ is calling us to learn the prophetic signs of Scripture. He also tells us clearly to not be troubled, but to be careful of those who would deceive others.

Leaders of faith called to service by the living God do not work strictly in the earthly realm. Our callings and service are inexorably linked to the future and to eternity. The reality of this life is that times are tough and will get tougher. We live in a world of spiritual warfare, and battles are occurring around us that we often cannot see. Many persons will claim to be leaders of faith who are not. They are deceivers sent to thwart the plan of God. True leaders of faith must be vigilant and aware.

Theologians argue with great emotion over Jesus' words in these passages. Yet we must concede to the spiritual truth that God controls the future. We should study and pray to be shown the ways and timing of God's hand in the world around us. As leaders of faith, we must prepare our congregations and organizations for the potential of both prosperity and austerity. We should become as wise and as frugal as necessary to be ready for the difficult times. We must able to survive the perils of both nature and man.

Leaders can learn the prophetic signs and teach those around us to value the things that are most important: our faith, family, friends, and communities. We should teach others to relish the small blessings and simple pleasures. We should develop giving hearts and openness to share our faith and love with those we encounter. We may not know what the future holds, but we know who holds the future. Christ tells us to hear Him and not to be deceived or troubled. Be prepared to love and lead others through the prophetic days ahead.

Our Prayer: *Lord Jesus, thank You for sharing the Word of God with us. Inspire us to study the Word and to grasp the meaning of the prophetic voice of Scripture. Reassure us and comfort us in these days as we try to lead others, often in very difficult circumstances. Give us Your peace and power to come through all the storms. Instill in us a sense of urgency to share our faith and love with all we meet through word and deed until the day You come again.* **Amen.**

Preparation Comes Before Great Leadership

"Unprepared Leaders Can Miss the Master's Opportunity"

"And five of them were wise, and five were foolish. They that were foolish took their lamps, and took no oil with them: But the wise took oil in their vessels with their lamps…. And while they went to buy, the bridegroom came; and they that were ready went in with him to the marriage: and the door was shut."

Featured Scripture: Matthew 25:2–4, 10

Background Scriptures: Matthew 25:1–13; and 1 Thessalonians 5:1–11

The parable of the ten virgins and the bridegroom holds much prophetic meaning about Christ and the Church. It can also teach a valuable lesson about becoming prepared servants. Leaders of faith who pray for new callings from God must first be sure that they are like the five wise virgins. Preparation can be very basic, like having enough oil for your lamp before embarking on a journey.

In haste and excitement, the five foolish virgins were so taken in the excitement of the coming of the bridegroom that they ran out to meet him without being fully prepared. They also leapt at the cry that he was coming before knowing if it was truly him. Leaders of faith, too, can leap out at seemingly real opportunities only to find that their timing was bad or that they were not prepared.

Preparation for a calling of leadership means we must have the basics of readiness completed. Not only should we have ample oil for our lamps, we should have built good habits of study and prayer. We should be humble of heart and resolute in our principles. We should be content in all our circumstances, knowing that the Lord is using our most humble work to accomplish His will. God will provide the provision for the call, but we must be ready and prepared to seize it when it comes.

Some leaders of faith have missed the call of the Master because when it came, they discovered they needed more education or training. By the time they realized they were unprepared, the task had been given to another and the door of opportunity was shut. Watch for the coming of opportunity. Be nimble and ready to travel. Keep your life and finances in order. Cut out unnecessary frivolities so that your time entanglements are few. Be lean in health and heart. Be prepared for the call of the Master.

The Scripture says we don't know the day or the hour of Christ's return. We also don't know the day or hour of Christ's special call to us for a task of leadership for Him. Be ready. Have oil in your lamp. Watch for the signs of the bridegroom.

Our Prayer: *Lord, we give thanks that You came to us and will come again. Help us to be wise and to watch for You. As leaders of faith, help us to prepare for the tasks and callings You have for us. May we study hard and live good lives. May we be lean and willing to hear Your voice. Bless us as we prepare and wait for the chance to serve You in a new way.* **Amen.**

Sheepherders Or Goatherders

"Incorporating the 'Least of These' Principles in All Leadership"

"For I was an hungered, and ye gave me meat: I was thirsty, and ye gave me drink: I was a stranger, and ye took me in: Naked, and ye clothed me: I was sick and ye visited me: I was in prison, and ye came unto me…. And the King shall answer and say unto them, Verily I say unto you, Inasmuch as ye have done it unto one of the least of these my brethren, ye have done it also unto me."
Featured Scripture: Matthew 25:35–36, 40
Background Scripture: Matthew 25:31–46; Proverbs 14:31; and Hebrews 6:10

Regardless of what we do in our organizations or congregations, our leadership journeys of faith must incorporate the "Least of These" principle. Whether we sell products or lead a group of volunteers, it is imperative that we become sheepherders, not goatherders. Jesus was clear: We are to be ministers to all people of need in His name. Jesus says those that do are like the sheep to be placed at His right side. Those who ignore or overlook those in need are like the goats He will judge. Our command as leaders of faith is to herd sheep, not goats.

Underlying the principle of the "Least of These" is the holy understanding that all persons are precious to God and made in His image. All life is precious. Jesus bestows His same love and providence in the lives of the impoverished, sick, and imprisoned that He does in the righteous and prosperous among us. Jesus wants us to not only value every human life, but to minister to them as if we were doing it unto Him. When we see Jesus in the hurting humanity around us, it is a great sign that the love and power of the Lord Jesus is manifested in us. Our ministry to others in His name is what it means to be a sheepherder.

How should leaders of faith incorporate the "Least of These" principle into our daily tasks? We should begin by valuing all those who work with us and for us, and all those we lead. Every organization or congregation will interface with people from every walk of life. How do we treat those who serve us in menial tasks? Do we see the silent and forgotten who till the soil, prepare the meals, clean the rubbish? Do we consider everyone we meet as though they were part of our own families? Are we too hasty to judge the plight of the homeless, prisoners, or addicted? God did not call us to judge or to make value statements of their worth. He called us to love and serve them. Before we can lead others by this principle, we must pray for and practice the act of service and humility and love to others. When this love and sense of obligation exists in the very fabric of our souls, others will seek to emulate our lives.

When you become a sheepherder for the "Least of These," God will bless you and those you lead in new and abundant ways. The very breath of Jesus will be upon your shoulders as you do.

Our Prayer: *Lord Jesus, make us aware of the worth and wonder in everyone around us. You made us all in Your image, and we belong to You. Give us the heart to love and serve the least of those persons around us. Let us not judge, but serve others with Your same passion. Let us be the sheep at Your right side. Make us sheepherders in our leadership journeys of faith.* **Amen.**

Leaders Set Priorities Others Don't Share

"TRUE LEADERSHIP IS BOLDLY SEEING THE FUTURE AS OTHERS DON'T"

"There came unto him a woman having an alabaster box of very precious ointment, and poured it on his head…. But when the disciples saw it, they had indignation, saying, To what purpose is this waste?... When Jesus understood it, he said unto them, Why trouble ye the woman? For she hath wrought a good work upon me…that this woman hath done, be told of a memorial to her."
FEATURED SCRIPTURE: MATTHEW 26: 7–8, 10, 13
BACKGROUND SCRIPTURES: MATTHEW 26:6–16; AND JOHN 12:1–8

Besides Christ, the real leaders in this story should be Jesus' disciples. After all, they had been chosen for the task of carrying on the message of the Gospel of Jesus. But in today's encounter, it was not the disciples who exemplified true vision and leadership, it was the woman who took of her own resources and anointed our Savior for His death. The Book of John tells us that this woman was in fact Mary, the sister of Lazarus. In certain situations of life, unlikely people are given a vision of purpose. They have God-given insights into what is the appropriate thing to do, and they take action.

Two lessons may be found here for leaders of faith. First, when we are the ones who have been given a God-sent vision, we should act upon it in faith. We should know that others will be critical, especially if they do not share that same vision. But if it is right and true, just like Mary in the anointing of Jesus, our decisions will be blessed.

The second lesson is that we, like the disciples, may be the designated leaders in the situation, but another unlikely leader can come along with an idea, vision, or bold priority that we do not understand at that time. In those moments, we need the discernment of Christ Himself, who sensed in the woman a holy purpose. We must never suppose as leaders of faith that we alone have all the good ideas and vision for our organizations. We should not chastise those who offer themselves up for service.

The cost of setting the right priorities may not only be the ridicule or criticism that it brings; it may, in fact, be the financial sacrifice of it. The cost of the spices and oil that Mary used on Jesus was the equivalent of the wages of a rural worker's pay for one year. The disciples could not fathom that Mary's act was worth the cost. They imagined how much food could be bought for the poor with that amount of money. Yet Jesus knew the symbolism of this act, and He understood that the financial sacrifice was part of her faith.

We, too, as leaders of faith must be bold in setting priorities of leadership. When we are called by God, it will always involve setting priorities that others may not share. But, like Mary, we must serve in boldness and certainty as we anoint others in Christ's name!

Our Prayer: *Lord Jesus, we are amazed at this beautiful act performed by Mary out of her love for You. We see the glory and love and faith as she made this act her priority of service to You. May we as leaders of faith have the same vision and sense of purpose to set priorities and to take action that is pleasing to You. Bless us, we pray.* **Amen.**

Fellowship With Those We Lead

"Appropriate Fellowship with Those We Lead Builds Strong Bonds"

"I will keep the Passover at thy house with my disciples. And the disciples did as Jesus had appointed them and they made ready the Passover. Now when the even was come, he sat down with the twelve… And when they had sung a hymn, they went out into the Mount of Olives."

Featured Scripture: Matthew 26:18–20,30
Background Scripture: Matthew 26:17–30

Many important events occurred during the Lord's Last Supper with His disciples. Christ laid before us the new sacraments of bread and wine to represent our remembrance of Him. He announced His betrayal. He washed His disciples' feet. But today's lesson focuses on another unique aspect of this night of celebration of the Passover. Jesus shows us the significance of intimate times of fellowship with those you lead.

As leaders of faith, we are indebted to our faithful followers and to those close associates with whom we entrust and share our mission. Many of these persons serve us with silent admiration and affection that they may not ever really disclose. Great leaders will sense the love and devotion others show in their work. We should be mindful that scheduling times of fellowship with those we lead is a powerful and necessary task of leadership.

Appropriate fellowship with those we lead, by way of a special meal or a casual gathering, validates the importance of those coworkers who serve in our callings. It sets forth an opportunity to show mutual respect and admiration. It gives us a chance to express our thanks and love. Fellowship is a time of intimacy that cannot occur in the hectic atmosphere of the formal workplace. Setting aside time after formal hours of work shows the importance of fellowship.

In this intimate setting in the Upper Room, Jesus entrusted the future Church to these disciples. He showed them that the Master was a servant and that they, too, must be servants. Each disciple had a different personality and different gifts. Judas would betray Christ. Peter would deny Him, but be reconciled. In fellowship times with our coworkers, we, too, will see the varying levels of affection and loyalty of those who serve with us. These times can build great memories and a deeper loyalty among team members. It also is a time to pray for special collective blessings for each other and for the collective work we do for others.

Strive in your leadership journey of faith to affirmatively set aside times and special places to fellowship with those who most closely serve you. It will build bonds that bind you together and further the mission God gives you to do. Our Scripture today tells us that Christ and the disciples sang a hymn together and then departed to the Mount of Olives. Let us sing and fellowship in praise together with those we leadand with those with whom we share our work for the Lord and Savior.

Our Prayer: *Lord Jesus, we give thanks for having shared the story of the Upper Room. Teach us to have intimacy and fellowship with those who serve with us. Help us to set an example of humble service in our leadership. Bind us together with those who freely give of their time and lives to help us succeed. May we sing and glorify You together in fellowship and love.* **Amen.**

The Cup That Will Not Pass

"GOD'S PLAN OFTEN TAKES US THROUGH NECESSARY SUFFERING AND SEPARATION"

"And he went a little further, and fell on his face, and prayed, saying, O my Father, if it be possible, let this cup pass from me: nevertheless not as I will, but as thou wilt. He went away again the second time, and prayed, saying O my Father, if this cup may not pass away from me, except I drink it, thy will be done."

FEATURED SCRIPTURE: MATTHEW 26:39, 42

BACKGROUND SCRIPTURES: MARK 14:36; LUKE 22:39–44; JOHN 12:20–33; GENESIS 3:15; PSALM 22:2; PSALM 22:14; DANIEL 9:26; ISAIAH 53:1–3; ZECHARIAH 11:12; AND 13:7

The time was nigh. Jesus had been born in a manger. The wise men had come and gone. The boy Jesus had taught in the Temple. John the Baptist had prepared the way of the Lord. Jesus was baptized. Water was turned to wine at the wedding at Cana. The disciples had been chosen. Many miracles and healings had been wrought. The greatest teachings of all time, describing the New Covenant of God and the Way, the Truth, and the Life, had been spoken. Finally, in Gethsemane, Christ came to His moment with God. He knew that His time of physical suffering for the sins of others and temporary separation from His Father had come, yet He prayed for the cup to pass; even more, He prayed for God's will to be done.

All four Gospel writers described the passion of this time of Christ. Jesus knew full well where His journey was taking Him. Old Testament prophecy described the death of Christ over thirty-six times from Genesis to Zechariah. But one last time Jesus went to Abba, Father to pray for the bitter cup to pass. Jesus clearly wanted to do the will of the Father. Luke wrote that Jesus sweat drops of blood as He prayed. Upon His accepting the will of God, an angel came and ministered to Him. Jesus knew what He had been called to do. It was the bitter cup, and He would partake of it.

For most who are called to a task of faith, there will be a bitter cup to drink along the way. Are you in the mind of Christ to drink of it? Like Christ, we want the difficult cup of our suffering in leadership to pass. We can surely pray for it to pass. Sometimes it may. Sometimes it will not. In the case of Christ, it did not. The plan and will of God must go forth. The Scripture must be fulfilled. Jesus in all things obeyed the will of the Father. How about you?

Our bitter cup may or may not bring us death or physical stress, but it may bring separation from friends and loved ones. It may involve some form of conflict. But God gives us our cup of leadership to drink for His Holy purpose. If your difficult cup will not pass, pray that God's will be done and that He give you the strength to overcome. The bitter cups we face in our journeys are in God's hands and can be used to change the lives of those we serve.

Our Prayer: *Lord Jesus, we praise and honor You right now for Your love for us and for Your obedience to the calling of God. You suffered for us even in Your deity and perfection. You endured our whippings, humiliation, judgment, and death. Thank You, Lord, for the gift of salvation by Your blood spilt for us. May we as leaders of faith follow Your example of obedience as we come face-to-face with our own bitter cup experience in service for You.* **Amen.**

Washing Your Hands Of A Bad Situation

"When Your Sense of Justice Is Overridden for Political Expedience"

"When Pilate saw that he could not prevail at all, but rather that a tumult was rising, he took water and washed his hands before the multitude, saying, I am innocent of the blood of this just person. You see to it."
Featured Scripture: Matthew 27:24
Background Scriptures: Matthew 27:11–26; and John 18:28—19:16

Leaders of faith should always be cautious before washing their hands of a bad situation. Pilate's action at Jesus' trial has been etched into folk language of modern history and become known as the euphemism: washing your hands of a bad situation. It may equate to shirking your responsibility to serve justice. It may equate to shortchanging or betraying a friend. It may equate to not confessing a sinful lifestyle when confronted by others. It may mean telling a small lie to avoid embarrassment.

Pontius Pilate was faced with a defining situation in faith and history on that day. He knew in his heart that Jesus had committed no crime and was no threat to the people. Trained in the Roman system of justice, Pilate must have had a burning desire to release Jesus and scold His accusers. The political collision of the Roman and Jewish worlds and the fulfillment of prophecy all came to a head with this trial and this Roman governor on this historic day. Not only did Pilate condemn an innocent man, he caved to the raucous crowd by changing a sentence of flogging to a sentence of death upon a cross. In a final effort to salvage some semblance of justice, Pilate offered an amnesty plan by proposing to pardon Jesus on this Jewish holy day; the crowd refused.

Pilate made the wrong decision for fear of the crowd. He shunned justice out of a greater concern for his own political future. Pilate's career did not last long after that as he eventually fell out of favor with the rulers in Rome. Tradition says that in his final days he lived a tormented life. Leaders of faith will all face moments when we will be confronted with extremely difficult public choices to make. The path of least resistance usually leads down the road of injustice and harms innocent persons. When we seek political expedience over the pursuit of fairness, we, too, are washing our hands of a bad situation.

God often allows leaders to be placed in the midst of controversial public choices. When we see only contentious outcomes, we should put our reliance on God to the test. God longs for us to go to our knees to Him in intercession and prayer. He wants us to pursue justice and mercy for His name's sake. When we allow ourselves to totally rely on Him in these moments of severe choices, He will open a third way that will lead to heavenly fruit. We may feel the thorns of our choices for a short while, but we will always prevail if we avoid washing our hands of a bad situation. Stand tall in faith and confidence as you make your tough choices today.

Our Prayer: *Lord Jesus, our passions and emotions rise and fall with You as we meditate on Your trial before Pilate. Never let us take the path of least resistance, Lord. Give us the courage to seek Your will and Your power to stand and make the right choices in the public eye. Forgive us when we, too, have failed You. Never let us wash our hands of a bad situation and shortchange the Kingdom of God.* **Amen.**

Choosing The Right Witnesses

"Those Who Love Us and Are Faithful to Us Will Bear Witness for Us"

"In the end of the Sabbath, as it began to dawn…came Mary Magdalene and the other Mary to see the sepulcher, and the angel answered and said unto the women, fear not ye: for I know that ye seek Jesus, which was crucified. He is not here: for He is risen…come see the place where the Lord lay. And go quickly, and tell his disciples that he is risen from the dead…and they went to tell his disciples."

Featured Scripture: Matthew 28:1, 5–7, 8
Background Scriptures: Matthew 28:1–10; John 20: 10—21

No account ever written is as valuable to mankind as the resurrection of Christ. The events of the resurrection are critical to our salvation and faith. But truly enlightening is to whom the reality of Jesus' resurrection was first shared. God chose the right witnesses to announce the fulfillment of prophecy and the promise of Christ's resurrection: the women whom Christ loved and who would now hear, see, and bear witness to an empty tomb and the resurrected Lord for all generations to come.

According to written Scripture accounts, Jesus made some eleven appearances over forty days after His resurrection and before His ascension to heaven. He primarily appeared to the women who loved Him, His disciples, including Peter and James, and a special multitude of about five hundred. In the years to follow, these persons would provide the eyewitness account to the physical, risen Lord.

The greatest story ever told is not left to priests, historians, media, and public officials to tell. Jesus knew that if people were to hear and believe in His resurrection, He had to have the right witnesses, witnesses who loved Him and believed in Him, who would cause the Passion story to spread. These women had the least clout in the formal legal and religious society of their day. Choosing the right witnesses often means choosing the most unlikely of persons to give testimony to your life and leadership.

Our earthly lives, and certainly our stints as leaders, are limited. Our message, purpose, and vision will certainly die with us unless we pass it along to a select few who can build upon it and bear witness to the values and ideals we represent. As we wane in our leadership journeys, it is important to find unlikely, but loyal loving brothers and sister, with whom we can share our values and stories.

The witnesses we choose should love us, even as we love them. If God has led us into positions of leadership, He will certainly provide loving witnesses and messengers to bear witness to our work so that it will not have been in vain. Surround yourself with meek, loving, and loyal friends and followers who will share your stories with others and bear witness to God's continuing love.

Our Prayer: *Heavenly Father, we give thanks and praise for a risen Lord who loves us and revealed Himself to us through witnesses and disciples of faith. Help us in our spiritual and leadership journeys to so inspire others to build on our vision of service to You and others.* **Amen.**

Unorthodox Leaders And Messages

"UNORTHODOX LEADERSHIP CAN BRING BOLD NEW MESSAGES TO STRANGE PLACES"

"John did baptize in the wilderness, and preach the baptism of repentance for the remission of sins…. And John was clothed with camel's hair, and with a girdle of a skin about his loins; and he did eat locusts and wild honey."
FEATURED SCRIPTURE: MARK 1:4, 6
BACKGROUND SCRIPTURE: LUKE 7:24–35

Preparing the way of the Lord as John the Baptist did was not done by conventional methods. John was not a refined, learned Jewish priest opining on the fulfillment of the Scripture from the Temple courtyard. He was a wilderness man, dressed in fur and a loincloth. He ate locusts and honey and preached a radically new Gospel of repentance from sin with a renewed call to baptism.

God ordained this unorthodox messenger for His express purpose. This voice crying in the wilderness was preparing the way of the Lord. The unorthodox leadership of John the Baptist developed such a following and power among the people that even King Herod and the Jewish leaders came to fear him. John gained many followers and disciples with his culminating act of the baptism of Christ Himself. Jesus declared the greatness of John the Baptist in Matthew 11:11: "That no man born of a woman was as great as John the Baptist."

Not all leaders of faith today are as bold or radical as John. Yet the great message of hope and deliverance can sometimes only be effectively delivered from unorthodox leaders armed with new and bold, God-inspired messages of repentance and salvation.

Has the old orthodoxy of your leadership journey made you ineffective? Have the old methods and the traditional approaches to leadership caused you to become stale? Are your followers and congregants leaving the fold? Is your organization stagnant with inactivity? Maybe God is calling you to become a new voice in the wilderness. Perhaps you, too, need to step out of the traditional boundaries and become bold in preaching a new message of hope in these times before Christ comes again.

John shows us that effectiveness in leadership is not about how we dress or what we eat or where we lead, but in whom we serve. John knew that God's task for him from his birth was to prepare the way of the Lord. His life and service would end with his martyrdom for Christ, and his work built a foundation for the Lord's ministry on earth.

We as leaders sometimes need to strip away the royal garments of pretension and orthodoxy and trade them for animal skins. We need to trade the old, stale messages of tradition for a new boldness and challenge to those we lead. Leave your comfort zone and go into a new wilderness of leadership with bold ideas that inspire others to action. We may bring scorn of critics, but we will earn the respect and trust of those we lead and serve.

Our Prayer: *God, we give thanks for John the Baptist. Instill in us that same passion and drive to fulfill Your calling. You often place us in strange places and circumstances of leadership. Give us courage to be bold for You by going into the wilderness and trying new, unorthodox ways of ministering to others. Sustain us and bless the work of our hands that we may prepare and lead others to Christ's love and salvation.* **Amen.**

News Travels Fast

"Your Ability to Heal Can Stifle Your Ability to Preach Salvation"

"And when they had found him, they said unto him, all men seek for thee. And he said unto them, let us go into the next towns, that I may preach there also: therefore came I forth. And he preached in their synagogues throughout all Galilee, and cast out devils. And there came a leper to him…and Jesus moved with compassion, put forth his hand, and touched him…be thou clean…and saith unto him, see thou say nothing to any man…but he went out and published it much…insomuch that Jesus could no more openly enter into the city, but was without in desert places…."

Featured Scripture: Mark 1:37–42, 44–45
Background Scriptures: Mark 1:35–45; Luke 5:12–16; and Leviticus 14

Jesus had the power to heal leprosy. In that day, this ghastly disease decimated the lives and families of people who contracted it . There was no medicine or cure in that day for leprosy, which sentenced a person to pain and banishment from society. But when Jesus encountered a leper, He was moved with compassion and healed him. Jesus told the healed man not to tell others but instead to immediately show himself to the priest. The healed man disobeyed Christ and greatly publicized the healing event. The news of the miracle traveled fast, and subsequent frenzied crowds would limit Christ's ability to openly preach in the cities.

Leaders of faith are called to perform specific tasks for God. Our positions of leadership often give us powers, credentials, and access to do things that others cannot do. Once those around us see our power, they may come to us, not to hear about God's love, but to receive a benefit. Leaders must guard against letting their primary callings be overwhelmed by secondary tasks, such as performing personal favors for those around us.

The leper who disobeyed Christ's request for discretion set forth a frenzy where people primarily sought Christ as a healer instead of the Messiah. Jesus' primary task of preaching became harder to perform because of it. Because the crowds were coming to Christ for the wrong reasons, He had to move on to other places.

Does our leadership status create a demand for our presence and services from those around us? Are you as a leader of faith able to separate acts of goodwill and compassion done for others from your greater calling to share Christ's love and salvation? Our good deeds do give testimony to our compassion and love, yet we must always guard against letting others misuse or misinterpret our true purpose as called leaders of faith.

Like Christ, we may have to retreat from the crowds and venues where people see us not as ministers of the Gospel, but as givers of favors. Jesus knew why He had come to this planet. He had the message of all time to share, and the gates of hell would not prevail against it. His preaching and life forever changed our world. He healed, but He also preached. He knew what was temporal and what was eternal. Don't let your ability to heal stifle your ability to share the Good News!

Our Prayer: *Lord Jesus, we need to be healed, but even more we need to hear Your voice and the Good News of salvation. As Your leaders called by Your name, help us to never let our focus of leadership stray from the message of salvation. Let us heal and serve others, but let us most of all preach Your love, grace, mercy, and salvation.* **Amen.**

Uncover Your Candle

"The Light and Calling Within You Must Be Set Apart to Shine"

"And he said unto them, is a candle brought to be put under a bushel, or under a bed, and not to be set on a candlestick? For nothing is secret, that shall not be made manifest; neither any thing hid, that shall not be known and come abroad…. Therefore judge nothing before the time, until the Lord come, who both will bring to light the hidden things of darkness, and will make manifest the counsels of the hearts: and then shall every man have praise of God."

FEATURED SCRIPTURES: MARK 4:21; LUKE 8:17; AND 1 CORINTHIANS 4:5
BACKGROUND SCRIPTURES: LUKE 8:16–21; AND 1 CORINTHIANS 4:1–5

Within most of us burns a passion, a secret dream, or a longing to pour our lives out for some greater cause. This pulling and tugging within us is God lighting our candle. Too often, however, this candle never burns its brightest. Our Scripture today tells us that the candle God lights within us must never be hidden or shaded. God is calling you in earnest to uncover your candle and shine brightly for the Kingdom today.

Leaders of faith hide their candles under many different bushels. We hide them from the winds of human conflict, fearing they will blow out our success. We hide it under our beds of insecurity and lack of self-confidence. We hide it behind the wall of procrastination or fear of being ridiculed by others. Christ tells us that we should never let His light or our call to proclaim His Word and love be hidden in any way.

Sometimes we cover our candles because the light of day seems bright enough, and we don't sense that others need to see our small torches. People long to see love and tenderness shown toward them, even if by a flicker of love through a small deed of kindness. Shining our light of humility and selflessness in our daily work can illuminate the way for the cynical and lost to find hope again. Our candle shines brightest in times of adversity. Even our small flames of light can lead others to the safety of Christ's grace and mercy.

Organizations and congregations have candles, too. Yet within the walls of our organizations, this light can become hidden by the listless traditions that fail to inspire others. Our congregants hide their candles when they fail to nurture, recruit, and affirm the talents and input of new members and new ideas. We blow our own candles out when we allow injustice and poverty to go unaddressed. God desires that we shed any habit, doubt, or obstacle that diminishes our candlelight. It may mean that we give up the bad habits that dim our candles' power. It may mean that we quit a profession or hobby that impedes our ability to shine the true light of God's love to those around us.

What is obstructing the holy light within you today? Give it over to God in prayer and confession. Let the power of the Holy Spirit remove the barriers that prevent you from shining God's love forth to others. Uncover your candle in a new way today. Let God shine through you!

Our Prayer: *Lord of light, we come this day beseeching Your power and intercession in removing the barriers that prevent our holy light from shining. Let us never be ashamed or timid to share Your love and Word to others this day. Uncover our candles in new ways, so we may share Christ more boldly.* **Amen.**

But Whom Do You Say That I Am?

"Polls, Perceptions, and Spiritual Truth"

"And Jesus went out, and his disciples, into the towns of Caesarea Philippi: and by the way he asked his disciples, saying unto them, Whom do men say that I am? And they answered, John the Baptist: but some say Elias; and others, one of the prophets. And he saith unto them, But whom say ye that I am? And Peter answered and said unto him, Thou art the Christ."

Featured Scripture: Mark 8:27–30
Background Scripture: Matthew 16:13–20

Christ posed the ultimate spiritual polling question of all time when He asked His disciples: *"Who do you say that I am?"* After a day's work, Jesus gathered His disciples around Him and questioned them about what the people were saying about Him. The disciples had taken an informal poll of the people, and they told Jesus that some believed Him to be another John the Baptist. Others thought He was Elijah or another great prophet. But the central challenge Christ posed was for all of His disciples, even today, to know Him in a more unique and personal way.

The question Christ asked His disciples many years ago still rings in the ears of each of us. A called leader of faith hopefully does know Jesus as the Christ. And while others may consider Him to simply be a significant religious historical figure, a prophet, or a holy man, we are called to a higher measure. We all must answer that spiritual polling question that Christ places before us today and serve Him in a way consistent with our answers.

Leaders are too often consumed with the opinions and the perceptions of others. We all want to be liked, and thus we seek the validation of those to whom we are accountable. Leaders are influenced by the traditions and customs of their upbringing. Leaders' opinions are also formed from educational and professional experience. But today Jesus is asking you a personal and very direct question. He does not ask "Who does your pastor say that I am?" or "What does your board of directors say that I am?" or "Who do the great religious scholars say that I am?" Jesus is asking you this moment: "Who do you say that I am?"

If you are to serve Christ effectively, you must get to know Him better. You must learn the Scriptures and seek Him daily in prayer and fervent study. You must get to know Him by feeding His sheep and tending to the hurts of the lowliest around you. You must follow His example of meekness, purity, and selflessness. You must become a suffering servant, forgiving those who persecute you. You must obey His commandments and claim His limitless power.

As we mature in our walk with Christ, we can more clearly answer the question of who He really is. It is incumbent upon each one of us to answer the question He poses to us today with greater clarity each time we are asked. If we know and serve Christ in the way He desires, then others will see Jesus shine through us. They will come to know Him also as they observe what we do and how we love and serve others.

Our Prayer: *Lord Jesus, You are the Christ. You are our hope and salvation. You give us life and are our sustainer and joy. Show us how to get to know You better and more intimately this day. Indwell us so that we yearn to serve You with gladness, joy, and limitless power. Let our works and service to others become the best definition of who You really are.* **Amen.**

Transfigured Leadership

"Leaving the Mortal Moment to See God's Glory and Eternal Plan"

"And after six days Jesus taketh with him Peter, James and John and leadeth them up into a high mountain apart by themselves: and he was transfigured before them. And his raiment became shining, exceeding white as snow…and there appeared unto them Elijah with Moses: and they were talking with Jesus…. And there was a cloud that overshadowed them: and a voice came out of the cloud saying, this is my beloved Son: hear him. And suddenly, when they had looked round about, they saw no man any more, save Jesus only with themselves."

Featured Scripture: Mark 9:2–4, 8
Background Scriptures: Mark 9:2–13; and Matthew 17:1–13

Jesus took His inner circle of disciples—Peter, James, and John—away with Him into solitude upon a mountain. On this day, the disciples would come to see their Master in a new light and be confronted with the reality of Christ's true glory. The human person of Christ whom they had toiled with in the faith vineyard for all these months would now be revealed to them in a new and miraculous way. The transfiguration of Christ and the appearance of Elijah and Moses gave notice to the disciples that their callings and lives were sacred.

Transfigured leadership can come to us when we yield our self-made plans to our heavenly calling from God. As leaders of faith who are called to perform eternal duties on this earth, we can have our own transfiguring moments. While we may not be visited by Elijah or Moses or hear God's voice from a cloud, if we allow God's Spirit to transform our souls and purpose for living, we, too, will become different leaders to those who observe us. When we become transfigured leaders, our priorities change. The way we deal with other people changes. Our demeanors become more loving and peaceful. Our prayer lives and interaction with fellow believers become richer and more loving. Those who follow us will suddenly know that we are part of a bigger, more holy mission. They, too, will seek transformation in their own lives. Our congregations and organizations will begin transforming as team members see God and the tasks we are given to do in sanctified and more glorified ways.

The transfiguration of our Lord was brief, but its impact on Peter, James, and John was lasting. On the mountain that day, after a few moments of glory, Jesus transformed back into the bodily form the disciples recognized. Yet, in a few shining moments of glory, Jesus chose to reveal Himself in a new way to His most trusted followers. In this act, Jesus allowed them to gain a glimpse of the majesty and importance of their calling.

We can't shine as leaders in every moment and situation, but we can carefully choose situations and moments when we reveal something deeper about ourselves and allow those who follow us to look more deeply into our souls. Share your testimony. Worship with others in full spirit. Confess your deepest feelings to your admirers. You will transform briefly in their eyes, and perhaps they, too, will see the greatness in the call to God's service.

Our Prayer: *Lord Jesus, in reading the Scripture we, too, can see You transfigure from a carpenter's son to the Son of God. We gain a glimpse of Your majesty and glory. Thank You for letting us share in this moment of holy contemplation. Transform us; transfigure us, O Lord, into holier and more sacred servants and leaders of faith. Help others see a change in our lives. Open our souls up in special moments so those around us can see God shine forth from our lives.* **Amen.**

Not What You Wanted To Hear

"SUCCESS IN OUR CALLINGS MEANS SACRIFICE AND CONFRONTING OUR REJECTIONS"

"There came one running, and kneeled to him, and asked him, Good Master, what shall I do that I may inherit eternal life?... Thou knowest the commandments...and he answered and said unto him, Master, all these have I observed from my youth. Then Jesus beholding him loved him, and said unto him, one thing thou lackest: go thy way, sell whatsoever thou hast, and give to the poor, and thou shalt have treasure in heaven: and come, take up the cross, and follow me. And he was sad at that saying, and went away grieved: for he had great possessions."

FEATURED SCRIPTURE: MARK 10:17, 19–22
BACKGROUND SCRIPTURES: MARK 10:17–31; AND MATTHEW 19:16–26

The word had gotten around the community that Jesus was passing by. The rich young ruler had also heard of it. His heart must have burned and caused him to seek out Jesus on this day; he even came running to Jesus, inquiring enthusiastically about becoming a follower of Jesus. In confronting Jesus, the rich young ruler asked the question many leaders of faith ask: *"What must I do to inherit eternal life?"* However, on this day he got an answer that was not what he wanted to hear.

Following Christ as a leader of faith is not an easy journey. When we answer God's call to perform tasks of heavenly significance, Christ will require acts of sacrifice that we did not anticipate. Not everyone we encounter will be as excited about our callings to leadership as we are—and we may experience this rejection. Like the rich young ruler, we, too, may receive the call to follow Jesus, only to find out the price is higher than we had imagined. We, too, may not hear want we want to hear as we begin to lead others in Christ's name.

Christ may, indeed, want you to sell all that you have in order to follow Him. Or Christ may simply want you to sell out all your assumptions and preconceived notions of what you are supposed to do and say on this journey for Him. Often the selling out of our own assumptions in leadership is the hardest thing to do. Giving up our safety nets and comfort zones means walking down new and unfamiliar roads with only our faith in Christ as a map. The rich young ruler wanted to follow Christ, but he received an answer to his question that he did not want to hear, and he mistakenly walked away from an eternal blessing because of it.

Did you receive a rejection this week? Did a superior or customer or coworker break your spirit by telling you something you did not want to hear? Is the price of your leadership journey of faith higher, more expensive, and more time-consuming than you had imagined? These disappointments are not the death of our calling, but merely Christ pushing us to a higher level of commitment and blessing. As we give up more, and suffer more, we become more available for Christ to take us into new territories of blessings. Follow your rejection and the answers you did not want to hear into the new light of Christ's shining opportunities in the Kingdom of Heaven.

Our Prayer: *Lord Jesus, You don't always give us the answer we want to hear. The cost of discipleship is high, but so are the rewards. Create in us obedient and surrendering spirits so we can pour all we have into Your service. Lead us through the rejection, disappointment, and insurmountable odds we face each day in our leadership walk. Show us a new silver lining of new mercy and blessing as we walk on in faith with You this very day.* **Amen.**

Right Hand, Left Hand, Bitter Cup

"THE PECKING ORDER OF REAL LEADERS IS MEASURED NOT BY STATUS, BUT BY SACRIFICE"

"They said unto him, Grant unto us that we may sit, one on thy right hand, and the other on thy left hand, in thy glory. But Jesus said unto them, Ye know not what ye ask: can ye drink of the cup that I drink of…and be baptized with the baptism that I am baptized with?"

FEATURED SCRIPTURE: MARK 10:37–38
BACKGROUND SCRIPTURES: MARK 10:35–45; MATTHEW 20:20–28; AND LUKE 22:23–38

How often the seeds of dissension are sown by the ambition of those we lead, followers who desire status, positions, and titles of greater power. The good ambition to serve others with increased responsibility can bleed into a desire to sit at the right or left hand of the seat of power. Jesus Himself was confronted with this situation in His own ministry from His own disciples. Many lessons of life and theology can be learned from this inquiry by Jesus' disciples and from His response to them. For all those who follow Jesus in leadership, there will be a bitter cup to drink on the path to our reward.

In our own leadership journeys of faith, we may all succumb at certain points to the intoxication or aphrodisiac of power and position. It is a powerful temptress and can prove our undoing unless we are tethered soundly to the humility of our calling. The disciples had seen the power and miracles of Jesus. They had seen the crowds and heard the Word of God spoken from the mouth of Jesus. They had been chosen out of all people on earth as one of the twelve disciples. But now they wanted more. They wanted the certainty of sitting at the right or left hand of Jesus in eternity. But coming up almost immediately for both Jesus and the disciples was the bitter cup of suffering.

Our role model in our leadership journeys is the Suffering Servant, Christ the Lord. How can any leader of faith, truly called by God; not be called to suffering? There will certainly be power, provision, and blessing. There will certainly be an eternal reward. But all of us will experience the bitter cup of disappointment, sacrifice, and even betrayal by those we love and trust. Christ said that the pecking order of heaven is ordained by God Himself and not for us to know. But rest assured our blessings will be beyond our wildest imagination. For the time being, we as leaders of faith should not look to be on the right or left, but squarely in the hands of our Lord as we drink of the bitter cup of salvation, sacrifice, and service.

When we have abandoned our wild ambition for status, position, and power, that is usually the very time when God deems us ready for a promotion. Keep moving forward in humility and service to others. God will grant the title and reward you deserve in His perfect way and time.

Our Prayer: *Dear Suffering Servant, we praise Your holy name. Thank You for choosing us to serve and suffer with You for the sake of others. Protect us, Lord, from blind ambition and the desire to obtain higher rank while losing sight of humble service. Bless every small and loving act of our hands that it may please You. Reward us with Your love and salvation.* **Amen.**

A Calm And Measured Response

"LEADERS SHOULD RESIST EMOTION AND EGO WHEN RESPONDING TO CONTROVERSY"

"There came to him the chief priests, and the scribes, and the elders, and say unto him, by what authority doest thou these things? And who gave thee this authority to do these things? And Jesus answered and said unto them, I will ask of you one question, and answer me, and I will tell you by what authority I do these things.... And they answered and said unto Jesus, We cannot tell. And Jesus answering said, neither do I tell you by what authority I do these things."

FEATURED SCRIPTURE: MARK 11:27–29, 33

BACKGROUND SCRIPTURE: MARK 11:27–33

It was Christ's great opportunity during this encounter with His detractors to unleash His true power and show His real authority. The very notion that these self-righteous leaders would challenge the Messiah and Son of God to reveal His authority should have prompted Jesus to immediate action. But it was the calm and measured response of Christ that showed who really did have the authority. For Christ to have revealed His glory to the religious authorities at this moment would have disrupted the grand plan of God. If Christ had let human emotion or His own indignity govern His response in the Temple that day, He could have destroyed the prophecy of thousands of years. Through Christ's confrontation with the chief priests, scribes, and elders, we learn that our callings are sacred, holy, and beyond the reach of men.

A calm and measured response in our own times of controversy and crisis demands that we be grounded in humility, true power, and singleness of purpose. We must exude the confidence of a higher calling and purpose when confronted by our rivals. To succumb to harsh words or to improperly unleash some institutional authority upon your critics at the wrong time may trivialize your ministry.

Jesus could have summoned a legion of angels to the Temple that day, blinding the hypocrites who dared question the authority of the Son of God. He could have physically transfigured Himself into the Godhead at that very moment and struck the contingent dead on the spot. The observers in the Temple would then have known the authority of Christ. But with that response, Jesus would have missed the suffering of the cross. The conquering power of His resurrection would have never taken place, and our path to forgiveness and eternal life would have been forever blocked. Jesus had many opportunities to display His power and reveal His true authority during His earthly ministry. He performed untold miracles, walked on water, and transformed into a glorified Messiah in front of His own disciples. He rose from the dead and appeared before many after His resurrection, and ascended to heaven before an assembly.

Jesus knew when and when not to show His authority. His calm and measured response at the critical junctures of His mission saved us all. Don't let your own mission and calling be disrupted by the dares of others to show your authority at a difficult time. Be calm. Be measured. Let the Spirit guide you and give you peace in all circumstances.

Our Prayer: *Lord Jesus, Your authority is unfathomable. Your power is immeasurable. Yet You showed us how to remain calm and measured when our callings and authority are questioned. Give us Your grace and poise in the tough situations so we, too, can conquer evil and fulfill Your purpose in our work each day.* **Amen.**

The Law And The Master's Words

"LEADERS SHINE CLARITY AND PURPOSE ON GOD'S COMMANDMENTS"

"And thou shalt love the Lord thy God with all thy heart, and with all thy soul, and with all thy mind, and with all thy strength: this is the first commandment. And the second is like, namely this, Thou shalt love thy neighbor as thyself. There is none other commandment greater than these."

FEATURED SCRIPTURE: MARK 12:30–31
BACKGROUND SCRIPTURE: EXODUS 20:1–17; DEUTERONOMY 5:1–21; AND MARK 10:17–25

The Ten Commandments were the central cohesive factor for the people of God. They were written with the very finger of God. These ten laws outlined the proper relationship between man and God. They set forth the fundamental responsibilities that persons have in living in a godly society. The rule of law of many nations borrows from the tenements of the Holy Law. Jesus Himself spoke of adherence to the Law as being central to the faith. But Jesus provided a New Covenant. He fulfilled and brought clarity and purpose to the Law. The Law and the Master's words are today the very words of Scripture and our own road map in the faith.

The people of Christ's day lived in a rigorous adherence to religious laws, customs, and traditions. The interpreters of those laws wielded great power and authority over the population. Many abused the privilege and selfishly manipulated others for selfish gain. The real path to salvation was often muted in the corruption and legal dicing of the central truths of God.

In His life and teachings, the Master's words opened the hearts of men to know the heart of God. Jesus knew that if we loved our neighbors as we loved our very selves, then we were in step with God. Jesus knew that if we loved God, we would give up the love of money and treasures of this life to follow Him.

In our own leadership journeys of faith, we, too, must be prepared to clarify the basic laws of God in everyday activities that we supervise. We can instill Christ's call to love of neighbor in our corporate creeds and business practices. We can assure that theft and adultery are not rewarded by celebrating honesty and purity. We can set forth policies that empower families and cause the respect of parenting to be lifted up. We can honor the Sabbath by facilitating our employees' ability to worship. We can create a culture where all persons are valued and rewarded and coveting a fellow worker's perks is no longer necessary.

As great leaders called by God for the holy tasks of leadership, we will make the Ten Commandments and the Master's words come alive to those we lead. Instead of a rigid and limited interpretation of faith, we can unleash love, power, and salvation to those we serve by loving them as we love our very selves.

Our Prayer: *Dear Father, we praise You for giving us the Law by Your very finger. We praise You for sending Your only Son to us to fulfill the Law. We are humbled that You have called us into holy service for Your heavenly purposes. Bestow on us the ability to make the Law and teachings of Christ come alive among those we lead. Help us to follow the commandments and to bring blessings through obedience.* **Amen.**

Leading When Others Make Bad Choices

"Christ's Love and Plan for Us Conquers All Our Bad Choices"

"Now at that feast he released unto them one prisoner, whomsoever they desired. And there was one named Barabbas, which lay bound with them that had made insurrection with him, who had committed murder in the insurrection…. But Pilate answered them, saying, Will ye that I release unto you the King of the Jews?… But the chief priests moved the people, that he should rather release Barabbas unto them."

Featured Scripture: Mark 15:6–7, 9, 11
Background Scriptures: Mark 15:1–20; and Matthew 27:11–26

The people whom leaders of faith are charged to lead can make poor choices that can have dreadful consequences. What is a leader to do when this happens? We have an obligation to lead on through the calamity of the bad choices of our followers. Oftentimes it will be us, the leaders, not out followers, who will be left with the consequences from such bad choices.

The innocence and majesty of the Savior, or the convicted criminal Barabbas; the choice was clear. But the people in the crowd that day chose to release Barabbas over Jesus. Christ, ever obedient to His calling, fulfilled Scripture and endured all of this rejection through His great love for us. He even forgave those who rejected Him. That same Christ lives with us today, loving us and forgiving us even as we shove Him aside through our bad choices in life.

When we are called by God to a special task of leadership, we become part of a heavenly purpose and plan. The people we serve and the peer group around us will invariably make incredibly poor choices at critical moments that may cause us great hardship. What should we do when this happens? Jesus never deviated from the plan. His heart broke, not for His fate, but for the failure of the masses to take freely the gift of salvation He offered.

In the crowd that day was most likely someone who had been healed by Christ. Maybe another had been present at the Sermon on the Mount. Maybe another was fed by the miracle of the loaves and fishes. Others had heard His incredible teachings in the Temple. But today, they voted wrong. They made a bad choice. Just as Christ loves us through our own bad choices, we, too, must love those we serve when they make bad decisions.

Leading through the bad decisions of others means you, too, will have pain and suffering. It means that others will blame the fallout from the decision on you. In these times, remember God's calling on your life. Know that God turned the rejection of Jesus into resurrection and salvation for all people for all times. God can take the scars of the bad choices of those we lead and turn them into glorious leadership success in His grand plan.

The people chose Barabbas. Jesus carried the cross. But in the end, even in the midst of all our bad choices, the way of the cross still leads home!

Our Prayer: *Lord Jesus, we praise and thank You for enduring the trials and mockery before Pilate. We sing praises of Your endurance of the cross for us. We shout "hosanna" that You were raised from death to life and offer us salvation. Help us to lead those You gave to us with faith and steadfastness, even when they make poor choices, for we know God's plan for us will trump the bad choices of others.* **Amen.**

When More Needs To Be Said

"Say and Do More, Even When It Appears All Is Said and Done"

"It seemed good to me also, having had perfect understanding of all things from the very first, to write unto thee in order, most excellent Theophilus, That thou mightest know the certainty of those things, wherein thou hast been instructed."
Featured Scripture: Luke 1:3–4
Background Scriptures: Luke 1:1–4; and Acts 1—5

In our leadership journeys of faith, we may encounter topics that seem to have been discussed and debated exhaustively. The rules and procedures of the organizations or congregations we lead may be steeped in tradition and appear to work well. It may seem that no more needs to be said or done to append their successful operations. But as leaders called by God, it is our good duty to set forth a more perfect work and understanding to others as God has given it to us to do.

Doctor Luke's writings in his Gospel and the Book of Acts, written to the Gentile leader Theophilus, came later than the writings of the other Gospels. Luke spelled out that there were other eyewitnesses and writers of the Word, but still he had something he must say. Luke told some of the same stories, but added others, and always gave a new and magnificent perspective. About half of the Gospel of Luke is new material not found in the other three Gospels. Acts is unique in all of Scripture.

As a champion leader of the faith, Luke stepped up and delivered some of the greatest accounts of the works of Christ and the early Church. Even with the writings of Matthew, Mark, John, and Paul already established, Luke sensed his calling by God to add greater understanding by recording his personal accounts. As a result, our faith is fuller and richer today. What do you feel called to say or do today? Are you burdened with the need to lend a unique perspective of a subject already familiar to those you lead? God could be calling you to write what has already been written, but to do it by your hand as He guides you.

Leaders of faith are called to make their organizations richer and deeper. While we stand on the shoulders of those we follow, we must make our own marks, tell our own stories. Challenge assumptions that others have made and contribute new work and new understanding to the old formulas of success. Who is your Theophilus? What diverse audience among your followers needs your unique understanding communicated to them? Go find them. Give them your best work and new words of understanding. Add to the Body of Christ, and God will bless your service.

Our Prayer: *God, we give thanks for Luke and Theophilus. Luke had his own story to tell, and You called him to pen great words and accounts of our Lord and the work of the Church. Give us, we pray, that same yearning to tell our stories in faith to others. Help us to build upon the foundations of knowledge and faith in our own leadership journeys so others can know the Master in a deeper, richer way.* **Amen.**

Woman, Behold Thy Son

"Parents Are God's Greatest Leaders of Faith"

"And the angel came in unto her, and said, Hail, thou that art highly favoured, the Lord is with thee: blessed art thou among women.... When Jesus therefore saw his mother, and the disciple standing by, whom he loved, he saith unto His mother, Woman, behold thy son! Then saith he to the disciple, Behold thy mother! And from that hour that disciple took her unto his own home."

Featured Scriptures: Luke 1:28; and John 19:26–27
Background Scriptures: Luke 1:26–56; Luke 2:39–52

Mary, the chosen mother of Jesus, was told by the angel that she was blessed among women. Mary had been entrusted with giving birth to and raising the Son of God. She never faltered in her task and remained with Him throughout His life and ministry. How she must have pondered in amazement as she saw how different He was from the other children. What burdens she secretly carried and blessings she must have harbored in her heart, as the Bible tells us she did. She saw the mighty acts and miracles He performed. She heard the teachings He gave from the Scriptures and in the Temple. But now she was watching her son die slowly on a Roman cross.

The phrase *"Woman, behold thy son,"* could have many meanings. It is one of the seven recorded utterances Christ spoke from the cross. Perhaps Mary knew that Jesus was completing His eternal task in that moment. Perhaps Jesus was expressing to Mary the ultimate love He held for her. But even in his agony, Jesus made sure that Mary would be cared for by entrusting her to John. Mary continued to be a tremendous servant of faith after Christ's ascension to heaven.

The quiet and gentle Mary had herself performed one of the greatest leadership tasks of faith of all time by quietly leading and nurturing her son, the Son of Man, to this agonizing moment on the cross. Mary's example of humble obedience to her tasks of motherhood still inspires the generations, showing us that parenting is our greatest and most noble leadership calling.

Mothers and fathers are society's true leaders. The home is the sacred workbench of God. In humble homes across the globe, young leaders are instilled with love and the knowledge of Christ. The world's great leaders are not found in boardrooms or seats of government; they are sitting at the heads of our kitchen tables saying a prayer of blessing for food, family, home, and health.

As we give thanks for Mary today, let us also give thanks to all mothers and fathers of faith, who, through godly parenting, have become the holy proxy of God. We as parents, or the children of great parents, should say a special prayer of thanksgiving for this special gift of God. Let us lift up the orphan and the struggling or estranged parent in our own leadership journeys. Let everything we do as leaders of faith help to uplift, empower, and equip both parents and children for success.

Our Prayer: *Lord, we thank You for Mary. She was obedient and faithful to the task of raising You and leading You to the cross. We give thanks for all the parents of faith who have led us. We pray for parents everywhere as they struggle to raise children amid the sin and distractions in life. Help them to be faithful. Give them strength and courage to face the hardships. Give them comfort as they see their children suffer in life and in service to You.* **Amen.**

Sanctity Of Life

"Five Women Lead by Giving, Cherishing, and Protecting Life"

"And it came to pass, that, when Elisabeth heard the salutation of Mary, the babe leaped in her womb; and Elisabeth was filled with the Holy Ghost: And she spake out with a loud voice, and said, Blessed art thou among women, and blessed is the fruit of thy womb."

Featured Scripture: Luke 1:41–42
Background Scriptures: Genesis 16; 17:15–21; 1 Samuel 1; Luke 1:26–56; and Luke 2:9–20

Our lesson today illustrates how five women become leaders of faith by cherishing the unborn lives within them. They have led all mankind by cherishing life and giving birth. The lives that they bore would forever change the faith of us all. Each of these five women revealed God's plan to the human race through their obedience to God's call and by cherishing the lives they brought into the world.

Three of these five women were considered too old or barren to conceive or give birth. Another was an unmarried teenage bride-to-be; and still another was a slave girl who served the jealous wife of her baby's father. How would God use these extraordinary circumstances to change history? He did it through the lives of Sarah, Hagar, Hannah, Elisabeth, and Mary.

God often uses the unlikely to do the impossible. It shows His power, and puts into play the need for leaders to exemplify faith in the face of scoffing and disbelief. The first reactions of the godly men in these stories were similar: Abraham laughed at the news brought by the angel that Sarah would conceive; Eli the prophet accused Hannah of drunken imaginings; Zacharias doubted the news from the great archangel Gabriel of Elisabeth's baby and was struck dumb; and Joseph, upon learning of Mary's conception, at first sought to send her away. Each of these men who initially doubted ultimately was obedient to the plan of God. But it was the character, faith, and fervent prayer of these heroines of faith that kept God's plan in place.

Each woman would experience both pain and blessing as a result of giving and cherishing life. But each knew that God's hand was upon the sacredness of life of the child to which they had given birth. The story of these five women is a tribute to the courage and faithfulness of mothers, and shows that with God, all things are possible. All life, born and unborn, is precious to the Creator, who breathes the essence of life into us all.

A lesson can also be learned of how persons of relative obscurity, but who possess great faith, can change history. Sarah and Hagar together became mothers to many nations. Hannah gave birth to a prophet who would guide Israel. And Elisabeth and Mary brought forth John the Baptist and Christ Himself, who would fulfill God's New Covenant for mankind.

Lead by cherishing all life, and by affirming that what exists in the lives of both the unborn and the born are the seeds of greatness for the Kingdom of God.

Our Prayer: *Dear God, all life is sacred, and we affirm You as the Giver of all life. Help us to cherish the born and unborn. Help leaders of faith to affirm the dignity and worth of all who are created by Your hand.* **Amen.**

The Meek Giving Testimony To The Mighty

"Revealing the Truth to the Humble Is the Best Way to Spread the News"

"And there were in the same country shepherds abiding in the field, keeping watch over their flock by night. And, lo, the angel of the Lord came upon them, and the glory of the Lord shone round about them.... And the angel said unto them, Fear not: for, behold, I bring you good tidings of great joy, which shall be to all people. For unto you is born this day in the city of David a Savior, which is Christ the Lord.... And when they had seen it, they made known abroad the saying which was told them concerning this child. And all they that heard it wondered at those things which were told them by the shepherds."

Featured Scripture: Luke 2:8–11, 17–18
Background Scripture: Luke 2:1–20

The shepherds are favorite characters in the Christmas story. Their gathering around the crib of the newborn Christ child is an indelible memory for so many of us. But our Scripture lesson today relays much more than a favorite Christmas story. It clearly shows us how God uses the humble, the meek, the lowly, and the most unlikely among us to bear witness to great spiritual truths.

King David was first a shepherd boy. Jesus Himself would come to be known as the Good Shepherd. And while lowly in the pecking order of society, shepherds had to possess many important skills as well as an unwavering commitment to the nurturing and protection of their flocks. On the night of Christ's birth, the angel of the Lord and a multitude of the heavenly host opened up before these shepherds in the fields outside of Bethlehem. The revelation of the deity of this newborn Savior of the world was given first to shepherds. The meek truly had been chosen to give testimony to the mighty.

The story of the shepherds should be a call to leaders of faith to value and cherish the potential of all those we encounter each day. The humble laborers and factory workers who silently toil away for meager wages are no less valuable to God than the shepherds. The tiny and bent bodies planting rice in a rural field are ready and capable to become great witnesses in our day. Who in your community is a shepherd? Have you sought them out to tell them about the Christ child and send them forth with this message of hope?

As leaders of faith we are called to serve others by spreading the miracle of Christ's love to every corner of this earth, and thus we have a special need to find new shepherds. We must see and develop the talent and potential of all those around us and help them to become full partners with us in sharing Christ's grace and mercy to a hurting and dying world.

Our Scripture says that "*when they had seen it, they made it known abroad the sayings which were told them concerning this child, and that all who heard wondered at those things told to them by the shepherds.*" The meek do give testimony to the mighty. Some of our greatest assets in our leadership journeys are the shepherds in our midst. Find them. Tell them. Train them. And empower them as you send them forth with the word and miracle of a Savior.

Our Prayer: *Lord Jesus, thank You for coming into our world as a child and rescuing humanity. We give thanks for the shepherds and all the meek over the years who have given testimony to Your love, might, and salvation.* **Amen.**

Attesting To Another Is Leadership

"God Can Use the Unlikely to Attest to the Almighty"

"And there was one Anna, a prophetess, the daughter of Phanuel, of the tribe of Aser…and she was a widow of about fourscore and four years, which departed not from the temple, but served God with fastings and prayers night and day. And she coming in that instant gave thanks likewise unto the Lord, and spake of him to all them that looked for redemption in Jerusalem."

FEATURED SCRIPTURE: LUKE 2:36–38
BACKGROUND SCRIPTURE: LUKE 2:21–38

The Scriptures are filled with examples of humble, faithful servants who waited their entire lifetimes to serve an express purpose of God. The plight of young widows in the time of Christ was bleak. If their next of kin or families did not take them in, they would become outcast. The prophetess Anna had been widowed at a young age after only seven years of marriage. But for the next forty-four years, Anna did not leave the Temple. Anna devoted herself solely to the humble tasks of the Temple and offered prayers with fasting to God each day.

The day that the Baby Jesus would be brought to the Temple for His circumcision and blessing would be the day that this faithful woman of God would attest to the authority and authenticity of Christ. God would use the unlikely person of an old widow to bring witness to the fulfillment of Scripture in Christ's incarnation. But Anna did not stop with this one-time validation of Christ. Our Scripture tells us that she spoke of Him to all who looked for redemption in Jerusalem. Even today, Anna's testimony speaks to us and reaffirms Christ's presence among us. Anna shows us of God's grace and mercy given in abundance to those in the lowly and unlikely circumstances of life. God uses the unlikely among us to attest to the living Lord.

In our leadership journeys, God often uses those persons around us who have gained the respect of others to attest to our callings and leadership. Like Anna the prophetess, when veteran leaders give endorsement and validation of us to their peers, they themselves become leaders through their attesting to our callings. Leaders of faith should be mindful each day of the old and wise followers in our midst. In our times of trouble and adversity, it may be an older, respected soul who steps forth to calm a tough crowd. It may be the quiet team veteran or congregational member who gives the one vote of confidence to our actions and moves an entire institution toward our leadership vision.

Who is the Anna among you? Finding others to attest to your leadership is invaluable. Just like He did for the Christ Child that day in Jerusalem, God has placed people carefully along your path to move you along in your journey. Value all the people you meet and touch each day. That lonely widow and poor ragged veteran may be your Anna. Embrace and pray for those who attest to others and lift them up as the leaders of faith.

Our Prayer: *Lord Jesus, we thank You for Anna. Even in her loneliness and loss, she stayed in the Temple to worship and help others. She gave of her poverty and humility to attest to the coming of the Prince of Peace. Let her memory and service motivate us to value all the humble servants and followers in our midst. We lift up those who attest to our own leadership as leaders of the faith.* **Amen.**

Fundamentals Of A Holy Calling

"HOLY FUNDAMENTALS OF FAITH IN ACTION FOR CALLED LEADERS TODAY"

"The Spirit of the Lord is upon me, because he hath anointed me to preach the gospel to the poor; he hath sent me to heal the brokenhearted, to preach deliverance to the captives, and recovering of sight to the blind, to set at liberty them that are bruised, to preach the acceptable year of the Lord."

FEATURED SCRIPTURE: LUKE 4:18
BACKGROUND SCRIPTURE: LUKE 4:14–30; AND ISAIAH 61

Jesus returned to Nazareth, the place of His upbringing, and He went to the synagogue on the Sabbath. But this day was not just a normal homecoming. Today, this hometown boy who had grown up and come back to fellowship with those He knew as a child would reveal Himself to the ages. Christ would rise, read the words of the Prophet Isaiah, and then declare the fulfillment of prophecy and begin the formal phase of God's calling for His life.

Jesus was the Anointed One, the Messiah. The reaction by those in Nazareth to Christ's declaration was not one of acceptance, but one of skeptical indignation and anger. So violent was the reaction of the people that they sought to cast Him off a bluff. In announcing the fundamentals of His calling, Jesus did more than fulfill Scripture; He set an example for future disciples and leaders of faith to follow.

The fundamentals of the holy calling include: preaching the Gospel to the poor; healing the brokenhearted; preaching deliverance to the captives; giving sight to the blind; serving liberty to the bruised; and declaring the coming of the Lord. These are part of the Great Commission for service to God. No leadership journey of faith would be complete without sharing the Good News through words and deeds. No leader could fulfill a calling without tending to the brokenhearted or seeking justice and deliverance for the oppressed and hurting souls around them. We can never be true to our callings unless we are clear in telling others that Christ will come again.

Christ was the Anointed One. He alone was the fulfillment of Isaiah's prophecy. But today we, too, must take the fundamentals of Christ's holy calling and make them our example and guide. We are Christ's new apostles and ambassadors. Sharing the Gospel of Christ by loving and caring for those entrusted to us makes us full partners in the building of God's Kingdom. Each of us as called leaders must measure our leadership success by how well we execute the fundamentals of the faith that Christ read boldly on that special day in the synagogue in Nazareth.

Let us find and minister to the prisoner and to those in the bondage of poverty. Let us seek out those who are strangled by life's cruel circumstances and lead them to a new hope in the faith. Let us practice the fundamentals of a holy calling as we serve Christ this very day.

Our Prayer: *Lord Jesus, we lift our hearts to You in thanksgiving and praise for the fulfillment of the Scripture in Your life and Your gift to humankind. By Your life, sacrifice, and example, we can all face tomorrow. Send the Spirit of the Lord upon us this very day so we, too, can preach, heal, rescue, and serve others in Your name. Help us to follow the holy fundamentals of faith as we fulfill our own callings for You.* **Amen.**

When The Crowd Comes To You

"A Crowd Is a Blessing and an Opportunity to Do Good As a Leader of Faith"

"And it came to pass on a certain day, as he was teaching, that there were Pharisees
and doctors of law sitting by, which were come out of every town of Galilee, and
Judaea, and Jerusalem: and the power of the Lord was present to heal them."

FEATURED SCRIPTURE: LUKE 5:17

BACKGROUND SCRIPTURES: LUKE 5:17–26; AND MARK 2:1–12

This scene as described for us in the Gospels of Luke and Mark represented a highlight in Christ's ministry. The energy must have crackled in the air as a packed crowd gathered around Jesus. News of Jesus and His miracles had traveled far and wide. The eyewitness accounts of His power, teachings, and healings had come to be known throughout the area. Here in this place on this day a crowd had gathered, including the hierarchy of religious leaders, sitting among common folk ready to hear this carpenter of Nazareth, now a proclaimed Messiah.

Following His baptism at the River Jordan and the calling of His disciples, the large and diverse crowds were now coming to see Jesus. So great was the faith in this crowd and on this occasion, that *"the power of the Lord was present to heal them."*

When the house became full, a group of four men showed up with a man stricken with palsy and, being unable to come in to where Jesus was sitting, they cut a hole in the roof and lowered the man down to Him. Jesus was confronted by an act of great faith from these men seeking healing. Jesus also must have felt the great skepticism from the legal and religious authorities gathered before him in the crowd to witness this event. The crowd had come to Jesus. He used this opportunity to declare the forgiveness of sin through a miracle that now lay before him.

There will come a time in your journey of leadership when the crowd will come to you. Chances are, you will have been successful or gained expertise or notoriety in your service that attracts others to want to hear what you have to say. At this point you, like Christ, must take the opportunity to share the greater truth clearly and without prejudice to those in attendance. A crowd is God's gift and an opportunity for a leader of faith to do good works and positively touch lives in the experience. Use it well and righteously.

Jesus knew the crowd included religious leaders of importance who were also His detractors. Christ could have merely performed a miracle of healing upon the palsy-stricken man, earning the crowd's amazement and inciting the crowd against the Temple rule. But on this day, Jesus looked beyond the physical and political to the spiritual. By offering forgiveness to this sick man, He made him both physically and spiritually whole. Jesus knew His words and works before the crowd this day would change the way we view sin, sickness, and salvation.

As a leader of faith, speak your truths clearly and boldly when the crowd comes to you!

Our Prayer: *Risen Lord, Forgiver of sins, we praise You for the gift of forgiveness and healing that gives us eternal life. We thank You for Scripture that puts us in that same room with You as You performed a miracle long ago. Help us as leaders of faith to know what to say and do when the crowd comes to us.* **Amen.**

New Wineskins For New Leadership

"New Dynamic Leadership Will Burst Stale Organizations"

"And no man putteth new wine into old bottles; else the new wine will burst the bottles, and be spilled, and the bottles shall perish. But new wine must be put into new bottles; and both are preserved."

Featured Scripture: Luke 5:37–38
Background Scriptures: Luke 5:36–39; Matthew 9:16–17; and Mark 2:21–22

Jesus was the new religion. His teachings and revelations would burst open the rigidity of old traditions. Salvation and the grace of God would come to all in this new religion. Jesus explained this new religion by use of the parable of the wineskins and new wine. Jesus and these radically new teachings could not be contained in the legalistic, formal religion of His time. A new Church would have to be built among all believers.

Leaders of faith who answer the call of Christ to service may experience a similar situation. New dynamic leadership equipped with a passion and burning to make a difference for God will burst open old, stale organizations if we try to execute our mission within them. We will encounter old organizations and entrenched systems that cannot withstand the strain of change and new ideas. In these times, we should invoke this parable for our own use. Sometimes leaders of faith have no choice but to make new wineskins before we pour our souls into a task.

Creating new wineskins may mean revamping a leadership team. We may need to set new goals and priorities for an existing organization. We may need to make hard choices and cast out spiritual diseases within our midst, like corruption and slothfulness. We may need to convince skeptical followers to try a new technique. If we pour our God-given callings into bad wineskins, we may never succeed. Leaders should pray for wisdom, courage, and especially patience, to build new structures before pouring out the wine of our callings. Change and the process of wineskin building will be painful for some and exciting to others. Once others catch the vision of your calling, they, too, will want to join in the work.

We often think we can "patch things up" without the pain and expense of building new foundations. Rebuilding an organization from scratch can bring us criticism, even persecution, most likely from those who have been in control. Jesus knew that the new religion He espoused would bring His own death and the persecution of many. That persecution continues even today. But the wineskins of Christ's new religion do not break. They are pliable and expand as new souls are added to the liquid of love. Pray for the courage to begin the process of making new wineskins for new leadership today.

Our Prayer: *Dear Jesus, we give thanks for the new religion of salvation that You poured out by Your blood and sacrifice. You made new wineskins to hold the new religion in which we share so richly. We pray for the wisdom, patience, and resources to make new wineskins to hold our own leadership calling. Help others to be attracted to our commitment so we can build new hope and fellowship for the Kingdom of God.* **Amen.**

Leading From Our Knees

"Solitary Places for Fervent Prayer Are Essential for Leadership Decisions"

"And it came to pass in those days, that he went out into a mountain to pray, and continued all night in prayer to God. And when it was day, he called unto him his disciples: and of them he chose twelve, whom also He called apostles...."

Featured Scripture: Luke 6:12–13
Background Scriptures: Matthew 14:23; and Mark 14:32–52

It was one of the biggest decisions Christ would make in His earthly ministry. Which of His followers would He choose to be His twelve disciples? We are not sure how Christ arrived at this decision, but we do know what He did immediately prior to announcing the twelve. He went alone to a mountain and prayed all night to God. Did heaven open to Him? Or did Christ merely receive the quiet confirmation from God the Father of His deepest feelings so that He was emboldened to make His final decision?

Jesus was both man and God. He had extraordinary power, vision, and the ability to do miracles. He saw into the future, and He knew things about people whom He had never met. Yet with all His supernatural abilities, Jesus set the example for all leaders of faith faced with a tough decision. He retreated to a solitary place and placed His decision before the throne of God in protracted prayer. He sought God's will in all things.

What leadership decision do you face today? Do you throw a prayer up to God on the way to a meeting, or do you retreat into your closet to lay it before to the Almighty Father in earnest prayer? Chances are, we can't go to a mountain to pray over every leadership decision we make. However, successful leaders of faith, when faced with decisions of major importance, should heed the example of Christ.

There were other times during His life and ministry that Jesus retreated for prayer, such as after feeding the five thousand. After this hard day of ministry, Matthew tells us, *"When he had sent the multitudes away, he went up into a mountain apart to pray and when the evening was come, he was there alone"* (14:23).

As He faced His final great task, the cross, Jesus fell on His knees in the Garden of Gethsemane, praying in all earnestness for the Father's will to be done.

Our Master teaches all of us as leaders that if we are going to lead, we must lead from our knees. No other way will do. In leading from our knees, we become vessels of the living God to complete the heavenly tasks ahead. Those tasks may involve suffering or a choice between bad alternatives; however, God will take our obedience and make something very special from it. Retreat into a solitary place, kneel, and pray...you will never stand as tall as a leader as when you are leading from your knees!

Our Prayer: *Loving Father, we praise our Lord Jesus for His life and ministry. We most especially thank Him for His gift, sacrifice, and offer of eternal life. Help us to follow His example of finding strength through solitary prayer with You. May we seek Your will and guidance in all we attempt to do as leaders, as we lead from our knees.* **Amen.**

The Fund-Raising Team That Traveled With Christ

"BEHIND ALL GREAT EFFORTS ARE THOSE WHO GIVE SELFLESSLY OF THEIR RESOURCES"

"And it came to pass afterward, that he went throughout every city and village, preaching and showing the glad tidings of the kingdom of God: and the twelve were with him, and certain women…Mary called Magdalene…and Joanna the wife of Chuza, Herod's steward, and Susanna, and many others who provided for him from their substance.…"

FEATURED SCRIPTURE: LUKE 8:1–3
BACKGROUND SCRIPTURES: MATTHEW 27:55–56; AND MARK 16:9

Jesus and the twelve disciples were on the move from village to village and town to town. They were preaching to all who would hear about the tidings of the Kingdom of Heaven. It took money for Christ and the team to buy food or rent a room. It took resources for them to buy a blanket or mend a tent. Our lesson today glorifies the contribution of the women and many others who traveled with Christ and gave to this ministry, not of their excess, but of their substance. The fund-raising team that traveled with Christ is to be hailed for their contribution toward spreading the Kingdom of Heaven. These women set a great example as they, too, were leaders of faith.

Rarely does a worthy cause, idea, or leader come along and succeed without raising the necessary funds and resources. You can usually measure the commitment level of those involved in a cause when discovering that they support the effort financially from their own substance. Giving of your substance means that you give from the core of your being and forgo pleasures and security. What would have happened if the ministry of Christ had been stifled by a lack of cash? What if our Lord had to stop preaching and healing in order to get a job as a carpenter to pay for His travels?

Mary, Joanna, Susanna, and the women of Jesus' team represent quiet leaders of faith who lead through sustaining God's work by giving of their own resources. For generations women of all descriptions have led movements and funded the cause. By partnering with these women in His own ministry, Jesus found a loyalty and faith that changed the world. Our lesson today teaches us that we should fold the great diversity around us into the investment of our enterprise. These women were unlikely heroines of faith. Each of them had a unique life story that should have prevented them from becoming part of the Savior's team. But God included them in the core of His ministry.

Their example of giving and sustaining Jesus' ministry with resources shows how God uses us all to accomplish the unthinkable. If you are to ever reach the pinnacle of success in your own calling, it will take money to accomplish it. Like Christ, reach out to unlikely sources and persons for help. It could be that your own Mary, Joanna, or Susanna has already been chosen by God to help you, and is simply waiting in the wings to be asked.

Our Prayer: *Precious Lord, thank You for being an inclusive God who places the right persons in the right places so they can contribute to the building Your Kingdom. Help us as leaders of faith to always reach out and extend an invitation to all people. Bring a Mary, Joanna, or Susanna into our paths this very day. We need them in order to share Christ with those we encounter. Thank You for these women and all heroines of our faith, O Lord.* **Amen.**

What To Do When Those You Lead Panic

"LEADING INVOLVES GETTING UP AND CALMING THE STORMS AROUND YOU"

"But as they sailed he fell asleep: and there came down a storm of wind on the lake; and they were filled with water, and were in jeopardy. And they came to him, and awoke him, saying, Master, Master, we perish. Then he arose and rebuked the wind and the raging of the water: and they ceased, and there was a calm. And he said unto them, where is your faith?"

FEATURED SCRIPTURE: LUKE 8:23–25
BACKGROUND SCRIPTURE: LUKE: 8:22–25; AND MARK 4:35-41

Most of us would not fault the disciples for panicking during this frightful boat ride. The storm was raging all around them. It was dark, their boat was taking on water, and their Master was asleep. The disciples awoke Jesus, not just because they were fearful, but because they knew He could save them. Christ arose from His sleep and addressed their concerns by calming the storm with His command. Upon calming the storm, Jesus rebuked the disciples for their lack of faith.

Christ is as ever-present in our journeys today as He was with the disciples during the storm. In leadership journeys of faith, our Lord reminds us that we have nothing to fear because He is in the boat with us. Jesus never feared the storm or death. Jesus calmly arose and did what He needed to do. He got up, stretched out His hand, and calmed the storm. In doing so, not only did He react to his followers' panic, but He showed each of them that they had much growing to do in their faith. They still needed preparation to be ready for the tasks He would later assign them to do. These same disciples in the boat with Jesus that day would go on to perform great miracles themselves. They would build Christ's Church and take the Gospel to other lands.

When those whom we lead in our own congregations and organizations break into unnecessary panic, how do we respond? Even though we know that the leadership storms will pass into the night, we, too, like Christ, must get up and bring calm to the situations around us.

By setting an example of leadership and confidence during a storm, we inspire those we lead to reach for greater dimensions of faith in their own walks with God.

On that day Jesus was most likely tired from a full day's ministry, and this lake journey was His opportunity to rest and reinvigorate Himself. By being awakened from needed sleep, His calming of the storm was yet another activity added to an already busy day. Like Christ in today's lesson, a leader's need to arise and bring calm to panic will often occur when we are ourselves tired and overwhelmed.

However, in calming the storm, Christ shows us that in these moments of crisis, we teach our followers how to stretch their own faith by trusting in God and by learning how to bring calm to their own storms of life.

Our Prayer: *Precious Lord Jesus, how often You calm the storms of our own lives. How often we fail to have the faith we need to get through the storm. We give praise and thanks that You are always in the boat with us, and that if we call, You will answer and bring calm and meaning to every situation.* **Amen.**

Mourning With Those We Serve

"Our Physical Presence with Those Who Hurt Helps Them Heal"

"While he yet spake, there cometh one from the ruler of the synagogue's house, saying to him, thy daughter is dead, trouble not the Master. But when Jesus heard it, he answered him… And all wept, and bewailed her: but he said, Weep not; she is not dead, but sleepeth."

Featured Scripture: Luke 8:49–50, 52

Background Scriptures: Luke 8:40–42, 49–56; and Matthew 5:4

As Jesus' ministry progressed, He was in great demand to not only speak and teach, but to heal and perform miracles. What is amazing about the Master is that not only did He heal, but He shared personally in the mourning of those whom He served. In fact, in Christ's Sermon on the Mount, he said, "Blessed are they that mourn: for they shall be comforted" (see Matthew 5:4).

Considering Christ had the power to heal disease or raise the dead, why did He also mourn that which He could fix? Was perhaps Christ teaching us a great lesson that mourning is part of healing? Mourning with others is part of our leadership service. Our love is enhanced as we make the pains of others our own, and we are empowered to become part of the healing process. We are definitely called to mourn with those we lead and serve, but we are also called to mourn with those we do not know or may not like. We are definitely called to mourn with those we lead and serve.

The daughter who was raised this day was the daughter of Jarius, a person of authority at the Temple. Jarius had originally come to Jesus to ask Him to heal his sick daughter, but in the meantime she died. They had come to ask Jesus to heal the child, and now He had come to hear their mourning. Mourners are not always easy to comfort. In this scene, some mourners scorned Jesus for going in to see the dead girl, not knowing or having faith in His power to raise her. Jesus raised the child to great astonishment, but He asked them to tell no man.

Even if we, as leaders of faith, cannot literally raise the dead, we can mourn with those who have suffered loss. It is our physical presence, empathy, prayer, and willingness to sit in silence with one who is hurting that can bring great power to the situation. In times of crisis and loss, people look to their leaders for comfort or meaning in their confusion and sorrow. Like Christ, we should not be there for show or for publicity, but because our participation in mourning is part of the process of healing.

Our Prayer: *Dear Jesus, You have the power to heal us, raise us up, and give us eternal life. For that, we praise You and thank You. You promised us that if we mourn, we will be comforted. Help us as leaders of faith to be present to mourn with those we serve, and in the process unleash God's miracles of healing and new life abundant.* **Amen.**

Looking Back Can Cause Leaders To Stumble

"When Given a Calling, Don't Doubt, Don't Dawdle, and Don't Look Back"

"And Jesus said unto him, No man, having put his hand to the plough, and looking back, is fit for the kingdom of God… And it came to pass, when they had brought them forth abroad, that he said, Escape for thy life; look not behind thee, neither stay thou in all the plain; escape to the mountain, lest thou be consumed."

Featured Scriptures: Luke 9:62; and Genesis 19:17
Background Scriptures: Luke 9:57–62; Genesis 19:15–26; and Matthew 4:17–25

Leaders of faith who are called by God accept a holy mission. Holy missions are pieces of eternal labor that are precious and valuable to God. The men Jesus encountered in our Scripture today asked Him about becoming His followers. Jesus' response was very frank about the seriousness of embarking on a task for the Kingdom of God.

Jesus told the first man that following Him meant that he would have no home and no earthly assets. Another man wanted to follow Christ, but he wanted to bury his father first and a funeral could last several days. Another man sought to follow Jesus, but he needed to go home and tell his family good-bye. Jesus rebuked them all.

When Jesus called Peter and Andrew, they were fishing. Jesus simply saw them and told them: "Follow me, and I will make you fishers of men" (Matthew 4:19). The Scripture says: "And they straightway left their nets, and followed him" (verse 20).. The same scenario took place when Jesus called James and his brother John: "And they immediately left the ship and their father, and followed him" (verse 22). Jesus' call to Peter, Andrew, James, and John was met with an explosive and immediate response. Unfortunately, to the men of today's lesson, Christ's call was perceived as a job offer that could be postponed until earthly business was handled. This was unacceptable to Christ.

Has Christ called you? Have you been praying for a new calling? Are you prepared for the Master to say "follow Me" to you today? Are you prepared to leave your job, friends, and family and take up the cross today? The call to leadership by God is serious business. It is not to be entered into lightly. Once we enter the calling, we should never look back. Those who looked back before they ever started immediately lost sight of the Master. Jesus Himself recalled how Lot's wife looked back, violating the instructions of the angel and the terms of safe passage. She turned to a pillar of salt. Don't let your calling turn to salt.

Looking back when Christ comes will cause a leader to stumble. Don't miss the call. Be resolute. Be faithful. Don't look back. Leap into the arms of Christ when He comes your way. Set your hand to the plough of leadership and make the furrow straight by going dead-ahead. Heal and help others by looking and straight into the eyes of the Master.

Our Prayer: *Lord Jesus, when You call, we must leave our lives behind and go. When we go to work for You, we must never look back. Give us, we pray, the courage to leap into Your arms. Give us the commitment to stay on task without looking back over our shoulders. Your calling for us is a holy one, and we must follow it with the zeal of eternal commitment. Thank You for calling the humble and unlikely, like us, to become servants.* **Amen.**

A Labor Shortage And The Call To Work

"The Burden Is on Leaders to Work and to Find Laborers for the Harvest"

"After these things the Lord appointed another seventy also, and sent them two and two before his face into every city and place, whither he himself would come. There said he unto them, the harvest truly is great, but the laborers are few: pray ye therefore the Lord of the harvest, that he would send forth laborers into his harvest."

FEATURED SCRIPTURE: LUKE 10:1–2
BACKGROUND SCRIPTURES: MATTHEW 9:35–38; LUKE 10:1–4; AND JOHN 4:33–42

The call of a leader of faith is simple: a call to fill the spiritual labor shortage. God's fields are ripe to harvest. We see fields of need around us every day. We see hurting souls and lonely people. We see poverty, crime, war, and oppression. We can sense the hopelessness of those we serve, even among those who seemingly have abundant possessions. Leaders of faith are called to assemble laborers for the tasks God has called us to do. By recruiting and training others for holy tasks and motivating them to tackle causes greater than themselves, we fulfill the real calling to leadership of faith.

We sense the emotion that exudes from Christ as He witnessed the masses and their needs. Christ saw not only the physical needs, but the emptiness and hunger of the human soul as people came from all places seeking healing and truth. But the Lord of the harvest knew He needed help. In commissioning an additional seventy apostles and sending them out two by two into the communities around them, Jesus was filling the labor shortage of faith. Our calling from Christ is no less important than that of the new chosen apostles who came before Him that day and received their call to labor. With a sense of urgency, Jesus not only tells us to go to work, but also to find more laborers.

Harvesting in the fields of need can be grueling. We will encounter ridicule and lack of resources. We will encounter rotted fruit among the ripe souls we harvest. We will become frustrated as we realize we cannot save every crop in the field. We will need to find and motivate new talent and new workers in our congregations and organizations, drafting the unlikely and the reluctant to new challenges of faith. We must encourage them and train them to attain new skills and a new sense of purpose so Christ's crop can be harvested.

The Lord of the harvest has called us to a specific field of harvest of His choosing. He stands with outstretched arms, sending us forth to rescue the perishing and care for the dying. What He has called us to do is an immediate and holy job. He will surely and mightily equip us with all the tools for the challenge ahead; may we not let the Master down.

Our Prayer: *Dear Lord of the Harvest, how plentiful are the fields of hurting hearts and souls who need tending. Make us shepherds of the hurting sheep, O Lord. Thank You, Lord, for giving us the opportunity to become part of the Kingdom of God. Motivate us and give us a sense of urgency to go to work and enlist others in the needed labor for the eternal harvest.* **Amen.**

Success And Rejection

"Preparing Those We Send for the Realities of Faithful Leadership"

"Go your ways: behold, I send you forth as lambs among wolves.... He that heareth you heareth me; and he that despiseth me despiseth him that sent me. And the seventy returned again with joy, saying, Lord, even the devils are subject unto us through thy name."

Featured Scripture: Luke 10:3, 16–17
Background Scriptures: Luke 10:1–20; and Matthew 10:16–42

The Son of Man certainly knew rejection. Even in all His power, even His deity, many people rejected and ridiculed Christ. Christ knew full well that those He chose to send forth with His message and power would experience both success and rejection. In fact, our lesson today teaches us clearly that as called leaders of faith and their followers will encounter the same.

Christ tells those whom He calls to go forth as lambs among wolves. While the true power of our callings is invincible, our purpose is meek, gentle, and subject to choice from those we serve. Jesus told the apostles that some would hear them, receive healing, and come to know God. Others would reject their help and send them away. The apostles no doubt experienced great celebration as the lame walked again and souls repented and came to God. But they also experienced hostile rebukes and stirred up controversy as they encountered the skeptics and scorners.

However, upon returning to Christ, the apostles marveled to Him of their newfound power in His name to rebuke devils and perform feats of healing. Christ told them that they would find even greater power than this as they went along their journey.

As leaders of faith, we, too, will send others into the roads of service. We need to prepare those in our care that they will have both success and rejection in the performance of their duties. Let them know that their success comes from Christ's power and the rejection they encounter is not a reflection on them, but rather on peoples' lack of faith and trust. In all of this, we are to carry on and keep serving others. God's power is freely available to us in all that we do.

You won't be successful every time. But how sweet when even one person is blessed and learns of Jesus' love for them. Rejection is part of success. Some people quit at the first sign of rejection. Christ warns us against becoming discouraged; instead we must pick ourselves up and keep on going. The next town and the next person we encounter may have been praying that we would bring hope, love, and provision to the needs in their lives.

Every great leader has known success and rejection. We have made and lost money. We have won and lost elections. We have seen congregations grow and parishioners leave our midst. We have known solidarity and division. But in it all and through it all, Christ is working in us. So keep the faith and keep constantly claiming His power. Then dust yourself off and keep going forth in Christ's power.

Our Prayer: *Lord Jesus, thank You for calling us and sending us forth among the wolves of our world. We are blessed and not afraid. You go with us and give us Your power and blessing. Help us to heal and serve others in Your name, and may many come to know You.* **Amen.**

Helping Those Who Can Never Repay You

"THE GREATEST ACTS OF LEADERSHIP ARE DONE WITHOUT EXPECTATION OF RETURN"

"But a certain Samaritan, as he journeyed, came where he was: and when he saw him, he had compassion on him, and went to him, and bound up his wounds, pouring in oil and wine, and set him on his own beast, and brought him to the inn and took care of him... Then said Jesus unto him, Go, and do thou likewise."

FEATURED SCRIPTURE: LUKE 10:33–34, 37
BACKGROUND SCRIPTURE: LUKE 10:25–37

The story of the Good Samaritan has crossed over from the faith community to the general population as it is heralded as an example of selflessness and noble human behavior. For leaders of faith, the lesson of the Good Samaritan has an even deeper meaning. There are people in need waiting for our help. Those in need may not only be physically hurting, but their souls may be wounded and in need of eternal hope. The most obvious sources of help for the wounded often pass them by. To many, the neediest among us are often invisible or dispensable.

Who is our neighbor? That is the question the legal authorities posed to Jesus. Jesus said the Good Samaritan is a person of another faith and race who helps a stranger when others would not. He helped someone that others passed by, someone who most likely could never repay him. He performed a great act of love for a stranger with no thought or expectation of return for his actions.

Leaders of faith should glean from this story our own calls to action. We have been called to holy tasks, like the Good Samaritan. We must seek out those who are hurting around us, those who can never repay us, and bring healing and hope to their lives. As leaders of faith we have a greater duty to do things for others who can never repay us. Those in authority who only render good works for the hope of reaping a political or financial return are not practicing faithful leadership or heeding the words of Christ.

Random acts of kindness and helpfulness to the most vulnerable among us unleashes God's power in unique and bountiful ways. Acts done by those with the institutional power and personal resources to effect great change for others can inspire entire organizations, congregations, and nations to act as well.

We don't know what the injured man did after being helped by the Samaritan. Most likely, his own life was changed. He probably told others about how the love of a stranger saved him. He most likely returned the gesture by helping someone else. The Good Samaritan most likely received a heavenly reward, and his selfless acts of love most likely convicted those who witnessed it to question their prejudices of people.

Leadership with love, practiced without thought of repayment or return, is what Christ commands us: *"Go, and do thou likewise."*

Our Prayer: *Lord, thank You for the story of the Good Samaritan. Help us to always seek out those in need around us, even if they are different, and in Your love bind their wounds. Help us to never practice acts of kindness with a motive to reap any reward save the thrill of keeping Your commandment to go and do likewise.* **Amen.**

When Not To Write A Speech

"TIMES WHEN LEADERS ARE TO RELY ON INSPIRATION ALONE"

"And when they bring you unto the synagogues, and unto the magistrates, and powers, take ye no thought how or what thing ye shall answer, or what ye shall say…. For it is not ye that speak, but the Spirit of your Father which speaketh in you."

FEATURED SCRIPTURES: LUKE 12:11; AND MATTHEW 10:20
BACKGROUND SCRIPTURES: LUKE 12:11–12; AND MATTHEW 10:16–20

As a leader are you ever lost for words? There are times in our leadership journeys when God controls this loss of words, so that we can become empty vessels through which God can speak. There will come a time in the life of every leader when the only words they will be able to utter will be the words given to them by the Holy Spirit. Sometimes you will be tempted to speak words that promote your own ego and bravado, but Christ commands us to yield and allow His words to be ours.

Leaders of faith should consider every opportunity to speak before others as holy, and be prayerful and yielding to the Spirit of the Father as to what we should say on every occasion. There have been situations when pastors and leaders of faith have beautifully researched and prepared a text to deliver, only to hear the voice of God prompt them to set it aside and speak in the Spirit. Some of the most powerful and memorable words of faith and history have been spoken this way. Sometimes the brevity of words, spoken with the emotion of deep conviction or pain, etches them into the conscience and hearts of the hearers.

People are capable of remembering only a fraction of what they hear each day. Many times it is not the words, but the great compassion and presence of the person speaking the words that communicate the greatest. A single word or phrase spoken in the Spirit can become an indelible marker in the human soul. God certainly calls us to preparation prior to speaking to others. But there will be moments when you feel the Spirit of God hearkening you to cast away your notes. Let your heart and mind become blank to God, and He will tell you what to say. It may be a great occasion or in the presence of a great audience, but let God move in your heart and give you the words to say.

To be a spokesperson for God means dying to your self-confidence and to your own words. It means you must be humble and open to listen to that small voice inside of you. Not every occasion will call us to set aside your plans; always be prepared. But your greatest preparation is your reliance on the power of the Holy Spirit within you. It will never let you down and will always work the will of God in the words you speak.

Our Prayer: *Lord Jesus, by the Spirit of Truth, may we speak the words that You would have us to speak. Help us to let go of our thoughts and rely solely on You. Give us the words to speak in every situation. Make our hearts and minds humble and brave to speak the truth that convicts and inspires others to seek Your light and glory. May the words of our mouth and the meditation of our hearts be always acceptable to You.* **Amen.**

Building Bigger Barns

"Contentment with Our Wealth and Accomplishments Can Bring Judgment"

"The ground of a certain rich man brought forth plentifully: And he thought within himself, saying, What shall I do because I have no room where to bestow my fruits? This will I do: I will pull down my barns, and build greater…and I will say to my soul, Soul, thou hast much goods laid up for many years; take thine ease, eat, drink and be merry. But God said unto him, Thou fool, this night thy soul shall be required of thee…."

Featured Scripture: Luke 12:16–20
Background Scripture: Luke 12:13–34

This parable of Christ sends a stark message to us all. As we are blessed with wealth and accomplishment, we must never lose our sense of thankfulness and total reliance on God. The rich man in this parable wanted more. He wanted to revel in his accumulated goods and eat, drink, and be merry. There is no thankfulness or burden to give his excess to others in need or to a cause greater than himself. His barns were full, but he wanted more. But God made a call on his soul and he was judged. What is the condition of your soul today?

This parable did not curse the bounty and the plenty. It did not curse the blessed man who had worked hard and saved. It cursed the man who did not understand that all blessing and provision comes from God. We are merely the temporary custodians of earthly possessions. Even our very life and breath are dictated by the Father above. Leaders of faith should always guard against a sense of pride and a need for more glory or wealth. As we build our congregations and organizations, be ever mindful that all increase is to be tithed and given back to God. We are to never believe that what we own or accomplish is by the sole work of our hands.

We can see the parable of this rich man played out in life every day. We see people of wealth take their riches and retreat to themselves, only to find failing health and loneliness. We see the excess of merriment lead to addiction and the breaking up of marriages and homes. We see the blind ambition of a successful enterprise take one too many risks in an effort to gain more wealth, and then witness the slow destruction of that organization. We see leaders who want greater power and position leave their sanctuaries and proper leadership roles only to find defeat and the loss of all power.

We do not have to follow this path if we surrender our lives to the call and purpose of Christ. Christ desires to bless us beyond our wildest imaginations. We will have all we need and enough to give away. We won't need to build bigger barns because our blessings will be sown among others as God's Kingdom grows in abundance.

Our Prayer: *Lord Jesus, make us content in the calling and blessing of the moment. May we always acknowledge that every gift and blessing comes from the Father above, and not of our own hand. Forgive us when we revel in our own talent, wealth, and accomplishments. Instill in us a burning desire to live and lead in humility and service to others.* **Amen.**

Confessing Our Leadership Failures

"As Our Measurement of Performance Is Greater, So Is Our Need for Confession"

"For unto whomsoever much is given, of him shall much be required; and to whom men have committed much, of him, they will ask the more. My brethren, be not many masters, knowing that we shall receive the greater condemnation. For in many things we offend all.... If we confess our sins, he is faithful and just to forgive us our sins, and to cleanse us from all unrighteousness."

Featured Scriptures: Luke 12:48; James 3:1–2; and 1 John 1:9
Background Scriptures: Luke 12:42–48; James 3:1–4; and 1 John 1:8—2:2

A life devoted to leadership can bring a heavy heart. To be chosen by God for leadership tasks of heavenly purpose brings with it a high expectation of success and performance, for unto whom much is given, much will be required. Furthermore, the more we attempt to do for God and the more we teach and lead others, the more likely it is that we will offend others unknowingly or fall short in many of our attempts to serve. As leaders of faith we must be constant confessors of our own leadership failures.

Confronting our shortcomings and our underperformance for the Master opens our hearts to hear God's voice and receive healing power for the new day at hand. The greater responsibility we gain as leaders of faith, the more likely it is that we will not perform a job at our full capacity or that we may hurt another by failing to fully acknowledge and appreciate our associates and co-laborers. God understands our predicament and wants to grant us clear minds and hearts for service. The more work we are given to do for God, the more often we must confess our weaknesses and failures to Him. This constancy of confession keeps us pure and strong.

When we confess often, we can more clearly see small hurts and confusion we may have caused as a leader. God will then equip us with the ability to make amends and in doing so lift others up to a new vibrancy and understanding of God. When we confess our bungling of great opportunities for God, He gives us other chances to serve and wipes away our feelings of despair and regret. God does not want His leaders of faith moping in the sadness of failure. Confess your failure, lay your shortcomings on God's throne, and let Him clothe you with a new garment of love and power.

We have been given much, and much is required of us. The more we are asked to do for God, the more likely it is we will fall short on many days. But confessing leaders of faith will be successful leaders of faith as we yearn to serve God and those around us in love and humility. Confess today, then arise and go in peace and new power as you embody Christ's constant love and grace.

Our Prayer: *Lord God, You have chosen us for Your service, yet we often let You down. Our hearts are heavy from missed opportunities and our underperformance in Kingdom. Cleanse us from our failures and offenses so we can arise again and do something edifying and wonderful for You. May our hearts be constantly confessing our weaknesses and failures to You so we can become better vessels of Your grace.* **Amen.**

Leadership Made For One Lost Sheep

"The Need of One Person Is Worthy to Great Leaders of Faith"

"What man of you, having an hundred sheep, if he lose one of them, doth not leave the ninety and nine in the wilderness, and go after that which is lost, until he finds it?.... I say unto you, that likewise joy shall be in heaven over one sinner that repenteth, more than over the ninety and nine just persons, which need no repentance."

Featured Scripture: Luke 15:4
Background Scriptures: Luke 15:1–10; and John 10:7–18

Leaders have many tough choices to make. Leaders often have to choose whether or not to cut their losses and move on to other matters. They may have to sacrifice one asset to protect another. In the political and organizational realm of majority rule, it is what is most important to the 50 percent plus one that becomes the priority for many leaders. Yet these standards of secular leadership are not what Jesus espoused in His Parable of the Lost Sheep.

To leaders of faith, every person, every voice, every hurt, and every need is important. In this parable, our Lord sets forth the value of the one lost sheep and sinner. Jesus even did risked assessment, saying it was worth leaving the ninety-nine sheep in the wilderness in order to find the one sheep that had strayed from the flock. How do we as leaders of faith reconcile such a risk? Resources are limited. To risk damage to our entire organization while we spend time on one person or project seems foolhardy.

But we can rest easy, for we are protected and guided by the Good Shepherd. When God calls us to a leadership task, we may have to leave our congregations to rescue that one lost child or hurting employee. The obedience we show in rescuing God's one sheep is our good work to the Lord. Others who observe our love for the lost sheep will come and search with us and offer assistance to the ninety-nine.

Have you encountered lost sheep in your own leadership journey of faith? Did you go searching, or did you leave it to someone else to reclaim them? Sometimes lost sheep or wayward followers don't want to be found or rescued. Lost sheep are not always people; they can be a church, congregation, or business. Those institutions may be lost in their own self-absorption and unable to be of value to those in need around them. We may have to leave our safe homes or the comfort of a stable job in order to rescue a congregation in peril.

Whomever the lost sheep or group may be, God is calling their name and asking us to join in the rescue. In love of heart and with a prayerful mind, obey Christ's command to rescue the lost sheep you encounter in your own leadership journey. Heaven will rejoice when you find even one who was lost.

Our Prayer: *Dear Great Shepherd, we know Your voice. Often we have been lost and You came looking for us. We want to obey Your command to find the lost souls among us. Let us be Your helpers in the search and rescue of the perishing and the dying. May we bring love, hope, and a sense of purpose to all those we encounter in Your name.* **Amen.**

Prodigal Leaders, Prodigal Followers

"When Leaders and Those They Lead Need Forgiveness and Restoration"

"I will arise and go to my father, and will say unto him, Father, I have sinned against heaven, and before thee, and am no more worthy to be called thy son: make me as one of thy hired servants. And he arose, and came to his father. But when he was yet a great way off, his father saw him, and had compassion, and ran, and fell on his neck, and kissed him."

Featured Scripture: Luke 15:18–20
Background Scripture: Luke 15:11–32

If you have lived long enough, you have been both a prodigal son and a loving father. The process of sin and restoration occurs countless times each day. Jesus gave us this parable to remind us that eternal love awaits those who hit bottom, repent, and come home in humility seeking forgiveness. This parable also has an institutional message for leaders of faith and those they lead. Leaders can easily take the power and assets they possess and use them for sinful or less than noble purposes, leaving the confines of our calling to go off to a distant place, and letting others down.

Those who follow can also abuse the relationship to the mission through lack of work or selfish indulgence in the prosperity of the moment. Followers may wrongly hold a leader in contempt for failing to go along with their folly. When leaders and followers violate a trust or waste the goodwill and inheritance of the organization, they need to confess and come home to each other. We need restoration with each other so we can once again get about doing the Lord's business of serving others.

No doubt the father knew his son would falter and waste the hard-earned resources. The father did not stop the son from leaving, but most likely thought of him and prayed for him each day. God's eternal love for us is much like this father's love for his son. God sees us going down the path of destruction. He sees the pitfalls ahead for us. Yet only when we are hungry, broke, and rooting among swine do we hear the call to repentance and restoration.

As leaders of faith we have a dual responsibility to both seek forgiveness when we err and offer forgiveness to others when we have been wronged. We will undoubtedly hurt others in the arduous process of leadership, and we will be unfairly hurt by others. Our response as leaders of faith will make the difference.

Our success will be measured by how much we love and forgive. God desires that families, congregations, and organizations be made whole and fellowship fully with love and forgiveness freely flowing one to another. Prodigal leaders and prodigal followers need only to confess, come home, and seek forgiveness for the healing process to begin. If you need to come home to God, He is waiting for you with open arms. In fact, He is running to meet you now.

Our Prayer: *Lord God, we need to come home. We need forgiveness and restoration with You and those we lead and serve. Make us whole again by Your healing power and love. Instill in us, O Lord, a forgiving heart so we can forgive the prodigal followers who have hurt us. Help us to ask for forgiveness when we have failed others. May our hearts be filled with love and forgiveness so we can bring our loved ones back into our arms again.* **Amen.**

Who Is The Lazarus Among Us?

"LEADERS SHOULD CONSTANTLY BE AWARE OF DIRE NEEDS AROUND THEM"

"There was a certain rich man, which was clothed in purple and fine linen, and fared sumptuously every day: And there was a certain beggar named Lazarus, which was laid at his gate, full of sores, And desiring to be fed with the crumbs which fell from the rich man's table: moreover the dogs came and licked his sores."

FEATURED SCRIPTURE: LUKE 16:19–21
BACKGROUND SCRIPTURE: LUKE 16:19–31

The story of the rich man and Lazarus is the only parable of Christ in which we are given the name of a particular person. The dire nature of Lazarus' circumstance is one we see in the world every day. Billions of people in our world have basic human needs that go unmet. Our own communities and neighborhoods are filled with hurting souls. Collectively as organizations and congregations, or even as a nation, we see our contemporaries and fellow institutions in "Lazarus-like" conditions. What do we do? How do we respond? Who is the Lazarus among us?

The second part of this parable is not about the poverty of Lazarus, for Lazarus died and was taken to heaven into Abraham's bosom. The judgment is upon the rich man, who saw the poverty and desperation of Lazarus right at his own gate and did nothing. The rich man was judged for his neglect of the need around him. Just as we ask, "Who is the Lazarus among us?" we must also ask, "Who is the rich man among is? Is it me? Is it my organization or congregation? Is it all leaders of faith?" The parables of Christ are pliable and speak lessons to us today.

Lazarus is, indeed, the poor and hurting around us. Lazarus is, indeed, the nations and communities of the world that are under duress and persecution. Lazarus is, indeed, the hungry, the sick, the imprisoned, the addicted, the lost, the lame, the depressed, and the oppressed. Lazarus is also a child of God and Abraham who is eternally loved. We are to love Lazarus, too. If we have more than we need at a given moment, then we are the rich man. If we have power or authority in an institution, we are the rich man. If we have the truth of the Gospel and the love of Christ, then we are the rich man. The rich man was not judged for being rich. He was judged for failing to reach out and meet Lazarus's most basic needs.

God sends Lazarus among us to test our hearts, to see if we recognize Jesus in the beggar, the sick, and the destitute around us. Great leaders of faith will always be aware of the Lazarus among them and will bring them into their care. The great challenge is not in having all the resources needed to help Lazarus, but in seeing him and being willing to help. Lazarus smells bad, and we may have to scare away the dogs that lick his sores. Lazarus is a different color and faith from us, and he has a criminal record. But God is waiting and watching us. Find the Lazarus in your midst, feed him, clothe him, and give him medicine in the name of Jesus.

Our Prayer: *Lord Jesus, thank You for Lazarus. We praise You for giving us this parable and command to find the Lazarus among us. Give us the spiritual ability to find the hurting and lost in our midst. Empower us to reach out beyond our comfort zones to help others in need. By Your power and in Your name, may we comfort Lazarus and find our own salvation in the process.* **Amen.**

Great Leaders Show Great Gratitude

"RECOGNIZING THE FAITH AND ACTS OF OTHERS UNLEASHES NEW POWER"

"And one of them, when he saw that he was healed, turned back, and with a loud voice glorified God, and fell down on his face at his feet, giving him thanks: and he was a Samaritan. And Jesus answering said, were there not ten cleansed? But where are the nine? There are not found that returned to give glory to God, save this stranger?"

FEATURED SCRIPTURE: LUKE 17:17–18
BACKGROUND SCRIPTURES: LUKE 17:11–19; AND JOHN 6:11

Ten men were healed of the horrific and life-altering condition of leprosy. Jesus heard their cries from afar, and by His words they were healed and became whole again. Yet only one man returned to praise God and show gratitude to Jesus. There is more to this lesson than the glaring ingratitude by those nine who received a miracle but failed to thank Jesus. This story represents the power and testimony that can be declared in giving gratitude to others.

One must wonder where the other nine healed lepers went. Were they so overwhelmed with their new, whole bodies that they went straight home to family or friends instead of giving Jesus their praise and gratitude? At least this one leper came back to Jesus to praise God and give thanks for the Master's grace and healing. Christ told this lone leper that he had been made whole because of his faith, then sent him on his way. The healing in this one man's life was more than the removal of his leprosy; it was the rebirth of his life in Christ's love.

Gratitude to others implies that we have faith in them and their abilities. The leper knew that Jesus had the capacity to make him whole again. Likewise, when leaders bestow responsibility and honor on their followers and reward their good work with gratitude, it instills into them a new power and confidence.

Leaders of faith often attain their own success through the talents and acts of others. Leaders win elections, contracts, or promotions not only through their own hard work, but usually through the contributions and skills of volunteers and coworkers. Too often we may act like one of the nine healed lepers. We can become so enamored with success that we fail to return and acknowledge the healing work rendered by those laboring in our congregations and organizations. Our failure to give adequate gratitude can be hurtful to others and slow our successful mission for God.

Leaders of faith are often the busiest people. However, if you as a leader will take the time to show gratitude to those around you, it will change lives. A handwritten note, a kind word, a thumbs-up, or the wink of an eye may be all the thanks a special person needs to feel loved and valued as a coworker in our Lord's vineyard of service.

Our Prayer: *Father, forgive us when we fail to praise and thank You for the many gifts of healing and blessing You bestow upon us each day. Create in us new hearts of gratitude and the commitment to acknowledge and appreciate those around us. May our faith in You and gratitude to those around us heal us and make us whole again.* **Amen.**

The Widow And The Unjust Judge

"Real Leaders Take Time for the Needs of Others, Especially the Weak"

"Yet because this widow troubleth me, I will avenge her, lest by her continual coming she weary me.... And shall not God avenge His own elect, which cry day and night unto Him, though he bear long with them? I tell you that He will avenge them speedily...."

Featured Scripture: Luke 18:5–8
Background Scriptures: Luke 18:1–8; and 2 Peter 3:8–9

Christ's parable of the widow and the unjust judge holds several great principles for leaders. It is first and foremost an affirmation that prayer—persistent prayer—works. God hears and tends to the needs of those who call upon Him.

A deep meaning can be found by looking at the widow and the judge. Widows in the day of Christ had few, if any, legal rights. For the woman of this parable to have appealed to a civil judge on any matter would most likely have been hopeless.

The unjust judge did not fear God; therefore, this civil leader had no compass beyond his civil obligation to render the duties of his job. This widow was tenacious in prayer and in pursuit of justice, and her persistence paid off by moving the judge to action. The judge's action was not based on his duty to God, the law, or his character, but rather the fact that solving her issue would cause her to depart from him.

How many times have we seen God-fearing, righteous leaders of faith fail to take time to tend to the needs of the weak? In our own leadership walk, the Holy Spirit often convicts us of having failed to tend to a real need or request of someone we did not know. Often, the meek may not seek leaders out with the tenacity of this widow. However, their need for justice and service is no less compelling. God's leaders should seek them out and minister to them.

Leaders of faith should go to the greatest effort to accommodate the needs of others, giving them time and a prompt response to their requests. God places leaders of faith in higher positions to provide others with the help they desperately need.

No doubt, God used this unjust judge to answer the prayer of a righteous widow. God uses both the just and the unjust to achieve His purposes. In our own leadership journeys of faith, let us become the answer to prayer of the many meek and tired souls who need justice, mercy, love, and attentiveness to their condition. Our time is a valuable commodity, but God placed us in leadership to aid the widows and all who need justice.

Our Prayer: *Precious Lord, we ought always to pray. Help us to value the power of prayer as You command. Avenge us when we are wronged; grant us mercy and justice in Your time and way. As leaders of faith, help us to be righteous judges and leaders who take time to solve others' problems. Make us aware that You placed us here to serve others and to become Your answer to their prayers.* **Amen.**

Slipping Into Self-Righteous Leadership

"SELF-EXALTATION BY A LEADER SOWS SEEDS OF SELF-DESTRUCTION"

"The Pharisee stood and prayed thus with himself, God, I thank thee, that I am not as other men are—extortionists, unjust, adulterers, or even as this publican. I fast twice in the week, I give tithes of all that I possess."
FEATURED SCRIPTURE: LUKE 18:11
BACKGROUND SCRIPTURE: LUKE 18:9–14

How often those of us in leadership have moments of temptation toward self-righteousness and self-congratulation. Sometimes we may feel a sense of our own piety and good works. In this parable Jesus gave a stark warning for each of us to get our hearts right in the presence of God. An inflated sense of self-importance can lead to trouble both in our walks with God and in our own leadership journeys.

In the day of Christ, both the government official (the publican, or tax collector) and religious leader (the Pharisee) were entrusted to serve others. Jesus made a stark contrast between the government official and the religious leader. Certainly the religious leader would show us the right method to pray, wouldn't he? He did not. It was his self-righteousness and confidence in his position and the keeping of religious laws that made him feel superior to others. Even in approaching the prayer table, the religious leader's heart was not pleasing to God. He failed to acknowledge his sin and shortcomings before his Creator.

In contrast, the government official was so overwhelmed by his own unworthiness at the table of prayer that he held his head low and beat his chest in humility as he asked God for forgiveness. It was this admission of failure and imperfection that pleased God. Jesus quickly let us know which man's sins were forgiven, which man would be exalted and which would be made low. This parable's lesson is also meant for congregations and organizations that have become pious and self-congratulatory. Those institutions we lead need to admit their shortcomings and admit frailty.

Leaders of faith must guard themselves each day from being sucked into the illusion of self-piety. They must set the example of humility by constantly examining their motives and by shunning the excessive praise of men. Leaders often get a sense of becoming indispensable to their organization. This tendency can lead to self-deception.

Too often, the accolades of peers and critics showered upon us can cause us (like the Pharisee) to begin to thank God that we don't have the sins and troubles of others. We consider our own stellar church attendance, mission work, and prayers for the poor, all while failing to see the corrosion building up in our own lives. In this we displease God.

Accountability is a great habit to practice—accountability to God and others. You may need a spouse or trusted friend to mentor you. Constantly pray that your heart and motives stay pure and that your eyes stay focused on the Savior and the people you are called to serve.

Our Prayer: *Dear Lord, we come to You today as impure, unfit servants with all our faults and failures. We have failed You often through both action and omission. Create in us humble spirits of service. Forgive us; purify us, so we can serve You by serving others with humility.* **Amen.**

A Leader In Need Of Redemption

"Putting Yourself in Position for an Encounter with the Master"

"And behold, there was a man named Zaccheus, which was the chief among the publicans, and he was rich. And he sought to see Jesus who he was; and could not for the press…and he ran before, and climbed up in a sycamore tree to see him: for he was to pass that way."

Featured Scripture: Luke 19:2–4
Background Scriptures: Luke 19:1–10; and Numbers 5:7

Zaccheus was not only a noted chief tax collector for the Roman government in Palestine, but he was also a Jew. The hatred of Zaccheus by the local population was, in large part, due to the fact that he was Jewish and was using the might of the Roman authority to earn a profit off of his own people. Zaccheus's actions had made him rich and powerful but also a sinful leader in need of restoration with God and his community. On this day a leader in need of redemption was in the right position to encounter the Master.

Repentance, salvation, and restoration came to Zaccheus courtesy of the Lord's presence that day. The chain of healing events was triggered because something in Zaccheus's heart told him that he needed to see Jesus.

The first step in repentance for any leader who has lost their way is to get into a position to encounter Jesus. Zaccheus had to run and climb a tree to get above the crowd. We may need to seek out a mentor, pastor, or congregation of faith that can show us how to encounter Christ. Maybe we just need to leave the bad crowd and invite Jesus to come home with us. When we earnestly seek Jesus, He will stop and come to visit. Jesus always finds the contrite heart. Draw close to Him and He will draw close to you.

Jesus' visit with Zaccheus brought great gossip among the people on that day. Jesus always wants to show us that the worst among us can be restored through His salvation. The mere fact that Jesus recognized Zaccheus and came to his home shows that everyone is covered by His redemptive grace. Once in the presence of the living Lord, one can only imagine how intense the confession of Zaccheus's sin and guilt must have been. Zaccheus received love and forgiveness. His redemption motivated him to give back all he had stolen, plus an amount four times that for the poor. What is it that you need to do to make it right with those you have hurt? Let Christ show you.

All leaders will make mistakes. Some may even betray those whom they are empowered to serve. However, Christ proved through this providential encounter with Zaccheus that His grace is sufficient to restore even the most broken among us. The path to restoration begins by seeking an encounter with Jesus and then getting into the right position. A new day can come to you by removing those obstacles that are blocking your view of the Master.

Our Prayer: *Dear Jesus, we thank You for redeeming those who have failed. Like Zaccheus, we long to be into a position to glimpse Your wondrous healing power. Help us to walk in a way that reflects Your love and mercy toward us.* **Amen.**

When Stones Cry Out

"WHEN THOSE WE LEAD CANNOT UNDERSTAND OUR MISSION"

"Blessed be the King that cometh in the name of the Lord: peace in heaven, and glory in the highest. And some of the Pharisees from among the multitude said unto him, Master, rebuke thy disciples. And he answered and said unto them, I tell you that, if these should hold their peace, the stones would immediately cry out."
FEATURED SCRIPTURE: LUKE 19:38–40
BACKGROUND SCRIPTURE: LUKE 19:28–48; AND PSALM 118:26

The triumphal entry of Jesus into Jerusalem on this day marks the modern commemoration of Palm Sunday. So important was this event that all four Gospels record it. Our faith is centered on this event and the events to come during the upcoming Holy Week. On this day Jesus looked around Him and saw the very people He came to save, but they did not know who He really was or why He had come. The most important mission of leadership in the history of mankind had seemingly been lost on the masses.

Centuries of prophecy had been written in the Scriptures. Signs and miracles had led to His birth. He had performed countless acts of healings and miracles. Many did believe in Him; others did not. But on this day of triumphal entry, the cries of "Hosanna" and "Blessed be the King that cometh in the name of the Lord" must have had a surreal ring in the ear of the Master. The Pharisees denied His deity completely, and many who cried out to Him thought Him to be a military and political liberator, not the Way, the Truth, and the Life.

Christ, in His majesty, knew that His life and ministry on earth would be understood for all ages, but what a rush of earthly emotion must have come over Him as He saw the people who had missed the purpose of His mission. Had no one acknowledged Him on this day, Jesus noted that the very stones would have cried out, in affirmation of this unspeakable gift to man. Jesus knew that for now the eternal meaning of His mission was hid from the eyes of many, but in time would be revealed to all men.

Leaders of faith can especially relate to the Savior in this moment. For many of us who have answered the call of God for leadership missions, we come to realize that many of those we serve do not recognize the significance of our work. Like our Master, we must never be discouraged, nor pause for regret. Every good work ordained by God will bear its fruit in time. Heavenly purposes are not always revealed to those we are called to serve, but our work is not in vain if it is dedicated to the Lord.

As the tens of millions of Christ's believers shout, "Hosanna, blessed be the King that cometh in the name of the Lord" on this Palm Sunday, the stones have no need to cry out. The great mission of all time was truly accomplished. May God give us the peace and assurance of victory as we complete our mission and calling in the name of that same Lord.

Our Prayer: *Hosanna to the Lord. We praise You, Jesus, that You answered Your call and completed Your mission. We praise God that He opened our eyes and hearts to receive the promise of salvation that You alone give freely to all. Help us as leaders of faith to not be discouraged in fulfilling Your purposes, whether those we lead fully understand it or not. May we always be confident in every task, large or small, You give us to do.* **Amen.**

A Lasting, Last-Minute Decision

"WHEN LEADERS ARE IN THE RIGHT PLACE TO MAKE THE RIGHT DECISION"

"And he said unto Jesus, Lord, remember me when thou comest into thy kingdom. And Jesus said unto him, Verily I say unto thee, Today shalt thou be with me in paradise."

FEATURED SCRIPTURE: LUKE 23:42–43
BACKGROUND SCRIPTURE: LUKE 23:39–45

The two thieves crucified alongside Jesus at Golgotha represent two aspects of humankind. One part ignores and rejects Jesus, and the other part seeks to know Him through pure, simple faith. Today's lesson focuses on a repentant thief who sensed the injustice being done to Jesus. This thief also rebuked the unbelieving criminal as he saw his own sin and Christ's power to save and asked Christ to remember him when He came into His Kingdom. Even in His greatest moment of suffering, our Master was listening, forgiving, and accepting. The repentant thief shows leaders of faith how to make a lasting, last-minute decision.

"Today, you will be with Me in paradise," Jesus answered. The repentant thief was truly under condemnation and judgment by Rome. He was being put to death for his transgressions. His time in this life was closing. He understood the righteous penalty of his actions, yet he made the last-minute decision to request something of the dying Lord. It was a raw act of faith and an affirmation of the deity of Christ. Jesus was swift to grant his request, promising not judgment, but grace and eternal life with Him in paradise.

As leaders of faith, we, too, encounter life-and-death moments along our paths. We are often are confronted with devastating circumstances, that, like the thief's, may be of our own making. We may feel as if we have no options, no way out. But the repentant thief shows that if we humble ourselves and place great trust in the Lord, our last-minute decisions need only be faithful requests to the Master for deliverance.

Neither thieves, nor leaders, should rely on deathbed confessions for salvation. We never know if we will have that chance. However, Jesus is really by our side all the time, even in our travail, waiting for us to realize our helplessness and ask Him for deliverance. We often fail to make good last-minute decisions because we fail the test of repentance and do not see the power in our requests. We also fail to recognize the constant willingness of the Savior to deliver us.

Jesus never asked the repentant thief a question, nor did He admonish him. Christ stood ready to grant his last-minute request in His pure love, grace, and forgiveness. Our lasting, last-minute decisions are always sound when they involve repentance and faith that Christ will take us where we need to go.

Our Prayer: *Jesus, we praise You for taking our transgressions upon Yourself on the cross. May we be ever mindful that redemption is ours by just repenting and asking You for it. May we as leaders of faith make good decisions, grounded in trust that You are next to us and will take us where we need to go.* **Amen.**

Seeking The Living Among The Dead

"Looking for the Wrong Thing in the Wrong Place"

"And they found the stone rolled away from the sepulcher. And they entered in, and found not the body of the Lord Jesus. And it came to pass, as they were much perplexed thereabout, behold, two men stood by them in shining garments: And as they were afraid, and bowed down their faces to the earth, they said unto them, Why seek ye the living among the dead? He is not here, but is risen...."

Featured Scripture: Luke 24:2–6
Background Scriptures: Luke 23:50–55; and Luke 24:1–12

Over the years I have developed a great love for the women of Easter. Their devotion, their bravery, and the loyalty of their love for Christ shines throughout the ministry of Jesus. After His death, the women went back to the tomb with spices to adorn the buried body of Christ. But even in their love for Christ, they were seeking the wrong thing in the wrong place. They sought the living among the dead.

They found the tombstone rolled away and two angels sitting in the empty tomb where Jesus had been laid. The angels spoke to them saying, "Why do you seek the living among the dead". The angels went on to remind the women of what Jesus had told them, that He would be delivered into the hands of sinful men, be crucified, and the third day rise again (see Luke 24:6–8).

How often do we miss the Master because we seek Him for the wrong reasons and in the wrong places? Had the women only remembered the words of Jesus about His resurrection, they might have gone to the Temple or to the Upper Room with the disciples and waited for Him to appear. Jesus will appear to us if we earnestly seek Him, but we must seek a risen, glorified Lord. We must seek a Lord of power. Leaders of faith need to seek Jesus every day in the midst of those we serve and in the most unlikely circumstances of the day.

In our own leadership journeys, we often seek to find newness of life and vibrancy among dead organizations and dead congregations, and we fail to seek new life and fresh potential among the humble who are willing to take new risks in faith. Renewed life is not always found in the paneled-wall buildings or in the monuments to the past. It may be found in the brightness and enthusiasm of our youth and in the wise counsel of our elders. It may be found in places of poverty and through people who are thankful for what blessings they have.

The glorified risen Lord still dwells among those who need redemption and who desire to change their lives for the better. Seek Him among those who practice selfless love and radiate kindness. Seek Him in the pages of Scripture and in anthems of praise. Seek Him in your own leadership sacrifice for others. Seek the living Lord and you will surely find Him!

Our Prayer: *O Risen Lord, we give praise and thanks for the empty tomb. You conquered death and are the giver of all salvation. We give thanks for the witnesses, those who told the story of Your resurrection. May resurrection to new life become more dynamic in our lives and our leadership journeys of faith. Help us to seek You in the right places, Lord.* **Amen.**

Fretting When Jesus Is Among Us

"How Our Preoccupation with Events of the Day Blind Us to the Master"

"And it came to pass, that, while they communed together and reasoned, Jesus himself drew near, and went with them. But their eyes were holden that they should not know him…. And it came to pass, as he sat at meat with them, he took bread, and blessed it, and brake and gave to them. And their eyes were opened, and they knew him; and He vanished out of their sight."

Featured Scripture: Luke 24:15–16, 30–31
Background Scripture: Luke 24:13–35

The encounter with the risen Lord on the road to Emmaus is one of the great moments in the faith story. Cleopas and a woman, perhaps his wife, were walking down the road to Emmaus on the third day after the crucifixion. Their hearts were heavy as they discussed the events that had occurred. Then what appeared to be a stranger joined them and inquired of the nature of their discussion.

This couple was walking and talking with the resurrected Savior of the world, and they didn't realize it. They walked a long while, and the couple recounted the events of Christ's trial and death. They told Him of the women at the tomb who found it empty. Their preoccupation with what had happened blinded them to the identity of the stranger.

Jesus asked them why they were slow to put the events together and to believe what had happened. Jesus then proceeded to teach them about the Scripture prophecies of His life, death, and resurrection. The night was coming, and they begged the stranger to come stay with them. As they sat for dinner, Jesus broke the bread, blessed it, and then vanished from their sight. It was then, in that moment of Christ's vanishing, that their eyes were opened and they realized they had been in the company of Christ the Lord.

Jesus is just as alive and involved in the events of our lives today as He was then. What might have happened if this couple had sensed the presence of the risen Lord a little sooner? They did encounter Him and gave a great witness to the resurrection, but did they miss even greater fellowship by fretting about recent events?

As leaders of faith, called by the same risen Lord, we are to always be aware that our daily business can involve the living presence of Christ. He can appear in the Spirit and in our hearts and minds. But if we fret about our circumstances, we may fail to recognize the presence of Jesus and His Holy Spirit until it is too late. We can walk with Jesus in our journeys each day. He wants to walk beside us and commune with us. Let us be ready to recognize and embrace Him when He appears.

Our Prayer: *Dear Risen Lord, we praise You and cherish the sacrifice and love You share with us. Help us to walk with You each day. Open our eyes that we may see You in the events and lives of others. May Your holy presence be felt in our hearts, minds, and souls.* **Amen.**

Predictions, Prophecies, And Stories

"TRUE LEADERS MUST LEARN THE PROPHECIES OF SCRIPTURE"

"Then he said unto them, O fools, and slow of heart to believe all that the prophets have spoken: Ought not Christ to have suffered these things, and to enter into his glory? And beginning at Moses and all the prophets, he expounded unto them in all the scriptures the things concerning himself."

FEATURED SCRIPTURE: LUKE 24:25–27
BACKGROUND SCRIPTURES: LUKE 24:13–35; LUKE 1:1–4; ACTS 7; AND LUKE 16:29

Woven throughout the Scriptures are the predictions, prophecies, and stories critical to our understanding of the faith. Leaders of faith should etch these truths of God into their hearts and be capable of sharing them with others. Jesus encountered two of His followers on the road to Emmaus after His resurrection. He was "unrecognized" by them as He expounded on the stories of faith beginning with Moses and expounding on the prophecies of the Messiah.

The resurrected Christ, even at this time of His appearance as the risen Lord, still needed to cover old ground with His followers. He showed them things that would come by sharing the predictions, prophecies, and stories of Scripture, which these followers should have read and known for themselves.

Just before his stoning, the new Church's first martyr, Stephen, gave a sermon to the high priests and recalled the stories of Scripture. Some scholars say there are 10,385 prophetic predictions in Scripture, consisting of over 165,000 words. From the calling of Abraham to the Second Coming of Christ, the predictions, prophecies, and stories are in the pages of Scripture for us to read. As a leader of faith, it is incumbent upon you to tackle the task of studying these truths for yourself. Don't neglect seeking new knowledge of the Spirit that is available to you through prayer, meditation, and careful study of Scripture.

Jesus seemed amazed that the prophecies of His, life, death, and resurrection were not recognized by His closest followers. Jesus would reveal them again and their eyes would surely open, but today, it is our duty and responsibility to seek them out for ourselves. Seeking out prophecies in Scripture is a calling for leaders of faith. Our work is heavenly work, and we are players in a spiritual realm that involves the fulfillment of God's promises. To fail to learn and know the predictions, prophecies, and stories of faith is to fail in our mission. Their unfolding significance sheds new understanding regarding the events happening around us each day.

Don't miss the power, glory, and joy of knowing the future. Pray today. Study today, and unleash the full portion of God's Holy Spirit through the incredible power locked in the pages of predictions, prophecies, and stories of Scripture. Just like the followers on the road to Emmaus, our eyes will be opened anew to a living Savior who walks with us on our road today.

Our Prayer: *Lord Jesus, open our eyes to You. Set a burning desire in our hearts to want to study Scripture and seek to learn the predictions, prophecies, and stories of God's plan. As leaders called by You, we become part of this living history. Endow us with discipline, open minds, and hearts to study and understand what it is You want us to know. Send us off prepared with knowledge for our task at hand.* **Amen.**

He Was The Word

"Knowing Our Beginning and History Is Essential for Leaders"

"In the beginning was the Word, and the Word was with God, and the Word was God…. All things were made by him; and without him was not anything made that was made. In him was life; and the life was the light of men. And the light shineth in darkness; and the darkness comprehended it not."

Featured Scripture: John 1:1, 3–4
Background Scriptures: John 1:1–18; Genesis 1:1; Colossians 1:15–20

Before leaders embark on a mission on behalf of an institution, they must become proficient in the genesis and history of that institution. Knowing the beginning and the history guides us as we make decisions and govern others on behalf of that institution. A leader of faith has an even greater responsibility to learn and understand the true beginning and history of the Holy One who calls us to serve. In the beginning was the Word. The Word, the Master, the Lamb of God, the Alpha, and the Omega are all the same Lord God who summons us to service today.

"He was the Word" is one of greatest revelations of our faith. Jesus, the carpenter from Nazareth, and Jesus, the Suffering Servant, was first and foremost the Creator of the entire heavenly and earthly realms. Every good thing came from Him and belongs to Him. There is nothing that is made that was not made by Him. Placing our Savior in His proper place of power and majesty is absolutely essential for leaders of faith. We cannot truly fulfill His call on our lives until we know the Word.

The love that took the Word from the throne of heaven to become a baby in a stable in Bethlehem is not just our history; it is our passion. Learning, knowing, and inculcating the truth of our faith into our everyday expression as servants and leaders should be a top daily priority for each of us. Likewise, to not know the essence and depth of the history of our own organizations, congregations, or communities robs us of every advantage as a leader. Knowing our history helps predict our future. Knowing our history helps us to avoid the mistakes of the past and gives us an advantage over our competition.

Whether we see it or not, the history of our faith and earthly institutions both limit and empower us. Become familiar with the foundations of your faith and congregation. Who poured the concrete? How was the first building financed? Who were the founders and patrons? What were the first storms and challenges? As we enmesh ourselves thoroughly with a true understanding of our beginning and our history, we will see Christ and our calling in a clearer and more brilliant light. The Word will manifest Himself in our lives in deeper and more effective ways. When we know the Word, we know that darkness will never overcome the Light.

Our Prayer: *Our Jesus, our Word, You are both our Creator and Savior. You are also our Friend if we love You and obey Your commandments. Instill in us a yearning to understand the truths of our history and faith as we study Scripture and learn of our earthly institutions. Empower us as we see ourselves and our purpose grow and become enriched because we knew the Word.* **Amen.**

Knowing Something About Others

"Leadership Begins When We Know Whom We Are Leading"

"Jesus saw Nathanael coming to him, and saith of him, Behold an Israelite in whom there is no guile! Nathanael saith unto him, Whence knowest thou me? Jesus answered and said unto him, Before that Philip called thee, when thou was under the fig tree, I saw thee…. The woman answered and said, I have no husband. Jesus said unto her, Thou hast well said, I have no husband; For thou hast had five husbands; and he whom thou now hast is not thy husband…."

Featured Scriptures: John 1:47–48, and John 4:17–18
Background Scriptures: John 1:35–51; and John 4:1–30

Some of the most powerful moments of Scripture take place when Jesus met someone for the very first time. Jesus met and called one of His disciples, Nathanael, with a personal vision. Jesus also met the Samaritan woman at Jacob's well and shared His knowledge of her life.

In both of these events, Jesus showed His power and deity by exhibiting miraculous knowledge about persons whom He had never met. Jesus proved Himself to Nathanael by knowing that he was an Israelite of good character. He proved Himself to the Samaritan woman by accurately describing her sinful life with multiple men. Before he even met them, Jesus knew something about them, and it changed their lives.

As leaders of faith, we don't have clairvoyant vision into the lives of others, but we do have a responsibility to learn about the needs of those we serve. In time, we need to get to know those whom we are serving in order to most effectively render leadership. Leaders of faith should seek to learn something unique and personal about the lives of those they lead.

By knowing something intimate about Nathanael and the Samaritan woman, Jesus gave evidence to His claim as the Messiah. He also gained two believers and followers who would tell others about the Christ.

When leaders of faith do their research and take the time to learn something special about those they lead, it unleashes power of another sort. People connect with leaders who bother to look into their souls, feel their pain, or desire to improve their lot in life. Leaders are most effective when they learn about the interests and families of their followers. Leaders need to know of the troubles in an employee's personal life that threaten to spill over into their work. By learning something about those we lead, it shows our love and care for others.

True, effective leadership in faith begins by knowing who it is we are called to serve. The Messiah we follow will grant to those leaders of faith a special empathy and power to gain disciples and change lives.

Our Prayer: *Lord Jesus, You know our hearts. You knew us when we were but babies in our mother's arms. You know our sins and our hearts. You know our potential to do great things. Grant to us as leaders of faith a curiosity and burning desire to know the hearts of the people You have called us to serve. May we serve them well in Your name.* **Amen.**

Leading Before You Are Ready

"PERFECT TIMING FOR LEADERSHIP IS ORDAINED TO ACHIEVE THE MOST FOR GOD"

"And both Jesus was called and his disciples, to the marriage. And when they wanted
wine, the mother of Jesus saith unto him, they have no wine. Jesus saith unto her,
woman, what have I to do with thee? Mine hour is not yet come."
FEATURED SCRIPTURE: JOHN 2:2–4
BACKGROUND SCRIPTURE: JOHN 2:1–11

The formal ministry of Christ from His baptism until His ascension to heaven lasted less
than four years. Jesus knew that the timing of His ministry on earth was critical to the Kingdom.
While Christ granted his mother's request and performed His first publicly recorded miracle, He
was fully aware that this wedding event was not the time to preach, share, or reveal too much of
Himself. Jesus knew exactly what to do and when to do it.

Leadership and the holding of formal office or position were never intended to be lifetime
appointments. Great acts of service are often performed by persons who were called for a single
act or a short burst of leadership. Great leaders know when to move and when to wait. Attempting to lead before you are ready can spoil your ability to do great things. Some are called early in
life and some are called later in the twilight of their years to a special task for God. Some are
called to a single task of leadership and others to a long career.

The Savior knew from the beginning of time what He needed to do and when He needed to
do it. However, as the imperfect children of God, we are often perplexed as to how to lead, when
to lead, or whether to lead at all. Many of us want to stand up and be heard too soon and too
often, thereby negating our potential effectiveness as a future leader. Some leaders-in-waiting,
unlike Christ, may want to give a speech at the wedding feast, when humbly pouring more wine
and staying quiet would serve God's purpose for the moment.

But leaders of faith need to be ready. They need to train and soak up life experiences. Some
need more time to incorporate their previous life success and failures into their worldviews.
Oftentimes it takes a tragedy or other negative event to coax certain people into leadership. God
expects us to be ready, but He also expects us to refrain from acts of leadership if we are not ready,
if we are unprepared, or if the circumstances are not yet right.

God's timing is perfect. As a leader of faith, you will be affirmed by the voice within and
know when you are ready for leadership. God will dictate the circumstances. Mentors and peers
will draft you into the lead as the resources and support systems are built. So remain in fervent
prayer and actively monitor your environment. Wait patiently in faith, and the Lord will anoint
you and show you the exact time and place to begin. Let the wedding feast continue for now.
And tomorrow, perhaps, your time to lead will come.

Our Prayer: *Thank You, Lord Jesus, for coming to lead us home to You. How we long to be with
You at the wedding feast in heaven. Help us, O Lord, to be patient and wait upon Your call and
anointing before we attempt to lead others. Show us the time and place to begin serving You by serving
others.* **Amen.**

A Leader Who Timidly Sought The Truth

"Even the Highest Officials Need to Find Real Truth at All Costs"

"There was a man of the Pharisees, named Nicodemus, a ruler of the Jews: The same came to Jesus by night, and said unto him, Rabbi, we know that thou art a teacher come from God: for no man can do these miracles that thou doest, except God be with him."

FEATURED SCRIPTURE: JOHN 3:1–2
BACKGROUND SCRIPTURES: JOHN 3:1–21; JOHN 7:45–53; JOHN 19:39–42

Nicodemus was a high priest and a Pharisee. In fact, Nicodemus was both a religious and a legal leader of his day. It would appear that Nicodemus was a man of wealth, power, and influence. Nicodemus appeared three times in the Gospel of John. Once he sought Jesus out secretly at night. Later he argued for due process for Jesus in a meeting of the chief priests and Pharisees. Finally, he was at the burial of Jesus, bringing myrrh and aloes to anoint the body of Jesus.

Whether Nicodemus had become a secret believer and follower of Christ is not certain. Some historians and tradition say that Nicodemus became a public follower of Jesus and was eventually stripped of all power and wealth and banished from Jerusalem. But what we do know is that Nicodemus recognized the miracles and power of Christ and sought to know more of Him, even if he came timidly by night.

As a leader of faith, regardless of our positions, we all must remain seekers of the truth. Nicodemus was timid and secretive in his quest, but he sought answers nonetheless. As a leader, you may pay a price for seeking the truth, especially if that truth can potentially weaken the position or authority of those you lead.

One can only hope that the secret curiosity of Nicodemus about Jesus, and his timid defense of Him before the high priest, became a burning public display of belief in the Messiah. Perhaps visiting the body of Jesus with spices after His crucifixion was that public display. If Nicodemus did become a believer, it most likely cost him everything that he had. Even so, if Nicodemus did seek the truth at all costs, he found it. He found the living Lord and reaped an eternal reward.

It is easy for leaders of faith to get into ruts of self-confidence, thinking that no new truth can be found. Leaders are often trapped by the institutional power structures that filter out truth. When leaders step outside those boundaries to find it, they can be punished. If God called you to lead, He certainly called you to be a seeker of truth, just like Nicodemus. Be bold and risk it all…you just might find the Master.

Our Prayer: *Lord Jesus, may we always seek You in boldness. Help us to seek the truth and light in our daily leadership journeys of faith. May we take risks to know the truth and be unashamed to declare it boldly. Give us courage and strength in our walk with You to be seekers of truth.* **Amen.**

Increasing By Decreasing

"A Leader's Greatness Is Often Achieved by Knowing When to Let Go"

"Ye yourselves bear me witness, that I said, I am not the Christ, but that I am sent before him… He must increase, but I must decrease…behold, I send my messenger…which shall prepare thy way…for I say unto you, among those that are born of women there is not a greater prophet than John the Baptist.…"
Featured Scriptures: John 3:28, 30; and Luke 7:28
Background Scripture: Matthew 3; 11

There is no sweeter love, nor synergy of mission, found in the Scriptures than that between John the Baptist and Jesus. Their mothers were pregnant with them at the same time. No doubt they grew up knowing each other. Jesus, the carpenter's son from Nazareth, was preparing for His ministry while John the Baptist was active in his own ministry: preparing the way of the Lord. It was John the Baptist whom Jesus called upon to perform His baptism. John the Baptist had his own disciples and a large following of believers. John the Baptist was a great leader and prophet of the faith, yet his greatest act of leadership was in knowing when to let go.

John the Baptist forever teaches leaders of faith that our greatest acts of leadership can be increasing by decreasing. Every calling has a timeline. We unknowingly are chosen and prepared for tasks for God. God then speaks to us in our hearts and life circumstances and calls us to perform leadership tasks of faith. We answer that call and begin the journey. Sometimes the journey is short and distinct; sometimes it is blurry and goes on for many years. But wise leaders know when a specific journey needs to end. And ending a journey empowers others to take over the holy tasks.

By preparing the way of the Lord, John the Baptist fulfilled prophecy. His mission was marked by eccentricities and bold proclamations. Even the religious authorities of his time feared him. John had popularity and sway over many people. Yet he began his descent at the peak of his power. By recognizing the beginning of Jesus' ministry with His baptism, John immediately began fading into the background to allow Christ to become the central focus of the faith. Had John the Baptist continued to seek the crowds and attention, it would have hampered Christ's mission.

How many times have you seen leaders hang on too long? They served well and effectively, but by staying in office or retaining power, they became a distraction to the very mission and institution they served so well for so long. By failing to decrease themselves, they hurt their organizations or congregations. John the Baptist's humility and willingness to step aside for Christ, solidified his ministry and place as the greatest prophet. By Christ's own declaration: *"Among those that are born of women there is not a greater prophet than John the Baptist."*

The true and lasting measurement of leadership rests in the changed lives of those we serve. Often our calling will be to prepare the way for others who will work the final miracles of success. Leaders of faith should always be prayerful, willing, and ready to increase by decreasing. That may become our greatest act and the one for which we are remembered the longest.

Our Prayer: *O Lord, create in me a humble heart. Destroy in me any ambition that is not seeded by Your will and purpose for my life. Once my service and call is completed, show me how to decrease and let others take over. May my decreasing have an increasing impact on the work of God.* **Amen.**

Mount Gerizim Or Jerusalem?

"Worshiping and Leading in Spirit and in Truth, Right Where You Are"

"But the hour cometh, and now is, when the true worshipers shall worship the Father in spirit and in truth: for the Father seeketh such to worship Him. God is a Spirit: and they that worship him must worship him in spirit and in truth."

Featured Scripture: John 4:23–24
Background Scripture: John 4:1–42

The capital cities and holy sites provide great history and tradition. We feel a sense of awe and reverence when standing in the midst of the great halls and cathedrals. Today's lesson, however, focuses on a central truth about worship that Christ revealed in His encounter with a Samaritan woman. The holiest places of worship are actually the places where the hearts of believers worship God in spirit and in truth.

Jesus made a conscious decision to take the longer route through Samaria on His way to Galilee. This decision by Christ shows that our best opportunities to share the Good News with others is by taking the path less traveled. In Samaria, at Jacob's well, Jesus encountered the Samaritan woman. In addition to offering her living water, Jesus shared one of the great revelations of our faith: God is a Spirit. He is everywhere and always waiting on us to encounter Him. We don't have to go to a holy mountain or religious city in order to find God.

Likewise, you are to lead and worship right wherever God places you. The Samaritans had built their temple to God on Mount Gerizim. The Jews built their holy Temple in Jerusalem. For generations, each tribe of people believed that their unique venue of worship was the only place where God dwelt. But in the coming of Christ among us, the holy sites and temples came to be wherever hearts of men and women were open to the Lord.

Many great leaders of faith begin their journeys from humble places. Some of the greatest leadership happens in small villages, on the banks of rivers, and in the slums of big cities. It is often in poverty or in war-torn encampments that we see the meek of the world worship God with the greatest fervor.

If the Spirit of the living God dwells in your heart as a leader of faith, then you are able to lead God's people in every place, time, and situation. The Spirit of God is not confined to churches or temples or mosques. The Spirit of God rests upon all those called to His purpose as they minister to people in need.

The Samaritan woman found the Spirit of God that day. She got the living water. Many in her Samaritan town came to believe on Jesus because He brought the message of salvation directly to them, right where they were. Will you lead in spirit and in truth? Will you take the long route through Samaria to get to Galilee so that those persons off the beaten path can encounter Christ? Give freely of the living water in spirit and truth wherever you are planted by God and watch lives change.

Our Prayer: *God, You are a Spirit. You are everywhere and available to us if we but seek You. We can worship You anywhere at any time in spirit and in truth. Help us as leaders of faith to know that we can lead for You, right where we are and in the most humble of circumstances. We praise You for Christ, for the gift of living water, and for calling us to lead.* **Amen.**

Perfecting Your Faith And Leadership Journey

"Searching the Scriptures for Wisdom unto Salvation and Good Works"

"Search the scriptures; for in them ye think ye have eternal life: and they are they which testify of me…. All scripture is given by the inspiration of God, and is profitable for doctrine, for reproof, for correction, for instruction in righteousness: That the man of God may be perfect, thoroughly furnished unto all good works."

Featured Scriptures: John 5:39; and 2 Timothy 3:10–17
Background Scriptures: 2 Timothy 3:10–17; Romans 15:4; and 2 Peter 1:20–21

Any person of faith not combing the Scriptures daily and devouring the Word of God with passion is not attaining the perfection of faith or reaching their potential. Perfecting the faith is a process we undertake, not a destination we reach. The apostle Paul wrote this loving letter to his son in the faith, Timothy, pouring out his wisdom and experience. God has used this divine writing to inspire all believers in the faith toward perfection.

Jesus Himself admonishes us to search the Scriptures. The divine inspiration of Scripture makes it a living and breathing guide for living. Leaders of faith under their own inspiration of the Holy Spirit can read and study these words and be given spiritual insights to virtually all of life's situations. As a life and leadership tool, the Scriptures are profitable for doctrine, for reproof, for correction, and for instruction in righteousness.

As we search and study Scripture, we will find the foundation of creation; the laws for living; and the teachings of the Old and New Covenants. We see the manifestation of God dwelling among us in Christ and the fulfillment of thousands of years of prophecy. We find Gospel teachings, proverbs, prophecies of future events, and a blueprint for every life challenge. A leader of faith can apply the teachings of Scripture to daily relationships and transactions in business, discovering how love, mercy, grace, and forgiveness can overcome all evil, bitterness, and tribulation.

Perfect your faith and leadership journey each day as you pray and devour the Word of God. Teach your children and inspire those who follow you to use its words as a guide to daily living. As we encounter suffering and other inexplicable events around us, we can seek solace in the salvation and providence of a Lord and Savior who loves us more than we even love ourselves. What men mean for evil, God can mean for good. Search the Scriptures. Perfect your faith through fervent study. Hone your leadership skills to their sharpest point through good works. Let God's power given freely to you become unleashed in your life in new ways as you strive for the perfection of your faith.

Our Prayer: *O Lord God, we give praise for the Scriptures and the divine inspiration You gave to the authors over so many centuries. Your Word lives in us today. Inspire us to appoint our minds and hearts to new understanding by searching and studying the Scriptures each day. Help us as leaders to strive constantly in the perfecting of our faith and to use its powers in service to others each day.* **Amen.**

It's What You Don't Do

"SHOWING MEASURED RESTRAINT IN A CRISIS MOMENT IS LEADERSHIP"

"This they said, tempting him, that they might have this to accuse him. But Jesus stooped down, and with his finger wrote on the ground as though he heard them not. So when they continued asking him, he lifted up himself, and said unto them, He that is without sin among you, let him first cast a stone at her. And again he stooped down and wrote on the ground."

FEATURED SCRIPTURE: JOHN 8:6–8
BACKGROUND SCRIPTURE: JOHN 8:1–11

History tells the tales of bold and daring acts of great leadership. Leaders take action in tough situations and make the news. However, Jesus teaches us several lessons in today's Scripture about restraint against taking an unadvised action. He shows us that it is often what we don't do that sets us apart as great leaders of faith.

The woman caught in adultery by the Scribes and Pharisees was taken before Jesus in the Temple, not in search of justice, but as a way to tempt Jesus into taking an action that would alienate people to His ministry. This crisis situation in the Temple was attended by onlookers who desired to see what Jesus would do in the face of sin, law, and religious tradition. In this moment of crisis, our Lord displayed the brilliance of His deity by turning the situation of one woman's adultery into a self-reflective examination of our own lives.

Jesus did not take action to judge the woman. In His own heart and mind, Jesus most likely knew the sins of all persons present. However, rather than leaping to judgment, Christ stooped down and wrote in the sand before rising to expound upon one of faith's greatest precepts: "He who is without sin among you, let him cast the first stone." Only Christ was sinless, and only He could choose to stone the accused woman. But in Christ's restraint, He teaches us that true judgment is God's alone, and that we should look at our own sins before publicly exposing another's.

In our own leadership journeys of faith, we will no doubt be placed in situations where our restraint and quiet refusal to take action against another person may become our greatest act. Our inaction may not seem like leadership, but it is. Often we lead best when we don't attack another or react violently against an apparent injustice. In situations such as these, it may be our calm demeanor and measured response that others see as godly leadership.

We may never know what Jesus scribbled in the sand with his finger that day. The power of His calm control and eternal wisdom claimed the moment. His refusal to condemn a sinner on this day is forever recorded in Scripture as a holy example. Leading others effectively often means stooping down in inaction rather than rising in judgment. It often means letting a guilty person go unharmed in order to convict others of their shortcomings. It means challenging others to live better lives rather than making a public spectacle of a rival's failure. It is often what you don't do that will forever define your leadership success.

Our Prayer: *Lord Jesus, only You are worthy to judge us this day. We have fallen short and have sinned and long for Your forgiveness. As You forgive us, let us forgive others. Help us to show restraint as You showed that day in the Temple. Show us how to lead by using restraint and mercy and love. We love You, Jesus.* **Amen.**

Born For Greatness

"Even in Our Imperfections, God Created Us for Greatness"

"And his disciples asked him, saying, Master, who did sin, this man, or his parents, that he was born blind? Jesus answered, neither hath this man sinned, nor his parents: but that the works of God should be made manifest in him."

Featured Scripture: John 9:3
Background Scripture: John 9:1–12

The prevailing thought in the day of Christ was that those afflicted with some disease or physical infirmity were unclean as a result of some sin they or their parents had committed. Jesus not only healed a man blind from birth, but He set forth a revolutionary fact of faith: Regardless of our life conditions, we are all born for greatness so the manifestation of God's hand in our lives can be shown to others.

As Jesus passed the blind man, He did not see infirmity or failure. Jesus saw a moment in which He could show God's power, grace, and mercy by making a blind man whole. He restored the man's sight as a manifestation of God's love. Even in our own frailty and imperfections, we are placed in certain situations so God's power can change us and show the world His love for us.

The act of restoring this blind man's sight required active participation by the blind man. Jesus told the blind man to go and wash the clay from his eyes at the pool of Siloam. He did and was healed. Others saw this miracle and no doubt the entire community heard of a life restored. God often requires our participation in our own miracles. He spits, makes the clay, and applies the compress, but we are to go in faith and wash away our own infirmities. Jesus wants others to see the change in our lives wrought by His own hand.

What life condition are you in today? Are you infirmed or stranded on the rocky cliffs of life? Is declining health or disease gripping you? Is your own leadership journey of faith stuck in the ditch? Perhaps you are here today so Christ can manifest God's love and power through your problems. Pray that Christ will make a clay elixir of healing for you. Take your blindness, brokenness, and impossible circumstance, then go in faith to the pool of Siloam and wash away the clay in the presence of others. Perhaps your pool of Siloam is a place of worship, or the home of a friend, or a door of opportunity upon which you have not knocked.

We are all moving toward greatness for God if we love and trust Him. Jesus desires that we have life and have it more abundantly. Our infirmities and problems today are merely setups for miracles, so that Christ can manifest His power in us and through us. You are already healed. Go and wash and tell others of Christ's love.

Our Prayer: *Lord Jesus, spit upon the ground and make the clay that will heal my infirmity. In my weakness and problems, make Your power and grace known to others. Heal me and restore me to full fellowship with You and those in my community. I go now in faith to wash the clay in the pool of Siloam. In my new sight, I will give praise and testimony to Your love.* **Amen.**

Jesus Wept

"WHEN YOUR HEART CAN WEEP FOR OTHERS, THEN YOU ARE READY TO LEAD"

"When Jesus therefore saw her weeping, and the Jews also weeping which came with her, he groaned in the spirit, and was troubled, and said, Where have ye laid him? They said unto him, Lord, come and see. Jesus wept."

FEATURED SCRIPTURE: JOHN 11:33–35
BACKGROUND SCRIPTURES: JOHN 11:1–44; AND LUKE 19:41–44

Many of us can smile as we remember, as children, memorizing the shortest verse of the Bible: "*Jesus wept.*" Ironically, the shortest verse of Scripture is also one of the most poignant. The reality of Jesus weeping with those He loved, weeping for the sorrows and loss of others, is a powerful lesson for those of us who feel a call to lead others in faith. Jesus' tears proved His unfailing love and kinship with us, as well as His desire to restore the dead to new life in Him.

The humanity of the Christ combined with His divine nature as the Son of the Trinity of God makes the story of Jesus unique in all of history. Jesus tarried as word came to Him of the imminent death of Lazarus. Lazarus, Mary, and Martha were dear friends to our Lord. Lazarus died as Jesus delayed coming to their home. Upon His arrival Jesus found not only a dead Lazarus, but remorse and a sense of lost opportunity from Mary and Martha. In their faith they knew that had Jesus come earlier, Lazarus would not have died. Christ's Spirit groaned for them, and Jesus wept. Jesus then performed a miracle by raising Lazarus from the dead.

Before we lead others and exhibit the power of our callings, we must be able to groan in our own spirits and weep in empathy with those we have been called to serve. Christ showed that real power comes from an abiding love and care for those God has entrusted to us. When friends hurt, we should hurt. By experiencing the pain, hurt, hopes, aspirations, addictions, shortcomings, and emotions of others, we become more uniquely equipped to serve them.

Before we can lead, we must be able to weep. We must wade into the pain and sorrow of our neighbor's toughest situation. We must go where others are experiencing trouble. We must experience the loss and pain of others so we can truly know how to comfort them. God will empower leaders of faith as they seek to comfort those who mourn and serve those who need new life and new opportunity. We must abandon the misguided effort to not let our emotions show. Leaders who can weep are leaders who can lead others to hope and faith in a better day and new life in Christ. Jesus wept; then Lazarus lived again.

Our Prayer: *Lord Jesus, weep with us this day. Our world needs healing and new life. Our own lives are wrought with pain, need, and despair. We believe that You can give us new life and new hope. Raise us up, O Lord, to a new and bold life centered in You. Instill in us the ability to groan and weep with others. Let our hearts be one with those who mourn. Unleash Your power in our lives today.* **Amen.**

Lust For Praise Of Others Leaves Us Empty

"SEEKING THE ACCEPTANCE AND ADULATION OF MEN
IN LIEU OF TRUTH LEAVES LEADERS EMPTY"

"Nevertheless among the chief rulers also many believed on him; but because of the
Pharisees they did not confess him, lest they should be put out of the synagogue:
For they loved the praise of men more than the praise of God."
FEATURED SCRIPTURE: JOHN 12:42–43
BACKGROUND SCRIPTURE: JOHN 12:37–50

Believing and confessing are separate acts of faith. Belief in the truth without a confession of
the truth still leaves us in chains. In the time of Christ, He experienced much rejection. This
rejection came not because people failed to witness the miracles or hear the words of Jesus and
believe. The rejection came when they could not turn their quiet belief into an open confession.
To those who believed but did not openly confess their belief, the allure of Christ was overcome
by their desire for acceptance by their peers. For them to confess their belief in Christ would
cause them to forfeit their station and status in life. Sadly, they walked away from the salvation of
the living Lord. Their lust for the praise and acceptance of others would leave them empty.

Often today we see this same lust for acceptance override the search for the truth in our own
lives. When leaders of faith begin a quest for the praise, acceptance, and adulation of others, it
can stifle their ability to see and confess the truths they need in leadership. If leaders of faith are
truly believing and confessing the truths of God each day, it will be noticed and blessed. Even the
greatest among us can slip into the temptation to search for the acceptance of our peers and
critics to the point of compromise. In moments of tough decisions, we may know what the right
course of action may be, yet we become fearful to act on it due to the personal and professional
loss it might bring.

In failing to confess the truth of Christ, the religious leaders in our Scripture today walked
away from attaining the peace that passes all understanding in Christ Jesus. When God places us
in positions of leadership and authority, He charges us to be seekers of the truth, lovers of
righteousness, repairers of the breach, and witnesses for the defenseless. When we know the
correct course of action, yet we don't follow it out of fear of personal loss, we have chosen the
acceptance of man over the praise of God. Who can truly measure what damage we inflict upon
our friends, families, and the organizations we lead by our failure to both confess and act on the
truth at hand?

Christ tells us that His truth is life everlasting. The truths that will set you free may often
bring pain, ostracism, and loss of friendships in this life. But confession and acting upon the real
truth leads to praise of God. For what greater purpose in life could we be called?

Our Prayer: *Heavenly Father, make me not only a believer of truth, but also a confessor of the
truth. Give me the courage as a child of God and as a leader to make bold stands for You. Help me to
confess the truth regardless of the earthly consequences. Let all that I do revolve around seeking Your
praise and life everlasting.* **Amen.**

Leading By Example

"Christ's Example in Washing the Disciples Feet Sets a Standard"

"Jesus knowing that the Father had given all things into his hands, and that he was come from God, and went to God; He riseth from supper, and laid aside his garments; and took a towel, and girded himself. After that he poureth water into a basin; and began to wash the disciples' feet, and to wipe them with the towel…. For I have given you an example, that ye should do as I have done to you."

Featured Scripture: John 13:3–5, 15
Background Scripture: John 13:1–20

Upon acknowledging that God had given all things into His hands, Jesus promptly stooped down to perform the menial task of a slave or servant. The washing of the disciples' dusty and dirty feet brought indignation from Peter. How could the Lord do such a task as this? Yet this act of Christ has come to forever symbolize the Servant-Savior. This act is a portrayal of Christ taking on the lowliness and humility of man in order to fulfill His calling. By meeting both the spiritual and physical needs of those around Him by washing His disciples' feet, Christ was leading by example.

To imagine the Son of God on His hands and knees performing this unpleasant task only hours before his arrest, trial, and crucifixion sends us the sobering message that leaders of faith are to rid themselves of pride and pretention in our service to others. Everything about the life of Christ on earth breaks the stereotypes of service: giving up glory and becoming human to rescue others; loving those who hated Him; forfeiting materialism for spiritual character; and associating with the lowliest of society.

Christ's act of washing the disciples' feet has been ceremoniously reenacted in the services of many faiths over generations. It is always a moving and awkward endeavor as a person attempts it for the first time, yet the participant literally lives the example of Christ in that moment. Jesus shows us that small acts done with great love and with sincere humility can impact others for eternity.

What tasks of lowly and humble service have you performed that would embody the example of Christ? Some of us may have worked with our hands in gratifying service to others by building, cleaning, sewing, or doing errands for someone in need. You may have read to a child; cleaned a bedpan; wiped the brow of a sick stranger; or visited a prisoner in your local jail. Christ calls all leaders of faith to His foot-washing example. We are to forgive others and lead by serving—not serve by leading. Service was a prerequisite to be on Christ's team.

Seek out the unwashed feet and the unsolved problems in your own community. Set aside your power and privilege for a while and kneel down to assist someone in need. Always lead others by example. By humbling yourself in menial and unpleasant tasks of service, you will unlock new spiritual power and a deeper kinship with our Lord. *"Do as I have done to you…if you know these things, happy are you if you do them."*

Our Prayer: *Lord Jesus, we feel as if we are in the Upper Room with You even now as we meditate on this act of humble service You performed. Motivate us, Lord, to humble ourselves as leaders and stoop down and perform menial tasks in love to those around us. Let our lowly service to others inspire all persons to want to know You better.* **Amen.**

No Greater Love

"Willingness to Die for Another Is the Greatest Love"

"This is my commandment, that ye love one another, as I have loved you. Greater love hath no man than this, that a man lay down his life for his friends.... Hereby perceive we the love of God, because he laid down his life for us: and we ought to lay down our lives for the brethren."

Featured Scriptures: John 15:12–13; and 1 John 3:16
Background Scriptures: John 15:11–17; and 1 John 3:14–18

Throughout the generations, we can count the soldiers, martyrs, servants and missionaries who have given the final, best gift of service to others. To give one's life up to death for another is the greatest act of love and service. Jesus tells us that there is no greater love. Jesus Himself was our example of sacrifice. He not only died for those who believed on Him, but also so that others could claim His love as a doorway to spiritual liberation.

First, we must pause this day and give thanks for the countless, faceless servants of old who gave their lives for others. Whether on the battlefield or in the daring rescue of another, we give honor and recognition to the souls of men and women who gave their last breath to defend a cause and the people they loved. As we answer the call to our leadership journeys of faith, we, too, should know that following Christ means we may be called to give that same final measure of love to others. We may be asked to die for others in one act or over time in service.

We should couch the reality of dying for others in terms of love for others. We should cover it with the words of Christ, which celebrate death for a brother as the greatest act of love. Dying for another or for a cause invokes the highest calling and the most potent form of love. Sometimes we may not die a physical death, but we die to our own time and desires in order to serve others. Dying to ourselves means we are giving up our lives in small increments for the work of God. It may mean leaving the safety of our own communities and traveling to dangerous places to carry out a mission. It may mean time spent away from the presence of family. It may mean giving up money and comforts of this world.

When we measure the love and sacrifice of others, it changes us. It changes how we lead others, and it changes the priorities of a nation or institution. It makes us value the lives of others in a new way. It makes us pause and not take for granted our liberty, freedom, and material blessings. It harkens us to never take lightly the death or loss of limb and innocence that so many have experienced in order to carry forth their duty and service to others. We pray and trust that God has an awesome reward waiting for those who give their lives for their friends. We pray that God will instill in us a fearlessness to serve without consideration to losing our own comfort or our own life. God's love is sufficient, and His glory will hold us in all eternity.

Our Prayer: *God of life and death, we pause to remember the servants of all time who literally gave their lives in service to those they loved. We give our ultimate praise and thanksgiving to Christ the Lord, who died and was raised from death for salvation. Instill in us the understanding and courage to face the sacrifice of leadership even until the final call of death. Never let us be discouraged or dismayed as we serve in the light of Your salvation and protection.* **Amen.**

Chosen For Vine And Branch Leadership

"True Leaders Are Chosen for an Inseparable Living Connection to Those They Lead"

"Ye are my friends, if ye do whatsoever I command you. Henceforth I call you not servants…but I have called you friends…. Ye have not chosen Me, but I have chosen you, and ordained you, that ye should go and bring forth fruit, and that your fruit should remain: that whatsoever ye ask of the Father in my name, he may give it to you."

Featured Scripture: John 15:14–17
Background Scripture: John 15:1–17

Jesus is the true vine, and we are the branches. We are but extensions of His power, calling, and commands. We have been chosen for special duty to Christ. Our Scripture today from John is a powerful lesson in the relationship between Christ and those He calls to serve Him. Jesus teaches how we should relate to Him and to those who serve us in our leadership quest. Vine-and-branch relationships are symbiotic. One cannot achieve its purpose without the other. But while branches can be pruned, die, and be cut away, the root and vine is the essence of the living plant. If we as leaders of faith stay plugged into the source of our nutrients, the vine, we will ultimately bear fruit. Likewise, we should recognize the branches of our leadership and appreciate them.

In this passage today, Christ bestows a new title upon those who are called and keep His commandments: *friend*. Master-servant relationships are more businesslike, more formal; but a friendship is intimate, with ingredients of greater love. Have you developed deeper relationships with those you lead? If you are the vine leader of your organization or congregation, have you reached out in true friendship to the branches of your group? If you do, you are following the example of Christ.

Loyal servants, who are devoted and play by the rules, are not just servants of an organization. They have bloomed from branch workers to trusted friends of the vine leader who leads them. As a leader of faith, make a new effort each day to find those persons and seek a deeper love and friendship with them. Their loyalty to the common cause indicates that perhaps they, too, are chosen by God to render service to the true vine. You can then pray together for what you need to achieve God's purpose.

Being chosen by Christ for service in His vineyard makes us special partners in a holy calling. In that calling, Christ gives us one of the greatest promises of all Scripture: whatever we ask in His name shall be given if it is according to His purpose. Those whom Christ has called to service and leadership are now His friends if we remain loyal to His commandments.

Go find the servants of your organization and call them into a new relationship with you. Vine-and-branch leadership watered with love and fertilized with obedience to Christ will yield abundant heavenly harvests. Those who love and serve Christ are now friends serving in His holy vineyard.

Our Prayer: *Dear Jesus, what a privilege to be called Your friend! Thank You for choosing us for a heavenly calling. May we, as Your branches in leadership and faith, remain grounded in Your Word and commandments. May we also seek to develop new relationships with those persons in our lives who serve us so well. May we show the love to them that You have shown to us.* **Amen.**

Praying For Those You Lead

"The Great Act of Leadership Is Intercessory Prayer for Your Followers"

"While I was with them in the world, I kept them in thy name…. I pray not that thou shouldest take them out of the world, but that thou shouldest keep them from the evil…. And for their sakes I sanctify myself that they also might be sanctified through the truth…. Neither pray I for these alone, but for them also which shall believe on me through their word…. And I have declared unto them thy name, and will declare it: that the love wherewith thou hast loved me may be in them, and I in them."

Featured Scripture: John 17:12, 15, 19–20, 26
Background Scripture: John 17

Few passages of Scripture so encapsulate the love and passion Jesus has for present and future believers as does the Intercessory Prayer of Jesus in John 17. Just before Christ's trial and death, He delivered an amazing prayer of intercession for the remaining band of believers He was leaving behind. Jesus not only passionately asked God to love them as God loved Him, but Jesus petitioned God to hold and protect each of us who would later come into a relationship with Him. Each of us today is covered by the prayer of Christ to the Father above.

Jesus desired and prayed for the highest good and heavenly love to come to those who would believe on Him. Protection and blessings of life everlasting have come to many as a result of this passionate intercessory prayer of Christ on our behalf. We should not only claim this blessing of prayer for ourselves as leaders of faith; it should set the high example of our own calling to pray for all those, present and future, whom God entrusts to us in leadership.

Leaders often lead from the written mission statements of their organizations. Our results and effectiveness as a leader are measured in growth of sales or membership. We are rewarded for victories and prosperity. Winning games and battles is often our sole focus. However, we can take on no greater endeavor than to pray for those we lead each day. Those who work with us and follow our leadership bring with them broken lives and sorrows aplenty. Many put on a good face, yet suffer secretly. Jesus' example calls us to pray.

Good leaders can discern when certain followers need the intercession of prayer. Jesus prayed for us to be blessed with the same intensity of love that God rained upon the very Son of God. Pray for your followers as you would your own family. Pray for the countless faces that rely on your leadership and decision-making each day. Pray that they will be loved and be safe. Pray for a cloak of protection over them from the evil of this world. Pray for provision and salvation so that all can be sanctified through the truth. Pray for them as Christ prayed: *"that the love wherewith thou hast loved me may be in them, and I in them."*

Our Prayer: *Lord Jesus, we give eternal thanks for the prayer of intercession that You made for your disciples and for each of us. We are unworthy but so thankful that You brought the love of the heavenly Father to us. You are in our midst even now. Help us as Your called leaders of faith to pray for those lives entrusted to us in leadership. Bless them and protect them and give us all a full measure of Your grace, love, and power. We long for the day we are united in heaven together.* **Amen.**

Remaining Calm When Subordinates Don't

"In Intense Situations, Great Leaders Take Charge, and Settle Others Down"

"Jesus therefore, knowing all things that that should come upon Him, went forth and said unto them, Whom seek ye? They answered him, Jesus of Nazareth.... Jesus answered, I have told you that I am he: if therefore ye seek me, let these go their way.... Then Simon Peter having a sword drew it, and smote the high priest's servant and cut off his right ear.... Then said Jesus unto Peter, Put up thy sword into the sheath: the cup which my Father hath given me, shall I not drink it?"
FEATURED SCRIPTURE: JOHN 18:4–5, 8, 10–11
BACKGROUND SCRIPTURES: JOHN 18:1–11; AND LUKE 22:39–53

Jesus had gone to the Garden of Gethsemane to pray. He told His disciples to go with Him. In this tense hour, Jesus knew all that was about to happen to Him and He was ready. But the disciples let Him down. Not only did Judas betray Him and lead the high priest to arrest Jesus, Peter reacted by pulling a sword out and violently cutting off the ear of the high priest's servant, Malchus. It was a moment when subordinates had come apart.

Jesus remained calm in it all. He faced the situation with dignity and gentle power. He gently rebuked Judas and chastised Peter for his hot-tempered and inappropriate response. Jesus even reached up and healed the ear of the servant of His accuser. Jesus mastered this tense moment and set the example for all leaders of faith.

Great leaders of faith seem to shine in moments of great drama. In these times, others around you will go astray. They will panic. They will invariably do things that can pull the entire group under. God gives perfect peace to those who are called by Him for special tasks. They will radiate His peace and confidence in these situations of danger. Jesus knew who He was and what it was that He was supposed to do. The unpleasantness of the arrest was part of the plan, but He would not let the panic of Peter upend Him.

One must wonder what the servant, Malchus, thought in future days as he remembered his ear being severed and then healed. Did this act of calm caring by Christ, even as He was being arrested, change Malchus's life? Can our calmness in tense moments also change lives?

When we exhibit calm and confidence in tense moments, our subordinates and our adversaries see in us a power that cannot be described. The leader should always know the task, the consequences, and the events that will unfold. Leaders of faith must always take charge of those who follow them and lead on, even if it is to an unpleasant place.

Our Prayer: *Sweet Lord, thank You for setting the example of confidence and for enduring the arrest and trial and tribulation for us. Help us to show the same courage as we face tough situations in the callings You have summoned us to. May we know exactly what it is we are to do and how to do it. May we become leaders who lead and take charge of those who panic around us. Bless the work of our hands, that it may glorify You.* **Amen.**

Speaking Your Truth Clearly

"LEADERS OF FAITH WHO KNOW THEIR CALLING SHOULD SPEAK IT CLEARLY"

"Jesus answered, My kingdom is not of this world: if my kingdom were of this world, then would my servants fight, that I should not be delivered to the Jews: but now is my kingdom not hence. Pilate therefore said unto him, Art thou a king then? Jesus answered, Thou sayest that I am a king. To this end was I born, and for this cause came I into the world to bear witness unto the truth. Every one that is of the truth heareth my voice."

FEATURED SCRIPTURE: JOHN 18:36–37
BACKGROUND SCRIPTURE: JOHN 18:28–37

In all situations Jesus knew who He was and what He was sent to do. Leaders of faith who have heeded the call of God should pray for this same self-assurance of their callings and for the specifics of their mission. Before Pilate, Jesus was not going to deviate from His calling or mission to bear witness to the truth.

The steadfastness of Jesus before Pilate would lead to ridicule by others and ultimately His death. This same steadfastness is the very spine of the miracle of the salvation story. How many times in your own leadership journey of faith have you stood before authority figures and ranking officials and been asked about own mission? Do you morph yourself into an image that they have of you in order to receive a promotion or a new assignment? The path of least resistance often includes the denial of our godly calling.

When we come face-to-face with those who doubt our calling or wonder how we survive the rigors of leadership, we must never be tempted to deny our commitment. Those around us should never doubt our steadfastness to our purpose. Jesus set the ultimate example for leaders of faith as He stood before Pilate.

By speaking our truths clearly, people can judge us on the merits of what we do. Our motives will not as likely be questioned, and our peers can more readily hold us accountable if we begin to stray from our calling or mission. We must constantly remain in prayer and communion with God to gain constant reassurance of His guiding hand in our lives.

Speaking our truths clearly and without reservation will also land us in tough situations. People will have unmet expectations. There may be persecution ahead for us. We may lose a chance for a promotion or higher office. But to fail to speak truth clearly and follow our calling to the end is to fail God. We, too, must bear witness to the truth that Jesus came to share with us as the Suffering Servant.

Our Prayer: *Dear Jesus, we praise You that You were the witness and bearer of the truth. Even enduring the ridicule of others, You fulfilled Your calling and in the process redeemed us all. Help us as leaders of faith to be bold to speak our truths clearly even in the face of adversity. If You called us to the task, it is a sacred responsibility. Give us the courage to endure for a while longer.* **Amen.**

It Is Finished

"When a Life and Mission Comes to a Conclusion, the Purpose of God Goes On"

"After this, Jesus knowing that all things were now accomplished, that the scripture might be fulfilled, saith, I thirst.... When Jesus therefore had received the vinegar, he said, It is finished: and he bowed his head and gave up the ghost."

Featured Scripture: John 19:28, 30
Background Scripture: John 17:4

Jesus had stepped out of the glory that was His in heaven to come to earth for this mission that God had sent Him to do. In His intercessory prayer before His crucifixion, Jesus declared that He had finished the work that God had given Him to do and He was ready to return to His glory in heaven. The last words of Christ on the cross, *"It is finished,"* meant more than just giving up the ghost of earthly life. It meant that this leg of His calling and His mission had been accomplished and that Scripture had been fulfilled.

The eventual resurrection of Christ and His multiple post-resurrection appearances tell us that Christ is still very much alive and involved with us, even after He uttered these last words from the cross. In the days following the resurrection, Christ appeared to His apostles and bestowed upon them the Holy Ghost. In the presence of His believers, Jesus ascended into heaven with a promise to return again. Jesus appeared many times to others after His ascension, including to Paul on the road to Damascus and to John as he wrote the Book of Revelation. He walks and talks with us even today.

Beyond the wonder and majesty of the theology found in today's text is the hope that exists for leaders of faith who claim Christ's promises. When our lives are finished, our work and accomplishments will continue to bless others. Leaders must endow their followers with truth and wisdom. When we build institutions and select new leaders to continue leading the mission, we are leaving good works behind. Become part of a mission wherever you are called. Be a good parent and a loving friend. It will yield eternal heavenly fruit.

Many of us will plant shade trees under which we will never sit. Did we give someone who was thirsty a drink of water in the name of Jesus? Did we share the stories of Jesus with a child during our lives? Did we silently and diligently pray for those friends and strangers who, by our lifted requests to God, were healed and saved? Did we lead our congregations humbly? Did we complete the mission God gave us to do even in our death? Did we write something worth reading?

Let us go to our heavenly reward with Christ knowing that we finished the work the Father called us to do. *It is finished!*

Our Prayer: *Lord Jesus, hallelujah! You were obedient to the call of the Father. By Your love and devotion, You completed the work God gave You to do, fulfilling all Scripture and bringing salvation to creation. We love You, Lord, and are so honored to share in our own small ways and lives the furtherance of Your purpose. As we come to the end of our earthly lives, may we say, "It is finished," and know that we, too, did what we were called to do.* **Amen.**

My Lord And My God

"When Our Doubt Causes Us to Miss a Blessing"

"And Thomas answered and said unto to him, My Lord and my God. Jesus saith unto him, Thomas, because thou hast seen me, thou hast believed: blessed are they that have not seen and yet have believed."

FEATURED SCRIPTURE: JOHN 20:28–29
BACKGROUND SCRIPTURES: JOHN 20:19–31; MARK 3:13–19; AND ACTS 1:12–26

Thomas, the disciple, has become known as Doubting Thomas because of his skepticism regarding Christ's resurrection. But after this encounter with Christ he remained a loyal disciple, and, according to some traditions, carried the Gospel to Persia and even India. Some believe that Thomas died a martyr's death for the Lord. But today, Thomas is primarily known for his doubt of the resurrection and his lost expectations after the crucifixion of the Lord he had served.

In the first appearance of our risen Lord to His disciples, Thomas was not present. Jesus showed the disciples there in that encounter the holes in His hands and feet from the nails of the cross. In that moment Jesus breathed on them and bestowed upon each of them the Holy Ghost. After Jesus left them and Thomas returned, the other disciples shared with Thomas about this miraculous encounter. In his doubt and disbelief, Thomas remarked that unless he saw it for himself, he would not believe, and in doing so, Thomas missed a blessing.

Jesus reappeared miraculously in a separate appearance to the disciples. Immediately, Christ turned to Thomas who was among them and confronted the disciple's disbelief. In this great encounter, Jesus made Thomas take the physical test—to touch and feel the scars of His hands and side so that he would believe. In the rush of his guilt and now his belief in the resurrection, Thomas' only words spoken in response are appropriate: *"My Lord and my God."*

How often have other leaders or fellow believers offered testimony to great miracles in their lives only for you to scoff (even quietly to yourself) in disbelief? Maybe they gave true testimony to answered prayer or changed lives, but you did not open your heart to believe. In that, your moment of disbelief, you may have missed a blessing from God. To practice faith that God fulfills His promises through the testimony of others is to open your soul up to receive a blessing.

In your leadership journey, don't let the Master catch you slacking in faith. By the time we see the physical manifestations of miracles and the fulfillment of God's prophecy and promises, along with the answers to prayers, it will be too late to receive the full blessing of simple faith. If you've prayed for it, believe it. If fellow believers give testimony, believe them. If God's Word says it, believe it. Don't let blessings be delayed or lost through your own doubt and disbelief.

Our Prayer: *My Lord and my God, forgive us all when we doubt and wallow in disbelief of the fulfillment of Your promises. Open our hearts to understanding and faith that if it has been promised, it will happen. Don't give up on us when we fail. Help us to gird ourselves with faith, hope, and a sense of anticipation that all good things will happen in time. We love You, Lord.* **Amen.**

Secret Followers

"LEADERS AND MOVEMENTS WILL GARNER SECRET FOLLOWERS WHO CONTRIBUTE"

"And after this Joseph of Arimathaea, being a disciple of Jesus, but secretly for fear of the Jews, besought Pilate that he might take away the body of Jesus: and Pilate gave him leave. He came therefore, and took the body of Jesus. And there came also Nicodemus, which at first came to Jesus by night, and brought a mixture of myrrh and aloes, about an hundred pound weight. Then they took the body of Jesus...."

FEATURED SCRIPTURE: JOHN 19:38–40

BACKGROUND SCRIPTURES: JOHN 3:1–21; JOHN 7:37–53; MATTHEW 27:57–66; LUKE 23:50–55; AND ACTS 1:21–25

Joseph and Nicodemus surface in the stories of Jesus as "secret followers." The curiosity and faith of these two men grew until they came onto the stage of the Passion Story in a major way. Both Joseph and Nicodemus were men of wealth, status, and official Jewish authority in Jesus' time. The fact that they had come to know and learn of Christ meant that they were risking their positions and lives if their proclivities became known. Our Scripture says they gave of their time and resources after the cross.

Joseph supplied the burial place for our Lord and went to Pilate after the death of Christ and appealed for the right to His body. Nicodemus, who had earlier approached the Rabbi Jesus to ask about being "born again," would bring expensive spices to anoint the body of Jesus for burial. These two secret followers show that the appeal of Christ had seeped into the formal setting of Jewish authority. These secret followers lent much significance to the holy events of the resurrection and show us that Christ's truth attracts diverse and unlikely followers.

In our own journeys of faith, we will encounter those persons from outside our core group of followers who will be attracted to the message we share. We may not even know that they exist until some special point in time. Some will fear retribution if they are discovered collaborating with us. Some may come from a competitor or from another faith. Some may see in us a freshness and integrity that attracts them. If leaders of faith remain true to the call and command of God, our leadership will surely attract the Josephs and Nicodemuses of our time. Secret followers will come in our midst and want to share in the joy and love we practice in serving others. They may even endow us with gifts.

According to tradition, Joseph and Nicodemus stayed with the faith but paid a dear price by losing wealth and religious status. Nicodemus was banished from the city and the Temple. Becoming a secret follower can lead to persecution. As a leader of faith, seek out your secret followers. Pray for them and coax them into a broader fellowship with your organization. God sends secret followers to lend credibility and assistance when we need it the most. Secret followers can themselves become bold messengers for the great missions of God.

Our Prayer: *Dear Jesus, the secret followers in Your holy time gave of their resources to assist You. The Scripture speaks of them. Send secret followers and benefactors to us who can benefit our heavenly call. Help us to seek them out and bring them into full service and fellowship with us.* **Amen.**

Mary...Rabboni

"The Power of Hearing Your Name from a Familiar Voice"

"And when she had thus said, she turned herself back, and saw Jesus standing, and knew not that it was Jesus. Jesus saith unto her, Woman, why weepest thou? Whom seekest thou? She supposing him to be the gardener, saith unto him, Sir, if thou have borne him hence, tell me where thou hast laid him, and I will take him away. Jesus saith unto her, Mary. She turned herself, and saith unto him, Rabboni...."

Featured Scripture: John 20:12
Background Scriptures: Genesis 3:1–4; Acts 9:1–6; and John 10:1–5

Great leaders master the art of remembering the names of persons around them. In giving speeches or in the recognition of volunteers, great leaders score loyalty from others by remembering names and calling people out for extraordinary service. The calling of names by God shows the intimacy and unique loving relationship He has for His children. The Good Shepherd calls His sheep, and they know His voice and follow Him.

One of the most personal and passionate scenes of the love of God is found in the story of the resurrection. Mary Magdalene had come alone to the tomb to see Jesus. She had found the tomb empty and encountered two angels who sat where Jesus had been laid. They asked Mary why she was weeping. She did not know she was about to become the first person to encounter the risen Lord. Mary loved Jesus and had been a faithful follower, even at the crucifixion. Her love was demonstrated in her presence at the tomb that day.

Mary turned and encountered what she believed to be the gardener as she wept. She then asked the stranger if he knew where they had taken the body of Jesus. With all the love and affection He had for Mary, Jesus called out..."*Mary.*" Immediately Mary turned to Him and, in recognition, responded..."*Rabboni.*" The power of hearing her name and the recognition of His loving voice was all it took for Mary to give an eyewitness account of encountering the Master.

In our own leadership journeys, we will encounter many faithful followers, coworkers, and volunteers who have followed our cause with great love and affection. What a thrill it is for those persons who have labored so hard for our cause to hear their names called by the voice of a leader. The very act of calling a name has power. To hear one's name is to personalize a relationship and to validate a person's value to the organization.

To learn names and to know faces is a sign that we truly value the worth and effort of every person. It means that we have taken the time to consciously incorporate a person's life into our missions of faith. God knows our names. We hear His gentle voice as we pray or walk or sleep. Our names are written in His Book of Life. We should strive each day to build relationships with those around us. As often as possible, we, too, should call others out by name with a voice of love and appreciation. Our efforts will blossom when others hear their own names called by our voices.

Our Prayer: *Rabboni, You are the great Master. Just as You knew and loved Mary, You love us today. We long to hear Your voice calling our names sweetly each day. Help us as Your servant-leaders to value and acknowledge all those entrusted to our care each day. Through our own voices and with Your power, may we call the names of those around us and serve as an example of Your love for us all.* **Amen.**

Come And Dine

"Using the Intimacy of Dining Together to Know and Lead Others"

"Jesus saith unto them, Bring of the fish which ye have now caught… Jesus saith unto them, Come and dine. And none of the disciples durst ask him, Who art thou, knowing that it was the Lord… And it came to pass, as he sat at meat with them, he took bread, and blessed it, and brake and gave to them. And their eyes were opened, and they knew him.…"

Featured Scriptures: John 21:10, 12; and Luke 24:30–31
Background Scriptures: John 21; Luke 24:13–35; and Mark 14:17–25

Come and dine. Christ used the intimacy of the meal to share many things about life and eternity with those He loved. The Holy Sacrament of the bread and wine are shared from a table of communion and fellowship with fellow believers. Jesus loved to go into peoples' homes and dine with them. Perhaps Jesus knew that sharing an intimate meal bonded us by our shared need for nourishment. In breaking and blessing bread, Jesus let us know that in His Presence we will never hunger again.

The resurrected Christ appeared to the disciples as they were fishing and invited them to bring their catch and dine with Him. Jesus issued yet another call to those He loved to fellowship with Him. The dining table can become a sacred place where Christ summons those He loves to give thanks and share love with each other. It is a small unit of time when we cease from our labors and our worries to share the bounty of food and celebrate the care put into preparing it. Leaders of faith should use every opportunity to enter into renewed fellowship and intimacy with those they lead by inviting them to *come and dine*.

When we invite others into our home to dine with us or when we visit another's home to dine with them, we break barriers and open new avenues of communication. In every generation and culture, the sharing of a meal in a home is a gesture of honor and respect. It can also become an opportunity to ask for forgiveness or invite others to join your cause. It can become a time when joy and laughter conquer tensions and bitterness. Preparing a meal with our own hands and serving another person is an act of love and humility and establishes a unique connection with them.

The love of Christ seemed to blossom as He sat around the dining table with others. Christ's theology of the dining table gives us something to emulate as we seek new fellowship and intimacy with those we lead and serve. When Jesus said He was going to prepare a place for us in heaven, we can only imagine that He is preparing a dining table of eternal fellowship where He will explain the mysteries of all time. Until He calls us there, we can seek His presence as we invite those around us to a deeper relationship around our table. *Come and dine.*

Our Prayer: *Lord Jesus, we come and dine at Your table of love and grace. We offer praise that You want us to dine with You. As we recall the times You dined with those You loved, we feel as if we are there with You. We give thanks for the daily blessings of food, water, family, and friends. Instill in us a yearning to become more intimate with those around us by using the theology of the dining table. Come and dine with us this day, O Lord.* **Amen.**

Feed My Sheep, Feed My Sheep, Feed My Sheep

"Redemption for the Rock of Leaders"

"He saith unto him the third time, Simon, son of Jonas, lovest thou me? Peter was grieved because he said unto him the third time, Lovest thou me? And he said unto him, Lord, thou knowest all things; thou knowest that I love thee. Jesus saith unto him, Feed my sheep."

Featured Scripture: John 21:17
Background Scriptures: Matthew 16:17–18; John 21:1–17; and Matthew 26:57–75

The arrest and trial of Jesus was not a time of glory for Simon Peter, the rock on which Christ would build His Church. Peter had pulled out the sword and cut off the ear of the high priest's servant, Malchus, which Jesus then healed. Later, during Jesus' trial before the religious leaders, Peter was identified three times as a follower of Jesus and three times he denied it; the cock crowed and thus fulfilled the prophecy of Christ.

Peter was still the rock, but he was a wounded and transgressed one. In His third appearance after rising from the dead, Christ was dining on the lakeshore with some of His disciples, including Peter. In this dramatic love scene between the Master and the Rock, we see the key to redemption and purpose in leadership. Not just once, but three times Jesus asked the same question of Peter, *"Do you love me?"* Three times Peter said, *"Yes."* And three times in response, Jesus said to Peter, *"Feed my sheep."*

Peter's example of the "rock in need of redemption" can be applied to all great leaders of faith. There lies within us the boldness, the insight, and the fire to serve Christ and those in need. But in all of us is also the propensity to make mistakes and to forsake on occasion the very reason and very persons we are called to serve. Our own denials of Christ and frequent failures in our missions would seem to eliminate us from useful leadership service to Christ. But that same loving, forgiving voice heard by Peter on the lakeshore is today calling our names to redemption…"feed My sheep; feed My sheep; feed My sheep." Each time Jesus said it, the sin of Peter's three denials was removed from him.

Just as Peter's fellowship with Christ was restored by his willingness to feed Christ's sheep, we are also empowered to do the next great thing for Christ. But who are the sheep Christ calls us to feed, and how will we feed them? Tell the stories of Jesus to people who have never heard. Boldly pray for healing and salvation in our world today. Give a cup of water to the thirsty and dying in Jesus' name. Visit the lonely and imprisoned. Through thought, word, and deed, let the love, mercy, grace, forgiveness, and salvation found in the resurrected Christ become the primary focus of our every act of service to others…now the sheep are being fed.

Our Prayer: *Lord Jesus, we love You, we love You, we love You. Help us to feed Your sheep each day. Help us to know we are redeemed as leaders of faith and ready to start anew. We are flawed but chosen. May we work each day so as to exude the love You have for us all. Forgive us and empower us with the Spirit as You did for Peter. Make us bold disciples and leaders of faith for the Kingdom of God.* **Amen.**

The Many Unwritten Acts Of Leadership

"Even the Unknown Acts of Leadership Have Eternal Value"

"And there are also many other things which Jesus did, the which, if they should be written every one, I suppose that even the world itself could not contain the books that should be written… And many other signs truly did Jesus in the presence of his disciples, which are not written in this book: But these are written, that ye might believe that Jesus is the Christ, the Son of God; and that believing ye might have life through his name."

Featured Scripture: John 21:25
Background Scriptures: Amos 7:10; John 20:26–31; John 21:24–25; and 2 Corinthians 3:1–3

There are some thirty-five recorded miracles of Christ in the Gospel stories beginning with the turning of the water to wine at the wedding at Cana. Yet John's Gospel account tells us that the wondrous works and signs of Christ that are not recorded would fill books the world could not hold. The disciple Matthew, on twelve occasions, stated that there were many more miracles than those recorded. The signs and miracles of Christ lend evidence to His deity and fulfill Scripture prophecy. We can only imagine in our own hearts the good works and miracles that Jesus did on earth and still does in our lives today.

Leaders of faith can often lose heart while performing tasks for the mission. Much of our obedient performance of duty will never be known to others. Does this unrewarded success cause us to pause and wonder if the hard work we do is worth the effort? The apostle Paul addressed this in his letter to the church at Corinth: *"Forasmuch as ye are manifestly declared to be the epistle of Christ ministered by us, written not with ink, but with the Spirit of the living God; not in tables of stone, but in fleshy tables of the heart"* (2 Corinthians 3:3).

Most of what we do in our journeys will not be written down or heralded by others. We may even come to forget our own acts of sacrifice and effort we made on behalf of others. Our unrecorded and uncommended acts of service are our offerings to God. Even small acts, carried out in love, will resonate for all eternity. The voluminous miracles, healings, and signs of Christ were never entirely written down and live only in our prayerful imaginings. Yet every expression and act of love and power of Christ is part of eternity. That example should be enough for leaders of faith today.

The days and months of seemingly unknown work that we do in our leadership callings can be celebrated as our holy tithe to God. Give all your own many unwritten acts of leadership to Christ. They may just unleash the very power and fulfillment of God that changes hearts and affirms your service to others in Jesus' name.

Our Prayer: *Dear Lord, most of what we do each day in our callings will never be known by historians or written into earthly commendations. Lord, we struggle some days to wonder why we do the things we do in obscurity. Lift us up, O Lord, and make every work of our hands and meditation of our hearts be something wonderful for You. Affirm us and encourage us as we go about the tasks You called us to do today.* **Amen.**

All The Power You Need

"God, Who Called You to the Task, Will Equip You with Great Power"

"But ye shall receive power, after that the Holy Ghost is come upon you: and ye shall be witnesses unto me both in Jerusalem, and in all Judaea, and in Samaria, and unto the uttermost part of the earth…. And suddenly there came a sound from heaven as of a rushing mighty wind, and it filled all the house where they were sitting. And there appeared unto them cloven tongues like as of fire, and it sat upon each of them. And they were all filled with the Holy Ghost…."

FEATURED SCRIPTURE: ACTS 1:8; 2:2–4
BACKGROUND SCRIPTURE: ACTS 2

Our Scripture today contains the last words of the risen Christ as He was about to ascend into heaven. Christ's earthly mission had been completed, and He was departing to His place in glory. He had charged his apostles and believers with tasks to do. But Christ did not ascend before leaving us with His last promise, that we would receive power!

Jesus did, indeed, send the Holy Spirit by way of cloven tongues to the assembly of believers at Pentecost. The believers there received supernatural powers, enabling them to do the signs and miracles of the faith and to promulgate the Gospel to all places.

The gift and promise of power given by Christ is universal to all believers who claim Him. As leaders of faith, we felt that call of Christ in our areas and realms of service. Our service may be a small task in our own Jerusalem, or it may be a bold initiative to the uttermost parts of the earth. But whatever our calling, however humble, and wherever that calling may take us, Jesus has promised to give us the power and provision to complete it.

Immense reservoirs of holy power go unused each day in the lives of believers! Like rushing waters lost over a steep dam, we fail to harness the full explosion of provision the Lord freely offers to us. What simple circumstances trip and befuddle leaders of faith each day because we fail to claim the power of the Holy Spirit!

We may not see tongues of fire in the unleashing of this power, but we will see the right people come into our lives at just the right moment. We may feel a sense of new confidence as an idea or vision rushes into our minds and hearts and we respond to the difficult challenges of life. We may awaken to find new circumstances and changed hearts as former adversaries or complete strangers come to our assistance. Small miracles in our own lives lend testimony to the presence of God's Holy Spirit working in our world. Our Lord promised that we would receive power. Let us claim it and use it for all things good and holy in Jesus' name.

Our Prayer: *Holy Spirit, come to us. Jesus promised it, and I claim it as an heir to His promise. Fill us, Holy Spirit, with power to perform any and all tasks that this journey of life requires of us. Help us to heal, build, earn, repair, and win victory in all life's circumstances. Stay with us until we come face-to-face with the risen Lord in our new home for eternity.* **Amen.**

After The Great Event

"Coming Together in One Accord to Go Forward"

"Then returned they unto Jerusalem from the mount called Olivet…. And when they were come in, they went up into an upper room, where abode both Peter and James, and John, and Andrew, Philip, and Thomas, Bartholomew, and Matthew, James the son of Alphaeus, and Simon Zelotes, and Judas the brother of James. These all continued with one accord in prayer and supplication, with the women, and Mary the mother of Jesus, and with his brethren…the number of the names together were about an hundred and twenty."

Featured Scripture: Acts 1:12–15
Background Scripture: Acts 1:1–15

The true and faithful followers of Jesus had just left the mountaintop and witnessed the ascension of the risen Lord into heaven. The last words of Christ spoken to them were a promise of power from the Holy Ghost and a command to be witnesses to Him in all places. Angels then told them that in the same manner Jesus had left, He would return again. This stunning and glorious event on the mountaintop came to a dramatic close. The great event was over. This remnant of the New Covenant would now have to come together in one accord and move forward.

The followers of Jesus went back to Jerusalem to an upper room and gathered together in prayer and supplication. Men and women alike were there. The disciples and Mary, the mother of Jesus, were there. Left in this upper room were the 120 witnesses to the faith who must carry on as the custodians of the message of Christ. Coming together after a great event and going forward is crucial to survival of any mission of faith. The emotions that stir in us after great events must become channeled into work and progress. To scatter is to fail.

Leaders of faith will encounter those moments when after a great event, the followers in our organizations or congregations find themselves on an emotional high. The "mountaintop experience" can lead to a crash of despair or confusion if leaders don't bring people together and show them how to move forward. The emotions running through these 120 followers of Christ in the upper room must have been palpable. When would Christ return? What was this power that Jesus promised, and when would it come? Would the angels appear to them again? What were they to do next? Peter, James, and others took charge and led, just as you must take charge and lead.

Coming together to go forward after a great event provides us with a chance to gain focus and set goals. It allows us the moment to build a commitment to a shared responsibility. In this time of togetherness, we must assign tasks and set timelines. We must share resources and lift each other up in prayer and supplication. We must hold each other accountable. These 120 persons built the foundation of faith forever. They showed us how to lead and follow after a great event. Let us come together and go forward as we lead others in a new spirit of Christ's love.

Our Prayer: *Lord Jesus, what a glorious event it must have been as You ascended to the Father. You promised to send us the power of the Holy Ghost and charged us to be witnesses all over the earth. Your call is as clear to us today as it was then. Bring us together as You brought Your disciples together long ago. Bless us and empower us to come together, go forward, and tell others of Your love and salvation that awaits all who believe.* **Amen.**

With One Accord In One Place

"Get in Place and Be Ready to Receive God's True Power"

"And when the day of Pentecost was fully come, they were all with one accord in one place. And suddenly there came a sound from heaven as of a rushing mighty wind, and it filled all the house where they were sitting. And there appeared unto them cloven tongues like as of fire, and it sat upon each of them. And they were all filled with the Holy Ghost, and began to speak with other tongues, as the Spirit gave them utterance."

Featured Scripture: Acts 2:1–4
Background Scriptures: Leviticus 23:15–22; Acts 1:8–9; and Acts 2

A great part of leadership is getting those you lead to come together in unison and create a singleness of heart and mind among them. When leaders of faith do this, they can accomplish great things for God. In our lesson today, the disciples and believers of the early Church had gathered for the observance of the second of the three great Jewish festivals, called Pentecost. It is also known as the Feast of Weeks, the Feast of the Harvest, or the Feast of the First Fruits. It was a celebration seven weeks after the Passover, a time to bring God the first fruits of the harvest.

For centuries the Jews had set this time aside as a time of thanksgiving and offering to God. The first and very best of what they gathered for their own sustenance was given to the Creator to show reverence, humility, and a sense of connectedness to God. The new believers of Christ, too, were gathered on this day and *they were all with one accord in one place.* Imagine the joy and anticipation that Peter and the other followers had on that day, longing for the time when they would see Jesus again.

The coming of the Holy Ghost upon the believers at Pentecost was the fulfillment of a promise Jesus made to them. Many present there had seen the Lord rise up into heaven. Their hearts were full and teeming with joy and anticipation. And as they gathered together the Holy Spirit came to them.

Leading others requires that we prepare our followers for the miracles God wants to send. Just like the early disciples, leaders of faith have similar congregations and organizations of followers who long to know God more deeply and who desperately need His abundant power to come into their lives. The power of the Holy Ghost that came upon the gathering at Pentecost that day is available to us. As leaders of faith we must create unity of heart and purpose and then gather our followers together to receive power.

The Holy Spirit is alive and ready to assist us. While we may not see flaming tongues of fire, we can see hearts change. We can see God's power move in worship and in prayer. We can see hopelessness replaced with holy purpose. The Holy Spirit moves among us in numerous and mysterious ways. So let us harvest that power so readily available to us by being with one accord in one place, serving others in Christ's name. The power of the Spirit is already on the way!

Our Prayer: *Lord Jesus, send Your Holy Spirit to us this day. Let us claim the power that is available to every believer with new boldness. May the Spirit guide us, nurture us, and show us how to live and serve with new power and dominion over evil.* **Amen.**

Holding Something Back

"When God Calls Leader to Task, They Must Give It Their All"

"But a certain man named Ananias, with Sapphira his wife, sold a possession, And kept back part of the price, his wife also being privy to it, and brought a certain part, and laid it at the apostles' feet. But Peter said, Ananias, why hath Satan filled thine heart to lie to the Holy Ghost, and to keep back part of the price of the land?...thou hast not lied unto men, but unto God."

Featured Scripture: Acts 5:1–4
Background Scriptures: Acts 4:32–37; and Acts 5:1–11

The fledgling flock of the early Church was the nucleus of the entire faith. God had chosen them to become part of the most incredible journey of faith ever known. They were the repository of the Good News of Christ. The Scripture says: *"The multitude of them that believed were of one heart and of one soul"* (Acts 4:32).

In response to this calling, this group voluntarily agreed to sell all their possessions and contribute them to the work of the early Church. The apostles received the tributes and made sure each person had the provision they needed in order to survive and preach the Gospel. It was a sacred vow, not only to their congregation, but to the Lord. But one couple held something back. Their calling was true, but their obedience and spirit was lacking. In their dreadful mistake is a great lesson for leaders of faith: When we are called by God to a task, we must hold nothing back.

Peter said that Ananias and Sapphira, by keeping part of the proceeds from the sale of their property for themselves, showed not only a lack of faith, but they lied to the Holy Spirit. As a result, both Ananias and Sapphira were overcome with fear and dropped dead in front of the apostles. In their moment to give it all up to God for the purpose of His calling, they had fallen short, and it left them lacking.

As leaders of faith, we are seldom asked to sell all our possessions and give them away, although that could be the case. More likely, our callings involve a full commitment to leave our comfort zones, perhaps even our professions or communities, in order to fulfill the missions God has given us to do. Our callings may involve new training or further education. They may involve changing our lifestyles or personal habits. They may mean the abandonment of old friends and places that hinder our purpose.

When God calls you to a mission, give it your all. Don't hold anything back. The Holy Spirit will not only multiply your gift and sacrifice, but God will bless you, keep you and your family safe, and make all your provisions sufficient when you sell out for God.

Our Prayer: *Dear Lord, what a blessing to be called to a holy task by You. Let us never hold anything back when You call us to Your service. Bless us with Your Holy Spirit and provide us with the courage, provision, protection, and peace we will need as a result of giving it all up for You.* **Amen.**

The Power To Heal, A Chance To Lead

"Healing the Hurts Around You Gives You a Chance to Lead in Faith"

"And by the hands of the apostles were many signs and wonders wrought among the people…. And believers were the more added to the Lord, multitudes of both men and women…. There came a multitude out of the cities round about unto Jerusalem, bringing sick folks, and them which were vexed with unclean spirits: and they were healed every one."

Featured Scripture: Acts 5:12, 14, 16
Background Scriptures: Luke 10:8–9, Acts 3:1–10; and Acts 5:12–16

"Silver and gold have I none; but such as I have I give thee: In the name of Jesus Christ of Nazareth rise up and walk" (Acts 3:6). This powerful passage tells of the encounter that Peter and John had with the crippled beggar at the Temple gate. The beggar had to be carried each day and laid at the gate to beg for alms. On this day, he got more than alms: He met the power of the living Christ and was healed.

The apostles' power to heal provided opportunities to lead others into the Kingdom of God. Even silver and gold, as precious and desired as they may have been, were mere commodities compared to the miraculous healing power the apostles offered the multitudes. If the beggar had gotten silver and gold from Peter, he would still not have been able to walk; more especially, he still would have failed to come to know the love, power, and eternal salvation of Jesus.

Christ has blessed you, as a leader of faith, with healing power, as well. Your healing power may be the ability to bring peace to a broken congregation. It may be the ability to inspire others through the spoken word. It may be the ability to create a vision of a better world and be able to convince others to give of their time and resources to make it happen.

The power to heal was the power to effect change in the lives of others, to confront the hurts, problems, and unmet needs of others. Many sick and hurting people in our communities await us and need the power we have to intercede on their behalf.

The healing power given to the apostles by the Holy Spirit was to be a sign of the loving grace and salvation offered through Jesus of Nazareth. As the apostles healed, they gave tangible testimony to the love and power of Christ. God has given you a very special gift to use in leadership. It has been given to you to draw a following so that Christ's love can be shared as you heal the pains of those you serve.

Silver and gold you may not have, but what you do have, share it with others in Jesus' precious name. If you do, the sick will be healed, and lives will be changed for eternity.

Our Prayer: *Lord Jesus, we praise You for the power of the Holy Spirit to heal and work miracles among us. Just as the apostles received power, we pray for that same power to do wondrous and great things for others in Your name. May the gifts You bestow upon us as leaders of faith be used to heal and bring others to You.* **Amen.**

Obeying God Rather Than Man

"Leaders Must Risk the Legal Consequences of Following God's Call"

"Then went the captain with the officers, and brought them without violence…they set them before the council: and the high priest asked them, did not we not strictly command you that ye should not teach in this name? And behold, ye have filled Jerusalem with your doctrine…. Then Peter and the other apostles answered and said, We ought to obey God rather than man…. Then stood there up one of the council, Gamaliel…now I say unto you…let them alone: for if this work be of men, it will come to naught: but if it be of God, ye cannot overthrow it.…"

FEATURED SCRIPTURE: ACTS 5:26–29, 34, 38
BACKGROUND SCRIPTURE: ACTS 5:12–42

Scripture clearly tells believers that we are to obey the laws of society and work within the rule of law and the ordination of government. Yet there comes a time when our call to share God's message compels us to confront human institutions. Peter and the apostles came to such a time. Their ministry and preaching in the Temple placed them squarely against the religious civic authorities. They were imprisoned. But through the act of an angel of the Lord, they were miraculously released from jail. And they immediately returned to preach the message to the people in the Temple. Confronted again by the authorities, Peter responded: "*We ought to obey God rather than man.*"

Many leaders of faith are called to service in lands where religious freedom is cherished and observed. We risk little to share our faith and put into practice our beliefs. Yet many of us live and work in societies that are hostile toward the faith of Christ, where the legal authorities punish those who practice and share the love of Jesus. But in all lands and at all times, leaders may be confronted with the situation of Peter and the apostles. We may have a stark choice to make, to obey man or obey God.

Leaders of faith are not called to overthrow governments. Jesus did not come to conquer Rome by the sword. We are called to love and to serve others through obedience to God's calling upon our lives. We should always strive to obey both God and the rule of man's law. Even Peter and the apostles, when caught preaching in the Temple for a second time, submitted themselves peacefully to the guard and to the civil council of authority. Nonviolent protest is appropriate in certain circumstances and has changed many institutions for the better. Yet we cannot always predict the outcomes or consequences of our civil disobedience.

The apostles were the recipients of divine intervention as the angel of the Lord sprang them from jail, and when the Pharisee Gamaliel made a wise appeal to the council for their release. God protects those who obey His commands. We may pay man's price through arrest or persecution, but we will always be cloaked in the eternal and holy covering of safety. Angels and the modern-day Gamaliels may come to our assistance in these times. But we must always obey God's certain call even when it collides with society; we must always peacefully submit to human consequences arising from our obeying God rather than man.

Our Prayer: *God, give us the courage to always obey Your calling and commands. Give us boldness of spirit to declare the Good News wherever we go. As leaders of faith called by Your name, we submit to Your call and are prepared to peacefully submit ourselves to the consequences of obeying You rather than man.* **Amen.**

Inviting Leadership Martyrdom

"Telling People the Truth They Don't Want to Hear"

"When they heard these things, they were cut to the heart… But he, being full of the Holy Ghost, looked up stedfastly into heaven, and saw the glory of God, and Jesus standing on the right hand of God. Then they cried out with a loud voice, and stopped their ears, and ran upon him with one accord, and cast him out of the city, and stoned him.…"

Featured Scripture: Acts 7:54–55, 57–58
Background Scripture Luke 4:14–30

Stephen is recorded the first martyr of the faith. Stephen is described in Acts as "a man full of the Holy Ghost" with "irresistible wisdom and spirit." Stephen was drafted into leadership as a deacon to better account for the funding and care of the widows in the community. Stephen was a grassroots leader of faith.

Stephen was outspoken and bold. His sermon just before his death, found in Acts 7, is the longest recorded sermon in Scripture. But by telling the religious and local authorities of his day what they didn't want to hear, Stephen set the stage for his own martyrdom. The leaders did, indeed, respond violently to Stephen's words and ultimately stoned him to death.

This account in Acts tells us that Stephen saw heaven opened up, with the "*glory of God, and Jesus standing on the right hand of God.*" Stephen's face became like that of an angel as he died, and Scripture describes his death sweetly as "falling asleep."

We may not face stoning from our leadership decisions or for speaking our words of truth clearly. But leaders of faith will many times see their careers, even their leadership positions, taken away for simply telling those they lead and the powers around them what they don't want to hear.

Being bold and true leaders ultimately means making hard, unpopular, or even radical decisions. It involves telling others that they are not walking in the light of truth, justice, or love. Your actions may mean that you invite your own leadership martyrdom.

The rewards of martyrdom may be great. Indeed, we may see God's very presence in our time of turmoil. But by speaking truthfully, we can attract others to our cause and leave a legacy, like Stephen, that cannot be extinguished.

Our Prayer: *Dear heavenly Father, we give thanks for the martyrs of our faith, like Stephen. In our own walks as leaders of faith, help us to never sacrifice the truth for fear of losing. Even if we lose power, position, life, or limb, help us to know that Your love, glory, and power will sustain us and promulgate our works far beyond our lives.* **Amen.**

The Right Place At The Right Time

*"Heeding the Call of God Puts You at the Right Place
at the Right Time to Achieve His Purpose"*

"And the angel of the Lord spake unto Philip, saying, Arise, and go toward the south unto the way that goeth down from Jerusalem unto Gaza, which is desert. And he arose and went: and, behold, a man of Ethiopia…then the Spirit said unto Philip, Go near, and join thyself to this chariot"

Featured Scripture: Acts 8:26–27, 29
Background Scripture: Acts 8:26–40

Success in life and leadership is often chalked up to simply being in the right place at the right time. Some call it luck, or fate. But for leaders of faith, being in the right place at the right time is more often than not the work and purpose of the almighty Father.

Success is also measured in great moments, encounters, and events. For us as leaders to truly be used by God, like Philip in today's lesson, we must follow God's call to go to a strange place without knowing the purpose. God is the God of circumstances, encounters, and events, and if we allow ourselves to let the Holy Spirit guide us in every moment, we can perform great feats for God.

We may not be visited directly by the angel of the Lord, like Philip was on that day, but God will speak to us through our friends, our relationships, our circumstances, and our own dire straits and failures. God often speaks to us in a small voice within our souls. It tugs gently on us until we respond. Being in the right place at the right time is being open to using our senses and holy instincts to make every situation an opportunity to share God's love to others through word, deed, and service.

Philip heeded the angel's call to go to the desert. In obedience, Philip went forth and as a result had an encounter with the Ethiopian eunuch. The eunuch was the treasurer of Queen Candace of Ethiopia and was a powerful person in a great land that had yet to hear the Good News of Christ. Philip approached the chariot of the eunuch and shared the Gospel story and the fulfillment of prophecy with this Ethiopian leader. The man believed, was baptized, and traveled home to spread the Gospel. A new missionary was sent.

This great story began with a call and the obedient answer of a leader who was willing to be placed in the right place at the right time for God. You, too, will get strange requests and invitations in your leadership journey. Life will present to you unusual circumstances to share with complete strangers the hope and the promise of a better way through Christ. It may mean staying an extra day in a strange city to perform an act of kindness for another. It may just mean striking up a conversation with an unlikely soul. But if we stay strong in the Spirit of God, we will inevitably find ourselves in the right place at the right time to lead and serve others in Christ's love.

Our Prayer: *Dear Lord, give us the heart of Philip to listen to what You ask us to do. Make us open to heed Your call to go to strange places, meet strangers, and bring hope and the Good News to the world. Protect us and gird us for these tasks; put us, we pray, O Lord, in the right place at the right time for You.* **Amen.**

Bearing Witness To A Leader's Conversion

"Being Obedient to God's Call to Bear Witness to the Bizarre"

"Then Ananias answered, Lord, I have heard by many of this man, how much evil he hath done to thy saints at Jerusalem…. But the Lord said unto him, Go thy way: for he is a chosen vessel unto me, to bear my name before the Gentiles, and kings, and the children of Israel…."

FEATURED SCRIPTURE: ACTS 9:13, 15
BACKGROUND SCRIPTURES: ACTS 9; AND ACTS 22:12

The conversion of Saul (Paul) on the road to Damascus is one of the great stories of the faith. Saul, the chief persecutor of the early Christians, was blinded by a great light and was converted in a direct encounter with the risen Lord. Paul was then taken to Damascus and after some time was transformed into the great missionary of the early Church. Paul's writings would ultimately comprise a major portion of the canonized New Testament. But before the great works of Paul, came a faithful leader bearing witness to a leader's conversion.

The success of this conversion experience lies in the obedience and good reputation of the apostle Ananias. The Lord knew that Ananias had the heart and character to effectively bear witness to Paul's conversion. The risen Lord came to Ananias in a vision, told him of Paul's conversion, and instructed him to go and meet Paul, put his hands upon him, restore his sight, and fill him with the Holy Ghost.

Leadership journeys of faith often involve something harder than conversion. They involve convincing others of things they may not want to believe. Leaders of good public standing and high rapport with others may be called upon to endorse a person, candidate, or cause that those we lead find dubious. But if we are called by God to bear good witness to a new leader, we must obey, just as Ananias obeyed this strange, but difficult request of Christ.

Acts 22:12 tells us: "And one Ananias, a devout man according to the law, having a good report of all the Jews which dwelt there…." Ananias was the credible witness God needed to confirm His calling on Paul. Ananias's faith had to be strong as he went to the house of Judas on the street called Straight, to inquire of Paul. After all, Paul was the persecutor of the Christians. Would Ananias be arrested; would the authorities be there to take him away? Could Ananias really heal and channel the Holy Spirit into a man who had killed so many of the early believers?

Jesus chose Ananias for this task because He knew Ananias understood that conversions can happen when people encounter the Master face-to-face. Just like Ananias, you as a leader of faith must rise up and give testimony to those persons who bring value to your cause. What great future saint is waiting for you to bear witness to their conversion experience?

Our Prayer: *Lord Jesus, You saw in the persecutor Saul, the apostle Paul. You can redeem anyone for Your service, even the most sinful among us. Thank You for Ananias and his obedience to Your call to provide a testimony for Paul. Help us to seek out those who need conversion or a mentor to prove them worthy for service.* **Amen.**

Resisting Adoration In Leadership

"SETTING FOLLOWERS STRAIGHT WHEN THEY WORSHIP THE MESSENGER"

"And when the people saw what Paul had done, they lifted up their voices, saying in the speech of Lycaonia, The gods are come down to us in the likeness of men. And they called Barnabas, Jupiter; and Paul, Mercurius, because he was the chief speaker…why do ye these things? We also are men of like passions with you, and preach unto you that ye should turn from these vanities unto the Living God, which made heaven, and earth and the sea, and all that are therein…."

FEATURED SCRIPTURE: ACTS 14:11–12, 15
BACKGROUND SCRIPTURE: ACTS14:1–20

The boldness of the Gospel that was being preached among the various communities brought the apostles of Acts into many volatile situations. Many who heard would come to believe in Christ, but many would incite the crowds against the apostles. The apostles were expelled from Antioch, were assaulted in Iconium, and had now fled to Lycaonia. In Lycaonia, Paul encountered a crippled man who was lame from birth. Paul saw him and commanded that he arise and walk. He did, and this miracle caused the people to want to worship Paul and Barnabas, not the living God by whose power they healed.

When Paul and Barnabas tried to set the people straight and refused their offerings and adoration, the people revolted and Paul was nearly stoned to death. The apostles once again had to leave a hostile place. Leaders of faith will encounter potential followers who don't want to hear the words we speak, but instead want to worship the messenger. They long for the simplicity of idol worship rather than the peace and power gained through repentance and surrender to God. A leader of faith who performs great acts among strangers can become godlike to simpleminded persons. Leaders of faith must never allow themselves to be held in higher esteem than they ought.

Some leaders become self-absorbed with their own polished words. Others become fascinated with their almost magical effects on those that follow them. Men and women of power can easily come to be set upon pedestals. Be careful to guard against adoration. Great leaders are humble leaders who give God the credit and glory. The power that God instills in you to lead should be used for the purposes of your heavenly calling. Like Paul and Barnabas, there will come a time when you, too, must set the people straight. Pastors, community leaders, and elected officials can often succumb to bouts of enjoying false adoration from congregations or organizations.

Stay focused. Keep your mind and heart centered on your call to serve others and tell them of the love, grace, and forgiveness found through the risen Lord. Speaking the truth plainly and powerfully may bring false adoration or even persecution. Never be deceived or discouraged, but let the light of heaven shine as God keeps you in the palm of His hand.

Our Prayer: *Lord, we give thanks for Paul and Barnabas and all the early apostles of faith. They knew their callings and remained humble and brave. Instill in us that same commitment and boldness. Forgive us when we allow our work to absorb us and others in false adoration. Protect us in our persecutions as we fulfill our callings for You. May our work and leadership bring others to a new understanding of You.* **Amen.**

Followers Are Fragile

"Legalistic Requirements for Followers Can Stifle the Spirit Among Us"

"And put no difference between us and them, purifying their hearts by faith. Now therefore why tempt ye God, to put a yoke upon the neck of the disciples, which neither our fathers nor we were able to bear? But we believe that through the grace of the Lord Jesus Christ we shall be saved, even as they."

Featured Scripture: Acts 15:9–11

Background Scripture: Acts 15:1–18

In the life of the early Church, the legalistic differences and the colliding cultural morays of the new believers threatened to break the unity of the congregation. Paul, Barnabas, and Peter clearly saw the fragility in the fledgling Church as the issue of circumcision and other legal doctrines became fodder for division. Their followers were fragile, and if they became divided over the legalism, it could destroy the love and unity found only in Christ Jesus.

The insistence on adherence to certain ways of expressing the faith can put a yoke upon those who follow our lead. When we restrain the simplicity and miracle of another's faith by insisting on legal adherence to a set of rules in order to be accepted into the fellowship of God, we can stifle our own callings. When others believe and accept the grace of Christ, they become part of the fellowship of God. We as leaders of faith should never break the beautiful and simple fellowship of a diverse congregation by insisting that hardened rules are followed.

No institution can survive without rules or boundaries. However, successful leaders are marked by the ability to recruit an abundance of different souls to the same task. Leaders should measure the hearts and humble spirits of those we bring into our fold. If our followers have pure intent and a sense of commitment to the purpose at hand, we should never allow our cultural and political differences to crush the new bond that we have formed.

The early Church survived and grew as its early leaders dealt quickly and assuredly with dissension over circumcision and Gentile acceptance. By making the grace and forgiveness of Christ the central and sole focus of faith in the new Church, the mission of service became supreme.

What issue of division do you need to confront today from those you lead? Are cultural or legalistic questions and divisions threatening your team? Has the criticism by the legalists in your profession sapped the spirit and drive from your own daily walk and calling? God is calling us to the simplicity and power of His plan for our lives. We are to simply walk in the light and grace of His salvation and purpose. We are to humbly, yet boldly declare His Word through our deeds and actions each day. Followers are fragile. Our own spirits can be fragile. Don't let the yoke of another's expectations steal your vision of the Master.

Our Prayer: *Lord Jesus, help me this day to affix my eyes solely upon You. Let me cease from the stress and striving of adherence to rules and procedures that stifle my spirit and calling. Forgive me when I allow legalism and high expectations to frustrate those who follow Your call to service. I pray for the courage and devotion to finish the tasks You have called me to do.* **Amen.**

When Saints And Leaders Disagree

"God Can Use an Impasse to Scatter Saintly Leaders for Greater Works"

"And the contention was so sharp between them, that they departed asunder one from the other: so Barnabas took John Mark…and Paul chose Silas.…"

FEATURED SCRIPTURE: ACTS 15:39–40
BACKGROUND SCRIPTURE: ACTS 15:36–40

Nothing can seem as painful or as catastrophic as when great friends disagree and split apart. When this involves leaders of faith, it can be seen as a setback for the work of God or the Church. In other organizations, splits of great leaders can portend failure or diminished value for investors. But leaders of faith who are called to special tasks should always know that God's plans are not always our own. Paul wanted to retrace some old ground in the second missionary journey that was covered in their first. But God had other plans.

Barnabas was determined to take John Mark with him and Paul on this journey. But God wanted their mission to scatter and spread. God wanted new territory to be evangelized. This disagreement among saints over John Mark caused them to divide and travel in different directions. It not only left John Mark on the mission trail, but added Silas, as well. From saintly disagreement, "*they departed asunder*." The apostles themselves had no idea that God was using this painful impasse as His providential tool to spread the Gospel and build the Church.

Leaders of faith will encounter disagreements with co-leaders and saints in our own congregations and organizations. The pain and discomfort we experience from an impasse may simply be God scattering us for His own purposes. Congregations split. Then they grow and multiply. Corporations and organizations split. Then they build and sell even more. Sometimes families split, but through forgiveness they can grow and prosper for God. In all that we do, let us be prayerful and obedient to our calls and to the voice of God.

Saints and leaders of faith should always try to overcome differences with Christian love and charity. We should allow our humility and self-sacrifice to be abundant in every encounter with others. However, sometimes leaders succumb to taking the path of least resistance during a disagreement. To follow this path can often bring danger.

If after prayer and supplication, you feel a great peace and resolve in your position at the time of an impasse with others, it may be time for a scattering to occur. Go to God in prayer. Ask Him if He wants you to "give in" or "dig in." Disagreements, impasses, and scatterings have always been part of the omnipotent hand of God. Even the saints and greatest leaders of our day cannot contain God and His limitless capacity to yield fruit from our disagreements. Let Him work through your impasse today and scatter us to show His glory to others.

Our Prayer: *God, even the greatest apostles and saints disagree. They often depart asunder and feel betrayal. Yet in it all is the providence of Your hand to build the Church and the Kingdom of God. Lord, use the impasses we encounter in our leadership journeys of faith to Your glory. Scatter us if it be Your will. Guide and direct us, and may we forgive those with whom we disagree. Empower us to work even harder for that glorious day of Your return.* **Amen.**

Leading By Opening Your Home To Others

"LEADING BY FAITH FROM YOUR OWN HOME"

"And a certain woman named Lydia, a seller of purple, of the city of Thyatira, which worshipped God, heard us: whose heart the Lord opened, that she attended unto the things which were spoken of Paul. And when she was baptized, and her household, she besought us, saying, If ye have judged me to be faithful to the Lord, come into my house, and abide there. And she constrained us."

FEATURED SCRIPTURE: ACTS 16:14–15
BACKGROUND SCRIPTURES: ACTS 16:11–15; GENESIS 19:1–3; HEBREWS 13:1–3

The home is a sanctuary for many; however humble, it can truly be the resting place of our hearts and lives. But for others, the home may be a place of pain and turmoil. It may be a prison of abuse. A sign of our wholeness in faith is our preparedness to open the privacy and sanctity of our homes to others, even strangers. Opening our homes to the work of God is a great act of leadership of faith.

Today, Lydia was the leader. Lydia was a merchant, a seller of purple dye in Thyatira. This woman who knew God was taught by Paul and his disciples. The Lord opened her heart to understanding. She and her entire household were baptized. In the opening of her heart by the Lord, she developed a boldness and zeal to the point that she became insistent that Paul and his disciples come and stay in her home. Paul was so overcome by her persistence and faith that he and his followers agreed to do so. For this period of time, Lydia's home was the headquarters of the Church.

The early hurch was built around the home. Even today, home churches and home Bible studies are part of the landscape of faith. In the great mission work of today, the humble homes of believers are flowing fountains of faith. Leadership of the home is also practiced when we allow friends and family to come into our midst. We are great leaders when we host special events and allow others to experience firsthand our love and commitment to God. The home is God's altar when we bring foster children, those who are homeless, or those in financial trouble into our inner sanctums. Or, as Lydia showed, we can shelter pastors, missionaries, or traveling evangelists in our homes.

Leaders of faith can lead at home by praying before meals and bedtime. The shelves of our home reveal the books and mementos that are sacred to us. The good behavior of our children is a sign that God is in our hearts. Laughter and singing with an abundance of love in a home is the best sermon most will ever hear.

Become an example of leadership by opening your home to others in Jesus' name. The Lord opened Lydia's heart to understand, and she opened her home to others. Pray for understanding of how you can best utilize the asset of your home for His sake.

Our Prayer: *Lord Jesus, thank You for Lydia. She set an example by opening her home to Paul and his disciples. Open our hearts to new understanding today. Help us to utilize all of our assets for You, Lord. Clean our lives and sanctify our homes so that they can become altars and sanctuaries of leadership in faith.* **Amen.**

To The Unknown God

"Leaders Must Lead Boldly Through the Arrogance and Ignorance of Philosophy and Idolatry"

"Then Paul stood in the midst of Mars' hill, and said, Ye men of Athens, I perceive that in all things ye are too superstitious. For as I passed by, and beheld your devotions, I found an altar with this inscription: TO THE UNKNOWN GOD. Whom therefore ye ignorantly worship, him declare I unto you…. Forasmuch then as we are the offspring of God, we ought not to think that the Godhead is like unto gold, silver, or stone, graven by art and man's device."

Featured Scripture: Acts 17:22–23, 29
Background Scripture: Acts 17:16–34

Paul found himself in Athens, and his spirit was stirred as he saw the idolatry throughout the city. Paul was burdened to share the Gospel story, and he set out into the city streets and markets to tell the powerful story of a resurrected Christ. Paul found his way to the heart of the stoic philosophers and the Areopagus, which was the high council in charge of religious matters. Paul stood upon Mars Hill, where the great debates took place in the city. There he boldly challenged all present to replace their monument of worship entitled TO THE UNKNOWN GOD with a true knowledge of a living God.

Paul preached the Gospel boldly and told of the One True God and Creator. He preached repentance of sin and the resurrection of the dead through Jesus. Many mocked him, and many questioned him; but a few came to believe. Paul's leadership journey of faith carried him into the bowels of philosophy and idolatry, yet he never flinched and was empowered to share the Gospel.

Leaders of faith today should also prepare to confront the skeptics among us. Some unbelievers will have open hearts and minds and will be curious to listen to a message of love, hope, and salvation. However, there will always be the scoffers and self-adulators whose supreme confidence in their own logic and debate will confront our message and our callings. The leaders of the young Christian faith after Pentecost were bold and unafraid. They would tell the truth boldly and let the Spirit move without fear of consequence. In today's world, we, too, must be bold and unafraid to lead others in spirit and in truth. We, too, may find ourselves among the scholar and the skeptic who will seek to shred our faith and purpose through confrontation.

The same Spirit of Pentecost that equipped Paul, Peter, Timothy, John, Silas, and the many saints is also ready to equip us today. Our challenge is to take the emptiness and hopelessness of and the worship of the unknown god and turn it into the hope of the salvation and liberation of a living Lord. Even among the philosophers and skeptics is a yearning to know the true God of all creation. Be bold, and be plain; lead on in the confidence of the Great *I AM*.

Our Prayer: *Lord, we shall encounter the idolatrous and the skeptic. We will surely face the scoffing of the philosopher and the learned as we journey in faith for You. Send Your Holy Spirit upon us so we will be bold and powerful to withstand the critic and the persecution we shall face. Plant the seeds of salvation in the scoffer and skeptic. May the love and power of a risen Savior rescue the perishing and care for the dying around us.* **Amen.**

Having Your Own Craft And Profession

"Leaders Equip Themselves by Having a Real Profession"

"After these things Paul departed from Athens, and came to Corinth; And found a certain Jew named Aquilla…with his wife Priscilla…and because he was of the same craft, he abode with them and wrought; for by their occupation they were tentmakers."

Featured Scripture: Acts 18:1–3
Background Scripture: Mark 1:16–18

The apostle Paul is one the great heroes of the faith, as the New Testament's greatest missionary and the most prolific author of Scripture, we might assume that being a faith leader was Paul's sole profession in life. Indeed, we know of Paul's great works of the faith, but little is known of his first craft, that of a tentmaker. Paul had a skill that could earn him a living outside of his ministry. Our call to leadership should not necessarily be our primary professions in life. Every leader of faith should learn and hone a skill and cherish their earthly professions.

Paul traveled to Corinth and met fellow Church leaders and tentmakers, Priscilla and Aquilla. Not only did Paul lodge with them, but he worked alongside them, making tents to sell. This kinship of faith and craft is found often in the Bible. God expects His leaders to be self-sufficient, able to make a living so that missions can be funded. Joseph, the earthly father of Jesus, was a carpenter. Most likely Jesus himself learned this trade. Leaders of faith should be industrious and hardworking earners of wages and profits. God expects us to pay our bills and debts.

The disciples James, John, and Peter were called from their fishing boats. The apostle Luke was a physician, and Matthew was a tax collector. Crafts and professions are part of the Gospel history. Today our earthly professions can bring great value to our leadership calling. We can draw from our education, training, work ethic, and peer networks to serve and help others. Many of the parables of Christ are derived from the workaday world of the people He encountered.

To prepare for leadership and to enhance your leadership abilities, you might seek a broader education. Learn a trade or craft that can earn you a good living. Practice the work ethic of our New Testament leaders.

Making tents or catching fish were necessary in biblical times; today they might compare to the practice of law or laboring on construction sites or factory floors. The skills and practice of our crafts and professions may propel us into leadership mission fields. Like the apostle Paul, we may need to cease leading for a while and make tents in order to keep the missionary journey alive. That may even be the way God means it to be.

Our Prayer: *Dear Lord, thank You for giving us professions and skills we can use to earn a living. Bless our work and leadership, however great or humble it may be. Instill in us a strong work ethic and yearning to learn a trade or profession. Help us through the works of our hands to find new opportunities to serve You.* **Amen.**

Giving Those You Lead Over To God

"Every Leadership Journey Will Come to an End"

"And now, brethren, I commend you to God, and to the word of his grace, which is able to build you up, and to give you an inheritance among all them which are sanctified…. And they all wept sore, and fell on Paul's neck, and kissed him."

Featured Scripture: Acts 20:32, 37
Background Scripture: Acts 20

The greatest self-deception a leader of faith can indulge is that a leadership journey will go on indefinitely. Every calling and appointment of leadership from God will have a limited life. Even the earthly ministry of Christ Himself lasted less than four years. In today's lesson, we see the passion and concern of the apostle Paul for the church at Ephesus. Yet it was time for Paul to leave. He would never see this fledgling congregation again.

Paul had held nothing back from them. He had been with them for three years. He had taught them well and poured his soul into the building of the Church there. He encouraged them to feed the Church by way of the Holy Ghost. He told them to support the weak. He knelt and prayed with them. But at the end of it all, he could only commend them to the grace of God. Paul had to trust in God's providence that the work begun there would yield fruit for the Kingdom of God.

Paul knew in his leaving that troubles would come to Ephesus. He said: *"After my departing shall grievous wolves enter in among you, not sparing the flock."* Paul knew also that deceivers would come and take some of the followers away with false doctrine. The early Church was fragile, and the leadership and divine doctrine of Paul's leadership had kept them from failing. But it was time for him to say good-bye and give them to God.

In our own leadership journeys of faith, we, too, give our lives to building congregations. We build not only organizations, but families of love. We invest all we have to see them grow, only for our portion of the journey to come to an end. Like Paul, many leaders of faith leave their followers with real concerns about what will happen to them. The fear of losing all we worked for can seep into our conscience. But if God sent us to build and lead, it is not us, but God who owns the work. Leaders of faith should never become so possessive of a task or group of followers that we believe our work is indispensible to its long-term success. Even the greatest leaders are but humble servants of God laying stones in an eternal wall of leadership.

Paul said: *"I commend you to God, and the word of his grace."* Paul's emotional departure showed the love and passion he had for this church and its leaders. It shows how attached we can become to our callings. But in the end, it is appropriate and positive that we pray, weep, and leave…giving it to God and the word of His grace, knowing we answered the call and gave it our all.

Our Prayer: *Dear God, help us to always understand that our leadership assignments are temporary and are gifts from You. We commend those whom we lead and those organizations we helped to build to Your grace and will. Protect those who lead in our absence. Bless them and protect them. Give us grace and mercy in the new tasks You have for us, O Lord, until You call us home.* **Amen.**

Telling Your Story In All Circumstances

"God Makes Our Duress and Bondage His Venues to Tell the Story"

"Then Agrippa said unto Paul, Thou art permitted to speak for thyself. Then Paul stretched forth the hand, and answered for himself: I think myself happy, king Agrippa, because I shall answer for myself this day before thee touching all the things whereof I am accused of the Jews…. Then King Agrippa said unto Paul, Almost thou persuadest me to be a Christian."

FEATURED SCRIPTURE: ACTS 26:1–2, 28
BACKGROUND SCRIPTURE: ACTS 25—26

Paul was once named Saul and was the persecutor of the early Christians. His life was changed forever after his encounter with the risen Lord on the road to Damascus. Paul had been a devout and learned scholar of the old religious traditions, but now was a leading missionary and planter of Christ's new Church. Paul's evangelism had landed him in trouble with authorities on many occasions, and in today's lesson he was held before Festus and King Agrippa.

In his duress and bondage Paul was given an unusual and lengthy opportunity to tell his story to the court of King Agrippa. He set forth the story of his faith, including his encounter with the living Lord. Paul's loss of freedom created unique opportunities for him to share his powerful story of spiritual liberation. Loss of personal liberty set up the venues for God to speak to others through Paul.

As leaders of faith, we may never be imprisoned in front of a king, but we may be put into unusual circumstances and venues to share our faith stories. Great leaders must be prepared to tell their stories in all circumstances. Like Paul, we must have the boldness to share the love of Jesus and the miracles in our own lives. We may risk losing friendships or experience social ostracism by telling our stories. We may risk a promotion or subject ourselves to ridicule. But God creates these circumstances to share our truths with others. These miraculous events may be the only place and time that others will ever hear the story of the faith journey.

When you find yourself in unusual circumstances, innocently accused of wrongdoing, or set before a high authority, pray that God will give you a word to say. Perhaps this is your moment to speak words of truth to others who would never hear them otherwise. It is not your freedom and liberty that is most important here; it is the sharing of the eternal hope and gift of Christ that matters most. Tell your story in all circumstances and let God do the persuading. God is the God of circumstances. Let His providence guide you in leadership and be ready in all contingencies to let your light shine.

Our Prayer: *Lord Jesus, we thank You for the apostle Paul and for the many brave missionaries and leaders of faith who told their stories with no regard for their own lives. Give us a portion of their courage. In our callings may we be bold to share our faith and stories with others. Forgive us when we are weak and fail. Create in us a purpose so strong that it drives us into every circumstance with a passion to tell the stories of Jesus and His love.* **Amen.**

Crisis On The Sea—From Prisoner To Leader

"GOD OFTEN SENDS OBSTACLES TO RAISE UP LEADERS FOR HIS CAUSE"

"And now I exhort you to be of good cheer: for there shall be no loss of any man's life among you, but of the ship. For there stood by me this night the angel of God, whose I am, and whom I serve, Saying, Fear not, Paul; thou must come before Caesar: and, lo, God hath given thee all them that sail with thee."

FEATURED SCRIPTURE: ACTS 27:22–24
BACKGROUND SCRIPTURE: ACTS 27

Your ship is wrecked. The water is cold. All those around you are in panic. A storm has demolished all your belongings and spoiled your well-made plans. The apostle Paul was one of several Roman prisoners aboard this ship, which ran into winds and trouble. Yet God meant this situation for His purpose. This crisis on the sea would transform Paul the prisoner into Paul the leader. God willed this incident at sea because He desired that Paul appear before Caesar in Rome.

God is the God of all situations. He uses them for His express purposes. Oftentimes we may find our lives resembling shipwrecks. Our long and well-conceived plans get derailed. Our lives tumble into turmoil. Our possessions, perhaps even our freedom, are lost. Yet in these times of crisis, God's plans can be revealed. Paul belonged to God. God had specific tasks for this leader of faith to accomplish. Even his imprisonment and transfer to another continent could not stop his ultimate purpose. On this special day, Paul would be sent to Rome. He would confront Caesar.

Our callings as leaders of faith may not hold such drama as the wrecking of a ship. But God's grip upon our lives can force major changes in our circumstances. Finding God's will in our callings may involve trauma. It may mean we encounter cold water and physical hardship. It may involve broken relationships and financial setbacks. It may mean we fail at certain challenges and lose status or position. But God is constantly positioning those He calls into greater service in His Kingdom.

God takes our personal crises or the dysfunction found in our congregations or organizations and turns them into opportunities to lead others for Him. Leadership is often situational. Certain times and situations literally transform ordinary folks into extraordinary leaders. God often uses our life's shipwrecks to breed into us the skills and courage we need to lead others to places we never imagined we would go.

Remain confident and steadfast in your faith in God in whatever station you find your life today. Have faith that God has laid forth the best plans for your life of service to Him. He is setting the course. It may involve a wreck or a change in direction, but your destination is set by a heavenly compass. In every imprisoning circumstance of life lies a divine journey of success if we will let the Almighty chart the course.

Our Prayer: *Lord God, our ships are wrecked and our courses are shot. We are in the cold water and await Your divine guidance. Take our situations and chart the course that You want us to travel. Take our current imprisonment and lift us into new roles of leadership and service for Your Kingdom. In every crisis, set a new course for us, a miraculous new beginning, we pray.* **Amen.**

We Glory In Tribulations

"OUR PERSECUTION AND TRIBULATION CAN BE CLAIMED AS OUR GLORY"

"But we glory in tribulations also: knowing that tribulation worketh patience; and patience, experience; and experience, hope: and hope maketh not ashamed; because the love of God is shed abroad in our hearts by the Holy Ghost which is given unto us."

FEATURED SCRIPTURE: ROMANS 5:3–5
BACKGROUND SCRIPTURES: ROMANS 5:1–11; AND 2 CORINTHIANS 4:7–14

If we are truly pushing the boundaries of faithful leadership, we will experience tribulation and persecution. Leaders of faith are called to be bold and obedient in completing the mission God has called us to do. Throughout Scripture, leaders of faith experienced persecution and affliction. Even in our days, we will experience trials and tribulations. God allows them in our lives so we can grow and attain spiritual maturity and oneness with Christ.

Our Scripture says we should glory in tribulations. Tribulation ignites a chain reaction within a believer. It creates patience, which leads to experience. Experience gives us hope. And hope makes us unashamed of the Gospel, because in our tribulation God's love shines forth in a supernatural way. The Holy Ghost takes our hardest and toughest moments, when others would buckle under the pressure or distress, and makes God's love come alive in us and shine forth in ways that attract others to Him.

If you are truly called by God to a leadership task, and if you are walking in His will each day; tribulation is coming your way. Do not fear it, but embrace it and glory in its arrival. Christ conquered all and indwells our hearts. God has bestowed the Holy Spirit upon His chosen ones and endowed each of us with immense power. Claim your power and God's promise when tribulation and adversity arrive. Tame them as you would a wild stallion. Ride adversity to the next phase of spiritual attainment that God desires for you.

Tribulation can come in many forms. It comes in the form of our own human failures from which we have to recover. It comes in compromised health. It comes in the form of scoffers and enemies who seek to destroy our life's work. It comes in the form of material need. We often see tribulation come in the form of war, abuse, and prejudice. Whatever form tribulation takes against us, our first reaction should be to fall to our knees and seek God's guidance, giving Him praise in all circumstances.

Any adversity can become God's stage for miracles, and a chance for His love to shine to broken hearts. When we glory in our times of hardship, we unleash new power and slay the very demons that carried the trials to our doorsteps. God tells us that we will never be ashamed in our tribulations. In the midst of our tribulations, God is working His plan for humankind. The glory of God's love for us is our reward. And even the toughest and darkest of days cannot bind the Spirit of Christ within us. So glory in your tribulation, and see what great things God has in store for you!

Our Prayer: *God of glory, we glory in our tribulations because Christ has already conquered all the hell this life could throw at us. Strengthen us and gird us for the tribulations that will surely come our way as we attempt to do Your will. Give us the patience, experience, and hope that accompanies hard times. Help us to grow and become more perfect in each hardship. Let us serve others in love and never be ashamed as we glory in our tribulations.* **Amen.**

The Holy Spirit Lifts And Rescues Leaders

"When We Are Down and Out, Our Advocate Is Alive with Intercession"

"Likewise the Spirit also helpeth our infirmities: for we know not what we should pray for as we ought: but the Spirit itself maketh intercession for us with groanings which cannot be uttered. And he that searcheth the hearts knoweth what is the mind of the Spirit, because he maketh intercession for the saints according to the will of God."

Featured Scripture: Romans 8:26–27
Background Scripture: Romans 8:18–30

God has called you into a holy duty of leadership. You are now a leader of faith. Did you know that you have a special advocate? To those whom God calls, and to those who serve Christ in faith and obedience, there is a special power available to us. Some of us fail to acknowledge it, and some of us don't even know it exists. What power we forfeit and what peace eludes us when we fail to claim and call on the assistance of the Holy Spirit in our lives.

Christ delivered flaming tongues of the Holy Spirit to the early apostles at Pentecost. Likewise, this power is sent to us and is among us today. The Holy Spirit is the third component of the Trinity of God. Not only does the Holy Spirit give us power and protection, He is a constant advocate and intercessor for us to the Father. The Spirit takes our confusion and exhaustion and searches our hearts to send messages to God. Even when we don't know what to pray for, the Holy Spirit knows. He senses our needs and, in holy groaning and utterances, expresses it to the throne of God on our behalf.

What praise we should have for such an advocate as the Holy Spirit within us. This Spirit is constantly calibrating our lives and actions to be in accordance with the will of God. It is constantly taking all the good and the bad and making it work for the good and glory of God. As a leader of faith, you should give thanks for this gift and allow the Spirit to unleash new vitality and power in your own leadership journey.

Let the Spirit move you to new heights in your times of prayer, meditation, and devotional study. Even as you read these pages today, allow the Holy Spirit to unlock a truth or purposes in the words you read and the prayer you recite. The Spirit longs for you to open yourself to the true power that Christ intended you to have.

The apostles of the early Church used their advocate and Spirit within to heal, preach boldly, find heavenly provisions, and escape peril. They used it for the purposes of their callings, and it helped their own leadership journeys of faith spread the Good News to many. That same power that established the early Church is available to you now. Call on it; even as you do, it is already healing your infirmities and being an advocate for you to the Father above.

Our Prayer: *Father, Son, and Holy Spirit, Great Trinity, You love and long for us to experience the blessings and power of heaven. We pray that the full power of the Trinity will be unleashed in our lives and in our work each day. As the early apostles used the Spirit, likewise empower us today, O Lord. May the Spirit continue to help with our infirmities and be our advocate as You search our hearts. All things work together for good to those who love You, O God.* **Amen.**

More Than Conquerors

"Claiming God's Power and Victory over All Things, Past and Present"

"What shall we then say to these things? If God be for us, who can be against us? He that spared not his own Son, but delivered him up for us all…. Who shall separate us from the love of Christ?…shall tribulation, or distress, or persecution, or famine, or nakedness, or peril or sword?…. Nay, in all these things we are more than conquerors through him that loved us."

Featured Scripture: Romans 8:31–32, 35, 37
Background Scripture: Romans 8: 28, 31–39

If God be for us, who can be against us? It is hard to imagine the leader of a starving, naked, dying regiment of followers as a conqueror. What can separate us from God's love and advocacy? Can perils of this life or the satanic demons of today's circumstances come between the Almighty God and His chosen children? To those of us who will claim the promise of God's victory over all things, we become conquerors of life. By answering God's call to leadership, you are already a success…you are more than a conqueror!

Tribulations come to us all. Death and disease come. Betrayal and distress and misfortune will seek us all and find us. Leaders of faith are part of the spiritual realm and thus subject to the battles of spiritual warfare. But the good news today is that we've already won. God intends for us to live our lives with the sacred security of knowing we are more than conquerors over all the events of life. So let us cast aside all fear and dread of the day ahead.

How should conquerors behave? As a conqueror, you must seek solace in the assurance that all things work together for good. Even our failures and tragedies can become building blocks of spiritual success. Conquerors should exude a quiet and holy confidence that they are Christ's immortal thread in the making of an eternal garment. If God is for us, whom should we fear? What do you need to claim victory today?

Life's circumstances will slam us to the ground many days. Hardships and burdens engulf us with complex problems to solve. To many, finding food, clean water, or medical care is a constant daily quest. Some are sidelined as they battle sickness, poverty, or abuse. Others of us battle the consequences of our own bad choices in life. By claiming God's power and providence over all things past, present, and future, we drive our demons away. For no creature, no heavenly or earthly authority, can stand against us as we claim the promise of our Scripture today.

Claim the victory over all events of your life today. Pray that God will show you the glimmer of heaven in the meek service you perform for others. Even amidst the chaos of a tough life situation, God is working through you. Nothing you face can change God's love, advocacy, and eternal reward for you. As you lead others, lead as more than a conqueror. The light of a conqueror will become a beacon of hope for others. Conquerors radiate the love and salvation of a most merciful Creator and redeeming Savior.

Our Prayer: *God, we are more than conquerors through You this day. Let us claim our victory over life and death and every circumstance we face. Instill in us confidence and power as holy conquerors. May our victory in Jesus give us the strength we need to lead and serve others with a greater zeal this day.* **Amen.**

Hearts Set To Hear

"Leaders of Faith Must Become Preachers of Faith"

"For with the heart man believeth unto righteousness; and with the mouth confession is made unto salvation…How then shall they call on him in whom they have not believed? And how shall they believe in him of whom they have not heard? And how shall they hear without a preacher? And how shall they preach, except they be sent?"

Featured Scripture: Romans 10:10, 14–15
Background Scriptures: Romans 10:1–15; and Isaiah 52:7

Many of us have answered a call to a leadership journey of faith. For some time, our hearts were heavy, and we felt the tug of God to do something new and bold in the name of Christ. The circumstances of our lives moved us to a moment when we stepped forward and tackled a new challenge for our Lord. Most of us felt called to lead, but probably not called to preach. However, if we are called to God's service, we must be prepared to tell others of God's love for them. Leaders of faith must become preachers of faith.

We will encounter unbelievers and persons who have concluded that they can follow their own conscience and sense of righteousness. Yet many of these encounters will reveal persons with open hearts and minds who yearn to know more about a relationship with the Master. But how will they ever know if we do not tell them? How will they ever come to believe and harness the eternal love, grace, and power of their Creator unless someone is sent to tell them? If you have been called to a leadership journey of faith, you must be prepared to share the word of faith to those you meet each day.

We don't need a crowd or a formal ordination to preach the Word of God. Most hearts come to an understanding of God through personal, one-on-one encounters with believers whose hearts burn with passion for Christ. Our leadership callings may be humble tasks of labor or quiet work with children or youth. But whatever the task we are called to do, we must be prepared to preach and share the living Word with others.

For leaders to become preachers is not a difficult transition. We simply let our love and light bleed into our words. We share our hearts and experience with those hurting and curious souls around us, those who long to know the truth and a better way of life. When we live and serve in full faith and obedience to God, our lives will shine and others will want to hear what we have to say. God will open opportunities for even the most challenged of us to share our faith and the love and grace of an eternal God with others.

Let your life and calling become a sermon. How will others believe if they have not heard? And how will they hear without a preacher? You can do it. Be prepared for God to open an opportunity for you to preach the faith to others today. Tender hearts are waiting to hear of God's love through the simplicity and power of your words.

Our Prayer: *Lord God, the hearts of Your children await to hear the words of salvation so they, too, can believe in You. The world needs preachers. As a leader called by Your name, make me a preacher and a teller of the stories of Jesus. Prepare me this moment to share the faith in both word and deed.* **Amen.**

Overcoming Evil With Good

"How Leaders Can Heap Coals of Fire on Their Enemies"

"Therefore if thine enemy hunger, feed him; if he thirst, give him drink: for in doing so thou shalt heap coals of fire on his head. Be not overcome of evil, but overcome evil with good."

Featured Scripture: Romans 12:20–21
Background Scriptures: Romans 12:14–21; Matthew 5:43–45; and Proverbs 24:29

Leadership rivalry at the top of the heap can become ferocious. Friends can become rivals, and mere opponents become mortal enemies. Competition becomes fierce when the stakes are high. Satan uses rivalry, gossip, and negativity as wedges against leaders of faith. By giving way to our darker instincts to punch back, go on the attack, or get even, we escalate competition to insane levels that are not edifying to the work of God. Jesus turned the old doctrine of an eye for an eye and a tooth for a tooth on its head. Christ commanded that leaders of faith overcome evil with good.

As leaders of faith, we are called to a higher realm of behavior and action. When leaders seek to repay evil with evil, a chain reaction occurs. Evil reproduces itself, infecting many innocent people. The core sins of pride, envy, and lust come to the surface during times of escalating evil, and our goals and missions become obscured.

The positive action of a leader of faith during a time of escalating evil can stop the chain reaction and re-instill order and sanity. When we show goodwill to our enemies, the power of the Holy Spirit is unleashed and persons are convicted of their sins.

Jesus expanded the commandment of loving your neighbors to loving your enemies: Bless them that curse you, do good to them that hate you, and pray for them that despitefully use you and persecute you. These spiritual precepts seem so foreign and unnatural to most people. Yet to believers and leaders of faith, they are our operating guidelines. They give us power over evil and our rivals. As love conquers evil, we gain a superior advantage in all circumstances. Praying for our enemies removes their leverage over us and gives holy authority in every situation.

When those whom you lead see you practice these principles in your organization or congregation, they will be drawn to know more about the love, grace, and mercy of Christ. The act of forgiveness is one of the greatest and most powerful forces in life. As we overcome evil with good, we become more and more successful as our witness shines to others. While you may not appear to win every earthly contest, the spiritual battles will be won and your mission to serve God and His creation will be fulfilled.

Our Prayer: *Heavenly Father, remove our sinful instincts of hatred and retaliation toward others. Instead, give us hearts of love and forgiveness. Give us the mind of Christ so that we can control all situations, dispensing good for evil and love for cruelty. Protect us as we become vulnerable to the attacks of evil persons. Let Your Holy Spirit indwell us and make bad situations perfect and whole.* **Amen.**

Serving God By Serving Society's Institutions

"Turning Secular Service into a Sacred Calling"

"Let every soul be subject unto the higher powers. For there is no power but of God: the powers that be are ordained of God…. Submit yourselves to every ordinance of man for the Lord's sake: whether it be to the king, as supreme; Or unto governors, as unto them that are sent by him for the punishment of evildoers, and for the praise of them that do well."

Featured Scriptures: Romans 13:1; and 1 Peter 2:13–14
Background Scripture: Romans 13; and 1 Peter 2:11–17

The call to leadership journeys of faith can take many forms. Because God allows and ordains the institutions of man, He calls persons according to His purposes into leadership and service in all places. As a leader of faith, your work each day can be an answer to God's calling. As such, your work in a secular institution of society becomes a sacred leadership endeavor.

The apostles Paul and Peter tell us that people are to submit to the powers of government and society. Those institutions have been given by God to provide order to our lives and to work His purposes. That does not mean that all leaders and institutions are righteous and noble; they certainly are not. In fact, many of those institutions persecuted the apostles and the early Church. However, as a leader of faith, you are to carry your character and the calling of your faith into every group, government, or institution you serve. God has a way of putting righteous people in tough and sometimes corrupt places.

If people of faith yield themselves to the power and authority of earthly institutions, they should actively participate in the organization, petitioning, and leadership of them. Public service and volunteer leadership can then become noble, as if anointed by God Himself. Leaders of faith are held to a higher set of principles, and as such are held to a heavenly accountability in their earthly leadership positions.

Leaders of faith should be people of love, discipline, honesty, and hard work. They should care for the needs of others and value the dignity of all persons. They should sense in every task, whether large or small, the nobleness of meeting the needs of others. When leaders of faith lead in spirit and in truth, what is secular becomes sacred, and the earthly institutions we serve become beacons of God's love and grace.

Wherever God has placed you, know that your institution is ordained by God if its mission is to bring order and service to society. Your leadership should be practiced with the commitment and zeal as if you are doing it unto God Himself.

Our Prayer: *God, You ordained government and the institutions of our society. We give thanks that You call people of faith into leadership journeys in these institutions. Help us as we serve to always be aware of Your hand upon us. May we endeavor to make secular service a sacred task of service to You and to our fellow man.* **Amen.**

To Whom This Day Belongs

"Giving Each Day, Each Task, and Each Situation over to God"

"One man esteems one day above another: another esteems every day alike…he that regards the day, regards it unto the Lord; and he that regards not the day, to the Lord he doth not regard it…for none of us live to himself, and no man dies to himself. For whether we live, we live unto the Lord; and whether we die, we die unto the Lord: whether we live therefore, or die, we are the Lord's."

Featured Scripture: Romans 14:5–8

Background Scriptures: Romans 14:5–12; Isaiah 38:18–22; Psalm 100:3; Psalm 118:24; and Proverbs 16:4

It is inescapable. Whether we live this day or die this day, we are the Lord's. These words from our Scripture lesson today need not be apocalyptic, yet they should be redeeming and empowering to all leaders of faith. Each day we live and each breath we draw is God's gift to us. We did not earn it nor did we create it. The time and tasks of this very day are God's alone. We are but time custodians of a blip of eternity. What plans do you have for this day today? Will what you do today be edifying to the Creator? Will it bring praise and thanksgiving? What will you do this day as a gift "to whom this day belongs"?

When we live each day as if it was God's precious gift to us, we are less apt to waste time and resources. When we give honor to God upon our awakening from sleep each morning, our days are branded for success. We all belong to God. We will return to the Creator, who gave us life. Our duty is to extract meaning and purpose from each day and every situation. Even mundane and routine tasks of life can be transformed by acknowledging our Lord in every situation. The adage, "nothing happens by chance", comes alive in light of our lesson today.

To whom does your day really belong? Do you make intricate plans for your time that are calibrated to the real purpose of your calling? Are your tasks carefully laid out so that they will allow you to give testimony or perform service to others? God wants our days to be full of joy, fellowship, and meaning. He wants us to have a laugh, a nap, and an occasional celebration with friends. But all we do must be conducted in respect and holy admiration for the One who brings us this day's precious gift of life.

To waste time damages eternity. Killing time with reckless abandon can prevent us from full fellowship with the God who never sleeps. Our time and tasks, even our struggles, should be given to God as our life offering. God will bless our fullness or our emptiness. He will bless our loneliness or joyful fellowship with others each day. In our faithful leadership, God will take the conflicts and controversy and transform them into a time for greater understanding. Whatever situation we face each day of this life, let us tithe the time to whom this day belongs.

Our Prayer: *Creator and Sustainer, You are the giver of each day and each breath. We give You praise and honor and thanksgiving for the day ahead. Let us strive to take every task and moment on this day and turn it over to Your providence and holy purpose. Bless this day, O Lord.* **Amen.**

Habits, Perception, And Stumbling Blocks

"Leaders Should Refrain from Certain Practices Around Others"

"Let us not therefore judge one another any more: but judge this rather, that no man put a stumbling block or an occasion to fall in his brother's way…. It is good neither to eat flesh, nor to drink wine, nor any thing whereby thy brother stumbleth, or is offended, or is made weak."

Featured Scripture: Romans 14:13, 21
Background Scripture: Romans 14:13–23

As the early Church grew, the faith of believers was influenced heavily by Jewish laws and traditions. It was also influenced by the cultural habits and morays of diverse communities where the Gospel was spreading. The apostle Paul and other early Church leaders were constantly differentiating the core and crux of the faith in Christ from false reliance on law, custom, and superstition. The food and drink referred to in Romans 14 may not have been judged to be wrong, but new believers of other cultures were skeptical of certain practices. Paul told us to refrain from habits and practices in the presence of others that could become stumbling blocks to others in their faith journeys.

The wisdom of Paul holds great value for leaders of faith in today's world. Leaders get noticed. Eyes are upon us each day as we perform our duties. People in and out of our congregations and organizations observe our lifestyles and habits so as to glean a direction for living their own lives. Sometimes our rivals or opponents will watch as well, carefully looking for private habits or subtle actions that could be construed as conflicting with our faith and beliefs. In this misrepresentation, they hope to stifle our effectiveness as leaders. To those who support us, the perception of bad habits can send a signal of endorsement for a bad lifestyle. It can even erode your effectiveness as a leader set apart for God's work.

Today it is still important to refrain from public displays of gluttony and drunkenness. It is also important in every way to live a life of discipline and purpose so that others can see and admire the good habits you display. For a leader, healthy diets and moderation in all consumption are good examples. Good habits of exercise and respect for your body are noticed by others. Respectful dress and grooming get noticed quickly by everyone you meet, even in private times and on holidays.

Taking a positive approach to this subject can lead us to set good examples by our politeness and cheerful demeanor. Sending handwritten notes of thanks, condolences, or congratulations is a tremendously good habit of a successful leader. Great leaders of faith set great examples when they are respectful to the meek around them and practice small acts of respect and goodwill to every person they encounter. We can lead others by both refrain and good practice of all habits in life. We are witnessing to others in all that we do. As many wise sage has said, a person would rather observe a good sermon than hear one any day.

Our Prayer: *Dear Lord, eyes and ears are studying us each day. You know our every thought, word, and intention. Help us, O Lord, to live lives of good habits. Help us to be conscious of our actions so as to never hinder others in their walks with You. Forgive us when we have lacked discipline and decorum in the practice of our daily routines. Empower us to use every action and habit as a testimony to the meekness and power of Your love for us.* **Amen.**

We Cannot Even Comprehend It

"GOD'S LOVE AND REWARD AWAITING US ARE UNFATHOMABLE TO OUR MINDS"

"But as it is written, Eye hath not seen, nor ear heard, neither have entered into the heart of any man, the things which God hath prepared for them that love him…. In my Father's house are many mansions: if it were not so, I would have told you. I go to prepare a place for you."

Featured Scriptures: 1 Corinthians 2:9; and Matthew 14:2
BACKGROUND SCRIPTURES: ISAIAH 64:1–4; AND MATTHEW 14:1–4

So much of the faith journey is discussed in terms of sin, sacrifice, suffering, salvation, hope, and love. Each of these characteristics of faith is part of the whole cloth of our spiritual lives. But in today's lesson, let your mind wander to a place you have never gone before. Imagine comfort; wealth; love; pleasure; acceptance; beauty; and the absence of pain, need, and sorrow. Imagine the most beautiful mountaintop or sunset you ever witnessed. Imagine restoration and reunion with all those you have ever known and loved. Imagine the successful accomplishment of every goal and ambition you ever had. Imagine the elimination of poverty, persecution, prejudice, and death.

When we ponder these things, you must give up. We have failed miserably. The rewards of loving Christ and accepting God's providence exceed all our abilities to comprehend. No sensation of sight, taste, or smell can compare to the new realm of the pleasure and reward the Scriptures promise. Nothing that ever entered into the heart of a human being could prepare us for the glory we will receive ahead. The apostle Paul penned these words, as did the prophet Isaiah. Christ Himself told us that part of His mission after His resurrection was to go and prepare our mansion for our arrival. Are you feeling a little better now?

Our lives today are full of difficulty and tribulation. The acceptance of the call to leadership in faith assures that you will become part of the spiritual warfare of this realm of life. It assures unending work and sacrifice. But whatever our plight, whatever our suffering on this day, we cannot even conceive of the eternal reward that awaits those of us who embrace the risen Lord.

This promise should reawaken even the most infirmed and most oppressed laborer in faith with a smile and new skip in your walk. Our work and callings are not in vain. The God we love and the God we serve is an awesome and gracious Creator who intends the best for those He calls His own. This future reward should inspire us to even greater service and sacrifice. This promise should trivialize the problems and challenges we face in our temporal situations of leadership. If ever we should doubt the price we pay or the call we received to serve Christ in this life, let us remind ourselves of the goodness of the One we serve. Glory! Hallelujah!

Keep dreaming and imagining the most incredible sensations of your heart and hear Christ's own voice saying…*you can't even comprehend it!*

Our Prayer: *Our Lord and our God, we bow in humility and praise for the promise of today's Scripture. You have already prepared an eternal reward for us beyond human comprehension. We are so unworthy. You have redeemed us and taken us as Your own. Instill this promise into the very fabric of our souls and may it motivate us to greater obedience, service, and thanksgiving with each new breath we draw.* **Amen.**

The Teamwork Of Leadership

"Great Leaders Play Their Roles and Share Tasks with Others for Success"

> "Who then is Paul, and who is Apollos, but ministers by whom ye believed, even as the Lord gave to every man? I have planted, Apollos watered; but God gave the increase. So then neither is he that planteth any thing, neither he that watereth; but God that giveth the increase."
>
> Featured Scripture: 1 Corinthians 3:5–7
> Background Scriptures: 1 Corinthians 3:1–9; Acts 9:1–32; and Acts 18:23—19:7

The growth of the early Church is a testimony to God's providence and to the devotion and teamwork of the early believers. The Gospel was spreading through a series of local churches and through the leadership of laypersons who were building grassroots networks and anointing new leaders and disciples. Paul was the great missionary chosen by Jesus Himself in his conversion experience on the road to Damascus. But another leader, Apollos, was described as a well-educated and fervent believer. Apollos was a gifted evangelist who preached with great power and brought many to the saving knowledge of Christ.

One great struggle of the early Church in its growth was the straying away from true doctrine by local believers. Another challenge was the tendency of new converts to cling to a particular teacher or preacher and fail to grasp the Savior in a personal way. In every growing enterprise, when many persons are contributing to the success of the organization, envy and "leader worship" can seep in and ruin a great movement.

Paul found such a situation as he came back to the church at Corinth where the great preaching of Apollos had paid dividends for God. Paul was quick to stifle any possibility that leaders should get credit over God for the salvation and growth of the Church. Subjugating Paul and Apollos as merely gardeners of the Gospel, who planted and watered, the potential of division in the growth of the early Church was put to rest.

"I have planted, Apollos watered; but God gave the increase." This phrase should be chiseled into the wall of any great organization that is led by leaders of faith. Subjugating ourselves to the principle that teamwork is leadership is critical to the success of our organizations, congregations, businesses, or governments. Even families must share the credit of success in daily life.

When we allow leaders to be given the credit for success rather than God, we can sow the seeds of evil and dissension within our groups. Strive in your calling to build teamwork of leadership through sharing the tasks. Also share the blame, the credit, and the accolades of success with others. But reserve all praise for the God who called you to service. Plant, water, or pull weeds as a leader, but let God give the increase.

Our Prayer: *Dear God, thank You for the teamwork of leaders in the early Church. Thank You for the teamwork in the movement of our faith today. Help us as leaders of faith to continually subjugate ourselves to only the roles You called us to play. Protect us against the need to take credit for the great works that only You can bring about. Help us to lead by building teamwork in faith.* **Amen.**

Blessing Our Unfinished Work

"Our Call and Unfinished Work Will Be Blessed If We Labor in Faith"

"According to the grace of God which is given unto me, as a wise master-builder, I have laid the foundation, and another builds thereon. But let every man take heed how he builds… Every man's work shall be made manifest: for the day shall declare it, because it shall be revealed by fire… Being confident of this very thing, that he which hath begun a good work in you will perform it until the day of Jesus Christ."
FEATURED SCRIPTURES: 1 CORINTHIANS 3:10, 13; AND PHILIPPIANS 1:6
BACKGROUND SCRIPTURES: 1 CORINTHIANS 3:10–14; AND 1 PETER 4:10–11

The great reality of any leadership journey of faith is that you will not finish the great tasks you have been given to do by God. But did you fail? Did you let God down? Today's lesson gives us an exhortation to work hard in faith and to be wise builders. But it also gives us solace that our unfinished work will be divinely completed. It will be forged by heavenly fire, and the final product will be revealed to us in our days in eternity with Christ.

God blesses our unfinished work. The fields are ripe for harvest, and the needs of the hurting are boundless. The tasks we are given to complete are enormous. In the scheme of eternity, our work may seem trivial. Many leaders attempt to build institutions and fail. Many missionaries minister and witness to the lost and hurting, only to see no fruit from their labors. Scholars and researchers pour themselves passionately into the sciences to solve problems of humanity, and yet they never solve the equation. We pray fervently for peace and for the blessing of the oppressed, only to see their burdens get heavier. But have we truly failed?

Whatever call to faith we answer and obediently fulfill will be completed and blessed by God. Every work we do will be burned in the heavenly judgment furnace and made into holy gold. The apostle Paul knew he was a master builder who could only lay a foundation for the Church that he would never see finished in his earthly life. Yet the early saints of faith set into action a chain of events that began with an answered call to lead others in Christ's name.

Each of us wrestles with dead-end projects that never seem to be successful. Our congregational membership has declined or stagnated. Sales are down and expenses are up, and our inclination is to suspect our product or service is fatally flawed. We may never know the lives that are changed as a result of our faithfulness in unfinished work. Don't lose heart. Give all your perceived failures and uncompleted tasks to God in prayer. Let the Holy Spirit attract others to complete the call you answered and finish all your unfinished tasks.

Be confident of this very thing: If God began a good work in your life, He will complete it and you will be blessed from it. No simple labor, humble prayer, or word uttered in Christ's name will ever fail or be forgotten. Don't let Satan discourage you in your unfinished work. Even as we fade away, another is picking up the trowel and hammer to finish God's temple, and the foundation we leave is solid indeed.

Our Prayer: *Lord Jesus, we labor away each day in obedience to our calling. We become tired and frustrated when we can't see the success or completion of certain tasks. Thank You for affirming us through Your promises in Scripture. Give us new energy to work even harder in the faith and the confidence that our callings and lives are not in vain.* **Amen.**

Casting Down Imaginations

"The Knowledge and Purposes of God Strike Down Our Self-Perceived Wisdom"

"Let no man deceive himself. If any man among you seemeth to be wise in this world, let him become a fool, that he may be wise. For the wisdom of this world is foolishness with God. For it is written, He taketh the wise in their own craftiness…. Casting down imaginations, and every high thing that exalteth itself against the knowledge of God, and bringing into captivity every thought to the obedience of Christ…."

FEATURED SCRIPTURES: 1 CORINTHIANS 3:18–19; AND 2 CORINTHIANS 10:5
BACKGROUND SCRIPTURES: 1 CORINTHIANS 3:18–23; AND 2 CORINTHIANS 1:10–31

Leaders of faith should fear the moment when they come to the conclusion that they are wise and correct. When we become self-congratulatory about our own ideas and earthly wisdom, we can unknowingly oppose the knowledge and purposes of God. The apostle Paul was very clear about a believer's self-appointed wisdom. God's thoughts and ways are beyond the comprehension of man, and God demands our constant obedience and searching in order for Him to use us to the fullest.

In order to truly follow our callings to leadership, we must continually cast down the imaginations of our own minds so we can yield to the promptings of the Holy Spirit within us. As we cast aside our own thoughts and wisdom and become vessels for the Spirit, we become wise and our thoughts become clear. Leaders who are obedient and who think and act by the Spirit will find themselves moving in directions that others find odd. Leaders of faith blaze new trails by bringing their thoughts into God's captivity.

In the early Church, Paul dealt often with counter-forces of self-appointed authorities and sage religious leaders. Paul even anointed leaders to subjugate themselves to God's voice. As leaders, we will find those in our own organizations and congregations who have anointed themselves with authority and portend to lead in earthly wisdom. Not only must we guard against our own proclivity to self-knowledge, but we must protect the flock we have been given from false leaders who can thwart the true purposes of God.

The act of casting down our imaginations begins with our own humility. It means practicing a fervent prayer life. It means staying grounded in the light of God's purposes and plans by methodically tackling the mundane tasks of each day with gladness. When we are serving others in love, it becomes harder for us to stray from God's providence. God wants us to learn and study and be bold in all of our actions; however, learning to submit ourselves in spiritual discipline to the voice of God requires incredible focus.

As leaders of faith called to a heavenly and eternal purpose for God, we are targets of temptation and spiritual attack. It is often not the temptation to be vile, but the temptation to become vain that trips good leaders. The wisdom of this world is foolishness to God. Let us become lowly so we can become wise. Let God's love and holiness hold us captive to our higher callings of service.

Our Prayer: *Heavenly Father, make us captives of Your wisdom, power, and purpose. Instill in us a humility and lowliness of spirit so we can become more pure vessels of service. Show us how to tame our success and temper our failures so we can faithfully and methodically lift others and shine Your love in our daily actions of leadership.* **Amen.**

Stewards Of The Mysteries

"CALLED LEADERS BECOME CUSTODIANS OF SPIRITUAL INSIGHT AND UNDERSTANDING"

"Let a man so account of us, as of the ministers of Christ, and stewards of the mysteries of God…. How that by revelation he made known unto me the mystery…. Whereby, when ye read, ye may understand my knowledge in the mystery of Christ. Which in other ages was not made known unto the sons of men, as it is now revealed unto his holy apostles and prophets by the Spirit.…"

FEATURED SCRIPTURES: 1 CORINTHIANS 4:1; AND EPHESIANS 3:3–5
BACKGROUND SCRIPTURES: 1 CORINTHIANS 4:1–5; AND EPHESIANS 3

Open your heart to understand. You already posses powers that you cannot even comprehend. As a called leader of faith, you are the modern-day holy apostle. Christ has selected you to carry out heavenly tasks for Him. The coming of Christ to the world was the revelation of God's mysteries to His chosen ones. The great missionary and apostle Paul wrote that he was a steward of the mysteries. Likewise, as God's ministers and leaders, we, too, become stewards of the mysteries of God.

In the time before the coming of Christ, the knowledge of God was limited to the words of the law and the prophets. But by Christ coming and living among us, and through the recording of His words and deeds, we can now gain new glimpses into the nature and purposes of God. Every person who lives in Christ and is called by His name is afforded the ability to experience these mysteries of the faith. We are given special insight into the Scriptures and new knowledge through fellowship with fellow believers. The Holy Spirit resides within us to guide us and to move our hearts and minds toward that deeper understanding of holiness through worship.

Leaders of faith are given special abilities to size up people and situations. We see hope and opportunity where others see defeat and destruction. We see the potential for redemption in a person's brokenness. We find love and decency amid war and poverty. We sense the risk in revelry and identify danger in complacency.

Our vision and passion for service was instilled into us by God. Leaders called by God are ordained to bring order and vision to our congregations and organizations. We can search and find new provisions for the tasks. We unlock the hidden talents in every follower and bring the lost back into fellowship. We interpret the events of each day in a way that brings clarity and purpose to our work and mission. Revealed mysteries and newfound knowledge come to us when we are humble, prayerful, and repentant. They come to us in greatest measure when we become more selfless, loving, and respectful toward others. As we slay our own ambitions by yielding to God, we open ourselves up to receive revelations and epiphanies that we never could have imagined. The love and knowledge of Christ passes all earthly understanding and transforms every small task into a holy work.

So seize the power and learn new mysteries this very day. Place your life and journey into His hands, and the peace that passes understanding will ordain you as a new steward of the mysteries of God.

Our Prayer: *Lord Jesus, we fall before You in praise and humility. We repent and rise to accept Your new knowledge of life. Make us Your stewards of all mysteries of our faith. Open us up to new knowledge so we can better serve and lead others by Your power.* **Amen.**

Leading Without Loving Is Worthless

"True Gifts of Leadership Showcased by a Great Love for Others"

"And though I have the gift of prophecy, and understand all mysteries, and all knowledge; and though I have all faith, so that I could remove mountains, and have not charity, I am nothing. And though I bestow all my goods to feed the poor, and though I give my body to be burned, and have not charity, it profiteth me nothing."

Featured Scripture: 1 Corinthians 13:2–3
Background Scripture: 1 Corinthians 13

It is always prudent to stop amidst the hustle and business of life and ask the eternal question: Why do we do what we do? What drives us? What motivates us to get up each morning and tackle the chores of our day? Often leaders of faith can be sucked into vortexes of responsibility and busy schedules so that our actions become instinctive reactions to solve problems rather than measured acts of love. Regardless of our talents or power, if we do not love those on the receiving end of our efforts, we are accomplishing nothing in the eyes of God.

We can be great managers and performers. We can be great orators and problem-solvers. But if our hearts are not attuned in love to the ones we serve and if our truest motivation is not sharing Christ's love for others, we are missing the mark. Many leaders may have started their journeys with purity of heart, but have morphed into calloused, routine leaders who are unconnected to the ones they serve. Our lesson today calls us to assess our actions and to constantly return to the source of real love and motivation. Let God refill our souls each day with a love and longing to serve others in Christ's name.

Some of us have reached pinnacles of success and power, yet we feel empty inside. Some days we are consumed with the confusion around us and end our days perplexed as to its meaning. If we go about our tasks and do not see the faces of the hurting and needy around us, we should step aside and question our calling. Losing the central focus of why we do what we do has sunk many a leader. We can experience worldly leadership success, receive the accolades of peers, and be given promotions without ever fulfilling our true callings to God. Where is your love? Where is your heart? Where are your true affections bidding you to go?

Serving others in true love does not mean that we must hold the highest office or attain the loftiest position. Serving and leading others may mean we give up some earthly title in order to attain a position of leadership. Leading others in true love means we seek new humility of rank and order. It means we seek the underserved and the unloved. It is when we shun man's power to serve others in need that God bestows real rank and power upon us. Find your love and answer your true call to service today.

Our Prayer: *Lord Jesus, teach me Your ways of love and service. Let my heart guide me and motivate me in my leadership journey. Never let me become self-absorbed in my own career or ambition to the point that the love fountain to others stops flowing from me. Motivate me by Your will each day to fulfill my leadership calling with true love and affection for others.* **Amen.**

Leaders Of Confusion And A God Of Order

"OUT OF OUR OWN CHAOS CAN COME GOD'S ORDERLY PLAN IN OUR LIVES"

"For God is not the author of confusion, but of peace…. Are not two sparrows sold for a farthing? And one of them shall not fall to the ground without your Father. But the very hairs of your head are all numbered."

FEATURED SCRIPTURES: 1CORINTHIANS 14:33; AND MATTHEW 10:29–30
BACKGROUND SCRIPTURES: ECCLESIASTES 3:1–11; AND ISAIAH 40:29–31

Any duty of leadership carries the great likelihood that confusion and chaos will come amidst the peace of our time. Sometimes leaders of faith inherit chaos from others. We can clearly see it as we begin our own journeys. Other times chaos comes to us like a storm in the night. We awaken only to find a sinking ship and mayhem around us. Other times chaos comes in slow drips until it has eroded away the foundation of our institution and it begins to crack and shift. In all its forms confusion and chaos can wreck lives and create panic among those we are given charge to serve.

Bringing order amidst confusion and chaos is one of the great callings into which God brings leaders of faith. God is a God of order, not confusion. The Scripture is filled with leaders, prophets, apostles, and saints who encountered these demons of confusion at every turn. Yet God used each of them to bring order and restoration to the broken. Our leadership journeys of faith today will see armies of death, the wrath of storms, and perpetrators of evil. We will see untold poverty, pollution, and human treachery. We will witness great human failure and the collapse of the man-made systems of order. Yet at every turn, God will anoint His leaders of faith with the tools of heaven to restore order again.

As the Author of peace, God knows when every sparrow falls to the ground. He knows the number of hairs on every head. Our Creator's eternal order is beyond our imagination or calculation. As we grow in faith and knowledge, God will slowly reveal His order to us. Sometimes it takes chaos to awaken the children of God to the need for the sovereign hand of God. There would be no ark without a flood. There would be no Promised Land without an Exodus and wandering in the desert. There would be no eternal salvation without a Roman cross.

As leaders of faith, we bring order to chaos by first kneeling and praying for the strength to endure. Enduring and surviving the chaos is the first step to restoring order. By invoking God's power and mercy, we see the clouds part. Leaders organize others around the mantle of hope and promise. We go to work and bring those we lead into a tighter fellowship and combined effort of restoration. We constantly give God praise and thanksgiving for each new mercy as we emerge from chaos to order. Out of man's confusions and chaos emerge God's order and plan. Restoration comes to those who wait upon the God of order.

Our Prayer: *Gracious God, You are a God of order. You long for us to live lives of peace and tranquility. Protect us from the sin of the world that creates chaos. Make us the restorers of peace and order when we find ourselves amidst chaos. Gird us with Your power, strength, and grace to weather any storm and endure any hardship. Bless us so we can be a blessing to others in every life circumstance.* **Amen.**

Not In Vain

"STEADFAST AND UNMOVABLE LABOR FOR GOD ASSURES ETERNAL VICTORY"

"O death, where is thy sting? O grave, where is thy victory? Therefore, my beloved brethren, be ye steadfast, unmovable, always abounding in the work of the Lord, forasmuch as ye know that your labor is not in vain in the Lord."
FEATURED SCRIPTURE: 1 CORINTHIANS 15:55, 58
BACKGROUND SCRIPTURE: 1 CORINTHIANS 15:51–58; AND 2 PETER 3:14–18

Oftentimes it is not the contest that defeats us; it is the frustration and weariness of the mundane work we do each day. When our daily tasks seemingly fail to yield the fruits and success we seek, we can doubt our calling or effectiveness for God. It is not necessary for Satan to defeat us if he can discourage us. Many a leader has stopped digging for gold only inches away from the prize because they thought their work was in vain. A heavenly call to a leadership task for God is not in vain. Our victory is already assured if we can just labor away each day in the steadfast and unmovable confidence that God's purposes are working through us.

Victory over death is assured through our Lord Jesus Christ, and that fear of dying and the grave should no longer limit us. When we are unafraid to die, we become unafraid to live life to its fullest measure. Moreover, if the tasks we are called to do are ordained by God, we cannot fail. Even if earthly measurements of our success don't show clear victory, if we are truly faithful to the most routine of tasks, God will bless our every action.

To be liberated from death and failure should embolden each of us as leaders of faith to take new risks for God. It should open our hearts and minds to endless possibilities. It should free us from having to measure our work against the standard measurements of man's limited worldview. Those measurements of wealth, power, and status are not necessarily part of God's plan and calling for us. God's measurements for success are infinite and boundless. Selfless acts done in the name and love of Christ have value beyond measure. The ability to love and pray for our enemies may seem unnatural, but it unleashes the Holy Spirit in the arenas of our earthly lives.

If all our efforts are cloaked in prayer and godly purpose, nothing we ever do shall be in vain. This concept of faith should not only lead us to new boldness, but should cause us to cherish and practice small acts of kindness. Sending a note of comfort or congratulations to a new acquaintance, or giving a gift of bread to a stranger, can take on new meaning when we know that nothing we ever do is in vain when we are called to God's purposes.

To live and work in Christ's victory and power is life's greatest blessing. Forgiveness and reconciliation are now abundant and all-encompassing. Failure is no longer inevitable, and nothing we do in Christ's name need ever be done in vain.

Our Prayer: *Lord Jesus, You are the victory over death and failure. Your holy sacrifice conquered sin and condemnation for all humankind. Lord, help us to live and serve with a new boldness and resolve that nothing we do as called leaders of faith shall be in vain. Even when we are frustrated and discouraged, let us think on Your power and claim the victory for ourselves.* **Amen.**

Praying For Our Own Victory

"WE ARE CALLED TO AN ETERNAL VICTORY UNMEASURED BY MAN"

"But thanks be to God, which giveth us the victory through our Lord Jesus Christ. Therefore, my beloved brethren, be ye steadfast, unmovable, always abounding in the work of the Lord, forasmuch as ye know that your labor is not in vain in the Lord.... For whatsoever is born of God overcometh the world: and this is the victory that overcometh the world, even our faith."

FEATURED SCRIPTURES: 1 CORINTHIANS 15:57–58; AND 1 JOHN 5:4
BACKGROUND SCRIPTURE: JOHN 17:15–21; AND LUKE 22:39–42

On the eve of a great contest or battle, is it appropriate for a leader of faith to pray for victory? Should a candidate who has felt God's call to service pray for triumph in an election? Should skilled athletes pray that they will vanquish their opponents? Praying for our own victories in this life should always be tempered with our humility and submission to the greater purposes for which we are called. While God's throne of grace is always open to us, it is imperative that we cast our hopes and ambitions solely on the cross of Christ.

A leader of faith may be called by God to a contest, but not called to win. Earthly battlefields have been littered with the bodies of martyrs and heroes for centuries. The history of our faith is replete with missionaries who labored and ministered to the lost and the hurting, only to never know the true confirmation of their work. Our greatest works for God can be accomplished in the shadows of apparent human defeat.

The tasks we undertake for God will invariably place us in the arena of human competition. Were we to measure our worth and success in sales made, games won, wealth amassed, or popularity achieved, we could easily become discouraged and tempted to quit. Our Scripture today tells us to be steadfast, unmovable, and always abounding in the work of the Lord. Our victories are to be measured in our obedience to God's call and commandments.

The life and mission of Christ could have looked like a failure to the earthly observer. The Son of God was rejected by many of His own followers, He was mocked and falsely accused by the religious and secular authorities of His day. He suffered humiliation and pain, only to die one of the most horrific deaths imaginable. But our victory, like Christ's, comes from the resurrection of life over death and good over evil.

Instead of praying for victory in your daily tasks, pray for strength and endurance. Pray for daily provision. Pray for your enemies and adversaries. Pray that God will take every oddly shaped event and sculpt it into an eternal masterpiece. Pray that God's will be done and not your own. Pray that God will reward you in due time, if not today. When you face your battles, contests, and elections, pray in this way. It will unleash unmeasured spiritual power and yank victory from the jaws of defeat. Pray especially that God's love will flow through your service to others in untold ways. After all, praying for victory isn't really necessary because the real victory has already been won.

Our Prayer: *Heavenly Father, the victory is already won through Christ. We face our own contests and are tempted to desire our own favorable outcomes. But we pray, Lord, not for our will, but Your will to be done today. Give us the strength to endure and the wisdom to see through all life's circumstances. Sustain us another day so we can serve others for Your sake.* **Amen.**

Simplicity And Sincerity

"Holiness in Leaders Is Marked by These Basics of Character"

"For our rejoicing is this, the testimony of our conscience, that in simplicity and godly sincerity, not with fleshly wisdom, but by the grace of God, we have had our conversation in the world, and more abundantly to you."

Featured Scripture: 2 Corinthians 1:12
Background Scripture: 2 Corinthians 1:12–23; and 1 Corinthians 2:1–4

Great leaders of faith are not marked by flamboyance or eloquence, but by simplicity and sincerity. Most calls of leadership are not given to the booming orators or handsome stars, but to the meek and humble. Through simplicity, sincerity, and humility, the Holy Spirit can speak to us and work through us. The apostle Paul knew this principle well, and he shared it with us generously throughout his writings.

In 1 Corinthians 2:4, Paul wrote: *"My speech and my preaching was not with enticing words of man's wisdom, but in demonstration of the Spirit of power: that your faith should not stand in the wisdom of men, but in the power of God."* As we lead others, we become vessels from which God's Spirit pours out to those who need to hear a message of hope. That spirit within us may be a special love and consideration for hurting and forgotten people in our communities. That spirit may be one of peacemaking and facilitating compromise among rival factions in our organizations. That spirit may be one of vision to lead others to see a mission they would never have dreamed.

When we are simple and sincere, people notice us and are attracted to us. God Himself is more able to use us when we are not bound to the earthly wisdom and worldly ways of practicing leadership. Shedding bad habits and the pretension of entitlement is a must for leaders of faith. It is hard to reach the spiritual plane of simplicity and sincerity when we are most concerned about the advancement of our own careers. It is necessary for us to find good role models, not only through Scripture, but in our communities today. Find the quiet and wise leader in your congregation or organization and observe them; note their simple and sincere power of persuasion.

Simplicity and sincerity are also marked by rejoicing and happiness. The meekness in our spirits allows the simple pleasures of friends, family, and daily life events to become sharper and more pleasurable. It opens our eyes to the Holy Spirit who will show us the deepness and richness of God's love and grace. More especially, the simplicity and sincerity of our character will reflect the presence of God in ways we can never imagine, and it will lead others to the light and salvation of the Prince of Peace.

Our Prayer: *Lord God, create in us hearts of simplicity and sincerity. May the Holy Spirit supplant our fleshly and worldly wisdom and desires with His own richness. Purge our character of the pride and ambition that can lead us astray. Bless us with newfound pleasures and appreciation of family, friends, and daily living. Make our character a vessel from which the light, love and power of Christ can flow.* **Amen.**

Whom You Hang Out With

"Leaders of Faith Should Find the Right Friends, Associations, and Mentors"

"Be ye not unequally yoked together with unbelievers: for what fellowship hath righteousness with unrighteousness? And what communion hath light with darkness? … Blessed is the man that walketh not in the counsel of the ungodly, nor standeth in the seat of the scornful."

Featured Scriptures: 2 Corinthians 6:14; and Psalm 1:1
Background Scriptures: 2 Corinthians 6:11—7:1; and Psalm 1:1–6

Our leadership journeys of faith will take us many places. We will meet many people and be exposed to evil as well as goodness. We must be willing to go where God wants us to go and deal with those persons He brings into our paths. We must bring goodness and light to every corner of darkness. We should love all manner of people in Jesus' name. But today's lesson isn't about our business and formal affairs, it is about those persons whom we choose to hang out with. Whom do you choose to associate with and select as friends, associates, and mentors?

Both David and Paul were clear about how righteous persons and leaders should conduct themselves in their personal associations. When we accept and embrace faith and become called leaders for Christ, we must carefully consider with whom we choose to spend our personal and professional time. Leaders of faith need to pray for God to send us friends, associates, and mentors who uplift us and validate our callings. We need righteous associations that help us grow in our character and spirituality. When we naïvely choose to spend our social time with persons who do not love or respect God, we set ourselves up to be led astray. Our witness and our reputation can be marked and send the wrong signals to those we are charged to lead.

Leaders of faith should guard carefully to never be mistakenly seen in the company of evildoers. God will send us good friends and associates. We all need wise mentors. We need peers and coworkers who can uplift us and hold us accountable to high standards of behavior and performance. We need spouses and family members who respect us and help us excel in our service to God and others.

We should never be judgmental of others or refuse to associate with persons outside our socioeconomic, geographical, or ethnic boundaries. Sometimes the most unlikely person can become our greatest righteous friend and ally. We need associates who will lift us up in prayer and seek our best interests. We need friends who forgive us when we fail and carry us over the rough spots in life. We, in turn, should be a godly friend and associate to others who may be desperately seeking righteous companionship.

When we love others in purity of heart and seek out associations in humility, God will bless us with the right friends. Pray for those you meet who need to know the grace, love, and mercy of God. Those we help rescue and those we serve may also become our newfound friends in Christ.

Our Prayer: *Lord Jesus, be our friend and mentor. We pray that You will also send us earthly friends, associates, and mentors who lift us up and encourage us. Lead us away from evil and sin. Forgive us when we have damaged our effectiveness as leaders by bad associations. Instill in us good judgment to make good choices. Help us to lead others to the light of Your love.* **Amen.**

Our Thorn In The Flesh

"Physical Ailments and Earthly Trials Lead Us Constantly Back to God"

"And lest I should be exalted above the measure through the abundance of the revelations, there was given to me a thorn in the flesh, the messenger of Satan to buffet me...."

Featured Scripture: 2 Corinthians 12:7
Background Scriptures: 2 Corinthians 12:6–10; and Galatians 4:12–15

The apostle Paul performed many great miracles in his day. He was arguably one of the greatest missionaries of our faith. Yet Paul, for all his power and faith, had his own ailment, or thorn in the flesh, that would not leave him. Even though Paul bathed his ailment in fervent prayer to the Lord three times, it was not taken away from him.

Some say his thorn was constant temptation or persecution wherever he went. Some believe it to have been epilepsy, malaria, recurring headaches, or blindness. Whatever the thorn in the flesh happened to be, it kept him reliant on the constant power of God as he quietly suffered it in humility and praise.

Paul was given many revelations of the Kingdom of Heaven. Paul was a repository of the new theology of the faith and received an abundance of revelations. The thorn in the flesh, however, tempered this special knowledge, lest Paul become too self-important. The constant pursuit of Paul by Satan appears to be meant for evil, but in all reality it kept him humble and longing for the end of the physical journey. Thorns that throb, hurt, and won't go away are constant reminders to us of our own frailty.

What is your thorn in the flesh? Leaders of faith often carry the burdens of thorns. These thorns cause us to constantly seek God's strength and provision. Is your thorn a physical disability, depression, or sickness? Is your thorn a wayward family member or friend? Is your thorn a temptation, addiction, or constant financial challenge? The more effective you become as a leader of faith and servant of God, the more likely you are to have a life challenge. If you have prayed for a thorn to be removed from your life and it won't go away, you may have Paul's thorn in the flesh.

Give your thorn to God today. If He will not remove it, pray that He helps you to endure it. Use your thorn as a constant reminder that you are chosen for a heavenly leadership task and that your weakness is His strength. This life's journey in comparison to eternity is short. The throbbing of your thorn in the flesh will not last long. Let God work through your thorns so that others can experience the grace of the living Lord.

Our Prayer: *Lord, we give thanks for Paul and all the heroes of our faith. Paul endured pain and persecution for the Gospel's sake. You chose us to be Your servants and to lead others in faith. We, too, will experience persecution and thorns in the flesh of this life. If You will not remove our thorns, give us the strength to endure them and use the pain to to serve You in a new and powerful way.* **Amen.**

When Others Question Your Call To Leadership

"Real Leaders Are Proven by Their Focus and Marks of Sacrifice"

"But I certify you, brethren, that the gospel which was preached of me is not after man. For I neither received it of man, neither was I taught it, but by the revelation of Jesus Christ… From henceforth let no man trouble me: for I bear in my body the marks of the Lord Jesus."

Featured Scriptures: Galatians 1:11–12; and Galatians 6:17
Background Scriptures: Galatians 1; and Galatians 6:11–18

Leaders of faith who profess to have a calling from God for a specific task will certainly feel the ridicule of others at some point in their journeys. We expect the ridicule from skeptics and those outside of the faith, but the real hurt and challenge can come when others in our faith or sphere of family and friends bring into question the authenticity of our call. What should we do? How should we respond?

The great apostle Paul dealt with this same criticism throughout much of his ministry. Once the persecutor of Christians and then a convert by the call of Christ, Paul's call to leadership was questioned by many Christians of his day. Paul preached that salvation is by grace, through faith alone. Those who disagreed with him sought to discredit him by questioning his status as a true leader of the Gospel.

Paul preached that the grace and gift of salvation through Christ alone was all-redeeming. His critics said that only keeping the Law of Moses and doing works in Christ earned salvation. What theological argument are you being dragged into that brings into question the validity of your leadership call?

Paul was resolute and certain of his calling. His ability to rise above the criticism of others and give glory only to Christ, all while bearing the suffering of Christ, was the only evidence he would provide to his critics. Paul prevailed in his mission because his devotion was to God alone and was confirmed by his call on the road to Damascus. Paul endured prison, beatings, and banishment. He was ultimately martyred for his fervent commitment to his calling. Paul closed his letter by telling the Galatians and any future critic: *"From henceforth let no man trouble me: for I bear in my body the marks of the Lord Jesus."* He would no longer let any criticism of his calling be entertained.

As you continue in your leadership journey of faith and feel the certainty of your calling by God, be resolute and carry on. Don't let the questioning, whispers, and mockery of others slow you down. You are not ultimately accountable to critics, but to God. Let others see in your daily sacrifices an evidence of your call. Let others see the stripes and scars of your selfless service to our Lord as evidence enough that Jesus lives in you and called you for His purpose.

Our Prayer: *Lord Jesus, thank You for converting Paul to Your service to spread the Gospel. Thank You for the letters and writings of Paul in the Scriptures. Give us the certainty of our own callings to leadership. Help us to know that we are ultimately accountable to You alone. Forgive others who mock and question our leadership callings. Help us to work hard and to endure all persecution to provide the evidence of our love for You.* **Amen.**

Called By Faith To Serve In Faith

"Called Leaders Falter When They Revert to Legalism Rather Than Faith"

"Received ye the Spirit by the works of the law, or by the hearing of faith? Are ye so foolish having begun in the Spirit, are ye now made perfect by the flesh? No man is justified by the law in the sight of God, it is evident: for, the just shall live by faith."

Featured Scripture: Galatians 3:2–3, 11
Background Scripture: Galatians 3

Leaders may begin their journeys with the certainty of a childlike faith in God. We answer the call to serve our Lord by ministering to others through a new vocation or in a new institution. Our calls may take us back to school or into new job training. We have traveled a long way by faith and met with much success. Yet somewhere along the way, we learned the rulebook of our trade and craft, and when confronted with new opportunities or new challenges, we may find ourselves reverting to the rulebook rather than the confidence of our faith.

God wants each of us to reach our full potential, and that usually requires acquiring new educational and vocational training. Yet the words of the apostle Paul remind new converts to faith that they were called to faith by the Spirit of God. Their faith journeys should be rooted in adherence to hearing God's voice and not a reliance on old religious legalisms. The just shall live by faith.

What does living and serving out our callings in faith truly mean? Does it mean that we abandon our earthly knowledge in solving problems? Does it mean we shun the advice of the veterans and sages around us? No! Living by faith means that we factor into our thought processes and actions a measure of godly wisdom. This wisdom comes to us through study, prayer, supplication, and fellowship with other believers. This wisdom feeds our faith. We measure each situation as our Savior would measure it and let the Holy Spirit guide us.

Serving in faith means that we will often take roads and paths that others deem foolish. We may encounter others who scoff at such a decision-making process and label us as naïve dreamers. Serving in faith may mean taking risks that others would not take. We may submit ourselves to dangers and to a chance of failure that others would never consider. Leading by faith may also mean we must bend rules and step outside of traditional legalistic boundaries of our institutions in order to achieve something great for God.

You were called by faith so serve in faith. Let the liberation of Christ's resurrection and the assurance of eternal victory embolden you to be justified by faith alone. Leading and serving by faith gives you the ultimate alibi in that all you are, and all you do in your journey is by Christ, in Christ, and for Christ. Living by faith means you will never be the same!

Our Prayer: *Lord Jesus, let us live by faith alone. May we never be trapped by the legalisms and the constraints of this life as we attempt to love and serve others in Your name. Empower us and strengthen us to endure trials and tribulations as we reach new heights of glory in faith.* **Amen.**

Building Teamwork Through Different Gifts

"Recognizing and Effectively Utilizing the Spiritual Gifts of Others"

"There is one body, and one Spirit, even as ye are called in one hope of your calling…. And he gave some, apostles; and some, prophets; and some, evangelists; and some pastors and teachers; For the perfecting of the saints, for the work of the ministry, for the edifying of the body of Christ."

Featured Scripture: Ephesians 4:4; and 11–12
Background Scriptures: Ephesians 4:1–16; and 1 Corinthians 12—13

The apostles of the early Church had a great challenge to build unity among believers. They needed all the talent available in the new church to effectively reach others with the Gospel of Christ. The apostle Paul saw the great challenge to help persons recognize their God-given gifts, all while encouraging each person to use that gift appropriately.

In our experiences as leaders of faith, we often see pastors who want to be prophets, and teachers who want to be pastors. We see some in our organizations who, from a lack of self-esteem or faith, fail to see that they possess any gift at all for service. We see the many talents of our congregants, but too often observe gifted members who drift into areas of work for which they are not equipped. The wrong spiritual gifts working in the wrong place destroys unity and knocks the team off balance.

How do we as leaders of faith recognize the gifts of those we lead and then channel them into the appropriate place to create confident teamwork? We start by having everyone acknowledge that any gift we possess is a blessing from God. We remind those we lead that the individual parts of the body cannot be interchanged, but to lose even one part hurts the whole body. We must play our special roles as leaders and encourage our followers to work in tandem with each other.

Leaders must prayerfully and carefully discern the spiritual gifts in those they lead and nurture the development of the fledgling gifts in others. The early apostles became mentors to the new believers and leaders of the early Church. They nurtured them, wrote to them, traveled with them, and taught them. They corrected them in love even as they gave them new responsibilities and sent them forth to do the work for which they were called. While they taught them a sense of humility, they instilled into them the hope and confidence of their calling and prayed for the Holy Spirit to fill them.

In our own leadership journeys of faith today, we, too, must discern the gifts in others and help them develop. We must put the right people into the right places. We must constantly mold and build the singleness of purpose for which God calls us. We must set the example of humility, meekness, longsuffering, and love in our own lives as the example for others to follow. The power of building teamwork through the different gifts of those we lead is our awesome task from God. There is one hope of all our callings. Use all gifts well.

Our Prayer: *Father, thank You for endowing each of us with a special gift and talent for service. May we be ever mindful of how we should develop and utilize those gifts for the service of Your Kingdom. Give us the discernment and patience to help create a winning team. Show us how to bring the right gifts into the right places of service for You and Your children.* **Amen.**

Children Of Light Become Leaders Of Light

"Redeem Our Time to Lead Others Away from Evil to the Light"

"For ye were sometimes darkness, but now are ye light in the Lord: walk as children of light: For the fruit of the Spirit is in all goodness and righteousness and truth; Proving what is acceptable unto the Lord."

Featured Scripture: Ephesians 5:8–10
Background Scriptures: Ephesians 5:1–17; and John 8:12

The struggle between good and evil is often depicted as a struggle between light and the darkness. The light denotes purity, love, righteousness, and salvation. Light represents goodness, forgiveness, and what is acceptable to the Lord. Christ describes Himself as the Light of the World.

The darkness of evil is described as filthiness, hate, idolatry, uncleanness, and covetousness. Evil is Satan himself. Evil is foolish talking and gossip and unfruitful works that lend themselves to darkness. Evil is all manner of behavior that seeks to thwart the purposes of God.

The apostle Paul told us that we should walk as children of light. Jesus describes children as "the Kingdom of Heaven." A child is resistant to hate, evil plotting, and hurtful gossip. Before we can become leaders of faith, we must become leaders of light. And before we can become leaders of light, we must become children of light.

Let each of us search deeply into our own lives and souls to make sure that the Light of the World has permeated us. It may mean that we become childlike, setting aside all pretension, position, status, and wealth in order to receive the light. Our outer garments of ambition and earthly power must be taken off in order for the warm rays of God's love and sweetness to seep into our skin. Leadership journeys of faith cannot be launched until we are fully bathed and saturated with the light of Christ. Unless our intentions and inner selves are innocent, selfless, childlike, and totally reliant on God, we should not pursue our callings.

Once we become children of light, we are ready to become leaders of light. Our callings to leadership will set us to sail into the darkest of waters, and we our leadership will become a beacon of light and hope for others. Our light will be proven in our works and the manner in which we lead in love and truth. Let us redeem the short time we have left to do the work of the Father by letting our light of leadership shine before all men.

Our Prayer: *Dear Jesus, Light of the World, make us as innocent as children so that we may receive the heavenly light. Give us the light of Christ so that we may become children of light and then leaders of light. Protect us from the darkness and let our light be sufficient to overcome the darkness of evil we will surely face. May all that we do shine light in the darkness so others may, too, find the love and salvation of the Prince of Peace.* **Amen.**

We Battle Not Against Partisans

"Spiritual Warfare Is Part of the Everyday Leadership Journey of Faith"

"For we wrestle not against flesh and blood, but against principalities, against powers, against the rulers of the darkness of this world, against spiritual wickedness in high places…. And when he was come out of the ship, immediately there met him out of the tombs a man with an unclean spirit…and said, what have I to do with thee, Jesus, thou Son of the most high God…?"

Featured Scriptures: Ephesians 6:12; and Mark 5:2, 7
Background Scripture Mark 5: 1–20

Discerning leaders of faith can sense when they are not merely facing a tough circumstance, but have become engaged in spiritual warfare. Evil is swapped for evil as we observe normally rational persons perform in a mean, irrational, and bizarre manner. We witness unpredictable events, the spiritual warfare of good and evil that has now become part of our own holy callings.

When we accept the call of God to tackle heavenly tasks for Him, we must realize our future battles will not just fall into the realm of partisan politics, congregational spats, or corporate competition; our eternal work will do battle with principalities and rulers of darkness. Leaders of faith should not be deceived into the naïvete that somehow the spiritual realms of good and evil do not find their way onto our leadership ground. They play out their battles against God and our service to Christ. Jesus was quite clear that His disciples should guard against evil. Paul was clear that we battle not against flesh and blood, but against principalities.

Leaders of faith should never worry or fear. The power of Christ in us is greater than all the evil the spiritual world can muster. However, we must remain in the Spirit and bathed in the Word of God. We must remain in the fellowship of believers and stand firm on the foundations and principles of faith so we will know when we are being besieged, not by circumstances, but by spiritual warfare.

Jesus and His disciples often encountered possessed persons who were proxies of evil spirits. When Jesus encountered a man possessed of many evil spirits, they recognized the presence of Jesus and cried out, *"What have we to do with thee, Jesus, Son of the Most High God?"* Jesus called the devils "Legion," for they were many that were in the poor man. He cleansed the man, and the evil spirits entered swine and ran into the sea to drown.

We should never seek to know the war, nor the reason for the battles we face. We only need to know the Master we serve and the calls we are given, and hold pure love for the people we serve. If we serve in total obedience to the Spirit and in God's power, we can claim every moment for Jesus. The evil will pass, and the situation will conclude as God ordained it.

Our Prayer: *Dear Jesus, hold our hands during times of spiritual warfare in the leadership tasks You give us to do. Be with us constantly and may our hearts be set on You. Help us to pray, fellowship with other believers, and know Your Word. Keep us, and those You entrust to us, safe from evil in Your bosom of holy protection.* **Amen.**

Incarcerated Leadership

"Leading Others by Faith in Every Incarcerating Life Situation"

"But I would ye should understand, brethren, that the things which happened unto me have fallen out rather unto the furtherance of the gospel; So that my bonds in Christ are manifest in all the palace, and in all other places; And many of the brethren in the Lord, waxing confident by my bonds, are much more bold to speak the word without fear."

Featured Scripture: Philippians 1:12–14
Background Scripture: Philippians 4:10–13

Paul was not only the great missionary of the faith; he was one of the most prolific authors of our Bible. Paul penned letters that comprise thirteen books of the New Testament. More astonishingly, five of these letters, Philemon, Colossians, Ephesians, Philippians, and 2 Timothy, were written while Paul was incarcerated. From these five books spring forth some our faith's most profound theology.

Paul was arrested and imprisoned several times in several places. His later imprisonments were harder and took a greater toll on the apostle. Paul's anguish at being separated from the saints, churches, and congregants he loved was overcome through his fervent prayers and letters to them. Paul shared the Good News in every place while in prison. He used this time of separation to allow the great truths of God to be revealed to him and shared in his letters to the fledgling churches of the new faith.

The separation and deprivation of incarceration can give birth to unique opportunities for leadership. Paul told us to give thanks in all circumstances of life because he knew that God could multiply His goodness and purpose for those He loved.

Paul said the thing that had happened to him led to the furtherance of the Gospel. As a leader of faith, Paul was not afraid to lead from jail. In fact, his confidence and fearlessness emboldened others to share the Gospel. In what prison do you reside today?

Leaders of faith can garner great confidence from Paul's life story. Our incarceration may be a prison of sickness or joblessness or loneliness, but we can still lead others if we remain grounded in Christ's truth. Earthly persecution may ostracize us from the fellowship of those we love and deny us many of life's privileges, but God will open new doors, even in our hardships, if we trust Him in our incarcerated leadership.

Leaders of faith will be both full and hungry. We will be abased and abound. We will know plenty and will suffer great need. But great leaders of faith see that all situations of life and apparent human entrapments are launching pads for glorious new service for our Lord. The opportunities and rewards to those who abide in the bosom of Christ's love will come in due time.

Our Prayer: *God, we give thanks for Paul and the great missionaries and writers of our faith. We give thanks for the early Church and the great confidence they had in success. In our leadership journeys, we, too, will face incarceration either through fault or no fault of our own. In each circumstance, Lord, give us the courage and will to allow Your power pnd Purpose to be unleashed within it.* **Amen.**

A Life-And-Death Matter

"Living for Christ and Looking Forward to Death Marks a Faithful Leader"

"According to my earnest expectation and my hope, that in nothing I shall be ashamed, but that with all boldness, as always, so now also Christ shall be magnified in my body, whether it be by life or by death. For to me to live is Christ, and to die is gain…for I reckon that the sufferings of this present time are not worthy to be compared with the glory which shall be revealed in us."

Featured Scriptures: Philippians 1:20–21; and Romans 8:18
Background Scriptures: Matthew 22:29–33; and Romans 12:1–2

You are not ready to live until you are ready to die. For leaders of faith, living and dying are both part of our service to the Savior. For the apostle Paul, daily life was all about living for Christ. And to die was only counted as gain. So whether Paul lived or died did not matter to him, for the centrality of his existence was Christ. When we make our callings life-and-death matters, we become more able to boldly share our faith.

Our present-day sufferings are to be counted as nothing compared to the glory we will inherit. As we are released from the fear of death, we will serve Christ with greater power. Being called by God for heavenly tasks on earth gives each day's actions eternal meaning. Life, and death given to life again, are marked as our blended yet timeless journeys toward our eternal hope and glory.

If you have accepted the call of God for leadership, you have become part of God's special team. Will the journey be tough? Yes. Will there be trouble and sorrow along the way? Yes. Will you become a target for spiritual warfare? Yes. But like Paul, Christ will be magnified in all that you do and all that happens to you if you will remain faithful in your service each day.

While Paul suffered and was imprisoned, he was also the beneficiary of great love, prayer, and fellowship from other believers. The Holy Spirit gave him holy insights, which he wrote down and are now shared with us as holy Scripture. Living for Christ is a sacred and honorable duty. Dying for Christ is the most noble act of all. Often the first death we must endure is dying to our own ways of life. We must die to sin and bad habits. We must die to selfish desires. We must die to those impediments that cause us to drift from God's holy path.

The physical death we face will bring us squarely into God's glory, majesty, and reward. So let living and dying in Christ become your wonderful adventure. When you lead without fear of life or death, you will begin serving others with more singleness of purpose. Your leadership journey will then unleash God's love and wonder in more magnificent and powerful ways.

Our Prayer: *Our Father and our Savior, we live and die to You. Instill in each of us a singleness of purpose to walk with You in a new way. Let every breath become more dynamic and rich as we cast away all fear of death and uncertainty. Let us make our callings to this leadership journey of faith a life-and-death matter.* **Amen.**

Honing Our Humility

"Constantly Seek to Be Humble and Unleash God's Power and Blessing"

"Let this mind be in you, which was in Christ Jesus: who, being in the form of God thought it not robbery to be equal with God: but made himself of no reputation, and took upon him the form of a servant…and being found in fashion as a man, he humbled himself and became obedient unto death, even the death of the cross…. Be subject one to another, and be clothed with humility: for God resists the proud, and gives grace to the humble. Humble yourselves therefore under the mighty hand of God, that he may exalt you in due time."

Featured Scriptures: Philippians 2:5–8; and 1 Peter 5:5–6
Background Scriptures: Philippians 2:1–11; Proverbs 18:12

To find true examples of humility, we don't have to look to prophets, disciples, apostles, or slaves. We can simply look to the Savior Himself. Christ demonstrates how humility and self-sacrifice unleashes God's providence and power. Christ emptied Himself from His rightful place of heavenly glory and took a frail human form. His humility and obedience to the call of God forever changed the eternal relationship of man to God.

Honing our humility means becoming more like Christ. It means shunning the outward trappings of power in order to more intimately know and love those we are called to serve. It means subjecting our own ideas and good works to the scrutiny and criticism of others. It means putting the rights and welfare of others before our own. Honing our humility is a process whereby we constantly resist sin and destruction through our pureness of heart and intention.

Leaders of faith must work at humility. Success and accolades showered upon leaders can bring satisfaction and a sense of well-being. But too much self-congratulation can bring overconfidence and pride. We can lose our mooring to God's throne of grace when our humility vanishes. Unfortunately, many leaders must rediscover their humility through a defeat or setback. Misfortune and loss of status are tools in which God teaches humility.

Honing our humility does not have to come through setbacks. True leaders of faith can cast their crowns of success at the feet of God and lay all our skills and talents upon Christ's lap. Love and humility are inseparable. In love, we lose ourselves as we serve others. And in service to others we lose selfish desires. Honing our humility therefore requires that we love others more intensely and serve others with greater passion. As we hone our humility, our power and influence over persons and situations grow exponentially. Humility disarms barriers and conflict. Humility does not suggest the lack of authority or blessing; it declares and magnifies it.

Christ could have come to earth as a conquering king or upon the flaming wings of judgment. Yet He came as a lowly child born to a virgin and grew up a carpenter's son. His stature and manner was humble and measured. But in all ways and in all things, Christ was victorious. Christ showed us how to hone our humility by pouring ourselves into the service of the Kingdom with pure love and purpose.

Our Prayer: *Lord Jesus, You are not only the Author and Finisher of our faith, but You are our example of humility and love. Teach us as leaders of faith to seek Your humility each day. Let humility become our tool to defeat evil. Show us how to hone our humility through Your power.* **Amen.**

Setting Aside Our Differences

"God Calls Us to Be of One Mind and to Put Away Our Petty Differences"

"I beseech Euodias, and beseech Syntyche, that they be of the same mind in the Lord. And I intreat thee also, true yokefellow, help those women which labored with me in the gospel, with Clement also, and with other my fellow laborers whose names are in the book of life."

Featured Scripture: Philippians 4:2–3
Background Scripture: Philippians 4:1–9

If our names are written in the Book of Life, why should we quarrel and why should we worry? The hope and glory of the Gospel should be enough to make us of a single mind. Yet even the saints and laborers of Christ will have our differences. Setting aside our differences for the sake and single purpose of Christ is our command from the lesson today. God desires that we be of one spirit in the love and fellowship of service.

The apostle Paul undoubtedly encountered every leadership challenge that we as leaders of faith face in our own journeys. Paul had great love and affection for the workers at the church of Philippi. The church there was obviously bearing much fruit. Yet even in the midst of their mission success, interpersonal strife rose up among the congregation. Strife among believers can cause pain to a leader of faith. Paul urged two of the ladies of the church to be of the same mind in the Lord. Their differences might not have been theological; more likely they were personal. Both ladies were important to the success of the faith in their community, but their differences concerned Paul enough that he called them out by name in his letter.

Who do you need to encourage today in your congregation or organization to quit quarreling and get along with one another? Your job as a leader of faith is to bring all the persons God has given you to lead into fellowship and harmony in Christ. We must confront the differences and disputes among our team members and resolve them. Strife between various employees or volunteers may seem trivial at first. But when leaders allow them to continue, they lead to greater problems that can become impediments to our success.

Oftentimes people become isolated among their peers. They may misunderstand their role within an organization, and this can lead to strife. Paul exhorted the believers at Philippi to help and encourage each other. Good congregations are marked by how well members nurture and lift one another up. Leaders should monitor the well-being of each parishioner. Satan can stall the work of good labor by creating dissension and disagreement. But the love of Christ brings singleness of purpose that overcomes human strife.

Be of one mind in the Lord. Beseech those persons in your care to remember why they do what they do each day. Encourage and lift every heart. Give credit and accolades from time to time. Let every soul who labors in your field of service know that they are valued and important. The differences will melt away, and our effectiveness in serving others will be sharpened for the good.

Our Prayer: *Lord, show us as leaders of faith how to bring people together. Help us to acknowledge the work of all the laborers and give them encouragement. Empower us with the ability to solve interpersonal conflict in our organization. Create in us all a singleness of mind and purpose that is rooted in Your love, mercy, and grace.* **Amen.**

Money For The Missionary

"EXAMPLES OF GIVING AND RECEIVING THAT BEAR HOLY FRUIT"

"But I rejoiced in the Lord greatly, that now at the last your care of me hath flourished again…. Not that I speak in respect of want: for I have learned, in whatsoever state I am, therewith to be content…. Notwithstanding ye have well done, that ye did communicate with my affliction…. Not because I desire a gift: but I desire fruit that may abound to your account…But my God shall supply all your need according to his riches in glory by Christ Jesus."

FEATURED SCRIPTURE: PHILIPPIANS 4:10–11, 14, 17, 19
BACKGROUND SCRIPTURE: PHILIPPIANS 4:10–23

Mission work is holy work. The execution and support of missions to spread the Gospel and to love and nurture people everywhere is part of our command from Christ. Paul is one of our faith's greatest missionaries. In his letter to the church at Philippi, he wrote intimately to the people there, thanking them for their financial gifts of support. This spiritual love letter between a missionary and a fledgling congregation sets forth for leaders of faith a two-pronged example of how we should both give and receive monetary gifts. The money for the missionary is about our collective partnership in planting and harvesting fruit for God's Kingdom.

The ceaseless preaching and teaching of Paul, combined with his many travels, were no doubt expensive endeavors. A scholar and tentmaker by trade, Paul probably suffered financially in his commitment to building the early Church. He had little time to earn income since he spent his days in relentless mission activity. Paul also endured several stints in prison. Paul indicated that he had known the poverty of this life. But Paul lavished love and appreciation to the parishioners of Philippi for sending a financial gift that helped to meet his personal needs. Paul hoped their gift to him would be multiplied back to meet their needs through Christ's glory.

Leaders of faith will become both givers and receivers of money and gifts. We may, be like Paul, performing our works on faith alone without knowing where our next provision will come from. We may be like the people in the church at Philippi, who in love and appreciation to their founder and mentor, sensed Paul's need and sent an unsolicited gift of money for his provision. The bond of love that this two-way act created is now part of holy Scripture. God's power is unleashed when we generously give and graciously receive provisions in Christ's name.

As leaders of faith we should seek out the financial needs of the members of our own congregations and organizations. We should help those who are humbly serving others to meet their personal needs. Unsolicited gifts to others in love can lift the heart of the giver and receiver. Likewise, we should pray for and seek blessings for those who help us financially. Some of us are called to help others through our gifts, while others are called to do the physical work in the field. Both givers and receivers are part of God's eternal plan to build the Church and to serve the least of those around us. Don't forget the money for the missionary. And missionaries, don't forget to bless those who bless you.

Our Prayer: *Lord Jesus, we give thanks for Paul and the church at Philippi. We relish the letters of Paul that are full of instruction and love. Help us to make giving gifts for missionaries a top priority in our lives. Make us generous givers and gracious receivers of blessings. Multiply the acts of love and generosity we participate in as we seek to serve You.* **Amen.**

Seeing Christ In A New Light

"The Christ We Serve Is the Creator with Dominion and Power"

"Who is the image of the invisible God, the firstborn of every creature: For by him were all things created, that are in heaven, and that are in earth, visible and invisible, whether they be thrones, or dominions, or principalities, or powers: all things were created by him, and for him: And he is before all things, and by him all things consist."

Featured Scripture: Colossians 1:15–17
Background Scriptures: Colossians 1:15–23; John 1:1–18; and Revelation 1:12–18

What mental image do you conjure when you think of Christ? Do you see a crucifix hanging on a wall? Do you see a bearded priest walking with disciples or holding children in His lap? Do you see a baby in a first-century manger hewn from a rock? All those images are accurate descriptions of His earthly life and ministry. The crucifixion and resurrection are central to our faith. Yet leaders of faith who are called to serve this Master need to see Christ in a new light in order to know Him, adore Him, and serve Him to the fullest.

The words of Paul to the church at Colossae tell the true story of the deity and dominion of Christ. Christ is the image of the living, but invisible God. He is the firstborn of all creation. Christ was active in the creation of all things that were made. By Him and for Him were all things made in heaven and on earth. All realms of spirits and principalities are subject to Him. He is before all things and all things consist for Him.

The Lordship and Godhead image of Christ is the true essence of Jesus. The bloodied and Suffering Servant is really the Glorified Creator. When we lead and serve others in His name, we should do so in full acknowledgment of His place and position in time and eternity. We also have at our disposal great powers we often don't claim because we don't truly grasp the essence of Christ. Moreover, this all-knowing and all-powerful Christ is our friend and guide. We can have conversations with Him and summon Him in our times of need and trouble. He is the One we praise and give thanks to for a blessing or a sunset.

Seeing Christ in a new light can lift our hearts, empowering us and those we lead to reach higher goals and to love others more deeply. It should motivate us to serve those in need around us with new tenderness and patience. The exalted Christ is also the One who has gone to prepare a place for us. This place will be our new home in eternity with Him. The Christ for whom all things were created and for whom all things consist has called us to His service and will summon us home to live with Him throughout time. What a call! What a blessing! Hallelujah! Let us sing new praises to Him and lead others with a new meaning on this glorious new day.

Our Prayer: *Lord Jesus, You are the firstborn of all creation, who has made all things. You make us perfect in You. You are also our Master and our friend. We give You praise and honor and thanks! Help us, O Lord, to constantly see You in a new light. Let us summon the power and glory that surround You into our own lives and service to others. We look forward to that day when we are called home to be with You.* **Amen.**

Uttering The Great Mysteries

LEADERS OF FAITH ARE GIVEN TO KNOW AND SHARE GOD'S MYSTERIES"

"Continue in prayer, and watch in the same with thanksgiving; withal praying also
for us, that God would open unto us a door of utterance, to speak the mystery of
Christ…. And the disciples came, and said unto him, Why speakest thou unto them
in parables? He answered and said unto them, because it is given unto you to know
the mysteries of the kingdom of heaven, but to them it is not given."

FEATURED SCRIPTURES: COLOSSIANS 4:2–3; AND MATTHEW 13:10–11
BACKGROUND SCRIPTURES: COLOSSIANS 4:2–4; AND EPHESIANS 3:2–4

You have been called to a holy task by God. You are chosen. Like Paul and the apostles, you,
too, are given power and knowledge of the mysteries of Christ if you will pray and claim the gift.
Part of any calling to the service of God and to those souls around us is for us to be active in
uttering the great mysteries of Christ, our Redeemer. When you were called of God for service,
the mysteries of heaven were set within your heart. Today those mysteries search for a door of
opportunity for you to share God's love with the perishing and dying of this world.

Uttering the great mysteries means living and working each day in the redemption and
power of Christ. Through prayer, study, and preparation, we have begun a journey of holy
service. The great mysteries of heaven were revealed in Christ's New Covenant and in the building of the Church. Each leader of faith is given a new and unique ability to unlock these mysteries
in our service and leadership to others. Some of us are given gifts to utter the mysteries of Christ
through teaching and preaching. Others, in quiet service of caring for the sick and oppressed,
reveal the mystery of Christ as a Great Physician and Suffering Servant.

We utter the great mystery through our example of righteous living and selflessness toward
others. We unlock the mystery of forgiveness when we show kindness to strangers and goodwill
toward our rivals. The mysteries of grace and mercy can be revealed to others as we lead and
serve in institutions that promulgate hope and peace in the midst of despair. Unlock the saving
power of Christ by giving others a copy of a Bible and invite them into a congregation of fellow
believers. Be a powerful example of humility and service to the poor and hurting around you.

Paul and the apostles of the early Church were given many doors to walk through so that
they could utter the great mysteries of salvation and eternal life found in a risen Lord. Whatever
your gift and calling may be, in prayer and supplication be prepared for that same door of
opportunity to open for you on this day. Now go and utter the great mysteries of God's love in all
you do today.

Our Prayer: *Our Lord and our God, we are humbled this day to know that we, too, may be
the living repository of the mysteries of the faith. Create in us a boldness to unlock these mysteries in our own lives so that we can share the love of Christ with all those we encounter. Show us
the doors of opportunity whereby we can utter these mysteries in word and deed to those we lead
and serve.* **Amen.**

Gentle Leadership That Makes The Sale

"Serving Others with Love, Purity, Selflessness, and Single Purpose"

"For neither at any time used we flattering words, as ye know, nor a cloke of covetousness: God is witness: nor of men sought we glory, neither of you, nor yet of others, when we might have been burdensome as the apostles of Christ. But we were gentle among you, even as a nurse cherisheth her children"

Featured Scripture: 1 Thessalonians 2:5–7
Background Scripture: 1 Thessalonians 2:1–12

The apostles Paul, Silas, and Timothy went to Thessalonica on their second missionary journey and established a church there. They were attempting to establish the Gospel in Europe, and they met with many new races, customs, and traditions and encountered great resistance from the authorities there. Even their host, Jason, was taken a prisoner to force them to leave.

Yet in all this great challenge and adversity, these apostles set an example of how to flourish in a mission among strangers and against seemingly overwhelming odds. First Thessalonians 2 demonstrates the qualities that real leaders of faith should exemplify.

First, they were bold to tell the Gospel story, even in the face of persecution. Their first priority was not to please men, but to please God. They did not use flattery or salesmanship to gain traction. They sought no glory and did not make authoritative demands upon their hosts at the fledgling church there. They were gentle, loving, and affectionate to those they met, even as a nurse cherishes her children.

What similar challenges do you currently face as a leader of faith? Are those persons you are sent to lead hostile to your message? Are their customs and traditions resistant in allowing you to serve them? God often places His most trusted leaders in these same circumstances as the early apostles. Let your gentleness be your boldness. Let love and purity be your witness. Let selflessness and your singleness of purpose for sharing the Good News shine through all you do.

Those whom you attempt to lead will sense your humility even as they witness your devotion to your message and task. A bold presentation made with gentle affection can be the recipe for leadership success. The apostles were honest, were blameless, and were hard workers. The people at Thessalonica sensed that the intentions of Paul, Silas, and Timothy were pure and that they wanted nothing for themselves except to share the great news of Jesus with those they met.

In any leadership situation you face, take the cue from these heroes of the faith. By leading with conviction of your beliefs in all uprightness, your industry and integrity will hold you blameless, and will bring many new persons to your call. Even small acts of leadership done with great love will pay great rewards. You can succeed in places and with persons no one thinks you can. And it will be gentle leadership that makes the sale.

Our Prayer: *God, give us, we pray, the qualities of leadership and the heart of service that Paul, Silas, and Timothy displayed in their missionary journeys. Help us to rely solely upon You for the word and service we give to others. Bless us in tough situations as we attempt to lead strangers with gentleness to a brighter way.* **Amen.**

Sending An Encourager To Exhort

"KNOWING WHEN TO SEND EMISSARIES TO TRAIN AND LIFT OTHERS"

"Wherefore when we could no longer forbear, we thought it good to be left at Athens alone; And sent Timotheus, our brother, and minister of God, and our fellow laborer in the gospel of Christ, to establish you, and to comfort you concerning faith...."

FEATURED SCRIPTURE: 1 THESSALONIANS 3:1–2
BACKGROUND SCRIPTURE: 1 THESSALONIANS 2:13—3:8

The fledgling church at Thessalonica was facing pressure from those in their community who wanted to squash this new faith in the risen Christ. Paul was writing to them with great passion. He sensed their pressures and knew that the persecution they faced was the same that was faced by the churches and apostles everywhere. Paul mentioned that he himself had wanted to come to them several times but the work of Satan had hindered him. At this critical juncture in the formation of this church, Paul sent Timothy as an encouraging emissary who could train, love, and exhort them in their faith.

As their congregations and organizations grow, leaders of faith will find that the challenges of managing this growth can overwhelm them. Just like the early Church, as the great acts of our service grow, problems will arise. Satan is still in our world today ready to thwart the plan of God. Just like the believers at Thessalonica, our followers need our presence and help in order to survive. In these times we must be willing to delegate and send encouragers to them. Timothy was trained and ready. He went to Thessalonica and ministered to the weary parishioners who were under duress and persecution because of their beliefs.

When we can't go ourselves, we should send an encouraging emissary. We must train surrogates in our organizations who can solve problems and travel wherever we need them to go. Many times these emissaries will need to resolve conflict among faithful followers. They need to train and encourage others to stay the course. Paul stayed in communication with the early Church by letters, which are now some of the richest words in modern Scripture. We, too, should send our letters and messages of encouragement to those we lead. Through prayer and in the Holy Spirit, leaders of faith will be given that "sixth sense" of knowing when our followers are hurting or in need of an encourager. Be constantly prayerful so as to hone that "sixth sense" of the Spirit and be ready to send your own Timothy to a crisis.

Travails and hardships will come as we grow and do God's work through our callings to leadership. Never be shy to place faith in others to do your bidding for you. Paul had a great ability to find and train new leaders to help him in the task Jesus called him to complete. Send an encourager of your own out into the midst of your network today to exhort others and bring new hurting souls into the light and love of God's grace.

Our Prayer: *O Lord, we are constantly pulled in many directions and know that those in our care may need our encouragement. Help us to raise up our own Timothy and be willing to delegate to others the task of encouragement and exhortation. Satan attempts to stop our work, but let every effort to thwart our calling only result in Your will being accomplished. Bless those in our care that they may remain in the light and love of Your Son.* **Amen.**

Quietly Paying Your Own Way

"Paying for Our Own Expenses So We Can Serve God and Help Others"

"And that ye study to be quiet, and to do your own business, and to work with your own hands, as we commanded you; that ye may walk honestly toward them that are without, and that ye may have lack of nothing…. Now them that are such command and exhort by our Lord Jesus Christ, that with quietness they work, and eat their own bread."

Featured Scriptures: 1 Thessalonians 4:11–12; and 2 Thessalonians 3:12
Background Scriptures: Acts 20:35; Ephesians 4:28; and 2 Thessalonians 3:7–8

The call to God's service will require money. Leaders of faith in all generations will find themselves in need of finances for expenses for living and travel and to help those who are hurting. The apostle Paul exhorted those he taught to work quietly with their own hands and to pay their own ways. Paul himself was a tentmaker and took time to work in his trade to pay his own way. Paul did not want the believers of the early Church to be a financial burden on others. Work is honorable, and servants of Christ are to be self-sufficient.

Most leaders of faith are called to short-term or part-time service for God. Their callings may be to work with others in a local organization or to travel as a short-term missionary to minister to those in need. Leaders of faith should have trades, businesses, or jobs. They should be industrious in business and commerce. The lesson is clear: We should be ready to pay for our callings and have funds left to meet the needs of others we encounter. Quiet industriousness is a timeless ethic for life. Paying our own way keeps us from becoming obligated to others. It also sets an example that we are committed to our callings by virtue of our financial investment in God's work.

Leadership journeys of faith will call on you to sacrifice financially. We will often find ourselves paying out our own funds for the sacred privilege to share Christ's love with others. Skeptics slowly become believers when they see our quiet sacrifice of time, money, and personal comfort. Quietly working in our jobs and business to earn extra funds for service keeps us grounded in humility and honesty. When we perform extra work with our own hands, in order to earn funds for our callings, it is an extra tithe to God.

God will bless leaders of faith who work to pay their way for His service. Unexpected blessings come to those persons who anonymously work in order to help others. In addition to working to pay our own way, we should be willing to make lifestyle changes that free up funds so we can help those in need. The titans of our faith were tentmakers, fishermen, and carpenters. They worked quietly and paid their own ways, even as they were boldly preaching and teaching the message of truth and salvation. What a wonderful example they set for us today. Now it is time for us to rise and go to work and earn, so we can pay our way in serving others this very day.

Our Prayer: *O Lord, we give thanks to You this day for our jobs and businesses. Give us a willing heart to quietly work even harder and longer so we can earn the resources to serve You and help others. We know that You will provide the opportunity and blessings when we step out in faith. Provide us with strong hearts and hands to labor for You. We offer our quiet work as an added offering to You and for the fulfillment of the Great Commission.* **Amen.**

Our Glory And Joy

"Giving Thanks, Encouragement, and Praise for the Persecuted in Faith"

"So that we ourselves glory in you in the churches of God for your patience and faith in all your persecutions and tribulations that ye endure…. Wherefore also we pray always for you, that our God would count you worthy of this calling…. For what is our hope, or joy, or crown of rejoicing?... For ye are our glory and joy."
Featured Scriptures: 2 Thessalonians 1:4, 11; and 1 Thessalonians 2:19–20
Background Scripture: 2 Thessalonians 1

A constant reality throughout the ages for the Church of Christ has been persecution. In every nation and in every generation, believers and congregations have encountered hostility and violence. Leaders of faith are often called to tasks that squarely place them into physical and spiritual battles. But the persecuted and oppressed in faith have a special call to receive glory and joy.

To many, the exercise of faith is not stressful. We worship freely and with great acceptance within our communities and cultures. Many leaders of faith are held in high regard and seldom feel the tugs of prejudice or condemnation. But for many others, to lead others in worship and service brings the wrath of neighbors and physical oppression to their followers. The courage and the faith of those leaders and institutions that face persecution and tribulation should become the focus of our prayers as well as our thanksgiving. The endurance of faith and leadership amid persecution unleashes the goodness and power of heaven itself.

As we lift up the oppressed in our leadership journeys of faith, we place high value on the worthiness of our own callings. By tithing and supporting the persecuted in faith, we transfer spiritual value to the building of God's Kingdom. When we confront violence and injustice around us and lift up the disadvantaged, we give praise to God. If it is we who are oppressed, we should remember that the saints and heavenly host are our advocates. Our endurance and boldness in faith brings righteousness to the hopeless and heavenly courage to those frozen in human fear.

Are you oppressed? Who are those oppressed around you? Have you sought out people of faith who are persecuted or facing tribulation? Our lesson today calls us to make them the very essence of our glory and our joy. We don't glory in injustice, but in the opportunity to unleash Christ's victory over evil. We don't joy in the hurting, but in the obedience to the call. Instill in your own prayer life and tithing habits the conscious inclusion of those who are persecuted in faith today. Make their plight and their answer to God's call your glory and joy and part of your praise to the Creator.

Let us strive each day to find glory and joy in the bad situations. Often the bad situations and the suffering around us are portals into amazing opportunities to serve others while we share the Good News of God's eternal love for all: *"for ye are our glory and joy."*

Our Prayer: *Lord God, we give thanks and intercession for the persecuted in faith. We lift up all those leaders and institutions that face tribulation for Your name's sake. Make us to be bold and more aware of the oppression of believers everywhere. Summon us to action and may they truly become our glory and our joy.* **Amen.**

Prayer And Supplication For Our Leaders

"WE ARE COMMANDED TO PRAY WITH CLEAN HEARTS FOR THOSE IN AUTHORITY"

"I exhort therefore, that, first of all, supplications, prayers, intercessions, and giving of thanks, be made for all men; For kings, and for all that are in authority; that we may lead a quiet and peaceable life in all godliness and honesty. I will therefore that men pray everywhere, lifting up holy hands, without wrath and doubting."
FEATURED SCRIPTURE: 1 TIMOTHY 2:1–2, 8
BACKGROUND SCRIPTURES: 1 TIMOTHY 2:1–8; AND ROMANS 14:1–8

Paul taught his apprentice, Timothy, a valuable principle of faith seen in our lesson today. Paul and the early Church were persecuted by the religious and political authorities of their day. The Roman emperor and famous torturer of Christians, the infamous Nero, was in power at this time. The authorities in the institutions that early Christians encountered were often more hostile than helpful to the fledgling Church. But Paul was very specific to teach us that we should pray for kings and for all those in earthly authority over us.

Paul said that prayer, intercession, and supplication for our leaders was *"good and acceptable in the sight of God our Savior who desires that all men be saved and come to the knowledge of the truth"* (1 Timothy 2:3–4). It is easier to criticize or condemn authority than it is to pray for those with power over us. Praying for leaders in authority means we may have to pray for our rivals and our enemies. It means we must pray for those with whom we disagree. It means that we may have to pray for a despot or tyrant in our generation. It does not mean we must pray for their continued success; rather, we should pray for God's hand to work in and through all authority. We should pray that hearts be changed. We should pray that leaders be given courage to do the right thing. Prayers to God for those in authority should always be done in a spirit of peace and humility.

As leaders of faith, we ourselves should desire and covet prayers for us from fellow believers. We need others seeking blessings from God for our provision, success, and strength in fulfilling our call of leadership. Do you ask for prayers that will give you new wisdom or increased stamina to complete a task for God? Your prayer request should always include a request for protection from the evil one and for power to resist the temptations of leadership. You may even need to ask others to pray that God would forgive you of your failures and shortcomings.

In the end of times, God will reveal the change in human events and the transformed lives of leaders that resulted from the prayers and intercession of believers on behalf of those in authority. Many small and obscure prayers offered by humble and holy persons for kings and authorities contain real spiritual power that sustains us. Let us pray that God will work His way through all authority, both good and evil, in these days.

Our Prayer: *God our Savior, we pray for our leaders and for those in authority over us at this very moment. We give thanks for those who pray for us in our leadership journeys. Instill in us a yearning that all men and women will find the miracle of Your love and mercy, O God.* **Amen.**

Nothing In And Nothing Out

"Leading Without Regard to Material Gains"

"But godliness with contentment is great gain. For we brought nothing into this
world, and it is certain we can carry nothing out.... For the love of money is the root
of all evil: which while some coveted after, they have erred from the faith, and pierced
themselves through with many sorrows."

Featured Scripture: 1 Timothy 6:6–7, 10
Background Scripture: 1 Timothy 6:6–21

The crooked path to a worldly view and a thirst for money and possessions often presents
itself to leaders of faith as they make small but certain missteps. As leaders of faith, our journeys
may begin with godly contentment rooted in love and obedient service, but we can err as we
become more successful and as financial prosperity begins to flow. Without even recognizing the
change that is taking place in our lives, our love for the tangible goods and power of this world
begins to overtake our leadership gardens like weeds. It begins to choke our purity of heart and
effectiveness to serve others in humility.

Our Scripture today tells us that *"the love of money is the root of all evil."* The blessings of
God's provision are not evil, but when the work of our callings begins to compete with our
affection for money and the accumulation of wealth, we begin to lose our bearings. The Scripture says that we pierce ourselves with many sorrows when we err from our true faith and calling
in search of riches. If your appetites for the things of this world seem to be growing, God may be
calling you to get back on the right track.

Our eternal reward and the unfathomable blessings God desires for us should be sufficient.
God desires that our needs in this life be met, but each of us must obediently labor in the
vineyard of our humble callings without a quest to accumulate earthly riches. Let earthly riches
that come our way be considered the byproducts of our faithfulness to God and not part of our
heavenly mission statements. Let us earn, save, give, and tithe as we use all our bounty to glorify
God and serve the needs of others.

Remain fervent in your prayer life. Constantly seek fellowship with other believers who
keep you grounded in the eternal framework of your daily activities. Find comfort in the simple
love and blessings of health, family, a spouse's laughter, playful children, and honest work.
Never let envy of wealth seep into your life. Be frugal and cherish every simple sensation of each
day. Long walks and good books can rival the great resorts of the world. The hard-earned savings
from the work of our callings bring greater satisfaction than lavish wealth obtained at the expense of others.

God wants to bless you and your work. Let Him do it in a way that protects you from any
diversion from your calling. Let us live and work in the knowledge that we brought nothing into
this world and will take nothing out except faith, love, and assurance of eternal life with the Lord
we have been called to serve.

Our Prayer: *Lord, we came from You and return to You. We brought no material things into this
world, and we take nothing out. Teach us, O Lord, to treasure our callings and the love and fellowship
of others. We know You will provide our every need. Create in us a contentment to answer our callings
and to serve obediently and humbly without lusting for the things of this world.* **Amen.**

Building And Trusting In The Right Treasure

"Spend Your Time in Ways That Accumulate Eternal Riches"

"Charge them that are rich in this world, that they be not high-minded, nor trust in uncertain riches, but in the living God who giveth us richly all things to enjoy…. Lay not up for yourselves treasures upon earth, where moth and rust doth corrupt…for where your treasure is, there will your heart be also…lay up in store for themselves a good foundation against the time to come that they may lay hold on eternal life."

Featured Scriptures: 1 Timothy 6:17; Matthew 6:19, 21; and 1 Timothy 6:19
Background Scriptures: Matthew 6:19–24; 1 Timothy 6:17–21; and Proverbs 22:1—23:4

Show me where a person spends their time, and I will show you what a person truly loves. Each of us must spend a portion of our time each day laboring at a job or craft that earns our sustenance. Each of us must spend time performing certain duties as a family member or caregiver. But each of us every day is given the free will to expend our mental energies and personal time toward efforts that accumulate some sort of treasure. Where are you spending your time each day? Where is your treasure being stored?

Some of us spend time building friendships and relationships. Some of us spend our time on hobbies that bring us satisfaction. Some of us spend extra hours earning money to afford a finer lifestyle or education or personal enrichment. Some of us spend time in study, prayer, and meditation. But all of us set a pattern in this life of spending time and accumulating a life savings account for good or bad.

Leaders of faith are to build eternal and heavenly savings accounts. Our limited time spent on this earth should be devoted to endeavors that lift Christ and serve others in love. Our Scripture cautions us against devoting too much of our time toward pursuit of monetary riches or personal vanity. The tsunami of the marketplace or the grim reaper of poor health and death can quickly wipe away our earthly treasures, personal beauty, and popularity.

Time spent teaching a child the lessons of Jesus yields rewards. Time spent serving our congregations or communities in humble ways will enrich lives and spread love to the hurting. Time spent building the richness within our own families forges strong bonds and personal character that will span generations.

Don't let your sole treasure become a bank account or a temporal reservoir of earthly pleasures. Let your time and effort spent in this life be spent accumulating the right treasures, treasure that will radiate God's grace, mercy, and love. Even the smallest acts and time spent in holy obedience and service to others in Christ's name will have an everlasting effect on untold lives and institutions. When we go to our reward in heaven, our savings accounts will be eternal and incorruptible. So spend your time wisely and eternally, and let your treasure be holy and praiseworthy.

Our Prayer: *Lord, our time is limited in this earthly life. Help us to save up treasure in heaven by spending our time and effort on things that have true meaning. Let us devote time each day to study and serve others in Christ's name. Let us pray for the hurting we have not met. Let our time and treasure be multiplied as we lead others in faith and service to Your Kingdom.* **Amen.**

A Legacy Of Faith

"Seeds of Greatness Are Often Sown by Generations Past"

"When I call to remembrance the unfeigned faith that is in thee, which dwelt first in thy grandmother Lois, and thy mother Eunice; and I am persuaded that is in thee also."

Featured Scripture: 2 Timothy 1:5
Background Scripture: Acts 16:1–5

Timothy became an apprentice to the apostle Paul and eventually a hero of the faith. From the mission work of Timothy and Paul, along with the other apostles of the young Church, the seeds of faith for millions in generations to come were planted. But before Timothy came to be an apostle, there existed Lois and Eunice, quietly rearing a son and grandson in the admonition of God.

In more cases than not, the readiness to a calling are set up beforehand by the leadership and loving instruction of family members who instill the seeds of faith. Lois and Eunice and many like them were every bit the builders of the new Church because they raised the great apostle-to-be Timothy in an environment of love and faith. Leaders of faith today can often track their most impressionable moments of development to the steady loving hand of a mother or grandmother who instilled into them a love for Christ, the Scripture, and a willingness to heed a call to missions.

The Apostle Paul developed a great love for Timothy and gave him much responsibility in the mission of the new Church. Paul was quick to acknowledge that Timothy was ready for this task because of the stock from which he came and because of his faithful rearing. Are you instilling this kind of faith into your own children? Have you taken time to give thanks to God for your Loises and Eunices? The greatness of leaders of faith often lies first in the hearts of the grandmothers and mothers of our world.

Recently I had the great pleasure of seeing a former Sunday school teacher from years ago who reminisced and told me the stories of my early days of faith instruction. She spoke with great pride and love of the potential that she saw in me. Often the values and abilities of a leader of faith are formulated in these humble, yet powerful times of instruction by our elders.

Our lesson on leadership today should call us to action on two fronts. First, let us all recall our own Lois and Eunice teachers/mentors who instilled in us the faith and stimulated our own readiness to accept leadership tasks. Let us thank them if they are alive, or give thanks to God for their souls if they have departed.

Second, let us resolve as leaders of faith to become a Lois or Eunice to our own young Timothys and pledge to instill into potential leaders hope, faith, and integrity so that the love of Christ can be known by all through their lives to come.

Our Prayer: *Lord, we give praise and thanks today for our own Loises and Eunices and the many heroines of the faith who led us, taught us, and instilled the love of Jesus into our hearts. May we resolve to find our own young Timothys to mentor so that they can lead others for You in the days to come.* **Amen.**

Lifelong Learners Can Be Lifelong Leaders

"Study Equips Leaders of Faith to Rightly Divide the Word of Truth"

"Study to show thyself approved unto God, a workman that needeth not to be ashamed, rightly dividing the word of truth."

Featured Scripture: 2 Timothy 2:15
Background Scripture: 2 Timothy 2:14–19; and Matthew 4:1–11

When Satan came to Jesus in the wilderness to tempt Him, he made calculating offers to Jesus in an attempt to get Him to deny His mission and purpose in God's redemptive order. In each instance of temptation, Jesus clearly and most effectively rebuked Satan with Scripture, by stating: *"It is written...."*

Jesus had studied the Scripture. He was found ready for the task. Even in His ministry, He went to the Temple, read Scripture, and set apart time to study, meditate, and pray. The apostle Paul shared a great command of the faith to all leaders of faith: *"Study to show thyself approved unto God."*

Leaders of faith who are called to heavenly tasks for God must study fervently, not only to know the mechanics of our trade that we must perform, but to be equipped so as to *"rightly divide the word of truth."* In Jesus' temptation, the devil also used the words *it is written.* Yet the context and meaning of Satan's words were meant to trick and deceive Jesus. Jesus had studied in spirit and in truth and could rightly divide the word of truth in just such a moment. Jesus would go on to rightly divide the word of truth as He was questioned by the Pharisees and Sadducees during His ministry.

In your own leadership journey of faith, you will face moments when only through dutiful study will you be able to rightly divide the word of truth. Knowing the real truth will help you make the right decision. Leaders who fail to study set themselves up for defeat. Lifelong learning yields lifelong leaders. Yet leaders who refuse to study are more easily tempted and deceived by darkness.

Careful, holy study of Scripture is a great start. Set aside the time for it. Plan times to travel to visit other cultures and other organizations that can enlighten you. Seek the advice of elders and successful leaders of faith. Devour new information and old truths. Bathe your learning experience in prayer so the Holy Spirit can inspire the truth and understanding that God places into every word and every experience. Don't continue your journey as a leader without a renewed commitment to study and become a lifelong learner of faith. By learning each day and seeking to rightly divide the word of truth, your leadership effectiveness will last a lifetime.

Our Prayer: *Dear God, instill in us the passion and discipline to study Your holy Word and to seek experiences and life events that will enrich our minds and souls. As we grow in knowledge, help us to become dividers of the Word of truth from false teaching and ignorance. Help us to use Your Word to rebuke Satan, as well as the temptation to make poor decisions without honest study.* **Amen.**

Ever Learning, But Never Knowing

"Not All Who Learn Truly Know God"

"This know also, that in the last days perilous times shall come. For men shall be lovers of their own selves…having a form of godliness but denying the power thereof…ever learning, and never able to come to the knowledge of the truth…they profess that they know God; but in works they deny him…".

Featured Scriptures: 2 Timothy 3:1–2, 5, 7; and Titus 1:16
Background Scripture: 2 Timothy 3:1–9; and Titus 1:10–16

The apostle Paul wrote to his faithful apprentices, Timothy and Titus, warning these young leaders that not all who are exposed to the faith actually become partners in the faith. In fact, those who have a form of godliness and who rise to leadership in the church, but whose hearts and spirits are not seized by the true knowledge and power of God, are actually dangerous. Their acts and works will prove that they are ever learning, but never knowing the power of the true God.

Each of us may have encountered similar persons who went to the same classes and learned the same lessons as we, but who never truly caught the fire and passion of the mission. Just because people train to be leaders of faith does not mean that God has called them to lead or that God's power and knowledge flows through them. In fact, those who outwardly resemble leaders, but who serve their own lustful passions are an abomination to God.

Our background Scripture gives us the signs to look for in these false leaders of faith. Pride, boastfulness, false accusations, loving pleasure, and denying God's true power are some of the characteristics we must watch out for in devious leaders. They profess to know God, but their works show disobedience to His commands. True leaders of faith should have discerning hearts and humble minds to root out false leaders. The Holy Spirit will give you insights and the good judgment of character of others in order to protect your own leadership flock.

In the last days and perilous times, we will see more and more persons who profess to know God, but who really deny Him in their congregations and organizations. Those ever learning, but never knowing persons who go through the motions of worship may actually be there to mock the simplicity and fervor of our trust in God. Some of these false leaders may outwardly be handsome and eloquent in style and speech, but their handiwork and lifestyles expose their true nature.

True leaders of faith must lead on and persevere even in the presence of false leadership. We must be gentle and always willing to teach others. We must be patient and kind and let our love for Christ radiate and overcome the lies and deception around us. Those whom God has given you to lead will want to follow you because they sense that real truth is found in your leadership walk of faith. Claim God's real power, then quietly lead others in service and love today.

Our Prayer: *Lord Jesus, we know in these perilous times that we will encounter those who profess to know You but don't. People will be seduced by false leaders. Give us pure hearts and discerning minds so that we can lead others away from sin and debauchery. Help us to rescue others from the grips of deception by Your love and power.* **Amen.**

Qualities Of Spiritual Leaders

"Qualities of Leaders of Faith Should Reflect Paul's List to Titus"

"Set in order the things that are wanting, and ordain elders in every city…. If any be blameless, the husband of one wife, having faithful children not accused of riot or unruly. For a bishop must be blameless, as the steward of God; not self-willed, not soon angry, not given to wine, no striker, not given to filthy lucre; but a lover of hospitality, a lover of good men, sober, just, holy, temperate; holding fast the faithful word…by sound doctrine both to exhort and to convince the gainsayer."

Featured Scripture: Titus 1:5–9
Background Scriptures: Titus 1:1–9; and 1 Timothy 3

As the early Church grew, Paul knew he must let his young apprentices go forth and find new spiritual leaders. Titus was like a son to the apostle Paul, and in this letter, he sent Titus forth into the cities of Crete to find persons to ordain as elders and bishops in the new Church. Paul listed the qualities that should be found in leaders of faith. The list is a tall order for sure, but for the faith to survive and grow in sound doctrine, the best citizens must be found and called to lead for Christ.

No doubt, many of us who are called to leadership journeys of faith would have a hard time measuring up to the strict standards of Paul and Titus. However, work in the Kingdom of God needs to be done, and just as the early Church needed elders and bishops in its cities to grow the faith, God needs workers in every city today. As a leader of faith, you may be called upon to go and find, recruit, and ordain new leaders.

What are the qualities to look for in finding new leaders? A stable family life is one sign of a healthy person. Good relationships at home are critical to healthy leadership in institutions. If our own home lives are lacking, maybe it is time to assess them and shore them up. Paul told Titus to avoid self-centered, quick-tempered recruits who were rowdy and prone to trouble. He told him to be careful of those who drank too much and sought quick and easy money.

Paul desired leaders who were of strong character and good hospitality so that others would respect them and want to be in their presence. Persons with good personal habits who loved the faith and exhibited humility and holiness were most desired. Leaders are forged by good doctrine, and they should possess the ability to share the faith effectively and turn hearts toward God.

Having our own home lives in order is the first sign we are ready to lead. Will Titus come knocking on your door? What door would you knock on to find a new spiritual leader? Becoming a leader of faith is a glorious honor and presents tall requirements. Look for the qualities of a good spiritual leader and continuously measure yourself and others by them.

Our Prayer: *Lord Jesus, we give thanks for Paul and Titus and the elders and bishops of our faith. Create in us the same qualities as those Paul desired in the leaders of the early Church. Help us to seek others of these same qualities in our leadership journeys. Make us stronger in our personal lives so we can better serve You and those in need of Your love.* **Amen.**

When Salvation Takes A Chance

"CHANGED PEOPLE SHOULD TAKE RISKS BASED ON THE CURRENCY OF SALVATION"

"I beseech thee for my son Onesimus, whom I have begotten in bonds…. For perhaps he therefore departed for a season, that thou shouldest receive him forever; Not now as a servant, but above a servant, a brother beloved, specially to me, but how much more unto thee, both in the flesh, and in the Lord? If thou count me therefore a partner, receive him as myself."

FEATURED SCRIPTURE: PHILEMON 10, 15–17
BACKGROUND SCRIPTURE: THE BOOK OF PHILEMON

The apostle Paul wrote this very personal letter to Philemon while a prisoner himself. Philemon was one of the believers and leaders of a home church that Paul had led. In Paul's imprisonment, he encountered Onesimus, who by all accounts was a runaway slave of Philemon. Onesimus had stolen from Philemon and was on the run; by God's providence, he met up with Paul in prison.

Paul had led Onesimus to Christ, and Onesimus had grown in the Lord, becoming a great brother and helper to Paul. Paul developed a love for Onesimus and now wrote on impassioned letter to Philemon and the fellow church members asking them to not only forgive Onesimus without recrimination, but to receive him as a brother equal in the Lord. Paul asked Philemon specifically to receive Onesimus as if he were receiving Paul himself. Paul even offered to personally pay for whatever damage Onesimus had caused.

In this encounter of love and leadership, salvation became the new currency. Paul staked his reputation as a leader of faith on Onesimus and guaranteed his debt. As a leader of faith, have you ever taken a risk for another person in trouble by staking your reputation on them? Leaders of faith have a currency that exceeds all the other tender of mankind. Fellow believers know that Jesus changes hurt and broken lives. They know that thieves can become saints and that runaways can return home triumphantly in Christ.

Paul took a chance on Onesimus. Onesimus took a chance with Paul, for the penalty of his previous acts could be death. Paul knew that with Onesimus's return, the Gospel would spread and that the currency of salvation would yield great dividends. We do not know if Philemon received Onesimus in the end. Some traditions state that he did and that Onesimus became a bishop in the church. In our lives and journeys, we should be open to receiving those who have changed and who need a new start.

Changed persons carrying the currency of salvation can be great witnesses and of great help to leaders of faith. Welcome them into your organization. God sends the most unlikely people to the most unlikely places to do the most incredible work for the Kingdom. By taking risks with the currency of salvation, the love of Christ multiples.

Our Prayer: *Dear Lord, salvation and the grace of forgiveness are the most powerful forces we know. Help us to use them wisely and to take risks with persons who have changed their lives through You. Make us advocates for fellow believers.. Help us to use our clout, like Paul, to do the right thing for others in Christ's love.* **Amen.**

True Rest From Our Labor

"True Rest Is Only Achieved Through Faith in God's Providence"

"For we which have believed do enter into rest…. For he spoke in a certain place of the seventh day on this wise, and God did rest the seventh day from all his works…. There remaineth therefore a rest to the people of God. For he that is entered into his rest, he also hath ceased from his own works, as God did from his."

FEATURED SCRIPTURE: HEBREWS 4:3–4, 9–10
BACKGROUND SCRIPTURES: HEBREWS 4:1–11; AND REVELATION 14:13

Whose work are you doing? Is the busyness of your life and work strangling your joy? Is your work thankless and repetitious? Does the lack of accomplishment or wealth created from your labor leave you feeling as if all you have been doing is in vain? God can offer true rest only to those who believe on Him and give their labor over to Him. True rest is not just a night of peaceful slumber. It represents the ability to cease from endless work and worry. Real rest comes through surrender of our vocation to God's purpose and by giving our tasks totally over to God.

Many great persons burn out in their careers. They give years of labor to an organization or congregation only to come to the end without a sense of rest and fulfillment. But God's children can enter into the joy and peace of his providence. Let God bless your labor each day. Just as God created the earth in six days, He has conceived us and ordained our work from the beginning of time.

True rest lies in our obedience to subordinate our lives and leadership tasks over to a greater purpose. God rested on the seventh day to relish and enjoy the beauty of His own creation. We find that same rest as we step back from the canvas of our life's work and see God's hand in the paint. We find rest by trusting in the promise that our work and callings will be blessed in the scheme of eternity.

Even called leaders of faith will not find true rest from their daily activities until they commit each undertaking to God through prayer and meditation. When we fully commit our work to God, we can conclude each day with the satisfaction that the Author and Finisher of our faith is also writing the text and plot of our lives.

If you cannot find true rest from your labor today, maybe you are in the wrong job. If your life's labor is robbing you of joy and satisfaction, go to God in fervent prayer and seek a new vocation that will bring God's rest and blessing.

Maybe you are laboring in the right vineyard of service, but you have lost your compass and godly bearings. Are you surrendering yourself each and every day to God's voice and call? The ability to find true rest from our labor is a sign we are doing the right work for the right reasons. Step back from your labor. Relax and bathe in God's glory and blessings.

Our Prayer: *Lord God, we believe in You and claim Your promise. Give us the right tasks and jobs to do in service to others. Let us work hard for the Kingdom, but give us true rest. Show us how to rest in Your arms today.* **Amen.**

Two-Edged Sword Of Leadership

"The Word of God Is a Leader's Weapon of Success"

"For the word of God is quick, and powerful, and sharper than any two-edged sword, piercing even to the dividing asunder of soul and spirit, and of the joints and marrow, and is a discerner of the thoughts and intents of the heart."
Featured Scripture: Hebrews 4:12
Background Scriptures: 1 Peter 1:22–25; and Revelation 1:12–16

All leaders of faith should undertake the constant and lifelong study of Scripture. Any leadership task of faith is a journey into spiritual warfare. And in every battle in which you engage, you should wield your two-edged sword. In the Book of Revelation, our Savior battles in the end days with the two-edged sword of God from His mouth. We fail as leaders when we fail to understand the power of God's holy Word.

The Word of God is quick and powerful. It cuts through ambiguity. It rightly decides controversy. It accurately discerns the true heart and true intentions of those we come into contact with. The Word is the Law, the commandments, the prophecy, the parables, and the way of righteous living. In the inspired Word of God lie history and lessons of leadership, including how to live and interact with others. It warns us of the perils of sin and spells out for us the abundance of grace and forgiveness available to us in Christ.

The Word of God gives us proverbs and poetry for living. It contains our old and new covenants for life. Our two-edged sword can slay temptation and unlock miracles of prayer. It is our hymnal of praise and our fountain of comfort when we grieve. It holds lessons for growth for the young and hope in dying for the old. It is the revelation of the future and the assurance of victory to all who claim and trust its words. When leaders of faith fail to harvest the abundance of the Word of God through reading, prayer, and study, we fail to harness power and authority over life. We become vulnerable to life's circumstances and uncertain in our daily decision-making. We fail to reach our God-given potential or fully fulfill all that God wants to do through our callings.

Christ used the Word of God to best the devil in the desert. Christ used the Word of God against the Pharisees and to teach His disciples. Even as our Lord used the Word of God in His ministry, we should use it in our own daily tasks of leadership. Set aside time to study the Word each day. Find mentors and seek out references. Let the words of Scripture become etched in your heart so the Holy Spirit can summon them quickly to your assistance in times of turmoil and emergency.

God longs for you to be successful in your leadership calling of faith. His two-edged sword awaits you. Train to use it effectively and with confidence as a warrior for love and justice in your world. It can lift the poor and hurting all around you. It can give life and victory to all who will wield it in Christ's name.

Our Prayer: *Lord God, we give praise and thanks for the Word of God. May we take the two-edged sword of truth and learn of its ways. Teach us the depths of its meaning and show us its true power. Instill in us a burning desire to study, learn, and seek the truth of Your Word in every situation of life. Unsheathe the Word of God in our leadership in a mighty way today, O God.* **Amen.**

When A Leader's Confidence Wanes

"Confidence Returns in Stillness, Rest, and Resumption of Good Works"

"Cast not away therefore your confidence, which hath great recompense of reward. For ye have need of patience, that, after ye have done the will of God, ye might receive the promise…. For thus saith the Lord God, In returning and rest shall ye be saved in quietness and in confidence shall be your strength…. And let us not be weary in well doing: for in due season we shall reap, if we faint not."

Featured Scriptures: Hebrews 10:35; Isaiah 30:15; and Galatians 6:9
Background Scripture: Hebrews 10:35–39

Leaders of faith can lose their confidence as they go about their many tasks. We will experience setbacks and failures. People will criticize us. We may think we are not making progress quickly enough or that our abilities are not sufficient for complex tasks. The sheer weight of responsibility overwhelms us as we solve new problems and sort through human conflicts each and every day. Our confidence as a leader may begin to wane.

When a good leader's confidence wanes, patience and judgment can go along with it. Leaders who lose patience lose their holy compass for good judgment and make mistakes that hurt the cause. Confidence wanes when leaders don't see the tangible success in their calls, even after years of work. When our confidence wanes, Isaiah tells us to retreat to quiet and rest. The author of Hebrews says to protect your confidence by exercising greater patience; then reward of doing the will of God shall come in time. In Galatians we are told to not become weary in well-doing, for in due season we shall reap, if we faint not.

When your confidence wanes, retreat to a quiet spot and let the burden of responsibility be lifted for a short while. Be prayerful and patient. As your patience returns, begin doing the good works you were called to do for others with a greater love and peace. Find trusted apprentices and delegate new authority to them. Seek the exhortation and affirmation of a trusted adviser or elder.

Satan usually attacks leaders of faith in times of weariness and frustration. Just as our confidence may not leave us in one swift moment, it may not return immediately. It sometimes takes prayer and the calm, repetitious performance of good tasks over time. Spiritual confidence is the reassurance that we are able, called, and equipped. For leaders of faith, the success and confidence in our work is found through the love and service we perform for others in Christ's name.

God has equipped leaders of faith for the long journey. Provisions may not always come when you want them, but always when you need them. When your confidence wanes, get away and get still. Through rest and holy silence followed by prayer, your patience will return. God will restore your confidence and instill within you a new enthusiasm for the tasks you are called to do. Stay confident on the road of faith; you are getting ever closer to the promised reward.

Our Prayer: *O God, we all lose our confidence from time to time as we grow weary and experience setbacks, even as we do good work for You. Give us the ability to recognize when our patience is growing thin. Send us to a retreat where our souls can refocus on the tasks You gave us to do. Restore our confidence as we resume doing good works of service to others in Your name.* **Amen.**

Substance And Evidence

"WHEN YOU HOPE BUT CANNOT SEE, ANSWERING THE CALL IS FAITH IN ACTION"

"Now faith is the substance of things hoped for, the evidence of things not seen. For by it the elders obtained a good report. Through faith we understand the worlds were framed by the word of God, so that things which are seen were not made of things which do appear."

FEATURED SCRIPTURE: HEBREWS 11:1–3
BACKGROUND SCRIPTURES: HEBREWS 11; AND GENESIS 12:1–2

Every great saint who answered a call from God had a common denominator. Their call came to them when their circumstances gave no clear evidence that God's promise would come to pass. The leaders of faith chronicled in Genesis and Hebrews were persons who claimed the substance of hope with the only evidence being God's eternal promise. True faith is grounded in the belief that all provision will come to us and that all the circumstances of life will bend to the will and purpose of God, if we remain true and obedient to our call.

God's called leaders of faith had to leave home and family and journey into unknown lands. Leaders had to begin building structures for events that people scoffed would never come. Leaders cast away possessions and earthly security and placed themselves into harm's way, in the simple hope that their work would not be in vain.

What hope burns within you? What end result can you see that no one else around you can? What evidence of future success can you touch that even your own friends and family pass off as impossible? Are you ready to do something without concern for your own well-being? It is by faith that we hear God and by faith that we are able to answer His call. Our faith is the substance and evidence of what we know God is placing upon our own hearts.

Beginning a journey without all the questions answered and without having enough money or assurances of help along the way is standard practice for leaders of faith. If every circumstance in our future were measurable and predictable, it would not be called a journey of faith. When we answer God's call to service, He goes before us moving mountains and changing hearts. God wants us to take His hand and hold it firmly as we walk in the shadows and darkness of the night. He desires that we leave our zones of physical comfort and seek circumstances that stretch us and test our abilities.

If you are feeling the hopeful substance of a call and seeing the spiritual evidence of its assured success, go to God in prayer and supplication. Answer His call, then get up and get going. New victories await you. New friends and hurting souls await your call to God's service.

Our Prayer: *God of all saints, we give You praise for calling leaders to service. The saints of our faith were brave and trusted the substance and evidence of calls others could not see. Create in us, O Lord, that same vision and courage to trust our callings and to step out in faith. Confirm in us the substance of our hope and the evidence of things unseen so we can take the hope of glory to all we encounter along the way.* **Amen.**

Chastening Purifies Leaders

"ALL LEADERS OF FAITH WILL EXPERIENCE DISCIPLINE FROM GOD"

"For whom the Lord loveth he chasteneth, and scourgeth every son whom he receiveth. If ye endure chastening, God dealeth with you as with sons; for what son is he whom the father chasteneth not…but He for our profit, that we might be partakers of His holiness."

FEATURED SCRIPTURE: HEBREWS 12:6–7, 10
BACKGROUND SCRIPTURES: HEBREWS 12:1–11; AND PROVERBS 3:12

A leadership journey of faith is a holy task. Those of us who are called to this task have embarked on missions of eternal significance and value. When we deviate from God's plan or commit sinful mistakes, we may experience the chastening of God. Chastening by God serves not to cast us away, but to purify us and make us more holy. Those persons whom God loves are those He chastens. We are God's children and occasionally, we need guidance and discipline from a holy Father.

Too often leaders view their time of punishment as a self-declaration of failure. That is not what the Scripture teaches. God will not take a repentant leader and throw him upon the trash heap of failure. Instead, God purges us and cleanses us for better and higher tasks. Often we may think we have been demoted or defeated, yet God desires us to move forward. We may be forced to endure hardship, discomfort, or even a loss of freedom for a while, but in this time of hardship, God removes the hard edges from our character and spirit to make us more holy and ready for service.

Submission to chastening is important. Prayer and repentance will surely bring forgiveness, but chastening is God's process of making us holy as He is holy. Leaders of faith get fired for mistakes. Leaders lose elections. Leaders set themselves up for public humiliation by their own sinful acts. Leaders engage in self-centered actions that hurt others. Leaders fail to heed advice or usher change when needed. Leaders seek greater power and glory and become callous to those around them. Every leader of faith can become a leader in need of chastening. God actually rescues us from our own destruction when He intervenes on our behalf.

The purification process during God's chastening may mean loss of status, office, or wealth. It may mean the temporary loss of respect from your peers. It may mean turmoil within your own family. It may mean facing up to a nasty addiction. Whatever mistake, failure, or challenge of your own making that you are facing today, God will get you through it. The chastening and purification process may not restore you to your previous earthly position, but it can make you more useful to God than ever before. God's process is to make you more like Him. When we become more holy and more pure, our ability to lead and serve others takes on new heavenly dimensions.

Our Prayer: *Lord God, we admit that we fail You from time to time. All of us fall short of Your holy standards. We know that You love us because we feel the chastening of Your hand. As You discipline us, please purify us for even greater tasks of service for You. Let us be repentant and constantly seek to do Your will. Protect us from the evil one, and let the sum of our lives and work be something that brings honor and glory to You, O Lord.* **Amen.**

Strangers And Angels

"Love and Care for Strangers Set Believers Apart"

"Let brotherly love continue. Be not forgetful to entertain strangers: for thereby some have entertained angels unawares. Remember them that are in bonds, as bound with them; and them which suffer adversity, as being yourselves also in the body."
Featured Scripture: Hebrews 13:1–3
Background Scriptures: Psalm 146:9; Luke 17:17–18; and Luke 10:25–37

Have you ever been lost, only to encounter a stranger who gave you directions to a destination? Have you ever found a person stranded without provisions and given them money or assistance to find their way home? One moment they are there, and the next moment they are gone, but you are left with the feeling that somehow your paths were meant to cross. Believers are to be kind and sensitive to strangers. Many a person has encountered strangers who were angels in earthly form; they were placed in our paths for a specific reason.

Not only are we to be kind to strangers, but we are to feel the pain of strangers in bondage. We are to suffer with those who face adversity in their lives, even those we have never met. The ability to love, connect, serve, and pray for strangers is a quality that leaders of faith must possess. As the love of Christ becomes a growing part of our character, we will find ourselves moved to help strangers. Strangers are God's children. Strangers in need are a leader's opportunity for service. Strangers are merely friends you haven't met yet.

Jesus met many strangers in His ministry. He fed multitudes of strangers miraculously on more than one occasion. Strangers with demons approached Him begging for relief, and He cast the demons out of them. Strangers marred by leprosy, blindness, and deformity encountered the Son of God and He healed them. The children of strangers lined up near a shady tree, clamoring to sit on the Master's knee, and Jesus let them come to Him. Jesus came to save the lost and rescue the stranger.

As a leader of faith, how do you treat strangers? Is your congregation or organization open to helping the needy around you? Do the homeless have access to your facilities and ministries? Is your membership exclusive, or is it open to strangers? While the strangers we encounter each day may not be angels, they are all observing us. When they see you, do they see kindness and openness? Do they see a leader and institution that includes the hard to serve and the hard to love? How we respond to strangers in our paths is God's litmus test to the limits of our faith and love.

We can love and pray for strangers whom we don't physically encounter. We know orphans and the widows exist all over the world. The incarcerated stranger who is locked away in our communities longs for our visits and prayers. Lonely, impoverished, and maimed strangers long for fellowship and ministry. As you begin to see Christ in every stranger, angels will follow to meet you.

Our Prayer: *Creator and Savior, all strangers are Your children. Help us, O Lord, to love and serve the strangers in our lives. Instill in us a capacity to love those whom others don't see and those the world forgets. Let the love and light of Christ shine in us and through us as we serve the seen and the unseen stranger.* **Amen.**

Good Marriages Nurture Good Leaders

"Good Marriages Shelter Leaders from the Winds of Life and Temptation"

"Marriage is honorable in all, and the bed undefiled…. Set me as a seal upon thine heart, as a seal upon thine arm: for love is strong as death.…"

Featured Scriptures: Hebrews 13:4; and Song of Solomon 8:6
Background Scriptures: Proverbs 18:22; 19:14; and Song of Solomon 8:5–14

The role and traditions of marriage have varied from generation to generation. The significance and reverence of marriage may vary in different cultures. But the institution of marriage and its benefits are clearly defined in the Scriptures. Leaders of faith would do well to take a new look at marriage as a gift of God, one of the greatest assets for happiness and achievement. Solid nurtured marriages can keep a leader from falling into the traps and mires of temptation.

The list of leaders who have fallen from power through acts of adultery, neglect, and violation of marriage are too numerous to count. When armies, kings, or pestilence could not subdue a leader, lust and wanton neglect of marriage did. God's ordination of marriage was meant as a gift and a sanctuary for life. It was meant as an ark of protection for families and children. But marriage is also a leader of faith's lifeline of protection from loneliness, lust, and error of judgment. Communion and communication with a spouse can tether a leader. Through love, affection, and the sharing of confidence, a leader and spouse can become a valuable team for God's service.

If marriages are nurtured and romance is kindled constantly, the resulting love and friendship of committed spouses cannot be cracked by outside influence. As leaders grow old, the comfort and love of a spouse is better than gold or wealth. The richness of marriage will grow over time even as the fleeting assets of youth fade. Carefully calculate the risks of losing a spouse from neglect or a wandering eye. Damage caused to marriage by infidelity or lack of judgment is not easily repaired.

For leaders who have failed in marriage or who long to find the true love of another, pray and work toward that goal. God is gracious when we seek companionship in purity of heart. Some leaders have lost the love of another through death or sickness. Pray for comfort and new blessings. Richly give thanks and cherish each day you experience love and the blessing of a happy marriage. Bad marriages can be repaired and restored with God's help and much effort. Encourage others in their marriages. Set a good example in your own marriage, or let others openly learn from your mistakes.

Let us all pray that marriages will be made strong and that God will bless leaders of faith with the meaningful love of a devoted spouse and better equip them to fulfill their call to service for others.

Our Prayer: *Dear God, thank You for marriage and the love of a spouse. We lift up the institution of marriage that You ordained for renewal of blessing. Forgive us when we have failed in marriage, and give us the chance to renew our lives through new chances at love. Bless those of us in strong marriages and keep us safe that we may grow. Comfort those who have suffered loss and need new friends and caring love. May the abundance of marriage make our leadership service stronger and more reflective of Your love for each of us.* **Amen.**

Patience And The Perfect Work

"Enduring Temptation Forges Leaders into the Perfect Work"

"My brethren, count it all joy when ye fall into divers temptation; Knowing this, that the trying of your faith worketh patience. But let patience have her perfect work, that ye may be perfect and entire, wanting nothing."
Featured Scripture: James 1:2–4
Background Scriptures: James 1:1–12; James 4:7–10; and Romans 5:1–5

How quickly temptation will come to new leaders of faith. How consistently it will come to all leaders of faith. Satan, the tempter, has many disguises, and temptation comes to us in many desirable packages. James tells us to resist the devil and he will flee. We are to be joyful when temptation comes to us. As we are tried and tempted and are victorious, we become forged into a stronger instrument for God.

The old English term of "divers" temptations means "various and diverse" temptations. One temptation that often comes to leaders of faith is yielding to expedience and quick results instead of practicing a slow building of their foundation and assets. The most common forms of temptation that find leaders are inclinations toward self-congratulatory pride and the desire for power. The more leaders beat back this beast, the more humble and respected they become. The temptations of the flesh also seek and find leaders of faith. The temptation of an innocent sexual encounter or an offer for an unearned benefit confronts many a leader. Leaders who yield to these temptresses can reap financial ruin, as well as the loss of family and the respect of those they lead.

Another dripping and eroding temptation is that of complacency in our work. We yield to this temptation without even noticing it. We can get into routines where our time spent in improving our organization or congregation is cut back or given over to leisure. We can become soft, ignorant to new techniques and new ways of our trade. We begin to make assumptions or stereotype persons or situations, and we lose the energy and excitement that was instilled in us at our callings. We can yield to the temptation of physical erosion through gluttony, addiction, or giving our bodies over to unfitness.

Great leaders of faith are those who identify temptation in all its forms and stay grounded in prayer, the study of Scripture, and the fellowship of fellow believers. Temptation is anything that prevents you from performing your best work for the Almighty God. Stay in shape to defeat temptation by building strong families and friendships and refraining from the venues of evil. Great leaders should remain humble, fit, and curious. When you encounter temptation, you should measure it and evaluate its source. You should always be fully cognizant of the consequences of succumbing.

As leaders of faith encounter and overcome temptation, they grow stronger, wiser, and more aware of the sinister imposter that Satan can be. Victory over temptation builds patient, experienced, hopeful leaders of faith who can then become living vessels of the Holy Spirit.

Our Prayer: *Lord, gird us and prepare us for the temptations of life and leadership. Help us to recognize these imposters in all their forms. Bless us and protect us as we face temptation, and grant us victory over it. As we defeat temptation, give us patience and endurance to finish the race. Craft us into holy, pure vessels who can lead others to Your light and love.* **Amen.**

Widows, Orphans, And Leadership

"TREATMENT OF THE MOST VULNERABLE IS THE BAROMETER OF GREAT LEADERS"

"Pure religion and undefiled before God and the Father is this, to visit the fatherless and widows in their affliction.... Learn to do well; seek judgment, relieve the oppressed, judge the fatherless, plead for the widow."

FEATURED SCRIPTURES: JAMES 1:27; AND ISAIAH 1:17
BACKGROUND SCRIPTURES: LUKE 18:1–8; AND HOSEA 14:1–4

Pure and undefiled religion before God is leadership action taken on behalf of the widows and orphans. Intervening for the least among us usually involves service to these neglected groups. In the time of Christ and throughout history, many widows became outcasts, relegated to poverty and banished to loneliness. Orphans are always among us as natural calamities, disease, war, and poverty claim the lives of parents in dozens of nations. Widows and orphans are precious to God, and our care of them is the very barometer of our success in any leadership journey of faith.

Leaders don't have to travel miles to find a widow or orphan in need. Vulnerable elderly citizens and children live among us in our own communities. They may frequent our churches or places of business. Many have quiet and unmet needs. But beyond their physical needs is their need to be loved and included in a family of faith and community. More often, widows and orphans need an advocate and an intercessor within the legal and institutional framework of our governments.

Even the unrighteous judge in Luke 18 gave justice to the widow because of her persistence. But the righteous leader should not need prodding to help the vulnerable. Any congregational or organizational structure we establish and its budgets should include a priority for widows and orphans. Have you volunteered as a layperson to help a child? Have you become a foster parent or adopted a child? Have you offered to visit the elderly who are homebound? Have you given of your financial resources to the myriad of causes benefiting the destitute around the world?

God harkens us to this calling of pure and undefiled religion. We can't go wrong when we find ways to assist others. We should pray for the vulnerable at every meal. We should advocate within our own places of worship for funds earmarked for the vulnerable. It is our righteous duty. Whatever we are called to do, we must incorporate the love and care for widows and orphans into our daily tasks. Become a friend to a lonely senior. Find a way to help clothe, educate, or provide mentorship to a disadvantaged child in your own child's school. Plan a mission trip of mercy to a new land.

The face of an orphaned child is the face of Christ. The feeble and wrinkled hand of the impoverish widow is the hand of the Master. The cry of the widow and orphan is the very voice of God calling us to pure and undefiled worship. Visit the fatherless. Plead for the widow. Relieve the oppressed.

Our Prayer: *Lord Jesus, the faces and voices of the widows and orphans are the essence of Your call to all of us today. Our response to their need and their presence among us is the purest form of worship. Instill in us a new awareness, desire, and passion to serve the least of these among us and lift the lives of those in need in our communities and around the world.* **Amen.**

A Tongue That Liberates Or Lays To Waste

"Taming the Tongue Is Key to Leadership Longevity"

"But the tongue can no man tame; it is an unruly evil, full of deadly poison. Therewith bless we God, even the Father; and therewith curse we men, which are made after the similitude of God. Out of the same mouth proceedeth blessing and cursing. My brethren, these things ought not so to be."

Featured Scripture: James 3:8–10
Background Scriptures: James 3:1–13; and Proverbs 15:2

The apostle James had great insight and wisdom into the potential of the tongue to be an instrument of both good and evil: *"Let every man be swift to hear, slow to speak..."* (James 1:19). Every leader of faith should post this quotation on their walls. Many great leaders of faith have been brought low because they were too quick to speak in a reactive or anger mode.

The tongue of a leader of faith can liberate or lay to waste the best-made plans. Leaders who have been raised in solid homes of discipline were taught that dirty speech and derogatory language were not permitted and when practiced was met with severe discipline. But it is not always the filthy or derogatory language of the tongue that stings. It is often the prideful remark spoken with haughtiness or a sarcastic tone of voice that hurts others most and damages your effectiveness as a leader.

First Corinthians 13 tells us that the motivation behind the tongue is what matters most: *"If I speak with the tongues of men and angels and have not love we are but as sounding brass and tinkling symbols."* Humility and holiness should guide the heart, and the heart should guide the tongue.

Great leaders are always great listeners. Before they speak out, they listen first to the thoughts and opinions of others. Sharp and brash tongues are often masks for a false sense of security that resides in arrogant leaders. Successful leadership involves ample input but measured output in communication. Habits of good communication can be built with practice over time. Greetings of goodwill can stop short of false flattery. Words of crushing criticism can instead become words of wisdom and helpful instruction if spoken firmly and in a caring way. Our reactions to the boisterous conversations of others should always be met with a measured, thoughtful response; or better yet, with silence.

Leaders of faith can never completely tame the tongue. But we must strive to do so. We must make sure our thoughts stay pure and that our minds get rest in order to keep the tongue in check. Don't speak on important subjects in haste, in anger, or during revelry. Be always prayerful that the Holy Spirit is within you before you speak out on any issue. Let your tongue be God's tool for the liberation of the captives, not a sword that lays us to waste.

Our Prayer: *Dear God, indwell our hearts and minds and may the Holy Spirit bridle our tongues. We pray that the Holy Spirit will temper any words that leave our tongues, so that all we say will be edifying for the Kingdom. Forgive us for the evil words that we've spoken. Help us to hear Your voice more clearly and more often, as we speak less.* **Amen.**

Envy And Strife Seep Into Leadership

"Real Leaders Must Confront Signs of Discord That Can Lead to Ruin"

"But if ye have bitter envying and strife in your hearts, glory not, and lie not against
the truth…. For where envying and strife is, there is confusion and every evil work."
Featured Scripture: James 3:14, 16
Background Scriptures: James 3:13–18; and Romans 13:13

As humility and meekness fade in a person's life, they are usually replaced by envy and strife.
No leader of an organization or congregation will be spared from dealing with the demons of
envy and strife, which lead to confusion and evil works. Envy and strife is in no way associated
with heavenly work. In fact, they lie against the truth. The corrosive effect of envy and strife can
render otherwise great and powerful people into confused, petty partisans who become unable
and unwilling to work in unity to achieve worthy goals.

Often envy comes when people don't feel valued or when they see unrighteous activity
rewarded in an organization. Anger and indignity can breed envy. Envy that lingers and grows
will inevitably lead to strife in relationships and institutions. Envy can also be sown by leaders
who fail to lead with gentleness, kindness, and meekness. Purity of heart in a leader is easily
recognizable. Those possessing it will be quick to forgive and prone to inclusion. Gentleness,
kindness, and meekness are not qualities of weakness in leaders; yet, they are the fertile soil in
which God's purposes can be planted and cultivated.

Followers and coworkers can easily succumb to envy and strife if leaders themselves are not
washed in prayer and humility. Leaders of faith must detect the early signs of envy and strife
among those we lead and confront it boldly in love. Those among us who would sow strife
should be expelled or contained. The envy and strife in our midst will stifle and paralyze our
activities. It will cause good people to make poor choices in anger. Innocent people will get hurt
as people exact retribution on each other. Evil deeds will lead to more evil deeds unless the core
root cause of envy and strife is identified and extracted from our team.

We guard against and tackle envy and strife when we practice the art of compromise and are
open to dialogue. We should be quick to forgive when others confess that they are sorry, and we
should seek the forgiveness of others when we know we have been in error. When we are fair,
evenhanded, and impartial, others will notice. Practice what you preach, and as a leader walk the
walk when it comes to following rules and procedures. Keep your word to others and never
allow yourself to be perceived as hypocritical; it can destroy your ability to contain envious and
strife-ridden persons. Keep your eyes on the cross and the Suffering Servant, who has already
conquered strife, envy, confusion, and evil on the hill at Golgotha. Cling to Him.

Our Prayer: *Lord God, You are not a God of envy and strife, but of meekness and peace. Protect
us from the demonic influence of these monsters in our own lives. Help us to keep our eyes focused on
Christ and on the call to love our neighbors as ourselves. Purge from us any longing to have or want
what others may possess. In the contentment of our faith, let us lead in purity of heart, being full of
mercy and bearing good fruit.* **Amen.**

Antidote For Strife And Envy

"Good Leaders Inoculate and Protect Against the Evils of Strife and Envy"

"For where envying and strife is, there is confusion and every evil work. But the
wisdom that is from above is first pure, then peaceable, gentle, and easy to be intreated,
full of mercy and good fruits, without partiality, and without hypocrisy."
Featured Scripture: James 3:16–17
Background Scripture: James 3:13–18; Romans 12:9–21; and Galatians 5:22–26

When the stakes are high, the clash of rivals in leadership can make the competition bitter.
Most leadership callings of faith involve competition. Our organizations and congregations compete for customers, votes, patronage, or membership. We compete for resources, funds, and
talent. We compete for elections and power. We compete for attention. Competition is not necessarily bad, but its tone and tenor can quickly change us for the worse. Envy and strife can
overcome otherwise sane and faithful persons, turning competition into confusion, strife, envy,
and evil works.

The fear of loss or of forfeiture of power often shocks leaders into a state of confusion. And
when leaders are confused, they make bad choices and begin returning evil for evil. This spiral-
ing digression destroys leaders of faith and the organizations they lead. How can leaders of faith
avoid confusion and protect against envy and strife? How do we inoculate our organizations and
congregations from the negative consequences of bitter competition?

Look inward with humility and in prayer and supplication. An honest evaluation of ourselves and the state of those we lead can yield immense return. We should find and mark the
wayward and fallen in our midst and deal honestly with them. We will find peace and gentleness
when we do not compete with others out of hypocrisy. Jesus says we cannot point to the splinter
in our rivals' eye when we have logs in our own. Hypocrisy is the greater sin. An honest admission of our own faults and impurities can anchor us, allowing us to compete with others in peace
and mercy without partiality and hypocrisy.

Envy and strife also indicate that our lives are not anchored in the harbor of God's peace.
Contentment in our callings means that we have confidence and humility to tackle the tasks
before us with the provision that God makes available to us. We need no glory, nor do we need
any accolades: save the praise of God and the service of others. We serve in love and truth and
without malice, needing only the love and affirmation of God. In this safe harbor, no envy or
strife will be found.

We are now ready to compete for the prize of salvation and the work of our callings from
God. Our envious and strife-ridden rivals will falter as they come against us in their own hypocrisy. Our efforts will yield fruits of righteousness that bless many and glorify God.

Our Prayer: *Lord, forgive us when our hearts give way to envy and strife. Purge the evil inclinations that can destroy our effectiveness as leaders. Create in us contentment in our callings. Help us
to be honest and humble by getting rid of our own impurities in leadership. Make us to compete in
love, truth, and gentleness as we let the hypocrisy in others become their undoing. May our works
always yield the fruit of righteousness according to Your holy plan.* **Amen.**

Righteous Leaders Are Peacemakers

"The Prince of Peace Calls Leaders to Missions of Peace"

"And the fruit of righteousness is sown in peace of them that make peace.... Blessed are the peacemakers for they shall be called the children of God.... Peace I leave with you, my peace I give unto you: not as the world giveth, give I unto you. Let not your heart be troubled, neither let it be afraid."

Featured Scriptures: James 3:18; Matthew 5:9; and John 14:27
Background Scriptures: Genesis 41:16; Numbers 6:22–27; Isaiah 9:1–7; and 1 Corinthians 7:15

The word *peace* is found dozens of times in the Scriptures from Genesis to Revelation. However, the word *peacemaker* is found only once, in the words of Christ in His Sermon on the Mount. Christ calls each of us as leaders of faith to become His *peacemakers* in our own callings and journeys. When we sow peace in the situations around us, it will bear righteous fruit.

Jesus Himself was prophesied to be the Prince of Peace by the prophet Isaiah. But what does peace really mean? Peace is not the absence of conflict, nor is it the abdication of fighting against evil. Peace is also not the absence of blood. Peace is not the absence of suffering, for it was Christ's calling to die in a gruesome act of Roman crucifixion. But true peace is that peace that Jesus left us and calls us to: the peace that passes understanding. Spiritual peace is found in the humble belief and assurance that we are redeemed and will be transformed through our trials in this life and upon our physical death. Peace is not a destination, but rather the constant process of shining forth the light of truth and justice in all situations. Peace is an act of restoration with your oppressors. It is the forgiveness for your enemy's crimes against you by way of Christ's mercy, grace, and love.

Bringing earthly peace means we find the conflicts that abound in our congregations and organizations. We uncover the simmering resentments and hard feelings that linger from past controversies. We confront the unhealthy rivalries and competitions among our followers that are escalating and causing our missions to drift. In prayer and through calm spirits, we must bring people together and find the holy ground. The Holy Spirit convicts the wrongdoers and guilty parties even as Christ's love and redemptive powers spring forth to bring peace to our situations.

Becoming a peacemaker means you must also confess your own sin. You must admit your wrongdoings that have caused strife and conflict. You must apologize to a family member or colleague and make amends for the hurt you caused them. Making peace means changing your habits, attitudes, and lifestyle. It means you must become more accepting and less strident and critical toward those you lead and love.

If you want to become a real leader of faith, you must become a peacemaker. It is your call. It is your vocation. And it is the example of our Lord. In our peacemaking lie our fruits of success as leaders. Even our attempts to make peace will unlock Christ's power and affirm us as children of God.

Our Prayer: *Dear Lord, thank You for giving us the peace that passes understanding. Your peace is available to all. Allow the inner peace we gain as Your children to shine upon the evil in our midst. Give us courage and help us to always seek peace in all situations. Plant Your love and power into every conflict and situation and let peace bear the righteous fruit.* **Amen.**

Failing By Asking Amiss

"WHEN LEADERS PRAY FOR THE WRONG THINGS OR IN THE WRONG WAY"

"Ye ask, and receive not, because ye ask amiss, that ye may consume it upon your lusts."

Featured Scripture: James 4:3
BACKGROUND SCRIPTURES: JAMES 4:1–6; AND PROVERBS 28–33

Leaders of faith vary in the effectiveness of their prayer lives. As we mature in our faith, our prayer lives become more intimate, more continuous. Every believer will hit walls in their prayer lives. We will experience mountains and valleys. Sometimes we will feel the very warm breath of God upon us as we pray, and sometimes we will feel as if we are mumbling only to ourselves. There are many prayer ailments that need different diagnoses, but one prayer ailment seldom addressed is praying for the wrong things or praying in the wrong way.

The apostle James called this ailment "asking amiss." Prayer should always begin with silence, with humility and respect. The silence gives way to awe, which gives way to confession. Confession brings a new clearness of heart, which gives way to praise. Praise gives way to thanks, which gives way to an openness to hear God's voice and to know His true will. Jesus gave us the perfect prayer, but sometimes we don't say pray it. As we grow in faith, we can begin to experience "merging of thought with the Creator." Sometimes we simply call the name of Jesus out loud when we need a spiritual hug. Sometimes we summon the full power of the heavenly Trinity when confronted by calamity, death, or fear.

Asking amiss can also mean asking for our own desired outcome rather than the will of God. Jesus Himself asked for the cup of pain and separation to pass, but He yielded to God's will in His prayer at Gethsemane. Asking amiss may also mean asking for victory before asking for power and courage. We might ask for our own blessings before asking for provision for the poor or our neighbors. We might pray for a position of power in lieu of a humble opportunity to help and serve others.

When leaders of faith pray the right way for the right things, showers of blessings come to them. We always underestimate God's love for us and His desire to give us the good things of this life and in eternity. As a wise sage once said, "You may not always get what you want, but you will always get what you need." A wise mother once said, "Be careful what you ask for; you might get it." Jesus told us that if we have the faith of a mustard seed, and ask God, we can move mountains.

What God wants to hear in our prayers is humility, confession, obedience, and a willingness to do His will. He wants to hear our selfless intercession for others. He wants us to have still minds and open souls. God expects us to ask for what we need. He already knows our problems, but when we ask and pray in the fullness of His love and grace, the results are immeasurable.

Our Prayer: *Father God, we kneel in stillness before You. We come to You in humility, confessing our sin and weakness. We praise You for calling us and for selecting us for Your service. We thank You for all blessings and for each breath we draw. We come to You in loving dependence for our provision. We lift up the needs of others. We pray for Your will to be done in our leadership journeys. Bless us, O Lord, in a mighty way today. Teach us how to pray and to never ask amiss.* **Amen.**

A Prayer Meeting

"GATHERING TOGETHER TO PRAY FOR EACH OTHER UNLEASHES POWER"

"Is any among you afflicted? Let him pray. Is any merry? Let him sing psalms. Is any sick? Let him call the elders of the church; and let them pray over him…. And the prayer of faith shall save the sick…confess your faults one to another, and pray one for another, that ye may be healed. The effectual fervent prayer of a righteous man availeth much…. For where two or three are gathered together in my name, there am I in the midst of them."

FEATURED SCRIPTURES: JAMES 5:13–16; AND MATTHEW 18:20
BACKGROUND SCRIPTURES: JAMES 5:13–18; AND ACTS 1:13–14

The sweetest and most powerful force on earth is a congregation of meek and humble people of God who have gathered to pray, praise, and petition the Almighty on behalf of each other and the world. Certain faith traditions set aside a day in the middle of the week for the congregation to gather to pray and sing. A prayer meeting of the faithful can unleash untold power from the throne of God.

As a leader of faith, you need to be a leader of collective prayer. Holding a prayer meeting does not have to happen exclusively within a faith congregation or a place of worship. Christ said that even when two or three of us gather in the name of Jesus, He is there, ready to hear us, comfort us, and listen to our petitions. But the habitual and affirmative gathering of congregations and organizations for the purpose of hearing needs, celebrating victories of life, and raising our collective voices to God is one of our highest duties as believers.

Who is sick among your group of friends and associates? Who has received a blessing? What is the greatest need of a congregant at this very hour? Call your team together to verbalize it and pray over it. Claim God's power and promise! How often we allow our lives to be full of anxiety and stress because we do not openly offer our needs to the power of group prayer. The combined prayers of righteous and humble people is the greatest weapon on earth against evil and pain.

Some of us are quiet and protective of our needs, sins, and shortcomings. Some of us celebrate our personal victories all alone. While not every need or praise must be subjected to collective prayer, don't ever underestimate the love and concern those close to you have for your well-being. Leaders of faith especially need the prayers of others. Too often leaders carry the heavy burdens of their institutions upon their own backs, thinking no one else cares or that no outside force could change the dynamics of our situation.

If you are in this mode of thinking, call those whom you lead or your elders and mentors together in Jesus' name. Let your praises and petitions be known before God as you lift collective hearts and voices to heaven. Healing, provision, protection, miracles, and blessings are already flowing down.

Our Prayer: *Lord Jesus, we gather together in Your name and bring our praises and petitions before Your holy throne. Forgive us and show us Your way. Shower us with eternal blessings by Your mercy, grace, and love. We pray for each other in humility. We know You are among us even now. Let your will be done, O Lord.* **Amen.**

Confronting Our Excess And Addiction

"ABUSE OF SUBSTANCES, PLEASURE, OR THE FLESH COMPROMISES LEADERS"

"For the time past of our life may suffice us to have wrought the will of the Gentiles, when we walked in lasciviousness, lusts, excess of wine, revellings, banquetings and abominable idolatries.... Wine is a mocker, strong drink is raging: and whosoever is deceived thereby is not wise.... For all that is in the world, the lust of the flesh, and the lust of the eyes, and the pride of life, is not of the Father, but is of the world. And the world passeth away, and the lust thereof: but he that doeth the will of God abideth for ever."

FEATURED SCRIPTURES: 1 PETER 4:3; PROVERBS 20:1; AND 1 JOHN 2:16–17
BACKGROUND SCRIPTURES: 1 PETER 4:1–6; COLOSSIANS 3:5–8; AND 1 TIMOTHY 3:1–7

Bad habits of good leaders can slowly but surely become webs of self-imprisonment. What begin as simple pleasures and daily enjoyment can morph over time into indulgent excess and addiction. Leaders of faith can become especially susceptible to the quiet retreats into personal pleasures that help assuage the daily pressures associated with leadership and responsibility. Leaders of faith should be vigilant and affirmative to confront their own excesses and addictions. Our excesses and addictions do not have to be illegal or even immoral. But we must realize that the lustful pleasures of this life are not of God. We deceive ourselves when we rationalize behaviors that are not healthy or edifying to God. These may involve hobbies, spending money, drugs, personal fitness, sex, or pornography, social events, grooming, food, alcohol, work, reading, or gossip. Our excesses may negatively affect those we lead and serve as they siphon our time and resources away from our leadership duties.

Any activity that separates you from fellowship with God and healthy relationships with others needs to be examined. What are your excesses and addictions? Some addictions have chemical and genetic causes, and we should seek professional assistance in confronting them. Other excesses result from our own lack of discipline or poor lifestyle choices. If you are not yet addicted to a bad habit, stay on guard that your own private activities or personal pleasures do not come to control you.

Leaders of faith who are called of God and commune with Him will be pierced and convicted often by the Holy Spirit as to those behaviors and actions in their lives that they need to confess. God is our intimate Creator, who understands us better than we know ourselves. He longs that we reach our God-given potential by living in a holy way. However, we should always be aware that God will hold us accountable for the un-confessed excesses and addictions in our own lives. Sometimes it takes a hard fall before leaders confess these types of sins to God and others.

Doing God's will in your life should be your highest and only addiction. Desiring to serve Him and fellowship with Him as you lead others each day should be all you need to bring satisfaction. Go to God in prayer and seek His help in reconfiguring your lifestyle with new purity. As your bad habits fade, you will be released into richer communion with a Lord who longs to have you completely.

Our Prayer: *Lord God, we confess our excesses and addictions of this life to You this day. Take charge of our minds and hearts and bodies. Forgive us when we have let seeking pleasure or practicing bad habits hurt our mission of faith or fellowship with You. Heal us and guide us as we strive to live purer and more holy lives.* **Amen.**

Not Lords, But Examples

"Great Leaders Lead Not by Power or Might, But by Example"

"Feed the flock of God which is among you, taking the oversight thereof, not by constraint, but willingly; not for filthy lucre, but of a ready mind; Neither as being lords over God's heritage, but being examples to the flock."

Featured Scripture: 1 Peter 5:2–3
Background Scriptures: 1 Peter 5:1–11; and 1 Timothy 3

Along with leadership positions usually come real power of authority and access to privileged information. With power and knowledge that others don't have, it becomes easy for a leader to manipulate or otherwise compel people to act. Peter set forth a list of what duties an elder or leader of faith should perform. Even though we may have a special calling, anointing, or ordination of faith and power, we should lead others in humility, not as lords, but by the example of how we live and work among those who follow us.

We are to feed the flock as a good shepherd. Leaders of faith are given a flock of followers for which to care. Some leaders are given nations to lead. Some leaders are given children to lead. Some leaders are given families to lead. Some leaders are given a flock of parishioners or constituents to lead. Whatever our flocks may be, we are first and foremost to meet their physical and spiritual needs. We are never to take advantage of them, and we are to walk among them setting the standard of good and ethical living.

Christ was the Good Shepherd. When the crowds followed Him into the countryside to hear Him preach and they became hungry, He fed them. When He encountered the lame, the blind, and the bereaved, He healed and comforted them. When He encountered the moneychangers and sinners, He called for repentance and forgave sins. When His own flock abandoned Him, He prayed and interceded for them. Like Christ, leaders of faith must pour themselves into their flocks, giving up their own well-being and privileges to the point of pain. A crown of reward awaits them in due time if they remain faithful to this call.

How can you change your behavior today to be a better example to those you lead? Can you give up an entitlement or perk? Can you arrive at work early and stay later? Can you value each person you meet in a new way today, striving to discern a hurt or need they may be holding? God gives grace to the humble leader of faith who pours his life into service to the flock. The less lord-like we are, and the more servant-like we become, the greater our effectiveness will be as leaders. God is watching and rewards such good shepherding. He says to cast our cares upon Him, for He cares for us. Our Good Shepherd was Lord indeed, but He showed us how to serve by His example. Let us strive to emulate Him and do likewise, not as lords, but by example.

Our Prayer: *Lord God, create in us humble spirits and shepherding instincts as we strive to care for those You have given to us in leadership. Help us to walk among them, leading by example. Let us pour ourselves out in faithful service, never claiming privilege of position or coercing others with wrong intent. We cast all our cares and concerns on You Lord, for we know that You care for us. Give us the strength to lead others.* **Amen.**

All In Good Time

"The Fruit and Blessing from Good Leadership Is Revealed in God's Time"

"Knowing that shortly I must put off this my tabernacle, even as our Lord Jesus Christ hath shewed me. Moreover I will endeavor that ye may be able after my decease to have these things always in remembrance…. But, beloved, be not ignorant of this one thing, that one day is with the Lord as a thousand years, and a thousand years as one day. The Lord is not slack concerning his promise…but is longsuffering towards us, not willing that any should perish, but that all come to repentance."

FEATURED SCRIPTURES: 2 PETER 1:14–15; AND 2 PETER 3:8–9
BACKGROUND SCRIPTURES: 2 PETER 1:12–21; 2 PETER 3:1–13; AND PSALM 90:4

The apostle Peter wrote this letter to believers just before his death. Peter would be martyred; his life was coming to an end. Even still, Peter was encouraging and instructing believers in the fundamentals of the faith. Moreover, Peter left a lesson for leaders of faith to learn and understand. Any good work that is called and ordained by God will be revealed in God's good time. The fulfillment of God's promises is revealed in God's time, not ours.

Often leaders of faith get discouraged when their labor and work does not seem to bear fruit or show clear signs of success. However, Peter is telling us today to be faithful and humble to the task we have been called to do. God will fulfill His perfect plan through the imperfect hands of the servants He has called. Peter was on the verge of death and would not live to see the explosive and expansive growth of the faith as a result of his work and writings. Yet Peter knew that God would manifest it all in His perfect time.

We should never let the prospect of unrealized success stop us from answering a call to leadership. Leaders may cultivate and plant without ever seeing the fruit or harvest of their efforts. Leaders of faith must succumb to the call of an eternal, timeless God, who makes all work of faith perfect in time. Like Peter, we may come to the end of our lives wondering what will be the real effects of our lifetime of work. We may go to our deaths without realizing the final pinnacle of success we hoped to achieve. But God gives us comfort as He promises all good works survive the fire of the end time of judgment.

Be faithful to the task to which you have been called. Don't let the lack of tangible achievement keep you from giving your all to God each day. Don't let others steal your dreams or discourage you with defeatism or regret. All works performed and prayers made in the purity of God's calling and through the love of Christ shall be reserved and redeemed in God's eternal glory.

Our Prayer: *God without beginning and without end, we bow humbly before You today and leave our works on Your altar. We know that Your time is not our time. Lord, help us to know that all deeds we do in Your name will be redeemed in eternity. Help us not to be discouraged or fainthearted as we labor each day in the vineyard where You called us to work. Let our struggles unleash light and salvation to others.* **Amen.**

The Fellowship Of Leadership

"A New Fellowship with God and Others Is Available to Leaders"

"That which we have seen and heard declare we unto you, that ye also may have fellowship with us…. But if we walk in the light, as he is in the light, we have fellowship one with another, and the blood of Jesus Christ his Son cleanseth us from all sin."

FEATURED SCRIPTURE: 1 JOHN 1:3, 7
BACKGROUND SCRIPTURES: 1 JOHN 1:1–7; ACTS 2:41–47; AND GALATIANS 2:9–10

With leadership callings of faith come challenges, tribulations, and a lonely sense of burden. Being called by God to leadership of any type is an awesome and daunting adventure. Our love for God and our desire to please Him can overwhelm even the strongest among us. But God sends a great gift to leaders of faith. It is called the fellowship of leadership. Not only does God enter into a more free-flowing daily fellowship with those He calls, but He also brings others into our lives to comfort, challenge, and encourage us.

Fellowship with other leaders is one of the most important activities we can undertake. Leaders of faith should always seek ways in which to meet and share time with those who have also been called to journeys of faith. Often we feel alone and discouraged in our daily challenges. It can be a great relief and comfort to hear the chuckle of another leader who has experienced the same problems and sailed through the storms. Elders and veterans will frequently offer to become special mentors and counselors to us, and we can learn from their experiences.

Be proactive to find a fellowship of leadership. Register for seminars and training sessions. Reach out to strangers. If you are a specialized leader, pastor, officer, or volunteer leader, locate the organizations and support groups you can attend. Never fail to pull aside a leader you admire and confide in them. God may have placed that very person in your path to help you solve a problem. Pray that God will send you new friends and colleagues who can nurture you.

The richest portion of the fellowship of leadership is the deepening friendship you can develop with our Lord. Jesus says if we keep His commandments, we are no longer His servants, but His friends! As you remain in fellowship with God, you can hear Him constantly whispering words of help and encouragement in your ear. God will always send the right people and circumstances into your life to validate His presence. So claim the fellowship of leadership. Let God bless you in a new way this very day.

Our Prayer: *Jesus, we praise You for choosing us for service in Your Kingdom. We know the trail of leadership will be long and hard. We pray for new fellowship in our leadership. Send friends, mentors, and blessings our way each day to equip and encourage us. We long for a deeper and more personal fellowship with You, Jesus. Open our hearts and minds so we can enter into Your love and fellowship in richer ways.* **Amen.**

Deed-And-Truth Leadership

"The Truth Is Manifested by Love and Deed, Not Empty Words"

"My little children, let us not love in word, neither in tongue; but in deed and in truth. And hereby we know that we are of the truth, and shall assure our hearts before him."

Featured Scripture: 1 John 3:18–19
Background Scripture: 2 Corinthians 4: 2; 13:7–10

Some persons exude truthfulness. By their countenance and by their reputation, you know that the truth lies within them. If they make a promise, they will keep it or fess up to the facts before them. The way of Christ became the truth. Jesus said, *"You shall know the truth and the truth shall make you free"* (John 8:32). For leaders of faith, the truth is not just the reality of a situation or a kept word or promise: the truth is a purity of purpose and life, of which no one should ever be ashamed. We must practice deed-and-truth leadership as our actions and lives exemplify the truth that is within us.

The apostle Paul has told us to renounce the things of dishonesty and craftiness. We are not to not handle the Word of God deceitfully. The truth is the truth. It is constant. It is honest and pure. We cannot pervert the truth without it finding us out. The truth is sent by God to edify, not to destroy.

In leadership circles, the falseness and manipulation of the ambitious will always be uncovered. Power, authority, position, and rank are aphrodisiacs that certainly attract the weak of heart to assault the truth for personal gain. Leaders of faith who are seekers and bearers of the truth are subject to be attacked when they defend the truth. Deed-and-truth leadership may make you look foolish to those around you. To harbor the truth in light of the reality of circumstances in an imperfect world may seem naïve and foolhardy. Some will tell you that to defend the truth at all costs and not bend to pragmatism is to endanger your organization.

All who stay the course of leadership over time will be confronted with those who bend the truth and shave the edges off the love and purity of our callings. This is when prayer and courage are needed. This is when the God of our calling checks our very constitution. Sometimes we ourselves have succumbed to shaving the truth, only to see others hurt. We can be forgiven, but we must return to the core of deed-and-truth leadership.

The truth is our light. It is our release of burden and guilt. Truth serves to edify, cleanse, and empower others to do God's will. The truth heals pain and is the jar of the salve of forgiveness and grace. Let your deeds reflect the truth that is in us all through the Spirit of Christ Himself.

Our Prayer: *Lord, let the truth be in us always. Let the truth be our light, and may that light be reflected in our deeds and words. Give us the fortitude and power to overcome the darkness of evil and deceit. Let our lives and leadership journeys reflect Your love and the truth of God's holiness and plan for us.* **Amen.**

Loving Those We Lead

"Leaders of Faith Are Leaders Who Love Others"

"Beloved, let us love one another: for love is of God; and every one that loveth is born of God, and knoweth God.... No man hath seen God at any time. If we love one another, God dwelleth in us, and his love is perfected in us.... If a man say, I love God, and hateth his brother, he is a liar.... And this commandment have we from him, That he who loveth God love his brother also."

Featured Scriptures: 1 John 4:7, 12, 20, 21
Background Scripture: 1 John 4:7–21

The ability to love others is the litmus test that proves God dwells in us. Leaders of faith are leaders who love others. Loving those we lead is not always easy. People can become boisterous and confrontational. Some who follow us wish secretly that we would fail, and they may even quietly work toward our demise. Loving those of us who are hard to love, and loving through adversity, is the truest sign that God has called us to a task of heavenly regard.

The apostle John was the "love author" of the New Testament. He wrote that the nature of God was that God is love. It is the essence of our theology. We love others because God's love and presence is in us and overwhelms all that we do. Unconditional love is found throughout the ministry of Christ. Even in Christ's dying moment, He asked God to forgive His tormentors because "*they know not what they do*" (Luke 23:34). Love begins with respecting and valuing the worth and dignity of every individual we encounter. Love begins with an acknowledgment that God created us all in His image and is no respecter of persons.

Leaders who love are not leaders who are soft. We live in a world of laws and rules. Leaders must adhere to and enforce proper codes of conduct. To love means to chasten, discipline, and instruct. But to exude God's love in our daily actions is to wield enormous power over every situation. Those who are motivated out of hatred and revenge shall surely fail. Those who are motivated out of selfish gain and constant partisan advantage shall fail. When leaders are anointed with God's love, to the point that it motivates all they do, people will sense it and follow them in extraordinary ways.

Soldiers on a battlefield give an extra measure of bravery and commitment to commanders who love and respect them. Congregants will go an extra mile in service for others when led by a pastor who loves them. Employees stay late at the office to complete a task for a boss who loves and values them. No measure of leadership training can match a leader who loves his or her followers. Abide in God's love as you lead. Pray for the strength to love the mean-spirited or your enemies. God is love. And as we truly love those we lead, others will see God in us.

Our Prayer: *God, You are love. Your essence and being exist in love. We love because You first loved us. You command us to love our neighbors as ourselves. Create in us, O Lord, an even greater capacity to love. We pray for the strength to love those who are hard to love. We pray for the courage and boldness to lead others in love and to bless others with an outpouring of Your love that flows through us.* **Amen.**

Bold, Fearless Leaders Driven By Love

"WHEN YOUR CALLING IS MOTIVATED BY LOVE FOR OTHERS, YOU ARE READY"

"No man hath seen God at any time. If we love one another, God dwelleth in us, and his love is perfected in us…. Herein is our love made perfect, that we may have boldness in the day of judgment: because as he is, so are we in this world. There is no fear in love; but perfect love casteth out fear: because fear hath torment. He that feareth is not perfect in love."

Featured Scripture: 1 John 4:12, 17–18
BACKGROUND SCRIPTURE: 1 JOHN 4

Many persons will feel the soft calling of God to leadership. For some, it seems as if they are haunted by the need to step out and do something in God's name. Many recruits to the leadership journey of faith have trouble knowing when is the right time to begin. Part of that answer may lie in the words penned by the apostle John.

When we no longer harbor a fear of failure, a fear of the unknown, or a fear of lack of provision for our journey, we may be ready. If these feelings are fed from a wellspring of love for God and our fellow man, and if those motivations are driven by a passion and love for the hurting, the profane, and the innocent, then love is being perfected in us and we are ready to begin. Perfect love casts out fear and makes us bold in fulfilling our calls.

When we embark on tasks for God, our love for Him and those we serve exudes out of us. Others will see the passion and sense of purpose we hold. By reaching out to and empowering the least among us, we wield heavenly power through Christ's example of love. Our boldness and fearlessness will disarm our foes, for they will sense we have something they don't have.

Leaders of faith are leaders of love. To remain in perfect love is challenging, but it is possible. We must remain grounded in love through fellowship with other believers. We must study the Scriptures and find new ways each day to encounter God. Jesus said if we seek Him each day, we shall surely find Him. We will always find God in the innocence and playfulness of children. We will find God when we practice random acts of kindness to strangers and see their reactions.

Practicing perfect love also means that we allow others to love us. We must open up, share, and even allow ourselves to become open to the constructive criticism of our peers. Perfect love also means stable lives at home. Let us renew our relationships with family members, spouses, and special friends. Perfect love means forgiving and asking for forgiveness.

The boldness and fearlessness of a leader of faith driven by perfect love may be the most powerful force for good on earth. If you feel this way today, go to work. If you are still lacking, keep praying and perfecting love. Keep your eyes upon Jesus and your cup will fill quickly.

Our Prayer: *Dear Lord, perfect Your love in us. Help us to love others even in difficult circumstances. Let our love eliminate fear and make us bold for the tasks You set before us to do. Help us to constantly seek Christ and walk in His blueprint of love.* **Amen.**

The Elect Lady And Her Call

"THE TRUTH OF OUR CALLING IS NOT A NEW COMMAND, BUT A TIMELESS ONE"

"The elder unto the elect lady and her children, whom I love in the truth.... And now I beseech thee, lady, not as though I wrote a new commandment unto thee, but that which we had from the beginning, that we love one another."

FEATURED SCRIPTURE: 2 JOHN 1, 5
BACKGROUND SCRIPTURE: THE BOOK OF 2 JOHN

Leaders of faith who feel they have been called to a high and holy task often complicate the purpose and meaning of their callings. When the elect of God sense the enormity of a particular task, they can put too much complexity into its mystery. But the truth of the calling of God's elect is always simple and plain: that we love one another.

John knew that God was love. Christ told us to love God with all our hearts and to love our neighbors as ourselves. This is the first and greatest commandment. Love toward others is the defining characteristic of the called leader. Leaders of faith who are truly walking in the call and purpose of God will exude love in all their thoughts, plans, intentions, and actions. The love they share toward others will prove that they are indeed the "elect lady" whom God has called.

The "elect lady" also represents our congregations and organizations. Our institutions should abide in simplicity by loving one another. This is not always easy. Sometimes it is easier to love the poor and dying far away than it is to love the disruptive team members working alongside us. It may be easier to love a competitor and rival than it is to love a superior whom we feel is not as competent as we are. While the old commandment to love one another is basic, timeless, and true, God knows that loving one another requires prayer, forgiveness, humility, and submission.

What are you doing as a leader to instill the call to love one another in your daily activities? How do you resolve conflict, and how do you keep those you lead from becoming too greedy and selfishly ambitious? As the leader of God's "elect lady," you must constantly stay focused on Christ, the Redeemer, who taught us how to love in a new way. He taught us to love our enemies and to deny ourselves and take up the cross daily. He taught us to grasp hold of suffering for His sake.

Even the most cantankerous and disruptive persons in our midst cannot resist the unlimited love of a leader who insists on overcoming evil with good each day. When we were called to leadership, we were not given a new set of commandments to follow. We were simply called to serve others in God's love. This love will conquer all and cover our leadership mistakes. Loving one another is the highest calling of any leader of faith. So go and love and serve and lead.

Our Prayer: *Lord Jesus, You taught us how to love in a new and eternal way. Instill in us the heart and power to love in all circumstances. May we and those You have given us to lead work each day with a renewed sense of love toward You and our neighbors. Forgive us when we have let selfishness or bitterness take us off course. Teach us anew how to love one another.* **Amen.**

Culling Connivers Is Part Of Leadership

"STRIPPING AUTHORITY FROM THOSE WHO SOW EVIL IN OUR ORGANIZATIONS"

"I wrote unto the church: but Diotrephes, who loveth to have the preeminence among them, received us not. Wherefore, if I come, I will remember his deeds which he doeth, prating against us with malicious words: and not content therewith, neither doth he himself receive the brethren, and forbiddeth them that would, and casteth them out of the church. Beloved, follow not that which is evil, but that which is good. He that doeth good is of God: but he that doeth evil hath not seen God."

FEATURED SCRIPTURE: 3 JOHN 9–11
BACKGROUND SCRIPTURE: THE BOOK OF 3 JOHN

Every leader of faith encounters the same situation as did the early Christians and their leaders. The apostle John wrote Gaius about being generous to those who are in the Church and to those traveling teachers. But even more, John was writing to set the record straight about Diotrephes, a person who had become a conniving and insolent influence to the detriment of the church family of Gaius.

Diotrephes had become cancerous to the organization, and John was using his leadership authority to address it. He wrote that we will know true persons of God by their works. If their works are good works, they are of God, but if their works are evil works, they are not of God. Evidently, Diotrophes had taken over the reins of this church by kicking out the teachers and not providing a loving welcome and sanctuary to the elect of God. His malicious and false chatter about John and the other leaders of the faith was not giving a true testimony of love of the Lord.

When we as leaders spot these same cancerous dissensions in our organizations, we must be strong and resolute to confront the connivers who would destroy the work of God. John wanted us to notice the self-conceit and evil works of our own Diotrepheses for ourselves. Those who are commended by others and speak the truth in all things are those whom we should follow.

John began this letter by sending good wishes to his fellow workers in the faith and an exhortation of his love and joy for their success. He encouraged them for walking in the truth of the Lord and commended them as "fellow helpers to the truth." John not only admonished Diotrephes, but he was certain to be a positive mentor first and foremost.

As a leader of faith, you, too, will come face-to-face with your own Diotrephes. The confrontation may be uncomfortable, but it is necessary to remove the evil influences from our ministries. The spirit and brotherhood of service can be very fragile, and we must cull the connivers in order to be true leaders in God's service.

Our Prayer: *Dear Lord, thank You for the apostle John and the many saints of the early Church who endured so much to keep the faith alive and to spread the Good News. Strengthen and embolden us as leaders of faith to identify the evil connivers of our own organizations who would try to wreck our witness. Help us to be discerning and bold to do what has to be done.* **Amen.**

Dealing With Evil Antagonists Appropriately

"Real Leaders Offer Simple Rebukes and Stay in a Spirit of Love"

"Yet Michael, the archangel, when contending with the devil he disputed about the body of Moses, durst not bring against him a railing accusation, but said, The Lord rebuke you…. But ye, beloved, building up yourselves on your most holy faith, praying in the Holy Ghost, keep yourselves in the love of God, looking for the mercy of our Lord Jesus Christ unto eternal life."

Featured Scripture: Jude 9, 20–21
Background Scripture: The Book of Jude

Jude, the brother of James, was a leader in the early Church in Jerusalem. He wrote a short book on the subject of false teachers who had sprung up amidst the growth of the early Church and were presenting challenges to its leaders.

False teachers were perverting the faith by redefining the material and spiritual realms. They were aggressively attempting to discredit the apostolic authority of the leaders of Christ's Body. Jude gave leaders of faith sound advice as to how to deal with antagonists appropriately. By heeding the advice of Jude, we may salvage our own fledgling leadership journeys.

We must first understand that false leaders will arise and claim our authority from time to time. Be ready for it. False teachers can be both subtle and corrosive or loud and confrontational. They may hatch and grow from within your own organization or they may come from the outside. Leaders of faith who bring the values of their own faith-based life experiences to a leadership task should be most able to spot false leaders. False leaders will attempt to undermine your God-given authority. They will promise to lead others with motivations based solely on their own lusts and vanity for power.

Jude speaks of gossipers, complainers, those who walk after their own lusts, and those whose mouths speak flattery to gain advantage over others. Have you met these persons in your leadership journey? Sure, you have, and you will encounter them all along the way.

When we encounter antagonists, we are simply to rebuke them in Christ's Spirit. Stay focused on Christ's call to purity. Constantly reevaluate your own motives in every leadership situation so that you are grounded in God's purposes and not your own. Pray fervently in the Holy Spirit, watch for Christ's mercy, and keep yourself bathed in God's love. Let all your service to others be grounded in selfless love and sacrifice.

To argue with or to validate the false and evil leaders of our day with too much direct confrontation sucks us into their vortex of evil. Being confrontational with antagonists can poison our hearts and harm our good witness. Even the archangel Michael knew the power of a simple rebuke of the Lord to the devil. Michael placed God's purposes first, as do we.

Our Prayer: *God, help us as leaders of faith to stay focused on the love and mercy seat of Christ. Help us to recognize false teachers and leaders who would pervert the nobleness of leadership for evil purposes. Help us to rebuke them in Your Spirit and to stay on Your course of service in prayer and love.* **Amen.**

When We Lose Our First Love

"Finding Our First Love or Risking Failure"

"Nevertheless I have somewhat against thee, because thou hast left thy first love. Remember therefore from whence thou art fallen, and repent, and do the first works; or else I will come unto thee quickly, and will remove the candlestick out of his place, except thou repent."

Featured Scripture: Revelation 2:4–5
Background Scriptures: Revelation 2:1–7; Ephesians 1:15–16

In Revelation 2 and 3, the apostle John wrote what Jesus Christ told him in their supernatural encounter, especially regarding the seven churches and their spiritual condition. Scholars take different positions about whether these instructions were allegorical and prophetic or were a true description of actual conditions in these actual seven churches.

What is clear is that while the church at Ephesus was doing good work, keeping the faith, and rooting out evildoers in their midst, the Lord sensed that they had abandoned their first works of eagerness, devotion, and love. Those works were the earliest trademarks of the Church. This church was functioning, but it had lost the zeal that made it truly special…it had lost the passion of its first love.

How often we see leaders and organizations that outwardly appear to be doing the work and mission they are responsible to do, but in reality, they have lost the inner passion and spark that brought them into power and service in the first place. In the years since their startup, something happened to dampen their devotion to their first love. It was substituted by other things.

A lost first love may be the loss of enthusiasm of your original calling to help others. It may be a lack of love and passion for helping the poor and hurting souls you used to see around you. A lost first love may be a loss of discipline and your failure to put in the long hours of extra effort for those you serve. Your first love can turn into drudgery and task-oriented monotony unless you are able to rekindle that God-inspired eagerness and boundless drive that launched you upon our original leadership journey of faith.

Jesus told the church at Ephesus to take an inward look, to admit that they had fallen short, and to repent of this condition. They were commanded to find their first love again. If they were able to overcome their loss of direction and rekindle their first love, all while doing the work they were already doing, Christ would bless them and allow them to eat of the Tree of Life.

If we as leaders of faith can confess when we, too, are burned out and have lost our first love, and if we seek God's grace to find it again, we can reignite the passion of our first love and serve with a new vigor. Organizations with leaders of faith and vision can do the same. Rekindle your first love and start anew. God is ready to bless you if you try.

Our Prayer: *Lord Jesus, even in the midst of our day-to-day leadership journeys, we can lose our first love. Help us to repent from the external influences that can so easily substitute themselves for true zeal and passion for service. Give us the strength to know when we have lost our first love and how to find it again.* **Amen.**

Lukewarm Leadership

"CHRIST REQUIRES PASSION, CONVICTION, AND LOYALTY FROM THOSE HE CALLS"

"I know thy works, that thou art neither cold nor hot: I wish you were cold or hot. So then because thou art lukewarm, and neither cold nor hot, I will spew thee out of my mouth."

FEATURED SCRIPTURE: REVELATION 3:15-16
BACKGROUND SCRIPTURE: REVELATION 3:14–22

The glorified Christ spoke these words through John to the church at Laodicea being quite clear about lukewarm followers of the faith. Christ preferred either a cold or a hot follower to the lukewarm believer who was blessed with the message but was blind and comfortable in the practicing of the faith. Contented and self-congratulatory leaders of faith will be spewed from God's providence.

Complacency in leadership can lull a congregation of followers into a false sense of security and stifle their fervor for God. We may be resting on our past accomplishments or spending too much time enjoying our wealth and earthly comforts. Leaders of faith are called to holy tasks that require immediacy and constant passion. We must constantly step out of our comfort zones for God. Lukewarm leaders become useless to God. They have a high calling, but they can become compromising and timid. If our days are too calm, we may be becoming lukewarm. Our works should be hot and bold and pushing new boundaries every day.

Leaders of faith set the tone and mood in organizations. When leaders are passionate, convicted, and full of loyalty to the mission, those we lead become infected with that same emotion. We are all guilty of lukewarm performance from time to time. If we are lukewarm leaders of faith, God will rebuke and chasten us back into shape because He loves us and wants us to have new fire for His service every day of our lives. He knocks on the door of our hearts each day, calling us out of our comfort zones and into the streets of service to others. Jesus knows our enormous potential to do great things for the Kingdom of God. Lukewarm leaders don't give the best testimony, nor do they do the best work in a world that is dying and in need of urgent care. Are you feeling lukewarm in your leadership journey? Are you dragging yourself out of bed each morning to begrudgingly tackle the problems and opportunities of the day? We should confess our lukewarm hearts to God. Christ wants to come into our lives and give us new excitement and passion for life again.

Let Christ turn your lukewarm leadership into a journey with new dreams and new goals. Let Him discipline your mind and body to get you into great mental and physical shape. Cast your spiritual complacency upon the throne of God and let Him transform you into an exciting leader again. God needs passionate leaders who yearn to rescue the perishing and care for the dying of this world. He will reward your passion, conviction, and loyalty as you boldly step out in faith today.

Our Prayer: *Jesus, make me come alive again with a fire and zeal to serve You and others. You chasten and rebuke me because You love me and want me to move from lukewarm leadership to passionate discipleship. Never let me rest on my past accomplishments or wait for the potential promises of the future. Help me serve You this day in a newness and freshness that will motivate and inspire others to find and serve You, as well.* **Amen.**

He Who Is Worthy Has Already Secured Our Future

ALL HEAVEN ATTESTS TO OUR LORD'S POWER AND OUR DELIVERANCE

"And they sung a new song, saying, Thou art worthy to take the book, and to open the seals thereof: for thou was slain, and hast redeemed us to God by thy blood out of every kindred, and tongue, and people, and nation; and hast made us unto our God kings and priests: and we shall reign on earth. And I beheld, and I heard the voice of many angels round the throne and the beasts and the elders: and the number of them was ten thousand times ten thousand, and thousands of thousands…"

FEATURED SCRIPTURE: REVELATION 5:9-11
BACKGROUND SCRIPTURE: REVELATION 5 AND MATTHEW 11:28

Try to fathom the sound of 100 million angels singing together a new song of glory to our Lord. Our Scripture today describes for us in detail this event and the unimaginable majesty and power of Christ. These verses reveal that the Lord who called us to lead is truly worthy of our full service, sacrifice and life. Jesus redeemed us and made us His partners in the heavenly purpose, so our future is now secured. Our life's work for the Lamb of God should reflect the same awe and worship that is displayed by the angelic heavenly choir.

There are many theological interpretations of the Book of Revelation; however, there can be no dispute about how the apostle John saw Christ in His glory and power. Too often we narrowly connote an image of Christ as the Baby Jesus in the manger, or, as the crucified Son of God at Golgotha. But our lesson today calls each of us to envision Christ in His eternal regality and to know that the power of the throne of God is freely available to each of us as called leaders of faith.

Our life and journey on this earth are tough. As we venture out into the streets each day to begin our work, we witness man's inhumanity to his neighbor, as well as an endless stream of human need and brokenness. Yet, our hope for the future should always reflect the certainty of our victorious outcome, even as we attempt to love and serve the hurting souls around us.

What challenge do you face today? Do you need to hear a choir of angels sing? *"He Who Is Worthy"* is also our own personal Savior who bids that we come to Him and give Him our weariness and heartbreak. Not only will He give us rest, but power. Always be mindful, not only of the eternal blessings already stored up for you, but of the power and provision Christ makes available for you this very day.

If you will start singing praises to the Lamb this day, then the angels will join you; because we are all part of that same great victory. So let us go and share that victory and the love and salvation of *He Who is Worthy* with those we encounter this day.

Our Prayer: *Worthy are You O Lord! In awe and praise we lift our hearts and voices to You this very day. With thanksgiving we come into Your presence and ask for the strength and provision to finish the earthly tasks that You have given us to do. We anxiously wait for that hour when we will join the choir of angels in heaven and sing new songs of praise to You.* **Amen.**

Patience Of The Saints

"Saints of God Will See Justice and the Fruits of Their Labor in Eternity"

"Here is the patience of the saints: here are they that keep the commandments of God, and the faith of Jesus. And I heard a voice from heaven saying unto me, Write, Blessed are the dead which die in the Lord from henceforth: Yea, saith the Spirit, that they may rest from their labors; and their works do follow them…. He that leadeth into captivity shall go into captivity: he that killeth with the sword must be killed with the sword. Here is the patience and the faith of the saints."

Featured Scripture: Revelation 14:12, 13; 13:10
Background Scriptures: Revelation 13:1–10; 14:9–13; and Hebrews 4:1–10

Some leaders of faith are called by God to lead in the toughest of times, places, and circumstances. Many leaders become martyrs or captives, or see gross acts of inhumanity perpetrated on the innocent people given to their care. Many leaders don't live long enough to see the fruits of their labor or justice done to their tormentors and enemies. But Christ tells us that if we are faithful and patient to keep His commandments, our work will follow us, and all the unrighteous who have hurt us will receive their just reward.

Patience requires that we go faithfully about the work of our calling in all circumstances. We may not see the results we desire each day, and we may very well see violence done against those we love. The voice from heaven told the apostle John to write the words of Revelation to give comfort to the saints. Go boldly forward this day with your work. Keep God's commandments. Love your friends and your enemies. Do unto others as you would have them do unto you. Serve the Lord with gladness even in your dire condition. Eternal power is at work in you this day.

The fear of many leaders is that they will go to their grave without seeing success or having wasted precious time facing overwhelming odds. Christ has said to let that fear go. Be obedient and never doubt. Those who torment God's people will perish with the very ferocity by which they have pursued you. Many missionaries worked years without seeing a convert. Many battlefield warriors never saw the victory they desired before falling by the sword. Many parents and pastors never live long enough to see the children and parishioners they raise and counsel become servants of Christ.

Many leaders may be imprisoned or maimed at life's end. Many leaders may become impoverished or incapacitated and never see fruit or blooms from their life's work. God tells us to not worry. In eternity we will see them. Our love of others and the small deeds we do in Christ's name are heavenly building blocks. Our fervent prayers have moved spiritual mountains we cannot see today. By turning the other cheek and praying for those who spitefully use us, we may have released angelic powers against evil. We will learn of it in our eternal rest. Don't become weary in following your call to Christ's service. The victory has been won. Rewards, justice, and peaceful rest await us in Christ's New Jerusalem.

Our Prayer: *Lord Jesus, praise and honor be given to You! The victory has already been won. Give us the strength to endure the trials and torture of this day, and may we obediently serve You in thought, word, and deed. Even when we cannot see the fruits of our work or justice done for the innocent in this life, let us keep leading others in faith and the assurance of Your promise to us. Give us a new confidence that all we do and all we endure for Your name's sake will be revealed and bring glory to You.* **Amen.**

Leading Through Song, Instrument, And Dance

"Raising Heart, Voice, Sound, and Movement in Leadership Praise to God"

"And they sing the song of Moses the servant of God, and the song of the Lamb, saying, Great and marvelous are thy works Lord God Almighty…. Praise him with the sound of the trumpet: praise him with the psaltery and harp. Praise him with the timbrel and dance: praise him with stringed instruments and organs. Praise him upon the loud cymbals: praise him upon the high sounding cymbals."

Featured Scriptures: Revelation 15:3; and Psalm 150:3–5
Background Scriptures: Exodus 15:2; Psalm 33:3; Lamentations 3:63; and 1 Samuel 16:14–23

Leading through song, instrument, and dance is found throughout the Scriptures, and the use of these arts as a form of leadership is ordained by God. They have a very special place for leaders of faith. Only certain leaders are called and gifted with the ability to lead in this way. Leaders without these gifts are wise to bring into their organizations and congregations the best artists and musicians possible.

Before David was the king of Israel, he was a harpist who soothed the torment of King Saul. Revelation 15:3 depicts the martyrs in heaven who are singing the song of Moses and the Lamb. The very praise of the heavenly throne is basked in sounds of music and song. The holy exhortation to leaders of faith is for us to sing a new song of faith.

The Psalms are full of leadership in worship and praise by way various instruments. True praise and worship of God would be difficult without the use of sound and movement. Some of the great messages of theology over many centuries have been shared through the pens and instruments used to create the great hymns of faith. Leaders of faith should be mindful to always lift up the traditions of hymns, liturgy, and instruments in times of praise and worship. The simple remembrance of a sacred hymn that is sung in a low voice in the early or late hours of a day can bring refreshment and new courage to our tasks.

Leaders of faith should always recognize the power that sound and movement have to unite the people we are called to lead. The singing of songs and the playing of instruments have a way of drowning out loud voices of discontent and feuding. Dance can eliminate the need to argue.

Great leaders should include in their repertoire of leadership tools the God-ordained use of song, instrument, and dance. Use them wisely and often in the performance of your heavenly calling. We can look forward to these same sounds and movements in our heavenly home!

Our Prayer: *Lord God, how often our hearts have been stirred by the sounds and movements of song and dance done in praise of You. Thank You for the gifts of song and instrument and dance. Give us the wisdom as leaders of faith to use them often and wisely in the execution of our tasks of calling for You.* **Amen.**

Angels And Fellow Servants

"Never Worship or Give Holy Praise to Any But God"

"And after these things I saw another angel come down from heaven, having great power; and the earth was lightened with his glory…. And I fell at his feet to worship him. And he said unto me, See thou do it not: I am thy fellow servant, and of thy brethren that have testimony of Jesus: worship God: for the testimony of Jesus is the spirit of prophecy."

Featured Scripture: Revelation 18:1; and 19:10
Background Scriptures: Revelation 18—19:16; and Acts 10:24–27

The apostle John's natural instinct upon encountering the angel of proclamation was to fall down and worship him. The angel, though beautiful, powerful, and shining with heaven's glory, was quick to correct John and bring the worship back to God. As called leaders of God, we are fellow servants with the angels. We are to worship no one except for our Lord alone. The apostles of the early Church also were put into predicaments of mistaken worship. When the apostle Peter encountered Cornelius, the man dropped and bowed before him in worship. Peter, the Rock of the Church and full of apostolic authority, quickly told Cornelius to stop and rise back to his feet. Worship only God, he told him, for they were both but men.

As leaders of faith, we will encounter holy and powerful persons. We may work with heroes and heroines of the faith. We may walk with evangelists, pastors, kings, prime ministers, and celebrities. We, too, may encounter an angel or a person overflowing with the power of the Holy Spirit. But we are not to fall into worshipful adoration of any being other than our Lord God. Our spiritual leaders and mentors are merely our fellow servants. We are all created for and called to give our praise to God alone.

Though we may not bow down before the holy and powerful, we must never allow ourselves to become too spiritually attached to those around us. We can and should harbor respect for and be subject to the earthly authority of those ordained above us. But save all your worship and praise for God. Regardless of how humble a task we have been called to do, it is the Lord God who has called us to His service. Beware of the beauty, glory and pageantry of power. It can take us from admiration to adoration.

Likewise, we as successful leaders must never let others hold us in too high of esteem. We want others' respect and should humbly be thankful for recognition and limited privileges, but we must never let others serve us with glowing adoration. Our own humility and commitment to serve and worship God alone should be our best example as leaders.

When angels, leaders, and followers together become servants of the Most High God, all praise and adoration rightly flows to the throne of God. Egos, jealousy, and dissension melt in our shared worship of our Creator. Strive in your own congregation and organization to bring both humans and angels into worship of an awesome God.

Our Prayer: *Our Lord and our God, You alone are worthy of our praise and worship. Never let us get so enamored with the majesty of power and glory of other holy servants that we give them any adoration that is Yours alone. Help us as leaders of faith to guard against letting any follower or friend to worship or adore us. Let us set an example of humility and focus all those around us on Your Throne.* **Amen.**

Faithful And True And Afflicted With Us

"Christ Shares Our Afflictions in All Ages unto Victory"

"And I saw heaven opened, and behold a white horse; and he that sat upon him was called Faithful and True, and in righteousness he doth judge and make war... In all their affliction he was afflicted, and the angel of his presence saved them: in his love and in his pity he redeemed them; and he bare them, and carried them all the days of old…. For our light affliction, which is but for a moment, worketh for us a far more exceeding and eternal weight of glory.…"

Featured Scriptures: Revelation 19:11; Isaiah 63:9; and 2 Corinthians 4:17
Background Scriptures: Revelation 1:5; 3:7; 19:11–16; and 2 Corinthians 4:13-18

In all times and in all ways, the Son of God has been in our midst both sharing our afflictions and bringing us eternal victory. Christ was present in world events from Genesis to Revelation, whether appearing first as the angel of the Lord to Hagar, or as the angel of His presence to Isaiah the prophet, or as Faithful and True to John in the vision of His Second Coming. And Christ is present with us even now. He is actively involved in the challenges of our callings of faith and has gone before us to prepare the victory.

Whatever your calling may be, and wherever that calling takes you, you have the assurance of an active advocate in Jesus. The apostle Paul told the church at Corinth that the afflictions of the present day are light, and lasts for just a moment compared to the eternal weight of the glory of our faithfulness. As a leader of faith, you may often find yourself overwhelmed with your responsibilities. Not only will you face physical and circumstantial challenges, you will be cast into bouts of spiritual warfare, in which you find yourself afflicted in ways others can never understand.

In these times of affliction, we should remain obedient to our callings and to the commandments of the faith. Jesus not only shares our afflictions, but He has redeemed us and saved us even when we were not aware of it. In His Second Coming, Jesus is called Faithful and True. All righteous judgment is His alone, and He holds the keys to eternity. We should never fear when following God's call with such an advocate as Christ.

We often forfeit power when we fail to acknowledge our advocate and our fellow bearer of affliction. Our lesson today should give each of us the courage to lead others in new ways and with renewed confidence. We often buckle under the pressures and afflictions of leadership. We let the controversy and the unending tasks of labor burden us and stifle our effectiveness. Christ wants us to give it all over to Him and allow Him to make war against the enemy on our behalf.

We have never been alone in our afflictions. Each day let us give praise to a God who loves us so much He cries when we cry and hurts when we hurt. Let us give our honor and devotion to a God who redeems us in the midst of our enemies and prepares a place in glory for us. Our afflictions this day are light and incomparable to the glory that awaits us. The Faithful and True has gone ahead of you and sealed the victory! Hallelujah!

Our Prayer: *Faithful and True, You are the King of kings and Lord of lords. We give praise and thanksgiving that You have shared our affliction in all ages and redeem us to Yourself. Give us the confidence that we can endure our present troubles and that we will share in the eternal glory of Your righteous victory!* **Amen.**

God And Living Waters

"Leading Others with a Newfound Respect for God's Life-Giving Water"

"And he showed me a pure river of water of life, clear as crystal, proceeding out of the throne of God and of the Lamb…. And it shall be in that day, that living waters shall go out from Jerusalem; half of them toward the former sea, and half of them toward the hinder sea: in summer and in winter shall it be."
Featured Scriptures: Revelation 22:1; and Zechariah 14:8
Background Scripture: Genesis 1:9–10; Isaiah 43:19–20; Joel 3:18; and Revelation 22:1–5

The image of a pure river flowing from the very throne of God makes us pause to wonder at the majesty of such a sight. The gift of living water should conjure more than our thanks for the provision of a cool drink of life-sustaining fluid. It should instill in leaders of faith an attitude of newfound respect for God's life-giving waters in our communities. Throughout Scripture God has used water to demonstrate His power to make life spring forth from dead and dry places.

The prophets Isaiah, Joel, Zechariah, and the apostle John all describe God's holy provision as a river of physical and spiritual life in the New Jerusalem at the time of Christ's Second Coming. The desert will flow again with God's life-giving water, water of the holiest source that will make all things new again. Just as God divided the waters at creation, He will make these living waters flow for the redeemed of the world.

God's relationship with His children is often marked by His leading them to water. He brought Abraham to water. He brought the captives of Egypt to new water. He brought His beloved Son to the river Jordan. Without water, life ceases. Leaders today should recognize their custodial and spiritual connection to God's water.

Throughout history, access to water has dictated the politics of nations. It has set the stage for battles and wars. It has marked the boundaries of republics and guided trade routes. When water becomes polluted and tainted by man's callous disregard for his neighbor, the glory of God's creation is diminished. Water is a precious resource. Virtually every leader of faith in the future will be challenged to take bold leadership positions on matters of water resources.

In light of Scripture, the custodial responsibility of water becomes a holy duty. Leaders of faith should set noble leadership examples of water stewardship through conservation, wise consumption, and water protection. The basic right of access to clean water should be considered a basic human right and a spiritual right. We must become advocates for the powerless, vulnerable, and poor who most often become sick or die from lack of access to clean water. We may have to take on powerful interest groups in order to assure that the least powerful among us can take a clean drink of water.

If the throne of God will supply the water to the redeemed souls in the glory His Kingdom to come, shouldn't we today become better leaders and advocates of life-sustaining water for all as our tribute to God? Let our lives of leadership include giving a cup of clean water to the world in Jesus' name.

Our Prayer: *God of heaven, You are the God of nourishing physical and spiritual water for all of creation. In those of us who have access to the fountain of Your Spirit and clean water to drink, create hearts of passion to become leaders who preserve and give Your living water to all we serve.* **Amen.**

Tears That Only God Can Dry

"Sorrow and Pain Shall Be No More As All Things Are Made New"

"And God shall wipe away all tears from their eyes; and there shall be no more death, neither sorrow, nor crying, neither shall there be any more pain: for the former things are passed away. And He that sat upon the throne said, Behold, I make all things new...."

Featured Scripture: Revelation 21:4–5
Background Scriptures: Revelation 21:1–8; 1 Corinthians 2:9–10

Some leaders of faith serve in the bowels of human suffering and misery. This service takes place on the battlefields, in the war zones, in abject poverty, and in the midst of emergency relief services. Some leaders deal daily with lives that are broken physically, mentally, and spiritually. Leaders of faith are often called to deal with human tragedy, whether it is caused by man or by nature.

In times of great crises, leaders of faith see the tears, death, pain, and sorrow that cannot be comforted by man. Despite this, we should not falter in doing good. Jesus will bring life and healing even in the depravity of humanity, as long as we let our light of love and service shine in us and through us. Regardless of how unspeakable the sin of man's inhumanity to man can be, or how destructive the occurrences of nature can seem, leaders can take solace that Jesus will make all things new. Sometimes we don't have the capacity to dry the human tears ourselves; these are the tears that only God can dry.

In these dire circumstances, we as leaders often attest to seeing the Holy Spirit through acts of decency and dignity even in the midst of untold human suffering. Our true hope is eternal. As leaders, we are called to serve God wherever His call takes us. It is our efforts in times of tribulation that can magnify Christ the greatest. And we must always remember: *"Eye hath not seen, nor ear heard, neither have entered into the heart of man, the things which God hath prepared for them that love him"* (1 Corinthians 2:9).

God can do more than dry the wettest tear or soothe the most horrific pain. No man has ever or will ever imagine in their hearts what good things He has prepared in eternity for those who love Him. Leaders of faith are often the final repositories of hope in dire human circumstances. But rest assured that the hope you offer those whom you lead and serve in times of sorrow for Christ's sake is not lost.

While we cannot dry every tear, we know that those who trust in the resurrected and glorified Christ will have all their pain, sorrow, and loss removed from them. And God shall wipe away all tears from their eyes, and there shall be no more death, neither sorrow, nor crying, neither shall there be any more pain: for the former things are passed away. Serve on in new confidence and faith.

Our Prayer: *Lord God, we know moments will come for some leaders of faith that will hold hurt, pain, sorrow, and unspeakable loss. Help us to always know that the pains and tears of this life will be wiped away forever for those who love You. Give us the courage to lead others in these situations by clinging to Your promises.* **Amen.**

Alpha And Omega

"The Author and Finisher of Our Leadership Journeys"

"And behold, I come quickly; and my reward is with me, to give to every man according as his work shall be. I am Alpha and Omega, the beginning and the end, the first and the last.... Looking unto Jesus the author and finisher of our faith; who for the joy that was set before him endured the cross, despising the shame, and is set down at the right hand of the throne of God."

FEATURED SCRIPTURES: REVELATION 22:12–13; AND HEBREWS 12:2
BACKGROUND SCRIPTURE: JOHN 17

Alpha and *Omega* are the first and last words of the Greek alphabet. Twice in the Book of Revelation Jesus referred to Himself as the Alpha and Omega. Jesus was present at the creation and is even now the Overseer of all things eternal. The apostle Paul referred to Christ as the Author and Finisher of our faith. As we take these two descriptions of Christ and incorporate them into our own lives and leadership journeys, we extract some profound theological meaning. As called leaders of faith we are specially woven into a timeless plan of eternal and holy dimension.

Leaders of faith will make decisions that profoundly affect the lives of others for years to come. Our decisions may involve our own family members or entire organizations. They may involve a community, business, or church. Our decisions might even affect the welfare and safety of thousands of people, even after we are gone. In all we do we are the custodians of the tasks given to us by a heavenly Father, and our work is of eternal significance.

In Christ's priestly prayer, He referred to His followers, both present and future, as *"those thou hast given me"* (John 17:24). As partakers in Christ's life and work, we are joined to the protection of Christ Himself. Christ wants to reward us for our service, and if our reward is eternal, then we should treat our work as eternal. If Christ is the Alpha and Omega of existence, then we become part of the holy middle as we lead and serve others in His name.

We are persons of great value and importance, not because of our leadership place or position, but because we belong to Christ. He has claimed us as His own. The work of our hands belongs to Him. Our leadership journeys belong to Him. And those we lead become part of the larger fabric of His Alpha and Omega purpose. We are to treat each person we encounter, each task we undertake, and each decision we make as if they are the holy patches of Christ's Alpha and Omega quiltwork.

The beginning and the end is already known to Him. He has overcome the world. The history of the faith has already been written. And we, as leaders of faith, should operate each day with the supreme confidence that all will be well because we know, are redeemed by, and belong to the Alpha and Omega, who is the Author and Finisher of it all.

Our Prayer: *Dear Jesus, it is done. You have already accomplished it. Help us to claim Your victory over life and death. We are loved and protected by You, and we give praise and thanks that we can live victoriously each day knowing that we are part of an eternal plan of blessing.* **Amen.**

O Man Of Sorrows, Come To Me

O Man of Sorrows, come to me. As I lie here broken, I look to Thee

Hopes do glimmer and joys do fade, even old pleasures my pain now jades

O Man of Sorrows, Acquainted with Grief, who knows my sorrows, which never cease

Hope of Glory, My Strength and My Song, my heavy heart need not wait for long

O Man of Sorrows, come to me; they gamble my robe away for all to see

Even when naked, they cast my lot; despised and rejected they esteemed me not

O Man of Sorrows, could it be Thee, an evil imposter has blinded me

The Balm of Gilead harkens me now

O Man of Sorrows, with blood well-spilt, a Sweet-Smelling Savor, a new creature is built

Joe Turnham, August 19, 2003

❖

Indexes

Subject

Bible Character

Calendar Event

Devotional

To order additional copies of

Leading From Our Knees

have your credit card ready and call
1 800-917-BOOK (2665)

or e-mail
orders@selahbooks.com

or order online at
www.selahbooks.com